CRITICAL SURVEY
OF
DRAMA

CRITICAL SURVEY
OF
DRAMA

REVISED EDITION
Fri-Jam

3

Edited by
FRANK N. MAGILL

SALEM PRESS
Pasadena, California   Englewood Cliffs, New Jersey

∞ The paper used in these volumes conforms to
the American National Standard for Permanence of
Paper for Printed Library Materials, Z39.48-1984.

**Library of Congress Cataloging-in-Publication
Data**
Critical survey of drama. English language series/
edited by Frank N. Magill.—Rev. ed.
    p.   cm.
Includes bibliographical references and index.
    1. English drama—Dictionaries. 2. American
drama—Dictionaries. 3. English drama—Bio-
bibliography. 4. American drama—Bio-bibliography.
5. Commonwealth drama (English)—Dictionaries.
6. Dramatists, English—Biography—Dictionaries.
7. Dramatists, American—Biography—Dictionaries. 8. Commonwealth drama (English)—Bio-
bibliography.
I. Magill, Frank Northen, 1907-   .
PR623.C75 1994
822.009′03—dc20   93-41618
ISBN 0-89356-851-1 (set)   CIP
ISBN 0-89356-854-6 (volume 3)

LIST OF AUTHORS IN VOLUME 3

CRITICAL SURVEY
OF
DRAMA

BRIAN FRIEL

Born: Omagh, Northern Ireland; January 9, 1929

Principal drama

A Doubtful Paradise (The Francophile), pr. 1959; *The Enemy Within*, pr. 1962, pb. 1979; *The Blind Mice*, pr. 1963; *Philadelphia, Here I Come!*, pr. 1964, pb. 1965; *The Loves of Cass Maguire*, pr. 1966, pb. 1967; *Lovers*, pr. 1967, pb. 1968; *Crystal and Fox*, pr. 1968, pb. 1970; *The Mundy Scheme*, pr. 1969, pb. 1970; *The Gentle Island*, pr. 1971, pb. 1973; *The Freedom of the City*, pr. 1973, pb. 1974; *Volunteers*, pr. 1975, pb. 1979; *Living Quarters*, pr. 1977, pb. 1978; *Faith Healer*, pr. 1979, pb. 1980; *Aristocrats*, pr. 1979, pb. 1980; *Translations*, pr. 1980, pb. 1981; *Three Sisters*, pr., pb. 1981 (adaptation of Anton Chekhov's play); *The Communication Cord*, pr. 1982, pb. 1983; *Selected Plays of Brian Friel*, pb. 1984; *Fathers and Sons*, pr., pb. 1987; *Making History*, pr. 1988, pb. 1989; *Dancing at Lughnasa*, pr., pb. 1990; *The London Vertigo*, pb. 1990, pr. 1992.

Other literary forms

Brian Friel has published two collections of short stories, *The Saucer of Larks* (1962) and *The Gold in the Sea* (1966). Two selections from these works have appeared: *The Saucer of Larks: Stories of Ireland* (1969) and *Selected Stories* (1979), reprinted as *The Diviner* (1982).

The short stories in these collections are gentle, well-turned tales of ordinary people caught, largely, in the toils of personal circumstances. They belong firmly in the tradition of pastoral frustration, to which the majority of modern Irish short stories belong. The narrative tone of Friel's stories is genial, quizzical, and often humorous, and it anticipates the affection and dignity that Friel's plays typically accord the common person.

Achievements

After a modest but assured beginning as short-story writer, Friel has grown, thanks to his plays, into one of the most important figures in the cultural phenomenon which will surely come to be known as the Ulster Renaissance. Like many other artists from the North of Ireland, Friel has had his work deepened and darkened by the history of his native province, yet it is also true that his willingness to face that history and its web of cultural subtexts has thrown into bolder relief the innate humanity of all of his work, rendering it all the more estimable.

Throughout his plays, Friel has persistently exposed stereotype, cliché, and narrowness of various kinds. In their place, he has substituted joy, openness, and individuality, qualities which enhance the human lot and for which his birthplace has not been noted. A deep sense of division informs both his characters and his dramatic practice, yet acknowledgment of division is an avenue to sympathy, not a recipe for impairment. Emphasizing with increasing vigor, range, and sophistication the value of spontaneity and the necessity of love, Friel's work is a moving—and stirring—statement of human solidarity in a dark time.

This statement is constantly renewed by the author's formal innovations. Friel's technical brilliance, however, does not permit him to break faith with the heritage of twentieth century Irish drama, its attachment to a sense of locale, its concern for the common lot, its resistance to institutionalized modes of thought. In fact, Friel makes these elements interrelate fruitfully and unexpectedly by subjecting them to the clear, unblinking light of his moral intelligence.

Historically and artistically, Friel's place as Ulster's most important dramatist ever, and as one of Ireland's most significant dramatists in the twentieth century, is secure. Friel's achievements have been acknowledged with numerous drama awards on both sides of the Atlantic, and in 1981, *Translations* received the Ewart Biggs Memorial Prize, instituted to recognize outstanding contributions to Anglo-Irish understanding. In 1992, Friel's play *Dancing at Lughnasa* won a New York Drama Critics Circle Award for best play of the 1991-1992 theater season. Also in 1992, *Dancing at Lughnasa* received a Tony Award for best play in addition to two other Tony Awards: for featured actress (Brid Brennan) and for director (Patrick Mason).

Biography

Order, industry, fixity, and quiet are the hallmarks of Brian Friel's life. He was born in Omagh, County Tyrone, Northern Ireland, on January 9, 1929, the son of a teacher. The family lived in Omagh for ten more years before moving to Derry, the second city of Ulster and the place which, along with its County Donegal hinterland, may be properly considered to be Friel's homeland.

Friel was educated at St. Columb's College, Derry, and at Maynooth, the Irish national seminary, where he was graduated in 1948, though it was not his intention to study for the priesthood. He attended St. Joseph's Teacher Training College, Belfast, from 1949 to 1950, and for the next ten years taught in various schools in Derry.

During this period, Friel began to write in his spare time, and from the mid-1950's, he was a regular contributor of short stories to *The New Yorker*. During this period also he turned to drama as a form, beginning with two radio plays, which were broadcast in 1958, and at the end of the 1950's, he branched out into staged drama.

In 1960, Friel resigned from teaching to devote himself to writing. The wisdom of that decision has been confirmed by the continuing string of international successes which has ensued. English and, particularly, American audiences have greeted his plays at least as enthusiastically as have Irish ones. Friel's rapid development as a playwright was decisively influenced by the celebrated director Tyrone Guthrie, at whose theater in Minneapolis Friel spent some months in 1968, in his words, "hanging around."

Beginning in 1980, a more public Friel has been in evidence as the moving spirit behind Field Day Productions, a theater company formed in collaboration, chiefly, with the actor Stephen Rea. Based in Derry, the company's objective is to renew the theatrical life of provincial Ireland by means of touring productions. Friel has also been instrumental in establishing Field Day Publications. This imprint has issued, most notably, an important series of pamphlets on Irish cultural matters by leading contemporary Irish poets and critics.

In 1991, the three-volume *The Field Day Anthology of Irish Writing*, edited by Seamus Deane, was published, extending and consolidating much of the range and interest of the Field Day pamphlet series and creating a landmark in the development of Ireland's conception of its literary culture. This publication coincided with the international success of Friel's play *Dancing at Lughnasa*, which played to packed theaters not only in Dublin but also in London's West End and on Broadway, and which brought its author a large number of theater awards.

Analysis

Brian Friel's dramatic output, wide-ranging in subject matter though it is, possesses a notable consistency of theme, tone, and attitude to the stage. Whether a Friel play's pretext is the mission of St. Columbia, Derry's patron saint, to the island of Iona in the sixth century *(The Enemy Within)*, or the living room of decaying gentlefolk *(Aristocrats)*, a hedge school in nineteenth century rural Ireland *(Translations)*, or the encampment of a traveling show *(Crystal and Fox* or rather differently, *Faith Healer)*, familiar themes recur. Their recurrence, however, is invariably fresh, given new life by the author's unfailing sympathy and the suppleness with which he shapes unexpected cultural nuances. Such flexibility and control may be seen as an expression of the author's essential good nature. In his plays, one can also see, however, one of his oeuvre's most consistent traits, his daring use of theater itself. Friel's work shows a marked flair for dramaturgical experimentation, but the experiments themselves are exclusively in the service of broader human concerns, revealing how hollow yet how inevitable ritualized behavior can be, for example, or economically contrasting characters' public and private spaces. A consummate orchestrator of theatrical space and (as is increasingly evident from his later work) the possessor of a light, though commanding, touch with ensemble work, Friel's is preeminently a writer's theater rather than a director's or a star's.

Foremost among Friel's broad human preoccupations is love—its persistence, its betrayal, its challenge. Few of Friel's characters manage to rise fully to the challenge of loving adequately. Their inadequacy is transmitted from one play to another, like a cynosure of frailty. What is significant, however, is not success but the apparent inevitability of exposure to a sense of human limitation and imperfection. Love generates many other important Friel themes. The affection for common people—uneducated, shrewd street-folk—which is unsentimentally present in all of his plays has a sympathetic loving-kindness in it which his characters themselves generally decline to embody. The destructiveness of family life, particularly the unhappy effects that parents may have on children—in Friel's world an unredeemable original sin—is also a feature of the author's preoccupation with love. Love likewise informs such concerns as fidelity to place and to cultural inheritance. A marked sharpness in attitude toward behavior which is determined by cultural institutions rather than by the vigor of the individual psyche is, again, motivated by Friel's concern with love. In fact, love has developed in Friel's work from being, in early plays, a matter of impossible romance, family bitterness, or sexual buoyancy to being the finely calibrated optic of a worldview. Friel's manipulation of the optic in later plays reveals love as a saving grace, not only personally but also culturally—and usually both, interdependently, offering at once the tolerance of charity and the zest of passion, a healing ethic and a moral force.

Yet division, symptomatic of love's failure, is very much in evidence in Friel's work. In *Philadelphia, Here I Come!* — his first and major international success—the dichotomy between self and world is given novel dramaturgical embodiment through the device of having two actors play different aspects of the protagonist, Gar O'Donnell: Public Gar and his alter ego, Private Gar. The world sees only the former, while the audience readily perceives that it is the latter who has the greater authenticity, by virtue of his ability to satirize Public's gaucherie and emotional timidity. (Gar O'Donnell is the most winning representative of the naïve, ardent youth, a type beloved of Friel, first seen as the novice in *The Enemy Within*.)

The action takes place on the night before, and early morning of, Gar's emigration to the United States, and consists less of a plot than of a tissue of what Friel in later plays calls "episodes." In effect, Gar's past life passes before him. The passage takes place in two dimensions—the public, by means of farewells, and the private, by means of Private's somewhat manic and mordantly witty analysis of that life's nugatory achievements. The only thing which will relieve life at home in Ballybeg of his abiding sense of depletion, as far as Gar is concerned, is an expression of affection by his father. It is never made; Gar is obliged to carry his incompleteness with him. In that case, staying or going becomes moot.

As in *The Enemy Within*, the conclusion is inconclusive. The difference is that in the earlier play, inconclusiveness was enacted in a condition; here, rather more satisfyingly, it is embodied in a character. *Philadelphia, Here I Come!* also benefits from having its cultural resonances localized, as well as having its treatment of division given clever dramatic form. This play launched Friel's mature playwriting career. It contains an affectionately critical characterization of restlessness and brio, as well as failed love and a lament for it, and longings for a fuller life and a fear of it.

Friel's preoccupation with love, familial relations, and romance is offered in a delicate, bittersweet blend in *Crystal and Fox*, one of his most effective works. Crystal and Fox, a man-and-wife team, own a traveling show of no particular distinction. When we first encounter it, audience response is poor and Fox, in a typical fit of recklessness, fires some of the players. The company is now reduced to four, one of whom is Crystal's ailing and incompetent father who is soon hospitalized. The traveling show, for so long an expression of Fox's restlessness, now attains a stasis, a condition which makes Fox mean and destructive. All that can save the situation is the unwavering romantic attachment, tantamount to worship, that Crystal and Fox have for each other. Into their impoverished encampment comes Gabriel, their son. Gabriel has spent years in England, like Cass in *The Loves of Cass Maguire,* the victim of a family row. Now, however, all is forgiven, and Gabriel is seen as an embodiment of renewal. He soon tells Fox that he is on the run from the English police, having, in desperation, committed robbery with violence. This information is kept from Crystal until Gabriel is arrested before her eyes. As a result, Crystal and Fox sell the show's remaining properties in order to help Gabriel, but en route to Gabriel's trial, Fox lies, telling Crystal that he informed on his son for the sake of the police reward. A demented Crystal leaves her husband, allowing the play to conclude with a statement from Fox about the motivation for his destructiveness. He wanted the whole of life to be reduced to one ardent form—namely, his romantic love of Crystal. Such a love, he believes, expresses the best in him. Everything else is tainted with contingency, incompleteness, mortality. Yet the finality and totality of his love for Crystal is what prompts treachery and ruin.

The play is satisfying on a number of levels. Its spare language complements its essentially violent action. Friel's metaphoric use of playing and roles is deeply ingrained in the piece's fundamental texture. Bleakness and joy are communicated with great clarity and economy. The need for romance—the desire that there be something more to life than the mere role one plays in it—is boldly established and subjected to an impressively unsentimental critique. In all, *Crystal and Fox* is a fitting culmination of Friel's early phase. From this point onward, his work, while not forsaking love as a theme or the family setting as its representative focus, has engaged more public issues and has placed less emphasis on individual destiny than on collective experience, a departure which has meant the virtual elimination of the often stereotyped minor characters present in his early work.

With *The Freedom of the City*, Friel began his major phase. Innovative dramaturgy, a marriage of private and public themes, a major renovation of the part played by love in human affairs, all make this play a work of notable theatrical events.

The city in question is Derry, and the play is inspired by, though it does not mimic, the events of Bloody Sunday, January 30, 1972, when British forces killed thirteen civil rights demonstrators. Friel opens the play's action by having his three protagonists flee from the violent disruption by army and police of a banned civil rights demonstration. They seek refuge successfully in the Mayor's parlor of the Guildhall (the ease with which they do so being one of the play's many ironies about "security"), and, with nothing better to do, they have a party. They drink the Mayor's liquor, smoke his cigars, dress up in ceremonial robes, and parody official ceremonies, including the conferring of the freedom of the city. Skinner, the most restless, deprived, and anarchistically inclined of the threesome, does a minimal amount of damage to property, stabbing a city father's portrait with a ceremonial sword. His opposite is Michael, a clean-cut embodiment of civil rights aspirations, who, without skepticism, wants nothing more than a fair chance to better himself. Between them stands Lilly, a blowsy mother of eleven, who approves of Michael's respectability yet is stimulated by Skinner's vitality. Eventually, summoned by military bullhorn to emerge, the three (now thought of, thanks to rumor, as forty) emerge from the circumscribed freedom of their refuge, to be shot in cold blood on the Guildhall steps.

The play's action, however, is only one of its levels. It is surrounded by frameworks of judicial and intellectual evaluation. Thus, from the outset, we are privy to the findings of the court of inquiry, which examines and distorts the protagonists' actions and characters. We are also periodically subjected to an analysis of the culture of poverty voiced by an American sociologist. These two framing devices—sophisticated revisions of an ironic use of omniscience, introduced in *Lovers* and used most tellingly in *Living Quarters*—help us appreciate the informal, living texture of the trio's activities, as it is that very quality which the processes of evaluation and formal discourse are unable to admit.

Perhaps the play is overloaded with framing devices. In addition to the two central ones mentioned, there are also two which derive from the trio's own cultural constituency, represented by the Church and by a ballad-singer. These two also distort what the characters embody. The aim to be comprehensive is no doubt laudable, and the resultant verbal range is an impressive feature of the play, but the ensuing emphasis on the distorting effects of objectification is overdone. At the same time, however, such an emphasis also draws attention to *The Freedom of the City* as a hymn to the theater, both in the value it implicitly locates in the spontaneous antics of the three victims and in the sense that the stage is large enough for spontaneity and formality to play opposite each other.

In *Volunteers,* Friel also uses an event and a set of issues from contemporary Irish history. The matter in question is the Wood Quay, Dublin, excavation, where, during groundbreaking for a new office block, invaluable remains of Viking Dublin were unearthed. Efforts to preserve the site on the part of local *bien-pensants* led to ugly clashes with the developers, the law, and Dublin's city fathers, and also, ultimately, to frustrated defeat for the preservationists.

Out of this volatile material, Friel fashioned a marvelous play. His volunteers are jailed social activists of a not very well-defined variety; inasmuch as they have a social philosophy, it generally seems to speak in favor of a more abundant life. (The play's one ideologue, a student radical who is one of the supervisors, in the end lets down the volunteers rather seriously.) The play is set in a hole in the ground, and the action takes place on the last day of the dig, a closing date which has been peremptorily hurried forward and which will leave the work unfinished. When this state of affairs is brought to the attention of Keeney and his fellow volunteers, it increases the audience's appreciation of the magnitude of their contribution as well as exposing the sterility of orthodox socially instituted planning. Indeed, the spontaneous gesture of volunteering has placed Keeney and his mates in danger of their narrow-minded fellow prisoners. Those who give freely, it seems, will be regarded with the most suspicion.

This conclusion is reinforced by the attitude of George the foreman. Superior to the volunteers in social status alone, his inability to have anything other than a master-servant relationship with them expresses insufferable moral smugness on the part of one who watches but does not dirty his hands. The only figure with whom the volunteers can feel kinship is the skeleton they have disinterred and named "Lief," and who seems to have been the victim of a ritual execution. Lief is the authentic representative of a past common to all in the play, a past which is only properly visible to the volunteers. Thus, Lief is to be cherished much more than the vase which George has assembled out of fragments rescued by the volunteers, and when one of them deliberately breaks the vase, the symbolic resonance is as great as that provided by their ceremonial reburial of Lief.

The volunteers, then, are those who come in closest contact with the texture of the past, its earthbound treasures and human blemishes—and this contact is all the more estimable for being freely given. Prisoners of the state, menaced by their own kind and by their masters, the volunteers give unlikely expression to *pietas,* which is in cultural terms what love is in personal affairs. Yet all this is communicated in anything but solemn terms; the breezy satire of *The Mundy Scheme* is here deepened and tightened almost beyond recognition. Finally, in Keeney, Friel has created a character who is in total command of himself and prepared to face whatever comes, a character whose abundant energies, verbal pyrotechnics, and keen mind equip him superbly to be the onstage director of what Seamus Heaney has memorably called "a masque of anarchy."

Friel's *Translations* is his finest achievement, as well as being, both intellectually and culturally speaking, his most ambitious. Set in the 1830's among the Irish peasantry, it discourses wittily, economically, and profoundly on the clash between the English and the Irish cultures, on language and its imprecision, on violence and its distortions.

The play opens with young adult peasants entering the hedge school of Hugh O'Donnell for their evening class in Latin, Greek, and arithmetic. In itself, such a scene is replete with noteworthy cultural resonances, being both a far cry from the stage Irishman and a vivid introduction to contemporary peasant life, down to the aging "infant prodigy" in the background who relishes Homer in the original. Hugh's son, Manus, takes the class this particular evening, because of his father's inebriation. One of the students is Manus' sweetheart, ambitious Maire, who is anxious for a fuller life for both of them. She plans to emigrate to America, while Manus, to some extent his father's prisoner, possesses a fierce loyalty to the local native life he loves so well.

In a sense, Maire resembles Manus' brother, Owen. He, too, desires a wider arena for himself, as is clear from his entry into the schoolroom with two well-disposed British soldiers, Captain Lancey and Lieutenant Yolland. These two are members of a detachment of troops engaged on an ordinance survey of Ireland, an enterprise which has as one of its features the translation of Irish place-names into English. Owen is employed in this work, under Yolland's supervision, and he is painfully aware of the offense against *pietas* constituted by the effective divorce of native tongue from native place which will inevitably result. His awareness is ironically contrasted with Yolland's onset of a vague, fashionable, romantic attachment to the locals, and Owen's situation is further underlined by the deft trick of showing that when the native characters speak among themselves, the soldiers do not understand them. In other words, at certain points, the audience must accept English to be Irish.

In the hope that the cultural conflict will not come to a head, Owen arranges for Yolland to attend a local dance. There, Yolland meets Maire, and despite linguistic barriers, hilarious at the time (Friel's flair for representing gaucherie is brilliantly displayed here), she seduces him. Having seen Maire home, however, Yolland is never seen again, and the play ends with peasant hegemony broken beyond repair by the threat of dire reprisal by Lancy, and by Manus' flight from the place whose main hope he was. The situation is left in the hands of Hugh, who is impotently eloquent about its linguistic implications, and Jimmy, the "infant prodigy," whom language has deluded to the extent of his announcing his impending marriage to Homer's *glaukopis Athene.*

The play's effectiveness is not solely derived from the novelty and richness of its cultural scenario: In addition, this scenario enabled Friel to marshal areas of interest which had hitherto existed separately in his works. Here one finds the intersection of public and personal history, the suffocation of love by unpromising family circumstances, the destructiveness and inevitability of passion, the author's devotion to the common people and to that sense of Ireland which Ballybeg connotes. The coalescence of these themes certainly makes *Translations*, in the words of the review in *The Times* of London, "a national classic." The play also sets the seal on Friel's reputation as the most resourceful, most engaging, and most serious voice in postwar Irish drama.

Friel's career throughout the 1980's has been more diverse than hitherto. Ranging from the farce *The Communication Cord* and its self-consciously parodic relationship to *Translations*, to an interest in adaptations and translations from the Russian (*Three Sisters* and *Fathers and Sons*, the latter a stage version of the Ivan Turgenev novel of the same name), to restrained and cerebral treatment of the genesis of history in language in *Making History*, the playwright's emphasis, more than ever, has been on the various types of relationships that can exist between time and thought, and on the ways in which those relationships are normalized publicly in culture and privately in identity. With its autobiographical basis and its inclusion, in the character of Jack, of a theoretical dimension, *Dancing at Lughnasa* may be regarded as a distillation of Friel's persistent probing of the connection between who people think they are and who they are thought to be. To discuss Friel's greatest international success since *Translations* in such terms is not intended to detract from audiences' keen enjoyment of a warmhearted play but is intended to be further evidence of the consistency and continual development of the theater of Brian Friel.

Other major works

SHORT FICTION: *The Saucer of Larks*, 1962; *The Gold in the Sea*, 1966; *The Saucer of Larks: Stories of Ireland*, 1969; *Selected Stories*, 1979 (reprinted as *The Diviner*, 1982).

RADIO PLAYS: *A Sort of Freedom*, 1958; *To This Hard House*, 1958.

Bibliography

Dantanus, Ulf. *Brian Friel: A Study*. London: Faber & Faber, 1988. A condensation and updating of the author's *Brian Friel: The Growth of an Irish Dramatist* (1985), which discusses Friel's career up to, and including, the production of *Fathers and Sons.* Through close readings of Friel's work, Dantanus focuses on the broad cultural and social issues that arise from it.

Deane, Seamus. "Brian Friel: The Double Stage." In *Celtic Revivals: Essays in Modern Irish Literature, 1880-1980.* London: Faber & Faber, 1985. A typically trenchant scrutiny of some of the "recurrent elements in a Brian Friel play." Most of Friel's major works are dealt with, including *Translations* and *Faith Healer.* The author is the leading Irish critic of his generation, a director of Field Day, and the editor of the *Selected Plays of Brian Friel.*

Maxwell, D. E. S. *Brian Friel.* Lewisburg, Pa.: Bucknell University Press, 1973. This brief study covers Friel's career as a short-story writer and dramatist up to *The Freedom of the City.* It conveys a firm sense of Friel's personal and historical background. The discussion of the individual texts is somewhat abbreviated.

O'Brien, George. *Brian Friel.* Boston: Twayne, 1989. An introductory survey of Friel's stories and plays up to *Making History.* The primary emphasis is on the character and quality of Friel's artistic vision. Surveys the whole of the Friel canon, including the early, unpublished stage and radio plays. Contains an extensive bibliography.

O'Connor, Ulick. *Brian Friel: Crisis and Commitment.* Dublin: Elo, 1989. A pamphlet by a well-known playwright and biographer. Addresses the problems of the writer's social and cultural responsibilities in times of civic crisis, using as its focus the work of Friel in the context of the crisis of authority in Northern Ireland.

Pine, Richard. *Brian Friel and Ireland's Drama.* London: Routledge, 1990. The most comprehensive, intellectually sophisticated, and theoretically ambitious reading of Friel's output up to and including *Dancing at Lughnasa.* Numerous stimulating and challenging connections are made between Friel and other Irish and international dramatists, and Friel is used as a means of focusing on the status and significance of drama in contemporary Irish culture.

George O'Brien

CHRISTOPHER FRY

Born: Bristol, England; December 18, 1907

Principal drama

The Boy with a Cart, pr. 1938, pb. 1939; *Thursday's Child*, pr., pb. 1939; *The Firstborn*, pb. 1946 (revised 1952), pr. 1948; *A Phoenix Too Frequent*, pr., pb. 1946; *The Lady's Not for Burning*, pr. 1948, pb. 1949; *Thor, with Angels*, pr., pb. 1948; *Venus Observed*, pr., pb. 1950; *A Sleep of Prisoners*, pr., pb. 1951; *The Dark Is Light Enough*, pr., pb. 1954; *Three Plays*, pb. 1960; *Curtmantle*, pr., pb. 1961; *Plays*, pb. 1969-1971; *A Yard of Sun*, pr., pb. 1970; *Paradise Lost*, pr., pb. 1978 (adaptation of John Milton's poem); *Selected Plays*, pb. 1985; *One Thing More: Or, Caedmon Construed*, pb. 1985, pr. 1986.

Other literary forms

Christopher Fry is well-known for his many translations of plays into English verse, which have had successful productions both for the stage and, in some cases, for the cinema. His first published translation was of Jean Anouilh's *L'Invitation au Château* as *Ring Round the Moon* (pr., pb. 1950), Fry's only effort in prose, followed by several translations, including *The Lark* (pr., pb. 1955; of Anouilh's *L'Alouette*), *Tiger at the Gates* (pr., pb. 1955; of Jean Giraudoux's *La Guerre de Troie n'aura pas lieu*), *Duel of Angels* (pr., pb. 1958; of Giraudoux's *Pour Lucrèce*), *Judith* (pr., pb. 1962; of Giraudoux's *Judith*), and *Cyrano de Bergerac* (pr., pb. 1975; of Edmond Rostand's *Cyrano de Bergerac*). Fry has also published critical prose, including *An Experience of Critics* (1952) and several important essays on the use of verse in drama. He has worked on television productions and screenplays, and his work for the British Broadcasting Corporation, *The Brontës of Haworth*, was published in 1975. His screenplay credits include *Ben Hur* (1959) and *The Bible* (1966). A family history, *Can You Find Me*, was published in 1978.

Achievements

Fry is one of the most popular and prolific of twentieth century English verse playwrights; only T. S. Eliot and William Butler Yeats exercised a greater influence on the development of twentieth century verse drama. Fry differs from Eliot and Yeats, however, in that he did not establish a reputation as a poet before turning to the stage: Fry began with an early and practical interest in the theater as an actor and director.

It is a fact worth noting that, with the exception of his translation of Jean Anouilh's *L'Invitation au Château*, all of Fry's plays are in verse in a century which has provided primarily a theater of realistic prose—a prose which Fry claims has lost all contact with anything other than surface reality. Fry insists that his use of verse is in the service of reality, that verse provides a medium for his attempt to shake the world alert again to the deeper reality of every human being's ability to experience afresh the eternal miracle of life—a reality at present obscured and staled by custom. In Fry's view, humankind has domesticated the enormous miracle of life and become deadened to the wonder which is everywhere available. Fry attempts to give voice to his sense of the miracle of life with the language of poetry; he derisively identifies prose on the stage with the tinkle of breakfast cups. In a 1951 article in *Saturday Review*, Fry makes it clear that "poetry is the language in which man explores his own amazement."

This worldview probably accounts for much of the adverse criticism Fry's plays have received, for his work sometimes rings false or hollow, irresponsibly separated from the world the theatergoer accepts as real. Sometimes the reader or viewer senses that Fry protests too much for a man firmly grounded in the "enormous miracle" of the world, and the atmosphere of his plays often has the unfortunate effect of sheer fantasy. The use of distant times and scenes adds to a sense of unreality, and it would seem particularly unfortunate that, if Fry's aim is to reestablish wonder in modern man, he should feel the necessity for setting his dramas in a world removed from the present by time and distance. *A Sleep of Prisoners* and *A Yard of Sun* are exceptions, and *Venus Observed* and even *The Dark Is Light Enough* can be viewed as fairly direct comments on the contemporary dilemma, but Fry's plays are never "modern" in the same sense that Eliot's, W. H. Auden's and Christopher Isherwood's, or Stephen Spender's are.

Fry seldom seeks to come to grips with the modern world by taking it as the arena of his explorations; rather, he works by indirection, indicating in the world of his plays the importance of the individual, the meaning of humanity, the futility and needless cruelty of wars, and the possibilities for redeeming life through love. Having demonstrated the vitality latent in the world, Fry believes that he has made sufficient comment on the modern situation. This approach is misleading in view of Fry's claim to be interested in the problems of his own time, for the emphasis in his work appears to be not on modern human beings, but on humankind, as if Fry thought he could best restore human life to its proper heritage not by showing the paltry thing it has become in the twentieth century, but by showing what it has been and yet may be. Thus, Fry's dramaturgy stems from his romanticism, which expresses itself in an undaunted humanism and draws its vocabulary from natural and biblical sources. In Fry, there is little of the peculiarly modern vocabulary that one finds in other contemporary playwrights; as a general rule, the science Fry draws upon for his images is that of alchemy or astronomy; his psychology is that of the theory of humors; his textbook, Robert Burton's *The Anatomy of Melancholy* (1621). It is not surprising, then, to find the charge of romantic escapism leveled against Fry: The dangers inherent in his approach are obvious.

Given his orientation, the problem Fry faces in terms of language is perhaps clearer when one considers that the mainstream of poetic idiom for the modern verse play is that established by Eliot and manipulated by Auden and others. This is an idiom, on the whole, expressive of the modern world as it has appeared to these poets, and such a language can be of little use to Fry. He needs a language not to embody the dreary failure and, at best, partially reclaimed successes of the modern world, but a language to carry as much as possible the wonder, the miracle, the exuberance of a world that, most likely, never was. Against Eliot's habitual understatement, Fry's project demands a language of overstatement, resulting in excesses: the riot of images which often impede the dramatic progress of a passage, the wit or whimsy which sometimes seems to exist for the sake of its own good nature, and the verbal coinages which can be effective theater for a time but begin to pall before the end of the third act.

Fry's linguistic debts have been traced to various and varying sources, and if all of the critics are right in their assumptions about sources, his verse has an impressive (but impossible) cosmopolitan paternity. Fry's work has been linked to that of the Georgians, but the Elizabethan playwrights as well as the Jacobeans, Francis Beaumont and John Fletcher, are most often named as his literary ancestors. Fry's desire to recapture a sense of life and wonder does suggest certain early seventeenth century parallels, as do specific literary borrowings from William Shakespeare's comedies. In this respect also, Fry's dominant rhythmic pattern is usually blank verse, although he makes extensive use of variations involving a four-stress line and the anapestic foot, which give his verse its characteristic speed.

Clearly, Fry's verse drama has taken a direction quite opposite from Eliot's, and one need only compare Eliot's *The Cocktail Party* and Fry's *Venus Observed*, both published in 1950 and both dealing thematically with the acceptance of limitations and the discovery of identity, to discern the differences in verse and treatment. In the Eliot play, the verse is submerged, approximating in general the common speech of modern man, rising to poetry only in moments of emotional intensity. In the Fry play, the verse is insistent throughout the play. Although both playwrights are concerned with the human being in his social context, the verse of *The Cocktail Party* seems much more solid, genuinely grounded in an action which in itself has a depth that the action in the Fry play lacks.

Fry, as a dramatist, has not consistently mastered the third voice of poetry identified by Eliot in "The Three Voices of Poetry" as "the voice of the poet when he attempts to create a dramatic character speaking in verse: when he is saying, not what he would say in his own person, but

only what he can say within the limits of one imaginary character address-
ing another imaginary character." Fry's characters, no matter how exor-
bitant their humors, generally reveal in their speech the voice of the poet,
slightly academic and a little self-conscious, and it is for this reason that so
many of Fry's characters sound alike.

Biography

Christopher Fry's work was virtually unknown to playgoers or readers
until the success of *The Lady's Not for Burning* in 1949, although he seems
to have been on his way to the creation of this play throughout most of his
life. Born Christopher Fry Harris, the son of an architect, Charles Harris,
Fry was reared in an intensely religious home. His father had been a lay
missionary in the Bristol slums and his mother was a devout Quaker. Fry
was still young at the time of his father's death, and his mother took in
boarders in order to send her only son to the Bedford Modern School. She
also did much to encourage his natural musical talents, translated, in his
later writing career, into an appreciation for the music of language. His
early performances as a solo musician may also have given him a taste for
the more multifaceted world of the professional stage toward which he
aimed his life. Fry did not pursue a university education but left school at
age eighteen to become a teacher, around this time beginning to use his
mother's maiden name, Fry—the name by which he has since been known.

Between periods of teaching, Fry joined the Bath Repertory Company.
His next experience with the theater was eight difficult years during which
he stubbornly tried to make a living with repertory troupes, performing in
plays by William Shakespeare, George Bernard Shaw, Oscar Wilde, Sir
James Barrie, and Noël Coward. When he moved to London in search of a
career at the center of England's dramatic activities, he found that economic necessity once again forced him to try other work—as an editor,
cartoonist, secretary, writer of children's plays, and even songwriter. From
1934 until its demise, he was director of the Wells Repertory Players at
Tunbridge Wells. According to Fry, through all of this time his desire to
write plays in verse never faltered.

Two years after his 1936 marriage, Fry received a small legacy from a
cousin which enabled him to begin sustained work on his plays. Shortly
thereafter his first published play, *The Boy with a Cart*, was conceived and
first performed as a pageant play for the fiftieth anniversary of a village
church, and *Thursday's Child* was produced in Albert Hall, London, with
the attendance of the queen at one performance. In 1939, Fry became director of the Oxford Playhouse, but, as a conscientious objector, he spent the
war years in civilian service, fighting fires and clearing bomb damage in
various parts of England.

In 1946, *A Phoenix Too Frequent*, the first of Fry's mature achievements in verse drama, was performed in London's private Arts Theatre Club, followed by sixty-four performances in a West End theater. The play, despite its success, drew critical reviews that saw it as too facile in its verse and too lightweight in its philosophical implications, in spite of the fact that Fry's original source was a tale from Petronius. The play, the first of Fry's to cross the Atlantic for a commercial performance, closed after only five nights in New York in April of 1950. New York critics almost unanimously condemned the play for being overwritten and too slight with regard to dramatic conception.

The Lady's Not for Burning was championed by John Gielgud for London production in 1948, a production in which Gielgud also had a hand in staging and a major character role in performance. This first of Fry's "seasonal comedies" brought him recognition and success on both sides of the Atlantic, and the play won the prestigious Shaw Prize as the best play of the year. *Venus Observed*, the "autumnal" play, followed the "spring" mood of *The Lady's Not for Burning* two years later when Sir Laurence Olivier successfully staged and acted in it. The "seasonal" round of Fry's intentions was interrupted by *A Sleep of Prisoners* published the year following, which was a religious festival play like *The Boy with a Cart* and *The Firstborn*. Published in 1955, *The Dark Is Light Enough* provided the "winter" comedy, and finally, in 1970, after slightly more than twenty years and the publication of *Curtmantle* in 1961, his Beckett play, Fry completed his expressed intention to write a play for each season of the year with *A Yard of Sun*, displacing *A Phoenix Too Frequent*, which some impatient critics had tried to take for the "summer" comedy needed for the cycle of the seasons.

As early as 1953, Fry wrote a script for a film of John Gay's *The Beggar's Opera*, followed by *Ben Hur* and *Barabbas* (1962). British television later saw his adaptation of Anne Brontë's *The Tenant of Wildfell Hall* (1968), a series of four plays on the Brontës (1973), a television play called *Sister Dora* (1977), and other mass media work.

After a gap of several years, Fry agreed to write a play about Caedmon, the unlettered peasant poet whose story is told in the Venerable Bede's *Ecclesiastical History of the English People* (731), titled *One Thing More*, on commission from the Chelmsford Cathedral. In 1987, in honor of Fry's eightieth birthday, *The Lady's Not for Burning* was televised by the British Broadcasting Corporation (BBC).

Analysis

A Phoenix Too Frequent and *A Sleep of Prisoners* are Christopher Fry's two most successful one-act plays, a length which Fry easily mastered, but of the two, *A Sleep of Prisoners* is the more interesting because it is one of the few plays in which Fry tries to deal with a contemporary setting, and it is, formally, the most experimental of Fry's plays. In many ways his most complex undertaking, *A Sleep of Prisoners* can be described as one of the most immediately modern of Fry's plays, not simply because it has as its characters four prisoners of war, and as its setting an interlude in World War II, but also because in this play, Fry draws on the experimental formal techniques of the modern theater. The scene of the play is a church converted into a temporary prison for four captured soldiers who, under the pressure of their surroundings, reenact biblical scenes in their dreams. Within this framework, Fry describes his intent and his design in the play's prefatory letter to Robert Gittings: "I have tried to make a more simple statement though in a complicated design where each of four men is seen through the sleeping thoughts of the others, and each, in his own dream, speaks as at heart he is, not as he believes himself to be."

This structure achieves a welding together of the spiritual history of humankind and the dreams of the four sleepers in an expressionistic fantasy which expresses the theme of the play. The dreams are made up of significant moments in the growth of vision Fry hopes to express, and the treatment of the material (the weaving of the patterns of the dreams and the final dream shared in common) suggests that the technique of the play owes more than a little to the Jungian idea of a racial memory, or perhaps to the tendency in modern poetry to suggest a composite experience and protagonist, as in Eliot's *The Waste Land* (1922) and in William Carlos Williams' *Paterson* (1946-1958).

The dreams of the four soldiers involve moments of passion, of suffering, of sacrifice, and the dream-lives of the men are determined by their temperaments, which are established in the brief exchange which opens the play. Peter Abel, outwardly easygoing, uncommitted, and even-tempered, is attacked by his friend, David King, whose nerves are frayed by the whole experience and by his concern for Peter's apparent untroubled acceptance of the situation in which they find themselves. In their subsequent dreams, these two reenact the conflict in the roles which their names and natures suggest—Abel and Cain, Absalom and David, Isaac and Abraham—until they finally join Corporal Adams in his dream, and the three of them become Shadrac, Meshac, and Abednego in the fiery furnace, the crucible of man's experience.

The creation of their dreams in terms of army life gives the whole play a sense of immediacy while underwriting the repetitive nature of history and the cumulative meaning of man's experience. The mixing of biblical situations and military terminology provides a very effective vocabulary for the verse of the play, creating the same kind of tensions which the larger design of the play encompasses.

The fourth character, Meadows, a man beyond the maximum age for enlistment, has accepted his involvement with humankind by the symbolic act of voluntary enlistment, and he provides the structural links between the waking and sleeping worlds. For the most part, as the other dreamers act out their passions, Meadows lies awake in his bunk; the others wake fitfully from time to time, and the waking men interact on the edge of their dreams. For example, after Adams, as Joab, has cut down Absalom with his tommygun, David (no longer the king) awakens, and in the anxiety of his guilt, which had been objectified by his dream, he asks Meadows, who has been awake, if he has heard a shout (the cry of the dying Absalom). Meadows' reply, "Nobody shouted," indicates the complexity of the formal convention of the dream, which is to be compared to the interior monologue technique in the sense that the world of the dream creates its own significant content and form although its larger setting is the external world.

There is a progression in the dreams which David and Peter enact, moving from the wrathful killing by Cain when Abel wins at dice to the meaningful but averted sacrifice of Isaac by Abraham. In the final experience of the furnace, when all three join in a single dream, Meadows appears as Man, who undergoes with the others the purgatorial fires in which humankind is tried. The fourth figure, the role which Meadows takes, is present in the biblical story and is traditionally identified with Christ; yet only if Christ is to be seen as a type of Everyman—not God but first of all Man, sharing the experiences of man—does this reading of the figure do no violence to accomplishment of the play.

In *A Sleep of Prisoners*, Fry deals more directly with the state of human beings in the modern world than in any of his other plays. David, for example, has the obsession Auden expressed in the 1930's, that the world is divided into "we's" and "they's" "ours" and "theirs"; "I've got to know which side I'm on./ I've got to be on a side." The intent of the play is to suggest, however, that sides and the wars and hatreds they represent offer no solutions, for no person is an island: "whatever happens on the farthest pitch,/ To the sandman in the desert or the island-man in the sea,/ Concerns us very soon." The involvement of man in his history is a purifying experience, just as the flames in the biblical furnace suggest the purgatorial nature of the dreams the men have endured. The flames in the furnace become human figures, the unquenchable fire of breath and blood, which "can only transform."

Fry comes closer in *A Sleep of Prisoners* to achieving a totally realized verse drama than in any of his other attempts. Fry's problem in moving toward longer plays was to find a form in which to put his particular kind of language into a sustainable relationship to the whole. The most critical problem encountered in the longer play, the three-act or the five-act, appears to be that of a structure in which verse can play an integral part and which will, in turn, justify the use of verse, for the problems of verse drama appear to be intensified and complicated by the necessities of the longer play. In the "seasonal comedies" and in *Curtmantle*, Fry stubbornly attacks the problem of the longer play in verse, only partially succeeding.

Fry's idea of a comedy for each season of the year is not a gimmick, but rather it belongs to the aesthetic notion that the "comedy of mood" or "comedy of seasons" can provide a unity of setting, time, and mood which will create the wholeness symbolized by the year itself.

Mood is everything in *The Lady's Not for Burning*. Two charming, young eccentrics—the rationalistic accused witch and the disenchanted soldier who wants to die—are pitted against two antagonists, one of which represents spring and all the forces of life, and the other the petty world of a society which claims that "The standard soul/ Must mercilessly be maintained. No/ Two ways of life. One God, one point of view./ A general acquiescence to the mean."

All in all, this spring comedy is determined to prove that April is *not* the cruelest month, that human beings can survive the birth pangs of self-knowledge, accepting finally even the burden of an unreasonable future and an imperfect world. Typically, love reclaims the characters for life and an intuitive recognition of the wonder of the universe. In the course of their reclamation, however, there is a good deal of sheer "talk" for its own sake of the kind that weakens rather than strengthens Fry's comedies. Even the eccentricity of the characters cannot excuse a language often so circuitously poetic that the most notable thing about it is its derivative quality. The verbal high jinks, the excesses of language and imagery are as obvious as the literary derivations, and although Fry intentionally does this sort of thing at times in a scheme of romantic mockery, the device does not always work, since he is quite capable of creating a passage bearing the same verbal characteristics when his intention is entirely otherwise.

Venus Observed, the autumnal comedy, is set in the declining season of the year, and its hero, the Duke of Altair, is well past the green age of youth; he has a grown son who becomes his rival in love and teaches him that he must accept the encroachments of age. At the beginning of the play, the Duke thinks that he has accepted the limitations imposed by his age, and he has gathered three of his former mistresses in his bedroom observatory to watch an eclipse of the sun through his beloved telescope. The Duke's son, Edgar, is to perform the Judgment of Paris for his father and present one of the three women with the symbolic apple, also appropriate to the day of the year, All Hallow's Eve, and to the autumn harvest. The apple is further to be identified with the legendary apple of the Fall of Man, so that through symbol and image, the scene of the play is extended to include the whole ruined Eden of the contemporary world, although there is no emphasis in the play on the modern situation.

The memory of Eden, of his first, unspoiled love, remains in the Duke, in spite of his autumnal resolves. When the eclipse has passed and the first renewed light of the sun reveals Perpetua Reedbeck standing in its rays, the Duke forgets that "'mellow'/ Is the keynote of the hour," and takes the apple to offer it to her youth and beauty. It is not until one of the Duke's aging mistresses destroys his observatory, which she sees as symbolic of the Duke's isolation and his invulnerability, that the Duke is brought to realize that so much he had "delighted in is all of ash." Out of the ash finally arises the Duke's acceptance of a love befitting his declining years. The action of the play brings the Duke into harmony with its autumnal mood— a mood which, like that of *The Cocktail Party*, leads all the characters to an examination of their limitations and to the adjustments necessary to make the best of the fading world in which they find themselves. In this respect, the play is close to the traditional function of comedy as a revelation of the follies and foibles of humankind, which brings human beings into an acceptable balance with society. As a part of this function, the speeches of certain characters (particularly of the Duke as Age pursuing lost Youth) are self-mocking, like those in *A Phoenix Too Frequent*, although Fry has achieved on the whole a quieter and less highly pitched verse.

The verse in this play shows, in general, a certain flexibility not achieved in the earlier comedies, and it is a verse that wears for three acts with much less friction than the verse of *The Lady's Not for Burning*. The language itself is closer to the contemporary idiom, and it is "poetic" in unobtrusive ways which involve concealed end-rhymes, internal rhymes, and alliteration. This is, on the whole, a more mature play than the earlier three-act comedy, and the language reflects this maturity. The verse almost entirely avoids the nondramatic philosophizing one ordinarily expects in a Fry play, and when such general comments do occur, they are part and parcel of the action or mood of the play.

The Dark Is Light Enough is a "winter comedy" presumable because it involves the physical decline and death (but spiritual victory) of its heroine, who triumphs in death as in life, not so much through her own action as through her influence on those about her. This is a comedy, not of manners, but of the spiritual fiber which informs the world of manners, even in a no-man's-land between two warring forces. As in *The Firstborn*, the play is held together by a single, commanding character, that of the Countess, and her sphere of influence is the area of the play, even in the final moments after she has suffered death and yet controls the action about to be performed. The language, as befits a winter comedy, is sober in comparison to that of the other comedies, but on the whole, it is undistinguished either by Fry's excesses or by his achievements. At its worst, the language of the play suffers from the same sentimentality that mars the whole work. At its best, it is a language which rises out of the situation to catch and hold the mood of the play, as when the dying Countess descends the stairs for a final Thursday evening with her devoted group of admirers and tells them, "We must value this evening as the one/ Thursday in the universe, for the rest/ Have gone, and no more may come,/ And we should be on our most immortal behaviour."

A Yard of Sun is set in an Italian summer during the first Palio to be celebrated following the conclusion of World War II. This ancient contest, with its religious and civic affirmations, becomes the fitting occasion for the trial of individual identity, which is a central action of all of Fry's plays. It is also the occasion to bring the characters into an acceptance of the flawed universe, the world that will not bend itself to their own conceptions and desires, but which is, in spite of this fact (or, more likely, because of it), worthy of acceptance and affirmation. In fact, Ernst Cassirer's definition of comedy in "An Essay on Man" seems to have been made for Fry. Cassirer sees comic art as possessing "in the highest degree that faculty shared by all art, sympathetic vision. By virtue of this faculty it can accept human life with all its defects and foibles, its follies and vices. . . . We live in this restricted world, but we are no longer imprisoned by it."

A Yard of Sun is set in the courtyard of an ancient Siena palazzo, and the scene is never varied, for in a technique reminiscent of John Millington Synge's *The Playboy of the Western World* (pr., pb. 1907), the news of the various stages of the running of the traditional horse race comes to the audience only by report. The contest, an occasion for family reunions, provides the heightened moment which unlocks the potentiality for the real challenges of the play.

The sun in this summer comedy seems to suggest to Fry the light before which the inner shadows of the characters must yield and modify themselves. The "heat of the day" (the original title of the play) is a time for clarity, and into the yard of the palazzo come nine characters, representing a variety of modern views and problems, each related to the others in ways which must be clarified before they can accept the ambiguities of their own experiences. Winning turns out, in the end, not at all to mean what the characters had thought it would.

The verse of *A Yard of Sun* is much more controlled and unobtrusive than in any of Fry's other plays. The people are more nearly people talking to one another than they are characters making poems on the stage, and the action of this play seems to fit its meaning with an ease never before achieved. There is nothing very original in the play itself, but it is original within the Fry canon in the sense that it does not strain toward either the condition of verse or the condition of drama.

The "seasonal" comedies, like all of Fry's plays, reflect his serious commitment to humanist and pacifist values and express the determined democracy of the individual spirit that is a legacy of Fry's Quaker heritage. Fry's insistence on the wonder of human life and the capacities of human beings, individually and collectively, for the growth of soul and conscience, has led him to some of the excesses of language and plotting for which he has been both accused and celebrated. Fry's career seems, ironically, almost a mirror of the effect of his best plays: a relatively brief and dazzling burst of light on the generally dark horizon of modern drama. He has persisted stubbornly through his original efforts and his translations of French playwrights to bring to what he sees as the contemporary theater's dreary realism a sense of delight and celebration that is nowhere else to be found and to wed this hopefully awakened sense of wonder to verse, a fit medium to oppose the dullness of the prevailing dialogue of contemporary realism. Fry's final reputation in the history of twentieth century drama may be that of one of the stubborn eccentrics he so loves to portray on the stage, but he will be respected for his desire to suggest a healthy—and very serious— alternative for his time.

Other major works

POETRY: *Root and Sky: Verse from the Plays of Christopher Fry*, 1975.

NONFICTION: *An Experience of Critics*, 1952; *Can You Find Me: A Family History*, 1978; *Death Is a Kind of Love*, 1979 (lecture); *Genius, Talent, and Failure*, 1987 (lecture).

SCREENPLAYS: *The Beggar's Opera*, 1953 (with Denis Cannan); *Ben Hur*, 1959; *Barabbas*, 1962; *The Bible: In the Beginning*, 1966.

TELEPLAYS: *The Canary*, 1950; *The Tenant of Wildfell Hall*, 1968; *The Brontës of Haworth*, 1973 (4 teleplays); *The Best of Enemies*, 1976; *Sister Dora*, 1977 (adaptation of Jo Manton's book).

CHILDREN'S LITERATURE: *The Boat that Mooed*, 1966.

TRANSLATIONS: *Ring Round the Moon*, 1950 (of Jean Anouilh's play *L'Invitation au Château*); *The Lark*, 1955 (of Anouilh's play *L'Alouette*); *Tiger at the Gates*, 1955 (of Jean Giraudoux's play *La Guerre de Troie n'aura pas lieu*); *Duel of Angels*, 1958 (of Giraudoux's play *Pour Lucrèce*); *Judith*, 1962 (of Giraudoux's play); *Cyrano de Bergerac*, 1975 (of Edmond Rostand's play).

Bibliography

Donoghue, Denis. *The Third Voice: Modern British and American Verse Drama*. Princeton, N.J.: Princeton University Press, 1959. A definitive study of verse drama, by no means kind to Fry's versification or his Aristotelian "action": "His permanent contribution to the theatre is likely to be slight. He is hardly as interesting as William Inge," Donoghue notes. The chapter entitled "Christopher Fry's Theatre of Words" is widely cited in all subsequent scholarship, but all chapters are pertinent to how Fry gets his poetic effects and where they fail. Index.

Fry, Christopher. *Can You Find Me: A Family History*. London: Oxford

University Press, 1978. A graceful remembrance of Fry's own childhood, but a reprise as well of his parents' and grandparents' lives and worlds (his father's last name was Harris, not Fry). Provides a strong descriptive account of the years surrounding World War I and its effects on Fry's life and art. Family trees and some photographs, but no index.

Leeming, Glenda. *Christopher Fry.* Boston: Twayne, 1990. After a brief chapter on Fry's life, the work offers a play-per-chapter discussion of the canon. It is much more a literary study of the drama than a performance study of the pieces as theater. Contains the first discussion of *One Thing More: Or, Caedmon Construed*, commissioned in 1986 by Chelmsford Cathedral and the BBC. Supplemented by a select bibliography, a chronology, and a skimpy index.

_____. *Poetic Drama.* New York: St. Martin's Press, 1989. Includes a long chapter on Fry's poetic drama, "in conventional setting." The work traces the language from early dramas ("assertive manifestation of the characters' thought") to later work ("the positive assertiveness of his language provokes critics to regard his work as like plum cake, too rich and too sweet"). Complemented by an index.

Roy, Emil. *Christopher Fry.* Carbondale: Southern Illinois University Press, 1968. From his success in 1948 ("A contemporary Shakespeare" said the press) to the inevitable comparisons to T. S. Eliot, Fry is examined to his 1961 play *Curtmantle*, one play per chapter. Attention is paid to the seasonal arrangement of his plays and to the religious view, dramatized in *A Sleep of Prisoners*, "that man can grasp hope through an endurance of suffering." Includes a bibliography, an index, a chapter on Fry's imagery, and an overview.

Salmon, Eric. *Is the Theatre Still Dying?* Westport, Conn.: Greenwood Press, 1985. *Curtmantle* and *A Phoenix Too Frequent* are treated in separate discussions around Salmon's thesis that the theater is in fact alive and well if people take "some aspects of the English-speaking theatre of the last eighty years and examine them for signs of life." Sees *Curtmantle* as "surely and safely theatrical" and laments its disappearance from the repertory. Bibliographical essay and index.

Spanos, William V. *The Christian Tradition in Modern British Verse Drama: The Poetics of Sacramental Time.* New Brunswick, N.J.: Rutgers University Press, 1967. A discussion of *A Sleep of Prisoners*, demonstrating its debt to Charles Williams' "sacramental doctrine of the Way of the Affirmation of Images." Sees Fry's "conception of human action as a figured dance that traces the outline of the mystery." Select bibliography and index.

Weales, Gerald. *Religion in Modern English Drama.* Philadelphia: University of Pennsylvania Press, 1961. Contains a chapter on T. S. Eliot and Fry, in which they are sharply contrasted: "In all of his [Fry's] work he celebrates the multiplicity of sensations that the world has to offer." Good description of Fry's theatrical apprenticeship, his relationship to words, and his achievements at religious dramatic revival. Complemented by an excellent appendix on the history of religious drama, a bibliography, and an index.

Donna Gerstenberger
(Updated by *Thomas J. Taylor*)

ATHOL FUGARD

Born: Middelburg, South Africa; June 11, 1932

Principal drama
No-Good Friday, pr. 1958, pb. 1977; *Nongogo*, pr. 1959, pb. 1977; *The Blood Knot*, pr. 1961, pb. 1963; *People Are Living There*, wr. 1962, pr. 1968, pb. 1969; *The Occupation*, pb. 1964 (one act); *Hello and Goodbye*, pr. 1965, pb. 1966; *The Coat: An Acting Exercise from Serpent Players of New Brighton*, pr., pb. 1967 (with Serpent Players); *Ten One-Act Plays*, pb. 1968 (Cosmo Pieterse, editor); *Boesman and Lena*, pr., pb. 1969; *Friday's Bread on Monday*, pr. 1970 (with Serpent Players); *Orestes: An Experiment in Theatre as Described in a Letter to an American Friend*, pr. 1971, pb. 1978; *Statements After an Arrest Under the Immorality Act*, pr. 1972, pb. 1974; *Sizwe Bansi Is Dead*, pr. 1972, pb. 1973 (with John Kani and Winston Ntshona); *The Island*, pr. 1973, pb. 1974 (with Kani and Ntshona); *Three Port Elizabeth Plays*, pb. 1974 (includes *The Blood Knot, Hello and Goodbye*, and *Boesman and Lena*); *Dimetos*, pr. 1975, pb. 1977; *A Lesson from Aloes*, pr. 1978, pb. 1981; *The Drummer*, pr. 1980 (improvisation); *"MASTER HAROLD" . . . and the boys*, pr., pb. 1982; *The Road to Mecca*, pr. 1984, pb. 1985; *A Place with the Pigs*, pr. 1987, pb. 1988; *My Children! My Africa!*, pr., pb. 1990; *Blood Knot and Other Plays*, pb. 1991; *Playland*, pr. 1992.

Other literary forms
Although Athol Fugard has written in a variety of literary forms, he is known primarily for his plays. *Tsotsi*, a long-lost novel written between 1959 and 1960 and abandoned until its publication in 1979, offers insight into Fugard's subsequent dramatic development. The eponymous antihero, known only by the South African generic label for thug or hoodlum, undergoes a week's journey into his past and present—only to have his future cut off through self-sacrifice. The novel is set in Sophiatown, then Johannesburg's black slum (where Fugard's first plays were set), and its characterization, graphic language, and sardonic humor foreshadow much in Fugard's drama.

Of Fugard's screenplays—*The Occupation* (1964), *Boesman and Lena* (1973), *The Guest: An Episode in the Life of Eugène Marais* (1977), and *Marigolds in August* (1982)—only the last three, under the superb direction of Ross Devenish, have been filmed and released. Published twice, once in 1964 as a screenplay and again in 1968 as a one-act play, *The Occupation* is a psychological tour de force in which four derelicts (three English, one Afrikaner) smash their way into an abandoned farmhouse and possess it. Their occupation is haunted, however, by the presence of a "native" outside and by the World War II memories of their leader, Cappie.

The film *Boesman and Lena* is Fugard's adaptation of his stage play. The opening shots of a bulldozer that levels the squatter's community make present what is known only retrospectively in the play. There are several other additions, and though Fugard himself portrayed Boesman, he prefers the play to the film. Nevertheless, it was a highlight of the Edinburgh Film Festival in 1973.

The Guest, an episode from the life of Eugène Marais, an early twentieth century South African naturalist, lawyer, philosopher, and drug addict, gave Fugard an opportunity to explore the life of someone who had long fascinated him and with whose addictive personality Fugard could identify. The film has been commended for Fugard's portrayal of Marais and for its stunning, at times almost surreal, cinematography.

Marigolds in August reunited Fugard with actors John Kani and Winston Ntshona for the first time since the three had collaborated in the plays *Sizwe Bansi Is Dead* and *The Island*. The film won the 1980 Johannesburg Film Festival Awards for Best Film, Best Director (Devenish), and Best Actor (Ntshona), as well as a special Berlin Film Festival Bear Award. In New York, the film received mixed reviews. *The Village Voice* charged Fugard with offering too pat a course in Empathy 101, but Vincent Canby in *The New York Times* argued that the film was "wise, tough, and theatrically effective."

Fugard's 1968 television script for the British Broadcasting Corporation, *Mille Miglia*—not published until 1984—explores in flashback the relationship between race drivers Stirling Moss and Denis Jenkinson, who won the last Italian one-thousand-mile race in 1955, and their preparations for the race. Fugard felt constricted by the factual material, and Moss and Jenkinson were not pleased with the telecast, but several critics and at least one major dramatist, Tom Stoppard, applauded Fugard's concern with the tyranny of time, the threat of death, and the game of life.

Finally, Fugard's *Notebooks 1960-1977* (1984) testify to the breadth of the influences upon him and his influence upon others. The notebook entries reflect his political engagement as well as his practical concerns as a dramatist; in addition, they are fascinating for what they reveal about the genesis of his plays.

Achievements

Fugard is South Africa's gift to world drama. Playwright, director, and actor, he is South Africa's most widely produced dramatist abroad. His plays, though rooted in one nation, have earned international acclaim. Like earlier dramatists whose work is identified with a particular region, Fugard meticulously details life in a remote corner of the globe yet raises compelling issues of general interest. Using what some consider to be the old-fashioned conventions of social realism, linear plot development, and naturalistic language graced by metaphor and symbol, Fugard has forged an impressive body of work for the theater, ranging from full-length plays to improvisational exercises for actors. These works from a self-styled white liberal constitute a crucible for South Africa's racially segregated society and for modern human beings, aliens in a world from which almost all security has diminished, the world of Jean-Paul Sartre, Albert Camus, and Samuel Beckett—Fugard's mentors. Theatrically sparse, with small casts and little, if any, reliance on elaborate sets, costumes, or props, Fugard's deceptively simple plays offer "infinite riches in a little room." They therefore have been read easily on radio and adapted frequently for television and film. On December 4, 1984, Fugard received the Common Wealth Award for Distinction in Dramatic Arts, an award which he shared with Stephen Sondheim.

Fugard's distinction as a playwright is inseparable from his contributions to and influences upon South African theater, as well as on the Yale Repertory Theatre. He has radically affected both the practice and purpose of serious drama in his native land. His interpretation of his world, his use of "poor theater" for its maximum effect, and his dedication to his actors, both black and white, have earned for him a critical respect accorded few modern playwrights. Early in his career, he chose to be a witness against what he called a "conspiracy of silence" about South Africa's apartheid legislation. That silence has been broken now, but Fugard has no illusions about his part in that. He considers theater to be no more—and no less—than a civilizing influence, one which may sensitize, provoke, or anger. He deplores the label "political playwright." He believes that if a playwright tells a story, a good one, the larger implications will take care of themselves. Since they are set in South Africa, Fugard's plays can no more ignore apartheid than William Faulkner's novels could ignore slavery and its aftermath, but Fugard's plays are not agitprop. Thus, aside from the message of his plays, critics and actors commend Fugard's craft, especially his attention to what he calls "carnal reality" and his ability to develop resonant images that repay repeated readings or performances.

Fugard's plays—and his actors—have been honored often. *The New York Times* voted *The Blood Knot* Best Play of the 1964 season. Fugard was elected Man of the Year in the Arts in South Africa in 1969. *Boesman and Lena* received an Obie Award for Distinguished Foreign Play from the *Village Voice* in 1971. Janet Suzman won the London *Evening Standard* Award for Best Actress in 1973 for her portrayal of Hester Smit in Fugard's *Hello and Goodbye*. *Sizwe Bansi Is Dead*, devised by Fugard with actors John Kani and Winston Ntshona, was chosen Play of the Year in 1974 by the London Theatre Critics. Kani and Ntshona went on to share Tony

Awards for Best Acting in the 1974-1975 New York season for *The Island*, another Fugard play devised with their help. In 1975, Fugard was commissioned by the Edinburgh Festival to write a new play, *Dimetos*, and in 1980 the Actors Theatre of Louisville (Kentucky) commissioned an improvisational work, *The Drummer*. (These works, along with *Mille Miglia*, a 1968 BBC television play, are not set in South Africa.) *A Lesson from Aloes* was awarded the New York Drama Critics Circle Award for Best New Play of the 1980-1981 season, while *"MASTER HAROLD"*... *and the boys* won both the Drama Desk Award and the Outer Critics Circle Award for Best Play of 1982, as well as a Tony Award for Zakes Mokae as Outstanding Featured Actor and the *Evening Standard* Award for Best Play of 1983. The play also won South Africa's largest cash award for theater: the AA Mutual Life/Vita Award for Best New South African Play, 1983-1984.

Moreover, Fugard has been given honorary doctorates by three South African universities—the University of Natal, Durban, in 1981; Rhodes University, Grahamstown, 1983; and the University of Capetown, in 1984. Two American universities—Yale, in 1983, and Georgetown, in 1984—have also honored Fugard with doctorates. According to the May 28, 1984, *The Washington Post*, the Georgetown degree lauded Fugard "for his compassion and his faith, for the compelling moral vision of his plays, for the quiet beauty of his craft, and for his struggle as an artist in South Africa to 'fly kites on rainy days'"—an allusion to a crucial incident and central metaphor in *"MASTER HAROLD"*... *and the boys*.

Fugard's reputation has grown with the world premieres of two plays written at Yale. Fugard finds a "beautiful irony" and "massive affirmation" in the fact that his artistic leader, Lloyd Richards, is a black man, according to *The New York Times*. Richards considers his friendship with Fugard "fascinating, strange, and subtle," but one that definitely affects "our theater, the theater." Richards is the only person to whom Fugard has ever shown rough drafts of his plays, yet Richards says, "I can't teach Athol anything; I just remind him what he already knows."

Fugard is also a gifted director; the range of his interests may be inferred from the plays he chose to direct at The Rehearsal Room in Johannesburg in the late 1950's and to stage with the Serpent Players in New Brighton from 1963 to 1973: Harold Pinter's *The Dumb Waiter* (pr. 1960), Samuel Beckett's *Waiting for Godot* (pb. 1952), John Steinbeck's *Of Mice and Men* (pb. 1937), and Jean-Paul Sartre's *Men Without Shadows* (pr. 1946) in Johannesburg; Niccolò Machiavelli's *Mandragola* (pr. 1520), Georg Büchner's *Woyzeck* (pb. 1879), Bertolt Brecht's *The Caucasian Chalk-Circle* (pr. 1948), Sophocles' *Antigone* (pr. c. 422 B.C.), August Strindberg's *The Father* (pr. 1887), Wole Soyinka's *The Trials of Brother Jero* (pr. 1960), William Shakespeare's *Coriolanus* (pr. c. 1607-1608), Albert Camus' *The Just Assassins* (pr. 1949), and Jean Genet's *Deathwatch* (pb. 1954) in New

Brighton. Fugard's talents as an actor have enabled him to perform in many of his own plays when they were first staged and now have earned for him "mega-extra" status in such films as *Gandhi* (1981, as General J. C. Smuts) and *The Killing Fields* (1984, as a United Nations official).

Fugard, preeminently a thinking playwright, is prolific. Still flexible, but wedded to telling stories with ambiguous outcomes and working from images rooted in his world, he defies categorization. His influence, national and international, is considerable, but it is too early to say what his final contribution to world drama will be. Like Helen, the reclusive seventy-year-old sculptor in and on *The Road to Mecca*, Fugard's works endure to challenge the silence and keep darkness at bay.

Biography

Harold Athol Lannigan Fugard (pronounced *fewgard*) was born June 11, 1932, in Middelburg, a town in the Great Karoo, a semidesert region of Cape Province, South Africa. The son of an Anglo-Irish father and an Afrikaner mother, Fugard is an ethnic hybrid. English is his first language, but, because of his mother's dominant personality, Afrikaner culture profoundly affected him. Fugard simultaneously honors and excoriates his Afrikaner roots. The two major abstractions of Fugard's work—love and truth—he saw fleshed out as he grew up in Port Elizabeth, a multiracial, industrial, windswept town on the eastern Cape to which his family moved when he was three.

Fugard's father lost a leg in a shipboard accident as a child, and in spite of successfully leading a series of jazz bands, he retired early, when Fugard was young, to a life of sloth and alcoholism. Fugard's ambivalent feelings about his father color much of his work, especially *Hello and Goodbye* and *"MASTER HAROLD"... and the boys*. His mother supported the family, first by running a boardinghouse, the Jubilee Hotel, and then by operating the St. George's Park Tea Room, the scene of *"MASTER HAROLD"... and the boys*. Early in life, Fugard thus learned about failed expectations, a major theme in his work, and about hard times.

As a schoolboy, Fugard, then known as Hally, shunned his peers and spent his free time with his mother's waiters, Sam Semela and Willie Malopo. (These men appear in *"MASTER HAROLD"... and the boys* under their real names.) Sam, in particular, though middle-aged, became Fugard's friend and his most influential adult figure. Fugard looked up to Sam as a man in the fullest sense of that word; while Sam taught Fugard about being a man, Fugard shared his schoolroom experiences and books with him. For some inexplicable reason, one day Fugard insulted Sam; he did not expiate his guilt for this act until he wrote *"MASTER HAROLD"... and the boys*. In real life, Sam Semela forgave Fugard almost immediately, and they remained friends until Sam died in 1983, shortly before the play in his honor opened in Johannesburg.

Fugard studied philosophy at the University of Cape Town from 1950 to 1953, but he quit immediately before his final examinations to hitchhike up Africa with a poet friend, deciding that the academic life was not for him. From 1953 to 1955, he traveled around the world on a merchant ship on which he was the only white crewman. He was married in 1956 to Sheila Meiring, who introduced him to the theater. When they moved to Johannesburg in 1958, Fugard was employed for three months as a clerk in the Fordsburg Native Commissioner's Court; then he began working with amateur black actors in Sophiatown, Johannesburg's black ghetto at that time. He also worked as a stage manager for the National Theatre Organization before he and his wife went to England and Europe in 1959.

The Fugards returned to South Africa in 1960, and the initial production of *The Blood Knot* in 1961 and its six-month tour around South Africa were crucial to Fugard's development as a playwright. In 1962, Fugard instigated a boycott of South Africa's segregated theaters by British playwrights, but by 1967 he had decided that even in such compromising circumstances, voices were preferable to silence. Fugard visited the United States briefly in 1964 and returned to England in 1966; both trips involved productions of *The Blood Knot*. His government withdrew his passport from 1967 to 1971. From 1963 to 1974, he directed and produced European plays as well as collaborating on indigenous South African material with the New Brighton actors known as the Serpent Players; many of these actors were arrested between 1965 and 1967. The Sharpeville Massacre of 1960, the Rivonia Treason Trial of 1964, the crackdown on all supporters of the banned African National Congress from 1963 to 1966, and the 1976 Soweto riots were major political upheavals which occurred while Fugard was writing. Since 1977, Fugard's reputation has been such that he divides his time between South Africa and the rest of the globe: America, Europe, Asia, and India. America, however, is the only place he could live, he claims, if he could not live in South Africa.

The early highlights of Fugard's life are many, but he has singled out some as of particular importance. For example, he says that his experience as a sailor cured him of any racial prejudice he might have had. His wife's prodding him into helping her establish a theater workshop in Cape Town, the Circle Players, in 1956 and 1957 led to the evolution of his lean, one-room dramaturgy. The move to Johannesburg and his work in the Commissioner's Court caused him to see the worst of apartheid legislation; there, an African was sent to jail every two minutes. Fugard turned this ugly nightmare to dramatic use when he devised *Sizwe Bansi Is Dead* with actors John Kani and Winston Ntshona in 1972; the play is an exposé of the passbook law, which requires every African over sixteen to carry an identity book that restricts both his employment opportunities and his movements inside South Africa.

The rejection of Fugard's scripts by the Royal Court Theatre in London in 1960, the hand-to-mouth existence the Fugards shared there, and Fugard's sense of isolation from his roots convinced him that he was a regional writer. Prior to the Fugards' return to South Africa in 1960, in response to the Sharpeville Massacre, they helped form—with Tone Brulin, David Herbert, and Clive Farrell—the short-lived New Africa Group, dedicated to the staging of original South African plays in Europe. Fugard played Okkie, the Greek who tries to pass for white, in Herbert's *A Kakamas Greek* (pr. 1960), which was set in the Karoo, Fugard's birthplace. This production won the Best Entry Award at the Festival of Avantgarde Theatre in Brussels in 1960 and toured thereafter in the Flemish part of Belgium, Holland, and Germany—performed in English. The question of racial identify in *A Kakamas Greek* also haunts Fugard's first critical success, *The Blood Knot*.

While he was writing, in solitude, *The Blood Knot, People Are Living There, Hello and Goodbye*, and *Boesman and Lena*, which detail claustrophobic relationships, Fugard was also experimenting with adapting European plays to South African life and with improvising from the raw material of his actors' lives. *The Coat* in 1967 and *Orestes* in 1971, which actress Yvonne Bryceland considers "the most important single thing" in Fugard's career, are examples of improvisations from life.

The "Statements" plays (*Statements After an Arrest Under the Immorality Act, Sizwe Bansi Is Dead*, and *The Island*), which secured Fugard's reputation outside South Africa, also evolved from collaborative theater. These plays together constitute Fugard's most outspoken indictment of apartheid. An early version of *Statements After an Arrest Under the Immorality Act* was the inaugural production in 1972 of The Space, an "open" theater in Cape Town that evaded audience segregation rulings. *Sizwe Bansi Is Dead* was next, followed by an early version of *The Island* in 1973. These two plays did not exist in written form until Fugard and actors Kani and Ntshona were safely in London, later in 1973, for the South African Season at the Royal Court Theatre. (A Beckett season ran concurrently, and Fugard finally met the playwright whom he most admires.) Nevertheless, in 1977 and 1978, Kani and Ntshona performed *Sizwe Bansi Is Dead* and *The Island* in Johannesburg at the Market Theatre, an "open" venue.

In 1974, after Fugard's success in London, *Three Port Elizabeth Plays*—including *The Blood Knot, Hello and Goodbye*, and *Boesman and Lena*—was published by Oxford University Press, with a detailed introduction by Fugard of excerpts from his then unpublished notebooks. This introduction, combined with that to *Statements After an Arrest Under the Immorality Act*, constituted the clearest summary of Fugard's aesthetics—as well as a biographical gloss on his plays—before 1984, when *Notebooks 1960-1977* appeared. In 1978, the "Statements" plays were performed and published in German; in 1979, *The Island* was translated and performed in French, while *Boesman and Lena* was translated and presented in Afrikaans in Cape Town.

Fugard returned to solo composition when *Dimetos* was commissioned by the Edinburgh Festival in 1975, but in spite of rewriting and a cast headed by Paul Scofield for the London West End run in 1976, *Dimetos* failed with critics and audiences alike. Its poetic allegory and nonregional setting are atypical of Fugard, yet the play remains one of his favorites. Like *Statements After an Arrest Under the Immorality Act*, another play that Fugard cherishes, *Dimetos* attempts to use prose musically and frequently becomes too elliptical and ambiguous.

Between 1978 and 1984, Fugard produced three major plays: *A Lesson from Aloes*, *"MASTER HAROLD"...and the boys*, and *The Road to Mecca*. Fugard's tenure at Yale, with which these plays are associated, began in January, 1980, and he later bought a house in rural New York State so that he could continue his hobby of birdwatching when he was not at the Yale Repertory Theatre.

In 1964, the Fugards moved from his mother's apartment in Port Elizabeth to a seaside cottage seven miles away. In a letter to his friend Mary Benson, Fugard wrote: "The sea is at our doorstep, there is enough land and need for the highly moral activity of tree planting and the beginning of a vegetable patch.... I've never realized fully how much of an Afrikaner I really am, until this moment when I kicked off my shoes and stood barefoot on the earth. I keep looking at my toes to see if roots haven't appeared." In *The Road to Mecca*, the pastor, Marius, enters with a basket of vegetables and proceeds sincerely to glorify a homegrown potato: "A pinch of salt and you've got a meal,... add a little butter and you have indeed got a feast." Fugard is kin to pastor Marius in his fervent embrace of nature—from snakes and aloes to men. Few playwrights know as much about plants and animals as he; his films *The Guest* and *Marigolds in August* exemplify this knowledge, but his work as a whole is pervaded by a reverence for life in all of its multiplicity. In this, as in other ways, Fugard's life and work are a testament to wholeness in a world of fragmentation.

Fugard's plays have constantly been revived and produced and have become staples of nonprofit professional theater in the United States and Great Britain. Fugard has continued to direct his own plays, both in the commercial British and in the nonprofit professional American theaters, such as his production of *My Children! My Africa!*, which enjoyed several venues, including the Lyttelton Theatre in London, the Perry Street Theatre in New York, the Yale Repertory Theatre in New Haven, and the La Jolla Playhouse in California. He also continued to act in his own plays on occasion, starring in *A Lesson from Aloes* in Los Angeles in 1991.

Analysis

Athol Fugard's plays satisfy a major criterion of good drama: the creation of vivid, lifelike characters. His characterization is immature in his early plays, *No-Good Friday* and *Nongogo*—with their black-ghetto gangsters, hustlers, musicians, whores, pimps, dreamers, and even a white priest—but these stereotypes foreshadow such fully developed characters in the 1960's plays as the half brothers in *The Blood Knot*, the landlady in *People Are Living There*, the siblings in *Hello and Goodbye*, and the destitute couple Boesman and Lena, in the play of that title. In the 1970's, Fugard created such powerful characters as the miscegenational lovers in *Statements After an Arrest Under the Immorality Act*, the urban and country blacks in *Sizwe Bansi Is Dead*, the prisoners in *The Island*, and the isolated Anglo-Afrikaner couple and their "colored" friend in *A Lesson from Aloes*. In his later plays, Fugard presents two black waiters and a teenage schoolboy (*"MASTER HAROLD" . . . and the boys*), and an elderly, reclusive sculptor, her young friend, and a local pastor (*The Road to Mecca*). Fugard's characters, who seem so specific and concrete as to personify South Africa, are at the same time universal in their humanity.

Most of these characters do little or nothing except validate their existence through words that cry out to be heard. Their language ranges from the harshly naturalistic to the eloquently poetic; their rhythms are acutely South African, yet they cross linguistic barriers just as Hamlet and Lear do. Fugard's *Notebooks 1960-1977* record the South African images from which his plays come: two brothers in a shack; a landlady who stays in her nightclothes for a whole day; a woman arriving with a suitcase and a man on crutches; a couple with their worldly possessions on their backs; six police photographs of two naked lovers; a self-confident black with a cigarette in one hand, a pipe in the other; two prisoners putting sand into wheelbarrows; a lonely man studying an aloe plant. Program notes for *"MASTER HAROLD" . . . and the boys* and *The Road to Mecca* provide images of ballroom dancing and a magical room of light and color. From such images, Fugard has crafted works of art as solid as steel, as fragile as china. Sturdy yet delicate, his plays wear well—the ultimate tribute to a master artist.

Fugard has long acknowledged his debt to Albert Camus and Samuel Beckett. In Camus, he found a kindred spirit for his worldview and his role as an artist; in Beckett, he found a dramaturgy of maximum import with minimum theatrical outlay. Confined to one room or space, two or three characters recollect, recriminate, role-play, and resign themselves to their existence in a world without meaning and little hope for change. They delude themselves with false hopes and dreams, amuse themselves with games to pass the time; such nobility as they possess comes in the fleeting, lucid moments when they acknowledge their condition—and their dependence upon each other. As does Camus, Fugard opts for a "courageous pessimism" born of the clear-sighted recognition of modern human beings' plight—trapped in a world as capricious as Ariadne's web and as mazelike as the Cretan Minotaur's labyrinth.

In his 1957 Nobel address at the University of Uppsala, Camus said, "To create today is to live dangerously"; he continued, "The suffering of mankind is such a vast subject that it seems no one could touch it unless he was like Keats so sensitive... that he could have touched pain itself with his hands." In an interview with Barrie Hough in 1977, prompted by *The Guest*, Fugard's film about Eugène Marais, Fugard commented that "one of the major Marais statements was that all living, survival, is grounded on pain.... It's really a theme that has gone through all my work; it's the string that holds all the beads together to make a necklace." Fugard has touched pain in his plays, as much as he has touched love and truth. He revels in the palpable, the tangible. In the realities of daily living—sore feet, tired bodies, arthritic hands, mounting stress, and cruel insults— Fugard reminds us that we are the sum of our pain. The whole is greater than the sum of its parts, but their interdependence is undeniable. Fugard forces us to recognize this interdependence preeminently in *The Blood Knot*, *Boesman and Lena*, *The Island*, *A Lesson from Aloes*, and *"MASTER HAROLD"* ... *and the boys*, the most representative of his plays, as well as in *The Road to Mecca*.

The two plays that began and ended Fugard's work in the 1960's, *The Blood Knot* and *Boesman and Lena*, illustrate his talent for full-bodied characterization, as well as his progression toward structural sparseness and multileveled, resonant language. The half brothers of *The Blood Knot*, bound inextricably in a union of opposites, reveal themselves completely in a long play of seven scenes that builds to a harrowing climax. The Nomadic outcasts and mixed breeds, or "Coloreds," Boesman and Lena, hover on the edge of life and death in what appears to be a cyclic pattern of eviction, of breaking and making camp, of Boesman's beating Lena, and of Lena's manic search for her identity, in two acts that are half as long as *The Blood Knot*. Unlike Beckett's tramps in *Waiting for Godot* (the closest analogue to *Boesman and Lena*), however, whose essence is not to change, Fugard's characters do change in the course of the play. Superficially, more happens in *The Blood Knot*'s shanty over a much longer period of time than the one cold evening under the stars of *Boesman and Lena*, but the latter's reduction in plot and stage business results in a thematic and symbolic complexity that allows for greater character revelation as well as greater character development.

In both plays, two characters diametrically opposite in temperament and goals explode in words and acts when confined in a small space. Such conflicts are the heart of Fugard's drama, beginning with *The Blood Knot*.

Morris, the light-skinned brother, suffers from agoraphobia—fear of open spaces—after wandering ten years trying to pass for white, while Zach, the dark-skinned brother, has suffered from claustrophobia ever since Morris returned to minister to him by ordering his life. In his notebook entry on the brothers, Fugard said, "Morris, if anything, hates himself. Zach hates the world that has decided his blackness must be punished. . . . Morris is the better equipped mentally for this last fight—also, weakened by thought and sympathy. Zach has the physical strength and impetus of hate. Zach wins." The tyrannical alarm clock that regulates the brothers' lives rings just in time to keep Zach's violence at bay. When Zach asks Morris for an explanation of why their game of black-white domination has gone awry, Morris responds, "I'll keep the clock winded, don't worry. One thing I'm certain is sure, it's a good thing we got the game. It will pass the time. Because we got a lot left, you know! Almost a whole life . . . stretching ahead. . . . I'm not too worried at all. . . . I mean, other men get by without a future. In fact, I think there's quite a lot of people getting by without futures these days." Condemned at birth to have no future, the brothers reconstructed a brief childhood reprieve in which they took an imaginary, wild, car ride—stopped only by a flock of butterflies—chased donkeys in the veld, climbed trees, teased girls, stole fruit, and caught birds. In contrast, the humor of their adult games is sardonic and menacing, their laughter double-edged. They are two particular South African brothers, yet avatars of Cain and Abel.

Like Morris and Zach, Boesman and Lena are locked in an intimate love-hate relationship as mates—one they have fallen into years before the play opens, and one which Lena chooses to reassert as the play ends, in spite of her open rebellion throughout. Motifs that recall *The Blood Knot*'s birds, donkeys, and aimless walking recur in the later play, while staccato, contrapuntal speeches are interleaved with poetic monologues in both. Lena's frenzied songs and dances on the mud flats parallel the brothers' childhood games, but the violence talked about in *The Blood Knot* actually happens in *Boesman and Lena*. Lena's bruises are real, and the old African whom she befriends dies before dawn; he literally becomes the white man's refuse that Boesman has said he and Lena are, and since they cannot dispose of him, they must resume walking. Though she threatens to remain behind, Lena prepares to follow Boesman; in response, he tells her the correct sequence of their journeys, which she had so desperately tried to get straight throughout the play—as if that knowledge would explain how she got where she is. "It doesn't explain anything," she says, but her parting shot, "I'm alive, Boesman. There's daylights left in me," is believable because she has demonstrated repeatedly her will to live.

Suicide is out of the question for Boesman and Lena. As absurd as their existence is, they endure it; they even tried to perpetuate it, but only one of Lena's babies was born alive, and it lived only six months. In recounting her past to the old African, who cannot understand her language any more than Boesman and Lena can understand his, Lena defines pain: "Pain? Yes! . . . One night it was longer than a small piece of candle and then as big as darkness. Somewhere else a donkey looked at it. . . . Pain is a candle *entjie* [end] and a donkey's face." Such metaphoric language typifies Fugard, as it does Beckett. Moreover, both have been accused of writing plays of despair or bitter comedy. Fugard defends Beckett against such charges, as many critics defend Fugard. Fugard finds Beckett's humor, combined with his love and compassion for man's "absurd and bruised carnality," positive and life-affirming; describing Beckett's humor to his wife, Fugard once said, "Smile, and then wipe the blood off your mouth." *Boesman and Lena* is Fugard's most pessimistic play, in mood and theme, but it is not morbid or maudlin; it is his most profound response to the world as he sees it, a world in which endurance and survival alone may be the only card human beings hold in a stacked deck.

In *The Island*, collaborative and improvisational in origin, Fugard experimented with the theories of Polish director Jerzy Grotowski, as he did in the unpublished *Friday's Bread on Monday*, in 1970, and *Orestes*, whose 1971 performance is described only in a letter. *The Island* is a tribute to actors' theater, but once written, it has stood on its own merits as a strong play for actors other than John Kani and Winston Ntshona, Fugard's original performers and collaborators. It reads as well as it plays. Unified structurally and centrally focused, it demonstrates Fugard's mastery of the one-act form. Its companion piece, *Sizwe Bansi Is Dead*, another virtuoso play for actors, comes closer to a stream-of-consciousness novella than to a drama built upon the classical unities of time, space, and action that Fugard observes in *Boesman and Lena* and his three subsequent critical successes. Yet Fugard has always practiced what he calls "actors' theater."

As early as 1962, Fugard defined the pure theater experience: "the actor and the stage, the actor *on* the stage. Around him is space, to be filled and defined by movement and gesture; around him is also a silence to be filled with meaning. . . ." The actor, space, and silence—Fugard continued exploring these dramatic requisites after a reading of Grotowski's *Towards a Poor Theatre* (1969) that validated the use of the actor as a creator, not simply as an interpreter. *The Island* could not have been written without Kani and Ntshona's experiences as South African blacks or without what they and Fugard knew of the Serpent Players, who had been sent to Robben Island, South Africa's hard-labor, maximum security prison primarily as political prisoners; some returned to tell their stories. (Kani and Ntshona have never been imprisoned on Robben Island, though they were arrested in 1976 before a performance of *Sizwe Bansi Is Dead* and imprisoned briefly until an international actors' protest secured their release.)

Fugard credits Grotowski with giving him the courage to "write directly into . . . space and silence via the actor," using the basic device of "challenge and response"; he also credits Brian Astbury, the founder of The Space in Cape Town, for his "vision and tenacity of purpose" in providing the venue for the "Statements" plays.

The Island, like *The Blood Knot* and *Boesman and Lena*, features two characters who are polar opposites in every sense. John and Winston (both the actors' actual names and the names of the characters) wrestle with fundamental questions of identity and purpose. The play opens and closes with the two convicts miming the futile labor of putting sand into wheelbarrows, pushing a barrow to where the other has been digging, and emptying the sand into that hole; the piles of sand therefore remain the same. A whistle blows, and the prisoners mime being handcuffed together and shackled at the ankles before the whistle blows again to send them off on a torturous three-legged run. They do not run fast enough to avoid being beaten. Bruised and bleeding, they collapse in their cell before uttering a word. After they nurse their wounds and curse their sadistic warder, John gives a news broadcast and weather report: "Black domination was chased by White domination. . . . Conditions locally remain unchanged—thunderstorms with the possibility of cold showers and rain. Elsewhere, fine and warm!" Soon, John begins to rehearse *Antigone* for a prison show. Winston does not want to play a woman, and his reluctance to appear as such is comic until the very end, when his identification with Antigone becomes complete. Condemned to life in prison, he faces the audience and cries, "Brothers and Sisters of the Land! I go now to my last journey"; he tears off his wig and confronts them with, "I go now to my living death, because I honoured those things to which honour belongs." (John had been sentenced for burning his passbook in front of a police station.)

The Island is more, however, than an anguished cry of defiance. Like all of Fugard's plays, it focuses on close human relationships; John and Winston are linked in a bond almost as indissoluble as that of Morris and Zach or Boesman and Lena—almost, because midway through the play, John discovers that he will be free in three months, while Winston must remain for life. Before receiving that news, they talked on an imaginary telephone to their friends in New Brighton, another funny game of the many that Fugard's characters play; after John's news, Winston re-creates John's release and welcome home. Ultimately, Winston recovers from his agony and, like Antigone, comes to terms with his fate. *The Island* is as compelling as Fugard's earlier plays because, once again, its particulars are transcended in a work of universal significance, a study of man's inhumanity to man and his capacity to endure that entrapment through a joy in embracing ideals—regardless of their consequences.

In *A Lesson from Aloes*, isolation, neurosis, and exile are the cost that

Fugard's characters must pay for their fidelity to the ideals of love and friendship; there is little laughter here. The three characters are Fugard's first attempt to portray his own kind: literate, well-meaning South Africans caught in their government's crackdown on dissent in 1963, which led many to flee the country. Every Fugard play can be seen as an exploration of the effects of public policy on individual lives, but *A Lesson from Aloes* is Fugard's most quietly anguished portrait of this phenomenon.

Aloes are thorny, spiky, cactuslike plants which survive without water in very harsh environments. Piet Bezuidenhout, a middle-aged Afrikaner, once an active member of an antiapartheid group that was silenced by the police, grows aloes in his back garden. Identifying them by name is his chief pleasure, other than reciting English poetry. Piet's English-speaking wife, back home after a stay in the Fort English mental home, and his "colored" friend and former comrade, Steve Daniels—preparing to leave South Africa on a one-way exit permit and just out of jail for breaking his banning order—are the other characters in this subtle but searing study of personal desolation. All three characters have internalized the shocks that their world has given them.

The first act opens with Piet trying to identify a rare aloe; this leads to a revelation of the bitterness that mars his relationship with Gladys. For her part, Gladys cannot forget the police seizure of her personal diaries during a raid prompted by Piet's political involvement; Piet broodingly wonders why his old friends suspect him of being an informer. Tension builds as Piet and Gladys await the arrival of the Daniels' family for a farewell celebration. When Steve does arrive, in the second act—without his family and a bit drunk—the party fails miserably. Playing a very nasty game, Gladys tells Steve that Piet had informed on him, but then she withdraws the charge. Piet refuses, however, to say anything: "Hell, Steve, you know why. If you could have believed it, there was no point in denying it." Apparently reconciled with Piet, Steve leaves. Gladys decides to return to the hospital, and Piet is left alone with his unidentified aloe. In spite of its explicit title and insistent metaphor, *A Lesson from Aloes* is not didactic. There are no clear-cut answers and few, if any, happy endings in Fugard's plays. Like Piet, Fugard cultivates a private garden with unidentifiable species.

In *"MASTER HAROLD" . . . and the boys*, Fugard returned to the humor associated with his earlier plays to underscore the point that personal choice and action define a life worth living. Set still further back in Fugard's past than *A Lesson from Aloes*, and his most autobiographical play, *"MASTER HAROLD" . . . and the boys* takes place in a Port Elizabeth tearoom one rainy afternoon in 1950. A long one-act play—too long perhaps—it opens with two black waiters, Sam and Willie, joking and practicing ballroom dancing for a contest two weeks away. Both men will compete if Willie can appease the partner whom he has recently beaten for not getting the quickstep right. Sam hits upon an ingenious solution for Willie's future practice sessions: "Give her a handicap. . . . Give her a ten-second start and then let Count Basie go. Then I put my money on her. Hot favorite in the Ballroom Stakes: Hilda Samuels ridden by Willie Malopo." As Sam demonstrates his superior skills, Hally, the teenage son of the tearoom owner, enters and applauds. Hally's long friendship with the waiters—especially with Sam—is soon apparent, but Hally is tense because of his father's imminent release from the hospital. Hally loves but is ashamed of his crippled, bigoted, alcoholic father and looks to Sam as a role model instead. Fugard lovingly re-creates Hally's camaraderie with the waiters; he focuses particularly on a kite that Sam made for Hally from scrap materials—a kite that miraculously flew. Nevertheless, Hally's "second family" cannot stand up against the demons of his first. These malign forces are unleashed in the play's climax, when Hally insists that the "boys" call him "Master Harold," tells them a crude racial joke, and, when Sam responds, spits in his face. Sam almost literally turns the other cheek, but Hally is too wracked with guilt to apologize. He leaves, and the curtain falls on the two waiters dancing once again—after Willie has used what was to be his bus fare home to start up the juke box.

A play about growing up and the real meaning of family as much as it is about racism, *"MASTER HAROLD" . . . and the boys* is at once exhilarating, sobering, exuberant, and wrenching. Like all of Fugard's plays, it relies upon resonant language; here, the governing metaphor is that of life as a ballroom dance, which leads Sam to dream of a world without accidents or collisions if people and nations can only get the steps right. The game that Hally and Sam play to identify "men of magnitude" who have benefited all humankind leads to some provocative choices by Hally—Charles Darwin, Leo Tolstoy, Socrates, Karl Marx, and Friedrich Nietzsche among others; Sam's choices are Abraham Lincoln, William Shakespeare, Jesus Christ, and Sir Alexander Fleming. Sam's poor-looking kite becomes the most splendid thing Hally has ever seen aloft, and the bench to which Sam ties it when he has to return to work becomes the "Whites Only" bench of Sam's final words to Hally: "If you're not careful . . . Master Harold . . . you're going to be sitting up there by yourself for a long time to come, and there won't be a kite up in the sky. . . . I reckon there's one thing you know. You don't have to sit up there by yourself. You know what that bench means now, and you can leave it any time you choose. All you've got to do is stand up and walk away from it." Avoiding sentimentality in a play that revels in sentiment is Fugard's rare achievement here; *"MASTER HAROLD" . . . and the boys* is a masterwork from a master craftsman.

Fugard's experiments as a dramatist have been within the confines of social naturalism or realism. His modes are representational rather than expressionist or surreal; his plots are convincing; his language is often poetic but rarely abstruse, colloquial but rarely vulgar. In short, Fugard is not an innovator but a conservator: He emulates the best of his predecessors, but he translates their voices and techniques into his own uniquely South African vision. Over the years—a quarter of a century—he has become inimitable, and no more so than in *The Road to Mecca*. A three-character play, like *"MASTER HAROLD"... and the boys*, *The Road to Mecca* is one of Fugard's most daring experiments.

The play is set in the autumn of 1974, and all three of its characters are white: two proud Afrikaners who live in New Bethesda (a village in the Great Karoo) and an equally proud young English-speaking schoolteacher from Cape Town. The plot is essentially uncomplicated. The young woman, Elsa Barlow, drives eight hundred miles for an overnight visit with her old friend, Miss Helen—a reclusive sculptor whom the local pastor, Marius Byleveld, wants to put in a nursing home for her own security. In the first act, the two women slowly reestablish their long-standing friendship, but Marius arrives at the opening of the second act and begins to undermine Miss Helen's confidence in her ability to cope and to create. Elsa briefly adopts Marius' point of view when he tells her that Miss Helen almost set her house on fire earlier. Finally, in a moving reverie about the purpose of her Mecca, Miss Helen becomes courageous enough to dismiss Marius and assert her right to live with the danger of her creative impulses. Disheartened by his failure to convert Helen—and to make her love him—Marius leaves. The play ends with the women trusting each other once again.

While this plot is fairly conventional, Fugard's choice of characters, the importance of the set, and the focus on the self-realization of the artist mark this play as a genuine advance for Fugard, a widening of his range. While women and their concerns crop up obliquely in other Fugard plays— especially in *People Are Living There* and *Boesman and Lena*—*The Road to Mecca* is Fugard's first attempt to fill space with two women talking, arguing, and nurturing each other. It is also the first time Fugard has dramatized the necessary isolation of the artist. Fugard's epigraph for *The Road to Mecca* is an Emily Dickinson poem: "The soul selects her own society/ Then shuts the door./ On her divine majority/ Obtrude no more." An extended metaphor for the artist's vision—its genesis and its consequences—*The Road to Mecca* may also be read as a parable about pain, the pain of loving and not being loved. Apartheid comprises only the subtext of the play, but Fugard's initial title was "My English Name Is Patience." These are the words of the young, barefoot Afrikaner woman whom Elsa befriends en route to Helen's house. This absent character pervades *The Road to Mecca* from beginning to end—like so many of Fugard's striking offstage presences, whose silences become virtually audible. What all of these silent characters share is a need for love.

Near the end of *The Road to Mecca*, candles flicker in mirrors and the light on the walls—a stunning witness to Fugard's belief that the "candle burns brighter because the night is dark" and an answer to his question, "Would the making of meaning be so moving without the eternal threat of chaos and nothingness?" Miss Helen's laboriously crafted garden of statues—all manner of animals, camels, wisemen, mermaids, and earth goddesses pointing East—does exist, at the home of the real Helen, Helen Niemand, in New Bethesda, South Africa. Created over a remarkable twenty years of Helen's life, from age fifty to seventy, by a small, slight woman using broken bits of glass and hand-mixed cement, the statues are mute witnesses to her courage, integrity, and imagination. Thought mad by her myopic neighbors, she persevered alone. In her life and work, Fugard found the perfect fusion of symbol and referent, fiction and fact. All artists try to give meaning to matter, form to the formless, but only rarely does an artist give meaning to beauty, truth, love, and trust in so magical a form as *The Road to Mecca.*

A Place with the Pigs, based on the actual story of a World War II deserter who hid for years in a pigsty, is a symbolic work that alludes to Fugard's own battles with alcoholism. *My Children! My Africa!*, also based on a true story, concerns the murder of an idealistic black South African schoolteacher by his own students. Significantly, one of Fugard's major concerns is the relationship between teacher and learner and the frequent shifts in their roles. To *The Road to Mecca*'s Miss Helen—his master teacher—Fugard gives the words that sum up his life's work: "Light just one little candle in here, let in the light from just one little star, and the dancing starts." Candles, stars, and dancing, healing images from art for a suffering world: Such is the theater of Athol Fugard.

Other major works

NOVEL: *Tsotsi*, 1979.

NONFICTION: "The Gift of Freedom," in *At the Royal Court: Twenty-five Years of the English Stage Company*, 1981 (Richard Findlater, editor); *Notebooks 1960-1977*, 1984.

SCREENPLAYS: *The Occupation*, 1964; *Boesman and Lena*, 1973; *The Guest: An Episode in the Life of Eugène Marais*, 1977; *Marigolds in August*, 1982.

TELEPLAY: *Mille Miglia*, 1968.

Bibliography

Benson, Mary. "Keeping an Appointment with the Future: The Theatre of Athol Fugard." *Theatre Quarterly* 7, no. 28 (1977): 77-86. A personal biography regarding Fugard's wife and daughter, his early career struggles, and his aesthetic debts to Jerzy Grotowski, Albert Camus, and others. Benson's interview is followed by some acting comments by and about Fugard. The entire issue is devoted to South African theater.

Fugard, Athol. "Athol Fugard's South Africa: The Playwright Reveals Himself to a Fellow Writer." Interview by André Brink. *World Press Review* 37 (July, 1990): 36-39. Excerpted from the Cape Town periodical *Leadership*, Brink discusses Fugard's "commitment to the search for meaning" in a warm interview following the opening of *My Children! My Africa!*. Fugard states that he regrets the time he must spend away from Africa, where his energies belong.

Gray, Stephen. *Southern African Literature: An Introduction.* New York: Barnes & Noble Books, 1979. A strong discussion of *Boesman and Lena*, "seen by more South African audiences than any other South African play," in its stage or film versions. Gray interprets the play as a "rewording of the myth" of Hottentot Eve: "The play is ultimately more about the strains of the marriage bond between her and her husband than the colour problem which aggravates it."

Green, Robert J. "Politics and Literature in Africa: The Drama of Athol Fugard." In *Aspects of South African Literature*, edited by Christopher Heywood. New York: Africana Publishing Company, 1976. Examines the "repressive and philistine, censorious and neurotically suspicious" nature of the society in which Fugard lives and which he reflects in his writing. Fugard dramatizes the change in a person from "a unit in a family structure to . . . a citizen."

Vandenbroucke, Russell. *Truths the Hand Can Touch: The Theatre of Athol Fugard.* New York: Theatre Communications Group, 1985. A full study of the playwright's life, work, and philosophies. Contains introductory material on South Africa and a concluding chapter on influences, crosscurrents, language, style, and critical reputation. Appendices offer the full text of *The Drummer*, an essay on *Dimetos*, and a production chronology. Bibliography and index.

Walder, Dennis. *Athol Fugard.* New York: Grove Press, 1985. A general survey and appreciation of Fugard's work to *"MASTER HAROLD" . . . and the Boys.* his plays speak "not only of the South African dimension of man's inhumanity to man, but also of the secret pain we all inflict upon each other in the private recesses of our closest relationships," Walder remarks. Plates and index, but no chronology.

Nancy Kearns
(Updated by *Thomas J. Taylor*)

CHARLES FULLER

Born: Philadelphia, Pennsylvania; March 5, 1939

Principal drama

Sun Flowers, The Rise, pr. 1968 (one-acts); *The Village: A Party*, pr. 1968 (retitled *The Perfect Party*, pr. 1969); *In My Many Names and Days*, pr. 1972; *Candidate*, pr. 1974; *In the Deepest Part of Sleep*, pr. 1974; *The Brownsville Raid*, pr. 1976; *Sparrow in Flight*, pr. 1978; *Zooman and the Sign*, pr. 1980, pb. 1982; *A Soldier's Play*, pr. 1981, pb. 1982; *Sally, Prince*, pr. 1988 (two parts of a projected five-part play, *We*); *Burner's Frolic*, pr. 1990.

Other literary forms

Charles Fuller is known primarily for his plays. He adapted his screenplay *A Soldier's Story* (1984) from his drama *A Soldier's Play*.

Achievements

Fuller is one of a growing number of African-American playwrights who have entered the mainstream of American drama. Previously, plays dealing with the black experience, such as Louis Peterson's *Take a Giant Step* (pr. 1954), Lorraine Hansberry's *A Raisin in the Sun* (pr., pb. 1959), and Ossie Davis' *Purlie Victorious* (pr. 1961), were rueful reproaches of white intolerance. Probably because of the period during which they were written (the early 1960's), they did not seek to stir up violent passions but rather to nudge the audience's sensibilities; as a result, they could enjoy a modest run in the commercial theater on Broadway. By the end of the 1960's, however, the Off-Broadway theater, which was always more daring (and less expensive), encouraged plays such as *Dutchman* (pr., pb. 1964) by Amiri Baraka (Everett LeRoi Jones), *Ceremonies in Dark Old Men* (pr. 1965) by Lonne Elder III, and *No Place to Be Somebody* (pr. 1967) by Charles Gordone, the first black playwright to win a Pulitzer Prize in 1970; these works paved the way for a more aggressive theater reflecting more militant times. As a result, when Fuller appeared on the scene, while he was able to dramatize the plight of African Americans for audiences that were more receptive than they had been in the past, he differed from his fellow playwrights in that he examined the effect of violence *among* black people as resulting from their environment.

Several of Fuller's plays deal with black-on-black murder and are constructed as mysteries; the hunt is on to discover not only the killer's identity but also the cause of the crime. His plays are less traditional in structure, freely moving back and forth in time with great fluidity. His characters often break the illusion of the fourth wall by actively engaging the audience in soliloquies, so that although his subject matter is realistic, his technique is expressionistic. In addition to his own screen adaptation of his drama *A Soldier's Play* (the film version is entitled *A Soldier's Story* and was a great success), he has contributed an adaptation of an Ernest J. Gaines story to public television and an original script to network television. He has also taught at Temple and Toronto universities. Fuller has been the recipient of two Off-Broadway awards (Obies), of Rockefeller and National Endowment for the Arts grants (both in 1976), of a Guggenheim Fellowship in 1977, of an Outer Critics Circle Award in 1982, and, also in 1982, of a Pulitzer Prize—the second awarded to an African-American playwright.

Biography

Charles Fuller was born in Philadelphia, Pennsylvania, on March 5, 1939. In the course of time, his parents gave shelter to twenty foster children, eventually adopting two of them. The family lived in a Philadelphia housing project until Fuller's father, a printer, went into business for himself and became one of the first African Americans admitted to the local printer's union. Soon, the family moved to a racially mixed neighborhood in North Philadelphia, where the Fullers, devout Roman Catholics, sent their children to integrated parochial schools.

As a young boy, Fuller became interested in books through helping his father correct galley proofs; when he was thirteen and had gone to the theater for the first time in his life to see Molly Picon performing in Yiddish (a language he did not even understand), he was so exhilarated that he was convinced he wanted to do nothing but write plays. In high school, he formed a lifelong friendship with Larry Neal, to whom he later dedicated *A Soldier's Play* and after whom he modeled its leading character, Captain Richard Davenport. Because Neal was also devoted to literature, eventually becoming a published poet and critic, the two young men buoyed up each other's ambitions. After graduation from high school in 1956, Fuller, an English major, attended Villanova University, where he was discouraged from writing because of his race. He left in 1959 to enlist in the army in Japan and South Korea, an experience he prefers not to discuss although it must have served as material for his plays. Returning to civilian life in 1962, he registered at La Salle College, studying at night while supporting himself by working as a bank loan collector in a loan company, as a student counselor at Temple University, and later as a housing inspector for the city. During this time, he kept alive his love for drama by helping to found and run the Afro-American Art Theatre in Philadelphia, creating a kind of street theater for ghetto inhabitants. After his first play was produced at Princeton's McCarter Theatre in 1968, Fuller left La Salle College without graduating and devoted himself full-time to his literary career. His plans include work on a musical and a cycle of plays concerning the African-American experience from 1866 to 1900.

Analysis

While the plays of Charles Fuller, like those of other African-American dramatists, explore the tensions in a society where the African-American minority is constantly exploited and repressed by the white majority, Fuller has set his sights on changing the way Western civilization perceives black people. At the same time, he attempts to avoid stereotyping whites, insisting that groups are formed of individuals, and all are different, some good, some bad. As a consequence, his characters have greater depth and complexity, and he avoids the clichéd situations that afflict so many problem plays. He is also deeply interested in telling a story, which is the point at which he usually begins his plays. First, what happened; then, to whom; and finally, why? Even after these questions appear to be answered, the results often raise greater issues that lead to even more perplexing questions. Ambiguity, not resolution, is at the heart of Fuller's work.

Fuller's major concern is not only the violence in today's universe and the way it erodes character but also the violence that black people employ against one another. Although they occupy a world originally shaped by whites who enslaved and abused them, African Americans continue to prey upon one another while accepting the role of victim at the hands of their oppressors. The cycle is always the same: sullen passivity that erupts into armed rebellion, followed by chaos, before subjugation and a relapse into bitter acceptance. All of his plays possess this rhythm, regardless of the difference in subject matter; artistically, they are a poignant echo of real life, of the race riots that have burned American cities since the 1960's. Yet, though Fuller's canvas is large, his use of the personalized grief of his characters gives the plays a human scale; he is never didactic.

In his first full-length play, *The Village: A Party*, he builds the story around a community composed of five interracial couples. When the black leader falls in love with a black woman, against all the rules of their society, disaster occurs. What is original here is the way Fuller turns accepted convention upside down: In real life, obstacles to marriage confront people of different races. If the play, however, is taken as a metaphor for the barriers encountered by slaves who were forbidden to marry, it becomes clear that Fuller is condemning any law that arbitrarily decides what is right or wrong without considering its effect on human beings. His next work, *In My Many Names and Days*, consists of six one-act plays about a black family, a structure he would adopt again when planning his five-play cycle of full-length dramas. *Candidate* represents his study of a black man's campaign to become mayor of his city and the struggles this entails, revealing Fuller's growing attraction to political themes. Since Fuller was becoming increasingly engrossed by the Civil War (he dates the African-American relation to the United States from the Emancipation Proclamation), he blended politics with history in his greatest success until then, *The Brownsville Raid.*

While working in New York with the Negro Ensemble Company, which had previously staged his first play for the group (*In the Deepest Part of Sleep*), Fuller showed the direction that his future plays would take. Using an event that had actually occurred, *The Brownsville Raid* dramatizes the story of a company of black soldiers who, in 1906, were wrongfully accused of causing a riot in Texas and shooting a man. Fuller in the play also explores the relationship between President Theodore Roosevelt and Booker T. Washington, who asks his black editors to play down the "incident" in order to preserve the peace. The soldiers are dishonorably discharged, and only sixty years later are they vindicated when the truth is discovered. For all of them, however, it is too late.

Although Fuller returned to a smaller-scale play with *Zooman and the Sign*, he again used the device of a murder investigation, which had already appeared in *The Brownsville Raid*, to propel the story. In addition, he began experimenting with the title character's soliloquies, which alternated with the general action, giving the play an abrupt, stop-start rhythm. The situation in *Zooman and the Sign* is one all too recognizable today: A twelve-year-old girl is accidentally killed in a fight between two street gangs, and the play charts the efforts of her anguished parents to discover the killer. Equally harrowing is the underlying theme: The father, in despair that none of his neighbors will come forward to identify the killer (because they are afraid that as witnesses they will have to deal with the police, though they themselves are innocent), puts up a sign outside his house proclaiming that his daughter's killers are free because of the community's indifference. The neighbors, in turn, are so incensed by the accusation that they threaten his life and attempt to tear down the sign. Their rage, in short, is turned against one of their own people; they have lost their sense of responsibility to one another because it has been destroyed by the very institution that should be protecting them: the law. Here, Fuller has touched on a universal theme, for in just such a way were Nazi concentration-camp monitors, though prisoners themselves, wont to ally themselves against their fellow captives because of their own brutalization. Meanwhile, the killer, Zooman, has proclaimed himself to the audience and in his soliloquies explains his way of life, noting that if a black man kills a black man and is not caught immediately, the authorities forget about it. In an ironic twist, the dead girl's uncle, unaware of the murderer's identity, accidentally shoots him, just as the niece was accidentally killed. When the parents look at the dead face of the "perpetrator," it is that of a teenage boy who, in his mind, has made virility synonymous with violence.

In his finest and most successful work, *A Soldier's Play*, which Fuller says was inspired by Herman Melville's *Billy Budd, Foretopman* (1924), he combines and perfects the themes and technique of his two previous dramas. Calling upon audience imagination, he sets his story in a space almost Elizabethan in its use: minimal scenery, few props, and areas that could be transformed from outdoors to indoors or from an office to a soldier's bunk. In addition, as one character is narrating an event in the present moment, by crossing from one side of the stage to the other, he moves into time past.

The play is a mixture of fact and fiction. It depicts an actual unit of black soldiers in the 1940's, stationed in a small Southern town while awaiting transfer to Europe. One of the ironies of the situation is the fact that while they are fighting for freedom abroad, they are still segregated at home. The play opens with true Elizabethan violence: A black sergeant is murdered by someone unseen, and he cries out in his death agony, "They still hate you," the sense of which is obscure until the pieces fall into place. The murder worries the white officer in charge of the group because of the suspicion that it was committed by the Ku Klux Klan, resentful that black soldiers had been quartered in the Klan's vicinity. A black officer, Captain Richard Davenport, who is also a lawyer, is sent to investigate; his presence disconcerts the white officers, one of whom confesses that he cannot accustom himself to the sight of an African American in charge. The black soldiers, who are pathetically proud of Davenport's status, are nevertheless unresponsive to his questions because, like the uncooperative neighbors of *Zooman and the Sign*, they are fearful that anything they reveal will cause trouble for them with the white authorities.

What finally emerges is the portrait of the murdered: He is the sadistic Sergeant Waters who, ashamed of being black, drove his men unmercifully, particularly one private, C. J. Memphis. Waters was infuriated by the good-natured, slow-moving, guitar-strumming C. J., who, he believed, prevented ambitious African Americans from moving ahead because he seemed to represent the traditional "nigguh" as seen by whites. Waters harassed C. J., first accusing him of a shooting in town, of which he was innocent, and then provoking him into a fight so that he can be arrested for attacking his superior. Unable to endure being imprisoned like a caged bird, C. J. killed himself; in revenge for what Waters has done, Private Peterson, the most intelligent and, therefore, the most rebellious man in the unit, shot Waters and fled, accompanied by his friend, Private Wilkie, who had witnessed the murder.

When the two are caught, Davenport asks why Wilkie stood by and did nothing while one African American murdered another; all Wilkie can stammer is that he was afraid. Before his death, Waters had gone on a drunken binge to erase the memory of what had happened to C. J.; encountering two white officers, Waters had found in alcohol the courage to speak disrespectfully to them. They, in turn, had beaten him brutally and left him on the road at the moment when Peterson found him, began an argument with him, and finally shot him. In Peterson's eyes, Waters is the real villain, not because he drove C. J. to suicide but because he was so full of hatred for his own blackness. The scene dissolves to the beginning, and suddenly, it becomes clear what Waters meant as he was dying: there is no use in struggling because no matter what black people do, white people will always hate them. At that moment, Waters becomes not a villain but the product of a society that has used him, first to destroy his fellow African Americans and then to turn his rage on himself. At the end, the unit is transferred to Europe, where, Davenport tells the audience, it was wiped out by a German advance. Grudgingly, the white captain admits that he will have to get used to the idea of African Americans having positions of authority.

Some black critics believe that Fuller softened the conclusion in order to make the play palatable to white audiences: The truth triumphs, the innocents are exonerated, the white captain apologizes, and the black captain has proved himself worthy of his assignment. This play, however, has no happier ending than a Shakespearean tragedy. There are resolutions, but they leave a bitter taste because there are no real winners, only an overwhelming sense of wasted lives.

Once more, Fuller moved back to American history. After watching the classic film *One Third of a Nation* (1939), with its infamous depiction of black-white relationships, Fuller decided to counter with his own perspective and planned his five-part opus, *We.* The first, *Sally,* concerns runaway slaves rebelling against the government's decision to pay them for their work three dollars per month less than whites; the second play, *Prince,* which reintroduces some of the same cast, tells the story of slaves following the Union army. Despite their liberation, they are still forced to pick cotton because of economic hard times. The mood of both plays is that of a trust betrayed. Both plays were produced by the Negro Ensemble Company but were not enthusiastically received. Nevertheless Fuller's five-part cycle is a form that attracted African-American playwright August Wilson. Fuller's determination to give his characters reality by providing them with a background, a history, and a past, his dogged honesty in exploring the results of racial conflict without once resorting to cartoonlike figures or simplistic solutions, and his bold experiments with space and time—all these elements, together with the passion that energizes his work, make him an impressive artist who has contributed a unique voice to the American theater.

Other major works

SCREENPLAY: *A Soldier's Story*, 1984 (adapted from his drama *A Soldier's Play*).

TELEPLAYS: *Roots, Resistance, and Renaissance*, 1967 (series); *Mitchell*, 1968; *Black America*, 1970-1971 (series); *The Sky Is Gray*, 1980 (from the story by Ernest J. Gaines).

Bibliography

Banham, Martin, ed. *The Cambridge Guide to World Theatre.* New York: Cambridge University Press, 1988. Errol Hill, a black writer and educator, contributes an article on the African-American theater, its history and development, which are important factors in the career of Fuller. Hill also discusses the playwright's two best-known plays in terms of their favorable reception by white critics and the more reserved attitude of black critics.

Boardman, Gerald. *The Oxford Companion to American Theatre.* New York: Oxford University Press, 1984. Contains a long and useful discussion of black playwrights in American theater, giving invaluable insights into the struggle of African-American artists, particularly playwrights, to find a place for themselves. How Fuller emerged from such a background is amply documented.

Fuller, Charles. "Pushing Beyond the Pulitzer." Interview by Frank White. *Ebony* 38 (March, 1983): 116. In this interview, Fuller appraises what the Pulitzer Prize has meant to him and discusses the kind of plays he wishes to write—broader in scope, freer in style. He offers some illuminating details about his association with the Negro Ensemble Company and his method of work with its director and playwright Douglas Turner Ward.

_____. "When Southern Blacks Went North." Interview by Helen Dudar. *The New York Times*, December 18, 1988, p. C5. This interview was conducted with Fuller after the two plays in his cycle, *We*, opened at the Negro Ensemble Company's theater. Fuller explains his plan to dramatize the lives of men and women as they moved North to escape slavery in the South. Fuller's goal has been to give literary permanence to black history that has been handed down largely through oral tradition.

Griffiths, Trevor R., and Carole Woddis. *The Back Stage Theatre Guide.* New York: Backstage Books, 1991. This important critical overview of the African-American theater not only discusses its beginnings and development but also compares it with the emerging Black Theatre in Great Britain. Although the problems are approached differently by American and English dramatists, the common thread of racism unites them. Includes a valuable assessment of Fuller.

Moritz, Charles, ed. *Current Biography*, 1989. New York: H. W. Wilson, 1989. The article on Fuller deals with his early career in the theater that he ran in Philadelphia. It also emphasizes his conviction that black-white relationships must be seen in all their complexity if they are ever to be understood.

Savran, David. *In Their Own Words: Contemporary American Playwrights.* New York: Theatre Communications Group, 1988. Includes one of the best and most comprehensive articles on Fuller. It offers a brief critique of his major plays and then records an interview held between Fuller and Savran in the former's apartment on November 28, 1986. In this free-ranging discussion, Fuller touches on everything from his taste in literature (Franz Kafka, Jean-Paul Sartre) to his experiments in dramatic technique and his experience in adapting *A Soldier's Play* for the screen. Photograph.

Mildred Kuner

JOHN GALSWORTHY

Born: Kingston Hill, England; August 14, 1867
Died: London, England; January 31, 1933

Principal drama

The Silver Box, pr. 1906, pb. 1909; *Joy*, pr. 1907, pb. 1909; *Strife*, pr., pb. 1909; *Justice*, pr., pb. 1910; *The Little Dream*, pr., pb. 1911; *The Eldest Son*, pr., pb. 1912; *The Pigeon*, pr., pb. 1912; *The Fugitive*, pr., pb. 1913; *The Mob*, pr., pb. 1915; *A Bit o'Love*, pr., pb. 1915; *The Little Man*, pr. 1915, pb. 1921; *The Foundations*, pr. 1917, pb. 1919; *Defeat*, pr. 1920, pb. 1921; *The Skin Game*, pr., pb. 1920; *A Family Man*, pr. 1921, pb. 1922; *The First and the Last*, pr., pb. 1921; *Hall-marked*, pb. 1921; *Punch and Go*, pb. 1921, pr. 1924; *The Sun*, pb. 1921, pr. 1922; *Loyalties*, pr., pb. 1922; *Windows*, pr., pb. 1922; *The Forest*, pr., pb. 1924; *Old English*, pr., pb. 1924; *The Show*, pr., pb. 1925; *Escape*, pr., pb. 1926; *Exiled*, pr., pb. 1929; *The Roof*, pr., pb. 1929.

Other literary forms

There are six multivolume editions of John Galsworthy's collected works; the most important and comprehensive is the thirty-volume Manaton edition (1922-1936). Galsworthy wrote prolifically, composing many novels, poems, stories, addresses, sketches, and essays.

Achievements

Galsworthy's literary reputation rests soundly upon his fiction, especially the novels and stories collected in *The Forsyte Saga* (1922). Adapted for television by the British Broadcasting Corporation, *The Forsyte Saga* appeared in Great Britain, Canada, the United States, and other countries during the late 1960's and early 1970's, reviving interest in his fiction.

Several of Galsworthy's plays gained critical and popular approval at the time of their first production or early revival in England, Europe, and America; they were translated into many languages, and their popularity in the 1920's contributed to the recognition which culminated with the Nobel Prize in 1932. Galsworthy wrote realistic, often almost documentary "problem plays," which focused on social problems far more impartially than was usual in contemporary social melodrama. Social issues such as labor unrest, prison reform, and anti-Semitism, all of which Galsworthy addressed dramatically, continue to be of great concern, but Galsworthy's plays, however much they spurred reform in attitudes or legislation in their own day, are now out of date. Their topicality and their uneasy tension between didactic moralizing and melodramatic theatricality have ensured that there is little interest in reviving his plays.

Biography

John Galsworthy was born August 14, 1867, at Kingston Hill, Surrey, to John Galsworthy, a kind, charming, and prosperous London lawyer and company director whom his son idolized, and Blanche Bartleet, an unimaginative, fussy, and religious woman to whom Galsworthy was never close. The Galsworthys were a newly rich, upper-middle-class family; their wealth came from house and shop rentals and from speculations and investments in real estate which were begun by Galsworthy's grandfather, a merchant who came from Devon to settle in London.

Because of the family's wealth, Galsworthy enjoyed a childhood of privilege and luxury; his family could afford the kind of education his father had not had, so Galsworthy was privately tutored before being sent at age nine to a preparatory school at Bournemouth. He went on to Harrow, where he distinguished himself as an athlete, and then entered New College, Oxford, where he seemed more interested in behaving like a gentleman of leisure, dressing well, and gambling on the horses than in studying. He was graduated in 1889 with a second-class degree in jurisprudence and continued to study law until 1894 at Lincoln's Inn in London; apparently, he wanted to please his father by following in his footsteps. He found the study and work boring and completed only one law case; he preferred hunting, shooting, and the company of a young singing teacher. His father disapproved of the infatuation and sent Galsworthy on several trips abroad to cure him of it. Sailing home from the South Pacific islands and Australia in 1893, Galsworthy met Joseph Conrad, then second mate on the *Torrens*; Conrad afterward became Galsworthy's lifelong friend. Galsworthy had undertaken the trip partly in the hope of meeting Robert Louis Stevenson, whose fiction he admired, but he showed no serious interest in becoming a writer himself for two more years.

In 1895, Galsworthy's acquaintance with his cousin Arthur's wife, Ada Nemesis Pearson Cooper Galsworthy, turned into an adulterous affair. Ada, the illegitimate daughter of Anna Pearson of Norwich, had been adopted by a Norwich physician, Emanuel Cooper, who provided for her and her brother in his will. Ada married unwisely; her escape from the unhappy marriage to Arthur had a profound emotional effect on her and on John Galsworthy, who transformed the episode into fiction several times, most notably into the marriage of Soames and Irene Forsyte in *The Man of Property* (1906). With Ada's advice and encouragement, and with support from a private income provided by his father, Galsworthy abandoned his abortive career at law and began writing fiction; his first stories appeared pseudonymously in 1897. Between 1895 and 1905, Galsworthy and Ada continued their affair, living separately in London but traveling together on vacations abroad. Galsworthy published three novels and two books of stories before his marriage to Ada in 1905 and made friends with a group of writers that included Conrad, Ford Madox Ford, Constance Garnett, and Edward Garnett, all of whom provided encouraging criticism of his work.

In 1906, Galsworthy scored a double success, publishing *The Man of Property* (the first and best novel of the Forsyte series) and producing *The Silver Box*, his first play. Staged at the Royal Court Theatre by the Barker-Vedrenne management, the play attracted favorable attention for its unsparing portrayal of one law for the rich and another for the poor. Its concern for issues of social importance set the tone for Galsworthy's best plays, *Strife*, *Justice*, *Loyalties*, and *Escape*. Galsworthy was soon spoken of, together with George Bernard Shaw, James M. Barrie, and Harley Granville-Barker, as part of a new renaissance in English drama.

Galsworthy's new literary prominence coincided with the social respectability he enjoyed by being married, and he soon felt able to speak out and to write pamphlets, letters, and essays on a number of subjects, such as humane slaughtering of animals, prison reform, and censorship in the theater. He told Ada that after coming down from Oxford to London and being sent to collect rents on some of his family's properties in poor neighborhoods, his social conscience had been awakened, and throughout the remainder of his life, he showed sympathy and concern for those less fortunate than he. He not only wrote on their behalf but also provided charitable assistance in the manner of his character Wellwyn in *The Pigeon*. Not a religious man, Galsworthy was disgusted with people who claimed to be Christians yet would not act charitably toward those in need. His novel *The Island Pharisees* (1904) portrays the rebellion of a young gentleman against upper-class social and religious hypocrisy. Particularly during his ten-year affair with Ada, during which he was ostracized from polite society, he seems to have felt strongly a sense of identity with social outsiders such as prisoners (he visited Dartmoor Prison to study conditions of servitude) and the poor.

After their marriage, the Galsworthys lived comfortably and pleasantly in London and in the countryside. Ada, plagued by illnesses during the English winters, liked to travel to warmer countries, and the Galsworthys made frequent and extensive trips abroad. Galsworthy seemed to be able to write copiously wherever they traveled. Yet success and comfort had their penalties: Though his books usually sold quite well, the quality of Galsworthy's writing did not improve significantly, and the onset of World War I severely shook his optimistic belief in the possibility of humanity's progress toward a better world.

After the war, Galsworthy's reputation grew with the publication of *The Forsyte Saga* and with the popular success of three plays, *The Skin Game*, *Loyalties*, and *Escape*. Galsworthy refused a knighthood but accepted many honorary degrees, the Order of Merit (1929), and the 1932 Nobel

Prize in Literature. He was an active member of PEN, the international writers' association, from 1921 until his death, probably caused by a brain tumor, on January 31, 1933.

Analysis

John Galsworthy's strengths and weaknesses as a dramatist both derive from his commitment to the ideas and methods of realistic drama. He was neither a religious man nor a political activist, and his plays spoke for no specific ideology or orthodoxy, but he believed that "every grouping of life and character has its inherent moral; and the business of the dramatist is so to pose the group as to bring that moral poignantly to the light of day." This meant, as he said in "Some Platitudes Concerning Drama," that "a drama must be shaped so as to have a spire of meaning."

Such a theory of drama attempts two mutually contradictory tasks: first, the objective, balanced, impartial depiction of reality, and second, the embodiment of the playwright's subjective, ethical, emotional response in the posing or shaping of a moral spire of meaning. Galsworthy's plays are secular morality plays; his gentlemanly didacticism issues in dramatic sermons which attempt to evoke sympathy and understanding for the human condition and which teach the humanistic creeds of civility, compromise, and fair play. In Galsworthy's plays, the sentimental or melodramatic pointing of a moral frequently undercuts the attempt to depict faithfully the problems of individual characters or social groups.

The realistic problem play was not a new form when Galsworthy took it up; its development in England can be traced back to the middle of the nineteenth century, when Tom Taylor and Thomas William Robertson attempted to leaven their melodramas with realistic settings and restrained social comment. (Robertson's *Caste*, produced in 1867 and notable for dramatizing a marriage across class lines, was Galsworthy's favorite play when he was at Oxford.) In the late nineteenth century, this English tradition drew strength from the influence of Henrik Ibsen's realistic social dramas, which were championed in England by William Archer and also by Shaw, who published *The Quintessence of Ibsenism* during this period (1891, 1913). Following Ibsen's example but lacking his genius, Henry A. Jones and Arthur Wing Pinero combined upper-middle-class marriage problems with the form of the well-made play; the result was a rejuvenation of English drama. Though he wrote comedy in the paradoxical mode pioneered by W. S. Gilbert and Oscar Wilde, Shaw's challenging and idiosyncratic variety of dramatic realism was also inspired by Ibsen. Shaw's plays and polemics helped to create an atmosphere of critical acceptance in England for the realistic theater of ideas and social problems. Shaw's *Candida* (pr. 1897) appeared in 1904 at the Royal Court Theatre as part of the Barker-Vedrenne management's effort to raise the level of English drama. When Galsworthy sent the manuscript of *The Silver Box* to Harley Granville-Barker, it arrived on a Saturday, was read by Barker and Shaw on Sunday, and was accepted for production at Shaw's urging on Monday.

In a letter, Galsworthy remarked that the "main idea" of *The Silver Box* was "that 'one law for the rich, another for the poor' is true, but not because society wills it so, rather, in spite of society's good intentions, through the mere mechanical wide-branching power of money." Galsworthy's play contrasts the unprincipled, propertied, and pragmatic upper-middle-class characters with their lower-class victims in the manipulation of the judicial system. The audience knows from the beginning who the culprits are in two related cases of petty thievery, but Galsworthy creates suspense through gradual revelation of their guilt to their families. The first thief is young Jack Barthwick, down from Oxford on vacation, who, while out drinking with a female companion, steals her purse containing seven pounds. The play opens as Jack returns to the Barthwick home with Jones, a drunken, unemployed groom. When Jack passes out, Jones steals the purse and a silver cigarette box. Jack's theft is revealed to his family but is concealed in court at Jones's trial until after Jones's sentencing, when he can only cry out in helpless frustration, thus giving the audience the "main idea" of the play: "It's *'is money* got *'im* off—*Justice!*"

The Barthwicks' cowardly hypocrisy is illustrated throughout the play, especially in one scene at the end of act 2. Jack's father, John Barthwick, a Liberal Member of Parliament, is so concerned that the scandal of a trial will damage his political and social reputation that he betrays his "Liberal" sympathy for the poor. One of the Jones children is heard sobbing outside the Barthwicks' window because the child cannot find Mrs. Jones, his mother and the Barthwicks' housekeeper (she has been wrongly accused, arrested, and imprisoned with her husband, even though he has admitted his guilt). The sound of the child's suffering moves Mrs. Barthwick to suggest that the case be dropped, but Mr. Barthwick says the matter is out of their hands and refuses to help; the curtain drops on a melodramatic tableau, as Mrs. Barthwick turns her back on the crying, Mr. Barthwick covers his ears, and a servant closes the window to shut out the noise of suffering.

Galsworthy teaches his dramatic lesson through contrasts and parallels, too. In order to illustrate further the disparity between the lives of rich and poor, he sets one scene in the Joneses' lodgings during their meager meal of potatoes and onions and contrasts it with the following scene of the Barthwicks' elaborate dinner. In act 3, the trial for theft is preceded by a hearing to remand the children of an out-of-work father to court custody. The court-ordered breakup of a family arouses Barthwick's liberal sentiments, but Galsworthy shows that liberal zeal for social reform is quickly sacrificed to self-interest as Barthwick seeks to suppress all evidence of

Jack's involvement in Jones's case.

In *The Silver Box*, Galsworthy attempts to portray realistically a serious issue of injustice without resorting to the heroics of melodrama. He imagines the characters as social types and describes their "keynotes" in a letter to Granville-Barker; the play has no hero, and if there is a villain, it is a social class rather than an individual. The drawback of this method was once its virtue, but the sense of recognition to be gained from its topical documentary realism has been lost, and one is left with a double overdose of obvious didacticism and melodramatic attempts to arouse pathos, as in the crying child scene.

The rise to real power of the English labor movement early in the twentieth century provided a subject suited to Galsworthy's realistic method: *Strife* comes closest, among his plays, to a work of lasting value. Through the careful dramatic opposition of ideas, characters, metaphors, and structural elements, the play presents the tragedy of two fanatically iron-willed leaders who battle against each other at great cost to themselves and their followers. The play takes place during six hours on a February afternoon and evening at the Trenartha Tin Plate Works on the English-Welsh border, where a strike has lasted for five months, crippling the company and bringing suffering, hunger, and a winter without heat to the laborers. The deadlock results from the conflict between the leaders of the opposing sides, David Roberts of the strikers and John Anthony of the company directors.

Galsworthy constructed the play so that its spire of meaning would arise from the dialectic of opposing concepts represented by Anthony and Roberts. In a letter to a director who wanted to revive the play in 1931, Galsworthy insisted that "the play's real theme" was not the battle between capital and labor but rather "*hubris*, or violence; *Strife* is, indeed, a play on extremism or fanaticism." Both Anthony and Roberts refuse to compromise their principles by giving in to the other side; their rigidity of purpose shows a kind of heroic intellectual vainglory, producing bitterness, suffering, waste, and death. Galsworthy once more created "type" characters, but Anthony and Roberts are types as extremists, not as members of any social class—such men may be found in any class.

Galsworthy imposes structural balance on the action to achieve the resonant effect of contrast and parallelism of idea, character, and situation. The confrontations of labor and management in the first and third acts balance each other, as do the separate meetings of directors and strikers in the second and third acts, in which each side rejects its leader's plan for action and decides to accept instead the terms for compromise proposed by the union representative. Galsworthy handles his large cast of characters with an almost schematic balancing of psychological and social types. He also uses settings, properties, and dramatic language appropriate to the theme of *Strife*: In several scenes, he contrasts the excesses of cold and heat, hunger and plenty, luxury and deprivation. Metaphoric language carries the idea that if Anthony and Roberts are like gods in their power over men, they are also like devils in the way they use power to cause suffering for the sake of their principles. The play has its melodramatic moments, such as the fight among the workers at the end of the second act, but overall, it is much less encumbered by the sentimentality and overly theatrical scenes which spoil many of Galsworthy's plays.

Strife, in an understated and bitter conclusion, neither celebrates nor condemns the opposing sides in the struggle of labor versus capital; instead, it portrays the need for civility and compromise in human affairs. The plan proposed by the union representative at the beginning of the play finally is adopted; Anthony and Roberts have a moment of mutual recognition after their followers have rejected the inhumanity of blind, proud adherence to principle. The theme of hubris is, if anything, too carefully and obviously portrayed in Galsworthy's systematic balancing of scenes, characters, and metaphors, and in the working out of a metaphoric dialectic of opposed ideas. *Strife*, nevertheless, remains Galsworthy's best problem play and the best realization of his theory of drama.

Galsworthy wrote in his diary for 1921: "During the summer *Loyalties* was written. . . . This was the only play of mine of which I was able to say when I finished it: 'No manager will refuse this.'" The play's popular success proved Galsworthy to be correct; he had adapted his realistic techniques to his audience's preference for entertainment instead of sermons. As in *The Silver Box*, he used a crime plot but spent far more effort creating a suspenseful modern melodrama which, along with his peek into the lives of the postwar, aristocratic, horse-racing set, includes a critique of upper-class anti-Semitism, hypocrisy, and misplaced loyalty to its own members. For the first time since *The Silver Box*, Galsworthy employed neither a pattern of recurrent imagery nor a central emblematic property or setting to underline his theme. The ideas in the play emerge in short speeches closely related to the action; the closest Galsworthy comes to a debate in *Loyalties* is the exchange between Ferdinand De Levis, a young, rich, Jewish social outsider, and General Canynge, the patrician elder statesman of Establishment values and taste. De Levis has (rightly) accused Captain Ronald Dancy, "a soldier and a gentleman," of stealing one thousand pounds. Canynge regards De Levis as an arrogant, insolent bounder and makes no secret of his distaste for De Levis' disregard of "the *esprit de corps* that exists among gentlemen." Other significant words or phrases, such as "unwritten code," "duty," and "honour," occur infrequently and unobtrusively; in context, they are appropriate to the plot and are not overly obvious guideposts to Galsworthy's moral. Just as Galsworthy does not unduly underline the theme of intolerance, neither does he follow his usual practice of overtly pointing up the merit of charity and unselfishness. Instead, the action embodies his theme of uncharitable Christians versus charitable non-Christians in implicit and understated ways.

The play's three acts emphasize three different kinds of loyalties in three appropriate settings. In the first act, at a country estate near Newmarket, De Levis' accusations against Dancy are attacked by Canynge and Charles Winsor out of personal loyalty, the code of the gentleman. In the second act, at a London club, social loyalty is the subject: Canynge and Winsor fear for the reputation of the club and the army; De Levis' loyalty to his race motivates him to refuse to sign an apology. In act 3, at the law office, loyalty to an institution, the profession of law, is emphasized. Finally, in the last scene, the Inspector embodies loyalty to a similar but more abstract institution, the Law itself.

Galsworthy appropriately structures the plot to carry the dramatic presentation of these types of loyalty and their conflicts. The controlled balancing of plot, character, and language which made *Loyalties* not only a popular success but also Galsworthy's best postwar social drama served him well again in *Escape*, which also places less importance on ideas than on action. In a series of ten episodes organized almost cinematically, an escaped prisoner evades capture, meets a variety of characters from all social classes, and eventually, acting out of conscience, gives himself up, having come to terms with the gentleman's code that Barthwick and Dancy betray in *The Silver Box* and *Loyalties*, respectively.

Throughout Galsworthy's dramatic works, there is a tension between oppressive moralism and melodramatic theatricality. As Allardyce Nicoll has observed, "Galsworthian realism and Socialist Realism tend to suffer from the same pathetic complaint—deplorable and even tawdry sentimentalism." In plays such as *Strife*, *Loyalties*, and *Escape*, however, Galsworthy successfully combined realistic representation with dramatic presentation of theme. His plays remain historically interesting because they embody his perceptions of English social and ethical attitudes in the early twentieth century. As examples of realistic drama, his plays have merit as the works of a sincere and careful craftsman who wrote in a tradition made great by the true artists who made it their own: Henrik Ibsen, August Strindberg, Anton Chekhov, and George Bernard Shaw.

Other major works

NOVELS: *Jocelyn*, 1898 (as John Sinjohn); *Villa Rubein*, 1900 (as John Sinjohn); *The Island Pharisees*, 1904; *The Man of Property*, 1906; *The Country House*, 1907; *Fraternity*, 1909; *The Patrician*, 1911; *The Dark Flower*, 1913; *The Little Man*, 1915; *The Freelands*, 1915; *Beyond*, 1917; *The Burning Spear*, 1919; *Saint's Progress*, 1919; *In Chancery*, 1920; *To Let*, 1921; *The Forsyte Saga*, 1922 (includes *The Man of Property*, "Indian Summer of a Forsyte," "Awakening," *In Chancery*, *To Let*); *The White Monkey*, 1924;

The Silver Spoon, 1926; *Swan Song*, 1928; *A Modern Comedy*, 1929 (includes *The White Monkey*, *The Silver Spoon*, *Two Forsyte Interludes*, *Swan Song*); *Maid in Waiting*, 1931; *Flowering Wilderness*, 1932; *Over the River*, 1933; *End of the Chapter*, 1934 (includes *Maid in Waiting*, *Flowering Wilderness*, and *Over the River*).

SHORT FICTION: *From the Four Winds*, 1897 (as John Sinjohn); *A Man of Devon*, 1901 (as John Sinjohn); *Five Tales*, 1918; *Captures*, 1923; *Caravan: The Assembled Tales of John Galsworthy*, 1925; *Two Forsyte Interludes*, 1927; *On Forsyte 'Change*, 1930; *Soames and the Flag*, 1930; *Forsytes, Pendyces, and Others*, 1935.

POETRY: *The Collected Poems of John Galsworthy*, 1934 (Ada Galsworthy, editor).

NONFICTION: *A Commentary*, 1908; *A Motley*, 1910; *The Inn of Tranquility*, 1912; *A Sheaf*, 1916; *Another Sheaf*, 1919; *Tatterdemalion*, 1920; *Castles in Spain*, 1927; *Candelabra: Selected Essays and Addresses*, 1932; *Letters from John Galsworthy, 1900-1932*, 1934 (Edward Garnett, editor).

MISCELLANEOUS: *The Works of John Galsworthy*, 1922-1936 (30 volumes).

Bibliography

Barker, Dudley. *The Man of Principle*. New York: Stein & Day, 1969. This book combines elements of autobiography and criticism, giving an impressive picture of the Victorian age and its mores and morals. It also shows how much Galsworthy's work was a reflection of his times, and it explores the relationship between him and his wife, Ada, as well as her influence on his work. Includes a frontspiece of the couple, a short bibliography, and an index.

Burgess, Anthony. "Seen Any Good Galsworthy Lately?" *The New York Times Magazine*, November 16, 1969, 57-64. When Galsworthy's novel *The Forsyte Saga* was adapted for British television and later shown in the United States and around the world, it was an immediate success and rescued Galsworthy from the neglect into which he had fallen since his death in 1933. In this essay, the distinguished British novelist Anthony Burgess paints a vivid picture of Galsworthy's past popularity both as playwright and novelist and reassesses a reputation that he considers inflated even for its day.

Dupré, Catherine. *John Galsworthy*. New York: Coward, McCann & Geoghegan, 1976. The importance of this biography lies in the new material that the author uncovered. Dupré was given access to Galsworthy's papers and was able to shed light on aspects of his life previously unknown. It is probably the best of the Galsworthy biographies in its psychological insights and is also useful because of its literary judgments. Contains a list of the complete works, an index, a bibliography, and many photographs.

Marrott, H. V. *The Life and Letters of John Galsworthy.* New York: Charles Scribner's Sons, 1935. Reprint. Clifton, N.J.: A. M. Kelley, 1973. The author, a close friend of Galsworthy, published this adulatory book with the assistance of Ada Galsworthy after the death of her husband. Mainly a source of biographical information, it offers no literary criticism but is valuable because it contains much material that no longer exists. Many photographs.

Morris, Mary. *My Galsworthy Story.* London: Peter Owen, 1967. Morris was a young dancer when she met and fell in love with Galsworthy, who had married his cousin's wife after her divorce. Galsworthy was torn between loyalty to his wife and devotion to Morris; finally, to protect his wife, he ended the affair. Galsworthy used himself and the two women as characters in one of his later novels, *The Dark Flower.* Photographs and a facsimile of his farewell letter to Morris are reproduced.

Sauter, Rudolf. *Galsworthy the Man.* London: Peter Owen, 1967. This slim volume is a personal reminiscence by the son of Galsworthy's sister, Lilian. It offers family insights into the daily lives of John and Ada, a discussion of their tastes and habits, their friendships, and their travels abroad. It is also a record of Galsworthy's working routine. Includes portraits, facsimiles, diagrams, and a bibliography.

Stevens, Earl E., and H. Ray Stevens, eds. *John Galsworthy.* De Kalb: Northern Illinois University Press, 1980. An annotated bibliography of writings, with contributions by Pierre Coustillas and others. A later, exhaustive bibliography of the author.

Philip E. Smith II
(Updated by *Mildred C. Kuner*)

GEORGE GASCOIGNE

Born: Cardington, England; c. 1539
Died: Stamford, England; October 7, 1577

Principal drama

Jocasta, pr. 1566, pb. 1573 (with Francis Kinwelmershe; translation of Lodovico Dolce's play *Giocasta*); *Supposes*, pr. 1566, pb. 1573 (translation of Ludovico Ariosto's *I suppositi*); *A Devise of a Maske for the Right Honorable Viscount Mountacute*, pr. 1572, pb. 1573; *The Glasse of Governement*, pb. 1575; *The Princely Pleasures at Kenelworth Castle*, pr. 1575, pb. 1576 (with others).

Other literary forms

In addition to his masques and plays, George Gascoigne wrote in a number of genres in verse and prose; whatever the genre, his style is generally direct, lucid, and idiomatic. Several of his works were the first of their kind in English literature.

Gascoigne's later moralistic writings, however, lack interest for most students of literature. In prose, these works include *The Droomme of Doomes Day* (1576) and *A Delicate Diet, for Daintiemouthde Droonkardes* (1576), and, in rhyme royal, *The Grief of Joye* (1576).

Two expository works in prose have special importance. Gascoigne's eyewitness account *The Spoyle of Antwerpe* (1576), originally written as a government report, is perhaps the best journalistic writing of the Elizabethan period, while his "Certayne Notes of Instruction Concerning the Making of Verse," included in *The Posies of George Gascoigne Esquire* (1575), is the earliest extant treatise on poetry in the English language.

Also included in that collection, and of even greater interest, is the prose narrative *The Discourse of the Adventures Passed by Master F. J.* (1573), revised and reissued as *The Pleasant Fable of Ferdinando Jeronimi and Leonora de Valasco* (1575). With lyric poems spaced throughout the prose, the experimental narrative tells the story of a young man's disillusioning love affair with a more experienced woman who is also having adulterous relations with her male secretary. The narrative, lacking in event, nevertheless deals slyly, often humorously, with courtly love conventions as they might apply in real life.

Gascoigne's best original compositions are his poems, numbering more than one hundred. Among the longer poems, two deserve to be singled out, for they share the skepticism toward life and society that is characteristic of much of his best writing: The part of *The Fruites of Warre* (1575) dealing with his own military experiences is lively reading, while *The Steele Glas, a Satyre* (1576) uses the device of a mirror to expose what the poet saw as the decline of social and moral responsibility in the Elizabethan world.

Gascoigne's finest poems, however, are to be found among the shorter poems in various forms published in *A Hundreth Sundrie Flowres Bounde Up in One Small Poesie* (1573), later revised as *The Posies of George Gascoigne Esquire*. Some of this volume's poems that are preferred by critics are "The Lullabie of a Lover," in which an aging lover sings to sleep his fading powers; "Gascoigne's Woodmanship," in which the poet likens his bad marksmanship to his other failures in life; and "The Praise of Phillip Sparrowe," a light celebration of the poet's pet bird. These and other of the poems may still delight and instruct a reader.

Achievements

George Gascoigne died in 1577, when a new generation of writers such as John Lyly, Sir Philip Sidney, and Edmund Spenser were beginning an outburst of literary creativity that lasted from 1578 to the start of the Commonwealth period in 1642. Comparison of Gascoigne's works to the great literature that followed shortly afterward causes Gascoigne to be considered, and perhaps correctly, a minor writer, but his literary achievements won recognition during his own time and strongly influenced the development of English poetry and drama; at least some of his pieces may still be read with enjoyment.

That Gascoigne achieved stature as a writer during his own time is shown by his dealings between 1572 and 1577 with some of the great nobility. He seems to have enjoyed at least some patronage from Lord Grey of Wilton, later a patron to Spenser. Recognition of his ability is implied by Gascoigne's having been asked by the family of Viscount Montague to provide the masque for the Montague-Dormer wedding, and even more by his being chosen by the Earl of Leicester to provide entertainment for the queen's visit to Kenilworth. The poet's appointment to government service very likely resulted from favorable notice by the queen herself.

Modern scholars continue to be interested in Gascoigne primarily because of his contributions to the development of English poetry and drama. During his lifetime, serious English writers, confronted by native and foreign traditions that differed radically, experimented in order to discover the means by which literature might best be created in the vernacular. "Certayne Notes of Instruction Concerning the Making of Verse," a pioneer work in literary criticism, provides insight both into the state of poetics at the time and into Gascoigne's own aims and methods. Consistent with his literary theory, most of his poetry uses plain English words directly and lucidly, maintaining in poetry a native English tradition bridging the gap between Sir Thomas Wyatt and such later poets as John Donne and Ben Jonson. In addition, *The Steele Glas, a Satyre* has historical interest both because it may be the first satire of the era and because it was the first original poem in English written in blank verse.

Literary historians have long recognized the importance of Gascoigne's contributions to the development of Elizabethan drama. As an example of the prodigal-son play, *The Glasse of Governement* has some historical interest but exercised little influence on later plays. Of greater significance was *Jocasta*, which was produced in 1566 and which Gascoigne, in collaboration with Francis Kinwelmershe, had translated from Lodovico Dolce's *Giocasta* (wr. 1549, an adaptation of a Latin translation of Euripides' *The Phoenician Women*, c. 411 B.C.). *Jocasta* was the first Greek tragedy produced on the English stage, though the text was not translated directly from the Greek. Using blank verse, a five-act structure, and dumb shows before each act, the tragedy reinforced the tendency toward the classical mode in tragedy established in 1561 by the production of Thomas Norton and Thomas Sackville's *Gorboduc*, also at the Inns of Court. *Supposes*, Gascoigne's translation of Ludovico Ariosto's *I suppositi* of 1509, exercised an even greater influence on English drama: It not only provided William Shakespeare with the idea for the Bianca subplot in *The Taming of the Shrew* but also helped to establish prose as the medium for comic drama and introduced Italian comedy to the English stage.

Biography

The life of George Gascoigne, probably the greatest writer of the early years of Queen Elizabeth's reign, illustrates some of the worst and some of the best aspects of the life of the Renaissance gentleman. An elder son of prosperous parents, young Gascoigne first undertook the study of law but then chose to pursue life at court. As presented and popularized by the Italian Count Baldassare Castiglione in *The Courtier* (1528), the ideal courtier was to be gracious, attractive, witty, intelligent, learned, wise, and skilled in warfare and in the arts and sciences; such a servant of the king was worthy of fame and fortune. In reality, few people had the character or ability even to approach such an ideal, and the extravagance and intrigue associated with life at court were not often conducive to strength of character. Gascoigne's adult life was characterized by legal difficulties, many of which were caused by his own financial excesses and strained personal relationships. His literary accomplishments, however, were extraordinary: He did much to prepare the way for the greater writers who followed him, and he earned a solid reputation as a lyric and satiric poet.

Relatively little is known about Gascoigne's early life, the period before his admission to Gray's Inn in 1555. His father, Sir John Gascoigne, had inherited a considerable estate at Cardington and had married Margaret Scargill, coheir to the estate of her father, Sir Robert Scargill of Yorkshire. Although Sir John served as a public official in his shire, legal records indicate that he and his men became violent with a neighbor over hunting rights, that Sir John was taken in adultery with a female servant, and that he could be unscrupulous in financial dealings. None of the father's failings, however, seems to have seriously damaged the family's fortune. The family could well afford the sort of education necessary to a young gentleman of prosperous family. Sometime between 1547 and 1555, George Gascoigne entered Trinity College, Cambridge. In 1555, he was admitted to Gray's Inn, to study and practice law. Probably while still pursuing a legal career, Gascoigne entered Parliament on January 20, 1558, and was probably present to hear announced the death of Queen Mary and the succession of Elizabeth. As a substitute for his father, Gascoigne assisted as almoner in the coronation proceedings. Soon afterward, he gave up the idea of a law career in order to take up life at court.

Apparently sharing some of his father's tendencies, Gascoigne seems to have spent money extravagantly and to have earned a reputation as a ruffian. In any case, he did not soon gain preferment at court, and his financial dealings led to expensive legal actions. His marriage to Elizabeth Bretton Boyes, the widowed mother of later poet Nicholas Bretton, did little to repair Gascoigne's finances, though she had inherited substantial wealth from her first husband. When she married Gascoigne she was still, at least in the eyes of the law, the wife of an Edward Boyes, who had in his possession property and money belonging to Elizabeth and her children by Bretton. Gascoigne became involved in even more conflict, both in and out of court. In 1562, as the legal actions multiplied, Gascoigne and Boyes and their retainers came to blows in Redcross Street in London. Probably needing to live more frugally, George and Elizabeth resided in Willington in 1563 and 1564, after which George returned to Gray's Inn, evidently to resume legal training; during this sojourn at Gray's Inn, however, he seems to have written much. In *A Hundreth Sundrie Flowres Bounde Up in One Small Poesie*, he published five poems written on themes provided by friends from this period. Both *Supposes* and *Jocasta* were staged at Gray's Inn in 1566. Soon, however, Gascoigne abandoned Gray's Inn again, to try his hand at farming at Cardington during 1567-1568, the latter the year of his father's death. Although Sir John seems on his deathbed to have considered disinheriting his elder son, George did receive a legacy, but it was not, evidently, sufficient to meet his obligations, for by April of 1570, he was in Bedford jail for debt.

At this low point in his life, Gascoigne redoubled his efforts and applied them in new ways: to win fame and fortune by volunteering to fight for William of Orange in the Low Countries and to gain patronage by exhibiting his writing in print. His military experience was disillusioning, though it provided material for his poetry, particularly *The Fruites of Warre*. In May, 1572, he departed from Greenwich with the first group of English volunteers but returned to England in the fall, after a disappointing campaign. His poetry at this point seems to have gained favorable notice from Lord Grey of Wilton, and Gascoigne was engaged to provide a masque for the Montague-Dormer wedding in October, 1572. He began preparing for the press *A Hundreth Sundrie Flowres Bounde Up in One Small Poesie*, which may include some lyric poems by other writers. The last material for the book was sent from the Low Countries, since he departed on March 19, 1573, for a second attempt in the wars. Worse than the first campaign, his second venture at war ended with his being imprisoned for four months by the Spaniards and abandoning the soldier's life. Upon his return to England in October, 1574, he discovered that *A Hundreth Sundrie Flowres Bounde Up in One Small Poesie* had created a scandal and had been seized by the authorities.

During the last three years of his life, Gascoigne did much writing, most of it repenting the sins of his earlier life. Almost immediately he began revising *A Hundreth Sundrie Flowres Bounde Up in One Small Poesie*; the revised version was published as *The Posies of George Gascoigne Esquire*, some copies of which were also seized by the authorities. Shortly afterward, he published *The Glasse of Governement*, an original play, and for the entertainment of Queen Elizabeth at Kenilworth in July, 1575, he provided most of the literary tribute later published as *The Princely Pleasures at Kenelworth Castle*. While performing the role of Sylvanus in one of his compositions for this entertainment, Gascoigne seems to have received favorable notice from the queen.

Even as Gascoigne was winning favor, his writing continued at a brisk pace. Shortly after April, 1576, he published in a single volume *The Steele Glas* and *The Complaynt of Phylomene*. In the same year, he published *The Droomme of Doomes Day*, a long repentance tract; *A Delicate Diet, for Daintiemouthde Droonkardes*, a temperance tract very like a sermon; and *The Grief of Joye*, a group of elegies which he presented to the queen as a New Year's gift. Also in 1576, he was appointed to government service by Sir Francis Walsingham and sent to Antwerp, where he witnessed and reported on the sacking of the city by the Spanish. *The Spoyle of Antwerpe* was originally written as a government report addressed to Lord Burleigh.

Ironically, Gascoigne did not live long enough to enjoy the success that his writing had brought him. During 1576, he had referred to his own ill health. On October 7, 1577, he died at Stamford, England.

Analysis

Both the state of development of drama during the 1560's and 1570's and the nature of George Gascoigne's dramatic efforts, including the masques and plays, mitigated against Gascoigne's achieving a level of art in drama equal to that in his better poems. His mastery of style may have been sufficient, if the lively prose dialogue of *Supposes* and the verse of his better poems are accepted as evidence, but the court masque, even at its best in the early 1600's, has generally been considered a minor form of art, existing primarily to grace a particular occasion and to honor powerful people. As for the plays, when *Supposes* and *Jocasta* were first produced in 1566, English playwrights had not yet learned how to combine native and classical traditions in order to create great drama. Indeed, much of the impetus behind the production of plays at the Inns of Court during the 1560's probably came from the desire of persons educated in the classical tradition to influence the development of English drama. Translations such as *Jocasta* and *Supposes* seem to have exerted a timely and beneficial influence, but the lesser art of translation, no matter how well done, does not evoke the sort of praise given creators of good original works of art. Gascoigne's one original play, *The Glasse of Governement*, has artful touches but lacks theatricality. An examination of the masques and plays may help to explain how Gascoigne's contributions to drama have earned for him a permanent place in literary history even though he is not regarded as a great playwright.

Performed in October, 1572, Gascoigne's first known attempt at the masque omits many of the conventional elements of the form, which usually included mumming, music, dance, verse spoken by more than one character, spectacular costumes and properties, and mythological characters. Of all of these elements, Gascoigne's *A Devise of a Maske for the Right Honorable Viscount Mountacute* uses only spectacular costumes and verse spoken by a single character.

The writer's preface suggests a cause for the masque's peculiarities. Eight men of the Montague family had decided to provide a masque for the Montague-Dormer wedding and had already purchased Venetian costumes. They asked Gascoigne to write something to be spoken by a professional actor that would give a pretext for the Venetian costumes. From the Montague coat of arms he gained information that served his purpose: There was an Italian branch of the Montague family.

In the masque, a boy actor, an imaginary descendant of the English Montagues, tells of his father's death and his own capture by Turks at the siege of Famagusta and of his rescue by Venetians, who are members of the Italian branch of Montagues. On the way to Venice their ship was driven ashore in England by a storm. After using 348 lines of poulter's measure to explain the presence of the Venetians, the boy presents them to the wedding party in ten lines, praises the newly married couples in eighteen lines, and speaks a two-line farewell that ends the masque.

It is true, as Ronald C. Johnson points out in *George Gascoigne* (1972), that the narrative moves well in *A Devise of a Maske for the Right Honorable Viscount Mountacute*, but except for its flattery of the Montagues, the boy's tale has little connection with the wedding. Further, the poet has relied too much on words, neglecting the dialogue, physical motion, and spectacle innate in drama, even in a form of drama as static as the masque.

By July 9, 1575, Gascoigne had learned more about courtly shows. The entertainment of Elizabeth commissioned by the Earl of Leicester and later published as *The Princely Pleasures at Kenelworth Castle* was a series of presentations written by Gascoigne and five other men, each of whose compositions was identified as such in the published text. At least two of the five, as Charles T. Prouty observes, had some experience with similar entertainments at court and therefore may have given Gascoigne valuable information.

Gascoigne himself spoke the first section he had written. As a savage man draped in ivy, he met the queen in the forest as she returned from hunting and spoke poetry expressing the natural man's admiration of the great people gathered at Kenilworth, especially flattering the queen and, fairly subtly, calling her attention to the Earl of Leicester, her suitor. Although this performance still relied primarily on recitation of poetry, Gascoigne made clever use of the character Echo, presumably hidden in the woods, to produce a special effect by repetition of endings of lines spoken by the savage man.

The second section composed by Gascoigne is a full-scale masque. It employs spectacular costumes, music, song, elaborate stage effects, and mythological characters that express a meaning. Diana, goddess of chastity, and four of her nymphs are passing through the forest when Diana remembers Zabeta, a favorite nymph who has abandoned her. Fearing that Juno has won Zabeta away from chastity, Diana sends her nymphs to find the lost follower. Through the help of Mercury, Diana learns that Zabeta is not yet committed to Juno. After Diana leaves, content to allow Zabeta to use her own judgment, Iris descends to earth and ends the masque by urging Zabeta to wed.

The masque was never performed, perhaps because its meaning was too clear: Zabeta was Queen Elizabeth, and she was being urged to marry the Earl of Leicester.

By order of the earl, Gascoigne also wrote a performance bidding the queen farewell. Again Gascoigne relied primarily upon recitation, this time a prose tale spoken extemporaneously. As Sylvanus, god of the woods, Gascoigne met the queen as she went out to hunt and told her the story as he walked beside her horse. Sylvanus' tale concerns the gods' sorrow at her departure and the good things they will shower on Kenilworth if she remains. An abrupt shift to the subject of a goddess who changes her followers into trees and shrubs leads to a holly bush from which Deep Desire speaks verse entreating the queen to stay, concluding the performance with a song lamenting her determination to leave.

The end of the presentation thus incorporates elements other than recitation, but Gascoigne as Sylvanus has depended on words to the point of excluding other desirable elements of the masque or pageant.

Gascoigne's place in the history of drama, however, was earned roughly nine years before the entertainment of Kenilworth, in 1566, when the translations *Jocasta* and *Supposes* were produced at Gray's Inn. The title pages of the plays, first published in *A Hundreth Sundrie Flowres Bounde Up in One Small Poesie*, provide the year and location of production, but there is no indication of precisely when the translations were done or of the order in which the plays were staged.

The tragedy *Jocasta*—its second, third, and fifth acts translated by Gascoigne, the first and fourth by Kinwelmershe—has much historical importance. Even though the title page states that the play is a tragedy written in Greek by Euripides "translated and digested into Acte," the translators actually worked from Lodovico Dolce's *Giocasta*. Still, *Jocasta* was the first Greek tragedy presented in England. By following the earlier *Gorboduc* in the use of five-act structure, blank verse, dumb shows before each act, and Senecan emphases, the play reinforced modes in tragedy that later served playwrights such as Thomas Kyd and Christopher Marlowe.

The translation of the particular play may have had bad as well as good effects on Gascoigne's development as a dramatist. As Johnson comments, *Jocasta* appealed to Elizabethans for several reasons, some of which are its concern with strife over succession to the throne, its use of dumb shows and long set speeches, and its dwelling upon accounts of violence and horror. There is no shortage of subject matter: The tragedy covers almost all the events in Sophocles' trilogy on the Oedipus myth. Scene by scene, the play shifts the focus from one major character to another, emphasis falling at different times on Jocasta, Servus, Antigone, Polynices, Eteocles, Creon, Tyresias, Meneceus, and Oedipus. The shifting causes a lack of focus; moreover, the play's use of long speeches may have encouraged a similar tendency in Gascoigne, primarily a maker of poems. The play, true to its origins in classical tragedy, persistently narrates action instead of showing it onstage.

Ariosto's *I suppositi* was a much better choice for translation than was Dolce's tragedy, and Gascoigne's treatment of the play reflects much skill with language. Carefully unified, Ariosto's comedy imitates Plautus' *Captivi* (c. 200 B.C.) and Terence's *Eunuchus* (161 B.C.) by having a master and slave exchange identities so that the master can enter the house of an attractive girl as a household servant. The young master (really Erostrato) comes to Ferrara from his home in Sicily in order to study at the university, bringing his servant Dulypo with him. Seeing the beautiful Polynesta, Erostrato exchanges roles with his servant and enters service in the house of Damon, Polynesta's father. Using the nurse Balia as an intermediary, Erostrato secretly becomes intimate with Polynesta and wishes to marry her, but her father is inclined to give her hand to Cleander, a rich but miserly old lawyer who offers a large marriage settlement. In order to delay the marriage, Erostrato has his slave pretend to court Polynesta, outbidding Cleander for her hand, but Damon demands that the younger suitor's father guarantee the arrangements. The crafty slave contrives to have a Sienese traveler pose as Philogano, the father of Erostrato. Just as the real Philogano arrives in Ferrara to pay a surprise visit to his son, the real Erostrato has been caught in intimacy with Polynesta and has been imprisoned. Through Pasiphilo, the parasite, the confusion about the father's and the son's identities is resolved, and Cleander discovers his lost son in Dulypo, the crafty slave. No longer needing a marriage to beget an heir, Cleander is happy at the end of the comedy when Philogano and Damon agree on a marriage between Erostrato and Polynesta. The comic resolution is complete and satisfying.

Unlike the masques and *Jocasta*, *Supposes* has sufficient action to appeal to a large audience, and Gascoigne's translation is in light, idiomatic style. He had access to both prose and verse versions in Italian but had the good judgment to opt for prose in English, influencing large numbers of later comedies. In addition, *Supposes* brought the first Italian adaptation of Roman comedy to the English stage, which would make use of many of Roman comedy's type characters and of such devices as disguise, mistaken identity, and love intrigue. If *Supposes* had been Gascoigne's original creation, the play would have earned for him literary immortality as a playwright.

Unfortunately, Gascoigne's one original play, *The Glasse of Governement*, lacks theatrical appeal even though it has interesting touches in characterization and structure. The first of Gascoigne's moralistic writings, the play is written in the tradition of the prodigal-son plays popularized by Dutch Humanists, a tradition to which Gascoigne was probably exposed during his military service in the Low Countries.

Structured in five acts, the story line is clear. Two rich citizens and neighbors of Antwerp, Phylopaes and Philocalus, have two sons each, paired by age with the sons of the other. Anxious for their sons to go to the university but wanting the boys to be prepared both morally and academically, the fathers entrust their sons to the teacher Gnomaticus, who teaches in accordance with the ideals of Christian Humanists. The two elder sons learn very quickly but are soon bored. They are easily lured to the house of Lamia the harlot by the parasite Echo. The two younger sons are slower to learn but eager to understand their morally based instruction.

Learning that their elder sons have been seen in bad company, the fathers consult Gnomaticus, who agrees that the four sons should be sent to the University of Douai so that the elder boys will be separated from evil company. Accompanied by the evil servant Ambidexter, the boys go to

Douai. Quickly the elder sons neglect their studies and, with Ambidexter, frequent taverns and brothels. The younger sons study. Hearing news of the elder sons' conduct, the fathers send the good servant Fidus to help them, but Fidus arrives too late. He returns with news that one elder son has been executed for robbery at the Palsgrave's court in the presence of his successful younger brother, who is now secretary to the Palsgrave. Another elder son has been publicly whipped and banished from Geneva for fornication, even though his younger brother, now a famous preacher there, tried to intercede on his brother's behalf. Thoroughgoing in its use of poetic justice, the play ends after all the evil characters have been punished by the law and the virtue of the two younger sons has been rewarded by social advancement.

For a play of its time, *The Glasse of Governement* has many good features. It is well organized by five-act structure, and the dialogue is in clear prose. Its greatest strength, however, lies in its characterization, which avoids mere stereotypes. The fathers are concerned and sympathetic; Gnomaticus is a kind and tolerant teacher with little practical knowledge of human nature; Severus is an officer of the law who refuses to punish offenders without firm evidence against them; and Lamia is a girl from a prosperous family who drifted into prostitution because she rejected her society's stifling restrictions on the conduct of proper young ladies.

Despite its virtues, the play seems not to have been produced, perhaps because of its untheatrical qualities. Its use of paired characters—fathers sons, and servants—offers theatrical possibilities through comparison and contrast, but there is little differentiation between the individuals in the sets of pairs. The play's heavy-handed didacticism poses more serious problems: It creates a mood more appropriate to a pulpit than to the stage; it leads to the oversimplified morality of poetic justice; and it results in static scenes in which Gnomaticus and, less frequently, the good sons recite extremely long and moral speeches. Finally, the focus of the action depicted onstage is misdirected. The elder sons' wild behavior and the younger sons' triumphs are merely narrated, whereas the lectures of Gnomaticus take place onstage. This misdirected focus prevents the conflict between good and evil from coming alive in the play.

Gascoigne's tendency to rely on long recitations in drama may suggest a weakness in his sense of the dramatic, or more likely may reflect the immature state of English drama during his time. In any event, George Gascoigne created no original work of lasting fame, but through his translations, particularly his *Supposes*, he did help to make possible the greatest age of English drama.

Other major works

NOVEL: *The Discourse of the Adventures Passed by Master F. J.*, 1573 (revised as *The Pleasant Fable of Ferdinando Jeronimi and Leonora de Valasco*, 1575).

POETRY: *The Fruites of Warre*, 1575; *The Complaynt of Phylomene*, 1576; *The Grief of Joye*, 1576; *The Steele Glas, a Satyre*, 1576.

NONFICTION: "Certayne Notes of Instruction Concerning the Making of Verse," 1575; *A Delicate Diet, for Daintiemouthde Droonkardes*, 1576; *The Droomme of Doomes Day*, 1576; *The Spoyle of Antwerpe*, 1576.

MISCELLANEOUS: *A Hundreth Sundrie Flowres Bounde Up in One Small Poesie*, 1573 (poetry and prose; revised as *The Posies of George Gascoigne Esquire*, 1575).

Bibliography

Johnson, Ronald C. *George Gascoigne*. New York: Twayne, 1972. An ample discussion of Petrarch and Gascoigne precedes separate chapters on the love lyrics and the other poems. *The Steele Glas* is discussed for its satire, *The Discourse of the Adventures Passed by Master F. J.* for its variety of narrative devices, and the three plays for their relationship to dramatic traditions. Includes a brief biography and a short annotated bibliography.

Orr, David. *Italian Renaissance Drama in England Before 1625: The Influence of Erudita Tragedy, Comedy, and Pastoral on Elizabethan and Jacobean Drama*. Chapel Hill: University of North Carolina Press, 1970. Orr compliments Gascoigne's skill in *Supposes* and finds the two plots neatly joined together, with "racy and readable prose." Recognizes the play's popularity and comments on Shakespeare's use of the comedy. Sees Gascoigne's tragedy *Jocasta* as neither skillful nor popular.

Prouty, Charles T. *George Gascoigne: Elizabethan Courtier, Soldier, and Poet*. New York: Columbia University Press, 1942. A full-length study of the life and works of Gascoigne, with attention to his military career and verses written for the court. The plays are treated too hastily, and *Supposes* is discussed mainly in connection with its sources and methods of translation. Emphasizes Gascoigne's great versatility throughout. Contains an appendix on Gascoigne's marriage to Elizabeth Bretton Boyes and another identifying the court ladies mentioned in Gascoigne's verse.

Sanders, Norman, et al. *The Revels History of Drama in English, 1500-1576*. Vol. 2. New York: Methuen, 1980. Of value to beginning students of Gascoigne. Considers three plays in connection with other English and continental plays in the dramatic traditions that they represent. Discusses *The Glasse of Governement*, for example, in the section on prodigal son plays. Contains compliments to Gascoigne's verse, a record of performances, and a valuable index.

Schelling, Felix E. *The Life and Writings of George Gascoigne*. 1893. Reprint. New York: Russell & Russell, 1967. A full-length older study, still of some value, by a scholar who is more interested in literary history than in literary criticism. It is readable and adequate on the life but is slight in the coverage of the plays, though it establishes the historical importance of *Supposes.* The bibliography is of little value. Index.

Millard T. Jones
(Updated by *Howard L. Ford*)

JOHN GAY

Born: Barnstaple, England; June 30, 1685
Died: London, England; December 4, 1732

Principal drama

The Mohocks, pb. 1712; *The Wife of Bath*, pr., pb. 1713, 1730 (revised); *The What D'ye Call It*, pr., pb. 1715; *Three Hours After Morning*, pr., pb. 1717 (with Alexander Pope and John Arbuthnot); *Dione*, pb. 1720 (verse tragedy); *The Captives*, pr., pb. 1724 (verse tragedy); *The Beggar's Opera*, pr., pb. 1728 (ballad opera); *Polly*, pb. 1729, pr. 1777 (ballad opera); *Acis and Galatea*, pr. 1731, pb. 1732 (libretto; music by George Frederick Handel); *Achilles*, pr., pb. 1733 (ballad opera); *The Distress'd Wife*, pr. 1734, pb. 1743; *The Rehearsal at Goatham*, pb. 1754; *Plays*, pb. 1760; *The Plays of John Gay*, pb. 1923 (2 volumes).

Other literary forms

In addition to his plays, John Gay is well known for his poetry, principally *Trivia: Or, The Art of Walking the Streets of London* (1716), the two series of *Fables* (1727 and 1738), and numerous songs and ballads. All of these writings are available in the 1926 edition of Gay's poetic works, edited by G. C. Faber, which also includes most of the plays, or in the two-volume *John Gay: Poetry and Prose* (1974), edited by Vinton A. Dearing with the assistance of Charles E. Beckwith. The entire canon, including all of Gay's dramatic works, is contained in the six-volume *Poetical, Dramatic, and Miscellaneous Works of John Gay* (1795, reprinted 1970). The poet's correspondence is collected in *The Letters of John Gay*, edited by C. F. Burgess (1966).

Achievements

Gay's abilities and significance as a dramatist have often been underestimated. Overshadowed by his more famous friends and sometime collaborators Alexander Pope and Jonathan Swift, Gay has generally been designated, as he was by Samuel Johnson, a poet of a "lower order." While his dramatic work may be uneven, it is generally well crafted and interesting; at its best, it displays originality, dramatic power, and a serious social concern. Gay's central theme is the corruption of English society, but while his criticism is often severe, his satire is more gentle and good-humored than that of his more famous literary friends. His work is also marked by a willingness to explore and reevaluate traditional forms, a practice which results sometimes in literary satire and burlesque and other times in experimentation and innovation. His experiments with mixed forms led him to the creation of a new dramatic type, the ballad opera, of which his masterpiece, *The Beggar's Opera*, is the first and finest example. While Gay's reputation rests principally on this unique work, his other plays abound with the same originality, good-natured satire, gifted lyric expression, and genuine comic spirit which have made *The Beggar's Opera* one of the few plays outside the Shakespearean canon to find a permanent place in the English theatrical repertory.

Biography

John Gay was born on June 30, 1685, at Barnstaple, in Devonshire. Apprenticed from 1702 to 1706 to a London silk mercer, Gay left the business world to make his living as a writer. For most of his life, he was plagued with financial problems, in part because of poor investments and in part because of difficulties in finding a long-standing patron. In 1712, he became secretary to the Duchess of Monmouth, and in 1714, he joined the household of Lord Clarendon, a position he kept less than a year. During these years, he became an active and well-liked member of the circle surrounding Alexander Pope and Jonathan Swift and remained close friends with both men all of his life.

In 1723, Gay received a government appointment which, along with an offer of lodgings at Whitehall, gave him a measure of financial security. His friendships with the royal circle, however, always made him hope for more substantial support, a hope which was perhaps unrealistic, since most of Gay's friends were Tories, and the Whigs, led by Prime Minister Robert Walpole, were in control of the government. Gay may have become concerned that the acceptance of a government post would mean the loss of his literary freedom, for in 1727, he turned down the offer of the position of Gentleman Usher to the two-year-old Princess Louisa.

Although Gay is consistently described as honest and congenial, and his works reflect his basically good-humored disposition, his struggles to achieve recognition and support left him somewhat disillusioned and disappointed. His dissatisfaction with the ruling party and with Walpole, whom he believed was responsible for blocking his own hopes, resulted in the strong vein of political satire which runs through his works. Walpole's displeasure with the satire in *The Beggar's Opera*, Gay's most financially successful play, led to the Lord Chamberlain's prohibition of its sequel, *Polly*, in 1728. The resulting squabble cost Gay his lodgings at Whitehall, and he spent the last years of his life, increasingly bothered by a chronic ailment, with his patrons, the Duke and Duchess of Queensberry. Gay died suddenly in London on December 4, 1732; he is buried in Westminster Abbey.

Analysis

John Gay's reputation rests primarily on *The Beggar's Opera*, to the extent that the rest of his work has gone largely unappreciated. Although none of his plays is as successful as *The Beggar's Opera*, a number of them show, in experimental form, the same characteristics that give Gay's masterpiece its unique form and spirit. Throughout his work, Gay is concerned with the emptiness and corruption of society, and his plays are distinguished by the innovative strategies he developed to present this theme: the use of pastoral forms to achieve a comparison between high and low classes, the inclusion of songs set to popular tunes, the use of literary satire and burlesque side by side with scenes of sincere feeling, the grafting of heroic qualities onto low characters, the use of carefully observed realistic detail, and the blending of several literary forms into a cohesive work. In those plays, principally the later ones, in which Gay is less innovative and more single-minded in purpose, there is a considerable loss of power. Gay's best plays—*The Beggar's Opera* and some of the earlier works—are characterized by a complex and original use of multiple dramatic forms which gives them a unique power and a surprisingly modern flavor.

Gay's interest in experimentation can be seen in his first two plays, *The Mohocks* and *The Wife of Bath*. Both plays have a clear literary ancestry, the first from Shakespearean comedy and the second from Geoffrey Chaucer's *The Canterbury Tales*. Described as a "tragi-comical farce," *The Mohocks* satirizes a group of bullies who roam London at night terrorizing the citizens. The aristocratic men of the gang are confronted by a group of watchmen strongly reminiscent of Dogberry's crew in William Shakespeare's *Much Ado About Nothing*. *The Wife of Bath* imagines the further adventures of Chaucer and some of the Canterbury pilgrims at a stop along their route. Both plays are essentially comic in form, ending in reconciliation and appropriate marriages. *The Mohocks* contains a great deal of literary burlesque, while *The Wife of Bath* gently mocks both Chaucer and the eighteenth century society from which its characters are drawn by a process of deflation, a technique Gay used in a more serious and sophisticated way in *The Beggar's Opera*. Both plays, with their combination of literary burlesque, topical satire, and farce and with their use of songs set to popular music, show Gay experimenting with techniques he later blended more effectively in *The Beggar's Opera*.

Perhaps the most complex and interesting of Gay's early plays is *The What D'ye Call It*. The play mystified its audience at first but eventually became a success. Its title, which recalls Shakespeare's *As You Like It* or *Twelfth Night*, leads one to expect literary parody, but that is only a part of the play's complex effect. Gay works here with the technique, also reminiscent of Shakespeare, of the play-within-a-play. A group of rustics are performing a tragedy, especially created for the occasion, before a country lord and his friends. The couplet verse and excessive sentiment of the tragedy are deflated by being delivered by the simple rustics. At the same time, the real problems and emotions of the lower-class characters are given a measure of dignity through their expression in poetic form. Gay uses the exaggeration of farce to create a blend of laughter and sympathy, an effect not unlike that of modern tragicomedy or Theater of the Absurd. This complex combination disorients the audience and destroys any idea it may have about the proper hierarchy or use of dramatic forms. At the same time, Gay resolves both inner and outer plays through a marriage that cuts across class lines and fittingly caps the play's social comment. With its combination of social satire and literary burlesque, its use of ballads, and its ability to contain and evoke genuine feelings, *The What D'ye Call It* was a major step on Gay's path toward *The Beggar's Opera*.

In his two verse tragedies *Dione* and *The Captives*, Gay abandoned his experiments with literary form to work in a single literary mode without questioning its conventions. Both plays are concerned with fidelity in love, a theme which also appears in *The Beggar's Opera*; they also examine the social conditions that affect fidelity and independence. In *Dione*, the shallowness and infidelity of Evander and the unhappiness of court life are contrasted to the fidelity of Dione and the simple goodness of the pastoral life. This contrast is developed more fully in *The Captives*, in which the imprisoned prince and princess, who have lost all wealth and power, remain faithful to each other and to those who have befriended them in the midst of a court characterized by lust, bribery, and political intrigue. The scheming queen, who uses the king's devotion and wealth to maintain her power, is not far removed from those characters in *The Beggar's Opera* who thrive on a system of bribes and payoffs.

In *The Beggar's Opera*, Gay brought to fulfillment both his experiments with dramatic form and his increasingly serious criticism of society. While it may be true that the initial idea for *The Beggar's Opera* lay in Swift's often quoted suggestion that Gay write a "Newgate pastoral," the actual work that Gay produced has a much more complex genesis. Certainly his central theme, the sameness of all men whatever their social position, was a logical development from his earlier works, especially *The What D'ye Call It*. The unorthodox form, a combination of pastoral, burlesque, satire, tragedy, and opera, was also a logical extension of his experiments with mixed form. The realistic detail of the criminal world and the inspiration for some of the major characters came from recent publicity surrounding the capture and execution of several notorious London criminals. In addition, *The Beggar's Opera* was designed as a response to the Italian opera, which, with its artificiality, unbelievable plots, and foreign music, was becoming increasingly popular in England. The innovative form of the ballad opera allowed Gay both to satirize the extravagance of the foreign opera and to offer a native entertainment as a replacement.

A final ingredient in Gay's dramatic mixture was political satire. Gay had criticized the corruption of city life previously, but before *The Beggar's Op-*

era, most of his criticism had been general. In *The Beggar's Opera*, he turned his wit directly on English politics through a sustained comparison between the London underworld and the British political system. Gay's turn to more specific and more biting political satire was probably a result of his gradual disillusionment with English society and his immediate disappointment over his own lack of recognition.

The Beggar's Opera, like most of Gay's plays, has its roots in the pastoral tradition. An essential element of pastoral is the comparison of upper and lower classes, a comparison Gay used in his earlier plays primarily to ridicule the upper class. In *The Beggar's Opera*, however, it is the similarities rather than the differences between the two classes that are stressed. The lower class is dignified by being portrayed as just as good as the upper. At the same time, the aristocrats are described as no better than the thieves and prostitutes of Newgate. In *The Beggar's Opera*, Gay pictures a society that is corrupt on all levels.

Gay's thesis is established in the opening scene of the play, a scene that also establishes the central organizing principle of both high and low societies. The inhabitants of this world are motivated solely by self-interest. Peachum protects the thieves as long as it is profitable to do so; when they are no longer useful, he turns them in for the reward money. Lockit similarly turns his charges over to the justices, or, if the criminals can offer a better deal, arranges for their release. When Polly announces that she has married Macheath, her parents' primary concern is for their own safety. Even Polly's attachment to Macheath is motivated in part by self-interest.

The one exception to this dedication to self-interest is Macheath, who displays a greater moral integrity than anyone else in the play. He is open and generous with his comrades, polite and considerate with women, and aloof from the vices of the gentlemen with whom he must associate. He is more than once referred to as a great man and is often given phrases reminiscent of Shakespearean heroes. His struggle for independence from the system controlled by Peachum gives him a kind of tragic stature; his dangerous attraction to women may be seen as his tragic flaw. He is genuinely surprised and disappointed by betrayal, first by Jenny and then by Jemmy Twitcher. The second betrayal is particularly disheartening, for it shows that there is no honor even among his comrades.

As engaging as Macheath's character is, Gay does not allow him to remain unblemished. His lack of courage as he faces death and the improbable appearance of four more wives with a child apiece seriously undermine the character's attractiveness. The deflation of Macheath's character also reduces Polly's stature somewhat, although her loyalty remains admirable. As Macheath approaches death, the author's and the audience's attitude toward him and Polly is ambiguous.

Macheath's execution is interrupted by the Beggar and Player, whose opening conversation introduced the play. The Player, voicing the audience's lingering sympathies for Macheath and Polly, protests Macheath's death. The Beggar, supposedly the author of the opera, points to the perfect poetic justice of his intended ending but agrees to a reprieve, since an opera must end happily, "no matter how absurdly these things are brought about." Thus, the "taste of the town" dictates not only an absurd ending, a thrust at the conventions of Italian opera, but also an immoral one, for none of the characters is punished. The way of the world will not allow Macheath a heroic end, but insists that he be drawn back into society and reduced to its level. The playwright cannot afford to take a moral stand; his integrity, like everything in the play, can be had for a price. Gay's final attack is not only against society but also, in a sense, against himself.

The Beggar's Opera was an instant critical and popular success; it has also had considerable influence on the English theater. Gay's attack on Italian opera is generally considered responsible for the decline in that genre's popularity during the next few years. Gay's innovative form, the ballad opera—a play including ballads sung to the tunes of popular songs—continued to be popular for many years and is one of the ancestors of the modern musical comedy. The success of the political satire in *The Beggar's Opera* encouraged other writers to attack the ruling party from the stage, leading eventually to the closing of the theaters and the Licensing Act of 1737. *The Beggar's Opera* remained popular during the eighteenth and nineteenth centuries and found new life in the twentieth century through Bertolt Brecht's adaptation of it, *The Threepenny Opera* (1928). While the play's initial success was partially the result of its treatment of contemporary art and politics, its lasting popularity attests both Gay's originality and his exploration of permanent and universal problems of human experience.

Perhaps to capitalize on the success of *The Beggar's Opera* and perhaps to answer criticism of the play's moral stance, Gay quickly produced a sequel, *Polly*, also a ballad opera. In it, Macheath, stripped of all heroic qualities, has been transported to the West Indies, where he lives with Jenny Diver as head of a band of pirates. Polly travels there to find him, but her quest is interrupted by a war between the pirates and the European planters and native Indians. Disguised as a boy, Polly captures Macheath, who is disguised as a black, and unknowingly sends him to his death. The play is more melodramatic and sentimental than *The Beggar's Opera*, but it contains some biting satire and clever literary burlesque. The contrast between high and low classes becomes a contrast between civilized and natural man, suggesting that the faults Gay finds in society are cultural, not part of man's nature. Unfortunately, Gay labors his moral point too heavily, and *Polly* never reaches the emotional or satiric heights of *The Beggar's Opera*.

Gay's final ballad opera, *Achilles*, is even more single-minded and less satisfying than *Polly*. To prevent her son from going to the Trojan War, Achilles' mother hides him, dressed as a girl, among the daughters of King Lycomedes. Gay exploits the farcical elements of the situation, but the characters never become fully human, and the play lacks the dramatic tension and ambiguities of Gay's more complex and experimental works. The same can be said of the comedy of manners *The Distress'd Wife*, another variation on the city-country comparison, but with little new to offer.

The short satire *The Rehearsal at Goatham* is more interesting and seems to refer more directly to Gay's own experiences with *The Beggar's Opera* and *Polly*; the Lord Chamberlain had prohibited the production of *Polly* without what Gay and his friends considered to be a fair hearing. Inspired by a scene in Miguel de Cervantes' *Don Quixote de la Mancha*, *The Rehearsal at Goatham* portrays a performance of the puppet show *Melisandra*. The performance is prohibited by the town aldermen because it supposedly contains material offensive to the local citizens. The townsmen agree to watch a rehearsal of the piece to see if it is acceptable and proceed to find scandalous references to themselves in the most innocent phrases of the play, thus exposing their own foolishness and misconduct. *The Rehearsal at Goatham* has some of the complexity of Gay's early works, with literary and social satire developed simultaneously, but it lacks the human characters and ability to evoke a full emotional response which characterizes *The Beggar's Opera*.

While Gay's reputation rests principally on *The Beggar's Opera*, his other plays are not without merit. He produced a number of delightful comedies, and his two verse tragedies are well crafted, if somewhat sentimental. The early plays show a development of theme and technique that leads directly to the powerful thesis and original form of *The Beggar's Opera*. The later plays, although weaker, continue to explore the central thematic concerns of Gay's masterpiece—the corruption of society and the difficulty of the individual, especially the artist, in maintaining his honor and independence. Gay's greatest achievement lies in his experimentation with traditional forms. This formal exploration, which gives even his less successful plays great complexity and vitality, led to the creation of a new dramatic form, the ballad opera, and one brilliant play which has had an important place in the English theatrical repertory for more than two hundred years.

Other major works

POETRY: *Rural Sports*, 1713; *The Fan*, 1714; *The Shepherd's Week*, 1714; *Trivia: Or, The Art of Walking the Streets of London*, 1716; *Poems on Several Occasions*, 1720, 1731; *To a Lady on Her Passion for Old China*, 1725; *Fables*, 1727, 1738; *Gay's Chair: Poems Never Before Printed*, 1820; *The Poetical Works of John Gay*, 1926 (G. C. Faber, editor; includes plays).

NONFICTION: *A Letter to a Lady*, 1714; *The Letters of John Gay*, 1966 (C. F. Burgess, editor).

MISCELLANEOUS: *Poetical, Dramatic, and Miscellaneous Works of John Gay*, 1795, 1970 (6 volumes); *John Gay: Poetry and Prose*, 1974 (2 volumes; Vinton A. Dearing with Charles E. Beckwith, editors).

Bibliography

Armens, Sven M. *John Gay: Social Critic.* 1954. Reprint. New York: Octagon Books, 1966. Armens examines Gay as a "serious" writer through an investigation of the reiterated themes in both his drama and his poetry. Armens contends that Gay was not merely the minor member of the Scriblerus Club or the writer of one successful but trivial play. Rather, he contends that Gay made a major contribution to eighteenth century literature, even though it was primarily through the pastoral lyric and the satiric and burlesque eclogue. Notes, index, and bibliography.

Gaye, Phœbe Fenwick. *John Gay: His Place in the Eighteenth Century.* London: Collins, 1938. Gaye provides a historical and literary context for the life and works of John Gay. This biography presents Gay's intellectual development simultaneously with his literary one. Contrary to what the title may intimate, however, Gay's "place" is not evaluated; it is only reported historically through the eyes of his eighteenth century contemporaries.

Irving, William Henry. *John Gay: Favorite of the Wits.* Durham, N.C.: Duke University Press, 1940. In this standard biography, Irving presents a well-researched, factual account of Gay's life and career. He includes a discussion of Gay's friendship with, and literary relationship to, his contemporaries, such as Jonathan Swift and Alexander Pope. Illustrations and index.

Lewis, Peter, and Nigel Wood, eds. *John Gay and the Scriblerians.* New York: St. Martin's Press, 1988. These ten essays, the result of the tercentenary of Gay's birth, are important in presenting later trends in the analysis and criticism of Gay's work. They focus on the dichotomies found in Gay's life and writings, the perplexing contradictions that now seem to have been purposefully and carefully constructed. These reevaluations of Gay's contributions will alter and color most future research and commentary. Notes and index.

Noble, Yvonne, ed. *Twentieth Century Interpretations of "The Beggar's Opera."* Englewood Cliffs, N.J.: Prentice-Hall, 1975. This brief collection of nine essays provides an excellent introduction to Gay's most important play and its relevance in the twentieth century in terms of its literary, musical, and theatrical contributions. In addition, the introduction places the play into its political and artistic contexts, increasing the reader's understanding of its historical impact and contemporary importance. Bibliography and side-by-side chronologies of Gay's life and times.

Spacks, Patricia Meyer. *John Gay.* New York: Twayne, 1965. Spacks explores Gay's struggle to find an appropriate poetic voice. Gay's development is traced chronologically, treating the poems and plays separately. The naïveté of the early poems slowly gives way to Gay's ability to deal with simplicities with great sophistication. Spacks also treats Gay's perceptions and his literary forms. References, annotated bibliography, and index.

Kathleen Latimer
(Updated by *Gerald S. Argetsinger*)

JACK GELBER

Born: Chicago, Illinois; April 12, 1932

Principal drama

The Connection, pr. 1959, pb. 1960; *The Apple*, pr., pb. 1961; *Square in the Eye*, pr. 1965, pb. 1966; *The Cuban Thing*, pr. 1968, pb. 1969; *Sleep*, pr., pb. 1972; *Barbary Shore*, pr. 1974 (adaptation of Norman Mailer's novel); *Jack Gelber's New Play: Rehearsal*, pr. 1976; *Starters*, pr. 1980.

Other literary forms

Most of Jack Gelber's plays have appeared in print. Gelber has also translated Franz Xaver Kroetz's play *Farmyard*, with Michael Roloff. The work was produced at the Yale Theatre in New Haven, Connecticut, on January 22, 1975, and published by Urizen the following year. In addition, the film version of *The Connection*, released in 1962, was based on Gelber's screenplay adaptation. The movie, directed by Shirley Clarke, was screened at the Cannes Festival (1961) and banned as obscene by New York State, though the New York State Supreme Court later found the language in the movie not to be obscene. Gelber's only nontheatrical literary endeavor has been a novel, *On Ice* (1964); some of the concepts that he deals with in this prose work reappear in *Sleep*.

Achievements

Whether fairly or not, Jack Gelber is primarily known for *The Connection*. The drama was popular enough to be made into a motion picture, and it achieved critical success as well, bringing the playwright the Obie, the Vernon Rice Award, and the New York Drama Critics Poll Award for most promising playwright of the 1959-1960 season. There were three reasons for the startling success of the dramatist's first play. First, and most obvious, are the nontraditional characters, setting, subject matter, and plot line. Gelber did in the American theater what John Osborne had done in the British theater with *Look Back in Anger* three years earlier; he exposed the theatergoing public to a new world, in this case, that of skid-row junkies waiting for their heroin connection to arrive with a fix. Second, the play's thematic content is important; it goes far beyond the dreary, desolate, frustrated life of the characters portrayed, for the addicts are really metaphors for modern mankind, much as Vladimir and Estragon are in Samuel Beckett's *Waiting for Godot*. Finally, Gelber's emphasis on improvisation has had a major impact on contemporary drama. Just as free verse has a special appeal to bad poets and is easily misused by them, this approach to playwriting can lead to horrendous results, but when used by someone with Gelber's ability, the improvisational ingredient reinforces one of the theater's basic strengths, its immediacy, and enhances the participatory nature of drama, involving the audience in a way that recalls, indeed reincarnates, the origins of the genre in public ceremonies.

Much of Gelber's writing since *The Connection* has been intended to broaden the theater's possibilities even further; it should never be forgotten that drama, even when based on a text and literary conventions, is essentially rooted in performance. Some of Gelber's subsequent efforts have extended the innovative strategies of *The Connection*, while others have moved in new directions. The dramatist continues to progress, but he has yet to equal the success, either popularly or critically, of *The Connection*.

Biography

Jack Gelber was born in Chicago, Illinois, on April 12, 1932, the son of Harold and Molly (née Singer) Gelber. The playwright has said that as a high school student, he passed the time playing the tuba and attending movies and burlesque shows, but he never went to the legitimate theater, that he did not even know the theater existed until he went to college. Even today, he mentions with respect the Russian novelists—Ivan Turgenev, Maxim Gorky, and Nikolai Gogol—who originally attracted him as well as Rainer Maria Rilke and the German Expressionists. He has also expressed an interest in Buddhism and in "religious states of being."

During the summers of his undergraduate years at the University of Illinois, Urbana, Gelber followed his father's trade as a sheet-metal worker; he has also been a shipfitter's helper in San Francisco and a mimeograph operator for the United Nations. Gelber was graduated from the university with a B.S. in journalism in 1953, and he wrote poetry before turning to dramaturgy. He became involved in Julian Beck and Judith Malina's Living Theatre, an experimental theater group, which mounted *The Connection* under Malina's direction for a run of 768 performances. *The Apple* was also written to be performed by the Living Theatre (sixty-four performances). These first two plays have been performed in a number of foreign countries, including Brazil, England, France, Germany, and Italy. *Square in the Eye* (thirty-one performances) was intended to be staged by the Living Theatre, too, though by 1965, the group was no longer based in the United States. Meanwhile, Gelber visited Cuba in 1963 and again in 1967, and *The Cuban Thing* (one performance) grew out of his experience in that country under Fidel Castro's rule. *Sleep* (thirty-two performances) followed in 1972, and *Jack Gelber's New Play: Rehearsal* was mounted in 1976.

In addition to writing for the theater, Gelber also has been active as a director. Besides his own *The Cuban Thing*, *Jack Gelber's New Play: Rehearsal*, and his adaptation of Norman Mailer's *Barbary Shore*, the dramatist has directed Arnold Wesker's *The Kitchen* (in 1966), Arthur Kopit's *In-*

dians (for the Royal Shakespeare Company at the Aldwych Theatre, in London, in 1968), Merle Molofsky's *Kool Aid* (in 1971), Frank Chin's *The Chickencoop Chinaman* (in 1972), Robert Coover's *The Kid* (in 1972), Tennessee Williams' *A Streetcar Named Desire* (in 1976), Miguel Rinero's *Eulogy for a Small-Time Thief* (in 1977), and Sam Shepard's *Seduced* (in 1979). In 1973, he received an Obie Award for his direction of *The Kid* the previous year. Gelber's experience as a director establishes him as a man of the theater in the fullest sense. More important, working as a director provides him with a wider perspective on the potentials and limitations of drama that he can apply in his writing.

In 1963, Gelber began alternating between fellowships and teaching to support his writing. In 1963, he received a Guggenheim Fellowship for creative writing for the theater; he was a writer-in-residence at the City College of New York from 1965 to 1966; he received a second Guggenheim Fellowship in 1966; from 1967 to 1972, he was employed as an adjunct professor of drama at Columbia University; in 1972, he was awarded a Rockefeller grant as playwright-in-residence at the American Place Theatre; and that same year he became a professor of drama at Brooklyn College of the City University of New York. In 1974, Gelber was the recipient of a Columbia Broadcasting System-Yale University Fellowship, and the following year he received a National Endowment for the Arts Fellowship. Gelber has lectured and organized workshops on the new play development circuit, notably at the 1983 Aspen New Play Festival in Colorado.

Analysis

In *The Connection*, his first, most famous, and best play, Gelber established himself as an innovative force in the American theater. His experimental approach to his themes wedded form and content far more successfully than would have been possible in a conventionally constructed drama.

The Connection is an exploration of universal human need, metaphorically expressed as a heroin fix; Gelber's play contains little action in any traditional dramatic sense. There is essentially no movement in the plot of this two-act play, since the characters are so desperate in their need that they remain in Teach's room, the only setting in the play, afraid to leave for fear that Cowboy, their dope supplier, might come while they are gone. This is not to say that nothing happens in the play or that no dramatic tension is created. Tension evolves out of the relationships between the room's inhabitants, the question of whether Cowboy will ever come, and the question of what will happen when he arrives. This atmosphere is reinforced by the emotions and physical discomfort displayed by the characters. More traditional plays have dealt with similar themes—Clifford Odets' *Waiting for Lefty* (pr., pb. 1935), Eugene O'Neill's *The Iceman Cometh* (wr. 1939, pr., pb. 1946), and even O'Neill's *Long Day's Journey into Night* (wr. 1941, pb. 1955, pr. 1956)—and invariably plays of this nature are condemned by imperceptive critics who demand constant action onstage. In this play, Gelber's form and content come together with an unexpected result. Following the approach of the Theater of the Absurd, the plot does not appear to be carefully and logically structured. Events that do not seem related (in an Aristotelian sense) occur one after another. Things simply happen onstage, and the feeling of improvisation that Gelber so carefully cultivates is very frustrating to those members of the audience who expect, or need, to have everything carefully spelled out in a strict format as the play progresses.

For other members of the audience, the mood of improvisation is intellectually stimulating; a sophisticated audience soon realizes that the supposedly random happenings and the tedious waiting reflect the drama's theme. If the audience feels frustrated by Cowboy's not coming, they can better imagine how the characters onstage feel (much as film director Michelangelo Antonioni bored the audience of his 1964 film *The Red Desert* for nearly three hours to demonstrate how boring life is for a certain class of Italians). The way jazz music is used here also serves to emphasize the playwright's theme: The essential character of jazz is improvisational, and the music in the play varies according to the musicians' moods rather than corresponding to events transpiring onstage, as would be expected in a musical. At the same time, the music itself provides some movement and a feeling of transition (though, again, in a nontraditional way, frequently increasing the audience's frustration and anxiety, since the changes that appear to be signaled by the musical breaks often remain unrealized).

In accordance with the stage directions, *The Connection* begins with the players coming onstage and arranging themselves around the set, giving the appearance of fourth-wall realism, which maintains the fiction of characters acting out their lives with no interaction between spectator and actor. As the actors move about, they are unhurried and seem to have no plans; they merely walk onstage and stand or sit randomly. Gelber emphasizes the spontaneity of the situation by indicating in the stage directions that "perhaps" there is a sign on the wall, or "perhaps" a painting or an orange-crate bookcase is in the room.

Two actors stroll down the theater aisle, and act 1 has begun. The first words are spoken by Jim Dunn, who introduces himself and Jaybird to the audience as the producer and author of *The Connection*, respectively. Those who feel that the play is about heroin should be alerted by these statements that Gelber wants the audience to be aware that they are watching a play, and that they should not take what happens onstage to be literally true. Throughout the play, one character or another directs his dialogue at the audience to make sure that they do not exercise a willing suspension of disbelief and accept the action onstage as real, even momentarily. Gelber does not want his audience to become absorbed in what is happening in the play; instead, he wants them to be constantly drawing analogies between what is transpiring in front of them and other areas in their lives. Moreover, to make sure that the audience understands exactly what the author intends, these asides clearly state the point that he wants to make. For example, Dunn announces that most recent studies of drug addiction, an "anti-social habit," have not had much to do with the subject of narcotics, per se.

As soon as the dialogue directed at the audience is completed, the Fourth Musician asks if Cowboy has come back yet, thereby immediately establishing the concept of waiting. Within a few moments, Jaybird interrupts the action to lecture the audience, reminding them that they are watching an art form, improvised theater, and noting that if they perceive a relationship between jazz and narcotics they are making their own "connection," not his.

Suspense is generated when there is a knock at the door of Teach's room, but it is not Cowboy who enters. Soon after this, two more characters enter, the First and Second Photographers. One is a black man dressed in a white suit, who is swift and agile; the other is a white man in a black suit, who moves slowly, "clodlike." During the course of the play, these two exchange their personalities and their clothing, piece by piece, as Gelber underscores the artificiality of his play so that his themes will receive more attention than the context in which they are presented.

The various characters are introduced by Dunn (Ernie is a "dope-addict psychopath," Sam is an "expert in folk lore," and so on), and the question about Cowboy's whereabouts is continually rephrased. Gelber continually reminds his audience that dope is not his subject, as when Sam, in a tirade attacking society, asserts that people who work and worry about money and new clothes are addicts ("chlorophyll . . . aspirin . . . vitamin") who are hooked worse than he is. Solly, the intellectual, agrees, commenting that everybody is looking for a fix, a fix of "hope"—to forget, to remember, to be sad, to be happy, to be. Later, he says that everyone is his own connection. At one point, Solly theorizes about Jaybird's intentions in writing the play. Sam ironically undercuts Solly's pronouncements, noting that Solly may be educated and know a lot, but that he is in the room waiting just as everybody else is. As the play progresses, a bit is revealed about the background and nature of most of the characters, yet when act 1 ends, Cowboy has still not appeared and everyone is still waiting for him.

Act 2 opens with a jazz break, and then Cowboy enters. Ironically, as Cowboy takes each of the characters into the bathroom to give them a fix, Sister Salvation visits with those remaining in the room, preaching religious salvation to them, unaware of what is going on about her. The men, including the Second Photographer and Jaybird, get stoned and begin telling stories, and again they turn to Jaybird intermittently to see if they have discovered the meaning that he is trying to convey. Teach takes an overdose, and this leads the characters to discuss why narcotics, particularly marijuana, are illegal. The play ends with Jaybird distressed that he has failed to get his characters to kick their habit, presumably because the actors have actually taken drugs onstage in their play-within-a-play. He has learned one lesson from this evening's experience: "It all fits together," and it fits together on the stage, he tells Dunn. By way of the final exchange in the play, Gelber has reiterated his two major themes—all people need a connection, and innovative theater is an excellent medium for expressing this message.

Besides these devices, Gelber extends the traditional boundaries of the stage in other ways. For example, during the intermission between the two acts, several of the actors mingle with the audience members in the lobby, panhandling, and later, an actor who is pretending to be a member of the audience engages an actor onstage in conversation. At first glance, the drama is chaotic. Underneath, however, it is a carefully structured work, much in the style of the early plays of Luigi Pirandello.

In Gelber's second play, *The Apple*, several of the devices employed in *The Connection* are extended to further blur the boundary between art and reality, as when the actors use their real names onstage, and when the painting that has been created onstage during the performance is auctioned off at the end of the show. Based on an incident involving cast members that took place in a nearby coffee shop during the time that *The Connection* was in rehearsal, this three-act drama is set in a "restaurant or coffee shop." Like *The Connection*, *The Apple* has no formal beginning; there is no curtain, and the actors and actresses move from the audience to the stage and begin to deliver their lines. Similarly, throughout the performance, the actors remind the audience that they are watching a play: Anna announces that she is in charge of the box office; Jabez comments on "control," stating that "art is precision." Gelber purposely confuses and misleads his audience as to the significance of the play's title; the audience tries to determine how apples operate symbolically in the play, but the numerous clues that the dramatist presents appear to be unrelated. In act 1, Anna enters with a bowl of apples, and Iris starts to eat one (which Ajax takes from her); in act 2, Iris tells Jabez that she is his apple; in act 3, Tom pulls a rotten, half-eaten apple out of Jabez's mouth and throws it at the mannequin that has been onstage for most of the play. The characters talk about acting the Adam and Eve story, and Ace concludes the play with the revelation that the apple "is a golden Chinese apple and stands for knowledge." It is likely that this is, indeed, what Gelber means for the fruit to symbolize, and this makes some sense within the various contexts in which apples are represented, but ultimately, the play is so disjointed that it does not seem to matter whether any meaning can be affixed to or drawn from the apples. The multiple possibilities of interpretation engender confusion, to the point that the audience becomes bored rather than gaining any insight.

The premise for *The Apple* is simple, even though its realization is muddled. In a coffee shop during rehearsals for a play, one of the actors goes mad. In act 1, the audience observes the madman; in act 2, the presentation is from the point of view of the madman; and act 3 again puts the audience in the observing position, with Ace trying to tie everything together. Gelber has said that the title of the play originally referred to New York City, but "now I just say it's a satire on death." Perhaps the death of individuality, art, society, and intellectuality, killed by prejudice and lack of understanding and human sympathy, is implied in the play, but none of this holds together very well.

Gelber is to be admired for trying to extend the limits of theater even further than he did in *The Connection*, through a combination of straight dramatic techniques, Theater of the Absurd devices, mime, blackouts, parody, slapstick, and masks, with frequent outright social commentary and philosophizing about the nature of art and the artist. Unfortunately, *The Apple* has neither the intensity nor the underlying structural stability of *The Connection*, and ultimately it fails, both as an intellectual statement and as a piece of theater.

Gelber's next play, *Square in the Eye* (which originally had the working title "Let's Face It"), is more conventional and more successful, up to a point. The play covers a multitude of subjects: life, death, sex, art, and relationships between husbands and wives, friends, lovers, parents and children, and teachers and students. It begins with traditional dramatic exposition, in which Ed tells the audience about his life, family, and work, but the exposition is delivered in an unconventional manner, because the actor enters from the auditorium and delivers his speech like a stand-up comedian. There are devices throughout the play that are reminiscent of experimental techniques used by Bertolt Brecht, Thornton Wilder, and Tennessee Williams—movies, still photographs, and so on.

Gelber has called *Square in the Eye* "a tale and instant replay, about art and artists, marriage and death." To make his point, the dramatist uses flashbacks, a technique that presents the plot out of chronological order. Scene 1 of act 1 takes place before Sandy's death, scene 2 is in the hospital immediately after her death, and scene 3 records Ed's second marriage, six weeks later. Scene 1 of act 2 flashes back to a time before Sandy's death, and scene 2 occurs on the day before her death. This play contains more humor than does Gelber's earlier work, and despite occasional confusion because of flashbacks, the narrative is basically straightforward. Unlike *The Apple*, *Square in the Eye* is about real people with whom an audience can sympathize, although some of the techniques used in it can be disturbing.

Some critics claim that Gelber's next work, *The Cuban Thing*, is not really a play but a political "happening." The production shows the effects of Castro's revolution on an upper-middle-class Cuban family from 1958 to 1964, as their alliance changes from Fulgencio Batista to Castro. On the night before the actual premiere of the play, the fifth of a series of preview performances was marred by the explosion of five powder bombs. The play was considered pro-Castro by many, and poor reviews, claims that the dramatist had researched his material poorly, threats to the actors, active opposition by Spanish-language television and newspapers, and audience fears about physical violence led to the drama's closing after a run of only one night. An example of the "theater of commitment" or the "theater of revolution," *The Cuban Thing* was presented as a happening, a free-form event popular in the early and mid-1960's. As part of a Cuban Action Night, the play was mounted during an evening of Cuban music, Cuban food, and various other activities centering on all aspects of Cuban culture (including politics). By all accounts, however, *The Cuban Thing* was anti-theater at its worst—bad writing that could not be salvaged by Gelber's own directing.

Square in the Eye was written during the playwright's first term as a Guggenheim fellow; *Sleep* was written while the playwright held a Rockefeller Foundation grant as playwright-in-residence at the American Place Theatre. Like *Square in the Eye*, *Sleep* is more conventional in form and content than those works that immediately preceded it. The play revolves around experiments into the nature of sleep conducted by two scientists, and one of the subjects of their experimentation, a young man named Gil. The play features a simple plot line and a good deal of humor as well as commentary on mind control (supposedly induced by means of sleep deprivation) and the role of the scientist in society. There are also dream sequences (the play-within-a-play technique) simulated within the framework of the experiment; several of the sequences bear some resemblance to *Interview* (pr. 1964), a revue sketch by Harold Pinter. For the first time, Gelber focuses on character rather than on events or abstract concepts, an extension of certain lines begun in *Square in the Eye*. In his novel *On Ice*, Gelber's protagonist has dreams that sometimes prove to be realities. In *Sleep*, Gil's dreams may not be identical to reality, but they reflect his reality outside the sleep laboratory more accurately than he perceives the reality that he experiences within the lab. Replacing the blackouts used to separate sketches in *The Apple* (particularly in act 2, the madman's act) are interruptions by the scientists as they check their subject between dream sequences. To some extent, the theme of appearance versus reality runs through all of Gelber's works, but in *Square in the Eye* it is dealt with on a conscious level and in an imaginative though relatively traditional way. The result is one of his most conventional and, ironically, most successful works.

Jack Gelber's New Play: Rehearsal depicts the casting, rehearsal, and, finally, the cancellation of a play about prison life (the stage author and one of the actors are convicts). Whereas *Sleep* was patently not about art and the theater, this play's subject is expressly the theater. The convicts are present merely as theatrical counters, not to provide a means to comment on convicts and prison life.

Like John Osborne, Gelber burst on the theatrical scene with a startling, innovative first play. In the years since then, he has not written much, and he has suffered several failures. He has also constantly tried to expand theatrical boundaries, and even his failures in this area have been important. When he has been successful, he has altered the nature of contemporary American drama.

Other major works

NOVEL: *On Ice*, 1964.

SCREENPLAY: *The Connection*, 1962.

TRANSLATION: *Farmyard*, 1976 (with Michael Roloff; of Franz Xaver Kroetz's play *Stallerhof*).

Bibliography

Brustein, Robert. *Season of Discontent: Dramatic Opinions, 1959-1965.* New York: Simon & Schuster, 1965. Contains a positive, descriptive review of *The Connection:* "It takes about ten minutes to realize that you are witnessing an extraordinary performance in which everything, including your initial response, has been planned with absolute precision. . . ." The text, Brustein states, "forms the basis for a brilliant theatrical occasion."

Cohn, Ruby. *New American Dramatists, 1960-1990.* 2d ed. New York: St. Martin's Press, 1991. A good reprise of Gelber's association with the Living Theatre, the pivotal place of *The Connection* in subsequent theater experiments ("the trumpet of the Off-Off Broadway movement"), and his place alongside Israel Horovitz, Jean-Claude van Itallie, Megan Terry, and María Irene Fornés, in "actor-activated" theater.

Gelber, Jack. "Jack Gelber Talks About Surviving in the Theater." Interview by Albert Bermel. *Theater* 9 (Spring, 1978): 46-58. A long, penetrating interview, touching on Gelber's views on staged readings (a process he has endorsed), the finances of playwriting ("pitifully small"), and the idea behind *Square in the Eye*, an attempt by Gelber to "expand my interests into multi-media."

Gilman, Richard. *Common and Uncommon Masks: Writings on Theatre, 1961-1970.* New York: Random House, 1971. "Bad Connection" is Gilman's opinion regarding the "disappointment" of *The Apple*, which he contrasts with *The Connection:* "Like *The Connection*, the play's cast is an abstract community" but "all that selling of coffee that's brewed on stage and the nightly auctioning off of the painter's work" were embarrassing.

Shank, Theodore. *American Alternative Theater.* New York: Grove Press, 1982. Describes *The Connection* in a chapter on the beginnings of the Living Theatre and the desire of Julian Beck "not merely to entertain but to affect the audience so deeply that it had a cleansing effect." Beck eventually thought of the play, however, as "deluding the audience." Bibliography and index.

Wellwarth, George. *The Theater of Protest and Paradox: Developments in the Avant-Garde Drama.* New York: New York University Press, 1964. Claims that Gelber looks at drug addiction "with a strong bias in favor of the addict." Disagrees with some critics' praise of the play: "Impressive, certainly, but hardly the way to write a play." Also mentions *The Apple*, judging it to be "totally without meaning."

Steven H. Gale
(Updated by *Thomas J. Taylor*)

WILLIAM GIBSON

Born: New York, New York; November 13, 1914

Principal drama

I Lay in Zion, pr. 1943, pb. 1947; *A Cry of Players*, pr. 1948, pb. 1969; *Dinny and the Witches: A Frolic on Grave Matters*, pr. 1948, pb. 1960; *The Ruby*, pb. 1955, pr. 1957 (libretto; as William Mass); *The Miracle Worker*, pr. 1957 (televised), pb. 1957, pr. 1959 (staged), pb. 1959; *Two for the Seesaw*, pr. 1958, pb. 1959; *Golden Boy*, pr. 1964, pb. 1965 (musical; adaptation of Clifford Odets' play, music by Charles Strouse, lyrics by Lee Adams); *John and Abigail*, pr. 1969; *American Primitive*, pr. 1971, pb. 1972 (revision of *John and Abigail*); *The Body and the Wheel: A Play Made from the Gospels*, pr. 1974, pb. 1975; *The Butterfingers Angel, Mary and Joseph, Herod the Nut, and the Slaughter of Twelve Hit Carols in a Pear Tree*, pr. 1974, pb. 1975; *Golda*, pr. 1977, pb. 1978; *Goodly Creatures*, pr. 1980; *Monday After the Miracle*, pr. 1982, pb. 1983; *Handy Dandy*, pr. 1984; *Raggedy Ann and Andy*, pr. 1984 (also as *Rag Dolly* and *Raggedy Ann*; music and lyrics by Joe Raposo).

Other literary forms

Although William Gibson is primarily a dramatist, his initial successes were as a poet and novelist. His first book, *Winter Crook* (1948), is a collection of his early verse, which is marked by complex use of nature imagery and metaphor to explore highly personal concerns. The novel *The Cobweb* (1954), a best-seller, introduced many of the themes important in his drama: the isolation of the individual, the potentially redeeming capacity of love to form bonds, and the power of language to define the self and its world. Set in a mental institution, the novel explores the relationships that develop among the psychiatric staff, members of their families, and the patients. As the image of the cobweb suggests, these relationships, while not always healthy, connect the characters in complex ways.

Gibson has also written several nonfiction "chronicles." The first of these, *The Seesaw Log*, an account of the writing and producing of his first successful play *Two for the Seesaw*, was published in 1959 with the text of the play. By chronicling the complexities of producing a play in mid-twentieth century America, Gibson demonstrates that a play, unlike a poem or novel, is a collaborative effort that both tests and invigorates the playwright, who has to work with producer, director, and actors, all of whom can truthfully call the play theirs.

Gibson's second chronicle, *A Mass for the Dead* (1968), is one of his most moving works. A mixture of poetry and prose loosely organized along the lines of the Catholic Mass for the Dead, the book recounts the lives of members of Gibson's family, especially his grandparents and their relatives as well as his mother and father. The book is Gibson's attempt to make sense of his ancestors' lives, tracing their progress from working-class roots to middle-class respectability.

In *Shakespeare's Game* (1978), Gibson turns his attention to practical drama criticism and critical theory. The book grew out of his experience in teaching a university course on playwriting—an experience which forced him to review all the basics of drama. As a result, he developed a terminology with which to discuss the craft and art of playwriting, and in *Shakespeare's Game* Gibson applies this terminology to the work of the greatest English-language dramatist. At the book's end, Gibson reveals the essentially psychological nature of his theory of drama, which has its roots in cognitive psychology. A play's structure, Gibson argues, like the human mind, works to achieve equilibrium; when in the uncomfortable state of disequilibrium, the play moves toward an object that promises relief. This movement dashes against barriers that prevent the easy relief of tension in the play and its characters. Using this theory, Gibson demonstrates how a single structure underlies all of William Shakespeare's best plays.

Achievements

Gibson will be remembered for his development of the popular biographical play; for his creation of strong women characters, many of whom have been portrayed by actress Anne Bancroft; and for his commentary on mid-twentieth century drama.

Gibson's most successful play, *The Miracle Worker*, was originally written for *Playhouse 90* and in 1957 won the Sylvania Award for the year's best television drama. This play pioneered the contemporary biographical drama. In it, Gibson exploited the dramatic qualities in Helen Keller's autobiography, centering on her discovery of the power of language under the tutelage of Annie Sullivan, a master teacher who transformed Keller from a wild animal into a human being. Part of the play's power derives from Gibson's ability to dramatize a historical event. Gibson continued developing this genre in later works, such as *American Primitive*, based on the letters of John and Abigail Adams, and *Golda*, based on the autobiography of Golda Meir, one of Israel's most famous prime ministers. While Gibson's subject matter in these plays is limited by his historical sources— in *American Primitive* the dialogue, except for some verse commentary that Gibson added, comes directly from the Adamses' letters—he uses modern stagecraft to make these lives significant.

Gibson will also be remembered for his creation of strong women characters in a period when such roles were the exception. In *Two for the Seesaw*, one of his most successful Broadway plays, the character of Gittel

Mosca, the Jewish girl from the Bronx, overpowers that of Jerry Ryan, the lawyer from Nebraska. As Gibson recounts in *The Seesaw Log*, Henry Fonda, who originally played Ryan, never felt comfortable in the role, partly because of Ryan's paleness compared to Gittel's fullness. *The Miracle Worker*, as well as its sequel, *Monday After the Miracle*, also developed strong women characters, as did *Golda*.

Finally, one of Gibson's most important contributions to the history of the theater is *The Seesaw Log*. By chronicling the composition and production of his play, he details how the mid-twentieth century American theater functioned, from the writing through the selling to the production of a Broadway play. Even though the chronicle is admittedly limited to Gibson's perspective, it re-creates for future audiences the texture and development of a work in progress as the producer, director, and actors, all with their own expertise, transform the playwright's initial creation into their own. Gibson has published other logs ("Preface: A Momento" with *Golden Boy* and "Notes on How to Turn a Phoenix into Ashes" with *Golda*), but none as detailed or as intriguing as *The Seesaw Log*.

Biography

William Gibson was born in New York on November 13, 1914, the son of lower-middle-class parents. The families of both parents were musical. Several of Gibson's maternal uncles belonged to the most famous banjo band of the early 1900's, and his mother's family operated a music school, where Gibson's mother had met his father, who was a talented popular pianist. Gibson himself mastered the piano and, in his late teens and early twenties, he tried to become a professional musician. This background explains his lifelong attraction to music, an interest reflected in his writing of pieces such as the libretto for the operetta *The Ruby* (which he wrote under the name of William Mass) and the text for the 1964 musical *Golden Boy*, a project that he finished for Clifford Odets, who died before it was completed.

Although Gibson was graduated at age sixteen from Townsend Harris Hall, a high school for academically talented boys that was affiliated with the City College of New York, he found college stultifying. He took his most rewarding classes at City College of New York from English professor Theodore Goodman, who encouraged his writing. After attending college sporadically for about two years, Gibson dropped out to educate himself, to become a musician, and to launch his writing career. During his years in college and immediately after, he became a Depression-era Communist and lectured on street corners to support this cause.

In 1940, Gibson married Margaret Brenman, a psychoanalyst, whom he had followed first to her graduate school and then to her psychiatric positions in Topeka, Kansas (where they married), and later in Stockbridge,

Massachusetts. His first literary success came as a poet when a group of his poems published in *Poetry* won for him the 1945 Harriet Monroe Memorial Prize. In 1954, he published a best-selling novel, *The Cobweb*, which he sold to Hollywood. The movie of the same name starred Lauren Bacall, Charles Boyer, and Richard Widmark and appeared in 1955 after Gibson helped rewrite the screenplay.

Gibson became interested in drama early in his career. After dropping out of college, he acted at the Barter Theatre in Abingdon, Virginia, where he wrote several unproduced plays. While in Topeka, Kansas, he acted in the community theater and wrote his first produced play, *I Lay in Zion*, which was staged at the Topeka Civic Theatre in 1943. His next play, *A Cry of Players*, a three-act drama about the young Shakespeare, won the Topeka Civic Theatre Award in 1947 and was staged in 1948. In the fall of 1950, Gibson met Clifford Odets, one of America's most important leftist playwrights, who admitted him to a playwright's seminar organized at the Actors' Studio. During this seminar, Gibson "learned more from him than I believed was possible from any man." After the course, while working at a psychiatric institution, Gibson directed Odets' *Rocket to the Moon* (pr. 1938) with a cast of mental patients. Odets saw this production and became a lifelong family friend.

Gibson's first national successes as a playwright were spectacular. In July of 1958, after an agonizing process (recounted in *The Seesaw Log*), *Two for the Seesaw*, which starred Henry Fonda and Anne Bancroft, opened at Broadway's Booth Theatre to enthusiastic reviews. The play ran for 750 performances and became one of the most successful plays of its era. It was also produced as a movie in 1962 starring Robert Mitchum and Shirley MacLaine. At about the same time, *The Miracle Worker*, which was originally written for television, became a Broadway hit in 1959, starring Anne Bancroft as Annie Sullivan and Patty Duke Astin as Helen Keller. These actresses re-created their roles in the popular 1962 film.

With the money he made selling *The Cobweb* to Hollywood, Gibson bought a house in Stockbridge, Massachusetts. In 1969, he cofounded and became the first executive officer of the Berkshire Theatre Festival in Stockbridge. There, *John and Abigail*, which he later revised as *American Primitive*, was first produced.

In 1971, Gibson almost died of a bleeding ulcer, an ailment from which he had suffered for years. This experience prompted him to reevaluate his life, and, during Christmas of 1972, he went to the Maharishi International University in La Antilla, Spain, to visit his son, who had enrolled in the University. There, Gibson studied under Maharishi Mahesh Yogi and was trained in the theory and practice of transcendental meditation. His interest in religion rekindled, he returned to the Catholic Church, in which he had been reared. He proceeded to write three liturgical dramas: *The Body and the Wheel*, a Passion play; *The Butterfingers Angel*, performed in Lennox, Massachusetts, in 1974; and *Goodly Creatures*, performed in 1980 at the Roadhouse Theatre in Silver Spring, Maryland.

Two major Broadway plays by Gibson that have been neither as critically nor as financially successful as his earlier works are *Golda* and *Monday After the Miracle*. In 1977, *Golda* was plagued by problems and closed after several months. In 1982, a similar fate befell *Monday After the Miracle*, the sequel to *The Miracle Worker*.

Handy Dandy, a two-person play, originally produced unsuccessfully in 1984, was revived in 1990 to slightly better reviews, with James Whitmore and Audra Lindley in the roles. Gibson's Christmas comic/tragic pageant, *The Butterfingers Angel*, which was first performed in 1974, has received several productions, notably at the Olney in Washington, D.C., in 1988, where it returned in 1989 because of popular demand. "A chronicle of hope . . . [which] poses some existential questions," was David Richards' assessment. He also noted that the play's full title, *The Butterfingers Angel, Mary and Joseph, Herod the Nut, and the Slaughter of Twelve Hit Carols in a Pear Tree*, is "a measure of the show's refreshingly antic spirit."

Analysis

William Gibson's plays are marked by impressive literary as well as dramatic qualities. Like much contemporary drama, they deal with existential themes, particularly the social and psychological isolation of the individual. To explore these themes, Gibson uses a variety of approaches, including a mixture of comedic and serious elements and an array of innovative production techniques, most notably the split stage to emphasize the psychological isolation of characters. Despite his emphasis on themes of isolation and loneliness, Gibson is not ultimately pessimistic: He shows that love has the potential to unite lonely individuals and that language sheds light on the human condition. Indeed, the consistent weakness in his plays is his tendency toward the sentimental.

Gibson's first major Broadway play was *Two for the Seesaw*, produced in 1958 and directed by Arthur Penn. Set in New York City, the play explores the relationship between Jerry Ryan, a Nebraska lawyer who is being divorced by his wife, and Gittel Mosca, a Jewish girl from the Bronx. Although much of the play's humor results from the cultural differences between the characters, the true conflict grows from the contrasts in their psychological makeup. Because of this psychological emphasis, *Two for the Seesaw* shares more similarities with Gibson's novel, *The Cobweb*, than with his later biographical drama.

Gibson uses *Two for the Seesaw* to explore one of his most important themes, the isolation of the individual and the need people have for human contact. The stage setting emphasizes this by creating two spaces. One is

Jerry's apartment, the other Gittel's. The lighting serves to isolate and emphasize one or the other, and the set registers the passing of time and changes in Jerry and Gittel's relationship. At the play's beginning, for example, Jerry's cheap apartment is bare and impoverished. As their relationship develops, the rooms begin to take on life because of Gittel's womanly touch. When Jerry moves into Gittel's apartment, his clothes and legal papers pile up in corners and on the table. Throughout much of the play, the two characters in their isolated areas are connected only by the telephone, which symbolizes the emotional distance between them.

The central problem of the play grows from the different needs that Gittel and Jerry have for each other, and this makes the play too clichéd to be completely successful. Gittel is a giving woman who allows herself to be used by men; Jerry, on the other hand, is used to taking from the people in his life. His career in Nebraska was successful largely because his father-in-law made him a law partner and bought him a fashionable home. Part of his reason for going to New York was his desire to escape from this kind of support. Because Gittel appears weak and vulnerable, she brings out in him for the first time the need to assist and care for others, and these nurturing feelings are intensified in Jerry when her stomach ulcer hemorrhages and he has to nurse her.

From the start, the play's problem is the unsympathetic nature of Jerry, which is heightened by the basic likability and charm of Gittel. Gibson's dialogue captures her character perfectly and infuses her with humor and spirit. Jerry, on the other hand, is too self-absorbed and self-centered to be likable. Henry Fonda, who originally played Jerry on Broadway, objected to the character's self-centered behavior, arguing that Gittel would have kicked him out rather than put up with his meanness. Although Fonda can be faulted for not understanding Jerry's psychological motivation—his attachment to his Nebraskan wife conflicts with his need for Gittel's support and love—Gibson was guilty of not infusing the male character with the lifelike qualities that Gittel possesses.

The play's ending exposes the imperfections of its characters and structure. Jerry decides to return to his wife, a wiser man because of Gittel's love. Although this desertion is believable, it makes Jerry distasteful, because it is clear that Gittel is left alone and pathetic. Gibson has her claim that she, too, has learned from the experience—she gives up her illusions of being a dancer, for example—but the audience has little hope that she will find a meaningful relationship. This bleak ending suggests that Gibson was uncertain whether *Two for the Seesaw* was to be comic or tragic, and the mixture of Gittel's comic antics and Jerry's morose irony further confuses the audience about the play's intentions.

Gibson's reputation rests on his second major Broadway play, *The Miracle Worker*, originally a television play. It opened on Broadway in 1959 under the direction of Arthur Penn and starring Anne Bancroft and Patty Duke. In 1962, after a long run, it was made into a United Artists motion picture starring Bancroft and Duke. Gibson's first major biographical play, *The Miracle Worker* is based on the lives of Helen Keller and her teacher, Anne Sullivan.

The characters and situation are perfect vehicles for two of Gibson's major themes, the isolation of the individual and the power of love to do good and harm. Because of Helen's afflictions—an early illness has left her blind and deaf—she has been cut off from all meaningful human contact. Because of her family's misguided love, she has been pampered and allowed to run wild like an untrained animal. It is only when Annie (as Sullivan is known in the play), herself partially blind, comes to live with the family and insists on disciplining Helen that progress is made.

Two major conflicts arise in the play. The first is between Helen and Annie. When forced to behave in a civilized manner, Helen rebels by attacking Annie, throwing food, and playing for sympathy from her parents. Eradicating this behavior is Annie's first job. The second conflict is between Annie and Helen's parents, Captain and Kate Keller. Captain Keller is an Alabama autocrat who expects Annie, a young Bostonian, to obey without question. His major concern is that she control Helen rather than educate her. Kate Keller feels guilty for Helen's condition and pampers the child. Annie, on the other hand, is a forceful woman who has grown up in terrible circumstances. After her mother's early death and the desertion of her alcoholic father, she was reared in a Massachusetts almshouse and blinded by trachoma. By strength of character and determination, she talked her way into an expensive Boston school for the blind, where she underwent nine eye operations in six years. She consequently has little patience with the Kellers coddling Helen.

One of the central symbols of the play is the water pump that stands outside the Kellers' home. It is there, after months of work, that Annie manages to make Helen recognize the connection between words and things, when she signs the word "water" on the girl's palm as actual water flows across it. It is language that allows Helen to become fully human, and this development is Annie's major triumph in the play. By sticking with her demanding teaching methods, by insisting that Helen learn the importance of language despite her parents' conviction that their daughter could never do so, Annie becomes, in Gibson's eyes, the perfect teacher.

One important theme that the play does not handle well concerns Annie's reactions to Helen's miraculous progress. Because of her horrible childhood, Annie, Gibson implies, has not learned to love, only to fight. At the end of the play, when she clutches Helen to her and proclaims her love for the child, the audience is not prepared for such a transformation in character. The ending does not grow out of the play and seems added to

give television viewers the warm glow they have come to expect.
Like many television dramas, *The Miracle Worker*'s answers to complex
questions are too pat. At the play's end, all problems are resolved, even
though in actuality Captain Keller later tried to charge the public an admission
fee to view his "freakish" daughter. Nevertheless, the play remains a
profound statement on the importance of faith and hard work and, in part
for this reason, has become one of the twentieth century's best-known
dramas.

Gibson takes up a darker strain in *Monday After the Miracle*, the sequel
to *The Miracle Worker*. Unlike the earlier play, which is comic in structure
because of its happy ending, *Monday After the Miracle* explores Annie's
and Helen's personal discontentments as Helen becomes internationally
famous, first as a writer and then as a lecturer. Gibson continues exploring
the nature of love, but in this play he examines the gloomier side of that
feeling.

The conflict in the play develops among its three major characters: Annie,
Helen, and John Macy. When the play opens, Helen, now in her
twenties, and Annie, now in her late thirties, have established a unique
bond. As "Teacher," Annie has created Helen much as an artist creates a
work of art. This project, her lifework, has both invigorated and limited
her: She has functioned as Helen's eyes and ears for almost two decades.
The love the two women feel for each other is powerful, but it also has
become a burden on Annie, who now longs for freedom. Macy complicates
matters when he completes the emotional triangle. He comes to help Helen
write, and he edits her first major work, her autobiography (Keller published
her autobiography, *The Story of My Life*, in 1902), which includes
selections from Annie's letters describing her teaching techniques. Both
Helen (who is closer to Macy's age) and Annie fall in love with him, and
this competition tests the women's relationship.

When Macy falls in love with and marries Annie, other conflicts develop.
First, Helen fears that Annie will desert her. This fear is confused by
Helen's certainty that Macy had been falling in love with her, not the older
Annie. Annie, on the other hand, must struggle with her feelings of guilt
about letting someone other than Helen into her life; at the same time, she
yearns for marriage, love, and children. After their marriage, Annie and
Macy must resolve the conflicts that arise when he becomes sexually drawn
to Helen. This situation develops not only because Macy and Helen live in
the same household and work closely together but also because Macy feels
neglected by his wife, whose major interest in life remains Helen. By the
end of the play, Macy's character has disintegrated because of heavy drinking
and his humiliating financial dependence on Helen's income from writing
and speaking.

If *The Miracle Worker* glorifies the power of love to connect people,

Monday After the Miracle, like *Two for the Seesaw*, exposes its power to harm and destroy people, especially those who are weak, such as Macy. The relationship between Annie and Helen survives all the pain and conflict, but that between Macy and Annie does not. Indeed, the failure of the marriage results in part from the intensity of Annie and Helen's love, which began with Annie's need to mold Helen into a full human being and which has become, for better or worse, the central passion of Annie's life.

Gibson is a popular Broadway playwright whose considerable dramatic talent allows him to fuse comic and tragic elements in a satisfying whole. While not always complete artistic and formal successes, his plays explore significant aspects of the human condition, especially the dangers and joys of love and the need humans have to connect with their fellows.

Other major works
NOVEL: *The Cobweb*, 1954.
POETRY: *Winter Crook*, 1948.
NONFICTION: *The Seesaw Log*, 1959; *A Mass for the Dead*, 1968; *A Season in Heaven*, 1974; *Shakespeare's Game*, 1978.
SCREENPLAY: *The Cobweb*, 1954 (based on his novel).

Bibliography
Atkinson, Brooks. "The Theatre: *Two for the Seesaw*." Review of *Two for the Seesaw*. *The New York Times*, January 17, 1958, p. 15. A glowing review among many good ones (only Walter Kerr has reservations). Atkinson states that Gibson has "a tender style of writing and a beautiful little story to tell" in this play, which starred Henry Fonda and Anne Bancroft. Concludes that Gibson "has looked inside the hearts of two admirable people" and thanks Gibson for his "thoughtful writing."
Gibson, William. "On the See-Saw." *The New Yorker* 33 (February 15, 1958): 23-24. A chatty interview with Gibson at home with his wife, Margaret Brenman. Contains much personal information in anecdotal style. Informative on unproduced plays and Gibson's offhanded attitude toward them, other thwarted projects, and his early theatrical experiences at the Barter Theatre in Virginia.
──────────. *The Seesaw Log: A Chronicle of the Stage Production, with the Text of "Two for the Seesaw."* New York: Limelight, 1984. Gibson's own journal of the ups and downs of Broadway theater production, a "balloon above the battlefield, into which I could climb to lick my wounds." *Two for the Seesaw* is his sixth play, but the first produced professionally. Generally negative tone, and the truth "was much worse."
Richards, David. "Holiday Pageantry." Review of *The Butterfingers Angel*. *The Washington Post*, December 2, 1989, p. C2. A review of the holiday play *The Butterfingers Angel*, with a few comments on Gibson's ability

to "depict the dark side of those long-ago events . . . a show for very nearly the whole family." Describes the "stumblefoot angel," jealous Joseph, and the feeble donkey, and says of Mary, "you may detect a faint radiance dancing about her head."

Simon, John. *Uneasy Stages.* New York: Random House, 1975. In these chronicles, Simon reviews his theater experiences in a conversational tone. Has something to say on the musical version of *Two for the Seesaw*, shortened to *Seesaw*, in the 1972-1973 season. The reader must know what year to look into, since Simon offers only seasons in the table of contents. Index.

Michael G. Moran
(Updated by *Thomas J. Taylor*)

W. S. GILBERT

Born: London, England; November 18, 1836
Died: Harrow Weald, England; May 29, 1911

Principal drama

Ruy Blas, pb. 1866 (in *Warne's Christmas Annual*); *Dulcamara: Or, The Little Duck and the Great Quack*, pr., pb. 1866 (based on Gaetano Donizetti's opera *L'elisir d'amore*); *Allow Me to Explain*, pr. 1867; *Highly Improbable*, pr. 1867; *Harlequin Cock Robin and Jenny Wren: Or, Fortunatus and the Water of Life, the Three Bears, the Three Gifts, the Three Wishes, and the Little Man Who Woo'd the Little Maid*, pr., pb. 1867; *The Merry Zingara: Or, The Tipsy Gipsy and the Pipsy Wipsy*, pr., pb. 1868; *Robert the Devil: Or, The Nun, the Dun, and the Son of a Gun*, pr., pb. 1868; *No Cards*, pr. 1869, pb. 1901 (libretto; music by Lionel Elliott); *The Pretty Druidess: Or, The Mother, the Maid, and the Mistletoe Bough*, pr., pb. 1869; *An Old Score*, pr., pb. 1869; *Ages Ago: A Ghost Story*, pr., pb. 1869 (libretto; music by Frederick Clay); *The Princess*, pr., pb. 1870; *The Gentleman in Black*, pr. 1870 (libretto; music by Frederick Clay); *The Palace of Truth*, pr., pb. 1870; *A Medical Man*, pb. 1870, pr. 1872; *Randall's Thumb*, pr. 1871, pb. 1872; *A Sensation Novel*, pr. 1871, pb. 1912 (libretto; music by Florian Pascal); *Pygmalion and Galatea*, pr. 1871, pb. 1872; *Thespis: Or, The Gods Grown Old*, pr., pb. 1871 (libretto; music by Sir Arthur Sullivan); *The Brigands*, pb. 1871, pr. 1889 (libretto; music by Jacques Offenbach); *On Guard*, pr., pb. 1872; *Happy Arcadia*, pr., pb. 1872 (libretto; music by Frederick Clay); *The Wicked World*, pr., pb. 1873; *The Happy Land*, pr., pb. 1873 (as F. Tomline, with Gilbert A' Beckett); *The Realm of Joy*, pr. 1873; *The Wedding March*, pr. 1873, pb. 1879 (adaptation of Eugène Labiche's *Le Chapeau de paille d'Italie*); *Charity*, pr. 1874; *Ought We to Visit Her?*, pr. 1874 (with Annie Edwards); *Committed for Trial*, pr. 1874, pb. 1930 (adaptation of Henri Meilhac and Ludovic Halévy's *Le Réveillon*, later revised as *On Bail*); *Topsy Turveydom*, pr. 1874, pb. 1931; *Sweethearts*, pr. 1874, pb. 1878; *Trial by Jury*, pr., pb. 1875 (libretto; music by Sullivan); *Tom Cobb: Or, Fortune's Toy*, pr. 1875, pb. 1880; *Eyes and No Eyes: Or, The Art of Seeing*, pr. 1875, pb. 1896 (libretto; music by Pascal); *Broken Hearts*, pr. 1875, pb. 1881; *Princess Toto*, pr., pb. 1876 (libretto; music by Frederick Clay); *Dan'l Bruce, Blacksmith*, pr., pb. 1876; *Original Plays*, pb. 1876-1911 (4 volumes); *On Bail*, pr. 1877, pb. 1881 (revision of *Committed for Trial*); *Engaged*, pr., pb. 1877; *The Sorcerer*, pr., pb. 1877 (libretto; music by Sullivan); *The Ne'er-do-Weel*, pr., pb. 1878; *H.M.S. Pinafore: Or, The Lass That Loved a Sailor*, pr., pb. 1878 (libretto; music by Sullivan); *Gretchen*, pr., pb. 1879; *The Pirates of Penzance: Or, The Slave of Duty*, pr. 1879, pb. 1880 (libretto; music by Sullivan); *Patience; Or*

Bunthorne's Bride, pr., pb. 1881 (libretto; music by Sullivan); *Foggerty's Fairy*, pr., pb. 1881; *Iolanthe: Or, The Peer and the Peri*, pr., pb. 1882 (libretto; music by Sullivan); *Comedy and Tragedy*, pr. 1884, pb. 1896; *Princess Ida: Or, Castle Adamant*, pr., pb. 1884 (libretto; music by Sullivan); *The Mikado: Or, The Town of Titipu*, pr., pb. 1885 (libretto; music by Sullivan); *Ruddigore: Or, The Witch's Curse*, pr., pb. 1887 (libretto; music by Sullivan); *The Yeomen of the Guard: Or, The Merryman and His Maid*, pr., pb. 1888 (libretto; music by Sullivan); *Brantinghame Hall*, pr., pb 1888; *The Gondoliers: Or, The King of Barataria*, pr., pb. 1889 (libretto; music by Sullivan); *Rosencrantz and Guildenstern*, pr. 1891, pb. 1893; *The Mountebanks*, pr., pb. 1892 (libretto; music by Alfred Cellier); *Haste to the Wedding*, pr., pb. 1892 (libretto; music by George Grossmith); *Utopia, Limited: Or, The Flowers of Progress*, pr., pb. 1893 (libretto; music by Sullivan); *His Excellency*, pr., pb. 1894 (libretto; music by Osmond Carr); *The Grand Duke: Or, The Statutory Duel*, pr., pb. 1896 (libretto; music by Sullivan); *The Fortune Hunter*, pr., pb. 1897; *Fallen Fairies*, pr., pb. 1909 (with Edward German); *The Hooligan*, pr., pb. 1911; *Gilbert Before Sullivan: Six Comic Plays*, pb. 1967 (Jane Stedman, editor); *Plays*, pb. 1982 (George Rowell, editor).

Other literary forms

Apart from his writing for the theater, W. S. Gilbert's principal literary accomplishment is *The Bab Ballads* (1869), whimsical verses which he illustrated himself. Originally published in comic journals such as *Fun* and *Punch*, they are generally regarded as the well from which Gilbert drew many of the songs and situations of his comic operas.

Achievements

The comic operas of W. S. Gilbert and Sir Arthur Sullivan are the product of one of the most successful collaborations in theatrical history, for while other teams of librettist and composer have achieved comparable distinction, in no other pair have the talents so complemented each other. Both chafed at the fact that their more serious accomplishments were less well regarded, and both tried, without great success, to work with other collaborators. Gilbert's whimsy and legalistic paradoxes would have been little more than quaint if they had not been humanized by Sullivan's melodies, and Sullivan's choral and orchestral virtuosity and his propensity to parody found their focus in Gilbert's preposterous plots. Their initial collaborations took place over a span of six years, during which they were engaged in other artistic enterprises as well. With the composition of *H.M.S. Pinafore*, however, they began a decade of enormous popularity, with virtually one new opera a year, each with a measure of uniqueness yet all derived from a recognizable formula. Although the later operas are somewhat more musically complex and more extravagantly plotted, these advances are less the consequence of artistic maturity than of technical confidence. Gilbert's not too serious social criticism, his tongue-twisting lyrics, and his gentle spoofs of romantic conventions appealed to a middle-class audience that had only recently been persuaded that the theater might be a respectable institution after all. The two operas Gilbert and Sullivan produced after the great breach that lasted from 1889 to 1893 are not sufficiently inferior to the others as to account for their unpopularity. The vogue of Gilbert and Sullivan had not ended, for the earlier operas continued to be revived. It is more likely that the collaborators had produced enough operas to keep their public happy. For almost a century, these operas have remained favorites on both sides of the Atlantic, kept alive largely by the D'Oyly Carte Opera Company, holders of the copyright, from whose elaborately stylized and insistently Victorian productions other professional and amateur renditions have been derived. Although changes in the company's finances forced its closure in 1982, interest in the operas was not noticeably diminished, with both Joseph Papp's 1980 revival and the 1983 film version of *The Pirates of Penzance* being well received.

Biography

William Schwenck Gilbert was born at 17 Southampton Street, Strand, London, on November 18, 1836, the son of a fairly well-to-do naval surgeon, who turned to a literary career at about the same time as young William did. At the age of two, while on holiday with his parents in Italy, Gilbert was kidnaped from his nurse and ransomed for twenty-five pounds. He later claimed to have a perfect recollection of the incident. At any rate, his plots frequently hinge on the removal of infants from their real parents.

Educated at Boulogne, France, and Great Ealing School, he then attended King's College, London, hoping to obtain a commission in the Royal Artillery. The sudden end of the Crimean War made a military career less appealing, and he obtained, by competitive examination, a clerkship in the Education Department of the Privy Council Office, a post he occupied from 1857 to 1862. Coming into an unexpected sum of money, Gilbert was able to free himself from that "ill-organised and ill-governed office." Having already entered the Inner Temple, Gilbert was called to the Bar in 1863. He did not thrive as a barrister, however, earning no more than seventy-five pounds in his first two years of practice. He never wholly abandoned either his military or his legal aspirations, for he held a commission in the Fifth West Yorkshire Militia, the Royal Aberdeen Highlanders, and, from 1893, was a justice of the peace for the county of Middlesex.

Gilbert's career as a writer had been launched as early as 1857, when he accepted a commission to translate a French song for a theater program. His first play to be produced, *Dulcamara*, a travesty based on Gaetano

Donizetti's opera *L'elisir d'amore* (1832), was followed in succeeding years by similar treatments of operas by Donizetti, Vincenzo Bellini, Giacomo Meyerbeer, and others. In 1867, Gilbert was confident enough of his abilities to marry Lucy Blois Turner, a woman fourteen years his junior. Despite the example of the tempestuous marriage of Gilberts' parents, his own irascibility, and his almost total absorption in his work, the union appears to have been a happy one. The 1860's were also the years of the composition of *The Bab Ballads.* In 1869, he became a contributor of short comic plays for the German Reed's Royal Gallery of Illustration, which provided a kind of family entertainment mixing song with improbable fable, presented without the elaborate trappings of the stage. He also began writing full-length comedies, such as *The Palace of Truth*, *Pygmalion and Galatea*, and *Broken Hearts*, whose plots involve the intervention of fairies or other supernatural agencies in human affairs.

The first meeting of Gilbert and Sullivan took place at the Gallery of Illustration and was brought about through a common friend. Though each knew the work of the other, it was another two years before Gilbert proposed that Sullivan set to music the draft of *Thespis* (the musical score has since been lost). Neither appears to have taken this first collaboration very seriously, and four years were to elapse before they worked together on another opera, a curtain raiser prodded into being by Richard D'Oyly Carte, then the manager of the Royalty Theatre, in the Soho district of London. The extraordinary success of this piece, *Trial by Jury*, prompted D'Oyly Carte to lease the Opéra Comique as the home of the Comedy Opera Company and to commission a third opera, *The Sorcerer.*

One success followed another. To frustrate theatrical piracy, a continuing problem as the popularity of their work increased, the premiere of *The Pirates of Penzance* took place in New York. By 1881, the trio of Gilbert, Sullivan, and D'Oyly Carte had opened their own theater, the Savoy, the first in the world to be illuminated by electric light. All of their subsequent operas were produced here. That two men so temperamentally different— Gilbert, robust and litigious, and Sullivan, frail and affable—should have collaborated at all is more remarkable than that their association became strained during the decade of their greatest artistic and commercial success. Each considered that he was being asked to yield too much to the other. These differences were precipitated by the famous "carpet breach." Believing that D'Oyly Carte had wrongly charged the theater's new carpeting as a cost of production of *The Gondoliers*, rather than as one of building maintenance, and that Sullivan and he were thereby aggrieved, Gilbert insisted on an immediate renegotiation of the agreement among them. When D'Oyly Carte demurred and Sullivan proved insufficiently vigorous in his support of Gilbert's demands, Gilbert became furious and actually took legal action against both of them. Although a compromise was eventually worked out, and two more operas followed the reconciliation, the heyday of the team of Gilbert and Sullivan was over.

Gilbert continued to be active with other collaborators in the 1890's, and he reverted as well to the fairy comedies of his pre-Sullivan days. Gout and other ailments, however, compelled him to lead a life of greater retirement. In 1907, some twenty-four years after Sullivan had received a similar honor, Gilbert was knighted for services to the theater—as a playwright rather than with the more prestigious designation he had craved, that of dramatist. Though rancor figured significantly in Gilbert's life, his death was gallant. Diving to rescue a young woman swimming in the lake on his estate, Sir William suffered a fatal heart attack on May 29, 1911.

Analysis

W. S. Gilbert has occasionally been called "the English Aristophanes"; however extravagant that designation, it may serve as a useful point of departure. Assuredly Aristophanic is Gilbert's capacity to create in his plays worlds in which recognizable institutions—the legal system, the military, the rigid caste system of Victorian society—are transformed into absurdities. In *Trial by Jury*, the legal wrangling between the counsels of the jilted Angelina and the flirtatious defendant are resolved by the judgment of the judge—to marry Angelina himself. In *The Pirates of Penzance*, a pirate must first serve an apprenticeship, as though he were an artisan or skilled mechanic; furthermore, the pirate gang is pardoned of all of their offenses because "they are all noblemen who have gone wrong." Also Aristophanic, though functioning in a different way, to be sure, are Gilbert's choruses—the sisters, cousins, and aunts of Sir Joseph Porter in *H.M.S. Pinafore*, the giggling schoolgirls of *The Mikado*, or the professional bridesmaids in *Ruddigore*—which serve to accentuate the ludicrousness of the situations.

The essential distinction, however, between the absurdities of Aristophanes and those of Gilbert is that for the Greek dramatist, the source of the comedy lay in some social or political aberration that he meant to expose, if not to correct. For Gilbert, on the other hand, though his plays are not devoid of social or political implications, the source of the comedy lies in the pursuit of some intellectual crotchet or paradox to its ultimate conclusion. The topsy-turviness of Gilbert's plays originates in legalisms and logic-chopping. As a slave of duty, Frederic, the hero of *The Pirates of Penzance*, feels that he cannot betray his pirate comrades, loathsome though their trade is to him, until he is discharged of his indentures on his twenty-first birthday. Having been born on the last day of February in a leap year, however, he discovers that he is, in terms of birthdays celebrated, only a little boy of five. Similarly, through an ancestral curse, each baronet of Ruddigore must commit a crime daily or perish in unutterable agony. Failure to commit a crime is thus tantamount to committing suicide, which is itself a crime. Not only are the dilemmas of the characters resolved by similar sophistry, but also it appears that the complications have been conceived with no other purpose in mind.

One Gilbert and Sullivan work that does not quite fit this description is *Princess Ida*. This opera, however, is essentially a reworking of an earlier Gilbert play, *The Princess*, a "respectful perversion" of Alfred, Lord Tennyson's poem of the same name (1847), that odd composition whose central subject is the education of women. Even here, however, Gilbert treats the topic not as a timely social issue but as an occasion to explore the comic implications of the attempted isolation of one sex from the other. To say that Gilbert's plays take place in artificial environments hardly accounts for the intense intellectual pressure that has gone into their formation. The clash between the fairies and noblemen in *Iolanthe*, for example, originates in the play on the words "peri" and "peer." The officers of the dragoon guards in *Patience* readily abandon their military garb and their military bearing to become aesthetic poets, because only in that guise can they successfully woo the chorus of rapturous maidens.

Each opera enunciates a topsy-turvy premise, which is then examined. In *H.M.S. Pinafore*, it is the notion that "love can level ranks"; in *Patience*, it is that true love is disinterested; and in *Iolanthe*, it is that a race of immortal and insubstantial beings can exhibit all the characteristics of human beings. All of these, it should be noted, are romantic notions derived very largely from literature. Gilbert's fancies are drawn as well from some of his own early works, particularly his parodies and *The Bab Ballads*. Very little seems to come from direct observation of life or reflection on personal experience, except for the minutiae, the little personal quirks and foibles that make a caricature. The result is a series of plays often quite rich in references or allusions to contemporary life but as remote from that life as animated cartoons are from the life of animals. The characters and plots have been reduced to formula.

Although some of the variations on them are quite subtle, the character-types encountered in Gilbert's plays are almost as rigid as those in classical New Comedy. In addition to the fresh and innocent heroine and her equally ingenuous hero, there is the fastidious and querulous authoritarian (who usually gets to sing the patter song)—Sir Joseph in *H.M.S. Pinafore*, Major-General Stanley in *The Pirates of Penzance*, the Lord Chancellor in *Iolanthe*, King Gama in *Princess Ida*, Ko-Ko in *The Mikado*, and the Duke of Plaza Toro in *The Gondoliers*—as well as the elderly, decayed contralto, who is physically repulsive yet longing for affection—Buttercup in *H.M.S. Pinafore*, Ruth in *The Pirates of Penzance*, Lady Jane in *Patience*, Katisha in *The Mikado*, Dame Carruthers in *The Yeomen of the Guard*, and the Duchess in *The Gondoliers*. The easy classification of roles in these operas makes them particularly attractive to repertory companies.

For all the variety of locales in Gilbert's works, the most frequent form of action involves what has been called the invasion plot. That is, the territory of a more or less settled group is overrun by another, the situation demanding some kind of compromise, if not retreat. Sir Joseph Porter and his female relations board H.M.S *Pinafore*; Major-General Stanley's daughters innocently decide to picnic in the pirates' lair; the procession of peers invades the Arcadian landscape in act 1 of *Iolanthe*, only to have the fairies troop in force to Westminster in act 2. There is actual combat between military units in *Princess Ida*, and in *The Mikado*, the imperial retinue sweeps into Titipu, demanding of its inhabitants the appearance of conformity to decrees from on high.

This reduction of character and plot to a formula, although it is more commercially palatable (thanks to Sullivan's music) than the insipid paradoxes of Gilbert's earlier straight plays, does not initially seem conducive to the generation of enduring art. Yet in at least two ways, it has secured Gilbert's place in the theater, even if not as a dramaturge. First, it provided a vehicle for some of the most versatile metrical and verbal extravagances in the English language. As a lyricist, Gilbert is unsurpassed in his ability to provide both singable *and* memorable words not only to arias, ballads, duets, and choruses but also to part-songs of considerable complexity and to patter songs for single and multiple voices. (Patter songs, which sound like tongue twisters sung at top speed, include "I am the very model of a modern Major-General," from *The Pirates of Penzance*.) The challenge produced the tuneful and rollicking songs familiar to almost everyone, such as "Faint Heart Never Won Fair Lady," from *Iolanthe*, or "For He Is an Englishman," from *H.M.S. Pinafore*. Yet it also produced tender and haunting songs, such as Ko-Ko's "The Titwillow Song" in *The Mikado* (which must surely have originated as a parody of Desdemona's "Willow Song" in William Shakespeare's *Othello*) and Jack Point's "I Have a Song to Sing, O" in *The Yeomen of the Guard*.

Moreover, it is in these lyrics, rather than in the large themes or preposterous situations of the operas, that Gilbert executes his greatest satiric thrusts. On the whole, like the audience for whom he wrote, Gilbert felt enormously pleased with the general state of things in the world around him and was vexed only by ideas, such as socialism or evolution, that threatened to rend society or by fads, such as aestheticism, that tended to distract it. Yet for all his conservatism, he did not wholly succumb to philistine complacency. In his songs, he frequently targets time-honored objects of satire: the abuse of privilege, the vanity in pride of ancestry, or the posturings of the *nouveau riche*. At the beginning of the second act of *The Mikado*, for example, Yum-Yum is adorning herself in preparation for her wedding day. She sings a song ingenuously identifying her with the world of nature, a song whose operation, like that of Alexander Pope's description of Belinda at the beginning of *The Rape of the Lock*, simultaneously elicits wonder and censure at the fair creature. As in this song, Gilbert's satire is often ironically self-deprecating, requiring a good deal of attention to be understood.

This demand for attentiveness constitutes Gilbert's second significant contribution to the English theater. He educated a generation of middle-class theatergoers to listen carefully to what was being said onstage and to expect paradox at every turn. Though himself unwilling or unable to use the stage for serious mockery of social institutions, he made it possible for others to do so. He prepared audiences to receive the witty comedies of Oscar Wilde and the more intellectually provocative plays of George Bernard Shaw.

Trial by Jury demonstrated that Gilbertian humor could successfully be translated to the operatic stage; *The Sorcerer*, that Sullivan could actually compose for Gilbert. In *H.M.S. Pinafore*, the collaboration attained its full flowering. The first and least complicated of their more popular operas, it is also the most familiar. The plot hinges on two threadbare conventions of comedy, a pair of lovers whose union is thwarted by their being of different social classes and a pair of babies, also of different classes, who have been switched in infancy. The discovery of the second circumstance conveniently resolves the difficulty of the first. Gilbert apparently believed in a fluid class structure: Josephine may marry up (although not too far up) but not down the social ladder, and Sir Joseph Porter, while his rise from office boy to First Lord of the Admiralty is a source of some amusement, is not repudiated, either as a cad or as a snob, for rejecting Josephine when she proves to be the daughter of a common seaman. His behavior is seen as quite understandable and serves to refute the absurd egalitarian sentiments he has uttered earlier, sentiments overwhelmed by the jingoistic sailors' chorus and glee. As is usual in Gilbert, the satire against the ruling class is mild. It manifests itself through the self-revelation of an authority figure who is on the whole rather likable, however pompous. In the final analysis, such satire is seen as secondary to the larger purpose of amusement. Sir Joseph and his retinue of sisters, cousins, and aunts are there to provide a complication and a chorus.

The Pirates of Penzance is, as many have observed, *H.M.S. Pinafore* brought to land. All the color of the nautical talk and the costuming has been preserved in the pirates, the female chorus of Sir Joseph's relations has become that of Major-General Stanley's daughters, and there is even an additional male chorus of policemen. Buttercup, who had been responsible for the mixup of babies in *H.M.S. Pinafore*, has metamorphosed into Ruth, whose blunder is to confuse words, apprenticing the young Frederic to a pirate instead of a pilot. There are distant echoes here of Shakespeare's *The Tempest* as Frederic, who has grown up knowing no women other than his nurse, Ruth, discovers the true nature of female beauty in Mabel. The complication is that, as a pirate, he is a sworn foe of legitimate authority, as represented by Mabel's father. Once again, the comic resolution undercuts any serious social criticism: Because they are really renegade noblemen, who owe fealty to Queen Victoria, the pirates surrender in her name and become suitable mates for the Major-General's daughters. There is far less occasion for criticism of social institutions in this opera, however, than in *H.M.S. Pinafore*. Rather, Gilbert takes delight in puncturing romantic myths. Instead of a band of lawless Byronic outcasts, Gilbert's pirates are a guild of credulous, tenderhearted incompetents, whose evil purposes dissolve at once if their intended victim claims to be an orphan (a weakness that Major-General Stanley is quick to exploit). Their antagonists, the local constabulary, prove to be as unheroic as the pirates are unvillainous. Major-General Stanley, like Sir Joseph Porter, is a mere functionary. In the modern world, Gilbert seems to be saying, romantic idealization is no longer tenable, and the conflict between good and evil dwindles into banality.

Although *Patience* appears to be one of the most topical of Gilbert's works, taking aim at the whole Aesthetic movement, the play's origins belie that contention. The central situation derives from "The Rival Curates," one of *The Bab Ballads*, in which two provincial clergymen compete for a title in abnegation or, in Gilbert's term, "mildness." Unlike the opera, the twenty-three-stanza ballad presents no motive for the eccentricity beyond that of a desire for reputation. The essential topsy-turvy premise of the opera, then, is that an affected mannerism extended to one's whole demeanor will excite admiration. Gilbert confessed that he had difficulty sustaining the conceit through the two acts of the opera without falling into bad taste or blasphemy, and this may account for the transformation of the rival curates into poets. The emergence of the young Oscar Wilde as a flamboyant exponent of Aestheticism made him appear to be a perfect prototype of Bunthorne, the fleshly poet, an association that proved profitable both for Wilde and the three partners of the D'Oyly Carte Opera Company. Love interest in the opera is supplied by Patience, a dairymaid sensible enough not to be attracted by bizarre behavior yet sufficiently innocent of passion to believe that love must be totally disinterested. It is through the characterizations of the fleshly and idyllic poets, however, that *Patience* achieved its popularity and has maintained its interest. Gilbert's attack was timely, to be sure, but somewhat off the mark. The eccentricity and languor of his poets are fair enough targets of satire, but he invests them as well with a kind of puritanism more appropriate to his curates. Elsewhere, Gilbert administers occasional mild jolts to middle-class complacency; in *Patience*, however, by portraying his poets not merely as fools but also as conscious hypocrites, he panders to philistine anti-intellectualism.

Iolanthe brings together the world of Gilbert's earlier fairy plays and the world of reality, particularly legal and political reality. As in *The Pirates of Penzance*, Gilbert insists upon looking at romantic matter in a matter-of-fact way. Like the Greek satirist Lucian, Gilbert endows his supernatural creatures not only with immortality, discretionary corporeality, and magical powers, but also with human emotions. The opening chorus of dancing fairies complains of boredom since the exile of Iolanthe for having married a mortal (Iolanthe is subsequently forgiven). The offspring of that union, the shepherd Strephon (a fairy from the waist up), is in love with Phyllis, the ward of the Lord Chancellor, who intends to marry her himself. Needless to say, both the young and the middle-aged lovers are properly sorted out by the end of the opera, but not before several clashes have taken place between the romantic and pragmatic worlds. Phyllis, seeing Strephon in the company of his very youthful-looking mother, is driven to jealousy; he, backed by the powerful influence of the fairies, takes over Parliament, where he proceeds to confound the whole political system by instituting competitive examinations for admission to the peerage and by eliciting assent to all of his proposals. *Iolanthe* is quite remarkable for the good-naturedness of its critical observations on parliamentary democracy. At the beginning of act 2, Private Willis' song ponders the division of people into parties, by which they relinquish their private intellects and submit to the discipline of a leader upon entering the House of Commons. Two songs later, Lord Mountararat extols the House of Lords for doing precisely nothing and doing it "very well": Britain's glory is contingent upon the assurance that "noble statesmen do not itch/ To interfere with matters which/ They do not understand." Taken together, the two songs seem to express Gilbert's belief that, however riddled with anomalies, the British system of government works very well indeed.

The Mikado signaled a change of direction for Gilbert and Sullivan. With the exception of *Thespis*, whose setting is Olympus, and *Princess Ida*, which, like Tennyson's poem, is laid in a legendary atmosphere, all of their operas up to *The Mikado* had been contemporary. However outlandish the premises or exaggerated the manners, they could be seen as obvious extrapolations of the familiar. Whether Gilbert felt that he had exhausted this vein or whether the possibility for more elaborate productions was the inducement, *The Mikado* initiated a movement away from the familiar. Though topical allusions abound, the last six operas all take place either in a locale definitely not English or at a time decidedly not the present. They are also characterized by more complicated plots. The simple invasion formula gives way to more intricate maneuverings, and the songs are made to carry a greater burden of exposition and development. Though *The Mikado* may be no less popular than *H.M.S. Pinafore* or *The Pirates of Penzance*, it is more difficult to unravel and its satire is more oblique. Most obviously, in its portrayal of excessive ceremony and politeness masking bloodthirstiness and tyranny, *The Mikado* sardonically congratulates Englishmen for choosing not to belong to any other nation and laughs at the Victorian fascination for things Oriental. It is equally obvious, however, that Gilbert's Japanese have no more authenticity than his fairies: The opening choruses of *Iolanthe* and *The Mikado* are strikingly similar. In both, the singers proclaim themselves creatures of artistic convention, doomed to perform antics they know to be meaningless. The world of *The Mikado*, then, is one of stylized behavior, in which the law no longer serves society but enslaves it. The Lord Chancellor in *Iolanthe* had proclaimed, "The Law is the true embodiment/ Of everything that's excellent," but it remains for Ko-Ko, the Lord High Executioner, to have "a little list" of society's offenders who can be dispatched whenever a victim must be found, and for the Mikado himself to invent cruel and unusual punishments to "fit the crime." The plight of the thwarted lovers, Nanki-Poo and Yum-Yum, is central; what is topsyturvy is their entire milieu, in which forms are preserved at the expense of substance.

The Yeomen of the Guard was Gilbert's response to Sullivan's repeated requests for more human situations, for characters less eccentric, and for songs whose sentiments were not continually undercut by irony. Though rich in comic turns, it aspires to the condition of grand, rather than comic, opera. It is quite likely that the setting—the Tower of London in the sixteenth century—with its potential for costuming and design, may have first suggested itself to Gilbert, and that only then did he begin to work on a plot. Sergeant Meryll, a yeoman of the guard, and his son, Leonard, and daughter, Phoebe, plan to effect the escape of Colonel Fairfax, who is destined to be executed on trumped-up charges of sorcery. Meanwhile, Fairfax, knowing nothing of their scheme, is resigned to dying, but desires to marry first and thus thwart the plan of his kinsman, who concocted the charges in order to inherit Fairfax's estate. A hasty marriage is concluded with Elsie Maynard, a strolling singer. Fairfax, disguised as young Meryll, disappears from his cell, and his jailer, Wilfred Shadbolt, who in his love for Phoebe Meryll has unwittingly assisted the plot, is in danger of suffering the penalty in his stead. Shadbolt allies himself with the jester Jack Point, who, as Elsie's lover, has also been discomfitted by Fairfax's disappearance, and together, they concoct a tale. Like that of Ko-Ko and Pooh-Bah in *The Mikado*, the explanation given for Fairfax's absence is filled with "corroborative detail, intended to give artistic versimilitude to an otherwise bald and unconvincing narrative," maintaining that Shadbolt shot Fairfax dead as he tried to escape. Phoebe, in love with Fairfax and in distress at seeing him woo Elsie in the guise of her brother, reveals his true identity to Shadbolt. As Phoebe and Shadbolt are now in possession of each other's secret, they agree to marry in order to purchase each other's silence. Fairfax, who has actually been reprieved, is genuinely attracted to the wife he has acquired out of convenience, Sergeant Meryll pairs off with Dame Carruthers, the housekeeper to the Tower, and only Jack Point is left pathetically without a mate at the opera's conclusion. The substitution of intrigue for topsy-turviness obviously distances *The Yeomen of the Guard* from *H.M.S. Pinafore*, yet the work is recognizably Gilbertian; for all their melodramatic pretensions, the characters have affinities with those of the other operas. Even Jack Point, who falls insensible as the curtain descends, is cousin to the Lord Chancellor and Ko-Ko. The plight of these characters, however, has been more poignantly imagined.

Composed in the midst of mounting strife between Gilbert and Sullivan, *The Gondoliers* is their last major theatrical success. In many ways it is the most colorful and lyric of the whole series. The richness of its foreign setting may be rivaled by that of *The Mikado*, but musically, it is unequaled; for this opera, Sullivan added to his usual array of arias, duets, part songs, and choruses the rhythms of Spain and Italy. Gilbert worked what must be the ultimate variation on the baby-swapping convention: Throughout the opera, the audience waits to find out which of the two gondoliers is the rightful king of Barataria, only to discover what may have already been guessed—that neither is. During the last few minutes of the opera, an even earlier switch is announced as having taken place, conveniently preventing the marriage of royalty with the lower orders. Indeed, it often appears that Gilbert is engaging in self-parody in *The Gondoliers*, for the situations of the earlier operas are here piled on one another. Topsy-turviness is present not merely in the mixup of the infants but also in the joint rule of the two gondoliers while they await the determination of their status and in their ludicrous attempts to introduce republican monarchy. In the antics of the Duke and Duchess of Plaza Toro, Gilbert is not repudiating the aristocratic ideal—the Grand Inquisitor sings persuasively of the need for degree in a stable society. Rather, Gilbert portrays in them examples of a decayed and venal aristocracy. Like Pooh-Bah in *The Mikado*, they have pride but no honor. For all of its sprightliness, however, *The Gondoliers* lacks the integrity of the earlier operas: Themes and characters are introduced capriciously because they have worked before.

Alone among the comic versifiers of his age—Lewis Carroll, Edward Lear, C. S. Calverley, Richard Barham, and others—Gilbert succeeded in converting comic verse to comic song, thereby transcending whimsy. For this, he certainly owes much to Sullivan. Yet in how many operas, comic or grand, does the work of the lyricist or librettist count for much? Gilbert has earned classic status not because he is timeless and universal, but because even after a century, he can impose a Victorian sensibility upon his audience.

Other major works

SHORT FICTION: *The Lost Stories of W. S. Gilbert*, 1982.
POETRY: *The Bab Ballads, 1869; More Bab Ballads*, 1873; *Songs of a Savoyard*, 1898.

Bibliography

Baily, Leslie. *The Gilbert and Sullivan Book.* London: Cassell, 1952. This examination of Gilbert and Sir Arthur Sullivan grew out of a series of British Broadcasting Corporation (BBC) radio broadcasts. Although knowledgeable, accurate, and complete, it maintains a popular quality, telling of the successes and failures of the team and commenting upon the two artists' works. Richly illustrated, bibliography, and index.

Darlington, W. A. *The World of Gilbert and Sullivan.* New York: Thomas Y. Crowell, 1950. Darlington provides the social context for the Savoy operas, providing a great wealth of local allusion, which should help the modern reader more fully to appreciate, understand, and enjoy Gilbert's scripts. Includes a dictionary-index of opera characters and a subject index.

Fischler, Alan. *Modified Rapture: Comedy in W. S. Gilbert's Savoy Operas.* Charlottesville: University Press of Virginia, 1991. Fischler begins his analysis with Gilbert's fiftieth theatrical work, *H.M.S. Pinafore*, because it both separated him from other Victorian playwrights and was the turning point in his comic dramaturgy. Gilbert's new approach to comedy appealed to bourgeois prejudices and provided his greatest popularity. Human law replaces providence. Law and authority emerge as the forces that mete out rewards and punishments in accord with the duty-based morality that the audience held so dear. Extensive notes and index.

Godwin, Augustine H. *Gilbert and Sullivan: A Critical Appreciation of the Savoy Operas.* Port Washington, N.Y.: Kennikat Press, 1969. Godwin's "critical appreciation" is possibly the first to examine the Savoy operas as a whole. It provides an excellent introduction to traditional Gilbert criticism, examining recurring themes, characters, and characterization, as well as staging and acting techniques.

Goldberg, Isaac. *The Story of Gilbert and Sullivan.* New York: Simon & Schuster, 1928. Goldberg's critical evaluations and biographies of Gilbert and Sir Arthur Sullivan focus on the political and social context of their works and lives. They do not represent either the era of William IV or that of Queen Victoria but are a bridge between the two. Illustrations, bibliography, and index.

Jones, John Bush, ed. *W. S. Gilbert: A Century of Scholarship and Commentary.* New York: New York University Press, 1970. This volume presents eighteen critical essays in chronological order from 1869 to 1968. Its value is in bringing together that period's leading commentaries on

Gilbert's work in a way that demonstrates the changing attitudes, approaches, and methodologies of literary and drama critics. Select bibliography.

Wilson, Robin, and Frederic K. Lloyd. *Gilbert and Sullivan: The Official D'Oyly Carte Picture History.* New York: Alfred A. Knopf, 1984. An excellent source for examining the aesthetic of Gilbert's work in performance. Hundreds of photographs and designs from the 107-year history of the D'Oyly Carte Opera Company trace the evolution of the Savoy operas on stage in both England and the United States. Brief introductions to each section include biographical and critical information on Gilbert as it pertains to the opera company. Illustrations, bibliography, and index.

Ira Grushow
(Updated by *Gerald S. Argetsinger*)

FRANK D. GILROY

Born: New York, New York; October 13, 1925

Principal drama

Who'll Save the Plowboy?, wr. 1957, pr., pb. 1962; *The Subject Was Roses*, pb. 1962, pr. 1964; *That Summer—That Fall*, pr., pb. 1967 (includes his teleplay *Far Rockaway*); *The Only Game in Town*, pr., pb. 1968; *Present Tense*, pr. 1972, pb. 1973 (4 one-act plays: *So Please Be Kind*, *'Twas Brillig*, *Come Next Tuesday*, *Present Tense*); *The Next Contestant*, pr. 1978, pb. 1979 (one act); *Dreams of Glory*, pr. 1979, pb. 1980 (one act); *Last Licks*, pr. 1979 (also as *The Housekeeper*, pr. 1982); *Real to Reel*, pr. 1987; *Marathon 1991*, pr. 1991 (includes *A Way with Words*).

Other literary forms

Frank D. Gilroy's career as a writer has been devoted primarily to drama, although he collaborated with his wife, Ruth G. Gilroy, on a children's book, *Little Ego* (1970), and he is also the author of two novels: *Private* (1970), a fictionalized account of his experiences in the Army, and *From Noon Till Three* (1973), a comical Western.

In addition, Gilroy has had an active career as a television scriptwriter and as a screenwriter. During the 1950's he was a contributor to many of the television programs that stimulated a new interest in drama in the United States: *Studio One*, *Kraft Theatre*, *U.S. Steel Hour*, *Playhouse 90*, *Omnibus*, *Lux Video Theater*, the *Armstrong Theater*, and *The Dick Powell Show*. Gilroy's screenwriting career developed initially out of his work for television. *The Last Notch* (1954), a Western drama he wrote for television, became the source of his first screenplay, *The Fastest Gun Alive* (1956). In the 1960's, he adapted two of his own plays for the screen, *The Subject Was Roses* (1968) and *The Only Game in Town* (1969). In the 1970's, Gilroy was the director as well as the writer of *Desperate Characters* (1971), *Once in Paris* (1978), and the film version of *From Noon Till Three* (1976).

Achievements

Gilroy's most impressive accomplishment has been his ability to master the techniques of three genres of drama, television, film, and the theater, and to gain recognition for his writings in each field. He not only wrote for television during its golden age; he was one of the playwrights who made it golden. As a screenwriter, Gilroy earned a national reputation for his adaptation of *The Subject Was Roses* as well as for his play. Patricia Neal was nominated for an Academy Award for her role as Nettie Cleary, and Jack Albertson won the Academy Award for Best Supporting Actor in the role of John Cleary. In 1971, Gilroy received international attention as writer, director, and producer of *Desperate Characters*, which won a Silver Bear Award at the Berlin Film Festival.

Gilroy's achievements and contributions as a writer for the stage are more substantial. His reputation as a dramatist is assured by the literary and theatrical merits of *Who'll Save the Plowboy?* and *The Subject Was Roses*. Not only have his first two plays been more highly regarded by critics and audiences than his later works, but also they continue to be produced. *Who'll Save the Plowboy?* won the Obie Award for the best American play produced Off-Broadway during the 1961-1962 season. *The Subject Was Roses* was the choice of many as the best play of 1964-1965; it won the Outer Circle Award (1964), the New York Drama Critics Circle Award (1964), the New York Theatre Club Award (1964-1965), the Antoinette Perry (Tony) Award (1965), and the Pulitzer Prize for Drama (1965). Gilroy received an honorary doctor of letters degree from Dartmouth College in 1966.

Gilroy has also been recognized by his fellow dramatists as a spokesman and advocate for the writing profession. His well-publicized campaign to get and keep *The Subject Was Roses* on the stage set an example for other playwrights in challenging the play-financing establishment and in having drama produced on the playwright's own terms. In 1965, he filed suit against two publishers, a television network, and two television production companies for misappropriating his property as a writer. When Gilroy won his case eleven years later (1976), his lawyer, Robert Ehrenbard, was quoted in *Publishers Weekly* as saying, "It is a very important victory for writers and supports their rights in a way that the law hasn't done before." It is evidently for efforts such as these that Gilroy was chosen to be a member of the Council of the Dramatists Guild and then its president (1969-1971).

Biography

Frank Daniel Gilroy was born and grew up in New York City. He was the only child of Bettina and Frank B. Gilroy. His father, like John Cleary in *The Subject Was Roses*, was in the coffee business. The family lived in an apartment in the West Bronx. Memories of his early family life and his relationship with his parents eventually provided material for *Last Licks* as well as for *The Subject Was Roses*. By the time Gilroy was graduated from DeWitt Clinton High School in 1943, he had shown an interest in writing but little promise as a student; his father was evidently willing to send him to college, but his grades were not good enough. Gilroy's autobiographical novel *Private* opens with an account of a visit to New Haven and the humiliating return trip to New York after Yale University had rejected his application.

Gilroy was drafted into the United States Army ten months after his high school graduation. He would say later that during his tour in the army his life underwent "some good and productive changes." In Europe, however, attached to the Eighty-ninth Infantry Division Reconnaissance Troop, he also faced degradation and the threat of death and witnessed the depravity of the final days of the war. *Private* records the indelible impression of his army experiences; war memories both trivial and serious also surface in *Who'll Save the Plowboy?* and *The Subject Was Roses.*

In 1946, Gilroy came out of the army with the determination to go to college and with the desire to write. He applied to forty colleges and was accepted by only two of them—Davis and Elkins, and Dartmouth. He chose Dartmouth and was graduated *magna cum laude* with a bachelor of arts degree in 1950. In college, he wrote stories and was an editor of the paper, but a playwriting course convinced him that drama was the form best suited to his talents. During his junior and senior years, he wrote and was accorded productions of two full-length plays and six one-act plays. In both years, he won the Frost Playwriting Award. Following his graduation, Gilroy attended the Yale School of Drama with the help of a scholarship, but his funds ran out after six months.

The growing popularity of television provided a new market for playwrights, and Gilroy began writing scripts for television in the early 1950's. To support himself during this period, he held a series of jobs—including messenger, trumpet player, and cabana salesman—but by the mid-1950's he was making a good living from television. He wrote regularly for two popular Western series, *The Rifleman* and *Have Gun, Will Travel,* in addition to having plays produced by the leading network drama programs. Only a few of his unpublished scripts can still be identified. He wrote at least three plays for *Studio One: A Likely Story* (1955), *Uncle Ed and Circumstances* (1955; adaptation of a story by Jackie Gleason), and *The Last Summer* (1958). Two of his plays appeared on *Kraft Theater: Run for the Money* (1954) and *Ten Grapefruit to Lisbon* (1956). *A Matter of Pride* (1957; adaptation of John Langdon's story "The Blue Serge Suit") was shown on the *U.S. Steel Hour.* For *Playhouse 90* he adapted two works by John P. Marquand, *Sincerely, Willis Wayde* (in 1956) and *Point of No Return* (in 1958).

In 1954, Gilroy married Ruth Gaydos, and by the time *The Subject Was Roses* was produced, ten years later, they had three sons and lived in upstate New York. For several years at the end of the 1950's, however, while Gilroy was employed as a studio screenwriter, California was his home. This experience was evidently the inspiration for *'Twas Brillig,* a one-act comedy about a writer's first day on a studio lot. In 1960, Gilroy collaborated with Beirne Lay, Jr., on *The Gallant Hours,* a biographical film about Admiral William Halsey, starring James Cagney. Gilroy's work for television and films gave him enough time and income to write for the stage and enabled him to complete *Who'll Save the Plowboy?* in 1957.

Gilroy moved his family back to New York in 1961, and in 1962, after searching for five years, he found a producer for *Who'll Save the Plowboy?* Although its reviews were generally favorable and it won an Obie Award, the play did not enjoy a long run—a month at the Phoenix Theatre and another month at the Orpheum Theatre. Its production at the Haymarket Theatre in the spring of 1963 introduced Gilroy's work to London audiences. On May 25, 1964, *The Subject Was Roses* opened at the Royale Theatre on Broadway, then moved to the Winthrop Ames Theatre on September 7, 1964. Although it ended up being Gilroy's longest-running drama and greatest achievement, he worked steadily for two years to get it produced and then faced the threat of an early closing. The play not only survived but also received 832 performances in New York, toured the United States, and was produced in a number of other countries. *The Subject Was Roses* won almost every award given for the best play of 1964-1965. In *About Those Roses: Or, How Not to Do a Play and Succeed* (1965), Gilroy gives a diary account of his struggles for the play from its completion in the spring of 1962 to its opening night in the spring of 1964. In a 1966 interview with Joseph Blank in *Reader's Digest*, Gilroy summed up the meaning of the experience for him: "It's amazing how much *can* be accomplished if you believe in what you want to do. The strength of your belief makes others believe."

In a story in *Life* three months after the opening of *The Subject Was Roses*, Tom Prideaux reported that Gilroy had become a "hot property" and had received offers "to adapt sixteen books into movies, to write four musicals and six TV pilot films." Gilroy may never have committed himself to any of these projects, but the decade between 1965 and 1975 was to become the most active period of Gilroy's writing career. In 1965, *Far Rockaway*, a very brief expressionistic play in thirteen scenes, was presented on National Educational Television. When it was printed with the Random House edition of *That Summer—That Fall*, Gilroy claimed that the little drama demonstrated that he was not exclusively dedicated to the "real." *That Summer—That Fall*, Gilroy's updated dramatization of the Phaedra story, opened on March 16, 1967, at the Helen Hayes Theatre in New York, and closed on March 25. The film of *The Subject Was Roses* was released in 1968, and on May 23, 1968, Gilroy's Las Vegas love comedy, *The Only Game in Town*, opened at New York's Broadhurst Theatre, only to close on June 1. The film of the comedy, for which Gilroy wrote the screenplay, was released a year later with Elizabeth Taylor and Warren Beatty as the lovers. *Little Ego*, the children's book which Gilroy wrote with his wife, Ruth, was published in 1970; the same year saw the publication of *Private*, Gilroy's autobiographical war novel. The novel is written in an impressionistic style, resembling in its form and its evocative power the interchapter vignettes of Ernest Hemingway's *In Our Time* (1924, 1925).

Gilroy produced, directed, and wrote the screenplay for *Desperate Characters* in 1971; the film was adapted from a novel by Paula Fox and starred Shirley MacLaine. A program of four of his one-act plays—*Come Next Tuesday*, *'Twas Brillig*, *So Please Be Kind*, and *Present Tense*, opened at the Sheridan Square Playhouse July 8, 1972, and closed July 23. Gilroy's Western novel, *From Noon Till Three*, was published in 1973. Its comic irony develops from two versions of a frontier romance told first by a lady and then by her outlaw lover. Gilroy adapted the story for the screen and produced and directed the film, which was released in 1976 and featured Charles Bronson and Jill Ireland in the leading roles. In the same year, Gilroy returned briefly to television to adapt stories by John O'Hara for *Gibbsville*, a short-lived series that he directed.

In 1976, Gilroy also realized a great profit, however indirectly, from another television play, *Who Killed Julie Greer?* (1961), which he had written for *The Dick Powell Show* fifteen years earlier. In the play, he created the character of Amos Burke, a wealthy detective, who became the main character in the television series *Burke's Law* two years later (1963). In 1965, Gilroy filed suit against two publishers, a television network, and two television production companies which had misappropriated the Burke character, and after eleven years of litigation a jury awarded Gilroy one million dollars in compensation and interest.

After that, Gilroy wrote the screenplay for *Once in Paris*, which he also produced and directed. His full-length play *Last Licks* focuses on the relationship between father and son and reveals an unhappy marriage and a family triangle in their past. With its autobiographical roots, the comedy is a sequel to *The Subject Was Roses*. *Last Licks* opened at the Longacre Theatre on November 20, 1979, and closed December 1. The plays that Gilroy wrote after 1964 have survived for only a short time on stage, yet Gilroy has retained a dramatist's interest in the theater and in theater groups devoted to developing and showcasing new plays. Two of his one-act plays, *The Next Contestant* and *Dreams of Glory*, were produced by the Ensemble Studio Theatre in its annual play festivals.

While Gilroy pursued a successful television and screenwriting career; he continued to write for the stage; his plays are frequently produced in regional and community theaters. The one-act play *A Way with Words* was produced by the Ensemble Studio Theatre in May, 1991, as part of a short-play marathon; *The Subject Was Roses* was revived on Broadway in June of 1991.

Analysis

Most of Frank D. Gilroy's plays—both comic and serious, full-length and one-act—may be identified by their development of themes and situations that are related to marriage or family problems and by their ironic style. Unhappy or failed marriages are directly or indirectly responsible for complications in *Who'll Save the Plowboy?*, *The Subject Was Roses*, *That Summer—That Fall*, *The Only Game in Town*, *Last Licks*, *So Please Be Kind*, and *Come Next Tuesday*. Family problems centering on the relationship between father and son or on an Oedipal triangle are sources of conflict in *The Subject Was Roses*, *That Summer—That Fall*, *Last Licks*, and *Present Tense*. Gilroy's realistic drama, like Henrik Ibsen's, is distinguished not so much by its verisimilitude in dramatizing these problems as by its mastery of irony. In each of his full-length plays, in the manner of Ibsen's *Hedda Gabler* (pb. 1890), Gilroy creates patterns of irony through triangular character relationships: in *Who'll Save the Plowboy?*, Albert and Helen Cobb and Larry Doyle; in *The Subject Was Roses*, John and Nettie Cleary and their son, Timmy; in *That Summer—That Fall*, Angelina and Victor Capuano and Victor's son, Steve; in *The Only Game in Town*, Fran Walker, Joe Grady, and Thomas Lockwood; and in *Last Licks*, Matt and Dennis Quinlan and Fiona (but also Matt and Dennis Quinlan and Margaret Quinlan, the dead mother). This triangular design allows for developments, in the relationship and dialogue between two characters, that are concealed from the third character but revealed to the audience. The complexities of the pattern may be expanded by shifts in the balance of the triangle that give each character a turn as the victim of irony.

The inciting action in *Who'll Save the Plowboy?* is deceptively simple, because only two of the characters who will form the ironic triangle are onstage when the play opens. An unhappily married couple, Albert and Helen Cobb, argue as they await the visit of Larry Doyle, Albert's buddy during the war. Larry risked his own life and was wounded in carrying out a miraculous battlefield rescue that saved Albert's life. Helen suspects that Larry is coming to ask for something, and, in an ironic way, he is. Albert, who considers Larry to be the best friend he ever had, anticipates an opportunity of some kind, perhaps a job offer. A bitter quarrel erupts when Helen balks at Albert's plan that they act like a loving couple and welcome Larry into a happy home. They exchange insults and threats, and Albert slaps his wife when she makes, fun of the "Plowboy" image he is reviving for Larry's sake. Before Larry arrives, Albert warns Helen not to mention the "farm" or the "boy."

Albert and Larry have not seen each other for fifteen years, but the joy of their reunion is quickly dissipated. Each man is surprised and disappointed by the changes in the other. Albert is made increasingly uncomfortable by Larry's questions about the "boy," the son who was named after Larry and is supposedly visiting relatives. Larry is evasive in speaking about his own life and work. Both men are disturbed by Helen's cutting remarks. The first scene ends in a violent argument between the two men after Albert reveals to Larry the sordidness of his life—the failure of the farm he bought after the war, his drinking problem, and his unfaithfulness to his wife. As Albert pleads with him to save the Plowboy again, Larry, disgusted, leaves the apartment but collapses on the stairs.

The first scene provides the exposition necessary to understand the relationships among the three central characters and the basic situation in the play, yet the scene is even more important in setting up the ironies that develop in the second scene of act 1 and in act 2. Before Larry arrives, the dramatic interest is created and sustained not by irony but by the strident verbal exchanges between Albert and Helen and particularly by Helen's sarcasm and ridicule of Albert. In her self-hatred ("Every night before I go to bed I hope I won't wake up in the morning") and in the destructive power of her words, she resembles Martha of *Who's Afraid of Virginia Woolf?*, the Edward Albee play that opened eight months after Gilroy's drama. After Larry enters, the first pattern of irony is introduced in the reversal of the two friends' expectations. Albert remembers Larry as a joking, hell-raising, hard-drinking woman-chaser, and he finds that Larry is serious, single, and no longer drinks. Larry discovers that Albert, who never took a drink, now drinks heavily. He finds it even harder to believe that the young man whom he had nicknamed the "Plowboy" and who had talked constantly about owning a farm is living in a run-down apartment in New York City and reading meters for a living.

In the second scene of act 1, Gilroy introduces the first of a series of discoveries that contribute to the ironic design which gives focus and dramatic force to the play. Mrs. Doyle, Larry's mother, reveals to the Cobbs her son's secret and his purpose in visiting them. Mrs. Doyle tells them that Larry has been in and out of hospitals for years and does not have long to live. He is dying of cancer that developed from the wound he sustained in saving Albert. Shortly after the war, when Larry discovered that his condition was terminal, he dropped out of medical school, where he was the top student, and broke off his engagement to spare the girl he loved. Mrs. Doyle lets Albert know that she blames and hates him for ruining her son's life. She also suggests that Larry has come to the Cobbs in the hope of proving before his death that Albert's life and family were worth the life and happiness he gave up. The scene ends with Albert, tormented by guilt, vowing to convince Larry that he is happy in his life and marriage. Helen agrees to join him in the masquerade and to pretend that Mrs. Doyle never called or told her story.

While the irony at the end of act 1 depends on the Cobbs's discovery of Larry's secret, the irony in act 2 is created by Larry's discovery of the Cobbs's secret, which provides both the climax and the resolution of the play. Larry's first discovery on the morning after his illness, however, merely develops the incidental irony that Helen has been just as unfaithful as Albert. After Albert has left the apartment to meet his boss, Larry tries to get Helen to tell him why she hates him. She breaks down, and when Larry plays the piano to get her to stop crying, she becomes even more upset. The trumpet player who lives upstairs appears at the door, and Larry deduces that Helen uses her piano as a signal for her lover. Promising not to reveal her secret yet unable to learn the reason for her hatred, Larry tells Helen that he intends to stay in New York until he meets the "boy" who bears his name. The "boy" is Larry's last hope of giving meaning to the life he sacrificed by saving Albert. Realizing that Larry will not heed her warning to spare himself by leaving, and "sick of lies," Helen reveals the secret about the "boy" that became a psychological cancer for her and Albert and destroyed their marriage: "I gave birth to a monster. . . . Not boy. Not girl. Not anything. . . . It took something in him and something in me. Something bad in the both of us to produce this thing." Helen's confession and the irony of its grotesque response to Larry's hope form the climax of the play. The monster child and its malignant effects on Helen, Albert, and their marriage are comparable to the imaginary child and its effects on George and Martha in *Who's Afraid of Virginia Woolf?* The monster would never have been born if Larry had not saved Albert, and that is why Helen has hated Larry. She suggests that Albert also regrets that he was not left to die.

In releasing her pent-up feelings, Helen inadvertently reveals that she and Albert know that Larry is dying. What follows this disclosure is one of the two moments of warmth and compassion in the play. After Larry tells Helen that the truth has drained away her hatred of him, she takes his head in her hands and kisses him on both cheeks and the forehead. The secrets that Helen and Larry now share and keep from Albert create the final ironies of the play's resolution. Albert returns with a boy whom he has picked up on the street and passes him off as his son. Although Larry is almost disgusted enough to spoil Albert's plan, he creates the second compassionate moment by accepting the boy as his namesake and, in effect, saving the Plowboy again. It is possible to interpret the close of the play as an act of compassion on Helen's part, as she answers "Yes" when Albert asks her if she thinks Larry believed the boy was their own. What makes the ending ambiguous and contributes the final irony is the sound of the trumpet in the background as Albert says, "Well, it was worth it. . . . He believed me. . . . I owed him that."

The Subject Was Roses is a more appealing play than *Who'll Save the Plowboy?*, and its three characters are more fully realized and more intrinsically interesting than Larry Doyle or the Cobbs. The irony, too, is more subtle and sympathetic and develops more directly from the characterizations of John, Nettie, and Timmy Cleary and from their relationships with one another. Although *The Subject Was Roses* is a "comedy drama," Gilroy's Cleary family may be compared with the Tyrones of Eugene

O'Neill's *Long Day's Journey into Night* (pb. 1955). Like Edmund Tyrone, Timmy Cleary overcomes his resentment of his father and his blind loyalty to his mother and achieves a better understanding of both parents. Like Mary Tyrone, Nettie Cleary was devoted to her father as a girl and feels that her marriage was a mistake—a comedown in class and something of a fall from innocence. She will not forgive John his past infidelities. John Cleary, like James Tyrone, grew up in abject poverty and is tightfisted with his money. Vital and gregarious as a young man, in his middle years he has trouble expressing his emotions and seems to be much more unfeeling than he actually is. Yet the form and substance of Gilroy's play has more to do with character relationships than with individual characterizations. A triangle is formed by the conflict between Nettie and John over Timmy, as each attempts to secure his love and allegiance. The shape of the triangle changes during the play as Timmy feels more strongly the pull of ties first to one parent and then to the other. It is only in the end that, in Timmy's eyes, all sides of the triangle are equal and the family relationships are balanced.

The first act of the play focuses on the realignment of family loyalties that begins when Timmy returns home after three years in the army. It is clear from conversations between Nettie and John and from Timmy's own remarks that in the years before he left home, he was much closer to his mother than to his father. In the exchange between Nettie and John that begins the play, John voices the hope that his relationship with his son will improve now that his son is a man, and everything that happens in the first act seems to support his hope, as Timmy displays not only a new understanding of his father but also similar personality traits. They drink together, take in a ballgame, and team up for an impromptu vaudeville routine after a night on the town. More important, they talk together, and for the first time Timmy is able to form his own impressions of his father. As a boy, he saw his father through his mother's eyes and accepted her judgments of him. Timmy gains a new appreciation of his father's humor, his fighting spirit, and his successful struggle out of poverty.

In the first act, as Timmy draws closer to his father, he pulls back gently but firmly from his mother. It is not that Timmy loves his mother less but that he realizes better his position at the center of his parents' conflict with each other. He is also aware that his identity is no longer defined solely by his role as a son and that he must claim his independence. Timmy's withdrawal from his mother's hold on him is dramatized in an emotionally intense moment in the first scene. When Nettie says she cannot believe he is home again, Timmy extends his hand and tells her to pinch him. His mother takes his hand, holds on, and will not let go until Timmy becomes agitated and "jerks" his hand free. Much of the irony in the first act comes as Timmy pulls away from his mother's grip on his life, and there is a reversal in her expectations of continuing their past relationship. Nettie is surprised and upset not only because Timmy is doing things with John instead of with her, but also because he shows signs of taking after his father—telling jokes, repeating John's favorite expressions, and drinking too much.

Act 1 concludes with a bitter argument between Nettie and John following the family's evening in New York. After Timmy has gone to his room, John grows amorous, and Nettie resists. Their struggle becomes ugly when John resorts to force; it ends with Nettie smashing the vase of roses she has been led to believe were a present from John. She has been moved by the roses, but she will not forgive his unfaithfulness—his "hotel lobby whores"—and refuses to renew their sexual relationship. In his frustration at the end of the scene, John tells her that the roses were Timmy's idea. What has appeared to be friction between them over their son is revealed to be a much more serious marital problem.

Nettie tells John that "what's wrong" between them "has nothing to do" with Timmy, but it does. The second act opens the morning after, and John, still smarting from Nettie's rejection, vents his anger on Timmy as well as Nettie. The scene suggests the tone of John's relationships with his wife and son before Timmy left home. His petulance gives way to outraged disbelief when Timmy declines to attend Mass with him because he no longer considers himself to be a Catholic. When Nettie defends Timmy's right as a man to choose for himself, John speaks bitterly of the "familiar alliance" between mother and son. Ironically, after John leaves the house, Timmy stands up for his father and tries to get his mother to admit that it was "always us against him." It is evidently the first time Timmy has ever argued seriously with his mother or sided with his father: "You, and him, and me, and what's been going on here for twenty years. . . . We've got to stop ganging up on him." Timmy also accuses Nettie of bolstering the alliance against John by maintaining close ties and daily contact with her mother and sister. The irony is doubled at the end of the scene when Nettie, angered by Timmy's accusations, thanks him for the roses and stalks out of the apartment with fifty dollars in coins which she has saved.

Irony is created in the second scene of act 2 in its reversal of one of the more melodramatic scenes of the Cleary's prewar family life. It is ten o'clock on a Sunday night, and it is Nettie, not John, who has not returned home. As the father and son wait and seek news of her, it is John who is frantic and Timmy who is drunk—but well aware of the irony of his father's position. He recalls for his father the dreaded ritual that was repeated throughout his childhood of lying awake listening for his father's return from a late-night adventure and for the argument between his parents that inevitably followed. The irony of the scene is complete when Nettie comes home but refuses to respond to John's angry demands for an explanation.

Instead, she uses John's favorite alibi of having been to a movie. Finally, as John presses her for an answer, Nettie insinuates that she has been with another man. She never reveals the truth of her absence to husband or son and will say only that her twelve hours away from them gave her the only "real freedom" she has ever known. Regardless of whether Nettie walked out with the intention of teaching her son a lesson, her rebellious act has that effect. Timmy's memories of his father's irresponsible behavior bring a further adjustment in his relationship with both parents.

The proof of a new evenness in Timmy's attachments to his parents is provided in the scene that follows. At two in the morning, Timmy and Nettie, who have been unable to sleep, talk together in the living room. Timmy tells his mother that he must leave home, and she accepts his decision. Nettie then tells Timmy the story of how she met and married John. Like Mary Tyrone, she describes her marriage in a litany of regret as the inevitable tragic turning point of her life. It is at this point that Timmy speaks of the shifts in his loyalties and of his new and more balanced view of his parents: "When I left this house three years ago, I blamed *him* for everything that was wrong here.... When I came home, I blamed *you*.... Now I suspect that no one's to blame.... Not even me."

The play ends as it began, by focusing on John and Timmy and on the final adjustment that ensures Timmy's balanced relationship with his parents and his own independence. Unsuccessful in his appeal to Nettie to persuade Timmy to stay, John himself tries to talk Timmy out of going. He tells him that he is willing to let him do as he pleases in the house, and, confessing that he was wrong in his treatment of Timmy in the past, he promises to change. Timmy insists that he must leave, but he gives his father an assurance of his love that makes his leaving bearable for both. Timmy tells his father of a childhood dream that he had dreamed again the night before—that his father would die without ever saying he loved him. Then, Timmy says, "It's true you've never said you love me. But it's also true I've never said those words to you.... I say them now—I love you, Pop." Timmy's declaration and what follows—the father and son in tears and embracing each other—provide the emotional climax of the play and a happy ending for Timmy, but there is no happy resolution of his parents' marital problems. Gilroy spoke openly of the play's roots in his own family life. In his interview for *Reader's Digest*, he explained that the play had been written several years after his parents' deaths as his "way of saying how [he] came to love them." By including unpleasant recollections as well as happy memories and by treating them honestly, Gilroy avoided the sentimentality that would have spoiled the play.

That Summer—That Fall, Gilroy's most ambitious drama, fails because it neglects the proven strengths of his first two plays—psychological realism and irony. Gilroy may also have made a mistake in taking the material for his play from a classical tragedy, turning away from his own experience. In another sense, however, the Phaedra story, with its unhappy marriage and its father-son conflict, was a logical choice for the author of *The Subject Was Roses*.

The play is given a contemporary setting in a run-down Italian neighborhood of New York City; with the exception of the opening and closing scenes in a playground, the action takes place in the apartment of Victor and Angelina Capuano. In his delineation of his characters and their relationships, Gilroy shows the influence of Jean Racine's *Phèdre* (pr. 1677) as well as Euripides' *Hippolytus* (428 B.C.). Victor, whose role is comparable to that of Theseus in the original story, is a successful restaurant owner in his mid-fifties. His wife, Angelina, who is thirty-six, is Gilroy's modern Phaedra and, like Racine's heroine, is the dominant character in the play. Angelina falls in love with Steve Flynn before Victor brings him home and identifies him as his illegitimate son. Steve resembles Racine's Hippolytus more closely than he does Euripides' chaste woman-hater. By the end of the play, he is dating Josie, a teenage neighbor girl who has fallen in love with him. Zia Filomena, Angelina's aunt, plays the part of go-between that Euripides assigned to Phaedra's nurse and Racine expanded for Oenone, the nurse and lady-in-waiting of his Phaedra.

The plot of *That Summer—That Fall* follows Euripides' tragedy more closely than Racine's. When the play opens, Angelina is already tormented by her secret passion for Steve. From papers his mother left after her death, Steve has discovered that Victor is his father, and he has hitchhiked from California to meet him. Victor accepts Steve as his son, all the more eagerly because he and Angelina are childless. A close, trusting relationship grows quickly between father and son, and they are soon working together as partners. At the same time, Angelina's desire and frustration are intensified by living with Steve under the same roof.

The turning point of the play comes on a night on which Josie and Steve have gone to a dance. Angelina attempts to dull her pain with wine, and in an inebriated stupor she confesses to Zia her love for Steve. The following morning, after Victor has told her that Steve will be staying, Angelina's thoughts turn to suicide. Zia realizes what Angelina plans to do and promises to help her. With the idea of bringing Angelina and Steve together to save her niece's life, Zia sends the young man to Angelina's bedroom.

The climax and resolution follow very quickly. Mistaking Steve's intentions in visiting her room, Angelina kisses him passionately and confesses her love. Steve is repulsed by her passion and tells her to go back to the playground and find another boy. When Steve returns to the apartment late that night, he finds Victor sitting alone in the dark. Angelina has killed herself, leaving a letter accusing Steve of raping her. Steve tells his father that the letter is a lie, but Victor will not believe him. After Steve runs out of the apartment, Victor confronts Zia with Steve's denial, and she finally confesses the truth—that Angelina loved Steve, "was dying for him," but that nothing happened between them. A hysterical Josie rushes in to tell Victor that Steve has crashed his car and is dying. The play ends with Steve, who lies dying in his father's arms, saying, "Raise me up," and Victor replying, "To heaven if I could."

Gilroy was upset by the hostile reception his play received and by its failure, and he offered his defense in a foreword to the Random House edition: "It was my intention that *That Summer—That Fall* should work both realistically and as ritual. Unfortunately, the latter element has, so far, escaped detection. . . ." The problems with *That Summer—That Fall*, however, have nothing to do with realism or ritual: The play lacks adequate plot development and convincing motivation for Angelina and Steve. At the end of the play, each crucial scene—from the moment that Steve enters Angelina's bedroom to the moment of his death—is unusually brief and is developed in dialogue that is monosyllabic and frequently stichomythic. As a consequence, there is little opportunity for the development of irony. Angelina's attraction to Steve comes across as lust, not love, since she registers her feelings most strongly whenever she sees Steve bare-chested. Unrequited lust is not a believable motive for suicide or revenge, and, since nothing happens, Angelina has no reason to feel guilty or sinful. Steve has even less motive for suicide, if indeed that is the way his automobile wreck is to be taken. He has no reason to blame himself for Angelina's death, and his father's wrongheaded rejection hardly seems motive enough to take his own life. Indeed, the best explanation of the motives of Angelina and Steve would seem to be that they behave as they do because that is the way Phaedra and Hippolytus behave.

The Only Game in Town is worth mentioning because it is Gilroy's only full-length comedy, and Gilroy is a talented comic writer—as is evident in *The Subject Was Roses* and *Last Licks*, as well as in the short comedies *'Twas Brillig, So Please Be Kind*, and *Dreams of Glory*. The plot complications in *The Only Game in Town* may be contrived, but the humor of the dialogue is as sharply honed and as quickly paced as Neil Simon's. The play also makes good use of comic irony to develop an idea that is treated seriously in Gilroy's other full-length plays: that marriage is a gamble at long odds. Appropriately enough, the comedy is set in Las Vegas, the action taking place in Fran Walker's apartment over a period of two years. Fran, one of the players in the love game, is a nightclub dancer who has not yet had the courage to bet on matrimony. It is revealed at the end of the play that she has feared and avoided marriage because her father deserted the family when she was ten years old. The other player is Joe Grady, a piano player who is also a compulsive gambler and a two-time loser at marriage. The first act traces the development of the relationship between Fran and

Joe from a casual sexual liaison into a love that each feels but conceals from the other. In the second act, having lived together for almost two years, Fran and Joe remove the obstacles to their marriage and reluctantly agree to wed. Joe licks his gambling problem, and Fran, although she is still "scared," finally takes a chance. The theme of the comedy and its underlying attitude toward marriage are expressed by Joe in proposing to Fran: "Granted that marriage is a most faulty, pitiful, and wheezing institution, right now it's the only game in town and *we're* going to play it."

As a realistic playwright in the 1960's and 1970's, Gilroy often faced the hostility or indifference of critics who were embracing the Absurdists and who dismissed realistic drama as dull and outmoded. Gilroy also found himself challenging the values of producers who dismissed as a bad investment any play that was serious and had no music or lyrics. He succeeded in overcoming the opposition of both groups by the sheer power of his writing in *Who'll Save the Plowboy?* and *The Subject Was Roses.* In these plays and occasionally in his later works, Gilroy has contributed to an evolving tradition in the best modern American drama, which refines and applies the techniques of psychological realism to a focus on the family and marriage.

Other major works

NOVELS: *Private,* 1970; *From Noon Till Three,* 1973 (also as *For Want of a Horse,* 1975).

NONFICTION: *About Those Roses: Or, How Not to Do a Play and Succeed,* 1965.

SCREENPLAYS: *The Fastest Gun Alive,* 1956; *The Gallant Hours,* 1960 (with Beirne Lay, Jr.); *The Subject Was Roses,* 1968 (adaptation of his play); *The Only Game in Town,* 1969 (adaptation of his play); *Desperate Characters,* 1971 (adaptation of Paula Fox's novel); *From Noon Till Three,* 1976 (adaptation of his novel); *Once in Paris,* 1978; *The Gig,* 1985; *The Luckiest Man in the World,* 1989.

TELEPLAYS: *The Last Notch,* 1954; *Run for the Money,* 1954; *A Likely Story,* 1955; *Uncle Ed and Circumstances,* 1955; *Sincerely, Willis Wayde,* 1956 (adaptation of John P. Marquand's play); *Ten Grapefruit to Lisbon,* 1956; *A Matter of Pride,* 1957 (adaptation of John Langdon's story "The Blue Serge Suit"); *The Last Summer,* 1958; *Point of No Return,* 1958 (adaptation of Marquand's play); *Who Killed Julie Greer?,* 1961; *Far Rockaway,* 1965.

CHILDREN'S LITERATURE: *Little Ego,* 1970 (with Ruth G. Gilroy).

Bibliography

Gilroy, Frank D. *About Those Roses: Or, How Not to Do a Play and Succeed.* New York: Random House, 1965. Printed with the text of *The Sub-*

ject Was Roses. Gilroy presents his personal reactions to the vicissitudes of Broadway production, day by day, with reviews (quite favorable, surprisingly to Gilroy) from New York critics. An interesting introduction to Gilroy's motives, work habits, and expectations.

Kerr, Walter. "Play: Gilroy Drama of Age, *Last Licks.*" Review of *Last Licks. The New York Times*, November 21, 1979, p. C11. This review of *Last Licks* provides an interesting examination of the genre problem caused by the incongruities of the first and second acts. Kerr questions whether the play is a comedy or "a deeply serious psychological snarl." In the second act, Kerr says. "[Gilroy] has . . . put an abrupt end to the pleasures that popped out of him while he was feeling his way."

Simon, John. *Uneasy Stages.* New York: Random House, 1975. A homage to Gilroy, whose *The Subject Was Roses* disappointed Simon. The ending, Simon remarks, "depended on a sudden and ephemeral paternal embrace, insufficiently motivated and unable to carry its load of hope—it was unearned." Simon describes Gilroy as "a product of television's Golden Age" and believes that Gilroy's plays belong on television, minus the sexual boldness.

Taubman, Howard. "Play by Frank Gilroy at the Royale Theater." Review of *The Subject Was Roses. The New York Times*, May 26, 1964, p. 45. Judges *The Subject Was Roses* to be "an impressive stride forward" from *Who'll Save the Plowboy?*, which Taubman says showed promise. Gilroy "knows the difference between sentiment and sentimentality and he is not betrayed into the latter." Martin Sheen, an unknown at the time, played the returning soldier in this production.

Weales, Gerald. *The Jumping-Off Place: American Drama in the 1960's.* New York: Macmillan, 1969. Weales treats Gilroy in a chapter entitled "Front Runners, Some Fading" and criticizes his work as suggesting television material rather than work for the stage: "It was neither the many scenes nor the suspicious length [of *That Summer—That Fall,*] that suggested television; it was the tone of the play." Good comments on the artificially happy endings, especially in *The Only Game in Town.*

Ted R. Ellis III
(Updated by *Thomas J. Taylor*)

SUSAN GLASPELL

Born: Davenport, Iowa; July 1, 1882
Died: Provincetown, Massachusetts; July 27, 1948

Principal drama

Suppressed Desires, pr. 1915, pb. 1917 (one act with George Cram Cook); *Trifles*, pr. 1916, pb. 1917 (one act); *The People*, pr. 1917, pb. 1918 (one act); *Close the Book*, pr. 1917, pb. 1918 (one act); *The Outside*, pr. 1917, pb. 1920 (one act); *Woman's Honor*, pr. 1918, pb. 1920 (one act); *Tickless Time*, pr. 1918, pb. 1920 (one act; with Cook); *Bernice*, pr. 1919, pb. 1920; *Plays*, pb. 1920 (includes *Suppressed Desires*, *Trifles*, *Close the Book*, *The Outside*, *The People*, *Woman's Honor*, *Tickless Time*, and *Bernice*); *Inheritors*, pr., pb. 1921; *The Verge*, pr. 1921, pb. 1922; *The Chains of Dew*, pr. 1922; *The Comic Artist*, pb. 1927, pr. 1928 (with Norman Matson); *Alison's House*, pr., pb. 1930; *Plays by Susan Glaspell*, pb. 1987 (C. W. E. Bigsby, editor; includes *Trifles*, *The Outside*, *The Verge*, and *Inheritors*).

Other literary forms

Susan Glaspell began her long career, which lasted almost four decades, writing short stories that appeared in such popular magazines as *Harper's Monthly*, *Good Housekeeping*, *American Magazine*, and *Woman's Home Companion*. The short stories, in the tradition of local-color writing, generally romanticized the Midwest and its people. Thirteen of her forty-three stories have been collected in *Lifted Masks* (1912). While she enjoyed success as a short-fiction writer and a playwright, Glaspell regarded herself primarily as a novelist. Her nine novels include *The Visioning* (1911), *Ambrose Holt and Family* (1931), *Norma Ashe* (1942), and *Judd Rankin's Daughter* (1945). In addition, she is the author of a children's tale, *Cherished and Shared of Old* (1940), several essays, and a biography of her first husband, George Cram "Jig" Cook, entitled *The Road to the Temple* (1926).

Achievements

Glaspell received recognition in three of the genres that she utilized. Several of her short stories were selected for E. J. O'Brien's yearly anthology, *Best Short Stories*: "Jury of Her Peers" in 1918, "Government Goat" in 1920, and "His Smile" in 1922. Her novel *The Morning Is Near Us* (1940) was a Literary Guild selection, and another novel, *Brook Evans* (1928), was made into the film *The Right to Love* by Paramount Pictures. In addition, she won in 1931 a Pulitzer Prize for her play *Alison's House*. Her greatest achievement, however, was the work that she did with the Provincetown Players, a group that she helped found. The Provincetown Players, whose stated purpose was to produce new plays by American playwrights, was extremely influential and changed the direction of modern American drama, providing a forum where none existed. From its inception to 1922, the group's theater produced ninety-three new American plays by forty-seven playwrights; all but two of these playwrights had their first plays produced by the theater. Glaspell, who wrote eleven of her fourteen plays for the group, was, after Eugene O'Neill, the group's most important playwright.

Biography

Born July 1, 1882, to Elmer S. and Alice Keating Glaspell, descendants of pioneer settlers, Susan Glaspell grew up in Davenport, Iowa, and attended public schools. She went to Drake University in nearby Des Moines, receiving her B.A. in 1899. While in college, she began writing stories and published her first one in the *Davenport Weekly Outlook* in 1896. After graduation, she spent two years working for *The Des Moines Daily News* and other newspapers as a reporter covering the court and legislative beats. She returned in 1901 to Davenport determined to become a writer. Her early stories, published in popular magazines, and her first novel, the best-selling *The Glory of the Conquered* (1909), were escapist, romantic, and conventional in form.

In 1907, Glaspell met Floyd Dell, future writer and social critic; George Cram Cook, a socialist writer; and Cook's feminist wife, Mollie. Cook and Dell established the Monist Society, a discussion group formulated to expose provincialism and to introduce avant-garde ideas to Davenport. Glaspell fell in love with Cook, encountered the disapproval of her friends and family, and in 1909, in an attempt to end the affair, she traveled to Europe, using the royalties earned from her first novel.

Upon returning to the United States, she spent time in Colorado, Davenport, Chicago, and Greenwich Village. She also finished her second novel, *The Visioning*, which shows Cook's influence in the seriousness of the issues it introduced—trade unions, evolution, and divorce, to name a few—and began a third, *Fidelity* (1915), which explores small-town life in the Midwest and examines the limits placed on women by traditional gender roles. In 1912, she published *Lifted Masks*, a collection of short stories based on her experiences as a reporter. She and Cook, who had divorced his second wife, were married on April 14, 1913, in Weehawken, New Jersey. As a result of being exposed to his ideas, she grew more radical and less conventional in her fiction. Her writing moved away from the sentimental and began to focus on more contemporary themes: the conflict between morality and individual freedom, the hypocrisy of small towns, and the evolution of the "new woman."

Glaspell spent the summer of 1914 writing and acting in plays with friends in Provincetown, and the following summer the Provincetown

Players was formed. Thus began a period of playwriting that lasted about fifteen years, from 1915 to 1931. She and Cook, who had a strong interest in drama, collaborated on the first play, *Suppressed Desires*, a satire on Sigmund Freud's ideas. Unable to get the play produced by the Washington Square Players, the first little theater in New York City, and encouraged by friends, Glaspell and Cook formed the Provincetown Players in 1915 as an outlet for American plays. In 1916, the group moved to Greenwich Village and, with its emphasis on new ideas and techniques and its support of new American playwrights, strongly influenced American drama. Cook became president and remained so until 1922, and Glaspell supported the endeavor primarily through writing plays but also through acting and directing, for the time being giving up her career as a novelist. She first wrote one-act plays; then in 1919, her first full-length play, *Bernice*, was produced, Glaspell performing the role of Abbie. As the Provincetown Players became more commercial, Glaspell and Cook grew disillusioned, and in 1922, they moved to Greece, fulfilling a lifetime desire of Cook, who wanted to live in the land where great drama began. There, in 1924 in the ancient town of Delphi, Cook died. During the years Glaspell spent with Cook, she wrote one novel, seven one-act plays, four full-length ones, and twenty short stories, the stories written to achieve some financial security. After her husband's death, she returned to Provincetown.

Later, traveling in Europe, Glaspell met Norman Matson, a writer, whom she married in 1925. In 1928, she returned to writing novels: *Brook Evans*, *Fugitive's Return* (1929), and *Ambrose Holt and Family*, the latter adapted from *The Chains of Dew*, the last play she wrote for the Provincetown Players. She also wrote *The Road to the Temple*, a biography of Cook, in which she allowed, as much as possible, Cook's own words, garnered from letters, diaries, and other sources, to speak for him. She collaborated with Matson on a play, *The Comic Artist*, and wrote *Alison's House*, which received a Pulitzer Prize. In 1932, Glaspell was divorced from Matson. Her last play, "The Big Bozo," was not produced or published, and no copies are known to exist.

Glaspell did not see herself as a playwright and, without the Provincetown Players' demand for new plays and without Cook's encouragement, she ceased writing plays, although she retained an interest in the theater. In 1936, she went to Chicago to direct the Midwest Play Bureau of the Federal Theater Project, where she selected plays and organized productions. Returning to Provincetown in 1938, she wrote three more novels: *The Morning Is Near Us*, *Norma Ashe*, and *Judd Rankin's Daughter.* She died on July 27, 1948, in Provincetown, of viral pneumonia.

Analysis

Although Susan Glaspell considered herself a novelist, she is best known for her plays. Her playwriting period lasted fifteen years, seven of which were during the time of her association with the Provincetown Players. In only one season, that of 1919-1920, did Glaspell not present at least one new play. While her work in short fiction and the novel is somewhat conventional, her work in the theater is not. She experimented, taking risks with her plays. She was an early advocate of expressionism, the use of nonrealistic devices to objectify inner experience. She experimented with language, sometimes incorporating poetry into the dialogue, and her plays are more often about ideas—feminism and socialism—than they are about characters and plot. The general critical response of her contemporaries to her plays was praise for her realistic ones and a reaction of confusion to her more experimental ones.

Her plays have a range of themes, but most concern the individual and the individual's need to find self-fulfillment. Specifically, she focuses on women who attempt to go beyond societal roles, searching for independence and autonomy. Often, however, these women pay a price: in love or acceptance by family and friends, in money, or, in the case of Claire Archer in *The Verge*, in sanity. Sometimes the search is for the "otherness" of life, that which makes life worth living and takes one beyond the trivial and the commonplace. This search is often aided by a guide or mentor who, some critics argue, is patterned after Cook.

Glaspell's best-known and most anthologized play is the one-act *Trifles*, written for the Provincetown Players' second season, 1916-1917, to fill out a bill with Eugene O'Neill's play *Bound East for Cardiff* (pb. 1916) and later rewritten as the short story "A Jury of Her Peers" (1917). In *The Road to the Temple*, Glaspell describes the origin of the play, writing that she sat in the empty theater until the image of a Midwest farm kitchen with its occupants appeared before her. *Trifles*, based on an event that Glaspell covered as a reporter in Des Moines, takes place in the kitchen of Minnie Wright, a woman accused of murdering her husband. Minnie Wright, in jail, remains offstage for the entire play. *Trifles* marked Glaspell's first use of the device of the absent protagonist, which would be employed again in other plays, most notably in *Bernice* and *Alison's House*. The play, with its grounding in realism and regionalism, is not representative of her later, more experimental plays, but it is said to be the best structured of her plays, and it is certainly the most often performed.

Trifles opens as five people enter a farmhouse kitchen. The three men—the sheriff (Mr. Peters), the county attorney (Mr. Henderson), and a neighbor (Mr. Hale)—are there to uncover evidence to link Minnie to the murder of her husband, John Wright, who was choked to death with a rope while he slept. The two women—the sheriff's wife and the neighbor's wife—are there to gather a few items to take to Minnie. As the men examine the kitchen, the bedroom, and the barn, the women remain in the kitchen. They notice the preserves Minnie had canned, the quilt she was sewing, things that the men belittle, but through their observations, the women solve the murder. The uneven stitching of the quilt indicates Minnie's anxiety, and when the women discover a canary with a broken neck, they know the motive. Minnie, who loved to sing as a young woman, was, in a sense, caged by John, cut off from her interests and isolated. She was figuratively strangled by John as the bird had literally been. After he killed what she loved, the only thing that gave her joy, she responded by choking him. Although the women have information that could convict Minnie, they remain silent. Mrs. Hale, the neighbor, had already failed Minnie by not visiting her when she knew that Minnie's life was bleak, and she will not fail her again. Mrs. Peters, the sheriff's wife, understands from her own experience—she had lost her firstborn—what loneliness is, and she, too, will support Minnie. In a sense, they are the jury of her peers, peers because only they can understand her loneliness and desperation. They try and acquit her. The play, thus, is about sisterhood and the importance of women's sustaining one another in a culture that is dominated by patriarchal attitudes, attitudes that trivialize women and the work—canning, quilting, baking—that they may do.

A more experimental play but one that also explores the limits placed on women is *The Verge*, a full-length play, produced in 1921 by the Provincetown Players. The play had a successful run at the New York MacDougal Street theater, but when it moved uptown to the Garrick Theatre, the audiences became more conventional and less receptive to the experimental and expressionistic play.

Claire Archer, a Faust-like figure, wants to create new life-forms, plants that transcend the boundaries of reality, reaching for "otherness." Claire has spent years in her laboratory developing her plants, but when one of them, the Edge Vine, regresses, she destroys it because it "doesn't want to be—what hasn't been." Similarly, when Claire's daughter Elizabeth accepts conventional attitudes, Claire rejects her, as she does with her sister Adelaide, who urges her to "be the woman you were meant to be." Tom Edgeworthy, one of Glaspell's mentors or guide figures, also fails Claire when he cannot commit to a complete relationship that would include both the spiritual and the physical. He does not reach for the "otherness" but instead attempts to restrain Claire: "I'm here to hold you from where I know you cannot go. You're trying what we can't do." She disagrees, "What else is there worth trying?" Because he refuses to accept the "otherness," she strangles him, destroying him as she did the Edge Vine. The play has strong feminist appeal in the character of Claire, who desires to go beyond the limits set by culture. She does succeed with her plant, the Breath of Life, but the price she pays is her sanity.

Glaspell's last produced play, *Alison's House*, presented by the Civic

Repertory Theater in 1930, received a Pulitzer Prize. As she had in earlier plays—for example, *The Comic Artist*—Glaspell developed the theme of the artist and his or her obligation to society. Alison Stanhope, whose story is loosely based on the life of Emily Dickinson, has died eighteen years earlier, but some of her poems, which obviously deal with a love affair, have recently surfaced. Her relatives are torn between destroying them because they would reflect negatively on the family—the love affair was with a married man—and publishing them because of the public's right to have access to them. The conflict is dramatized by the poet's brother, who wants the poems to remain unpublished, and his daughter Elsa Stanhope, who argues for publication. Elsa, who also had an affair with a married man, is forgiven by her father as they reach the decision that the publication of the poems should not be denied because of small-town morality and hypocrisy. In addition to these themes, the play exhibits other features common to Glaspell's plays: the absent main character and the setting of the small midwestern town.

While Glaspell did not see herself as a dramatist, the contribution she made in this area affected the future of modern American drama. Her willingness to experiment introduced American audiences to more than the traditional Broadway fare and encouraged other playwrights to follow her lead and to take risks.

Other major works

NOVELS: *The Glory of the Conquered: The Story of a Great Love*, 1909; *The Visioning*, 1911; *Fidelity*, 1915; *Brook Evans*, 1928; *Fugitive's Return*, 1929; *Ambrose Holt and Family*, 1931; *The Morning Is Near Us*, 1940; *Norma Ashe*, 1942; *Judd Rankin's Daughter*, 1945.

SHORT FICTION: *Lifted Masks*, 1912.

NONFICTION: *The Road to the Temple*, 1926.

CHILDREN'S LITERATURE: *Cherished and Shared of Old*, 1940.

Bibliography

Ben-Zvi, Linda. "Susan Glaspell's Contributions to Contemporary Women Playwrights." In *Feminine Focus: The New Women Playwrights*, edited by Enoch Brater. New York: Oxford University Press, 1989. Argues that Glaspell's plays represent the female experience and that through their structure, characters, and language, the plays help to create a woman-centered drama.

Bigsby, C. W. E. Introduction to *Plays by Susan Glaspell*. Cambridge, England: Cambridge University Press, 1987. Contains good biographical information and focuses on Glaspell's development as a playwright. Provides insightful critical comments on four of Glaspell's plays: *Trifles*, *The Outside*, *The Verge*, and *Inheritors*.

Dymkowski, Christine. "On the Edge: The Plays of Susan Glaspell." *Modern Drama* 1 (March, 1988): 91-105. Examines Glaspell's theme of "otherness," of taking risks in order to fulfill one's potential.

Ozieblo, Barbara. "Rebellion and Rejection: The Plays of Susan Glaspell." In *Modern American Drama: The Female Canon*, edited by June Schlueter. London: Associated University Presses, 1990. Explores why a playwright as influential as Glaspell had been to her contemporaries is excluded from many studies of drama and concludes that Glaspell was ignored because of her challenge to patriarchal attitudes.

Sarlós, Robert Károly. *Jig Cook and the Provincetown Players: Theatre in Ferment.* Amherst: University of Massachusetts Press, 1982. While the focus of this book is on George Cram Cook, the author presents much useful biographical material about Glaspell. Good discussion of the influence of the Provincetown Players.

Waterman, Arthur E. *Susan Glaspell.* New York: Twayne, 1966. Primarily a critical-analytical study of Glaspell's novels and plays but also contains relevant biographical information. A chapter on the Provincetown Players describes the importance of the group and Glaspell's contribution to it. A bibliography contains both primary and secondary sources.

Barbara Wiedeman

OLIVER GOLDSMITH

Born: Pallas, County Longford(?), Ireland; November 10, 1728 or 1730
Died: London, England; April 4, 1774

Principal drama
The Good-Natured Man, pr., pb. 1768; *She Stoops to Conquer: Or, The Mistakes of a Night*, pr., pb. 1773.

Other literary forms
Although best remembered as a dramatist, Oliver Goldsmith is also known for his work in several other genres. His only novel, *The Vicar of Wakefield* (1766), the comic and sentimental tale of a village curate's attempts to guide his children through the tribulations of growing up, remains a minor classic. *The Citizen of the World* (1762), a recasting of Charles de Montesquieu's *Persian Letters* (1721), is a collection of fictitious letters, purportedly written by a Chinese philosopher who is living in London, describing English customs and English society from an outsider's point of view.

Goldsmith's poetry was often comic as well (as in his parodies of "An Elegy on the Death of a Mad Dog," of 1766, and "An Elegy on the Glory of Her Sex: Mrs. Mary Blaize," of 1759), but when his sympathies were touched, he produced some creditable serious poems, the most notable of which is *The Deserted Village* (1770), a protest against the economic and social conditions that were forcing a massive shift of the populace from small villages to cities.

Like other eighteenth century authors, Goldsmith earned his living by writing whatever publishers thought would sell: histories of Rome and England, biographical sketches, epilogues for the plays of others, translations, and introductions to the natural sciences as well as plays, novels, and poems. The best modern edition of Goldsmith's varied canon is *The Collected Works of Oliver Goldsmith* (1966), in five volumes, edited by Arthur Friedman for Oxford University Press.

Achievements
Goldsmith's success rate as a dramatist is virtually unmatched: two plays written, the first very good, the second a masterpiece. Goldsmith was the preeminent English comic dramatist in the period of almost two centuries between William Congreve and Oscar Wilde. Only his contemporary Richard Brinsley Sheridan—who wrote more plays and had better theatrical connections—came close to matching Goldsmith's talent.

The qualities which make *The Good-Natured Man* and *She Stoops to Conquer* wonderful theater are the qualities that mark all Goldsmith's writings: an eye for human foibles, a knack for creating the scene or situation in which such foibles can best display themselves, and a willingness to laugh at folly rather than to be irked by it. Goldsmith expresses his comic vision of human experience in language that induces the reader's continuing attention and seduces the reader's affection.

Goldsmith was a writer who believed that it was his duty to entertain his audience. Like a stage performer, he used every device, trick, and resource which gives pleasure. No reader finds Goldsmith's prose a chore to read; no theatergoer finds his plays too long.

Biography

Tony Lumpkin in *She Stoops to Conquer* is one of those classic ne'er-do-wells in English literature who would rather eat, drink, and play a merry prank than work for a living. Tony may have been Oliver Goldsmith's favorite male character in the play; at the very least, he was a kindred spirit, because the playwright himself had lived a ne'er-do-well's existence before successful authorship brought him some stability and an income, however irregular it may have been.

Goldsmith began life as the second son in the large family of an Anglo-Irish clergyman. What limited wealth the family had was destined to become part of his older brother's inheritance or of the dowry for an older sister who "married above herself"; nothing much was left for Oliver. Goldsmith seems to have been equally slighted by nature: He was a sickly child, badly disfigured by smallpox contracted at age seven, and he was considered dull by his first teachers. From this inauspicious background, it took a number of years for Goldsmith to discover his niche in the world as a writer.

Goldsmith was graduated from Trinity College, Dublin, in 1749, after fitful periods of study that were punctuated by riotous parties and pranks, clashes with administrators, and attempts to run away. Two years later, he applied for ordination in the Church of England, but the red trousers he wore to the interview seem not to have made a favorable impression on the local bishop. Goldsmith's uncle, the Reverend Thomas Contarine, gave him the money to study medicine, first at the University of Edinburgh and then at the University of Leyden, but the fledgling physician preferred to spend the time and money otherwise, wandering the Continent as a tourist. In 1756, when Goldsmith returned to London, he found it hard to support himself. His casual medical knowledge was no help in obtaining a doctor's commission in the Royal Navy (which at the time appointed as "surgeon" almost anyone who could wield a scalpel without self-mutilation). Goldsmith tried teaching, but he proved less disciplined than the young boys he was supposed to instruct.

Not until he began work as a proofreader for novelist-printer Samuel

Richardson did Goldsmith find a task that focused his energies. Drawing upon his Continental wanderings, the proofreader turned author in 1759 when his *An Enquiry into the Present State of Polite Learning in Europe* was published with some success. His achievement brought Goldsmith freelance assignments from other publishers, and he contributed essays, reviews, and poems to several periodicals. From these, Goldsmith gained popular applause, the recognition of fellow writers, and a modest though unsteady income. The most notable sign of his success was his admission to the Literary Club in the early 1760's. There, Goldsmith dined and conversed with the most prominent London intellectuals, among them the painter Sir Joshua Reynolds, the politician Edmund Burke, the actor David Garrick, and the writer-critic Samuel Johnson. In the Literary Club, Goldsmith found and immersed himself in a sophisticated version of the lively fellowship Tony Lumpkin enjoys at the Three Pigeons Tavern.

Club members helped channel Goldsmith's efforts in new literary directions. When Goldsmith was threatened with arrest for nonpayment of rent, Samuel Johnson sent the unfinished manuscript of *The Vicar of Wakefield* (on which Goldsmith had been working intermittently for several years) to a publisher, who bought it for sixty pounds. Because Goldsmith did not get along with David Garrick, who was manager of the Drury Lane Theatre, Reynolds wrote a letter of recommendation to Garrick on behalf of Goldsmith's recently finished first foray into drama, *The Good-Natured Man*. Though Goldsmith was no doubt anxious to become a playwright, with a chance of making hundreds of pounds if his play ran until the third night (which was the performance known as the "author's benefit"), *The Good-Natured Man* was not produced until two years later. Garrick and Goldsmith had argued over revisions and payments; eventually, Goldsmith had to take the play to another theater.

The profits from his first play were enough to provide Goldsmith with new quarters, new furnishings, and several new coats; they also whetted his desire to repeat his success. By 1771, he had finished a second comedy, *She Stoops to Conquer*, which was produced by a recalcitrant theater manager who procrastinated over the production for more than a year until Johnson again intervened. Through his reasoned arguments and bearlike presence, Johnson convinced the manager to put the play into production, and from the moment it opened on March 15, 1773, it was a huge success. Goldsmith, however, would have only thirteen months left in which to enjoy these financial rewards.

Even after he turned novelist and dramatist, Goldsmith never stopped racing from literary project to literary project. He continued to write essays, biographies, and general histories as well as to compile translations and anthologies. Despite his remarkable output in the last decade of his life, he was never far out of debt. Fortunately, publishers were always eager for his services, because they knew that Goldsmith's name on the title page increased their chances of a brisk sale.

Goldsmith wrote almost until the hour of his death. His last effort was the poem "Retaliation," a verse response to Garrick's epigrammatic remark (that Goldsmith "wrote like an angel, but talk'd like poor Poll"). Goldsmith died on April 4, 1774, the victim of both a fever and the remedy prescribed to cure it.

Analysis

The Good-Natured Man and *She Stoops to Conquer* were written to spite the prevailing taste in comedy. In an essay written just after he completed the second play, Oliver Goldsmith explained that the comedy of his time, which he called sentimental comedy, was a degeneration of a genre that had been clearly defined since the days of Aristotle. Comedy, Goldsmith lamented, had become a kind of tragedy that sought to influence the audience by appealing to its sympathy.

Sentimental comedy was a dramatic subgenre that developed at the beginning of the eighteenth century. The Restoration comedy of manners, which had delighted audiences with contrasting manners, sharp wordplay, and sexual innuendo, had been attacked by Jeremy Collier and others as immoral. To save drama, some writers began to make sure that every rake reformed by the fifth act and that sober, sensible lovers got as much attention as witty, scandalous ones. Sir Richard Steele, in the influential *The Conscious Lovers* (pr. 1722), had shown that lovers could be entangled in plots of parental opposition and mistaken identities so complicated that only the playwright could untie the fifth-act knots. Audiences, it seemed, would watch good people suffer through complex but manageable difficulties and would cheer when the protagonists swept all before them. Sentimental comedy was a part of Sensibility, a movement which characterized much literature after 1740. Sensibility invited readers and audiences to prove their humanity by sympathizing with the plight of fictional or dramatic heroes and heroines; it promised that their sympathy would be rewarded because all would work out in the end, leaving viewers with emotions stirred, teased, and satisfied.

In his essay on "laughing comedy," Goldsmith described the typical sentimental play

> in which the virtues of private life are exhibited . . . and the distresses rather than the faults of mankind made our interest. . . . In these plays almost all the characters are good, and exceedingly generous; they are lavish enough of their *tin* money on the stage; and though they want humor, have abundance of sentiment and feeling.

Whatever claim to merit such plays have is reduced by the fact that they—like modern television situation comedies—are too easily written. Goldsmith scoffed that in sentimental comedies, it was enough

> to deck out the hero with a riband, or give the heroine a title; then to put an insipid dialogue, without character or humor into their mouths, give them mighty good hearts, very fine clothes, furnish a new set of scenes, make a pathetic scene or two, with a sprinkling of tender melancholy conversation through the whole. . . .

The essay concludes with a lament on the art of making audiences laugh, an art that Goldsmith thought had disappeared with plays of Sir John Vanbrugh and Colley Cibber at the start of the eighteenth century. Determined to show that whatever delight sentimental comedies gave, laughing comedies gave better, Goldsmith submitted his own two plays as evidence.

The Good-Natured Man, which debuted while Hugh Kelly's latest sentimental play, *False Delicacy* (pr. 1768), was dominating theatrical London, teased contemporary taste in two ways. First, Goldsmith created scenes which are ironic, farcical, or witty enough to generate laughter. Second, he delineated—that is, in traditional terms, offered up to ridicule—the folly of a culture hero of the age, the "good-natured man." The good-natured man is the sentimental hero, the one who thinks with his heart rather than his head and who leaps to help solve life's smallest distresses. This generous instinct, Goldsmith's good-natured man discovers, has its limitations: One so inclined to sympathize with others may be in danger of losing himself. The twin purposes of the play—literary and moral—actually work together because the laughter which the play generates makes the lesson easier for the audience to accept.

The Good-Natured Man traces Sir William Honeywood's attempt to test and reform his nephew and heir, whose easy generosity (that is, good nature) has led him into extravagance and foolishness. Sir William's plan is to involve young Honeywood in enough fictitious distresses that he will be jailed for debt. Young Honeywood, then, the uncle reasons, would learn a valuable lesson by seeing which of his friends come to his assistance and which of them have only been taking advantage of his generosity. Sir William willingly admits that his nephew's universal benevolence is "a fault near allied to excellency," but as far as Sir William is concerned, it is still a fault to be corrected.

Sir William's plot is intended to demonstrate the need for the sentimental, good-natured man to be shown his follies, and most of the play's other characters reinforce the same idea. Sir William himself is a not very subtle mouthpiece for the dramatist, expostulating precisely and exactly upon the hero's mistakes. Honeywood's friend Croaker is the exact opposite of Honeywood; as a man who sees everything gloomily and selfishly, he lets the audience see the defects of the other extreme. Another friend, Lofty, is a character who counterfeits benevolence (pretending to use influence at court on his friends' behalf) in order to puff himself up in the eyes of the world. Lofty is a conscious pretender, while Honeywood is sincere, but the latter comes to see that "in attempting to please all," he "fed his vanity" as much as Lofty did.

Once Honeywood has been arrested for debt, Sir William is pleased to learn, Miss Richland, a woman of independent fortune and a close friend, has secured his release. Honeywood, however, does not need his uncle's conniving to find himself in difficulties. His benevolence, good nature, and sensibility generate other problems, one of the most knotty being his relationship with Miss Richland. Honeywood loves her deeply, but he is content to be only a friend. "Never let me harbour," he proclaims sentimentally, "a thought of making her unhappy by a connection with one so unworthy her merits as I am." In addition to being modest about his worth to her, Honeywood fears that he could never please her guardians, Mr. and Mrs. Croaker. Rather than tackle such obstacles directly, as would the witty hero of a Restoration comedy, Honeywood is content to sigh and wring his hands in distress.

Circumstances, however, refuse to let Honeywood remain uninvolved. Honeywood must watch while Croaker tries to marry his son, Leontine, to Miss Richland, despite the fact that Leontine is really in love with Olivia, an orphan whom he has brought to England from France in place of the long-absent sister he was sent to fetch. Honeywood must not only watch Croaker's matchmaking, but he must also intercede for Lofty's wooing of Miss Richland. Lofty, pretending to sentimental friendship, calls upon Honeywood to court the young heiress for him. Honeywood is on an emotional rack, stretched between the desire to please a friend and the agony of speaking love in another person's name: "What shall I do! Love, friendship, a hopeless passion, a deserving friend! . . . to see her in the possession of another! . . . Insupportable! But then to betray a generous, trusting friend!—Worse, worse."

Honeywood's dilemmas are solved in the last two acts by accident and by Sir William's intercession. He lends money to Leontine and Olivia that they may elope, but when Croaker intercepts what he thinks is a blackmail letter, Honeywood accidentally sends him after the "blackmailer" to the very inn where the lovers are hiding. Catching his son and "daughter," Croaker praises Honeywood for his help and Leontine damns him for his apparent betrayal. Meanwhile, in speaking to Miss Richland on Lofty's behalf, Honeywood coaxes an admission of love from her. Not realizing that the one she confesses to loving is himself, Honeywood decides that "nothing remains henceforward for me but solitude and repentance."

As the characters gather at the inn for the last act, Sir William sets all to rights on his nephew's behalf. First, he persuades Croaker to accept Olivia as Leontine's bride: She is, Sir William testifies, the daughter of an old acquaintance, of good family, and an orphan with a fortune. Next, Sir William exposes the pretentions of Lofty so that Honeywood sees he is no friend. Now that his sentimental dilemma between love and friendship is understood to be no dilemma after all, a pleased but surprised Honeywood receives Miss Richland's hand in marriage. The events have been a lesson for the good-natured man, who closes the play with the promise that "it shall be my study to reserve pity for real distress, my friendship for true merit, and my love for her, who first taught me what it is to be happy."

Goldsmith generates "laughing comedy" in the play by several devices: a farcical scene in which a bailiff and his deputy dress as gentlemen, humorous characters such as Croaker and Lofty whose foibles are played upon repeatedly, and dialogue at cross-purposes. Dialogue at cross-purposes is one of Goldsmith's favorite comedic devices, one of several dialogue strategies that had made the Restoration comedy of manners so rich in wit. When characters speak at cross-purposes, they manage to hold what appears to be a logical conversation although each is talking about a different subject. The result is confusion among the characters onstage and delight for the audience, which appreciates the ironic interplay of one attitude with another.

The best of these scenes in *The Good-Natured Man* are Leontine's marriage proposal to Miss Richland in act 1, Honeywood's plea on Lofty's behalf in act 4, and Honeywood's interview with the Croakers in act 4. In the first instance, Leontine twists himself into verbal knots as he tries simultaneously to convince his father that he is making an ardent proposal and to make it lukewarm enough to ensure that Miss Richland will reject it. In the second, Honeywood pleads so eloquently for another that Miss Richland is convinced he speaks for himself. In the third, Honeywood counsels Croaker on how to forgive the eloping lovers—counsel which the old man mistakes for advice on how to treat a blackmailer.

What Goldsmith does well in *The Good-Natured Man*, he does brilliantly in *She Stoops to Conquer*. The second play dispenses with the mouthpiece figure of Sir William, offers more entanglements more dexterously resolved, and satirizes sentimental comedy more subtly. *She Stoops to Conquer* has no thesis at all in the usual sense. It is a play that is not *about* something; instead, it is a play that *is* something: a recipe for laughing comedy.

Talking about *She Stoops to Conquer* is somewhat like trying to explain a joke. *She Stoops to Conquer* is an inventory of dramatic tricks for making comedy: juxtaposing high-class and low-class characters, creating farcical situations, putting witty dialogue in the mouths of several characters and having them converse at cross-purposes, establishing several good intriguers to initiate the action, and adding a generous helping of mistaken identities. *She Stoops to Conquer* is one of the purest pieces of entertainment ever written; it stands above its time and historical circumstances to such a degree that it has been a theatrical staple since its first production. To enjoy Goldsmith's comedy, an audience needs no special knowledge or moral perspective; it needs only a willingness to react instinctively to high spirits, confusion, and surprise. The play is a delight for actors as well as audience because all the principal characters are good roles; it is a play for an acting company rather than a vehicle for one or two stars. Although there are two plots, they are so nicely balanced that no audience wishes to see one enhanced at the expense of the other.

Goldsmith manages throughout the play to keep the audience informed of all that occurs while the characters onstage usually act under some mistaken impression. By constantly shifting who-knows-what-about-whom, Goldsmith keeps the plot throttle on "full ahead," the characters in unexpected predicaments, and the audience wide awake. Casting the whole in clever dialogue adds to the delight. In the hands of actors capable of playing the physical comedy broadly, *She Stoops to Conquer* becomes three hours of fast-paced merriment.

So much seems to be occuring simultaneously that *She Stoops to Conquer* is a difficult play to summarize. Perhaps reviewing the *dramatis personae* and sketching the action of the two plots best reveals Goldsmith's dexterity at introducing contrasting parts while keeping the whole moving forward. This dramatist is a theatrical juggler of rare skill; once set into motion, no character, action, or situation falls from his hand.

"The mistakes of a night" occur at the country residence of Mr. and Mrs. Hardcastle, a mismatched couple, each of whom is married for a second time. Mr. Hardcastle loves the country and its old-fashioned ways; Mrs. Hardcastle yearns for the city and the latest styles. Like another literary couple grown accustomed to each other's hobbyhorses, Mr. and Mrs. Bennet in Jane Austen's *Pride and Prejudice* (1813), each Hardcastle takes an independent path while poking fun at the spouse's preference.

Living at the Hardcastle residence are three young persons on the verge of independence and love. First, there is Tony Lumpkin, Mrs. Hardcastle's son by her first marriage. He is about to turn twenty-one and come into his own estate. Mr. Hardcastle regards him as a lazy and useless child, while Mrs. Hardcastle dotes on him, one minute sure he has the makings of a scholar and the next worried that he is consumptive. Tony prefers to ignore both parents and to concentrate on drinking and singing at his favorite tavern, the Three Pigeons. Here he entertains his fellows with practical jokes and lyrics that make clear his values:

> Let schoolmasters puzzle their brain
> With grammar, and nonsense, and learning;
> Good liquor, I stoutly maintain,
> Gives genius a better discerning.

Tony, the alehouse hero, is rather a bold protagonist for Goldsmith to portray to audiences accustomed to central male characters dressed in fine linen and attentive to providing themselves with life's essentials: a pretty wife and a sufficient income.

The second resident is Constance Neville, Mrs. Hardcastle's orphaned niece. Constance is treated with as much restraint as Tony is indulged. She is anxious to marry George Hastings but cannot, because her dowry, a substantial sum in jewels, is closely kept by her aunt. Mrs. Hardcastle is reluctant to give the jewels into Constance's care because she hopes to force her niece to marry Tony. Mrs. Hardcastle's matchmaking is having no luck: The sober Constance and the lighthearted Tony thoroughly dislike each other. Constance is a typical dramatic heroine of the time: pleasant but not especially bright, rich but without control of her fortune, and restless but not very disobedient.

The third person is Kate, Hardcastle's daughter by his first marriage. She and her father get along much better than do mother and son or aunt and niece. They are honestly affectionate with each other and speak frankly to each other; they care enough for each other to indulge each other's preferences. Kate, for example, who shares her stepmother's interest in fashion, moderates her indulgence by dressing for one half of the day in current styles and the other half in a plain country style that pleases her father. Mr. Hardcastle, in turn, has allowed Charles Marlow, the son of an old friend, to become Kate's suitor only after knowing that he is financially sound, handsome, and modestly spirited. As the play begins, Kate anxiously awaits her first look at this prospecting and prospective husband.

When young Marlow and Hastings (the man Constance loves), arrive at the Hardcastle house, they mistakenly believe that they are at a public inn. This false impression is entirely Tony's fault. Tony recognizes the two London beaux when they stop to ask for directions at the Three Pigeons. Irritated by their affected manners, desirous of playing a trick on his stepfather, and anticipating no consequences but a solid embarrassment, Tony directs them to his stepfather's house, telling them that he is sending them to the best inn of the neighborhood. This first mistake of the night begins a series of events that will turn the household topsy-turvy.

Expecting the modest young men described by his old friend Sir Charles Marlow, Hardcastle greets the two weary travelers generously and familiarly. Surprised at the supposed innkeeper's behavior, Marlow and Hastings react with hauteur and sarcasm. To Hardcastle's every offer of hospitality, they respond with increased demands. This scene (act 2, scene 1) is a classic instance of Goldsmith's spectacular handling of dialogue at cross-purposes.

Soon afterward, Hastings encounters Constance and learns how Tony has deceived him and Marlow. The reunited lovers plan to elope as soon as Constance can gain possession of her jewels; to protect their plot, they

decide to keep Marlow in the dark about where he is. They introduce him
to Miss Hardcastle as if she had just alighted at the inn. Throughout the
play these two couples will maintain distinct characteristics. Constance and
Hastings, whose mutual affection is a given, will struggle against external
obstacles; Marlow and Kate, having just met, will try to discover what mutual affection, if any, exists between them.

Kate is anxious to meet the man who has come to court her. In a complete reversal of the bold, brash character that he showed to Mr.
Hardcastle, Marlow becomes shy and stuttering in Miss Hardcastle's presence. It seems that proper young ladies of rank intimidate Marlow with
their genteel and sentimental conversation. He bumbles his way through a
conversation saved only by Kate's promptings:

> MISS HARDCASTLE: You were going to observe, Sir—
> MARLOW: I was observing, Madam—I protest, madam, I forget what I was going to
> observe.
> MISS HARDCASTLE: . . . You were observing, sir, that in this age of hypocrisy—some-
> thing about hypocrisy, sir.
> MARLOW: Yes, madam. In this age of hypocrisy, there are few who upon strict in-
> quiry do not a-a-a-
> MISS HARDCASTLE: I understand you perfectly, sir.
> MARLOW: (*aside*) Egad! and that's more than I do myself.
> MISS HARDCASTLE: You mean that in this hypocritical age there are few that do not
> condemn in public what they practise in private, and think they pay every debt to vir-
> tue when they praise it.

While Constance enlists Tony's help to get the jewels from his mother
and thus free both of them from her matchmaking, Kate and Mr. Hardcastle try to decide who is the real Marlow: the overbearing puppy who insulted his host or the tongue-tied dandy who courted the daughter? The
mystery begins to clear a little when Kate, now wearing her plain country
dress, meets Marlow a second time. The young man makes his second mistake of the night. Not recognizing Miss Hardcastle in what appears to be a
barmaid's outfit, Marlow is immediately and frankly attracted to the pretty
servant. He proves not shy at all in the presence of lower-class women.
With them he can wittily compliment, flirt, and steal a kiss. When Mr.
Hardcastle sees Kate receiving this impudent attention, he is ready to
order Marlow from his house. Kate, however, having seen what a charming
wooer the young man can be, protests that this is the same modest man
she interviewed earlier. She asks her father for the chance to show
Marlow's real character; he begins to wonder if the usually sensible Kate is
not now afflicted by that same malady that makes all young people
undecipherable by their elders. At a second interview, Marlow begins to
fall in love with the girl he assumes to be a household servant.

For one frantic moment the two plots intertwine before going separate ways. Tony filches Constance's jewels from his mother's bureau and gives them to Hastings. To get them out of sight, Hastings hands the jewels to Marlow. Thinking that such valuable gems must not lie around unguarded, Marlow gives them to Mrs. Hardcastle for safekeeping. Mrs. Hardcastle, alerted by the odyssey of the jewels that something is afoot, is quickly suspicious when her illiterate Tony receives a letter. Neither Constance's extemporaneous excuses nor Tony's obstinacy can prevent Mrs. Hardcastle from snatching the letter and discovering instructions from Hastings about the elopement. Determined to frustrate her niece and Hastings, Mrs. Hardcastle orders her carriage made ready for a trip to London: Constance is going to be taken where she can be better watched.

Thus, by the end of act 4, Goldsmith has every character's fate up in the air. The dramatist who knotted things into such a delightful tangle, however, has enough legerdemain to unravel the confusion. Goldsmith will not have to step in to rescue the characters: Kate by her stooping and Tony by his prankstering will set all to rights.

Kate has quite a tangle to undo: first, her father's impression that Marlow is a rude guest and an inconsiderate lover; second, Sir Charles' fear that the son he thought to be honest and modest is really the lout that Hardcastle has described and an indifferent lover to his friend's daughter; third, Marlow's belief that he can be gallant in the pantry but *must act* standoffish in the parlor. She accomplishes all three ends by having the fathers witness the third interview of Kate the maid and Marlow. He professes his love for her—and learns to his shock that he has wooed the redoubtable Miss Hardcastle as well as the pliant Kate.

Meanwhile Tony has been frustrating his mother's flight to London. In the darkness, he has led her carriage on repeated rounds of the estate before driving it into a pond; Mrs. Hardcastle is convinced that she is stranded "forty miles from home." Determined to torment her further, Tony leads his mother into a gloomy thicket where even Mr. Hardcastle, out for a walk in his yard, may look like something more sinister. Although Tony's prank is soon exposed, he at least has had the pleasure of exhausting his mother.

Tony has exhausted the eloping lovers as well. Constance and Hastings decide it will be easier to talk Mrs. Hardcastle into compliance than to escape her this evening. All the cold and sore wanderers in the night return to the house and find Kate and Marlow engaged while the fathers stand beaming. When Mrs. Hardcastle threatens revenge on Tony and Constance, Mr. Hardcastle breaks another surprising bit of news: Tony has already reached the age of majority. The Hardcastles had kept this fact secret to keep the irresponsible Tony from squandering his inheritance, but Mr. Hardcastle now resents his wife's misuse of her authority. Tony's first act as an independent gentleman is to renounce any claim to Constance.

George Hastings quickly grabs the marriageable hand that Tony surrenders. Everyone except Mrs. Hardcastle now sees that the mistakes of a night have turned out happily indeed.

Even this account of the play omits some of its brighter moments: Hardcastle's amusingly futile efforts to turn rough farm laborers into stylish drawing-room valets; the rousing but innocent debauchery of Tony's friends at Three Pigeons; and Kate's dumb-show wooing that quickly heals Marlow's embarrassment after his mistakes were revealed. Actually nothing but reading or viewing can give a complete idea of the brilliance of *She Stoops to Conquer*. It is a rare play, in which no situation is unexploited, no detail wrong, and no word wasted.

Even without the historical interest, many readers still find Goldsmith enjoyable for his prose style and his sense of humor. He is one of the masters of the middle style; his informal, almost conversational prose and his humane and humorous observations of individuals make his work accessible and pleasurable even to those who have never met a lord or made the Grand Tour. Goldsmith's characters and comments are rooted in universal experience.

Other major works

NOVEL: *The Vicar of Wakefield*, 1766.

SHORT FICTION: *The Citizen of the World*, 1762 (collection of essays first published in *The Public Ledger*, 1760-1761).

POETRY: "An Elegy on the Glory of Her Sex: Mrs. Mary Blaize," 1759; "The Logicians Refuted," 1759; *The Traveller: Or, A Prospect of Society*, 1764; "Edwin and Angelina," 1765; "An Elegy on the Death of a Mad Dog," 1766; *The Deserted Village*, 1770; "Threnodia Augustalis," 1772; "Retaliation," 1774; "The Captivity: An Oratoria," 1820 (written in 1764).

NONFICTION: *An Enquiry into the Present State of Polite Learning in Europe*, 1759; *The Bee*, 1759 (essays); *Memoirs of M. de Voltaire*, 1761; *The Life of Richard Nash of Bath*, 1762; *A History of England in a Series of Letters from a Nobleman to His Son*, 1764 (2 volumes); *Life of Bolinbroke*, 1770; *Life of Parnell*, 1770; *An History of the Earth, and Animated Nature*, 1774 (8 volumes; unfinished).

MISCELLANEOUS: *The Collected Works of Oliver Goldsmith*, 1966 (5 volumes; Arthur Friedman, editor).

Bibliography

Danziger, Marlies K. *Oliver Goldsmith and Richard Brinsley Sheridan.* New York: Frederick Ungar, 1978. In this comparative study of the two authors, Danziger maintains that Goldsmith and Sheridan are important for more than restoring "laughing" comedy to the stage of their time. Their best plays, he argues, have a universal quality and are also entertaining.

Goldsmith's conservative nature is contrasted with Sheridan's irreverent, mocking spirit, particularly in the early plays. Danziger also responds to critics who accuse the two authors of "sentimentality" and "safety." Illustrations, chronology, bibliography.

Kirk, Clara M. *Oliver Goldsmith.* New York: Twayne, 1967. This brief study of Goldsmith focuses on the major works. Discusses such topics as the balance of reason and imagination in the works and the author's attempt at self-realization—an attempt underlying all of his writing. Kirk attempts the complex task of relating Goldsmith's life to his writing. Contains a chronology and a bibliography.

Rousseau, G. S., ed. *Goldsmith: The Critical Heritage.* Boston: Routledge & Kegan Paul, 1974. This book is divided into two parts. Part 1 presents the critical heritage of Goldsmith's seven most important works; part 2 incorporates a chronological assortment of statements concerning the author and his works. The eighty-six items have been gathered from many different sources: reviews, diaries, memoirs, letters, autobiographies, biographies, and prefaces and brief introductions to the editions of Goldsmith's works. The section devoted to Goldsmith's drama focuses on *The Good-Natured Man* and *She Stoops to Conquer.* Includes a chronology.

Sells, A. Lytton. *Oliver Goldsmith: His Life and Works.* New York: Barnes & Noble Books, 1974. Despite the wealth of published material on Goldsmith, this study raises and addresses significant, still-unanswered questions about the life and career of the author. New source material is incorporated. In the section devoted to the author's works, Sells discusses Goldsmith as critic, journalist, biographer, novelist, poet, dramatist, and translator. Also contains illustrations, appendices, and a select bibliography.

Swarbrick, Andrew, ed. *The Art of Oliver Goldsmith.* Totowa, N.J.: Barnes & Noble Books, 1984. This insightful series of essays on Goldsmith's works attempts to restore serious critical attention to those classics created by Goldsmith as well as the certain areas of his life and work previously disregarded. The complex personality and the stylistic simplicity of the author are discussed. Balances literary criticism with studies of more general aspects of the author, such as his political inclinations, his classical inheritance, his place within certain eighteenth century literary traditions, and his lack of originality. Chronological table.

Robert M. Otten
(Updated by *Genevieve Slomski*)

HARLEY GRANVILLE-BARKER

Born: London, England; November 25, 1877
Died: Paris, France; August 31, 1946

Principal drama

The Weather-Hen: Or, Invertebrata, pr. 1899 (with Berte Thomas); *The Marrying of Ann Leete*, pr. 1902, pb. 1909; *Prunella: Or, Love in a Dutch Garden*, pr. 1904, pb. 1906 (with Laurence Housman, music by Joseph Moorat); *The Voysey Inheritance*, pr. 1905, pb. 1909; *A Miracle*, pr. 1907; *Waste*, pr. 1907, pb. 1909; *The Madras House*, pr. 1910, pb. 1911; *Rococo*, pr. 1911, pb. 1917 (one act); *The Morris Dance*, pr. 1913 (adaptation of Robert Louis Stevenson and Lloyd Osborne's play *The Wrong Box*); *The Harlequinade*, pr. 1913, pb. 1918 (with Dion Calthrop); *The Dynasts*, pr. 1914 (adaptation of Thomas Hardy's verse drama); *Vote by Ballot*, pr., pb. 1917 (one act); *Farewell to the Theatre*, pb., pb. 1917; *Three Short Plays*, pb. 1917 (3 one-acts; *Rococo, Vote by Ballot*, and *Farewell to the Theatre*); *Deburau*, pr. 1920, pb. 1921 (adaptation of Sacha Guitry's play); *The Secret Life*, pb. 1923; *His Majesty*, pb. 1928; *The Collected Plays of Harley Granville-Barker*, pb. 1967; *Plays*, pb. 1987 (edited by Dennis Kennedy).

Other literary forms

Harley Granville-Barker's concern for a serious drama, and for a serious theater to interpret that drama, informs much, if not all, of his prose writings. With William Archer, Granville-Barker compiled *A National Theatre: Scheme and Estimates* (1907, revised by Granville-Barker in 1930), a working blueprint for a national repertory theater. *The Exemplary Theatre* (1922) presents Granville-Barker's conception of the theater from the perspective of a director-actor-playwright. His other writings on the theater, *On Dramatic Method* (1931), *The Study of Drama* (1934), *On Poetry in Drama* (1937), and *The Use of Drama* (1945), focus primarily upon his conception of a theatrically viable drama. This particular concern is evident as well in his famous series *Prefaces to Shakespeare* (1927-1947) and in its predecessor, the various prefaces and introductions Granville-Barker wrote for the volumes of *The Player's Shakespeare* (1923-1927). The remainder of Granville-Barker's literary works comprises a handful of articles on drama and on the theater; six short stories, of which only three have been published; and numerous translations.

Achievements

In addition to his full-length plays, Granville-Barker wrote three one-act plays, *Rococo, Vote by Ballot*, and *Farewell to the Theatre*. "Agnes Colander" (wr. 1901) and the unfinished "The Wicked Man" (wr. 1910-1914) were never published or produced. Also never published were the four plays Granville-Barker wrote in collaboration with Berte Thomas between 1895 and 1899. Two of his other collaborations, however, *Prunella: Or, Love in a Dutch Garden*, with Laurence Housman, and *The Harlequinade*, with Dion Calthrop, were published. The remainder of Granville-Barker's dramatic writing consists of translations or adaptations, most notably a translation of Arthur Schnitzler's *Anatol* (pr. 1911) and an adaptation of Sacha Guitry's *Deburau*. He also translated plays by Jules Romains and, with his wife, Helen Huntington Barker-Granville, by Gregorio Martínez Sierra, and by Serafín and Joaquín Álvarez Quintero.

Granville-Barker's reputation as an *homme de théâtre* began to suffer a decline after he left active theater work and became a "mere professor." His plays, already looked upon with suspicion by his contemporaries, suffered an even greater decline. Although Granville-Barker's plays were lauded by such fellow dramatists as George Bernard Shaw, John Masefield, and Gilbert Murray, external factors, such as the growing dominance of Shaw and changes in dramatic and theatrical styles, hastened the decline of his plays into obscurity. Recent years, however, have seen a revival of interest in the plays of Granville-Barker (*The Madras House*, for example, was produced for television by the British Broadcasting Corporation). This revival of interest betokens Granville-Barker's significance as a dramatist.

The Granville-Barker play is singular among plays of the Edwardian period in its use of heterosexual relationships to define the worth of human actions and to signify the larger moral concerns that are the prime concern of his plays: the necessity of what he termed "the secret life," the inner reality that puts into perspective the trivialities of everyday life. Granville-Barker was lauded by his fellow dramatists not only for the superb "actability" and polish of his plays but also for his dramatic portrayal of the real, vital dilemmas of human sensibility and of absolute morality beneath the superficialities of daily existence. Granville-Barker's greatest achievement as a dramatist, and his significance as a dramatist to our age, lies in his successful deployment of heterosexual relationships as signs of our fragile hold on our essential selves and our humanity.

Biography

Harley Granville-Barker was, in a manner of speaking, born into the theater in 1877. Granville-Barker's mother, Mary Elizabeth Barker, formerly Bozzi-Granville, was a professional entertainer. The family traveled around together to her engagements, and young Harley was brought up to appear and to recite poetry with her professionally. Little is known of the extent and the nature of his formal education, but, at the age of fourteen, he was enrolled in Sarah Thorne's theatrical school at the Margate Theatre. During his six-month sojourn at the school, Granville-Barker met Berte Thomas, with whom he collaborated in the writing of his first four plays.

Granville-Barker's first major acting job was touring with Ben Greet's Shakespeare Company, which included Lillah McCarthy, whom he was later to marry. In 1899, at the age of twenty-two, Granville-Barker took the main role in William Poel's Elizabethan Stage Society production of William Shakespeare's *Richard II.* Poel's production led Granville-Barker to become involved in the newly founded Stage Society, for which he functioned as both an actor and a director. One of the results of his involvement with the Stage Society was his long and close friendship with George Bernard Shaw and, through his involvement with Shaw, his membership in the Fabian Society.

Another, more significant result of Granville-Barker's work with the Stage Society was the revolutionary Vedrenne-Barker management at the Court Theatre from 1904 to 1907; J. E. Vedrenne acted as business manager, and Granville-Barker directed all the plays and acted in many. The Vedrenne-Barker seasons at the Court Theatre were revolutionary not only in the plays they presented (by John Galsworthy, Henrik Ibsen, Maurice Maeterlinck, Gerhart Hauptmann, and Shaw, to name a few) but also in their format of repertory. In 1906, Granville-Barker married Lillah McCarthy, who also had been involved in the Vedrenne-Barker productions. Following the Vedrenne-Barker management, Granville-Barker's involvement with the theater took the form of efforts to establish a repertory theater in London. Such efforts defined the nature of his management of the Duke of York Theatre in 1910 (a venture backed by the American impresario Charles Frohman), the McCarthy-Granville-Barker management of the Little Theatre in 1911, and the Granville-Barker management of the St. James Theatre in 1913. In 1912, Granville-Barker gave his last performance as an actor, preferring to devote his time and his energy to directing, to the establishment of a repertory theater, and to the writing of plays.

On a trip to America in 1914, Granville-Barker met Helen Huntington, his future second wife. Upon his return to England, Granville-Barker became involved in World War I, serving with the Red Cross. He later enlisted in the Royal Horse Artillery and was soon transferred to Army Intelligence. Lillah McCarthy and Harley Granville-Barker were divorced in 1917, and the following year he married Helen Huntington; it was also at this time that he hyphenated his name. Granville-Barker's second marriage marked the beginning of the end of his friendship with George Bernard Shaw. Moreover, the new Mrs. Granville-Barker's dislike of Shaw in particular and theater people in general, coupled with Granville-Barker's own disillusionment with the theater, led to his retirement from active theater work in 1921.

Beginning in 1922, Granville-Barker devoted himself entirely to the program of writing that he began with his first attempts at playwriting. In 1930, the Granville-Barkers moved to Paris, where they lived until the German invasion of France. They spent the remainder of the war years in New York, where Granville-Barker worked for the British Information Services until 1942. After the war, the Granville-Barkers returned to England and then to Paris, where Granville-Barker died in 1946, a few months before his sixty-ninth birthday, of arteriosclerosis.

Analysis

Harley Granville-Barker's early dramatic efforts—his apprentice plays—reveal that from the beginning, his plays were preoccupied with, if not generated by, the question of how a heterosexual relationship delineates and nurtures that moral strength or secret life essential to confront absolute moral dilemmas. The protagonist of a Granville-Barker play (Shaw preferred "worm" to "protagonist" in his letters to Barker) is thrust into a moral dilemma through a conflict between his outer, public life and his inner, secret life. The dramatic action of the play, then, is ordered by this conflict between the inner and the outer life of the protagonist. Granville-Barker heightens this basic conflict by means of his deft interweaving of theatrical symbol, dialogue, and theme. The dialogue itself, condensed, close-textured, and elliptical to the point of appearing disjointed, further underscores the central conflict of the play. In addition, much of the power of a Granville-Barker play is generated by what is implied through theatrical symbol rather than what is verbally stated. Granville-Barker's stage directions are decidedly Shavian in their wealth, precision, and breadth of detail and description. In *The Madras House*, for example, much of Jessica Madras is revealed through the description of her as "the result—not of thirty-three years—but of three or four generations of cumulative refinement. She might be a race horse!"

The basic conflict inherent in all the plays naturally imposes a similar structural pattern upon them. The protagonist is faced with a moral dilemma in which he is opposed by a figure of authority, refuses the negative examples of his close associates, and ends by accepting a mate under his own difficult conditions. The crucial point in this pattern is the protagonist's great refusal to accept the prevailing conditions and the prevailing wisdom in favor of his own conditions and his own wisdom. This great refusal invariably involves a sexual conclusion—that is, a consideration by the protagonist and his mate of how to continue in a world made difficult by the action of the inner life upon the outer. The element of sex in Granville-Barker's plays is not the "farmyard world of sex" denounced by Philip Madras but the relationship that prevails between the sexes, as in the case of Ann Leete and Abud, in the new world that the protagonist strives to create.

In *The Marrying of Ann Leete*, the conflict of the inner and the outer life takes the form of marriage. Carnaby Leete, a parliamentarian out of favor with his party, attempts to revive his career through the marriage of his daughter Ann to Lord John Carp, as he had once before salvaged his career by marrying his daughter Sarah to a member of the opposite party. Sarah's marriage, now falling apart in acrimonious mutual contempt, is a negative example for Ann. Her brother George provides another negative example of marriage; in defiance of his father, he has married a woman beneath his station who reveals herself to be little more than a vulgar social climber. Although Ann presumes that she will be married, she refuses to permit her father to sell her into marriage.

When Carp tells Ann he loves her, she responds: "It suddenly occurs to me that sounds unpleasant." For Ann, marriage is the union of male and female in the service of life; it requires no metaphysical justification. Her decision to marry John Abud, the gardener, is a manifestation of her inner life, of her need to forge a sexual relationship that is true to the fundamental moral purpose of men and women. The reference to Ann as a "new woman" and as the "new generation" underscores not only her determination not to repeat the marital mistakes of her brother and sister but also the role she forges for herself: the new Eve who will bring the future into the world. Ann's marrying, however, is left at the play's close as a frail gesture against the unlivable present. The class suspicions that emerge in the wedding scene, along with Ann's recognition of the experimental nature of her marriage, suggest that whatever the private significance of Ann's marrying, its public significance is minimal. Ann's marital experiment must bear fruit in the private life before it can be recognized by the public life.

Although *The Voysey Inheritance* also ends with a marriage, the focus of the play is not upon marriage per se. The central conflict of the play is structured in terms of capitalism and creativity. The elder Voysey, like his father before him, has placed the family's small solicitor's firm on the brink of ruin by systematically defrauding clients' accounts for personal profit through financial speculation. Moreover, the elder Voysey has managed this fraud with an artistic flair and a brilliance that ensures not only the prolongation of the game but also the temporary well-being of his clients. The elder Voysey's death pitches his son and heir, Edward Voysey, into the moral dilemma of continuing the family "practice" or turning himself in to the authorities, thereby atoning for the family's financial sins.

Edward is persuaded into accepting his inheritance by his potential wife, Alice Maitland. She encourages Edward to persist in his father's game of fraud to rectify the past and to ensure the economic future of his clients and of his firm. Although he never approaches the elder Voysey's talent for creative fiscal management, Edward's inheritance does save him from the morally flaccid existence of the "well-principled prig" and from the morally compromising positions of his brothers: the cold legality of Trenchard, the moral conventionality of Booth, and the uncontrolled creativity of Hugh.

In the final scene, a new Edward, with his new fiancée, Alice, charts the implications of their new life of benevolent fraud and of mutual help. Moreover, the final scene strongly suggests that Edward Voysey's inheritance is not the moral dilemma of financial corruption but the moral resolution of an admixed creativity and capitalism, the merging of the inner life with the outer.

Of all Granville-Barker's dramas, *Waste* is the most concerned, outwardly, with politics; its inner subject, however, is again the sexual relationship that unlocks the secret life. In fact, *Waste*'s open reference to sex—an abortion—prompted its censorship until 1936. Henry Trebell's suicide superficially results from his disappointment in the loss of a cabinet seat and in the rejection of his life's work by his party. In reality, his suicide is the direct result of his lack of a secret life. A meaningless sexual encounter with a married woman that culminates in her death in a back-alley abortion forces Trebell to a recognition of his own back-alley act of spiritual abortion: His angry hatred of women and his powerful reason (he is described at various times as a machine) have killed his human sensibility, his secret life, before it was born.

Trebell's lack of a secret life, his incapability of loving another human being, is matched by that of his mate of the moment, Amy O'Connell, who is incapable of accepting the fact of life and of her womanhood without the placebo of love. Without a secret life and without a sexual means of engendering a secret life, Trebell is destroyed by the assumption of the void within him by his outer, political life. The motif of waste in the play achieves its final, most powerful resonance in the waste of Trebell. Without the supportive strength of the secret life, Trebell becomes the plaything of the Edwardian political oligarchy that controls government policy by Machiavellian infighting and that deliberately uses the bogey of public morality to destroy the threat posed to it by the able man with the good cause.

Implicit in all of Granville-Barker's plays is the question of the social and moral position of women. This question is made explicit in *The Madras House*, becoming, in fact, the dominant theme of the play. The play's action proceeds in a documentary fashion that suggests the simultaneous existence of contrasting groups of women within the great Edwardian middle class. Each act shows a different kind of woman and a different perspective—familial, marital, and professional—upon women's economic dependence upon men. Act 1 counterpoints Mrs. Huxtable, the paragon of that respectability that inhibits all spontaneous impulses and reduces life to domestic conventions, to her six, no longer young, daughters. This particular gaggle of spinsters is indistinguishable. The Huxtable daughters have no expressive language of their own, only a code of verbal behavior imposed upon them that governs them and threatens all who approach them. Act 2 presents the economic slavery of the independent woman. Most of the employees of Huxtable and Roberts and of the Madras House live on the premises under the morally vigilant eye of Miss Chancellor. When it is discovered that Miss Yates, one of Miss Chancellor's charges, is pregnant, an inquisition into her morals is held. Miss Yates's secret life, which has its source in her pregnancy, permits her to scoff at the world's equation of virtue with gainful employment. Her ability to rise above her moral dilemma throws into relief the pathos of Miss Chancellor, whose life has been stunted by the conventional morality imposed upon her spirit by thirty years of economic slavery to the drapery firm of Huxtable and Roberts.

Act 3 is the antithesis of act 1, as it presents a male banquet of articulateness in a fantastic seraglio setting. The masters of the drapery trade, enthroned in the "Moorish" rotunda of the Madras House, are shown engaged in the business of reducing women to sexual automata for economic exploitation in haute couture. Mr. State, an American millinery magnate, idolator of the "woman-spirit" and admirer of the women's movement as womanly sartorial self-expression, defines the middle-class woman as "one of the greatest Money Spending Machines the world has ever seen." The only women to appear in the act are barely women at all. The grotesquely dehumanized fashion mannequins, members of the industrial seraglio, are present only because actual automata are inefficient and uneconomical in comparison to flesh-and-blood automata.

The fourth and final act of the play attempts to bring to a resolution the question of womanhood delineated in the preceding acts. Philip Madras, the play's connecting character, by rejecting a position in the Madras House, rejects the prevailing conceptions of womanhood. Rather than exploit women, and through them, men, Philip chooses to change prevailing conditions by joining the County Council. Jessica Madras, the epitome of the Edwardian middle-class lady, supports her husband provided that he, in his new world, creates a meaningful place for her by his side. More disgusted than her husband by the farmyard world of sexual games symbolized by the Madras House, Jessica yearns for a world in which men and women can be friends. The play closes with the unresolved, because it is unresolvable, discussion between Philip and Jessica as to the place of woman in this new life. Like Ann Leete and John Abud, Philip and Jessica Madras must make their marriage the testing ground for the moral dilemma represented by their redefinition of the sexual relationship and their need to realize the secret life of both man and woman.

The Secret Life, written after Granville-Barker left the theater, is his finest, fullest dramatic exploration of sexual relationships and the secret life. *The Secret Life* is an exploration of the potential hazards of middle age, with its loss of purpose and of conviction, its desires that fail to come to fruition, and the extreme difficulty of bringing the inner life to bear upon the outer. As in *Waste*, to which it is the natural pendant, the outer life of the play unfolds in the political arena. Evan Strowde, who left politics years ago to write a multivolume industrial history, is being wooed back into politics at the start of the play by his parliamentarian friends. Strowde himself is attempting to renew his courtship of his old love, Joan Westbury. Evan and Joan are presented throughout the play as antithetical yet complementary. Strowde, like Trebell, has a full outer life but no inner life, whereas Joan, stripped of her outer life by the deaths of her husband and her sons and by the destruction of her home, has a rich inner life. Although Strowde needs Joan to kindle his inner life and she needs him to structure her outer life, Joan refuses to commit herself to him. Such a commitment would destroy her inner life and, by extension, herself: "I couldn't have lived my love for you, Evan . . . it would have killed me." Joan's secret life is based upon her love for the unattainable in Evan, and its existence depends upon the sanctity of that unattainability. Union with Strowde would make external her secret life, would reduce her secret life to an everyday triviality, and would leave her an empty shell.

Because Joan, like Amy O'Connell and Trebell, refuses to risk her happiness in what is, essentially, a commitment to the absolute morality of life, she condemns herself and Strowde to death. Strowde loses himself in his renewed political career, and Joan loses herself in death. Although Joan's great refusal of life destroys both herself and Strowde, it does provide the play's youth, Oliver and Susan, with a negative example of the power of the secret life. In the play's final scene, Oliver, Strowde's illegitimate son, and Susan, Joan's alter ego, reveal the potential to make the great commitment demanded by the conflict of the inner life with the outer life.

Other major works

NONFICTION: *A National Theatre: Scheme and Estimates*, 1907 (with William Archer), 1930 (revised by Granville-Barker); *The Exemplary Theatre*, 1922; *The Player's Shakespeare*, 1923-1927 (prefaces and introductions); *Prefaces to Shakespeare*, 1927-1947; *On Dramatic Method*, 1931; *The Study of Drama*, 1934; *On Poetry in Drama*, 1937; *The Use of Drama*, 1945; *Granville-Barker and His Correspondents*, 1986 (edited by Eric Salmon).

TRANSLATIONS: *Anatol*, pr., pb. 1911 (of Arthur Schnitzler's six playlets); *The Romantic Young Lady*, pr. 1920, pb. 1923 (with Helen Granville-Barker, of Gregorio Martínez Sierra's *Sueño de una noche de agosto*); *The Two Shepherds*, pr. 1921, pb. 1923 (with Helen Granville-Barker, of Martínez Sierra's *Los pastores*); *The Kingdom of God*, pr., pb. 1923 (with Helen Granville-Barker, of Martínez Sierra's *El reino de Dios*); *Wife to a Famous Man*, pb. 1923, pr. 1924 (with Helen Granville-Barker, of Martínez Sierra's *La mujer del héroe*); *Six Gentlemen in a Row*, pr., pb. 1927 (one act, of Jules Romains' *Amédée et les messieurs en rang*); *The Women Have Their Way*, pb. 1927, pr. 1928 (with Helen Granville-Barker, of Serafín and Joaquín Álvarez Quintero's *Pueblo de las mujeres*); *A Hundred Years Old*, pb. 1927, pr. 1928 (with Helen Granville-Barker, of the Álvarez Quintero Brothers' *Papa Juan: Centenario*); *Fortunato*, pb. 1927, pr. 1928 (with Helen Granville-Barker, of the Álvarez Quintero Brothers' play); *The Lady from Alfaqueque*, pb. 1927, pr. 1928 (with Helen Granville-Barker, of the Álvarez Quintero Brothers' *La consulesa*); *Take Two from One*, pb. 1931 (with Helen Granville-Barker, of Martínez Sierra's play); *Love Passes By*, pb. 1932 (with Helen Granville-Barker, of the Álvarez Quintero Brothers' *El amor que pasa*); *Peace and Quiet*, pb. 1932 (with Helen Granville-Barker, of the Álvarez Quintero Brothers' *La escondida senda*); *Doña Clariñes*, pb. 1932, pr. 1934 (with Helen Granville-Barker, of the Álvarez Quintero Brothers' play).

Bibliography
Henderson, Archibald. *European Dramatists.* Cincinnati, Ohio: Stewart & Kidd, 1913. Henderson wrote six essays, considering Granville-Barker along with August Strindberg, Henrik Ibsen, Maurice Maeterlinck, Oscar Wilde, and George Bernard Shaw. He describes Granville-Barker's prominence with theatrical production and then praises his plays for their originality and for enlarging the boundaries of drama by breaking new ground, thereby creating new laws of drama.
Kennedy, Dennis. *Granville Barker and the Dream of Theatre.* Cambridge, England: Cambridge University Press, 1985. A detailed examination of Granville-Barker's work as a producer and director of theater. If focuses on how he influenced drama, for example, through his introductions to William Shakespeare and in the legitimization of George Bernard Shaw. It concludes that his dream was realized by the establishment of a national British theater, which he championed during his life. The volume is richly illustrated and contains a comprehensive listing of his productions and an index.
McDonald, Jan. *The New Drama, 1900-1914.* Basingstoke, England: Macmillan, 1986. Examines the "new drama" movement in the British theater, its theaters and major playwrights, Granville-Barker, John Galsworthy, and John Masefield. Provides a brief biography and extensive discussion of each of Granville-Barker's major plays. Bibliography and index.
Mehra, Monmohan. *Harley Granville-Barker: A Critical Study of the Major Plays.* Calcutta: Naya Prokash, 1981. Considers Granville-Barker's experience in theatrical production as the background to his work as a playwright. His merit lies in his ability to create vividly drawn characters while subordinating plot to political and social themes, but without

preaching. Emphasizes Granville-Barker's characters who revolt against the social conventions of sex and politics. Index.

Morgan, Margery M. *A Drama of Political Man: A Study in the Plays of Harley Granville Barker.* London: Sidgwick & Jackson, 1961. A dramaturgical examination of the plays, referring to theoretical essays, other writings, and biographical and performance information only as they shed light on the scripts. By examining the plays in terms of performance, Morgan concludes that Granville-Barker's works are enriched by his sensitivity to the feelings and political philosophy of his age. Index.

Purdom, C. B. *Harley Granville Barker: Man of the Theatre, Dramatist, and Scholar.* London: Rockliff, 1955. The standard chronological biography of Granville-Barker. It was written with the cooperation of his first wife, Lillah McCarthy, and reflects a bias toward her point of view. Purdom discusses the scripts, but more as artifacts along the path of the playwright's life, rather than as viable stage plays. Includes complete listings of characters he portrayed, plays he produced and directed, and his extensive writings. Index.

Salmon, Eric. *Granville Barker: A Secret Life.* London: Heinemann Educational Books, 1983. Salmon examines the various aspects of Granville-Barker's life as independent entities. He attempts to find the proper balance between these various aspects. Salmon freely points out what he perceives as flaws in the writings of C. B. Purdom and Margery M. Morgan (above) and concludes that Granville-Barker's greatness was in his imaginative perception. Illustrations, chronology, bibliography of works by Granville-Barker, and index.

Stella Maloney
(Updated by *Gerald S. Argetsinger*)

SIMON GRAY

Born: Hayling Island, England; October 21, 1936

Principal drama

Wise Child, pr. 1967, pb. 1968; *Dutch Uncle*, pr., pb. 1969; *Spoiled*, pr. 1970 (staged), pb. 1971 (televised 1968); *The Idiot*, pr. 1970, pb. 1971 (adaptation of Fyodor Dostoevski's novel); *Butley*, pr., pb. 1971; *Dog Days*, pr. 1975, pb. 1976; *Otherwise Engaged*, pr., pb. 1975; *Molly*, pr. 1977, pb. 1978 (revision of Gray's television play *Death of a Teddy Bear*); *The Rear Column*, pr., pb. 1978; *Close of Play*, pr., pb. 1979; *Stage Struck*, pr., pb. 1979; *Quartermaine's Terms*, pr., pb. 1981; *Tartuffe*, pr. 1982 (adaptation of Molière's play); *The Common Pursuit*, pr., pb. 1984; *Otherwise Engaged and Other Plays*, pb. 1984; *The Rear Column and Other Plays*, pb. 1985; *Plays: One*, pb. 1986; *Melon*, pr., pb. 1987 (revised as *The Holy Terror*, pr. 1989 as radio play, pb. 1990, pr. 1991 as stage play); *Hidden Laughter*, pr. 1989, pb. 1990.

Other literary forms

Simon Gray is primarily known as a stage dramatist, but he began his playwriting career as an author of television scripts: *The Caramel Crisis* (1966), *Death of a Teddy Bear* (1967), *A Way with the Ladies* (1967), *Sleeping Dog* (1967), *Pig in a Poke* (1969), *The Dirt on Lucy Lane* (1969), *Style of the Countess* (1970), *The Princess* (1970), *The Man in the Sidecar* (1971), *Plaintiffs and Defendants* (1975), and *Two Sundays* (1975).

Besides being a successful dramatist, Gray has also published novels: *Colmain* (1963), *Simple People* (1965), *Little Portia* (1967), and *A Comeback for Stark* (1968). This last novel was published under the pseudonym Hamish Reade; Gray has also used the pen name James Holliday.

In 1975, the playwright wrote the screenplay version of his play for the film *Butley*, directed by Harold Pinter and starring Alan Bates, re-creating his stage role as the title character. The movie was made as part of the American Film Theatre series.

Finally, Gray became editor of *Delta* magazine in 1964, and he coedited with Keith Walker an anthology entitled *Selected English Prose* that was published by Faber in 1967.

Achievements

Gray has received many of the highest awards for dramatists. *Death of a Teddy Bear* won a Writers Guild Award, *Butley* received the *Evening Standard* (London) Award for Best Play of the Year in 1972, and *Otherwise Engaged* was voted Best Play by the New York Drama Critics Circle. Moreover, the filming of *Butley* and the option taken to film *Death of a Teddy Bear* are indicators of the dramatist's popularity.

Biography

Simon Gray was born on Hayling Island, Hampshire, England, on October 21, 1936, the son of James Davidson and Barbara Celia Mary (née Holliday) Gray. The elder Gray was a pathologist and first-generation Canadian of Scottish ancestry, and when World War II began, Simon Gray was sent from Great Britain to his grandparents' home in Montreal. He returned to the United Kingdom for a while after the war and then moved back and forth between England, Canada, France, and Spain. He married Beryl Mary Kevern, a picture researcher, on August 20, 1964, and they have one son, Benjamin.

Gray, a lecturer in English, taught at Trinity College, Cambridge, from 1965 through 1966 and was on the faculty at Queen Mary College of the University of London from 1965 to 1984. This experience, together with his educational background, serves as the source of many of the dramatist's subjects (and characters) and his literate style alike. He attended the Westminster School in London, and he received a B.A. (honors in English) from Dalhousie University in Canada in 1958, and another B.A. (again with honors in English) from Cambridge University in England in 1962. Between the awarding of his two bachelor's degrees, Gray served as a lecturer at the University in Clermont-Ferrand, France. He resided in France from 1960 to 1961 and in Spain from 1962 to 1963.

In 1987, Gray's play *Melon* was produced in London, and that same year saw the production of his screenplay *A Month in the Country. Hidden Laughter* was produced in Brighton in 1989, and in London a year later. *The Holy Terror*, a revision of *Melon*, was broadcast in 1989 on the British Broadcasting Corporation's radio and was published in 1990. The 1991 Arizona production was its premiere as a stage piece.

Analysis

Two important elements in Simon Gray's playwriting career evolved directly from his educational background. The Cambridge experience was clearly an important one. In a sense, when Gray reports, "I went to university when I was seventeen and I never left," he is speaking metaphorically as well as literally. His postgraduate life has been spent in academia, but it is obvious that there are symbolic connections with his everyday life that reappear in his plays. During Gray's tenure at Cambridge, there was an extraordinarily gifted group of other students also in attendance. The intellectual atmosphere was stimulating; a number of undergraduates wrote and acted in satiric revues on campus and then moved on to the London stage immediately afterward (and sometimes even while still pursuing their studies). Peter Cook, a contributor to the immensely successful *Beyond the Fringe* (1959), was one such. Novelist Margaret Drabble, television personality David Frost, actor Derek Jacobi, and Christopher Booker, a cofounder of *Private Eye* magazine, were among Gray's contemporaries. Furthermore, director John Barton was a don at King's College and poet Sylvia Plath lived in the town of Cambridge.

Besides the literary climate of the present and the long line of literati connected with the university in the past, Gray was also exposed to literary and dramatic traditions in his course work. Many of his characters, settings, and plot situations derive from this aspect of his life. The numerous literary allusions that are characteristic of his style are direct outgrowths of Gray's Cambridge experience. Finally, the many references to Cambridge, typically related to the concept of class distinctions, are similarly attributable to this period in his life.

The second element is Gray's experience as a teacher. A number of the aspects of his writing that can be traced to his university days extend to his professional career as well; the origins of several of Gray's dramatic works reflect the attitude of an academic mind.

Unlike many contemporary playwrights who began writing dramas while in college, Gray actually became a dramatist as a young man after he was graduated and while he was trying to write short stories and novels. He had already published two prose volumes, *Colmain* in 1963 and *Simple People* in 1965, when he adapted a short story that was primarily dialogue and sold it as a television script. The piece, entitled *The Caramel Crisis*, was televised in 1966, and within a year *Death of a Teddy Bear*, *A Way with the Ladies*, and *Sleeping Dog* were also televised. *Death of a Teddy Bear* was an award-winning script, and *Sleeping Dog* was well received for its examination of the elements of domination and submission in the British national character (represented by Sir Herbert, a retired colonial administrator, who imprisons Claud, a black homosexual, in the basement of his manor house—the theme of ambiguous sexuality is also introduced).

Wise Child was written for television, too, but it was reportedly considered "too bizarre for home viewing," and it became Gray's first play to be staged in the theater (at the Wyndham on October 10, 1967). The play is usually considered Gray's best early effort, and it has been favorably compared with the work of Joe Orton. The plot revolves around a criminal who is wanted for a brutal mail robbery and is hiding from the police by disguising himself as a woman (creating a sort of black comedy version of Brandon Thomas' 1896 farce *Charley's Aunt*) while his accomplice poses as his son. After the pair murder their homosexual landlord, the older man reverts to wearing men's clothing, and the younger man dons the maid's clothes. Gray was fortunate that one of the finest actors of all time, Sir Alec Guinness, took the lead role. The "son's" part was played by Simon

Ward, who would appear in later plays by Gray. Harold Hobson, drama critic for the London *Sunday Times*, was impressed by the piece.

Dutch Uncle followed *Wise Child* and was considerably less successful. Mounted by the Royal Shakespeare Company at the Old Vic in London, the drama shows the academic turn of mind characteristic of Gray's later works. The play was inspired by the case of police constable Reginald Christie, a mass murderer who did away with his wife, the wife of his upstairs lodger, and several other women. (Christie walled up the corpses in his kitchen. Gray's play *Death of a Teddy Bear*, written a few years earlier, was similarly based on an actual murder case.) In *Dutch Uncle*, the main character, Mr. Godboy, tries to murder his wife to attract the attention of Inspector "Manly" Hawkins. His motivation is a homosexual obsession for the policeman. Unfortunately for Godboy, he proves ineffectual as a murderer—his wife blissfully and unknowingly avoids his trap—and when the inspector finally becomes interested in the household, it is because the upstairs tenant is the Merritt Street rapist. The play was not well received, and Gray himself described it as a failure "as witless as it was macabre. . . . [It] would goad an audience into an irritated restlessness." He goes on to claim that the London opening was "the worst night in the British theatre." Nevertheless, the husband's distaste for his role as a husband and the dramatist's exploration of the themes of domination and submission (also dealt with in *Wise Child*) mark the play as a contemporary work. It was probably these elements that attracted Harold Pinter to Gray's work.

Next came *Spoiled*, a realistic domestic drama that was televised in 1968 and then adapted for the stage in 1970. The play, which premiered at the Close Theatre Club in Glasgow, Scotland, on February 4, moved to London's Haymarket Theatre on October 31 of the following year. It is about the relationships among a high school French instructor, his pregnant wife, and a young male student. During the course of tutoring the teenager, the teacher seduces him, and the play evolves into a straightforward study of the "unthinking abuse of trust and power." *Spoiled* also serves as a companion piece to *Butley*; both plays involve student-teacher relationships in an academic setting, as well as failed marriages and homosexual activities. There are also some parallels with *Otherwise Engaged*. In contrast with the latter play, however, in which Simon Hench is too detached to be able to maintain a human relationship, Howarth, the teacher in *Spoiled*, falls tragically because he is too emotionally involved.

Butley, one of Gray's most successful dramas, premiered at the Oxford Playhouse on July 7, 1971, and then moved to the Criterion Theatre in London exactly one week later. The first of Gray's works to be directed by Pinter, it starred Alan Bates in the title role. Subsequently the play moved to the Morosco Theatre in New York City, on October 31, 1972.

All the action in the two-act play takes place in Ben Butley's office in a college of London University. Act 1 opens at ten o'clock in the morning on the first day after the midterm break, and the second act begins about two hours later, "shortly after lunch."

Butley is an English teacher at the University. He shares an office with Joseph Keyston, whom he calls Joey. Joey is also an English instructor, a former student of Butley and his current lover.

From the play's beginning, it is clear what kind of person Butley is— even the office set reflects the nature of his mind. His desk, for example, "is a chaos of papers, books, detritus" in contrast to Joey's neat, almost bare desk. Similarly, Butley's bookcase is "chaotic with old essays and mimeographed sheets scattered among the books." Butley's attitude toward his profession is certainly evident, as is the unsettled state of his mind. The photograph of T. S. Eliot indicates the kind of literature that interests Butley and is a visual reference to the source of some of the literary allusions that embellish Butley's conversations. The smeared and curled corner shows that what was once important enough to Butley that he put it on his wall no longer has his attention and has become damaged (and not repaired) as a result. The lamp that will not work for Butley is further evidence of the lack of connections in his life, the way that things no longer work for him.

Butley's egocentrism and the tactics that he uses to isolate himself from others and from his responsibilities are evident in his very first speech. He tells the head of his department, who has called him on the telephone, that he cannot talk at the moment because he is "right in the middle of a tutorial"—and all the while the audience can plainly see that Butley is sitting alone in his office. In a sense, there is dramatic irony involved here, too, and not only because the audience is aware of something that one of the characters (the caller, in this case) is not. Throughout the play people try to get in touch with Butley, and he rejects their attempts; he constantly uses the false tutorial excuse to avoid contact. The comic touch of Butley taking a squashed banana from his pocket and throwing the peel on Joey's desk seems to lighten the effect of Butley's lie, but it soon becomes evident that this is merely another indication of Butley's sloppy habits, his lack of consideration for others, and his conscious attempts to belittle everyone. The piece of toilet paper stuck to his chin to stop the blood from a cut sustained while he was shaving is a parallel to the banana. Obviously Butley does not demonstrate much respect for himself, and he shows even less for those with whom he comes in contact.

In the first act, Gray introduces most of the rest of the characters who play major parts in the protagonist's life. In essence, there is no action and no traditional plot. Joey appears first, and through his conversation with Butley, the various levels of their relationship are exposed, as is Butley's estrangement from his wife and the possibility that Butley is about to be replaced in Joey's life by Reg Nuttall.

The word games, wit, literary allusions (often in the form of direct quotations), and cruelty that characterize Butley are also revealed. Butley emerges as a sad, lonely man who wants some sort of relationship with someone, preferably Joey, but who is unable to give enough of himself or accept enough from anyone else to allow them to penetrate his sarcasm to create a truly emotional relationship. Instead, Butley retreats behind a wall of sterile intellectualism.

Miss Heasman, a minor character, makes an appearance, serving as a bit of comic relief (and creating dramatic irony) when Butley purposely misunderstands her request and then lies about her duties (the audience already knows about his treatment of a student with a similar request previously). There is also a confrontation between Butley and his wife, who informs him that she has decided to take up with an acquaintance of theirs.

In his dealings with all of these people, Butley is consistently sarcastic and offensive, he knows where his victims are most vulnerable, and he sticks the knife in with sadistic pleasure and precision. He jokes about homosexuality, frequently by using double entendres or literary allusions. Other literary allusions (to Eliot, William Blake, Gerard Manley Hopkins, and others) provide further insight into Butley's character (unwittingly on his part), as he uses them as weapons. Butley's use of literary allusions is effective because the other characters in the play recognize their sources; this is an essential part of his game-playing. Also indicated is the probability that patterns are being repeated, implying that they have all engaged in the activity before—and this is reinforced by Butley's expressed appreciation for good comebacks by his targets. One of the games that he plays revolves around Joey's constant use of the tag "in point of fact." When Joey says that Reg's family lives "in a place just outside Leeds, in point of fact," Butley pretends that he thinks that "point of fact" is the name of a suburb. This becomes a running joke in the play and serves a dual purpose by simultaneously drawing attention to Reg's lower-middle-class background. The situation concerning Gardner is prepared for, too.

In act 2, the only major character not met in act 1 appears when Reg comes to collect Joey (and, incidentally, to make sure that Butley does not adversely influence the younger man's decision to leave). Beyond this, about all that happens is a continuation of the lines self-destructively developed by Butley, leaving him as he was when he first came onstage—alone and ineffectually trying to turn on the lamp. Butley's nonstop allusions (to Eliot, nursery rhymes, John Donne, D. H. Lawrence, John Milton, Sir John Suckling, Richard Lovelace, and Beatrix Potter, among others), his use of a Northern dialect to denigrate Reg's social background—all of this epitomizes his hollowness.

In her essay entitled "Literary Allusion as Satire in Simon Gray's

Butley," Sophia B. Blaydes discusses this important aspect of the writer's technique and demonstrates how the allusions may provide insight into Butley's self-image as an individual "beset by betrayal and mediocrity," a tragic figure rather than the pitiable, "irresponsible, wasted man" that the characters in the play perceive him to be. The truth probably lies somewhere between: Butley is, indeed, surrounded by foolish people, but he cannot see beyond their flaws to their common humanity.

Otherwise Engaged, also directed by Pinter and featuring Bates in the part of Simon Hench, was first presented at London's Queen's Theatre on July 30, 1975. In February, 1977, the production was transferred to the Plymouth Theatre in New York City, with Tom Courtenay making his long-awaited Broadway debut in the lead role.

The setting for *Otherwise Engaged* is more elegant than that of *Butley.* As in the earlier play, the action is limited to the events that transpire in one room, in this instance over a period of time equivalent to the running time of the drama. That room is Hench's living room in London. The plot has been described as the depiction of a series of events that occur during an afternoon that Hench wishes to spend listening to a newly acquired phonograph recording of Richard Wagner's opera *Parsifal* and which prevent him from accomplishing his goal; that is a bit like saying that *Butley* is about a teacher who is not interested in teaching.

In act 1, Hench, a book publisher, is discovered preparing to listen to his new purchase. He is interrupted by Dave, a dull polytechnic student who is renting a flat from him. This is only the first of a series of interruptions. Hench no sooner gets rid of the young man, who is seeking advice on his love life and money, than Hench's brother, Stephen, enters to expose fears and self-doubts about his professional status. Hench is witty, sociable, and somewhat supportive, but his rather obvious wish is to return to his recording. This pattern is repeated throughout the play.

The next interruption comes in the form of Jeff Golding, a dilettantish literary critic who seems not to be particularly attractive either as a critic or as a person. He confesses, for example, that he does not like literature, and his own description of how he mistreats women is damning. Next, Jeff's current mistress, Davina, appears, searching for her lover, whom she immediately dismisses. After Jeff leaves, Davina tries to seduce Hench. She is unsuccessful, but he does agree to consider for publication a book that she has written.

Hench then records a message on his telephone answering machine to inform anyone who might call that he is "otherwise engaged" for the rest of the day. Bernard Wood enters. Hench and Wood attended Wundale School at the same time, a place where both men engaged in homosexual activities. Wood accuses Hench of seducing his fiancée, Joanna, and Hench admits to the transgression as the curtain falls.

Act 2 opens where act 1 left off; in the continuation it becomes clear that Hench does not consider the seduction as a serious transgression. Wood wants to know if Hench's wife is aware of his activities; the audience soon learns that Mrs. Hench is involved in an affair and that she is considering leaving her husband. Hench finds her choice of partners tasteless, but sees the affair, like his, as posing no threat to their marriage. Wood, on the other hand, has a history of being unstable, and he calls to leave a message on the telephone recorder: He is going to shoot himself in the head because he is despondent about the Hench-Joanna affair, and he wants the act recorded so that Hench can hear it. Hench switches the machine off the instant before Wood squeezes the trigger. The play ends with Jeff returning to sit with Hench, listening to *Parsifal*.

The theme of *Otherwise Engaged* is again that of a man incapable of sustaining human relationships. Unlike *Butley*, however, Hench does not even seem to desire a meaningful relationship. He is comfortable in his marriage—whether he or his wife, Beth, actually have engaged in affairs is less important to him than his desire that they remain together, mainly because breaking up is a tiresome process, and staying together makes life easier, especially since he does not wish to become emotionally involved with anyone, including his wife, anyway.

There are some contradictory pieces of information provided by the dramatist. In act 1, Hench refuses to be seduced by the attractive Davina, even though she is aggressively willing and he admits that "I fancy you because of your breasts" (which she has exposed by removing her shirt). This scene is in direct contrast with Wood's claim that Hench seduced his fiancée. Additionally, in spite of Stephen's protests to the contrary, Hench does seem to have an interest in his brother's well-being. Finally, there is the ironic counterpointing between Hench's apparent attempts to remain emotionally disengaged from those intruders who surround him and his pleasure (and possibly his retreat) into Wagner's *Parsifal.* Wagner's music is lush and romantic in nature, full-bodied and emotional. If Hench enjoys this kind of music, it would indicate that he, too, has a romantic, emotional nature. His seeming lack of concern for Wood or Beth may stem either from his sense of hurt and betrayal, or from his realization that there may be little that he can do to alter the circumstances, or both. On the other hand, it may well be that he has no feelings for people and that he seeks emotional release in the safety of music—which can make no demands upon him, and which does not interrupt his privacy. Somewhat like the characters in *Close of Play* four years later, those in *Otherwise Engaged* are so wrapped up in their own problems that they think that all action focuses on them, and they are insensitive to and inconsiderate of others.

Stylistically, the play is entertaining. Gray is at his witty, literate best, and he handles the language masterfully. There are some echoes from

Pinter's plays, particularly _The Caretaker_ (pr. 1960), _The Collection_ (pr. 1961), and _The Homecoming_ (pr. 1965), and there are some amusing plot twists. The repetition of certain tags ("Not as stupid as he seems," for example) and other stylistic devices used in _Butley_ reappear in _Otherwise Engaged_. Structurally, the interweaving of reappearing characters, motifs (egotism, fidelity, dominance, sexuality, and so forth), and images (drinks thrown in people's faces) all combine to give the play an operatic texture.

Gray's subsequent plays did not immediately develop his earlier themes and style. In _Close of Play_ (presented at the National Theatre's Lyttleton Theatre in London on May 24, 1979). Gray returned to an intellectual setting, of sorts. Jasper, a retired academic, sits silently while his wife, children, grandchildren, and assorted in-laws reveal the desperate nature of their lives. _Close of Play_ is a dark, mature drama, yet it breaks no new ground for the playwright. With _Stage Struck_ (Vaudeville Theatre, London, November 21, 1979), the dramatist tried his hand at a stage thriller in the vein of Ira Levin's _Deathtrap_ (pr. 1978) and Anthony Shaffer's _Sleuth_ (pr. 1970). In 1981, _Quartermaine's Terms_, his play about an ineffectual upper-class teacher who is fired by his school's new principal, opened at Queen's Theatre, London, on July 28. In New York, the Long Wharf Theatre presented the drama at Playhouse 91 in February, 1982. _Quartermaine's Terms_ earned wide praise; critic John Simon noted the play's powerful mixture of laughter and melancholy and raved over its "understatedly heartbreaking ending." _The Common Pursuit_ focuses on a reunion of 1960's campus rebels who have become 1980's sellouts. The play manipulates time in a fashion that reminded some critics of Pinter's _Betrayal_ (pr. 1978); Gray, though, explained that his source for the technique was an older television drama.

Gray has shown the potential to become a major playwright, but so far he has not achieved that status. His plays are interesting, witty, and well structured, and his characters are believably drawn. Furthermore, he uses language well, and it is clear that the use of language in his later works has been influenced by Pinter's dramaturgy, improving an already good product.

The major weakness in Gray's dramas is in their subject matter. While he deals with problems of interpersonal communication and the difficulties involved in establishing or maintaining meaningful relationships, his plays are primarily character sketches. They are superficial portrayals of self-destructive people, and they lack the depth of Pinter's plays or the dramas of other contemporary British dramatists.

If Gray's plays lack profound thematic significance, they nevertheless excel in stagecraft and technique, and his works have entertained audiences at home in England and abroad. He does not contend that his plays are meant to convey a message, but he does work at his writing rigorously; _Otherwise Engaged_, for example, required thirty-five drafts. Combining this attention to craftsmanship with a flair for witty dialogue, Gray has achieved both critical acclaim and popular acceptance.

Other major works
NOVELS: *Colmain*, 1963; *Simple People*, 1965; *Little Portia*, 1967; *A Comeback for Stark*, 1968 (as Hamish Reade).
NONFICTION: *An Unnatural Pursuit and Other Pieces*, 1985; *How's That for Telling 'Em, Fat Lady?*, 1988.
SCREENPLAYS: *Butley*, 1975; *A Month in the Country*, 1987.
TELEPLAYS: *The Caramel Crisis*, 1966; *Death of a Teddy Bear*, 1967; *Sleeping Dog*, 1967; *A Way with the Ladies*, 1967; *Pig in a Poke*, 1969; *The Dirt on Lucy Lane*, 1969; *The Princess*, 1970; *Style of the Countess*, 1970; *The Man in the Sidecar*, 1971; *Plaintiffs and Defendants*, 1975; *Two Sundays*, 1975; *After Pilkington*, 1987.
ANTHOLOGY: *Selected English Prose*, 1967 (editor with Keith Walker).

Bibliography
Blaydes, Sophia B. "Literary Allusion as Satire in Simon Gray's *Butley*." *Midwest Quarterly* 18 (Summer, 1977): 374-391. Discusses the academic setting of *Butley* and concentrates on explicating some of the more obscure literary allusions: "Butley's skill is verbal . . . yet he manages to create a distance so that ultimately he is isolated from us, too." Includes an end note on the making and distribution of the film version in 1975.
Burkman, Katherine H. "The Fool as Hero: Simon Gray's *Butley* and *Otherwise Engaged*." *Theatre Journal* 33 (May, 1981): 163-172. As a reflection of the malaise of the twentieth century, these two plays portray the characters of Ben Butley and Simon Hench, fools whose "wit becomes a weapon to be used in the world in which the fool is hero [but] without a Lear to admonish." Burkman states that these two characters deserve the sympathy of the audience not only because they are social critics but also because they are entertainers.
_____, ed. *Simon Gray: A Casebook.* New York: Garland, 1992. An introduction and a chronology are followed by fourteen essays, a bibliography, and an index. This volume is the first book-length exploration of Gray's work, from *Wise Child* to *Hidden Laughter*. Contains single-work essays, overviews, and articles on adaptations. *The Holy Terror*, a revision of *Melon*, which was produced in Arizona in 1991, is mentioned in the chronology but is not dealt with in the essays.
New, William H. "Household Locks: The Plays of Simon Gray." In *Dramatists in Canada: Selected Essays.* Vancouver: University of British Columbia Press, 1972. New discusses the novels and teleplays before examining *Sleeping Dog*, *Wise Child*, *Dutch Uncle*, and *Spoiled*. He provides

literary criticism and character study and sees a broadening of social views as the canon progresses.

Rich, Frank. "Stage: Simon Gray Play, *The Common Pursuit.*" *The New York Times*, October 20, 1986, p. C17. This first play since *Quartermaine's Terms* is about Cambridge "litterateurs from twenty years ago." Rich provides some history of the play's New Haven tryout and change of directors, one of whom is Gray himself. Includes a strong description of the play's staging.

Shafer, Yvonne. "Aristophanic and Chekhovian Structure in the Plays of Simon Gray." *Theater Studies* 31/32 (1984/1985): 32-40. Deals extensively with *Otherwise Engaged* (whose central character is "a solitary searcher for order and peace in a chaotic world") and *Quartermaine's Terms*, with a Chekhovian atmosphere and a "central character moving through a landscape of incipient disaster, unable to take any action to save himself." Comparisons are made with Anton Chekhov's *Vishnyovy sad* (pr., pb. 1904; *The Cherry Orchard*, 1908).

Steven H. Gale
(Updated by *Thomas J. Taylor*
and *Robert McClenaghan*)

PAUL GREEN

Born: Lillington, North Carolina; March 17, 1894
Died: Chapel Hill, North Carolina; May 4, 1981

Principal drama

Surrender to the Enemy, pr. 1917; *The Last of the Lowries*, pr. 1920, pb. 1922; *The Long Night*, pb. 1920; *Granny Boling*, pb. 1921 (revised as *The Prayer Meeting*, pb. 1924); *The Old Man of Edenton*, pr. 1921, pb. 1925; *Old Wash Lucas (The Miser)*, pr. 1921, pb. 1924; *The Lord's Will*, pr., pb. 1922; *Blackbeard*, pr. 1922, pb. 1925 (with Elizabeth Lay Green); *White Dresses*, pb. 1922, pr. 1923 (one act); *Sam Tucker*, pb. 1923 (revised as *Your Fiery Furnace*, pb. 1926); *Wrack P'int*, pr. 1923; *Fixin's*, pr. 1924, pb. 1934 (with Erma Green); *The Hot Iron*, pb. 1924 (revised as *Lay This Body Down*, pb. 1959, pr. 1972); *In Aunt Mahaly's Cabin: A Negro Melodrama*, pb. 1924, pr. 1925; *The No 'Count Boy*, pr., pb. 1924; *The Lord's Will and Other Carolina Plays*, pb. 1925; *The Man Who Died at Twelve O'Clock*, pr. 1925, pb. 1927; *Quare Medicine*, pr. 1925, pb. 1928; *The End of the Row*, pb. 1926; *In Abraham's Bosom*, pr., pb. 1926 (one-act version), pr. 1926, pb. 1927 (full-length version); *Lonesome Road: Six Plays for the Negro Theatre*, pb. 1926; *The Man on the House*, pb. 1926; *Supper for the Dead*, pb. 1926, pr. 1954; *The Field God*, pr., pb. 1927; *Unto Such Glory*, pb. 1927, pr. 1936; *Blue Thunder: Or, The Man Who Married a Snake*, pb. 1928; *Bread and Butter Come to Supper*, pb. 1928, pr. 1954 (as *Chair Endowed*); *The Goodbye*, pb. 1928; *In the Valley and Other Carolina Plays*, pb. 1928; *Old Christmas*, pb. 1928; *The Picnic*, pb. 1928; *Saturday Night*, pb. 1928; *Tread the Green Grass*, pb. 1929, pr. 1932 (music by Lamar Stringfield); *The House of Connelly*, pr., pb. 1931; *Potter's Field*, pb. 1931, pr. 1934 (revised as *Roll Sweet Chariot*, pr. 1934, pb. 1935; symphonic drama; music by Dolphe Martin); *Shroud My Body Down*, pr. 1934, pb. 1935 (revised as *The Honeycomb*, pb. 1972); *The Enchanted Maze*, pr. 1935, pb. 1939; *Hymn to the Rising Sun*, pr., pb. 1936 (one act); *Johnny Johnson: The Biography of a Common Man*, pr. 1936, pb. 1937 (music by Kurt Weill); *The Southern Cross*, pr. 1936, pb. 1938; *The Lost Colony*, pr., pb. 1937 (symphonic drama); *Alma Mater*, pb. 1938; *The Critical Year*, pb. 1939; *Franklin and the King*, pb. 1939; *The Highland Call*, pr. 1939, pb. 1941 (symphonic drama); *Out of the South: The Life of a People in Dramatic Form*, pb. 1939; *Native Son*, pr., pb. 1941 (with Richard Wright; adaptation of Wright's novel); *The Common Glory*, pr. 1947, pb. 1948 (symphonic drama); *Faith of Our Fathers*, pr. 1950; *Peer Gynt*, pr., pb. 1951 (adaptation of Henrik Ibsen's play); *Serenata*, pr. 1953 (with Josefina Niggli); *The Seventeenth Star*, pr. 1953 (symphonic drama); *Carmen*, pr. 1954 (adaptation of the libretto of Georges Bizet's opera); *Wilderness*

Road, pr. 1955, pb. 1956 (symphonic drama); *The Founders*, pr., pb. 1957 (symphonic drama); *The Confederacy*, pr., pb. 1958 (symphonic drama); *The Stephen Foster Story*, pr. 1959, pb. 1960 (symphonic drama); *The Thirsting Heart*, pb. 1959, pr. 1971; *Five Plays of the South*, pb. 1963; *Cross and Sword*, pr. 1965, pb. 1966 (symphonic drama); *The Sheltering Plaid*, pb. 1965; *Texas*, pr. 1966, pb. 1967; *Sing All a Green Willow*, pr. 1969; *Trumpet in the Land*, pr. 1970, pb. 1972; *Drumbeats in Georgia*, pr. 1973; *Louisiana Cavalier*, pr. 1976; *We the People*, pr. 1976; *The Lone Star*, pr. 1977.

Other literary forms

An extremely prolific writer, Paul Green produced work in all the main literary genres. Related to his numerous stage plays is his work in other dramatic forms. Some of the screenplays he wrote for Hollywood include *Cabin in the Cotton* (1932; adaptation of Harry Harrison Kroll's novel of the same title), *State Fair* (1933, with Sonya Levien; adaptation of Phil Stong's novel of the same title), *Dr. Bull* (1933; adaptation of James Gould Cozzens' novel *The Last Adam*), *David Harum* (1934; adaptation of Edward Noyes Westcott's novel of the same title), *Time Out of Mind* (1947; adaptation of Rachel Field's novel of the same title), and *Black Like Me* (1963; adaptation of John Howard Griffin's novel of the same title).

Green's fiction includes two novels, *The Laughing Pioneer* (1932) and *This Body the Earth* (1935), and several collections of short stories: *Wide Fields* (1928), *Salvation on a String and Other Tales of the South* (1946), *Dog on the Sun* (1949), *Words and Ways* (1968), *Home to My Valley* (1970), and *Land of Nod and Other Stories* (1976). Green's verse appeared in *The Lost Colony Song-Book* (1938), *The Highland Call Song-Book* (1941), *Song in the Wilderness* (1947), *The Common Glory Song-Book* (1951), *Texas Song-Book* (1967), and *Texas Forever* (1967).

Nonfiction by Green includes a critical work, *Contemporary American Literature: A Study of Fourteen Outstanding American Writers* (1925, with Elizabeth Lay Green); a book about teaching, *Forever Growing: Some Notes on a Credo for Teachers* (1945); and four collections of writings on the theater, *The Hawthorn Tree* (1943), *Dramatic Heritage* (1953), *Drama and the Weather* (1958), and *Plough and Furrow* (1963).

Achievements

Early in his long career as a playwright, Green was hailed as the promising young Eugene O'Neill of the South. The New York drama critics were encouraging and so was a Pulitzer Prize for *In Abraham's Bosom* in 1927. Green's promise, however, was never quite fulfilled, although he continued to write for the New York stage up until World War II. Both Green's initial success and his ultimate failure in New York can be attributed to his folksy images of the South—images which, upon examination, and with repetition and age, proved stereotypical, especially in comparison with the work of more substantial Southern writers, such as Thomas Wolfe and William Faulkner. Green wrote too prolifically for his work to attain consistent quality: In particular, his characters, usually meant to be realistic, tend to be one-dimensional (or, when he tried to make them complex, merely inconsistent), and, for a student and teacher of philosophy, Green's lack of philosophical depth is disappointing.

When the romance with New York waned, Green, who had a down-home lover in the Carolina Playmakers and who had flirted with German experimental drama and with Hollywood, went in other directions. These other directions constitute his main achievement. Along with such groups as the Carolina Playmakers, Green helped to expand the material, techniques, and audiences of legitimate drama in the United States. He brought in more folk and historical material, music, and stylized techniques, and his "symphonic" plays (historical plays usually with patriotic themes), performed in outdoor theaters recalling the original Greek drama, brought drama to the people, particularly in the South. Immensely popular, great tourist attractions, some of the symphonic dramas continued to be performed, including the first one, *The Lost Colony*. Unfortunately, the setting, ritual, and spectacle of the symphonic dramas do not cover up Green's tendency toward stereotypes, which became even more pronounced with the historical material.

Of Green's prodigious output, his best work includes *White Dresses* and *Hymn to the Rising Sun* among the one-act plays, *In Abraham's Bosom* and *Johnny Johnson* among the full-length plays, and *Wilderness Road* among the symphonic dramas.

Biography

Paul Eliot Green was a product of the Cape Fear River farming region of eastern North Carolina. His paternal grandfather, John Green, had owned a plantation and slaves before the Civil War, and his maternal grandfather, William Byrd, was a preacher, singing teacher, and composer of hymns. Green's parents were William Archibald and Betty Byrd Green (William's second wife). His father owned and operated a large farm, where, with the other Green children, Paul played, worked, and got to know the sharecroppers, black and white. This rural background provided a rich source of material for Green's future plays.

After attending public elementary school, Green entered Buie's Creek Academy (now Campbell College) and benefited from the teaching of the academy's dedicated founder, James Archibald Campbell. Upon graduation, Green earned money to attend college by working for two years as the principal of tiny Olive Branch School and as a professional baseball player for the Lillington Cats. (He was an ambidextrous pitcher—a fact in which some critics of his plays might see a symbolic fitness.) He entered the University of North Carolina, Chapel Hill, in 1916, the same year as Thomas Wolfe, but his university studies were interrupted by volunteer service (1917-1919) in the United States Army Engineers. After serving at the front during World War I and in Paris afterward, attaining the rank of second lieutenant, Green left the engineers to resume his university studies. During Green's absence, Frederick Koch had come to the University of North Carolina and established the Carolina Playmakers. Koch and the Playmakers, with their emphasis on folk drama, exercised a profound influence on Green and his subsequent career, although at the university Green majored in philosophy.

Through Green's involvement with the Carolina Playmakers, he met his future wife, Elizabeth Lay, who had written the first play produced by the Playmakers and continued to work for them after her graduation in 1919. She helped produce some of Green's early one-act plays and collaborated with him in writing *Blackbeard*. They were married in 1922, between two years of graduate study in philosophy for Green, first at North Carolina, then at Cornell. In 1923, they returned to Chapel Hill, where they made their home and reared four children and where Green taught at the university, as lecturer and then associate professor of philosophy (1923-1939), as professor of dramatic arts (1939-1944), and as professor of radio, television, and motion pictures (1962-1963).

Green's 1927 Pulitzer Prize for *In Abraham's Bosom* was followed in 1928 by a Guggenheim Fellowship allowing him to study theater for two years in Germany and England. In Berlin, Green was particularly impressed by Alexis Granowsky's stylized productions in the Yiddish Theater (including the actors' imitation of puppets) and by the "epic theater" (deliberately theatrical, didactic drama) of Bertolt Brecht. Also influential was Green's intermittent screenwriting work in Hollywood (1932-1936, 1942, 1964). Finally, in the last part of his life, Green's successful production of patriotic outdoor dramas received further stimulus when he was frequently called upon to represent the United States officially and unofficially: Among other such activities, he was a United States delegate to UNESCO (1950-1952), lectured for UNESCO in Asia (1951), and attended the International Conference on the Performing Arts (Athens, 1962). He received the Freedoms Foundation George Washington Medal three times (1951, 1956, 1966).

Analysis

Paul Green's playwriting career is usually divided into three phases: an early phase when he wrote one-act plays about the South; a middle phase when he advanced to full-length plays, at first traditional but then experimental in form, mostly set in the South but including other settings; and a final phase when he concentrated on historical outdoor plays, the so-called symphonic dramas, still mostly set in the South. Another division scheme is suggested by a surprising break in his career around World War II, when for five years (1942-1946) this prolific playwright produced no work for the stage (though he was writing for Hollywood). The five-year break effectively divides Green's period of concentration on indoor drama from his period of concentration on outdoor drama.

During the five-year period, Green apparently reassessed his dramatic career and emerged not only with a new form but also with new material and new attitudes. Before the break, Green relentlessly criticized social injustice in the United States, particularly the Southern parts, but the born-again Green celebrated the patriotic *Faith of Our Fathers* and became a member of the United States Executive Committee and member of the National Commission, UNESCO (1950-1952). The onetime antiwar playwright filled the stage with battles. Green can be accused of inconsistency here—or at least of going for the popularity by merely reflecting changes in social climate from the 1930's to the 1950's. In his defense, however, it should be noted that his development was dictated, in part, by the opportunities available to him (which perhaps, in turn, were influenced by the prevailing social climate).

More important, the gulf between *Native Son* and *The Common Glory* is not as great as it first appears. The uniting strand is Green's democratic belief in human rights, expressed in a negative, critical form before World War II and in a positive, celebratory form after the war. Green's emphasis changed, but his beliefs remained the same, as can be seen most clearly in his consistently sympathetic portrayal of black Americans. His consistent development is demonstrated by the following analysis of his best work during the various phases.

The one-act plays *White Dresses* and *Hymn to the Rising Sun* both depict brutal social conditions in the South early in the twentieth century. *White Dresses* focuses on the relationship of a white landowner and his black female tenants, while *Hymn to the Rising Sun* shows guards and convicts on a chain gang. Both plays are expository in nature, with little plot, the action serving to demonstrate a sordid condition—the cruel dominance of one party and subjection of another, as though the South knows no other pattern.

In *White Dresses*, the mulatto girl Mary McLean has likings for young Hugh Morgan, the white landlord's son (with whom she has apparently had sexual relations), and talks of going to New York and passing for white. Her aspirations in both directions are crushed by the landlord, Henry Morgan, who forces her to marry another black tenant, Jim Matthews; otherwise, he will evict her sickly old grandmother. Henry Morgan comes across as a Simon Legree, but, as the eye-popping conclusion reveals, he has at least one good reason for preventing a liaison between Hugh and Mary— Mary is Hugh's half sister. Also, because it is Christmas Eve, Henry delivers Mary a present, apparently from Hugh: a white dress matching the one Henry gave Mary's mother to bribe her. The dress is a powerful symbol of Mary's crushed hopes and the cycle of degradation from which she had hoped to escape.

Hymn to the Rising Sun, the chain-gang drama, is also set on an ironic date, the Fourth of July. All the action takes place between dawn's first light and sunrise of another hot Southern day, the nearest thing to Hell in the life of the chain-gang members (black and white here are treated equally). The state legislature and judges have decreed "hard labor" for the convicts, and Captain, the head guard, is there to see that the decree is carried out. A stereotype of the Southern sheriff or "boss" (fat, sombrero-crowned, wearing a whip curled up in one boot), Captain obviously takes pleasure in his work, although he denies it. His easygoing humor loaded with sinister threats, Captain rules by intimidation and sadism. To celebrate the holiday, Captain has the guards blast off their shotguns, makes a speech to the convicts on his concept of democracy (law is of, by, and for the Establishment), and forces the convicts to sing a verse of "America." He then proceeds to routine matters: whipping Bright Boy for talking too much and releasing Runt from eleven days in the sweatbox (unfortunately, the man is dead).

Both *White Dresses* and *Hymn to the Rising Sun* have social implications beyond their immediate themes of race and penal servitude, although Green does not push these wider implications to the fore. *White Dresses* shows the paternalistic economic system by which the few control the many, and *Hymn to the Rising Sun* shows what happens to those who step out of line: They are given a few basic civics "lessons." The chain gang, hired out by the governor to build the railroad, is a microcosm of the whole system, and Captain, with his Mussolini-style harangue on "democracy," in particular suggests the system's totalitarian nature.

Like Mary McLean in *White Dresses*, Abraham McCranie of *In Abraham's Bosom* is a mulatto who hopes to break out of the cycle of Southern degradation. Unlike Mary, Abe aspires to lift his whole race with him. He is, therefore, a much more dangerous character than Mary; Mary only wanted to go to New York, but Abe wants to teach blacks to read and write. A heroic figure who first struggles to teach himself, Abe is feared by both blacks and whites, with the exception of Goldie, a mulatto who becomes his devoted wife, and Colonel McCranie, a white landowner and Abe's father. Although the stereotypical old Colonel whips Abe onstage (because Abe throws the Colonel's mean white son, Lonnie, into a brier patch), he genuinely likes Abe, encourages him, and eventually helps him to open a school for black children. Unfortunately, when the Colonel dies, the children stop coming, and Abe is run out of town. Eighteen years later, Abe returns and tries to open his school again, but he is beaten by a white mob and, after he kills the abusive Lonnie, he is gunned down in the doorway of his home.

One of the many depressing aspects of *In Abraham's Bosom* is the way other blacks oppose Abe's aspirations. His sarcastic old aunt, Muh Mack, constantly derides him, and his fellow turpentine workers consider him up-pity; they are convinced that blacks are hewers of pine trees and pickers of cotton, and they resent any effort to prove otherwise. Such is the heavy weight of oppression upon the blacks that they have internalized white at-titudes toward them. Another psychological inversion is represented by Douglass, Abe and Goldie's son, who, though named after a great black leader, turns out no-good and stirs up the white mob against his father. He embodies Abe's self-defeating anger and frustration, which boil forth occa-sionally (although too abruptly and awkwardly) and lead to Abe's killing of Lonnie, his white half-brother. To complete the Cain-Abel parallel, Abe sometimes thinks, in this cycle of waste and defeat, that even God is against him. In the sense that God has abandoned Abe, the play's multi-faceted title seems sardonic, a theological mockery.

Although some of Green's plays might be considered dated, such is not the case with *Johnny Johnson*, an outstanding antiwar satiric comedy. The play is as timely now as when it was written, and audiences have grown more receptive to antiwar themes. In addition, Green's technique in *Johnny Johnson* caught American audiences and critics by surprise in the 1930's; now they should be more prepared. The early critics thought they should pan *Johnny Johnson* for its rambling plot and mix of harsher mate-rial with comedy; nevertheless, they felt a strange affinity for the play. The play is in the "epic theater" style of Bertolt Brecht (whose work Green had admired on his German theatrical tour, 1928-1929), complete with music by Brecht's partner, Kurt Weill, who had fled Adolf Hitler's Germany. Besides songs, other Brechtian features include emblematic settings and scenes, folk sayings, signs, vaudeville tricks, and stereotypical characters (here Green's penchant for stereotypes served him well).

Although Johnny Johnson is a Southern bumpkin, he has enough sense to know that peace is better than war. He would rather stay home and marry his girl than fight in the war. His girl, Minny Belle, has other ideas: Swept up by patriotic fervor, she demands his complete sacrifice. Persuaded by President Woodrow Wilson's words that this is the war to end all wars, Johnny finally enlists. Wounded on the Western Front (actually, shot in the behind), he steals a cylinder of laughing gas from the hospital and reduces the Allied High Command to silly ninnies. Having elicited from them orders to stop the fighting, he dons the American commander's cap and coat and, with the spontaneous assistance of like-minded German soldiers, halts World War I. Soon, however, the ruse is discovered, Johnny is arrested, and the war resumes. Johnny is confined in an insane asylum for ten years, during which time Minny Belle marries his rival, the prospering owner of Crystal Mineral Springs, Anguish Howington, whom the army rejected on medical grounds.

An early example of black humor, *Johnny Johnson* mixes farce and horror, but its main components are irony and satire. War is announced at a small-town ceremony to unveil a peace monument, and the populace instantly switches gears. Recruits are enticed by a phonograph blaring "Democracy March," and they are immediately introduced to military dehumanization by a brutal physical examination. The insane asylum's debating society, solving problems and prescribing world order, sounds like Congress or the United Nations. The overriding irony is that the common man, Johnny Johnson, has better sense than his leaders but is declared insane.

As Howington's prosperity shows, war is good for some people's business. As the war hysteria shows, war also encompasses the nature of bloody ritual. War's cyclic nature is suggested by the play's ending, set in the 1930's, that shows the pacified Johnny Johnson selling homemade toys in front of a crowded stadium from which martial noises (music and shouted slogans) are issuing. Along comes Minny Belle, fat and fur-swathed, accompanied by her son, Anguish Jr., who wants to buy a toy soldier. Johnny, however, whom Minny Belle fails to recognize, does not make toy soldiers.

The theme of war as insane ritual and the Cain-Abel theme of brother against brother continue in *Wilderness Road*, Green's symphonic outdoor drama of the Civil War. Named after the road carved into Kentucky by struggling early settlers, *Wilderness Road* was commissioned by Berea College, a distinguished Kentucky college established in 1855 for poor people, black and white. The founding of Berea College (by abolitionists) is closely linked to the action of the play, set in the Kentucky hills nearby. Influenced by Berea's founders, John Freeman struggles to establish a school for mountain children. At first the community supports him, but some of his slave-owning neighbors do not like his radical notion that "God hath made of one blood all nations of men" (Berea's motto). To these fearful neighbors, led by the politician Jed Willis, education itself is a subversive idea. Against such forces, in the midst of brewing civil war, Berea's founders and John Freeman have to travel a "wilderness road," like Abraham McCranie of *In Abraham's Bosom* or like Jesus walking "that lonesome valley" (in the Appalachian hymn so prominent in the play). Eventually, the school board withdraws its support from John; he is beaten and the school vandalized by the hooded Knights of the White Star, also led by Jed Willis.

When civil war comes, the divided community, like neutral Kentucky as a whole, sends men off to both sides. Both sides whoop it up, but, as the dead and wounded come home, the whoops change to lamentations. Performed on three adjacent stages and summarized by the play's narrator, the Civil War panorama unfolds in swift, emblematic scenes like movie montages, but the audience gets a taste of stunning realism from the fireworks going off all around and the sound effects of shells whizzing overhead. Altogether, Green leaves little doubt that war is hell.

A pacifist, John Freeman stays out of the action until the community is overrun by Southern forces, again led by Jed Willis, who gloats that the new social order will reflect his ideas. Willis' temporary triumph provides a shocking glimpse of the totalitarian society which might have emerged if the South had won the Civil War. Faced with this possibility, John Freeman joins the Union forces, leads a raid to destroy a key railroad bridge near his home, and is killed in action. On the railroad bridge, which supplies Southern forces, hangs the fate of Kentucky and, to some extent, the Union; thus, by his death John Freeman strikes a decisive blow for freedom. He leaves behind Elsie Sims, a girlfriend who will now marry his brother and rival, Davie (on the vast outdoor stage, the initial love interest in the play can hardly compete with the cannon fire). Also surviving, minus a leg, is Neill Sims, Elsie's brother and John's best student, who will carry on the school.

To a great extent, *Wilderness Road*, the best example of Green's work in his most successful form, represents the culmination of his development as a playwright. Here his interests in the folk, in music, and in history are integrated; so also are the influences of Brecht and the movies. *Wilderness Road*, in addition, shows the coming together of Green's various themes. Through his portrayal of civil war, of brother against brother, Green comments on the nature of all war: If God has made of one blood all nations of human beings, then all war is civil war. For purposes of persuasion, Green much preferred education to warfare, yet, as John Freeman illustrates, there are some things worth fighting for: One such thing was whether, as Lincoln said, the United States would be defined as free or slave—a very close call in American history. Green, in his life and work, was still struggling to establish the definition of freedom in the United States. A man of the South and of the folk, Green contributed more than his share to the cause.

Other major works

NOVELS: *The Laughing Pioneer*, 1932; *This Body the Earth*, 1935.

SHORT FICTION: *Wide Fields*, 1928; *Salvation on a String and Other Tales of the South*, 1946; *Dog on the Sun*, 1949; *Words and Ways*, 1968; *Home to My Valley*, 1970; *Land of Nod and Other Stories*, 1976.

POETRY: *The Lost Colony Song-Book*, 1938; *The Highland Call Song-*

Book, 1941; *Song in the Wilderness*, 1947; *The Common Glory Song-Book*, 1951; *Texas Forever*, 1967; *Texas Song-Book*, 1967; *This View from Above*, 1970.

NONFICTION: *Contemporary American Literature: A Study of Fourteen Outstanding American Writers*, 1925 (with Elizabeth Lay Green); *The Hawthorn Tree*, 1943; *Forever Growing: Some Notes on a Credo for Teachers*, 1945; *Dramatic Heritage*, 1953; *Drama and the Weather*, 1958; *Plough and Furrow*, 1963.

SCREENPLAYS: *Cabin in the Cotton*, 1932 (adaptation of Harry Harrison Kroll's novel); *Dr. Bull*, 1933 (adaptation of James Gould Cozzens' novel *The Last Adam*); *The Rosary*, 1933; *State Fair*, 1933 (with Sonya Levien; adaptation of Phil Stong's novel); *Voltaire*, 1933 (with Maude T. Howell); *Carolina*, 1934 (adaptation of his play *The House of Connelly*); *David Harum*, 1934 (adaptation of Edward Noyes Westcott's novel); *Time Out of Mind*, 1947 (adaptation of Rachel Field's novel); *Broken Soil*, 1949; *Red Shoes Run Faster*, 1949; *Roseanna McCoy*, 1949 (adaptation of Albert Hannum's novel); *Black Like Me*, 1963 (adaptation of John Howard Griffin's novel).

RADIO PLAY: *A Start in Life*, pr., pb. 1941 (also as *Fine Wagon*).

Bibliography

Adams, Agatha Boyd. *Paul Green of Chapel Hill.* Edited by Richard Walser. Chapel Hill: University of North Carolina Library, 1951. Adams traces Green's early development, education, and plays. She then discusses the plays' themes that demonstrate Green's concern with the plight of rural inhabitants of the South and their struggles with life. Provides a full consideration of *In Abraham's Bosom* and Green's other major works.

Clark, Barrett H. *Paul Green.* New York: Robert M. McBride, 1928. This twenty-five-page monograph presents an enthusiastic introduction to the then unknown Southern farmer-playwright who seemed to come out of nowhere to win the Pulitzer Prize for *In Abraham's Bosom*. It provides a brief biography, traces the themes of Green's early plays, and examines his influences. While criticizing Green's philosophizing, Clark commends his writing and emphasizes that Green's career is only beginning. Contains a complete listing of all Green's published and unpublished writings from 1916 to 1928.

Free, William J., and Charles B. Lower, eds. *History into Drama: A Sourcebook on Symphonic Drama.* New York: Odyssey Press, 1963. The finest source for information on and about symphonic drama as developed and practiced by Green. It contains a wide variety of essays on theory and performance, the complete text of *The Lost Colony*, and four performance photographs.

Kenny, Vincents. *Paul Green.* New York: Twayne, 1971. Kenny discusses how Green's abiding faith in human nature fuses the common person, the outdoors, and the United States into a working democracy. Green's plays are divided into three categories: white-folk literature dramatizing the bitter lot of the tenant farmer, black-folk literature dramatizing the plight of the farmer's struggles with the soil and society, and the later development of the outdoor symphonic drama. Notes, references, annotated bibliography, and index.

Lazenby, Walter S. *Paul Green.* Austin, Tex.: Steck-Vaughn, 1970. This forty-four-page monograph provides a brief commentary on the development of Green's plays simultaneously with his development as a writer. Green's early plays are motivated by compassion for the lowly and by the troubling aspects of the South. *In Abraham's Bosom, The Field God,* and *The House of Connelly* are given in-depth analysis. Lazenby then turns to the outdoor symphonic dramas, devoting primary attention to *Potter's Field* and *The Lost Colony.*

Harold Branam
(Updated by *Gerald S. Argetsinger*)

GRAHAM GREENE

Born: Berkhamsted, England; October 2, 1904
Died: Vevey, Switzerland; April 3, 1991

Principal drama

The Heart of the Matter, pr. 1950 (adaptation of his novel, with Basil Dean); *The Living Room*, pr., pb. 1953; *The Potting Shed*, pr., pb. 1957; *The Complaisant Lover*, pr., pb. 1959; *Carving a Statue*, pr., pb. 1964; *The Return of A. J. Raffles: An Edwardian Comedy in Three Acts Based Somewhat Loosely on E. W. Hornung's Characters in "The Amateur Cracksman,"* pr., pb. 1975; *For Whom the Bell Chimes*, pr. 1980, pb. 1983; *Yes and No*, pr. 1980, pb. 1983; *The Collected Plays of Graham Greene*, pb. 1985.

Other literary forms

Graham Greene tried his hand at every literary genre. He was poet, reporter, critic, essayist, pamphleteer, dramatist, screenwriter, short-story writer, biographer, and autobiographer. His near compulsion to travel led to published accounts of his numerous journeys. His established place in literature, however, is the result of the worldwide acclaim that has greeted most of his twenty-odd novels. Critics have noted a strong autobiographical element in his fiction and have charted the development of his philosophical, religious, and political thought through his career. Certain themes recur in a recognizable pattern: human beings as aliens at home and abroad, oppressed by evil in a violent world, flirting with suicide as an answer to their despair, seeking salvation, perhaps finding it at last, through the grace of God. Since *Brighton Rock*, published in 1938, most of the novels are decidedly the work of a confirmed Roman Catholic, but Greene himself rejected the label "Catholic writer." Acknowledging his Catholicism as a point of reference, Greene, borrowing the title of one of his novels, preferred to think of himself as a writer exploring the human factor.

From 1929 to the early 1960's, Greene's works, with few exceptions, were published in Great Britain by William Heinemann. From the mid-1960's, his British publisher has been the Bodley Head, a firm in which he served as a director from 1958 to 1968. In 1970, the two British publishing houses became jointly involved in issuing a uniform edition of his collected works, for which Greene wrote new introductions. In the United States, his works have been published by the Viking Press and Simon and Schuster.

Achievements

Greene, most highly regarded for his work as a novelist, was not a distinguished dramatist, nor was he an innovator in dramatic form. His first dramatic work was not even meant for the stage; *The Great Jowett*, a character study of Benjamin Jowett, the late nineteenth century educator and head of Balliol College, Oxford, was written as a radio play for the British Broadcasting Corporation and broadcast in 1939. One of Greene's early plays, for which no manuscript survives, was accepted by a theatrical firm but never reached production. Only five of his plays—*The Living Room*, *The Potting Shed*, *The Complaisant Lover*, *Carving a Statue*, and *The Return of A. J. Raffles*—have been produced in London. Two later plays, *Yes and No*, a curtain raiser consisting of a comic dialogue between a director and an actor, and *For Whom the Bell Chimes*, a black farce in the manner of Joe Orton, have been produced in the provinces.

Greene's major plays—*The Living Room*, *The Potting Shed*, and *The Complaisant Lover*—suggest the influence of the well-made play as they recall the work of Henrik Ibsen in his realist phase. As in Ibsen's work, the present dilemma in which the characters find themselves has been dictated by the irrevocable events of the past. Tradition, superstition, and religion all take their toll on characters torn between a sense of duty and the urgings of love. Despite their serviceable structure and moving content, Greene's plays generally echo his superior fiction without deepening its themes.

Biography

Graham Greene was born on October 2, 1904, in Berkhamsted, a small town twenty-eight miles northwest of London, and was the fourth of six children. His father, Charles Henry Greene, was a teacher, and later headmaster, at the Berkhamsted School. Being the son of the headmaster created difficulties for the sensitive youngster. He was victimized, or so he believed, by his schoolmates and made the butt of their jokes. His bouts of depression led him, at an early age, to several attempts at suicide, which, in later years, he understood to be merely disguised pleas for attention and understanding rather than serious efforts to end his own life. In his teens, he was determined to be a writer, to demonstrate to his schoolmates and to the world that there was something at which he could excel, and several of his stories were printed in the school paper, some even finding their way into the local newspaper.

When Greene was sixteen, his older brother, then studying medicine, suggested to his father that Graham needed psychiatric help. Agreeing, his father sent him to live in London for six months with an analyst, Kenneth Richmond, who helped the boy make some necessary social adjustments. During this period, Greene developed an interest in dreams and the subconscious. He also read widely and later claimed that the works that most influenced him were the melodramatic adventure stories of Anthony Hope, John Buchan, and H. Rider Haggard. Marjorie Bowen's *The Viper of Milan* (1917) enabled him to recognize evil as a force to be dealt with in his everyday life.

From 1922 to 1925, at Balliol College, Oxford, Greene involved himself in the literary life of a great university. He edited the *Oxford Outlook* and published a book of verse, *Babbling April: Poems* (1925). The depression of his early youth was replaced by a boredom which plagued him for much of his life and was the impetus for his frequent travels. His method of relieving boredom during his Oxford days was to engage in excessive drinking, even some Russian roulette, this time the result of an urge to gamble rather than a desire to kill himself. At Oxford, he met Vivien Dayrell-Browning, who wrote to him objecting to his reference in a film review to Catholics "worshiping" the Virgin Mary.

Unsure of his next move, but determined not to be a teacher, Greene applied for work with *The Times* of London but could find employment only with the Nottingham *Journal*. Interested in Vivien, whom he was still seeing, he sought out a Father Trollope in Nottingham to give him Catholic instruction in order to understand her better. As a result, in February, 1926, he converted to Catholicism, a decision which influenced all of his subsequent writing but which first appeared as a thematic concern in the novel *Brighton Rock* in 1938. In 1926, he also became subeditor for *The Times*. Greene and Vivien married the next year and had two children, a son and a daughter. A few years later, the couple separated. Thereafter, Greene protected his family's privacy by maintaining silence in regard to their relationships.

After the publication of *The Man Within* in 1929, Greene expected to support himself as a novelist; the failure of his next works, *The Name of Action* (1930) and *Rumour at Nightfall* (1931), which he later suppressed, proved a setback. In 1932, however, *Stamboul Train: An Entertainment* began a string of successes for Greene. For a time in the 1930's, he supplemented his royalties by serving as film critic for the *Spectator* and *Night and Day*. During the 1930's, he also began a series of extended journeys, such as a walking trip across Liberia which led to *Journey Without Maps: A Travel Book* (1936) and a trip to Mexico which led to both a travel book, *The Lawless Roads: A Mexican Journal* (1939), and a work of fiction, *The Power and the Glory* (1940).

In 1940, Greene became literary editor for the *Spectator* and two years later worked in Sierra Leone, Africa, for British Intelligence under the authority of Kim Philby, who later defected to the Soviet Union. In 1948 and 1949, Greene worked with director Sir Carol Reed on the films *The Fallen Idol* and *The Third Man*, gaining a sound preparation for his coming theatrical endeavors. Before seriously undertaking his own plays for the theater, in 1950 he adapted his novel *The Heart of the Matter* (1948) for the stage with director Basil Dean. Another of his novels, *The Power and the Glory*, was made into a play, but Greene had no hand in its adaptation. His three most significant plays—*The Living Room, The Potting Shed*, and *The*

Complaisant Lover—were all produced in the 1950's.

A trip to Indochina in 1954 and 1955 bore fruit in the publication of *The Quiet American* (1955); likewise, a trip to the Belgian Congo led to the publication of *A Burnt-out Case* (1961). *The Comedians* was published in 1966 following a trip to Haiti, and later trips to Paraguay and Chile laid the foundation for *The Honorary Consul* (1973). A strain of anti-Americanism is apparent in some of these works, perhaps traceable in part to a libel suit involving Greene's references to the nine-year-old Shirley Temple as a sexual tease, a contretemps that developed while he was writing film criticism for the short-lived comic weekly *Night and Day*. He also felt harassed by the State Department when, on more than one occasion, his visas for travel to the United States were delayed. He was vociferous in his condemnation of the United States' actions in Vietnam as well.

Greene was awarded an honorary doctorate from Cambridge University in 1962, was made a fellow of Balliol College, Oxford, in 1963, and was named Companion of Honour by Queen Elizabeth in 1966.

Though he never received the Nobel Prize many expected for him, Greene remained a productive and well-regarded writer into his eighties. Such critically successful novels as *Doctor Fischer of Geneva: Or, the Bomb Party* (1980) and *Monsignor Quixote* (1982) showed that age had not blurred his literary vision. In his final years, he turned increasingly to writing a lengthy journal of his dreams. When he died in Switzerland at the age of eighty-six, he was universally regarded as one of the century's major writers.

Analysis

In the introduction to the 1974 edition of his first thriller-novel, *Stamboul Train*, Graham Greene confesses to an early passion for playwriting. While his earliest attempts at that genre have never come to light, the idea of shaping scenes dramatically informed much of his work as a novelist. Greene admitted that he sometimes found it essential to escape the liquidity of the novel to play out a situation, a confrontation between two characters perhaps, within the narrow confines of a space approximating the dimensions of a stage. This dramatic method within the form of the novel reached its climax in *The Honorary Consul*, in which most of the story takes place in a hut where the kidnapped victims are held hostage.

Whereas dramatic form has influenced Greene's novels, the theme of what may be his most popular novel, *The End of the Affair* (1951), pervades his most ambitious plays: *The Living Room*, *The Potting Shed*, and *The Complaisant Lover*. Frequently thought of as a Catholic novelist, Greene, who may have converted to Catholicism out of an intellectual need to find answers to questions ignored by the Anglican Church, makes his most explicit statements about the relationship of God and human beings in *The*

surprisingly informative review of theater conditions in the West End from the mid-1940's to 1960, Greene's active theater years. The notes serve as a source for continued inquiry.

Albert E. Kalson
(Updated by *Thomas J. Taylor*
and *Robert McClenaghan*)

ROBERT GREENE

Born: Norwich, Norfolk, England; c. July, 1558
Died: London, England; September 3, 1592

Principal drama

Orlando Furioso, pr. c. 1588, pb. 1594; *A Looking Glass for London and England*, pr. c. 1588-1589, pb. 1594 (with Thomas Lodge); *Friar Bacon and Friar Bungay*, pr. c. 1589, pb. 1594; *John of Bordeaux*, pr. c. 1590-1591 (fragment); *James IV*, pr. c. 1591, pb. 1598; *Complete Plays*, pb. 1909.

Other literary forms

Although Robert Greene is perhaps most respected today for his contribution to English drama, it was as a writer of prose fiction that he was best known to his contemporaries. His novellas made him England's most popular writer of fiction in the 1580's. Among his early works, showing the influence of Italian writers, are *Mamillia: A Mirror or Looking Glass for the Ladies of England* (part 1, 1583; part 2, 1593), *Morando: The Tritameron of Love* (part 1, 1584; part 2, 1587), *Arbasto: The Anatomy of Fortune* (1584), and *Planetomachia* (1585). Turning to the pastoral romance in 1588, Greene published such novellas as *Alcida: Greene's Metamorphosis* (1588), *Pandosto: The Triumph of Time* (1588), *Ciceronis Amor* (1589; also known as *Tullies Love*), and *Menaphon* (1589). Pastorals featuring repentance as a major theme include *Greene's Never Too Late* (1590), *Francesco's Fortunes* (1590), *Greene's Mourning Garment* (1590), and *Greene's Farewell to Folly* (1591).

Greene created still another literary fashion in the last two years of his brief life, as he cultivated another form, the rogue, or "connycatching," pamphlet. His *A Notable Discovery of Cozenage* (1591), *A Disputation Between a Hee Conny-catcher and a Shee Conny-Catcher* (1592), and *The Black Book's Messenger* (1592), as well as other small books in the series, combined London street argot with satire of middle-class greed to produce a form that appealed to all levels of society.

Greene's untimely death in 1592 sparked the publication of two alleged "deathbed" pamphlets, *Greene's Groatsworth of Wit Bought with a Million of Repentance* (1592) and *The Repentance of Robert Greene* (1592), both usually attributed to him but neither closely resembling his style and thus probably spurious. The one surely authentic posthumous work, *Greene's Vision* (1592), follows the pastoral penitent style of 1590 and was probably written during that most fruitful year of his career.

Achievements

Greene's accomplishments as a playwright have always been greatly overshadowed by those of his younger contemporary, William Shakespeare. Still, it is accurate to say that Greene created in comedy the form on which Shakespeare worked his greater miracles, just as Thomas Kyd and Christopher Marlowe led the way for Shakespeare in tragedy. The form Greene developed, the English romantic comedy, as demonstrated most clearly in *Friar Bacon and Friar Bungay*, *James IV*, and the fragmentary *John of Bordeaux*, is strikingly different from its predecessors. Departing from the morality tradition still current on the London stage, Greene chose as his principal theme romantic love between princely men and beautiful women. The popularity of this approach was greatly enhanced by Greene's ability to weave the love plot into a tapestry of affairs of state—usually events from English history—and to convey in dialogue the varied atmospheres of court, city, and countryside.

Greene's most immediate influences were his own prose romances, in which his heroes and heroines become embroiled in the wars of love through their pride, only to be chastened by the disasters they occasion and thus eventually brought to repentance and reconciliation. These romances, in their lengthy, intense monologues and conversations between lovers, created in the 1580's a drama of character, as it were, well before Marlowe's *Tamburlaine the Great* lit up the stage in 1587. The vision of Greene's romances and plays differed from, even opposed, Marlowe's vision of the individual will able to dominate society and bend morality to its own consciousness. Through his thoroughly comic perspective, Greene saw individual attempts to conquer or dominate as ineluctably limited by an inherent human need to form communities and by the ideals of peace and the orderly succession of generations.

The few contemporary assessments of his work that have survived praise Greene as a "plotter of plays." Certainly, his ability to move characters across a stage and from scene to scene is unmatched before Shakespeare, who no doubt profited from Greene's example. Indeed, Shakespeare learned more from Greene than plotting: Greene was also the first English playwright to vary verse and prose significantly in order to imply differences in rank or tone; he also varied rhyme and blank verse for tonal effects. Moreover, Greene was the first to create memorable female characters in English drama (the women in his romances are usually more interesting and important characters than his men). Greene's Margaret, Dorothea, and Ida worthily precede Shakespeare's Rosalind and Viola. Perhaps Greene best prepared the way for Shakespeare by peopling his plays with individuals who could also represent the various levels within a society. In this way, Greene could create for the spectators the illusion that they were witnessing the reactions of an entire nation to critical events.

Though not a satiric dramatist, Greene also influenced the comedy of Ben Jonson and Thomas Middleton through his connycatching pamphlets of London life. These works created a tremendous vogue for tales of the exploits of thieves and confidence men. In these dramatic narratives, Greene brought such figures to life through dialogue rich with the patois of the city. Shakespeare's Falstaff and Autolycus, as well as the rogues of London comedy after 1600, take much of their inspiration from Greene's connycatchers.

Biography

According to the best, albeit sketchy, evidence, Robert Greene was born in Norwich, Norfolk, in 1558, of a saddler and his wife. It is certain that this ambitious son of bourgeois parents went on to St. John's College, Cambridge, in 1576 on a sizar's appointment (a sort of work-study position by which scholars earned their keep, usually as valets for sons of aristocrats). Though Greene's record at St. John's appears to have been undistinguished, he did take his baccalaureate in 1580. Greene continued his studies at Cambridge and received his master of arts degree from there in 1583, the same year in which his first prose romance, *Mamillia: A Mirror or Looking Glass for the Ladies of England*, was published. A second master's, from Oxford, came in 1588; this degree was more a formality than the result of further study. There is no evidence that after 1583 Greene intensely pursued any course other than the winning of a large, eager audience in London for his romances, plays, and pamphlets.

Concerning Greene's no doubt adventurous life as a writer in London from 1583 until his death in 1592, there is much rumor and rancor but little solid fact. His publication record indicates that he was immensely popular; his title pages from 1588 onward include his name within the titles themselves, as in *Greene's Mourning Garment* and *Greene's Never Too Late*. His friend Thomas Nashe declared that printers felt "blest to pay him dear for the very dregs of his wit." Nevertheless, since the London publishing industry, still in its infancy, provided large returns for printers but no royalties for authors, even great popularity guaranteed no security. Thus, Greene survived on the speed of his pen. Curiously, there is no indication that he seriously vied for the relative stability of noble patronage, nor does he seem to have written for the pay of either the Anglican Establishment or their Puritan opponents, as did many, including Nashe and Marlowe.

Perhaps more because of the persistent theme of repentance in his writings than because of his actual life, Greene at his death left a considerable reputation as a rakehell, albeit a penitent one. His vitriolic companion Nashe wrote that he cared only "to have a spell in his purse to conjure up a good cup of wine with the poet Gabriel"; Harvey, whom Greene had insulted in a pamphlet, called him "A rakehell, a makeshift, a scribbling fool/ a famous Bayard in city and school." Gentler wits, such as the critic Francis Meres, ignored the gossip and merely noted Greene's achievement as one of the "best for comedy" among the playwrights.

Of Greene's allegedly bitter feelings toward the acting companies which bought his plays, much has been echoed through four centuries. In the posthumous tract *Greene's Groatsworth of Wit Bought with a Million of Repentance*, there is a thinly veiled attack on the players, one "Shake-scene"—no doubt Shakespeare—in particular. Careful studies, however, have concluded that another, most likely Henry Chettle, the author and printer, wrote these words and passed them off as Greene's. That the playwright's dealings with the actors were not always cordial is certain; Greene himself admits, for example, that he sold the same play, *Orlando Furioso*, to rival companies. Nevertheless, that at least five of his plays were produced in London between 1588 and 1591 attests largely amicable relations between the author and his clients.

Analysis

The most obvious common feature of Robert Greene's two best-known plays, *Friar Bacon and Friar Bungay* and *James IV,* is the love plot, the romantic battle of strong male and female personalities. The women in both plays are particularly striking; it is no wonder that critics have focused much attention on them and that they see Greene's principal dramatic impulse as romantic. Nevertheless, what joins all five of Greene's known plays is not the love interest but rather the playwright's exploration of the individual's role within society; in those plays in which it is central, the love plot is merely one overt vehicle by which Greene asks his characters to choose between the desire to dominate others and the desire to live in harmony.

Greene found a locus for his first known dramatic handling of this theme within Ariosto's long narrative epic, *Orlando Furioso* (1516, 1521, 1532). Greene's play of the same title centers on the affection of the epic hero for Angelica, daughter of the King of Africa. In the play, Orlando, a warrior but not a king, contends with monarchs for the heroine. When he wins her, it is the victory that means everything to him; Angelica herself means nearly nothing to him. So little does he know or trust her that he eagerly believes the lies of Sacrapant, here a minor court attendant, that she has betrayed him with one Medoro. Orlando goes mad with jealousy; he runs wild through a stage forest, killing and dismembering. Symbolic of his ignorance of Angelica is his failure to recognize her when they meet in the forest; rather, he speaks his rage to a dummy (or a clown) made up to look somewhat like his beloved. Only after a woodland priestess, Melissa, is brought in to heal his madness can Orlando understand his fault and beg Angelica's forgiveness.

In *Orlando Furioso*, Greene paints with bold and none too careful strokes his typical portrait of the proud hero who slights his lover, suffers disasters, and comes to repentance. The audience cannot take the ranting Orlando seriously, though he might be more likable than the unbearably pompous kings who are his rivals; before the final scene, Orlando does virtually nothing to win the audience's hearts, nor does the audience sympathize with the slighted Angelica, who (albeit in the fragmentary version of the play that has survived) shows none of the depth of Greene's later heroines. Greene's heavy hand is deliberate here, however, for *Orlando Furioso* is an out-and-out parody of Marlowe's hero, Tamburlaine, the second part of whose history had appeared a few months earlier than Greene's play. Greene had attacked Marlowe's thumping verse and arrogant hero in the preface to his romance *Perimedes the Blacksmith* (1588), and here he burlesques Tamburlaine's megalomania as mere insanity. Critics have misjudged the play as Greene's failed attempt to match Marlowe as a bombastic tragedian; since Greene throughout his prose and verse shows consistent antipathy to the conqueror type, there is no reason to see *Orlando Furioso* as anything other than satire.

If *Orlando Furioso* is misjudged as a serious but inept attempt at what might be called tragicomedy, then it is difficult indeed to account for the skill and sensitivity apparent in Greene's next play, *Friar Bacon and Friar Bungay*, produced most likely in 1589. This play is still only beginning to be appreciated for its plotting, its use of verse and prose structures, and its study of ideas, though scholars have long recognized it as the prototype of English romantic comedy.

As in *Orlando Furioso*, the love story is the primary vehicle for Greene's exploration of the individual's relationship to society. Here, the love intrigue has social consequences that every member of Greene's audience could easily appreciate, particularly in the year following the invasion of the Spanish Armada. Greene sets his play within the reign of Henry III (1216-1272) and focuses his plot on the Prince of Wales, Edward, who must choose between honoring an arranged marriage with Eleanor, Princess of Castile, and pursuing the affections of the beautiful Margaret, an English country maid. The first third of the play is devoted to Edward's stratagems for securing the maid as a mistress, including his hiring the great English scientist (popularly considered a magician) Roger Bacon to use the "art" to win Margaret. When Edward fails to appear at court, his father and the royal Habsburg visitors grow nervous and set out to find him. When the prince is stymied in his illicit suit by Margaret's falling in love with Edward's best friend, Lacy, Earl of Lincoln, the tension almost provokes bloodshed. Finally, however, the deep, honest love of Margaret and Lacy cures Edward's fury. He heads back to court, once again knowing his duty to king, nation, and conscience.

Nevertheless, the play is only half over. The second half beautifully juxtaposes two stories. One is Bacon's attempt to rise at court, at first by overmatching the Habsburg magician in a test of powers, then by conjuring a wall of brass to surround England and thus ward off potential invaders (the audience would have immediately thought of Spain). The other story is Lacy's attempt to assure himself of Margaret's constancy to him despite her being ceaselessly flattered and bribed by rich suitors. Both Bacon's and Lacy's attempts are proved shameful. Not only would Bacon's wall destroy the harmony of nations promised in the marriage of Edward and Eleanor, but also, as Bacon comes to see, the conjuring requires the aid of evil powers. On Lacy's part, his test of Margaret gravely insults her; moreover, his hesitancy to ask her hand leaves her at the mercy of two boorish suitors, Lambert and Serlsby, who grow so incensed at her refusal to choose between them that they fall to swords; both are killed. The tragedy is compounded—and the two plots brought strategically together—when the sons of the combatants, both scholars at Bacon's college in Oxford, witness their fathers' duel through one of Bacon's conjurations, a "perspective glass." The sons turn enemies, and they, too, wound each other mortally. By juxtaposing these plots, Greene allows his audience to see that both Bacon and Lacy have been blinded by their desire for control, Bacon's over the power of magic, Lacy's over the power of Margaret's beauty.

When Lacy eventually gives up the stupid test and comes to claim her, Margaret forgives him heartily, even though he fails to see how much he has hurt her. Then, in the final scene, which celebrates the double wedding of Edward and Eleanor, Lacy and Margaret, this country lass, now Eleanor's attendant, offers to all the royalty present an example of humility and thanksgiving. By stating her thanks to "Jove" rather than to the favor of the court, she implicitly reawakens the awareness of all, especially Edward and Lacy, to the dangers which have providentially been averted. She places the emphasis of the closing scene where it belongs, on the sanctity of marriage rather than on the euphoria occasioned by a successful political match. Friar Bacon, now penitent, is also on hand to lend further solemnity to the celebration.

The final impact of the play is intensified by what might be called the delicate power of Greene's verse. His ability to evoke in diction and line the flavor of the English countryside has been amply noted by critics, but the varying of this accent with the equally accurate rendering of the courtly and academic atmospheres is perhaps just as remarkable. The play affirms the power of language to embody the spirit of place and person. That Greene's style shifts easily from blank verse to Skeltonics to prose, and from images of "butter and cheese, cream and fat venison" to those of "cates, rich Alexandria drugs" helps to create an environment as magical as Bacon's spells or Margaret's beauty. In such an atmosphere, rich with promise, one easily believes in the magic of love to soften hearts and heal wounds of the spirit.

Written in collaboration with the playwright and romance writer Thomas Lodge, *A Looking Glass for London and England* explores England's relations with other countries in a form quite different from the romantic comedy. Neither tragedy nor comedy, *A Looking Glass for London and England* is a dramatic sermon, Greene and Lodge's quite faithful retelling of the biblical story of Jonah and the Ninevites. An enduringly popular play in printed form and on the stage, it was one of the last and best of the religious dramas of the 1570's and 1580's that had developed out of the morality and mystery play traditions. Like *Friar Bacon and Friar Bungay*, *A Looking Glass for London and England* urges the audience to consider ethically its attitudes and actions toward foreign neighbors. The particular focus of the play is on the moral state of nations basking in victory over foreign foes. Though the censure is only implied in the parable of Nineveh, Greene and Lodge judged England to be on the verge of losing its ethical perspective in the wake of its defeat of the "invincible" Armada. Reminiscent of *Orlando Furioso*, the play's opening scenes ring with pompous speeches by vainglorious nobility; these court scenes are juxtaposed to scenes of the merchant and laboring classes lost in greed, drunkenness, and adultery.

One of Greene's presumed contributions to the play (it is impossible to determine each author's influence exactly) is the light touch with which much of the dissipation among the commons is handled. Greene's romances of these years show his increasing skill in creating clowns and cityfolk with whom his audience could identify, and this talent is used here to draw characters who can lull an audience into feeling that all of these dangerous excesses are mere jests and good fun. Having trapped the audience, however, Greene suddenly turns the plot so that dire consequences result; the most dramatic incident of this kind is the jovial drinking bout that leads to a brawl—which in turn leads to murder. Greene uses these scenes not only to prove the prophet Jonas' point about the perils into which the society can fall, but also to compare the typical evils of the populace with the even more dangerous behavior of the nobles, who are expected to lead society.

James IV, probably written shortly after *A Looking Glass for London and England*, retains some of the former play's sermonizing tone while replacing the parabolic structure with that of a masquelike fairy tale. One of Elizabethan drama's most imaginative spectacles, *James IV* combines authentic British history with materials adapted from Italian romance and then invests the story with sweetness and light by means of fairies, clowns, and balladlike verse. As in *Friar Bacon and Friar Bungay*, Greene here uses the pleasing form to move his audience gently toward accepting a controversial political stance, in this case the rightful succession of the Scots king, James VI, to the English throne.

Greene sets his play a century back in history, to the reign of James IV, another Scots monarch who had roused English ire. With the aid of a romance on the same theme by Cinthio (1504-1573), he twists the chronicle to create another love story in which the hero's injury to his beloved leads his nation to the brink of disaster. James, married to Dorothea, daughter of the English king, falls in love with a young gentlewoman, Ida, a peerless beauty. Urged on in his adultery by Ateukin, a Machiavellian adviser who secretly desires the King's overthrow, James banishes Dorothea, whom Ateukin accused of plotting against her husband. When news of the banishment reaches England, King Henry leads an army against James, whose demoralized forces wither before the English. Thousands of soldiers die and many towns fall; then, just as the climactic battle is about to commence, Dorothea, who has lived like a hunted animal, appears on the battleground. She begs her husband and father to throw down their arms. James, at last overcome by his injustice, implores her forgiveness. She replies with renewed vows of obedience to him. Again, the Greene heroine sets the example of humble love.

As in *Friar Bacon and Friar Bungay*, the fairy tale works because several poetic and structural devices conspire to create a magical atmosphere. One key element is the subplot involving Ida and an English officer, Eustace, whose courtship occasions the tenderest wooing scene in Greene's dramatic canon. Their love makes all the more painful the estrangement of James and Dorothea; it also sustains the audience's faith in the potential of romantic relationships to engender love and fidelity. Also vitally important to the fairy-tale magic is Greene's poetry, particularly the frequent alternation between blank verse and ballad stanzas. The rhyme provides minstrel-like distance between the harsh events being portrayed and their poetic evocation by Greene. Particularly in the dialogue between the banished Dorothea and her trusty servant, Nano, the rhyme enhances the poignancy of the situation. Greene's technique is put to a purpose far different from that in *Friar Bacon and Friar Bungay*, in which rhyme forms had been used satirically by Miles, the clown.

In *A Looking Glass for London and England*, Greene and Lodge had used another plotting device, the frame, as a means of relating the Ninevite parable to contemporary England. In the frame plot, a second prophet, Oseas, comments on the action. In *James IV*, Greene again turns to the frame plot to focus the audience's attention on a key issue in the play. Here, two antithetical types, a dour Scots cynic, Bohan, and an immortal optimist, Oberon, King of the fairies, observe the historical pageant as a test of their opposing views of human nature. Though for them the play will merely confirm or deny a point of view, these objective onlookers become more and more emotionally involved as the action proceeds. The intent is obvious: Greene again wants to move the audience to understand how the power of compassion can affect even the most resistant spirits. If even the cynic and the fairy king can feel for these characters, the audience is supposed to ask, how can love not prevail? Though Greene provides many devices to heighten the artifice of this pseudohistory, the patriotic appeal in *James IV* is even more obvious than that of *Friar Bacon and Friar Bungay*, with its direct references to England's defenses. The marriage of James and Dorothea would have immediately reminded the spectators of the recent marriage of James IV to Anne of Denmark, while the English-Scottish alliance in the play directly foreshadows the likely advance of James VI to the English throne upon the death of Elizabeth. Greene's presentation of James's character indicates the author's sympathy for the fears of the English public toward the current king's suspected reliance on untrustworthy ministers. The romantic ambience of the play, however, and the happy resolution of the plot are meant to ease the fears of the audience. Moreover, the horrors of war depicted in the play are intended to keep spectators aware of the inevitable outcome of opposition to the succession. Thus, the political presentation is balanced, not partisan. Greene's interest, as in his earlier plays, is to encourage in the theatergoing public the same faith in the power of love that his romances tried to evoke in his readers.

Scholars have attributed to Greene various plays otherwise anonymous, since these plays bear some distinguishing marks of Greene's style. Long thought a Greene play is *Alphonsus, King of Arragon* (pr. c. 1587, pb. 1599), which bears the name "R. Green" on its 1599 edition, the only extant; the play itself, however, is little like anything Greene is known to have written, so the attribution is doubtful. A more plausible case can be made for the bitterly satiric *A Knack to Know a Knave* (pr. 1592, pb. 1594), which emphasizes a Greene-like concern for the moral health of the different levels of society and which vividly portrays some of the tricks of characters doubtless drawn from Greene's connycatching pamphlets. *A Knack to Know a Knave* gradually degenerates, however, into a brutally vengeful depiction of the punishments of wrongdoers. Certainly antithetical to Greene's philosophy of forgiveness, this play, as it exists, may be a revision by another writer, perhaps the violent-tempered Nashe, of a work left unfinished by Greene at his death.

The only anonymously produced play definitely of Greene's authorship is *John of Bordeaux*, a sure sequel to *Friar Bacon and Friar Bungay*. Loosely based on the chivalric romance *Duke Huon of Bordeaux*, this play features Roger Bacon, who had renounced his magic in the earlier play, here using his powers to free beggars from prison, relieve their suffering, and confound their enemies. The play seems a perfect vehicle to rehabilitate this popular character from his relative ignonimy at the close of *Friar Bacon and Friar Bungay*. As one might expect, the friar shares center stage with a chaste and loyal woman, Rossalin, the wife of Bordeaux. Her warrior husband gone and feared dead, the constant Rossalin is wooed by a tyrant, then banished, penniless, when she rejects him. Eventually, her endurance, Bacon's magic, and Bordeaux's return win a happy ending.

The appeal of this play is more social than political. Rather than supporting a particular view of a specific national situation, it attempts to move the audience to identify with the poor folk portrayed onstage. In the most affecting scene of the play, Rossalin and her children beg from passersby, who probably resemble members of the audience; they scorn her pleas as the ruses of a begging thief or give her the cold comfort of pious warnings about the wages of sin. That chance can reverse the places of rich and poor is one message of the play, a message which Greene hoped to insinuate through his characteristic appeal to the finer emotions of his audience. *John of Bordeaux* illustrates once again that Greene's way in drama, as in prose, is not to threaten or lecture his audience on their duties to one another, but to create characters of sympathy and courage, humility and humor, who might win their hearts and set examples to follow.

Other major works

FICTION: *Mamillia: A Mirror or Looking Glass for the Ladies of England*, 1583, 1593 (2 parts); *Arbasto: The Anatomy of Fortune*, 1584; *The Mirror of Modesty*, 1584; *Morando: The Tritameron of Love*, 1584, 1587 (2 parts); *Planetomachia*, 1585; *Euphues His Censure to Philautus*, 1587; *Penelope's Web*, 1587; *Alcida: Greene's Metamorphosis*, 1588; *Pandosto: The Triumph of Time*, 1588; *Perimedes the Blacksmith*, 1588; *Ciceronis Amor*, 1589 (also known as *Tuilies Love*); *Menaphon*, 1589; *Francesco's Fortunes*, 1590; *Greene's Mourning Garment*, 1590; *Greene's Never Too Late*, 1590; *Greene's Farewell to Folly*, 1591; *Greene's Vision*, 1592; *Philomela: The Lady Fitzwater's Nightingale*, 1592.

POETRY: *A Maiden's Dream*, 1591.

NONFICTION: *The Spanish Masquerado*, 1589; *The Royal Exchange*, 1590; *A Notable Discovery of Cozenage*, 1591; *The Second Part of Conny-catching*, 1591; *The Third and Last Part of Conney-Catching*, 1592; *The Defense of Conny-catching*, 1592; *A Disputation Between a Hee Conny-catcher and a Shee Conny-catcher*, 1592; *The Black Book's Messenger*, 1592; *A Quip for an Upstart Courtier*, 1592; *Greene's Groatsworth of Wit Bought with a Million of Repentance*, 1592; *The Repentance of Robert Greene*, 1592.

MISCELLANEOUS: *Life and Complete Works in Prose and Verse*, 1881-1886.

Bibliography

Bevington, David. *Tudor Drama and Politics: A Critical Approach to Topical Meaning.* Cambridge, Mass.: Harvard University Press, 1968. Dismisses the early heroic plays as mock Christopher Marlowe. Praises

Friar Bacon and Friar Bungay but still discerns "mockery through caricature." Analyzes *George à Greene* (pr. before 1593, pb. 1599), even though its authorship is uncertain, stressing how this figure of "the virile, bluff, typical English yeoman" embodies "the ideals and prejudice of his class."

Dyce, Alexander. "Some Account of Robert Greene and His Writings." In *The Dramatic and Poetical Works of Robert Greene and George Peele, with Memoirs of the Authors and Notes.* New York: George Routledge and Sons, 1883. Dyce's account of Greene should be supplemented by later research, but Dyce lards his commentary with passages taken from Greene's contemporaries and quotes at length from Greene's prose. The many notes are well worth perusing.

Ellis-Fermor, Una. "Marlowe and Greene: A Note on Their Relations as Dramatic Artists." In *Studies in Honor of T. W. Baldwin*, edited by Don Cameron Allen. Urbana: University of Illinois Press, 1958. Ellis-Fermor establishes an order in which Christopher Marlowe's and Greene's plays might well have been written and then stresses the influence of Marlowe on Greene. *Alphonsus, King of Arragon*, for example, is a "crude response" to Marlowe's *Tamburlaine the Great* (pr. c. 1587), and Greene's *Orlando Furioso* is a parody of that same play. *Friar Bacon and Friar Bungay* is a triumphant continuation of Greene's reaction.

Greene, Robert. *The Plays and Poems of Robert Greene.* Edited by J. Churton Collins. 2 vols. Oxford, England: Clarendon Press, 1905. Collins' sixty-nine-page introduction in volume 1 is invaluable. Surveys all the problems of the biography, including a discussion of the autobiographical elements in the novels, and weaves in an account of the works. Moreover, each play receives a full introduction, and all are supplied with notes.

Gurr, Andrew. *The Shakespearean Stage, 1574-1642.* New York: Cambridge University Press, 1970. Devotes only two pages specifically to Greene but provides a clear exposition of "the material background to Shakespearean drama, a picture of the society in which the drama flourished, of the acting companies, their theatres, and their acting and staging." A twelve-page appendix lists several hundred plays by author, title, date, company of performers, and playhouse. An excellent source.

Muir, Kenneth. "Robert Greene as Dramatist." In *Essays on Shakespeare and Elizabethan Drama in Honor of Hardin Craig*, edited by Richard Hosley. Columbia: University of Missouri Press, 1962. All the extant plays come late in Greene's life, Muir says. Muir accepts as Greene's work only the four plays conclusively ascribed to him and *A Looking Glasse for London and England*, written with Thomas Lodge. Finds that *A Looking Glasse for London and England* is "much more competent" than *Alphonsus, King of Arragon*, and that some of the verse in *Orlando*

Furioso is "not without eloquence." *Friar Bacon and Friar Bungay* and *James IV* "mark a great advance."

Sanders, Norman. "The Comedy of Greene and Shakespeare." In *Early Shakespeare*, edited by John Russell Brown and Bernard Harris. New York: St. Martin's Press, 1961. Sanders finds "evidence of their kinship" (but no influence) throughout the comedies of Greene and Shakespeare and explains "the value of farcical comment on and irreverent contrast with the fervour of the lovers" in *Alphonsus, King of Arragon* and *Orlando Furioso*. Romantic love, everywhere in human life, is central to both Greene and Shakespeare. Shakespeare had greater range, subtlety, and depth, but they were alike in kind.

Christopher J. Thaiss
(Updated by *Frank Day*)

LADY AUGUSTA GREGORY

Born: Roxborough, Ireland; March 15, 1852
Died: Coole Park, Ireland; May 22, 1932

Principal drama

Spreading the News, pr. 1904, pb. 1905; *The Rising of the Moon*, pb. 1904, pr. 1907; *Kincora*, pr., pb. 1905, pr. 1909 (revised); *The White Cockade*, pr. 1905, pb. 1906; *Hyacinth Halvey*, pr., pb. 1906; *The Canavans*, pr. 1906, pr. 1907, pb. 1912 (revised); *The Gaol Gate*, pr. 1906, pb. 1909; *Dervorgilla*, pr. 1907, pb. 1908; *The Jackdaw*, pr. 1907, pb. 1909; *The Workhouse Ward*, pr. 1908, pb. 1909 (with Douglas Hyde; revision of *The Poorhouse*, pb. 1903, pr. 1907); *Seven Short Plays*, pb. 1909; *The Travelling Man*, pb. 1909, pr. 1910; *The Image*, pr. 1909, pb. 1910; *The Full Moon*, pr. 1910, pb. 1911; *Coats*, pr. 1910, pb. 1913; *The Deliverer*, pr. 1911, pb. 1912; *Grania*, pb. 1912; *Damer's Gold*, pr. 1912, pb. 1913; *The Bogie Men*, pr. 1912, pb. 1913; *Irish Folk-History Plays*, pb. 1912; *New Comedies*, pb. 1913; *The Wrens*, pr. 1914, pb. 1922; *Shanwalla*, pr. 1915, pb. 1922; *The Golden Apple*, pb. 1916, pr. 1920; *Hanrahan's Oath*, pr. 1918, pb. 1922; *The Jester*, wr. 1918, pb. 1923; *The Dragon*, pr. 1919, pb. 1920; *Aristotle's Bellows*, pr. 1921, pb. 1923; *The Story Brought by Brigit*, pr., pb. 1924; *Sancho's Master*, pr. 1927, pb. 1928; *Dave*, pr. 1927, pb. 1928; *Selected Plays*, pb. 1962 (Elizabeth Coxhead, editor); *The Collected Plays of Lady Gregory*, pb. 1970 (4 volumes: Ann Saddlemyer, editor).

Other literary forms

Lady Augusta Gregory would have been a significant figure in Irish literature even if she had never written any plays. Her earliest writing centered largely on the life and correspondence of her deceased husband, Sir William Gregory. In 1894, two years after his death, she completed the editing of *An Autobiography of Sir William Gregory*, and in 1898 she published *Mr. Gregory's Letter Box*.

Lady Gregory also did a number of translations, most notably of Molière's plays. Her plays were published in various collections throughout her lifetime and were collected in 1970 in *The Collected Plays of Lady Gregory*. A selection of nine plays can be found in *Selected Plays*, edited by Elizabeth Coxhead.

Lady Gregory's most valuable work for literature and Irish culture, however, was the gathering and publishing of the myths and legends of Ireland, a love for which began early in her life and lasted until the end. Traveling from village to village and cottage to cottage (including trips to the Aran Islands at the same time as John Millington Synge), she devoted herself to the recording of an oral tradition that she felt was central to the future as well as to the past of Ireland. The first of these numerous collections appeared as *Cuchulain of Muirthemne* in 1902, and the last, as *Visions and Beliefs in the West of Ireland* in 1920.

Lady Gregory also wrote for and about the Irish Renaissance itself, particularly about the dramatic revival. In 1901, she edited a book of essays, *Ideals in Ireland*, that called for a renewal of Irish culture and criticized English domination. Her account of the rise of Irish drama and the struggles at the Abbey Theatre are given in *Our Irish Theatre* (1913).

Lady Gregory's other nondramatic writings grow largely out of her personal life. In 1921, she published *Hugh Lane's Life and Achievement*, a memorial to her beloved nephew who died with the sinking of the *Lusitania*, and in 1926 *A Case for the Return of Hugh Lane's Pictures to Dublin*, part of a futile battle to get his French Impressionist collection returned from England. Others oversaw the publication of some of her private thoughts and reminiscences in *Coole* (1931) and *Lady Gregory's Journals, 1916-1930* (1946).

Achievements

The achievement of Lady Gregory is not to be found in awards and prizes given to her, but in the gift of her life, possessions, and talents to the literary and cultural awakening of modern Ireland. She would be a significant figure for any one of her contributions, but the sum of them makes her central to one of the most important movements in modern literature.

Lady Gregory's initial contribution to what has been called the Irish Renaissance (or Irish Literary Revival) was the early collecting of the myths and folktales of the Irish people. In so doing, she was participating in the discovery of the richness of so-called primitive cultures that was only beginning at the end of the nineteenth century to engage the interest of the earliest anthropologists and ethnologists. These efforts not only served an important historical function but also became a part of both her own plays and the poetry and plays of William Butler Yeats, and contributed significantly to the Irish people's rediscovery of and pride in their own past.

Lady Gregory's plays, while not greatly influential on other playwrights, were important in their contribution to what has come to be called the Irish dramatic movement (especially in its primary expression, the Abbey Theatre) and as works of art in their own right. They broke new ground, for example, in the mixing of the fabulous with the realistic and in the transformation of peasant speech into successful dramatic dialect. Lady Gregory perfected the one-act play; she also led the way in demonstrating that the lives and speech of peasants could be the stuff of dramatic art— and, in fact, the popular success of her plays helped sustain the Abbey Theatre during years of great struggle.

Perhaps her most important and most widely acknowledged achievement was as a motivating and sustaining force behind the Irish dramatic movement. As cofounder, with Yeats and Edward Martyn, of the Irish Literary Theatre at the turn of the century, later to become the Abbey Theatre, she worked tirelessly as director, fund-raiser, playwright, and defender in what seemed times of endless trouble.

Lady Gregory's contribution, however, extended beyond the dramatic movement itself. She also played the important role of encourager, comforter, guide, provider, and friend to fellow writers and laborers in the cultural renewal of Ireland. The symbol for this was her country estate, Coole Park, near Galway in the west of Ireland, where she graciously provided spiritual and material sustenance to many, most famously to Yeats.

Biography

Lady Augusta Gregory was born Isabella Augusta Persse on March 15, 1852, at Roxborough in County Galway, the twelfth of sixteen children. Her staunchly Protestant family was thought to have come to Ireland in the seventeenth century at the time of Oliver Cromwell's suppression of Ireland. The intellectual and aesthetic sterility of her childhood was relieved by the storytelling and quiet nationalism of her Catholic nurse, Mary Sheridan.

An avenue out to the larger world of which she longed to be a part was provided by her marriage in 1880 to Sir William Gregory, a man of sixty-three who had recently resigned as governor of Ceylon and returned to his country estate at Coole Park, not far from Roxborough. As the new Lady Gregory, she found a large library, a kind and intelligent husband, and the beginning of an outlet for her incipient talents.

It was to be many years before Lady Gregory would think of herself as a writer. Her first efforts consisted largely of editing the autobiography and letters of her husband, who died in 1892. Of more importance to her career, however, was the publication in 1893 of both Douglas Hyde's *Love Songs of Connacht* and Yeats's *The Celtic Twilight.* These two books sparked her own latent interest in the tales and speech of the Irish peasant. She was drawn to their lyric beauty, imaginativeness, and rich spirituality, and she made it her task for much of the rest of her life to record this rich oral tradition.

Lady Gregory first discussed with Yeats in 1894 the possibility of launching a theater devoted to the writers and plays of Ireland. Their dream became a reality in January, 1899, with the founding of the Irish Literary Theatre. This movement was to be the central concern and accomplishment of her life.

Initially, Lady Gregory's contribution was largely practical. She was an organizer, fund-raiser, encourager, and occasional collaborating playwright; it was she who first argued that the theater should be in Dublin, not London, as Yeats proposed. Within a few years, however, she was writing plays of her own, initially, she said, to provide some brief comic relief from Yeats's more esoteric works. These one-act plays proved to be more popular with the Dublin audiences than were Yeats's, and her career as a playwright was well, if late, begun.

The early years of the literary movement also saw the publication of a series of her collections of Irish myth and folklore, beginning with *Cuchulain of Muirthemne* and followed in rapid succession by *Poets and Dreamers* (1903), *Gods and Fighting Men* (1904), *A Book of Saints and Wonders* (1907), and *The Kiltartan Wonder Book* (1910). These were important books because they offered a single coherent telling of previously scattered tales (especially of the mythic hero Cuchulain) and, in so doing, made this heritage more widely known not only in Ireland but also abroad.

The single phrase which sums up all that Lady Gregory aimed for and achieved was her own oft-repeated observation to her fellow laborers that "we work to add dignity to Ireland," and work she did. As one of the directors of the Abbey Theatre (initially with Yeats and Synge), she was involved in constant battles—artistic, political, financial, and personal—to preserve the dramatic movement. As an Anglo-Irish Protestant with strong nationalistic convictions, she was suspected and attacked by both sides in the increasingly politicized and polarized Ireland.

The symbol of all this was the famous riots early in 1907 over Synge's *The Playboy of the Western World*. Considered a slur against Ireland by the ardent nationalists, and immoral by some quarters of the Catholic Church, the play evoked a series of riotous confrontations within the theater and an ongoing controversy without. Lady Gregory defended the play with all of her energies at the time and during a subsequent tour in America in the winter of 1911 to 1912, even though she personally disliked it.

Lady Gregory's skill as a dramatist grew rapidly, and her works were increasingly important to the financial solvency of the Abbey Theatre (especially since she collected no royalties for her plays). The first of a number of collections of her dramas, *Seven Short Plays*, came out in 1909, followed later by *Irish Folk-History Plays* (1912) and *New Comedies* (1913).

The beginning of World War I marks a tragic turn in the life of a remarkable woman who became a central figure in the literary life of a nation, a woman who did not write her first imaginative work until she was fifty. Lady Gregory's beloved nephew, Hugh Lane, died in the sinking of the *Lusitania*. His death left her with the task of trying to get his important collection of French Impressionist art returned from England to its rightful place in Ireland, a battle into which she futilely poured her declining energy until her death. In January, 1918, her only child, Robert Gregory, was killed while flying for the Royal Flying Corps. These personal tragedies, combined with her grief for the suffering of Ireland during the prolonged bloodshed of that nation's struggle for liberation, cast a darkness over Lady Gregory's declining years.

The 1920's were still years of effort on behalf of the Abbey Theatre, however, and they were brightened for a time by Lady Gregory's special role in the discovery and encouragement of Sean O'Casey. That undertaking also took a sad turn, as O'Casey broke relations with her and the Abbey Theatre over their rejection in 1928 of *The Silver Tassie.*

Lady Gregory's last years were spent in poor health and growing loneliness, but she maintained her aristocratic dignity up until her death at Coole Park in 1932.

Analysis

Lady Augusta Gregory's beginnings as a dramatist were modest. Her first efforts involved contributions of pieces of realistic dialogue and plot to Yeats's early poetic drama. Even when she began to write her own plays, she claimed that they were only to serve as brief comic relief from the more serious work of the poet. This situation, however, did not last long. Lady Gregory's plays soon became important in their own right to the Abbey Theatre and to the Irish dramatic movement, and they remain a significant part of one of the most seminal periods in modern literature.

The central motivation behind all that Lady Gregory did is found in her statement that she and others worked "to add dignity to Ireland." Some of the ways in which her plays contributed to this lofty goal are suggested in her remarks on the desired impact of her historical plays, comments which at the same time give telling clues to the nature of her own work:

> I had had from the beginning a vision of historical plays being sent by us through all the counties of Ireland. For to have a real success and to come into the life of the country, one must touch a real and eternal emotion, and history comes only next to religion in our country. And although the realism of our young writers is taking the place of fantasy and romance in the cities, I still hope to see a little season given up every year to plays on history and in sequence at the Abbey, and I think schools and colleges may ask to have them sent and played in their halls, as a part of the day's lesson.

One sees here much that finds dramatic expression in Lady Gregory's plays: the desire to have her work both spring from and appeal to the common people of Ireland; the intention to recover and respect Irish history, particularly as it is found in the stories and songs of the people rather than in the books of academics; the unapologetic combination of didacticism and entertainment; the wish to preserve romance, myth, and imagination in an increasingly skeptical, political, and materialistic age; the hope that Irish drama could be a natural part of the education and life of the Irish people.

These desires find expression in each of the three categories into which

Lady Gregory's plays are usually divided: comedy, tragedy and tragicomedy (including the historical plays), and plays of wonder and the supernatural. Lady Gregory's first plays were comedies. Like most of her drama, they were largely one-act works which combine a skillful command of structure, plot, and dialogue with genuine insight into human nature.

The recurring locale for Lady Gregory's comedies is the rural community of Cloon, a fictional version of the real town of Gort, near which Lady Gregory lived on her estate, Coole Park. The poor peasants and only slightly less impoverished townspeople with whom she mingled from her earliest childhood became her characters. She tried to capture not only their speech and mannerisms but also the quality of their lives that transcended their poverty and sometime clownishness. That quality had to do with their closeness to the spiritual heart of life, to myth and legend, to a sense of the past and of community, and to other dimensions of reality which Lady Gregory feared were disappearing from Ireland and from the world.

These characters are not idealized. They are often fools, simpletons, and ne'er-do-wells. Hers are not the heroic poor of some literature, yet beneath their gullibility, love of gossip, and simplemindedness is a closeness to the core of life which Lady Gregory admired and tried to capture. This accounts for the consistent sympathy for her comic creations. Lady Gregory laughed with, not at, her characters, and she did not set herself apart from the human foibles that they portray.

One of those foibles, both a weakness and a strength, is the Irish love of talk. This very human desire to share lives manifests itself comically (and sometimes tragically) in Lady Gregory's plays in an unquenchable thirst for gossip, a penchant for exaggeration and misrepresentation, a disposition to argument for its own sake, and an irrepressible urge to know their neighbor's business. This foible is at the heart of two of her most successful works, *Spreading the News* and *The Workhouse Ward*.

The skillfully structured *Spreading the News* turns on the eagerness of a man's neighbors to hear and believe the worst about him. Poor Bartley Fallon, a man convinced that if something bad is to happen it will happen to him, finds that his innocent attempt to do a good deed becomes the basis, through a series of outrageous misunderstandings of everyday speech, of the universally believed story that he has murdered his neighbor and plans to run off with the neighbor's wife. The humor of the situation grows exponentially as each new person who happens on the expanding story embraces it eagerly and adds to its enormity in passing it on. The comic tension builds even beyond where it seems it must be released as the appearance in good health of the supposedly murdered man only prompts the police to arrest him along with Bartley as they set off to find the body of the "real" victim, whom he is assumed to be impersonating.

The Workhouse Ward also turns on the Irish love of talk. Two old men in a poorhouse argue viciously with each other until the sister of one, whom he has not seen for five years, arrives to offer to take him into her home (for largely selfish reasons). He is eager to leave his pitiful surroundings until he learns that his roommate cannot come with him. After the sister leaves, the two old men resume their fighting, hurling objects as well as words at each other.

Both comedies illustrate Lady Gregory's ability to capture the rich dialect of the Irish peasant in all its color, cadence, and natural metaphor. One of the old men in *The Workhouse Ward* responds to the charge of the other in typical fashion: "To steal your eggs is it? Is that what you are saying now? . . . Isn't it a bad story for me to be wearing out my days beside you the same as a spancelled goat. Chained I am and tethered I am to a man that is ransacking his mind for lies!"

As with most of Lady Gregory's comedies, these two reveal her interest in something more than laughter. The condescending and uncomprehending attitude of the English magistrate in *Spreading the News* is a clear if commonplace indictment of Ireland's oppressor, and his repeated references to his earlier duties in the Andaman Islands indicate that Ireland too is simply another of England's exploited colonies. Both plays also reveal Lady Gregory's fondness for symbolism and near allegory. She later said she wanted the two old men in *The Workhouse Ward* to be seen as symbols of Ireland itself, suggesting that the Irish, as with any family, feel free to fight among themselves but do not desire the interference of outsiders, especially hypocritical ones whose apparent benevolence is only thinly disguised exploitation.

Although it was her comedies that were most popular and are most likely to last, Lady Gregory herself preferred to write tragedy. Her work in this form ranges from the highly condensed power of *The Gaol Gate* to one of her most ambitious works, the three-act *Grania*. One finds in the tragedies the clearest expression of the idealism, patriotism, and respect for the noble lost cause that are so much a part of Lady Gregory's own character. The tragedies generally center on people who have refused to be the passive pawns of circumstance, and who, in insisting on acting independently, come to grief against the harsh realities of life.

In *The Gaol Gate*, the man who has acted thus is dead before the play begins. Refusing to inform on his friends, he is hanged for a political murder he did not commit. The action of the play centers on the discovery of his fate by his wife and mother. As they approach the prison, unaware that he has been executed, they agonize over the rumors that he has in fact informed against his friends. His wife makes excuses for him in preparation for the possibility that it may be true, but his mother, with a longer memory of the suffering of the people, will not tolerate the idea of a son who is not faithful to his neighbors. On learning that her son has died for his loyalty, the mother breaks into a shocking celebration that reveals simultaneously the strength of the code of honor of the nationalist, the woman's own selfish desire to triumph over her son's false accusers, and the mental strain of a grief too great to bear; the latter is reminiscent of Maurya's break with reality at the end of Synge's *Riders to the Sea* (1903).

Given the nature of Irish history, it is fitting that Lady Gregory's historical plays are found among the tragedies and tragicomedies. This is true both of plays based on Ireland's mythological history, such as *Grania*, and of those based on more verifiable history, such as *The White Cockade*, an idiosyncratic account of James II and that infamous turning point for Ireland, the Battle of the Boyne. In *Grania*, a play which Lady Gregory never allowed to be produced during her lifetime, one finds in the treatment of the legendary love triangle between Grania, Diarmuid, and Finn perhaps her most sophisticated exploration of psychological motivation. As a strong woman whose determination to live intensely rather than conventionally leads her into a lifetime of turmoil to which she never succumbs, Grania perhaps contains more elements of Lady Gregory than she herself was ready to make public on the stage.

The third major category comprises the plays of wonder and the supernatural. Here Lady Gregory explored most directly that realm of folk spirituality she loved and valued so much. It was this sense of the spiritual (in both a figurative and literal sense), underlying and giving meaning to the physical, that Lady Gregory feared was disappearing from the modern world. Her plays of wonder and the supernatural, many of them written for children, portray that world where reality is multilayered and the physical world is suffused with beings of another dimension.

The Travelling Man is a case in point. Giving the Christian tradition of entertaining angels, or Christ, an Irish setting, Lady Gregory adapted a story told her by an old peasant woman about a destitute girl who had been directed by Christ to the house of her future husband, but who herself failed years later to show charity to Christ in the guise of a traveling beggar. In the play, the woman readies the house, as she does each year on the anniversary of her rescue, for the possibility that her Saviour from long ago, the King of the World, will return as He had promised. She is so absorbed in preparing only the finest for what she assumes will be His dignified and impressive return, that she turns furiously against the poor beggar who interrupts her preparations, and who, of course, is Christ Himself. In this play, as in many others, Lady Gregory demonstrated her interest in the deeper reality that infused the life of the Irish peasant with a significance that transcended physical deprivation.

This need for a spiritual sustenance to redeem the tragic physical and political burden that had long been Ireland's is the overarching theme of

Lady Gregory's plays. She valued, above all, the mythmakers of Ireland, whether the anonymous poets of ancient legend, or Raftery, the blind wandering poet of the early nineteenth century, or a political mythmaker such as Charles Parnell. She wanted the Irish Renaissance to be a revival of mythmakers, herself among them. The potential for all this rested, she believed, in the Irish people themselves, particularly the peasants, with their natural mythmaking reflected in their common stories, their conception of the world about them, and their very speech.

In their formal character, Lady Gregory's plays can most readily be understood, following critic Ann Saddlemyer, as classical treatments of largely Romantic subject matter. The plays demonstrate economy and balance, are very linear and simple in construction, and generally observe the classical unities of time, place, and action. The tendency to sameness and predictability in structure is relieved by her storyteller's gift for local color and suspense, and by her effective adaption to the stage of the Irish-English dialect that she called Kiltartan (after the district in which she and her peasant models lived).

Lady Gregory was not a great playwright. She was not considered so at the time, by herself or by others, and is only in recent years being rescued from the oblivion into which her reputation fell following her death. She deserves great respect, however, as one of a lesser rank who made a significant contribution at a crucial time and in so doing served both her art form and her country well.

Other major works

NONFICTION: *An Autobiography of Sir William Gregory*, 1894 (editor); *Mr. Gregory's Letter Box*, 1898 (editor); *Ideals in Ireland*, 1901 (editor); *Our Irish Theatre*, 1913; *Hugh Lane's Life and Achievement*, 1921; *A Case for the Return of Hugh Lane's Pictures to Dublin*, 1926; *Coole*, 1931; *Lady Gregory's Journals, 1916-1930*, 1946 (Lennox Robinson, editor).

FOLKLORE EDITIONS: *Cuchulain of Muirthemne*, 1902; *Poets and Dreamers*, 1903; *Gods and Fighting Men*, 1904; *A Book of Saints and Wonders*, 1907; *The Kiltartan History Book*, 1909; *The Kiltartan Wonder Book*, 1910; *The Kiltartan Poetry Book*, 1919; *Visions and Beliefs in the West of Ireland*, 1920 (2 volumes).

Bibliography

Adams, Hazard. *Lady Gregory.* Lewisburg, Pa.: Bucknell University Press, 1973. A brief, incisive introduction to the complete range of Lady Gregory's writings. The study opens with a biographical summary, following which the author examines, in turn, Lady Gregory's retelling of the ancient Irish sagas, her plays, and her folklore writings. Includes a chronology and a brief bibliography.

Coxhead, Elizabeth. *Lady Gregory: A Literary Portrait.* London: Martin Secker & Warburg, 1966. A revised and enlarged edition of a 1962 work that uses a biographical approach to concentrate on Lady Gregory's writings. Lady Gregory's so-called collaboration with other leading writers of the Irish Literary Revival, such as William Butler Yeats, John Millington Synge, and Douglas Hyde, are examined. The study also contains a checklist of Lady Gregory's writings.

Gregory, Lady Augusta. *Lady Gregory: Interviews and Recollections.* Edited by E. H. Mikhail. London: Macmillan, 1977. A selection of excerpts from memoirs, newspapers, and other contemporary sources that provide a composite portrait of Lady Gregory's public life. Among the accounts selected are those by Sean O'Casey, Yeats, George Moore, and Hallie Flanagan. Glimpses are also provided of Lady Gregory's celebrated home, Coole, and her estate, Coole Park.

Kohfeldt, Mary Lou. *Lady Gregory: The Woman Behind the Irish Renaissance.* New York: Atheneum, 1985. A narrative biography that provides information about Lady Gregory's early personal life as well as a thorough account of her involvement with the Irish Literary Revival. While the work's main emphasis is on the literary personalities among whom Lady Gregory spent the influential part of her life, use is also made of archival material.

Saddlemyer, Ann, and Colin Smythe, eds. *Lady Gregory: Fifty Years After.* Totowa, N.J.: Barnes & Noble Books, 1987. A substantial collection of essays that provide a comprehensive scholarly treatment of Lady Gregory's life and times. Her playwriting and involvement with the Abbey Theatre provide the volume with its central focus. Also included is a considerable amount of material pertinent to an evaluation of the overall cultural significance of Lady Gregory's career.

Daniel Taylor
(Updated by *George O'Brien*)

JOHN GUARE

Born: New York, New York; February 5, 1938

Principal drama

Universe, pr. 1949; *Theatre Girl*, pr. 1959; *The Toadstool Boy*, pr. 1960; *The Golden Cherub*, pr. 1962(?); *Did You Write My Name in the Snow?*, pr. 1962; *To Wally Pantoni, We Leave a Credenza*, pr. 1964; *The Loveliest Afternoon of the Year*, pr. 1966, pb. 1968; *Something I'll Tell You Tuesday*, pr. 1966, pb. 1968; *Muzeeka*, pr. 1967, pb. 1969 (one act); *Cop-Out*, pr. 1968, pb. 1969; *Home Fires*, pr. 1968, pb. 1969; *A Play by Brecht*, pr. 1969 (libretto; music by Leonard Bernstein; lyrics by Stephen Sondheim; based on *The Exception and the Rule* by Bertolt Brecht); *A Day for Surprises*, pr., pb. 1970; *The House of Blue Leaves*, pr., pb. 1971; *Two Gentlemen of Verona*, pr. 1971, pb. 1973 (with Mel Shapiro; music by Galt MacDermot; adaptation of William Shakespeare's play); *Marco Polo Sings a Solo*, pr. 1973, pb. 1977; *Optimism: Or, The Misadventures of Candide*, pr. 1973 (with Harold Stone, adapted from Voltaire's novel); *Rich and Famous*, pr. 1974, pb. 1977; *Landscape of the Body*, pr. 1977, pb. 1978; *Bosoms and Neglect*, pr. 1979, pb. 1980; *In Fireworks Lie Secret Codes*, pr. 1979, pb. 1981; *A New Me*, pr. 1981; *Gardenia*, pr., pb. 1982; *Lydie Breeze*, pr., pb. 1982; *Women and Water*, pr. 1984, pb. 1990; *The Talking Dog*, pr. 1986, pb. 1987 (one act; based on a story by Anton Chekhov); *Moon over Miami*, pr. 1988; *Six Degrees of Separation*, pr., pb. 1990; *Four Baboons Adoring the Sun*, pr. 1992, pb. 1993.

Other literary forms

John Guare's short teleplay *Kissing Sweet*, a satirical pastiche about pollution, appeared as part of New York's WNED-TV program *Foul!* on November 25, 1969. His 1971 screenplay for director Miloš Forman's *Taking Off* was actually a revision of a script by Forman and Jean-Claude Carrière. His screenplay *Atlantic City* (1981) was Guare's original work. The 1986 revival of *The House of Blue Leaves* resulted in a Public Broadcasting Service (PBS) televised version on the *Great Performances* series; similarly, the British Broadcasting Corporation (BBC) broadcast on radio a version of *Women and Water* in October of 1988.

Achievements

Although Guare has been recognized from early in his career as one of the United States' best playwrights Off-Broadway, the distinction of success on Broadway was late in coming. He has been the recipient of numerous awards and honors, among the early ones being Off-Broadway's Obie

Freydis to hide from him; Elliott becomes a woman. The changes are effected through technology, the agent of the submerged violence in this play: Elliott's sex-change surgery, Skippy's electronic impregnation, and the prosthesis of Larry Rockwell, for whom Diane buys marvelous electronic legs after she crushes his real legs in a car accident. Promising improvements, all these operations end up hurting and alienating.

Rich and Famous, as its title suggests, continues Guare's exploration of the manifold effect of fame on culture. Like *Marco Polo Sings a Solo*, it was first produced in a regional theater, then brought to New York in a revised form a few years later (1976). Like most Guare plays, *Rich and Famous* sports autobiographical elements: The protagonist, Bing Ringling, is a writer of autobiographical plays, 843 of them unproduced. Bing is elated to have his 844th attempt actually produced, and by the great Veronica Gulpp-Vestige, who has never had anything but hits. He is crestfallen, however, when Veronica tells him that she chose his play to be her first flop so that she could have a comeback—and flop it does.

The rest of the play is Bing's vain, surrealistic attempt to understand his failure by interviewing the myriad individuals in and out of show business (all played by one actor and one actress) connected with his career. His parents are supportive until they discover that their son is a flop: They, too, want only the "Rich and Famous," and when their son is neither, they look for a surrogate son in Bing's childhood friend Tybalt Dunleavy, now a successful actor. For Tybalt, too, fame is more important than life. When his agents convince him that suicide would increase his fame, he jumps to his death—off of a billboard image of himself.

Landscape of the Body was a departure for Guare in many ways, and an indication of the future of his drama. For one thing, Guare's odd balance of tragedy and farce, both lauded and deplored by critics, is tipped in favor of tragedy. The darkness that had been an undercurrent in previous plays is now the mainstream, with only eddies of comedy here and there. The violence is now central to the plot. The pivotal event is the murder and decapitation of the only son of the protagonist, Betty Yearn. The story is told as a flashback in the police interrogation room, where Betty is trying to convince Captain Marvin Holahan that she is not the murderer.

Joining in the flashback are the ghosts of other people in Betty's life who have recently died: her sister Rosalie, who sings hauntingly inappropriate songs by Guare; her boss, Raulito, who died in a prank played by Betty's son Bert; her childhood friend Mavis, who died of cancer. As in previous plays, the plot development in *Landscape of the Body* is alternately narrative and dramatic. This time, however, the alternating technique arises naturally out of the framing scene in the interrogation: Betty is *supposed* to be telling her story. Much more of the narration, however, goes to the ghost of Rosalie. The detachment from the play that results from a direct address of the audience is all the more appropriate for mirroring Rosalie's metaphysical detachment from the world of the living.

Bosoms and Neglect can be considered an updating or expansion of Guare's falling-in-love-by-chance plays such as *The Loveliest Afternoon of the Year* or *A Day for Surprises*. In *Bosoms and Neglect*, however, the plot has a more mature tone. The lyrical zaniness of young people in love develops an ugly side and is shown to be only a manifestation of an unstable personality. The lovers here are Scooper, a computer analyst, and Dierdre, who runs a mail-order used-book business. They meet because they both have the same psychiatrist. Like the characters of Guare's earlier romances, Dierdre spins ludicrous fantasies about her past and her family, and Scooper is involved with another woman when he begins the relationship. Instead of providing comedy, Dierdre's tales evoke sympathy for her need to lie; instead of heightening the drama, Scooper's infidelity is shown to be a symptom of his pervasive selfishness. The violence of the earlier plays had a whimsical side; here, it is too real, too integral a part of the characters to be slapstick. Dierdre and Scooper become vicious at the end of the first act: She stabs him, and he hits her.

Yet the background of this romance is seen in the prologue and the second act: Scooper's discovery that his mother, Henny, has been hiding cancer sores on her breast for more than two years. The "neglect" of the title is not only her neglect of cancer, allowing it to spread, but also Henny's and Scooper's mutual neglect of each other. Dierdre, it appears, has a similar relationship with her father, leading to her ridiculous stories about him, as well as her penchant for "neglected authors." Since neither Dierdre nor Scooper can deal with the other-gender parent, neither has success in relating to the opposite sex. The play ends with both of them going off together, leaving the audience purposely unsure whether that is a good idea.

The 1980's became for Guare the decade of his most ambitious project: a tetralogy of plays tracing the complex interrelationships of several characters in New England in the late nineteenth century. Known as the *Lydie Breeze* cycle, the plays were conceived as a unit, and three of the four were written and produced in the 1980's; *Women and Water*, *Gardenia*, and *Lydie Breeze*. The last to be written, though third in the series, *Bullfinch's Mythology*, was long in writing: "I haven't let that play go yet," Guare wrote in 1990.

The complex story begins on the eve of the American Civil War, in 1861, and ends in 1895 with a second generation exorcising the personal violence that came out of that time. The central character is Lydie Breeze. Daughter of a ship's captain whose white crew mutinied to protest his equal treatment of black crewmen, she, too, came to embody freedom, rejecting the traditional role of wife and mother (though she became both) and starting a commune near her ancestral home in Nantucket. In the more than thirty years spanned by the plays, she becomes a nurse and privateer in the Civil War, marries a dashing young socialist named Joshua Hickman, maintains a previous relationship with another war privateer named Dan Grady, and commits suicide years after her husband is sent to prison for killing Grady.

The *Lydie Breeze* plays are ambitious in more than just scope: They are Guare's first sustained attempt at realism and his first serious historical drama (*Home Fires* is historical but not too serious). After successfully capturing the language style of his generation in the 1960's and 1970's, Guare achieved equal success in imitating the rhythms and vocabulary of the second half of the nineteenth century. By turns poetic and conversational, the plays establish the form of poetic drama that Guare seems to have been seeking in his career. The infectious comedy is gone (and missed), but the *Lydie Breeze* plays by themselves earn for Guare a major place in contemporary drama.

Guare continued developing in new directions in the 1990's, while touching base with his traditional themes. In *Six Degrees of Separation*, the motif of fame drives the plot. The idolization of celebrity by the main characters, Flan and Ouisa Kittredge, allows a man named Paul to bilk money from them by convincing them that he is the son of famous actor Sidney Poitier. Paul's character (based on a real-life con artist who posed as "Paul Poitier" in the early 1980's) is fluid: In later scenes, he poses as Kittredge's neglected, illegitimate son.

In *Four Baboons Adoring the Sun*, Guare returns to one of his ideas in *Muzeeka*: an attempt to resurrect the Dionysian spirit of the ancient Etruscans. In doing so, he reaches for the roots of Western theater, for ancient Greek drama began in revels sacred to Dionysus. The god at the center of *Four Baboons Adoring the Sun* is Eros, who provides commentary and transitions through songs in Guare's familiar style. The main characters, Penny and Philip McKenzie, are newly married anthropologists on a dig in Sicily; each has several children, from previous marriages, whom they are trying to meld into a family. The eldest children, Penny's daughter and Philip's son, become closer than siblings, brought together sexually by Eros in an attempt at transcendence ending in the son's death.

Though reviewers, including those who had championed Guare's earlier work, were not kind to *Four Baboons Adoring the Sun*, and though it was not a commercial success, it served as a sign that Guare would not abandon his earlier zany style, with its sometimes uncomfortable combination of farce and tragedy, realism and fantasy. Furthermore, combining fantasy and myth added a new dimension to Guare's drama, maintaining his position as a major force in the American theater at the close of the twentieth century.

Other major works

SCREENPLAYS: *Taking Off*, 1971 (with Miloš Forman and Jean-Claude Carrière); *Atlantic City*, 1981.
TELEPLAY: *Kissing Sweet*, 1969.

Bibliography

Bernstein, Samuel J. *The Strands Entwined*. Boston: Northeastern University Press, 1980. A survey of contemporary drama, this volume includes an excellent chapter on *The House of Blue Leaves*, which also touches on Guare's other plays. A particularly helpful feature of this book is the summary of and quotation from major reviews.

Guare, John. "The Art of Theater IX." Interview by Anne Cattaneo. *The Paris Review* 34 (Winter, 1992): 68-103. A wide-ranging interview that provides valuable insights into Guare's working methods and his conception of theater. "I love the part of playwrighting [sic] that is a craft to be learned continually," Guare remarks, "The *-wright* part, like *shipwright* or *wheelwright* or *cartwright*." He deplores the dominance of naturalism in American drama: "How we *escape* naturalism always seems to be the key." Particularly interesting are Guare's comments on the journal he has kept for many years, a resource frequently mined for his plays.

_____. "Preface to the Plume Edition." In *The House of Blue Leaves and Two Other Plays*. New York: NAL Penguin, 1987. Intended as an introduction to *The House of Blue Leaves* after its successful revival in 1986, this essay by Guare also touches on *Bosoms and Neglect* and *Landscape of the Body*.

Markus, Thomas B. "John Guare." In *Contemporary Dramatists*, edited by James Vinson. 3d ed. New York: St. Martin's Press, 1982. This article offers a brief summary of Guare's career and works, with equally brief critical comments, and is a good starting point for the beginning student. Includes production information on all Guare's plays up to 1981.

Rose, Lloyd. "A New American Master." *The Atlantic* 253 (March, 1984): 120-124. Anticipating the production of a third *Lydie Breeze* play, this article not only reviews the previous two but also provides a succinct and illuminating retrospective on all Guare's previous works.

Savran, David. *In Their Own Words: Contemporary American Playwrights*. New York: Theatre Communications Group, 1988. This volume, consisting of a series of interviews with leading American playwrights, includes an insightful interview with Guare. In it, he discusses *The House of Blue Leaves* revival, the *Lydie Breeze* cycle of plays, and autobiographical elements in his plays.

John R. Holmes

A. R. GURNEY

Born: Buffalo, New York; November 1, 1930

Principal drama

Three People, pb. 1956; *Turn of the Century*, pb. 1958; *Love in Buffalo*, pr. 1958; *The Bridal Dinner*, pb. 1961, pr. 1962; *The Comeback*, pr. 1964, pb. 1966; *The Open Meeting*, pr. 1965, pb. 1968; *The Rape of Bunny Stuntz*, pr. 1966, pb. 1976; *The David Show*, pr. 1966, pb. 1968; *The Golden Fleece*, pb. 1967, pr. 1968; *The Problem*, pb. 1968, pr. 1969; *The Love Course*, pb. 1969, pr. 1970; *Scenes from American Life*, pr., pb. 1970; *The Old One-Two*, pb. 1971, pr. 1973; *Children*, pr., pb. 1974 (based on John Cheever's short story "Goodbye, My Brother"); *Who Killed Richard Cory?*, pr., pb. 1976; *The Middle Ages*, pr. 1977, pb. 1978; *The Wayside Motor Inn*, pr. 1977, pb. 1978; *The Golden Age*, pr. 1981, pb. 1984; *The Dining Room*, pr., pb. 1982; *What I Did Last Summer*, pr. 1982, pb. 1983; *The Perfect Party*, pr. 1985; *Another Antigone*, pr. 1986; *Sweet Sue*, pr. 1986; *The Cocktail Hour*, pr. 1988, pb. 1989; *Love Letters*, pr. 1988, pb. 1989; *The Old Boy*, pr. 1991; *The Snow Ball*, pr. 1991 (adapted from his novel).

Other literary forms

Albert Gurney has written for television and film as well as for the stage; in addition, he has published the novels *The Gospel According to Joe* (1974), *Entertaining Strangers* (1977), and *The Snow Ball* (1984).

Achievements

Gurney is often labeled the dramatist of the WASP (white Anglo-Saxon Protestant) enclave. He laughs at, ridicules, even satirizes WASPs but at the same time understands them and in some ways sympathizes with them. Being born and reared a WASP, he knows his material. His characters live and breathe. They vividly represent a passing culture. Their motivations are clearly depicted, along with their frustrations and emotional tensions. Never really damnable, they are bored, fenced in, stifled. They crave freedom and self-realization. Gurney's mastery of concise form reflects his classical bent. His plays are brief and to the point. They exemplify glories of artistic structure similar to those of the sonnet or sonata form. No excesses mar their impact. They abound with thrilling resonance of offstage events.

Gurney is in like manner a master of dramatic dialogue. The clichés and literary reflections of his characters are consonant with their status and emotions. Like Henrik Ibsen's plays, Gurney's are well wrought. Stage settings, props, and costumes are carefully detailed. Following in the tradition of such American innovators of drama as Eugene O'Neill, Arthur Miller, Tennessee

Williams, and Edward Albee, Gurney loosens space, opening up the stage. Hamlet-like, his characters address the audience, who at times even become participants in the play. The rueful humor of Gurney's highly polished, smoothly crafted plays makes for entertaining theater, despite the underlying pessimism of his work.

Biography

Albert Ramsdell Gurney, Jr., nicknamed "Pete," was born in Buffalo, New York, on November 1, 1930, the son of Albert Ransdell Gurney, Sr., a dealer in real estate and insurance, and Marion Spaulding Gurney. The young Gurney grew up in the exclusive suburbia he depicts in his plays. From St. Paul's school he went to Williams College, where he was graduated in 1952 with a B.A. degree in English literature. After graduation, he served three years (1952-1955) in the navy as an officer and then attended the Yale School of Drama, where he earned the M.F.A. degree in 1958. In 1984, he was awarded an honorary D.D.L. degree. In 1960, he began a long, distinguished career as teacher of literature and humanities at Massachusetts Institute of Technology (MIT).

In June, 1957, Gurney married Mary Forman Goodyear; they have four children: George, Amy, Evelyn, and Benjamin. They lived in Boston until 1983, when Gurney moved his family to New York to be near the theater, television, and publishers while he was on sabbatical from MIT. All this time he was concerned with the contrast between the values instilled in him as a youth and those of the world he was experiencing.

From early childhood, he had a passion for drama. He wrote his first play in kindergarten. His passion was fostered by his aunt, who liked to attend matinees but could find no one to go with her. It fell Gurney's lot to go, and he enjoyed every minute of the saturation. He also liked to listen to dramas on the radio and through them learned the importance of sound to drama, especially the spoken word. He developed an accurate ear for the kinds of things certain kinds of people say. While at Williams College, he began his writing career by creating college revues. In the Navy, as special services officer, he wrote and produced revues on a grander scale. Finally, in drama school at Yale, his playwriting career began in earnest, and he published his first drama, the one-act play *Three People*, in 1956.

While teaching he had little time to write, but he always had writing on his mind. As he lectured and read, ideas for drama would come to him; during summer vacations, he would write. Following this routine, he managed to publish more than fifteen plays between the late 1960's and the early 1980's.

Gurney has received many notable awards. In 1971, he was the recipient of the New York Drama Desk Award, and in 1977, the Rockefeller Playwright Award. In 1987, he received the Award of Merit from the American

Academy and Institute of Arts and Letters, and he won a Lucille Lortel Award in 1989.

The National Endowment for the Arts bestowed on him the Playwriting award for 1981-1982. He is a member of the Dramatists Guild (council) and the Writers Guild. His *Three People* was included in *The Best Short Plays of 1955-56; Turn of the Century* appeared in *The Best Short Plays of 1957-58; The Love Course* was selected for *The Best Short Plays of 1970;* and *The Open Meeting* was anthologized in *Best American Short Plays, 1991-1992.*

Gurney's first major success came in 1982 with *The Dining Room.* He continued to turn out commercially successful dramas throughout the 1980's, though critics found many of these plays to be somewhat slender.

In a brief prolific period near the decade's end, Gurney wrote *The Cocktail Hour, Love Letters, The Old Boy* and *The Snow Ball* (from his novel of 1984), all of which enjoyed success in New York as well as in the regional theater circuit. During a sabbatical from MIT, Gurney began adapting *Love Letters* for the screen.

Analysis

Albert Gurney crafts his plays about the people he knows—WASPs. The setting of most of his plays is New England suburbia. The stage is never crowded with actors or furniture; rather, Gurney's sets suggest moods and situations. Often the audience become participants, and offstage actions, sounds, and characters are central to the play. Though writing with classical constraint, he is innovative in staging. In several plays, multiple scenes go on simultaneously. Music is also an integral part of many of his plays; Gurney deftly employs songs for atmosphere and tone. His plays are notable for their structure and polish; not a word is wasted.

Gurney's first published play, *Three People*, written while he was in the Yale School of Drama, deals with his major theme: freedom. Two of the three characters—a university professor and his wife—are sympathetically presented in their struggle to accept the fact that their child is mentally deficient. They struggle magnificently with their broken dreams. The tragedy of this tightly knit one-act, one-scene play is that the third character, the baby, gets very little consideration as a person. Gurney manages the pathos of the situation without being morbid or sentimental. The baby is never onstage. He is talked about and tended to, but he is never seen. Much dialogue is exchanged from the offstage nursery as the wife talks to her husband from the nursery. The characters are honestly and sympathetically drawn, each encased in a tragic plight from which there is no release.

Gurney's first three-act play, *The Bridal Dinner*, is typical of his classical restraint of setting and time. All action takes place in one room where a bridal dinner is held during an evening and a morning in June. The characters are also typical of Gurney: high livers in high society, concerned with money and status, acting out their lives of boredom. Gurney masterfully presents a play-within-a-play wherein the bride and groom look into themselves and their future. WASPish standards are humorously, satirically, and delightfully paraded before the bridal party and the audience. The play is full of telling vignettes and repartee as the young couple feel alone, isolated, apart—all the links broken. They recognize the empty ritual of the bridal dinner for what it is and discard symbolic relics of the past. The problem, ever-present in Gurney plays, is what to do next. Are they strong enough to cast off the old armor and face up to a new and challenging future? Where can they go from here? They feel wobbly, so they decide to dance. This parody of marriage in a "rotten world" has enough reality to make the caricature believable. As the characters themselves admit, it smacks of Thornton Wilder, Luigi Pirandello, and "the worst from Broadway"; still, it is delightful and thought-provoking. As in most of Gurney's plays, literary references abound, and clichés and old saws are subversively employed. Finally, reflecting Gurney's patriotic theme in the 1960's, the marriage assumes global scope with a vision of world peace through the marriage of nations in love. Gurney's wit saves the play from melodrama by posing the question, "But can she cook?"

Gurney continued in this seriocomic vein in *The David Show*, where he sets the biblical story of the coronation of King David in a modern television studio. This one-set, one-scene, five-character parody is good fantasy. The characters are catchy, if a bit overdrawn. David is portrayed as a Madison Avenue type who uses people for his benefit; Bathsheba, with her cliché-studded dialogue, is a combination of charm and clowning. She comes across as a true philistine, while Jonathan is a playboy seeking only "the good life." Gurney's characterization is vivid and entertaining, and the dialogue sparkles. Clichés are cleverly sprinkled throughout; there is much witty wordplay. Undergirding the spoof is Gurney's usual seriousness. Problems of war, the good life, moral fiber, and ethnic groups are aired until in contrast with the surface hilarity, David is forced to face up to the reality that Goliath is David himself: his own rotten soul looming larger than life. Though not always successful onstage, this satire laced with wit and underlying seriousness is good reading.

Scenes from American Life, as the title indicates, is a montage depicting the upper-middle-class society that Gurney knows so well. Like most of his plays, this one lends itself to easy production. The set is attractive, simple, and functional, with the action flowing around a burnished baby-grand piano. To achieve this feeling of flow, no curtain is used and few blackouts; one scene blends naturally into the next, with the actors setting up the stage and carrying on and off their props and costumes. Music plays an integral part in this drama, establishing the time and tone of each scene. Props, accessories, and costumes also help anchor the date of a particular scene.

The play is set in Buffalo; the time fluctuates from the early 1930's of the opening scene to the mid-1980's. One character, Snoozer, serves to unify the diverse vignettes. From the opening scene of his christening to the final scene, when, inebriated, he participates in the burning of a canoe, the play depicts the passing of an old order of Americanism. Four male actors and four female actors are all that are required for producing these vignettes. These eight characters may act various roles in the various scenes, with the stipulation that the same actor and actress play the father and mother in the first and last scenes. In the intermittent scenes, sons play fathers and mothers play daughters so as to keep the play from appearing to be about only one or two families. A sense of virtuosity prevails. Here is a kaleido-scope of scenes from America.

Here again, Gurney satirizes upper-middle-class society. The characters are self-centered, modish, pampered, misguided, opinionated, and bored. They speak in clichés and find their world disappearing. Like an unmoored boat, they float along. At times the satire is more biting than in Gurney's earlier plays, but the message is clear and the entertainment delightful.

The language, typical of these characters, helps reveal their plight. A toast to the Father, the Son, and the best gin ever smuggled across Niagara River is followed by chatter about a pusher and manners at meals. The characters' names underscore the satire. Snoozer earns his name by sleeping through everything; Grace, Snoozer's godmother, to the tune of "The Star Spangled Banner" boozily proposes a one-word toast to Snoozer, "responsibility." From the Depression days of Franklin D. Roosevelt to an apocalyptic vision of a Fascist America in the 1980's (a decade in the future when the play was produced), Gurney depicts a vapid society that lacks any moral foundation.

In one of the drama's strongest scenes, a father takes his son, who is in trouble for draft evasion, out for a day's sailing. Quoting his own code of honor, which is anachronistic to the boy, the father tries to persuade his son to stand trial and go to prison. His son tells him off with one epithet. In another scene typical of Gurney's dramas, a Yale graduate dictates a letter to a classmate declaring that he will not contribute to the alumni animal fund; midway into the letter, however, he resorts to the usual clichés, sending his wife's regards and an enclosed check. Gurney's recurring theme of freedom and coercion is evident in a luncheon scene with a mother and daughter. The mother says that the daughter may do as she pleases, choosing between a coming-out party and a college education, yet in spite of the daughter's pro-tests in favor of an education, the mother ultimately decides on the party.

Not surprisingly, Gurney has often been compared to novelist and short-story writer John Cheever, the rueful chronicler of suburbia. Gurney's play *Children*, based on Cheever's story "Goodbye, My Brother," is another satire on the old gentry as they conduct themselves when they come face-to-face with the upheavals of the present. *Children* provides actors with a number of splendid roles, but, as in several other Gurney plays, the characters who motivate much of the action are never seen onstage. These include Pokey, scion of the genteel family at the center of the action, who stands ominously in the shadows offstage; his braless Jewish wife, who holds a doctoral degree; and their uninhibited child. Also unseen but significant to the action is the rich local builder, who once worked as a yard boy for the WASP family.

Set in a summer house on an island off the Northeast coast during a Fourth of July weekend in 1970, *Children* includes four characters who appear onstage: an affluent, attractive mother; her daughter, Barbara, a divorceé; her son, Randy; and his wife, Jane. Though a slight disruption threatens and slight violence erupts, the play ends in unrelieved, unenlightened stasis. The characters prefer withdrawing into their status quo, staying put, deeply embedded in the customary ground of their past. Here, as in *Scenes from American Life*, Gurney presents intelligent entertainment for a wide audience, offering an ironic portrait of a classic WASP family that is losing its identity in a changing America. Subversive forces are undermining what is eventually revealed as the hypocrisy of an entire way of life.

The Wayside Motor Inn, like *Scenes from American Life*, is composed of scenes that flow into each other. Five separate subplots take place simultaneously in one room of a suburban motor lodge outside Boston during the late afternoon and early evening of a spring day in the late 1970's. Like other Gurney plays, *The Wayside Motor Inn* deals with decadent Americans. Each of the five plots dramatizes the plight of WASP society, underscoring the characters' inability to escape to freedom. Such key words as "door," "escape," and "choose" hint at a choice, but the characters cannot bestir themselves to act decisively. They are not so much enthralled as self-entrapped. They and their language ring true to themselves and to life. They mirror, enlighten, and entertain.

A Willy Loman–type father confronts his Biff-like son to no avail, while a couple pondering divorce look out from the balcony at the world, then come back inside for a drink. A traveling salesman bitterly chafes under the domination of the computerized world, while a young college couple can make love only when hyped up by dope and a hot tub. Another couple snap at each other between fits of sympathy, contempt, and boredom. The television in the background amplifies and extends the drama of ordinary life. These ten ordinary people find themselves at the wayside of their lives, wondering which turn to take. Their difficulties and conflicts are commonplace, but Gurney succeeds in giving them resonance by presenting them side by side, simultaneously, onstage, thereby making the ordinary seem somehow extraordinary. The diverse scenes flow into an organic whole, commenting on the dark undercurrents of modern life.

Gurney scored his greatest hit with *The Dining Room*. In this play, the din-

ing room becomes a metaphor for the continuity of bourgeois values, challenged by the younger generation in the latter part of the twentieth century.
The space of the dining room itself—and the changing use of the space as
scenes from different time periods are going on simultaneously—dramatizes
the ways in which these values have been distorted. Through a humorously
poignant series of vignettes, Gurney dramatizes the changing role of the classical, formal dining room through the course of three generations of WASPs.
The changes are bittersweet—in some ways inevitable, but lamentable—a
combination of continuity and change. Like Gurney, the little boy in the play
views his great aunt's Waterford crystal finger bowls with fascination, seeing
in them the habits of a vanishing culture, a neurotic obsession with clean-
liness that is associated with the guilt of the last stages of capitalism. In
its combination of moral critique, satiric wit, and humane sympathy. *The
Dining Room* epitomizes Gurney's contribution to contemporary American
drama.

Gurney's work in the wake of *The Dining Room*'s success continued to
explore the suburban WASP life-style and its decay. *The Perfect Party* centers on the efforts of a fiftyish college professor to host a social event that
will rise to the level of great art; Gurney's Oscar Wilde-style repartee won
wide praise (the critic John Simon, however, demurred that the playwright
had written nothing more substantial than "a two-act play entirely in *New
Yorker*-caption cartoons.") In *Sweet Sue*, Gurney experimented with the simultaneous onstage use of two actors for each of the two central roles, but
the doubling of the characters struck most reviewers as little more than an
unnecessary special effect. *Another Antigone* is notable chiefly for its portrait of yet another middle-aged scholar, Henry Harper, an uncompromising
classics professor fighting a rearguard action against the decay of Western
civilization. An idealistic anachronism, Harper is a moving figure emblematic of many of Gurney's characters, doomed to endure the extinction of a
culture they cherish.

Gurney's 1993 comedy *Later Life* is again set in New England and centers on Austin, a divorced and WASPish Boston banker in his late middle
age who one night unexpectedly meets an old woman friend. The woman,
Ruth, whom Austin had met about thirty years before as a serviceman on
the Italian island of Capri, happens to be present at a cocktail party that
he attends. Ruth is still attractive and single, and the two almost spend the
night together. Austin, however, acting on a presentiment that something
bad is going to happen to him in the near future, kisses Ruth good-bye.

With the future now drawing nearer, the plot centers on the intriguing
premonition that Austin felt and on whether the couple will this time grab
the chance for happiness that is at their fingertips. *Later Life*, which is
partly inspired by Henry James's *The Beast in the Jungle* (1903), once more
demonstrates the playwright's talent for satirizing New England WASPs and

his ability to bring his audience not only to laugh at his characters but also to sympathize with them.

Other major works
NOVELS: *The Gospel According to Joe*, 1974; *Entertaining Strangers*, 1977; *The Snow Ball*, 1984.
SCREENPLAY: *The House of Mirth*, 1972.
TELEPLAY: *O Youth and Beauty*, 1980 (based on a short story by John Cheever).

Bibliography
Barnes, Clive. "Wasps, No Sting." *Post* (New York), May 6, 1991. The Playwrights Horizons, a tryout house for much good work in New York, presented *The Old Boy*, to the disdain of Barnes: "The whole cast goes flat out . . . but the play, for all its evident demonstration of skills, just goes flat." Good synopsis, however, of the play's themes and plot.

Gurney, A. R. "Here's to Playwright A. R. Gurney." Interview by Daryl H. Miller. *Daily News* (Los Angeles), April 13, 1990. The Canon Theatre's production of *Love Letters* coincided with previews of *The Cocktail Hour* at the Doolittle Theatre in Hollywood. This biographical interview brings both plays, and Gurney's successful *The Dining Room*, into perspective. *The Cocktail Hour* "examines the differences between the new and the old WASP," Gurney remarks.

Rizzo, Frank. "A Gentle Man, a Civil Man, and Theater's Favorite Playwright Wasp." *Courant* (Hartford, Conn.), February 10, 1991. Based on informal interviews during rehearsal breaks for the Hartford Stage Company's production of *The Snow Ball*, this piece discusses Gurney's involvement with the Dramatist Guild's dispute with the League of Resident Theatres (LORT), examines his WASP image, and reports his screenplay work for *Love Letters*.

Skinner, M. Scot. "Playwright Keeps It All So Civilized." *Arizona Daily Star* (Tucson), November 26, 1989. During previews of *The Cocktail Hour* at the Arizona Theatre Company, Gurney talks about newspaper criticism of his plays, the connection between *The Cocktail Hour* and the earlier *The Middle Ages*, and the cool British reception of his work: "They want to hear . . . Mamet and Shepard, something more anarchistic and outrageous."

Welsh, Anne Marie. "Things 'Snow Ball' for Gurney." *The San Diego Union*, May 5, 1991. When the Old Globe Theatre premiered *The Snow Ball*, Welsh caught Gurney in an expansive mood. Gurney discusses his busy schedule, especially his decision to write screenplays from his works, rather than sell them outright to Hollywood.

Winn, Steven. "'Letters' Notes Change in Star System." *San Francisco*

Examiner, December 17, 1989. Praising the "deft and graceful script" of *Love Letters*, Winn describes the performance (here with John Rubinstein and Stockard Channing) as "a beautifully tooled vehicle for pure acting," unlike the big "ensemble" shows of Broadway, such as *Phantom of the Opera* and *Cats.*

Helen H. Naugle
(Updated by *Thomas J. Taylor*)

WILLIS HALL

Born: Leeds, England; April 6, 1929

Principal drama

The Long and the Short and the Tall, pr. 1958, pb. 1959; *A Glimpse of the Sea and Last Day in Dreamland*, pr. 1959, pb. 1961; *Billy Liar*, pr., pb. 1960 (with Keith Waterhouse; adaptation of Waterhouse's novel); *Chin-Chin*, pr. 1960 (adaptation of François Billetdoux's play); *A Glimpse of the Sea: Three Short Plays*, pb. 1961 (includes *Last Day in Dreamland* and the teleplay *Return to the Sea*); *Celebration*, pr., pb. 1961 (with Waterhouse); *England, Our England*, pr. 1962, pb. 1964 (musical, with Waterhouse; music by Dudley Moore); *The Sponge Room*, pr. 1962, pb. 1963 (one act, with Waterhouse); *Squat Betty*, pr. 1962, pb. 1963 (one act, with Waterhouse); *Yer What?*, pr. 1962 (revue, with others; music by Lance Mulcahy); *Come Laughing Home*, pr. 1964 (with Waterhouse; originally as *They Called the Bastard Stephen*, pb. 1965); *Say Who You Are*, pr. 1965, pb. 1966 (with Waterhouse); *Joey, Joey*, pr. 1966 (musical, with Waterhouse; music by Ron Moody); *Whoops-a-Daisy*, pr. 1968, pb. 1978 (with Waterhouse); *Who's Who*, pr. 1971, pb. 1974 (with Waterhouse); *Saturday, Sunday, Monday*, pr. 1973, pb. 1974 (with Waterhouse; adaptation of Eduardo de Filippo's play); *The Card*, pr. 1973 (musical, with Waterhouse; music and lyrics by Tony Hatch and Jackie Trent; adaptation of Arnold Bennett's novel); *Walk On, Walk On*, pr. 1975, pb. 1976; *Filumena*, pr. 1977, pb. 1978 (with Waterhouse; adaptation of de Filippo's play); *The Wind in the Willows*, pr. 1984 (musical; music by Denis King; adaptation of Kenneth Grahame's story); *Treasure Island*, pr. 1984 (musical; music by King; adaptation of Robert Louis Stevenson's novel); *Lost Empires*, pr. 1985 (musical, with Waterhouse; music by King; adaptation of J. B. Priestley's novel); *The Water Babies*, pr. 1987 (adaptation of Charles Kingsley's novel); *Budgie*, pr. 1989 (musical, with Waterhouse).

Other literary forms

Willis Hall has become familiar to English audiences through a variety of media and genres. He and Keith Waterhouse, with whom he regularly collaborates, are highly regarded for their screenplays; some of their more notable efforts are *Whistle Down the Wind* (1961) and *Billy Liar* (1963). With Wolf Mankowitz, Hall has adapted for the screen *The Long and the Short and the Tall* (1961). Hall has also worked extensively in television, writing for programs such as *The Fuzz* and *Secret Army*, coauthoring half a dozen other series with Waterhouse, and writing a number of television plays, often for children. Hall has written musicals—*England, Our En-*

gland, with music by Dudley Moore, was reviewed with great praise—
books on sports, the text for a documentary, pantomimes, novels, award-
winning adaptations of foreign drama, and scripts for television series. The
sheer bulk of Hall's work and its rich variety testify to his artistic strength
and durability.

Achievements

It is difficult to find any single descriptive category or term under which
Hall's achievements as a dramatist will fit with accuracy. *The Long and the
Short and the Tall* (commissioned by the Oxford Theatre Group for the
Edinburgh Festival of 1958, and winner of the *Evening Standard* Drama
Award for Best Play in 1959), associated him with the new drama appear-
ing in the wake of John Osborne's *Look Back in Anger* (pr. 1956), and
comparisons have often been made between Hall's Private Bamforth and
Osborne's Jimmy Porter. At the same time, Hall's early collaborations with
Keith Waterhouse have been considered in terms of regional realism, as
authentic representations of life in the North of England. Plays such as
Billy Liar and *Celebration* reflect their authors' feel for the idiosyncrasies
of regional language, serving as reminders that Hall and Waterhouse often
draw with success upon their shared Yorkshire background. These descriptions are somewhat helpful; yet with plays such as *The Sponge Room* or
Squat Betty they plainly break down, since these are expressly nonrealistic
plays. Such descriptions also do not apply well to later plays, such as *Say
Who You Are* and *Who's Who*, which move away from realistic Northern
themes and introduce elements of farce.

If Hall's work resists any single-phrase summary, this in itself is perhaps
an indication of his achievement as a writer. He has directed his efforts
toward a wide variety of literary ventures in a variety of genres, each
demanding its own kind of discipline, and he has performed with some success in all of them. Further, his writings with Waterhouse represent the
foremost dramatic collaboration in England today, and both are admired
for their professional competence and consistency. In addition to their own
work, they have been successful adapters of two plays by Eduardo de
Filippo, *Saturday, Sunday, Monday*, which starred Sir Laurence Olivier and
Joan Plowright, and *Filumena*, which enjoyed a two-year run in England.
On his own, Hall has written and staged a successful adaptation of François Billetdoux's *Chin-Chin*. Hall, then, has written on his own and in
collaboration, for children and adults, for the stage and for the radio and
screen.

While praising Hall's versatility and the range of his work, reviewers and
critics have at times questioned its depth, and indeed it is difficult to avoid
feeling that some of the plays are too light or are perhaps dominated by an
adept dramatic technique that masks other and more profound limitations.

One might say simply that the aims of the plays are sometimes modest but that they achieve those aims with delightful flair and insight and offer genuine rewards for their readers.

Biography

Willis Hall was born on April 6, 1929, in Leeds, England, the son of Walter and Gladys Hall, and was educated in Leeds at the Cockburn High School. As a youth, he became friends with Keith Waterhouse, with whom he worked on a youth-club magazine and collaborated on a wide variety of projects for the stage, television, film, and radio. That friendship was interrupted in 1947 by Hall's five-year stint in the British Regular Army, during which time he served in the Far East as a radio playwright for Forces Radio. The military provided the background for Hall's first major stage success after his return to England, *The Long and the Short and the Tall*, which included Peter O'Toole and Robert Shaw in the cast. Hall resumed his friendship with Waterhouse, and together they adapted Waterhouse's novel *Billy Liar* for the stage in 1960, a highly successful production that established Albert Finney and Tom Courtenay, each of whom had a turn at the title role, as exceptionally gifted actors.

From that time on, Hall has occupied himself with a remarkably prolific and consistent literary life. With more than two dozen stage plays to his credit, some written with Keith Waterhouse, Hall has successfully experimented in more commercial forms as well. In addition to an active career writing and adapting for television, Hall has contributed *The A to Z of Soccer* (1970), the first of several "football" books in the 1970's. He has written much high-quality children's literature, including *Spooky Rhymes* (1987), *Dr. Jekyll and Mr. Hollins* (1988) and its companion piece *Henry Hollins and the Dinosaur* (1988), and *The Vampire's Holiday* (1991). He is an avid amateur magician and a member of several magic societies.

Analysis

Many of Willis Hall's plays (including those he coauthored with Keith Waterhouse) concern the discrepancy between the real world and the world that people invent for themselves. Again and again one comes upon figures who have created their own drama about the world and their own part in it, only to find that reality is an entirely different drama which proceeds indifferent to its characters. This theme lends itself to a variety of treatments: In a play such as *Billy Liar*, it can create a pathetic character whose imagination defends him from the world and masks his lack of courage, and who, when he sees beyond the veil of his own private fictions, knows that he is alone and insignificant; it can also produce the lighthearted farce of a play such as *Who's Who*, in which the distortions of reality create a complex series of mix-ups and mistaken identities culminating in comic disclosures, admissions, embarrassments, and reconciliations. In many of the plays, the imagination is a kind of obstacle to a character's growth, for it substitutes the satisfying (and effortless) vision of distant success and security for any real development.

The Long and the Short and the Tall, Hall's first major success, is a realistic war drama about a small unit of British soldiers in the Malayan jungle, set during the Japanese advance on Singapore in 1942. It seems at first to have little to do with the themes or subjects of Hall's subsequent work, but much of the play's conflict grows out of the soldiers' storybook ideas about war, their visions of themselves as heroic and moral men defending the side of good—visions that are denied by the reality of the war as it quickly closes in on them. This theme is suggested in an early scene. As the men rest in a deserted store-hut where nearly all of the action takes place, Private Evans sits reading the serial story in an issue of *Ladies Companion and Home* (his mother sends it to him each week), a romantic tale about a second lieutenant who must leave his girl behind when he is posted overseas. The story takes its hero through a variety of exciting and fantastic adventures, the last installment having left him in the hands of some Bedouins who have bound and suspended him above a roaring fire. Evans is puzzled, though, because the current issue finds the hero inexplicably escaped from the Bedouins and enjoying a honeymoon in Brighton with the girl he had left behind, who has waited faithfully for him. The events of the play contradict everything about this kind of story. The petulant Private Bamforth quickly questions the fidelity of Evans' own girl, taunting him with the suggestion that by now she has probably found a variety of substitutes for him. Bamforth also rejects the heroic ideal of the magazine story by describing his plans for a fast exit in the event of a Japanese invasion. Often, Bamforth's remarks have a disturbing edge of reality to them that deflates the *Ladies Companion and Home* image of war, and this is one reason that he is often at odds with his comrades, who still cling to that image. At the play's conclusion, that image is finally destroyed. Far from effecting any miraculous escape, the men are surrounded by the Japanese and killed, except for Corporal Johnstone, who is wounded and surrenders.

The romantic view of the war is attacked in the second act of the play by Sergeant Mitchem, in his speech on women. The context of that speech is important. The unit has captured a Japanese soldier, separated from his patrol, who has wandered into the hut, and in the initial struggle several of the men find that they are unable to kill the soldier when called upon to do so, largely because they realize for the first time that war involves killing men very much like themselves. "He's human at least," Private Macleish later explains to Mitchem after the captured soldier has shown them a picture of his family; for Mitchem, however, the point is obvious: "What do you want for your money? Dracula?" He is annoyed by the naïve assumptions about war that the men have brought with them to battle, and he lays the blame on "bints," on women, who give a man a heroic image of himself in uniform as he heads gallantly off to war. "Few weeks after that," Mitchem concludes, "he's on his back with his feet in the air and a hole as big as your fist in his belly. And he's nothing." This remark might just as easily have come from Bamforth's mouth, for he shares with Mitchem an unflinching sense of the truth that lies covered by the men's self-deceiving fictions.

The Long and the Short and the Tall examines the nature of war, the ways in which it changes the moral relations between men, the almost unbearable demands that it makes upon the human conscience. Hall demonstrated, in this play, his skill with dialogue and pace; he also demonstrated a subtlety in his handling of theme that often goes overlooked. At its heart, the play is a study of the fundamental human tendency to believe and act according to the stories we tell ourselves about life and the problems that arise when these stories are contradicted by the sometimes harsh facts of the world.

In Billy Fisher, the main character of *Billy Liar*, this storytelling tendency is taken to an extreme. Billy is a conscious fabricator who deceives his family, his friends, his employers, and perhaps most of all himself, for reasons so obscure that one is tempted to agree with his friend Arthur in saying that Billy's condition is pathological.

Billy Liar is set in the industrial North of England, and the play's action describes the affairs of the Fishers, a lower-middle-class household whose father, Geoffrey Fisher, has recently lifted his family above his own working-class background through his success as a garage owner. The father is plainly expecting something of the same initiative from Billy, his nineteen-year-old son, but as one meets him in the opening moments of the play, he seems an unlikely successor to his father. He has risen late from bed, and comes downstairs in his pajamas and an old raincoat. Billy is also pressured by his mother, Alice, and by her mother, Florence Boothroyd, who is living in the Fisher household and who habitually directs her remarks to the sideboard. The house is decorated in poor taste, and this contributes to the tense and oppressive atmosphere, in which Billy is almost constantly derided by his father for being lazy and also for mismanaging his affairs. In some sense, it is understandable that Billy retreats into the worlds created by his imagination.

Billy is in a bad position from the very start of the play. His job with Shadrack and Duxbury, Funeral Furnishers, is in jeopardy because he has been absent on days when he was supposed to have been at work (including the day on which the play takes place); he has also apparently been taking money from the firm, and he has failed to mail the company's

Christmas calendars as he has been asked to do. The calendars are crammed into a cupboard that Billy uses for his "private" things, but which he opens for Arthur when Arthur asks him about the calendars. In the cupboard, also, is a letter from Alice Fisher to the host of a radio show called "Housewives' Choice," asking him to play an old favorite for her. She concludes the letter with a postscript saying that her son also writes songs but that he probably will amount to little in that line because he lacks the training. She ends with a remark about the family being just "ordinary folk," and upon reading this Billy abruptly tosses the letter back into the cupboard, denying the limitations his mother seems to be putting on his abilities. One senses in this scene that Billy's stories and fantasies are part of an effort to escape from the mediocrity of his life, an attempt to be something more than ordinary. One soon discovers, however, that he lacks the courage to make any significant break with his environment and that his only escape is to change his world by inventing it anew in his own mind. When Billy threatens to make some practical effort to change his life by quitting his job, Arthur recognizes the characteristic bravado that masks a deeper fear of change and he scoffs at Billy's threat by saying that he has heard it before.

At first, Billy's fictions strike us as wonderfully absurd, as flashes of life in a generally dull existence. He has apparently told his parents and others that his friend Arthur's mother is pregnant—a lie—and this story has gotten back to her. When Arthur's mother threatens to come and see Mr. Fisher about it, Billy complains to Arthur that she cannot do that, because Billy has since told his parents that she has had a miscarriage to prevent his own mother from delivering a present for the baby. This is good fun, but it suggests other more serious problems that will confront Billy later. Often his stories have significant effects on people around him, and his insensitivity to the problems he may be causing for others reveals a certain self-centeredness.

Billy also seems unaware of the problems he may be causing for himself when the real world breaks through his artifice; his stories have a way of turning on him, as, for example, in his relationships with women. He is expecting a visit in the afternoon from Barbara, a girl to whom he is supposedly engaged and whom he plans to try to seduce by dropping some "passion pills" in her drink. He also needs to convince her to return her engagement ring to him for a time, since he needs it to give to another girl—Rita—to whom he is also engaged. The plan backfires when the passion pills prove worthless and Barbara refuses to give up the ring, and when Rita suddenly appears at the Fishers' door demanding her engagement ring there is an angry and embarrassing exchange among the saucy Rita, Barbara, and the astonished Mrs. Fisher. In this scene, Billy has lost control over events that his lies set in motion; he is clearly to blame for the situation, and any comic element in it is overshadowed by his apparent indifference to the feelings of others and his inability to foresee the consequences of his actions.

Billy nevertheless wins a measure of sympathy in the play's conclusion, where we see him as a frustrated dreamer whose imagination is marvelously agile but who is unable to get beyond that agility to the more profound courage required by genuine growth and maturity. In the third act, he meets an old girlfriend, Liz, a much more levelheaded and insightful girl than are the others, and with her Billy at least approaches self-recognition. By this time, his deceptions have landed him in a complicated mess that even involves a physical threat from Rita's brother, and Billy for the first time seems to sense that he has only himself to blame. His fantasies become visions of self-extinction, and he imagines going to London with Liz to lose himself, to become "invisible." Liz plainly shares his feelings, and they arrange to meet at the train station at midnight to run off to London. The vision, however, succumbs to reality, and the play closes with Billy's silent return to the house after his parents are in bed. Just why he cannot bring himself to go is left to the reader's judgment. Billy may realize that a life of invisibility is as much a lie as is the life that he is living now, or it may be that he is lured back by the prospect of manipulating the world, in the hope that someday it may match his own desires. In any case, the fertility of his imagination is inextricably tied to his frustrations and his lack of growth, and the play's ending leaves little hope for any immediate change in his life. The last line of the play, appropriately, is Rita's, shouting from outside the Fisher house that she will be back in the morning for her ring, her angry voice an emblem of the world outside Billy's imagination, demanding satisfaction.

Last Day in Dreamland is a shorter and less ambitious play than *Billy Liar*, but it illustrates how deftly Hall can establish atmosphere and mood and how, even in a short play, his attention to language can give solidity to half a dozen different characters. The play is related to *Billy Liar* in dealing with characters who seem trapped in an unsatisfying way of life, powerless to take the actions that might create some real change.

Like *Billy Liar*, too, *Last Day in Dreamland* is set in the North, but in a seaside town. It centers on the owner and operators of an amusement arcade during what turns out to be the last day of the season, though none of them knows this at the start. Still, they know that the end of the season is very near and that they will soon be out of work again until the next season comes around, and it is this atmosphere of melancholy anticipation that hangs over the action throughout, ironically heightened by the backdrop of festivity.

The play begins with a strong sense of pattern and repetition, a strong sense that each of these characters has been at his job for countless years, for they move about with a clear understanding of both their own responsibilities on the job and their relationships to the other workers. In his production notes to the play, Hall emphasizes its "group construction" and the importance of each actor's studying the parts of the others, because the mood of the action depends on a complete familiarity among the characters and on their displaying the sense that they have done all of this hundreds of times before. Tich Curtis' question about whether today is their last day is met with affectionate scorn by the manager and mechanic, Coppin, who has heard the same question for fourteen years from Curtis when the season comes to an end. Though he is young, George Fentrill is already noted by the others for claiming that each year at the arcade is his last, and each year Sailor Beeson seems to come closer to losing his job because of his tardiness. The repetition, the sameness, helps to give these figures identity, yet it is an identity that each of them might willingly forsake for a different life.

Coppin's history is representative of the others'. One of the younger members of the crew, Harry Lomax, announces that he plans to leave and try his hand at lorry driving after this season, and Coppin responds by recalling his own youthful dreams. He had, he says, planned to open his own shop, repairing wirelesses, but like the others, Coppin's dream simply slipped away. "So what happened?" Lomax asks, and Coppin's response gives us some insight into his sympathies with the men who work under him: "Nothing. That's all—nothing. For years I talked about having that shop—the summers I've spent in here dreaming about that joint don't bear thinking about. So one day, before you know where you are, you're fifty-two and all you've got is a screwdriver, a fistful of loose change and six months' work a year." In some ways, the speech recalls Sergeant Mitchem's in *The Long and the Short and the Tall*, because it breaks through the haze of dreams and fantasies to a level of reality that few of the characters are willing to face. In the end, Coppin's description of his own life proves to be true for the others; both Lomax and Fentrill hedge their plans to get away at the end of the season, and the audience is left with a strong sense—as in *Billy Liar*—that despite the dreams of the characters, a new season at the arcade will find all of them there, lacking the will to escape.

In other plays, Hall has allowed his form to echo these themes, so that while their characters avoid reality by arranging their own worlds of fantasy, the works become less realistic. This is true of plays such as *The Sponge Room* and *Squat Betty*, which, as Hall and Waterhouse observe in their production notes, depend on a "mood of suspended disbelief in which the audience will be ready to go along with the incongruities of the plot while at the same time appreciating the basic truths about loneliness, fear and fantasy." *The Sponge Room* in particular puts the audience in a situation somewhat analogous to that of the characters: The young "lovers" are also suspending their disbelief by pretending to plan an intimate rendezvous, though neither really wants to carry it out. "The play is about three dreamers," say the authors, "who will never have the courage to carry out their dreams—for the dreams themselves are a substitute for courage." The later farce, *Who's Who*, is another example of this nonrealistic treatment. The play's two acts are divided by a discussion between the two actors playing Bernard White and Timothy Black in which they agree to reenact the events of the first act with some important changes in the scenario. In some ways, the play represents a comic flip side to *Billy Liar* in that Black, like Billy, runs his life on deception, but without the kind of consequences suffered by Billy. It is a highly stylized, artificial play, but, as in *The Sponge Room*, the technique seems curiously appropriate here, applied as it is to a work about that fundamental human drive to orchestrate the events of one's life and re-create a world according to one's desires.

The Sponge Room and *Who's Who* demonstrate the diversity of Hall's talents, and his longevity and consistency as a writer must in some degree be attributed to his skill for finding new and varied methods of handling his subjects. Though they depart from the earlier, more conventional techniques, they share with Hall's other plays the insight and feeling that make his art worth experiencing. It is an art full of sympathy for its characters, perhaps because Hall sees in the human urge to dream, to fantasize, to imagine a world and to believe in it, an impulse very much like the dramatist's.

Other major works

NOVEL: *The Fuzz*, 1977 (novelization of television series).

NONFICTION: *The A to Z of Soccer*, 1970 (with Michael Parkinson); *The A to Z of Television*, 1971 (with Bob Monkhouse).

SCREENPLAYS: *The Long and the Short and the Tall*, 1961 (with Wolf Mankowitz); *Whistle Down the Wind*, 1961 (with Keith Waterhouse); *The Valiant*, 1962 (with Waterhouse); *A Kind of Loving*, 1963 (with Waterhouse); *Billy Liar*, 1963 (with Waterhouse); *West Eleven*, 1963 (with Waterhouse); *Man in the Middle*, 1963 (with Waterhouse); *Pretty Polly (A Matter of Innocence)*, 1967 (with Waterhouse); *Lock Up Your Daughters*, 1969 (with Waterhouse).

TELEPLAYS: *Air Mail from Cyprus*, 1958; *Return to the Sea*, 1960; *On the Night of the Murder*, 1962; *Happy Moorings*, 1963 (with Waterhouse); *How Many Angels*, 1964 (with Waterhouse); *That Was the Week That Was*, 1964-1965; *The Ticket*, 1969; *The Railwayman's New Clothes*, 1971; *The Villa Maroc*, 1972; *They Don't All Open Men's Boutiques*, 1972; *Song at Twilight*, 1973; *Friendly Encounter*, 1974; *The Piano-Smashers of the Golden Sun*, 1974; *Illegal Approach*, 1974; *Midgley*, 1975; *Match-Fit*, 1976 (from Brian

Glanville's story); *A Flash of Inspiration*, 1976; *Danedyke Mystery*, 1979 (from a work by Stephen Chance); *National Pelmet*, 1980; *Christmas Spirits*, 1981; *Stan's Last Game*, 1983; *Return of the Antelope*, 1986 (with Waterhouse).

CHILDREN'S LITERATURE: *The Play of the Royal Astrologers*, 1958 (play); *The Gentle Knight*, 1964 (radio play); *Kidnapped at Christmas*, 1975 (play); *Christmas Crackers*, 1976 (play); *A Right Christmas Caper*, 1977 (play); *Worzel Gummidge*, 1980 (play, with Waterhouse); *The Inflatable Shop*, 1984 (novel); *Dragon Days*, 1984 (novel); *The Return of the Antelope*, 1985; *Spooky Rhymes*, 1987; *The Antelope Company at Large*, 1987; *Dr. Jekyll and Mr. Hollins*, 1988; *Henry Hollins and the Dinosaur*, 1988; *The Vampire's Holiday*, 1991.

Bibliography

Elsom, John. "Willis Hall." In *Contemporary Dramatists*, edited by D. L. Kirkpatrick. 4th ed. New York: St. James Press, 1988. Elsom discusses Hall's and Keith Waterhouse's common Yorkshire background (being born in the same year and same city), their eventual collaboration, their professionalism, and their writing styles. Contains a lengthy discussion of *Celebration.*

Lesniak, James G., ed. "Willis Hall." In *Contemporary Authors.* Vol. 36. Detroit: Gale Research, 1992. This entry in the New Revision series provides some biographical information and separately lists Hall's writings, his published plays (without the collaboration of Keith Waterhouse), those published with Waterhouse's collaboration, and his unpublished plays, all in chronological order. Also lists his screenplays, teleplays, radio plays, and edited work, with dates of appearances.

Matlaw, Myron. *Modern World Drama.* New York: E. P. Dutton, 1972. Although Hall has written a large number of plays, screenplays, teleplays, and children's books, little has been published about him and his work. This short entry mentions some of his plays and the influence of John Osborne on his work, and briefly traces his switch to light comedy.

Taylor, John Russell. *The Angry Theatre: New British Drama.* Rev. ed. New York: Hill & Wang, 1969. In an epilogue, Taylor puts Hall among the "old-style professionals to emerge in the middle of the new drama," a category that includes Robert Bolt. Discusses *The Long and the Short and the Tall*, *Last Day in Dreamland*, and *Billy Liar.* Praises some television work, notably *That Was the Week That Was.*

The Writers Directory, 1980-1982. New York: St. Martin's Press, 1979. Contains a brief entry that provides a chronological list of Hall's publications.

Steven Reese
(Updated by *Thomas J. Taylor*)

LORRAINE HANSBERRY

Born: Chicago, Illinois; May 19, 1930
Died: New York, New York; January 12, 1965

Principal drama

A Raisin in the Sun, pr., pb. 1959; *The Sign in Sidney Brustein's Window*, pr. 1964, pb. 1965; *To Be Young, Gifted, and Black*, pr. 1969, pb. 1971; *Les Blancs*, pr. 1970, pb. 1972 (edited by Robert Nemiroff); *The Drinking Gourd*, pb. 1972 (edited by Nemiroff); *What Use Are Flowers?*, pb. 1972 (edited by Nemiroff); *Les Blancs: The Collected Last Plays of Lorraine Hansberry*, pb. 1972 (includes *Les Blancs*, *The Drinking Gourd*, and *What Use Are Flowers?*).

Other literary forms

As a result of her involvement in the civil rights movement, Lorraine Hansberry wrote the narrative for *The Movement: Documentary of a Struggle for Equality* (1964), a book of photographs, for the Student Nonviolent Coordinating Committee (SNCC). Because she died at such a young age, Hansberry left much of her work unpublished, but her husband, Robert Nemiroff, the literary executor of her estate, edited and submitted some of it for publication and, in the case of *Les Blancs*, production. In addition, he arranged excerpts from Hansberry's various writings into a seven-and-a-half-hour radio program entitled *To Be Young, Gifted, and Black*, which was broadcast on radio station WBAI in 1967. This program was later adapted for the stage, opening at the Cherry Lane Theatre in New York on January 2, 1969, and becoming the longest running production of the 1968-1969 season. Many readers know Hansberry through the anthology of her writings edited by Nemiroff, *To Be Young, Gifted, and Black: Lorraine Hansberry in Her Own Words* (1969), a book which has enjoyed very wide circulation.

Achievements

Hansberry's career was very brief, only two of her plays being produced in her lifetime, yet she recorded some very impressive theatrical achievements. She was only twenty-nine when *A Raisin in the Sun* appeared on Broadway, and its great success earned for her recognition that continues to this day. When *A Raisin in the Sun* was voted best play of the year by the New York Drama Critics Circle, she became the first black person as well as the youngest person to win the award. In 1973, a musical adapted from *A Raisin in the Sun*, entitled *Raisin* (with libretto by Nemiroff), won a Tony Award as best musical of the year (1974). She was respected and befriended by such figures as Paul Robeson and James Baldwin, and she helped in an active way to further the work of the civil rights movement. Though her later work has received far less recognition than her first play, *A Raisin in the Sun* continues to enjoy a broad popularity.

Biography

Lorraine Vivian Hansberry was born on May 19, 1930, in the South Side of Chicago, the black section of that segregated city. Her parents, Carl and Mamie Hansberry, were well-off; he was a United States deputy marshal for a time and then opened a successful real estate business in Chicago. Despite their affluence, they were forced by local covenants to live in the poor South Side. When Hansberry was eight years old, her father decided to test the legality of those covenants by buying a home in a white section of the city. Hansberry later recalled one incident which occurred shortly after the family's move to a white neighborhood: A mob gathered outside their home, and a brick, thrown through a window, barely missed her before embedding itself in a wall.

In order to stay in the house, to which he was not given clear title, Carl Hansberry instituted a civil rights suit against such restrictive covenants. When he lost in Illinois courts, he and the N.A.A.C.P. carried an appeal to the United States Supreme Court, which, on November 12, 1940, reversed the ruling of the Illinois Supreme Court and declared the local covenants illegal. Thus, Lorraine had a consciousness of the need to struggle for civil rights from a very young age. Her father, despite his legal victory, grew increasingly pessimistic about the prospects for change in the racial situation, and he finally decided to leave the country and retire in Mexico City. He had a stroke on a visit to Mexico, however, and died in 1945.

Hansberry's uncle, William Leo Hansberry, was also an important influence on her. A scholar of African history who taught at Howard University, his pupils included Nnamdi Azikewe, the first president of Nigeria, and Kwame Nkrumah of Ghana. Indeed, William Leo Hansberry was such a significant figure in African studies that in 1963, the University of Nigeria named its College of African Studies at Nsakka after him. While Lorraine was growing up, she was frequently exposed to the perspectives of young African students who were invited to family dinners, and this exposure helped to shape many of the attitudes later found in her plays.

Lorraine, the youngest of four children, was encouraged to excel and was expected to succeed. After attending Englewood High School, she enrolled in the University of Wisconsin as a journalism student. She did not fare very well at the university, however, and felt restricted by the many requirements of the school. After two years, she left Wisconsin and enrolled in the New School for Social Research in New York, where she was permitted greater leeway in choosing courses.

Once in New York, Hansberry began writing for several periodicals, including *Freedom*, Paul Robeson's monthly magazine. She quickly became a reporter and then an associate editor of the magazine. In New York, she met Robert Nemiroff, then a student at New York University, and they were married in June of 1953. By this time, Hansberry had decided to be a writer, and while the bulk of her energies went into writing, she did hold a variety of jobs during the next few years. When Nemiroff acquired a good position with music publisher Phil Rose, she quit working and began writing full-time.

Hansberry's first completed work was *A Raisin in the Sun*, which, after an initial struggle for financial backing, opened on Broadway at the Ethel Barrymore Theatre on March 11, 1959. The play, starring Sidney Poitier, Ruby Dee, Louis Gossett, Jr., and Claudia McNeil, was an enormous success, running for 530 performances, and in May, winning the New York Drama Critics Circle Award.

Soon thereafter, Hansberry and Nemiroff moved from their apartment in Greenwich Village to a home in Croton, New York, in order for Hansberry to have more privacy for her work. At the same time, her success made her a public figure, and she used her newfound fame to champion the causes of civil rights and African independence. She made important speeches in a variety of places and once confronted then Attorney General Robert Kennedy on the issue of civil rights.

It was not until 1964 that Hansberry produced another play, *The Sign in Sidney Brustein's Window*, and by that time she was seriously ill. The play opened at the Longacre Theatre on October 15, 1964, to generally good but unenthusiastic reviews, and Nemiroff had to struggle to keep it open, a number of times placing advertisements in newspapers asking for support, accepting financial support from friends and associates, and once accepting the proceeds from a spontaneous collection taken up by the audience when it was announced that without additional funds, the play would have to close. On this uncertain financial basis, production of the play continued from week to week.

Hansberry's life continued in much the same way. While the play struggled, she was in a hospital bed dying of cancer. She once lapsed into a coma and was not expected to recover, but for a brief time she did rally, recovering all of her faculties. Her strength gave out, however, and on January 12, 1965, she died. That night, the Longacre Theatre closed its doors in mourning, and *The Sign in Sidney Brustein's Window* closed after 101 performances.

Analysis

Lorraine Hansberry claimed Sean O'Casey as one of the earliest and strongest influences on her work and cited his realistic portrayal of character as the source of strength in his plays. In *To Be Young, Gifted, and*

Black, she praised O'Casey for describing

> the human personality in its totality. O'Casey never fools you about the Irish . . . the
> Irish drunkard, the Irish braggart, the Irish liar . . . and the genuine heroism which
> must naturally emerge when you tell the truth about people. This . . . is the height of
> artistic perception . . . because when you believe people so completely . . . then you
> also believe them in their moments of heroic assertion: you don't doubt them.

In her three most significant plays, *A Raisin in the Sun*, *The Sign in Sidney Brustein's Window*, and *Les Blancs*, one can see Hansberry's devotion to the principles that she valued in O'Casey. First, she espoused realistic drama; second, she believed that the ordinary individual has a capacity for heroism; finally, she believed that drama should reveal to the audience its own humanity and its own capacity for heroism.

Hansberry claimed that her work was realistic rather than naturalistic, explaining that "naturalism tends to take the world as it is and say: this is what it is . . . it is 'true' because we see it every day in life . . . you simply photograph the garbage can. But in realism . . . the artist . . . imposes . . . not only what *is* but what is *possible* . . . because that is part of reality too." For Hansberry, then, realism involved more than a photographic faithfulness to the real world. She sought to deliver a universal message but realized that "in order to create the universal you must pay very great attention to the specific. Universality . . . emerges from truthful identity of what is." This concern for realism was present from the very beginning of Hansberry's career and persists in her work, though she did occasionally depart from it in small ways, such as in the symbolic rather than literal presence of "The Woman" in *Les Blancs*, that character symbolizing the spirit of liberty and freedom which lives inside man.

Essential to Hansberry's vision of reality was the belief that the average person has within him or her the capacity for heroism. Hansberry believed that each human being is not only "dramatically interesting" but also a "creature of stature," and this is one of the most compelling features of her drama. Like O'Casey, Hansberry paints a full picture of each character, complete with flaws and weaknesses, yet she does not permit these flaws to hide the characters' "stature." Perhaps she expressed this idea best in *A Raisin in the Sun*, when Lena Younger berates her daughter Beneatha for condemning her brother, Walter Lee. Lena says, "When you start measuring somebody, measure him right, child, measure him right. Make sure you done taken into account what hills and valleys he come through before he got to wherever he is." For Hansberry, each character's life is marked by suffering, struggle, and weakness, yet in each case, the final word has not been written. Just as Beneatha's brother can rise from his degradation, just as Sidney (in *The Sign in Sidney Brustein's Window*) can overcome his ennui, so each of her characters possesses not only a story already written but also possibilities for growth, accomplishment, heroism. Hansberry permits no stereotypes in her drama, opting instead for characters that present a mixture of positive and negative forces.

Hansberry's realistic style and her stress on the possibilities for heroism within each of her characters have everything to do with the purpose that she saw in drama. As James Baldwin observed, Hansberry made no bones about asserting that art has a purpose, that it contained "the energy that could change things." In *A Raisin in the Sun*, Hansberry describes a poor black family living in Chicago's South Side, her own childhood home, and through her realistic portrayal of their financial, emotional, and racial struggles, as well as in her depiction of their ability to prevail, she offers her audience a model of hope and perseverance, and shows the commonality of human aspirations, regardless of color. In *The Sign in Sidney Brustein's Window*, she takes as her subject the disillusioned liberal Sidney Brustein, who has lost faith in the possibility of creating a better world. After all of his disillusionment, he realizes that despair is not an answer, that the only answer is hope despite all odds and logic, that change depends upon his commitment to it. So too, in *Les Blancs*, Hansberry gives her audience a character, Tshembe Matoseh, who has a comfortable, pleasant, secure life and who seeks to avoid commitment to the cause of African independence, though he believes in the justness of that cause. He learns that change comes about only through commitment, and that such commitment often means the abandonment of personal comfort on behalf of something larger.

Hansberry's earliest play, *A Raisin in the Sun*, is also her finest and most successful work. The play is set in the South Side of Chicago, Hansberry's childhood home, and focuses on the events that transpire during a few days in the life of the Younger family, a family headed by Lena Younger, the mother; the other family members are her daughter, Beneatha, her son, Walter Lee, and his wife, Ruth, and son, Travis. The play focuses on the problem of what the family should do with ten thousand dollars that Lena receives as an insurance payment after the death of her husband, Walter Lee, Sr. The money seems a blessing at first, but the family is torn, disagreeing on how the money should be spent.

The play's title is taken from Langston Hughes's poem "Harlem" and calls attention to the dreams of the various characters, and the effects of having those dreams deferred. The set itself, fully realistic, emphasizes this theme from the first moment of the play. The furniture, once chosen with care, has been well cared for, yet it is drab, undistinguished, worn out from long years of service. The late Walter Lee, Sr., was a man of dreams, but he could never catch up with them, and he died, exhausted and wasted, worn out like the furniture, at an early age. His family is threatened with the same fate, but his insurance money holds out hope for the fulfillment of dreams. Lena and Walter Lee, however, disagree about what to do with the money. Walter Lee hates his job as a chauffeur and plans to become his own man by opening a liquor store with some friends, but Lena instead makes a down payment on a house with one-third of the money, and plans to use another third to finance Beneatha's medical studies. After the two argue, Lena realizes that she has not permitted her son to be a man and has stifled him, just as the rest of the world has. In order to make up for the past, she entrusts him with the remaining two-thirds of the money, directing him to take Beneatha's portion and put it into a savings account for her, using the final third as he sees fit. Walter Lee, however, invests all of the money in a foolhardy scheme and discovers shortly thereafter that one of his partners has bilked him of the money.

The house that Lena has purchased is in a white neighborhood, and a Mr. Lindner has approached the Youngers, offering to buy back the house—at a profit to the Youngers—because the members of the community do not want blacks living there. Walter Lee at first scornfully refuses Lindner's offer, but once he has lost all the money he is desperate to recoup his losses and calls Lindner, willing to sell the house. The family is horrified at how low Walter has sunk, but when Beneatha rejects him, claiming there is "nothing left to love" in him, Lena reminds her that "There is always something to love. And if you ain't learned that, you ain't learned nothing." Lena asks Beneatha, "You give him up for me? You wrote his epitaph too—like the rest of the world? Well, who give you the privilege?" The epitaph is indeed premature, for when Lindner arrives and Walter is forced to speak in his son's presence, Walter gains heroic stature by rejecting the offer, telling Lindner in simple, direct terms that they will move into their house because his father "earned it." It is a moment during which Walter comes into manhood, and if it has taken him a long while to do so, the moment is all the richer in heroism.

The theme of heroism found in an unlikely place is perhaps best conveyed through the symbol of Lena's plant. Throughout the play, Lena has tended a small, sickly plant that clings tenaciously to life despite the lack of sunlight in the apartment. Its environment is harsh, unfavorable, yet it clings to life anyway—somewhat like Walter, whose life should long ago have extinguished any trace of heroism in him. Hansberry gives her audience a message of hope.

Hansberry also reminds her audience of the common needs and aspirations of all humanity, and she does so without oversimplification. None of the characters in the play is a simple type, not even Lindner, who might easily have been presented as an incarnation of evil. Instead, Lindner is conveyed as a human being. When asked why she portrayed Lindner in this manner, Hansberry replied "I have treated Mr. Lindner as a human being merely because he is one; that does not make the meaning of his call less malignant, less sick." Here is where Hansberry calls her audience to action. She reminds the audience of what it is to be human and enjoins them to respect the dignity of all their fellows.

An interesting subtheme in the play, one that would be developed far more fully later in *Les Blancs*, is introduced by Joseph Asagai, an African student with a romantic interest in Beneatha. Some of the most moving speeches in the play belong to Asagai, and when Beneatha temporarily loses hope after Walter has lost all the money, Asagai reminds her of her ideals and the need to keep working toward improvement in the future. When Beneatha asks where it will all end, Asagai rejects the question, asking, "End? Who even spoke of an end? To life? To living?" Beneatha does not fully understand Asagai's argument at the time, but its meaning must be clear enough to the audience, who will see at the end of the play that Walter's victory is not an end, but rather one small, glorious advance. There will be other trials, other problems to overcome, but, as Asagai says, any other problem "will be the problem of another time."

Hansberry's second play, *The Sign in Sidney Brustein's Window*, never matched the success of her first, but it, too, uses a realistic format and was drawn from her own life. Instead of South Side Chicago, it is set in Greenwich Village, Hansberry's home during the early years of her marriage with Robert Nemiroff, and the central character is one who must have resembled many of Hansberry's friends. He is Sidney Brustein, a lapsed liberal, an intellectual, a former insurgent who has lost faith in his ability to bring about constructive change. As the play opens, Sidney moves from one project, a nightclub that failed, to another, the publication of a local newspaper, which Sidney insists will be apolitical. His motto at the opening of the play is "Presume no commitment, disavow all engagement, mock all great expectations. And above all else, avoid the impulse to correct." Sidney's past efforts have failed, and his lost faith is much the same as Beneatha's in *A Raisin in the Sun*.

The surrounding environment goes a long way toward explaining Sidney's cynicism. His wife, Iris, has been in psychoanalysis for two years, and her troubled soul threatens their marriage. Iris' older sister, Mavis, is anti-Semitic, and her other sister, Gloria, is a high-class call girl who masquerades as a model. Sidney's upstairs neighbor, David Ragin, is a homosexual playwright whose plays invariably assert "the isolation of the soul of man, the alienation of the human spirit, the desolation of all love, all possible communication." Organized crime controls politics in the neighborhood, and drug addiction is rampant; one of Sidney's employees at the defunct nightclub, Sal Peretti, died of addiction at the age of seventeen, despite Sidney's efforts to help him. Faced with these grim realities, Sidney longs to live in a high, wooded land, far from civilization, in a simpler, easier world.

The resultant atmosphere is one of disillusionment as characters lash out in anger while trying to protect themselves from pain. One of the targets of the intellectual barbs of the group is Mavis, an average, settled housewife who fusses over Iris and pretends to no intellectual stature. When the wit gets too pointed, though, Mavis cuts through the verbiage with a telling remark: "I was taught to believe that creativity and great intelligence ought to make one expansive and understanding. That if ordinary people . . . could not expect understanding from artists . . . then where indeed might we look for it at all." Only Sidney is moved by this remark; he is unable to maintain the pretense of cynicism, admitting, "I *care*. I care about it all. It takes too much energy *not* to care." Thus, Sidney lets himself be drawn into another cause, the election of Wally O'Hara to public office as an independent, someone who will oppose the drug culture and gangster rule of the neighborhood.

As Sidney throws himself into this new cause, he uses his newspaper to further the campaign, and even puts a sign, "Vote for Wally O'Hara," in his window. Idealism seems to have won out, and indeed Wally wins the election, but Sidney is put to a severe test as Iris seems about to leave him, and it is discovered that Wally is on the payroll of the gangsters. Added to all of this is Gloria's suicide in Sidney's bathroom. Her death brings Sidney to a moment of crisis, and when Wally O'Hara comes into the room to offer condolences and to warn against any hasty actions, Sidney achieves a clarity of vision that reveals his heroism. Sidney says, "*This world*—this swirling, seething madness—which you ask us to accept, to maintain—has done this . . . maimed my friends . . . emptied these rooms and my very bed. And now it has taken my sister. *This* world. Therefore, to live, to breathe—I shall *have* to fight it." When Wally accuses him of being a fool, he agrees: "A fool who believes that death is waste and love is sweet and that the earth turns and that men change every day . . . and that people wanna be better than they are . . . and that I hurt terribly today, and that hurt is desperation and desperation is energy and energy can *move* things." In this moment, Sidney learns true commitment and his responsibility to make the world what it ought to be. The play closes with Iris and Sidney holding each other on the couch, Iris crying in pain, with Sidney enjoining her: "Yes . . . weep now, darling, weep. Let us both weep. That is the first thing: to let ourselves feel again . . . then, tomorrow, we shall make something strong of this sorrow."

As the curtain closes, the audience can scarcely fail to apply these closing words to themselves. Only if they permit themselves to feel the pain, Hansberry claims, will it be possible to do anything to ease that pain in the future. James Baldwin, referring to the play, said, "it is about nothing less than our responsibility to ourselves and to others," a consistent theme in Hansberry's drama. Again and again, she reminds the audience of their responsibility to act in behalf of a better future, and the basis for this message is her affirmative vision. Robert Nemiroff says that she found reason to hope "in the most unlikely place of all: the lives most of us lead today. Precisely, in short, where *we* cannot find it. It was the mark of her respect for us all."

Hansberry's last play of significance, *Les Blancs*, was not in finished form when she died and did not open on stage until November 15, 1970, at the Longacre Theatre, years after her death. Nemiroff completed and edited the text, though it is to a very large degree Hansberry's play. It was her least successful play, running for only forty-seven performances, but it did spark considerable controversy, garnering both extravagant praise and passionate denunciation. Some attacked the play as advocating racial warfare, while others claimed it was the best play of the year, incisive and compassionate. The play is set not in a locale drawn from Hansberry's own experience but in a place that long held her interest: Africa.

Les Blancs is Hansberry's most complex and difficult play. It takes as its subject white colonialism and various possible responses to it. At the center of the play are the members of the Matoseh family: Abioseh Senior, the father, who is not actually part of the play, having died before it opens, but who is important in that his whole life defined the various responses possible (acceptance, attempts at lawful change, rebellion); in addition, there are his sons, Abioseh, Eric, and, most important, Tshembe. Hansberry attempts to shed some light on the movement for African independence by showing the relationships of the Matosehs to the whites living in Africa. The whites of importance are Major Rice, the military commander of the colony; Charlie Morris, a reporter; Madame Neilsen, and her husband, Dr. Neilsen, a character never appearing on stage but one responsible for the presence of all the others.

Dr. Neilsen has for many years run a makeshift hospital in the jungle; he is cut in the mold of Albert Schweitzer, for he has dedicated his life to tending the medical ills of the natives. It is because of him that all of the other doctors are there and because of him too that Charlie Morris is in Africa, for Charlie has come to write a story about the famous doctor.

Whereas Charlie comes to Africa for the first time, Tshembe and Abioseh are called back to Africa by the death of their father. Abioseh comes back a Catholic priest, having renounced his African heritage and embraced the culture and beliefs of the colonialists. Tshembe too has taken much from the colonial culture, including his education and a European bride. He has not, however, rejected his heritage, and he is sensitive to the injustice of the colonial system. Though he sees colonialism as evil, he does not want to commit himself to opposing it. He wants to return to his wife and child and lead a comfortable, secure life.

For both Charlie and Tshembe, the visit to Africa brings the unexpected, for they return in the midst of an uprising, called "terror" by the whites and "resistance" by the blacks. Charlie gradually learns the true nature of colonialism, and Tshembe, after great struggle, learns that he cannot avoid his obligation to oppose colonialism actively.

While Charlie waits for Dr. Neilsen to return from another village, he learns from Madame Neilsen that the doctor's efforts seem to be less and less appreciated. When Tshembe comes on the scene, Charlie is immediately interested in him and repeatedly tries to engage the former student of Madame Neilsen and the doctor in conversation, but they fail to understand each other. Tshembe will accept none of the assumptions that Charlie has brought with him to Africa: He rejects the efforts of Dr. Neilsen, however well-intentioned, as representing the guilty conscience of colonialism while perpetrating the system; he rejects Charlie's confident assumption that the facilities are so backward because of the superstitions of the natives. Charlie, on the other hand, cannot understand how Tshembe can speak so bitterly against colonialism yet not do anything to oppose it. Tshembe explains that he is one of those "who see too much to take sides," but his position becomes increasingly untenable. He is approached by members of the resistance and is asked to lead them, at which point he learns that it was his father who conceived the movement when it became clear that the colonialists, including Dr. Neilsen, saw themselves in the position of father rather than brother to the natives and would never give them freedom.

Still, Tshembe resists the commitment, but Charlie, as he leaves the scene, convinced now that the resistance is necessary, asks Tshembe, "Where are you running, man? Back to Europe? To watch the action on your telly?" Charlie reminds Tshembe that "we do what we can." Madame Neilsen herself makes Tshembe face the needs of his people. Tshembe by this time knows what his choice must be, but is unable to make it. In his despair, he turns to Madame Neilsen, imploring her help. She tells him, "You have forgotten your geometry if you are despairing, Tshembe. I once taught you that a line goes into infinity unless it is bisected. Our country needs *warriors*, Tshembe Matoseh."

In the final scene of the play, Tshembe takes up arms against the colonialists, and Hansberry makes his decision all the more dramatic by having him kill his brother Abioseh, who has taken the colonial side. Yet, lest anyone misunderstand the agony of his choice, Hansberry ends the play with Tshembe on his knees before the bodies of those he has loved, committed but in agony, deeply engulfed by grief that such commitment is necessary.

Les Blancs is less an answer to the problem of colonialism than it is another expression of Hansberry's deep and abiding belief in the need for individual commitment, and in the ability of the individual, once committed, to bring about positive change for the future, even if that requires suffering in the present. Surely her commitment to her writing will guarantee her work an audience far into the future.

Other major works

NONFICTION: *The Movement: Documentary of a Struggle for Equality*, 1964 (includes photographs); *To Be Young, Gifted, and Black: Lorraine Hansberry in Her Own Words*, 1969 (Robert Nemiroff, editor).

Bibliography

Freedomways 19 (1979). This special issue is devoted to a reassessment of Lorraine Hansberry's work. Contains a bibliography.

Gomez, Jewelle L. "Lorraine Hansberry: Uncommon Warrior." In *Reading Black, Reading Feminist*, edited by Henry Louis Gates, Jr. New York: Meridian, 1990. Gomez believes that the commercial success of *A Raisin in the Sun* caused critics to overlook Hansberry's "redefinition" of black American women as "active and responsible participants in our political future." She calls Beneatha, Walter's sister in *A Raisin in the Sun*, Hansberry's "most autobiographical" character.

Lester, Julius. Foreword and afterword to *Lorraine Hansberry: The Collected Last Plays*, edited by Robert Nemiroff. New York: New American Library, 1983. Lester states that Hansberry's work was not consumed by anger but motivated by it. Makes the point that "her commitment was to people, not to ideology."

Miller, Jordan Y. "Lorraine Hansberry." In *Poetry and Drama*. Vol. 2 in *The Black American Writer*, edited by C. W. E. Bigsby. Baltimore: Penguin Books, 1971. Miller presents the standard view of white critics of the time and discusses *A Raisin in the Sun* and *The Sign in Sidney Brustein's Window*. Also praises Hansberry's ability to make people care about her characters and examines her use of traditional realistic structure.

Nemiroff, Robert. "A Critical Background." In *Lorraine Hansberry: The Collected Last Plays*. New York: New American Library, 1983. Nemiroff discusses both the intellectual and the emotional impetus that led Hansberry to write *Les Blancs*, *The Drinking Gourd*, and *What Use Are Flowers?* He describes her struggle to finish *Les Blancs* as she fought against the cancer that killed her and his synthesis of the unfinished script that she left and its production in 1970. Discusses the refusal of Columbia Broadcasting System (CBS) to produce *The Drinking Gourd*, suggesting that part of the problem was that both African Americans and whites were presented as victims. Also included is the genesis of the brief one-act *What Use Are Flowers?*, which was inspired, Nemiroff states, by Samuel Beckett.

Russell, Sandi. *Render Me My Song: African-American Women Writers from Slavery to the Present.* New York: St. Martin's Press, 1990. In a chapter entitled "Urban Realities," Russell discusses Hansberry's work together with other African-American women writers of the 1930's through the 1960's in the context of the struggle to find and free their own voices.
Weales, Gerald. *The Jumping-off Place.* New York: Macmillan, 1969. In "The Negro Revolution," Weales discusses *A Raisin in the Sun* and *The Sign in Sidney Brustein's Window* in the context of his chapter title, along with Ossie Davis (*Purlie Victorious*, pr. 1961), Amiri Baraka (*Dutchman*, pr. 1964), and others. "Miss Hansberry is unique in this chapter, the only Negro playwright who attempts to write about a society larger than the Negro community, one defined in terms other than black-white relations," Weales states.
Wilkerson, Margaret B. Introduction to *Lorraine Hansberry: The Collected Last Plays*, edited by Robert Nemiroff. New York: New American Library, 1983. Wilkerson, a professor of African-American studies and women's studies at the University of California at Berkeley, deals with Hansberry's work in the context of her own experience with it as director and teacher. She discusses Hansberry's "insistence upon a thorough probing of the individual within the specifics of culture, ethnicity, and gender."

Hugh Short
(Updated by *Katherine Lederer*)

THOMAS HARDY

Born: Higher Bockhampton, England; June 2, 1840
Died: Dorchester, England; January 11, 1928

Principal drama

The Dynasts: A Drama of the Napoleonic Wars, pb. 1903, 1906, 1908, 1910 (verse drama), pr. 1914 (abridged by Harley Granville-Barker); *The Famous Tragedy of the Queen of Cornwall*, pr., pb. 1923 (one act).

Other literary forms

Thomas Hardy is best known for his fiction. He was the author of fourteen novels, four collections of short stories containing more than forty tales, and several volumes of poetry comprising some nine hundred poems, as well as a large assortment of nonfiction prose, prefaces, and essays. His letters, diaries, notebooks, and private papers have survived, despite Hardy's intention that this material be destroyed. Several volumes of his correspondence have been published. In addition, there are two books of autobiography, *The Early Life of Hardy* (1928) and *The Later Years of Thomas Hardy* (1930), which Hardy dictated to his wife.

Achievements

While Hardy's achievements as a novelist and poet are widely recognized, his achievements as a playwright are less well-known. Hardy's training as an architect has been taken to explain his intricately plotted novels, and it might also be seen as the reason Hardy liked the conventions of dramatic structure. Hardy had a lifelong interest in drama and the theater, and it was his original literary ambition to be a playwright, although he did not produce any plays until near the end of his career and then wrote only two. Although he was sometimes tempted by London theatrical agents and friends to turn his talents to the stage, he largely resisted the lure of stagelights, being unwilling to compromise with the demands of actors and directors in the commercial theater, a position he explains in an essay, "Why I Don't Write Plays" (1892). Alternately fearful of the limitations and fascinated by the possibilities of drama, Hardy finally wrote his first "play," *The Dynasts*, which is something of a composite literary form. Intended for a mental rather than a real stage, it is epic in size and scope. This immense verse play, about which one might remark, as Samuel Johnson did of John Milton's *Paradise Lost* (1667, 1674), "none would wish it longer," has attracted some critical attention, but it has never drawn many readers from the general public. As a closet drama, it is a major artistic accomplishment, and it rivals Leo Tolstoy's *War and Peace* (1865, 1869) as a work that most vividly chronicles the defeat of Napoleon's dynastic ambitions. Hardy's hope of reviving interest in the verse drama, however, was not fulfilled with *The Dynasts* or with his second verse play, *The Famous Tragedy of the Queen of Cornwall*, which was conceived for actual stage production. The one-act *The Famous Tragedy of the Queen of Cornwall* was a coda to Hardy's brief career as a playwright; an extremely different type of poetic drama from *The Dynasts*, it shows what Hardy might have been able to do with stage conventions had he kept to his early ambition "to write a few fine plays."

Biography

Thomas Hardy was born on June 2, 1840, in a thatched-roof cottage at Higher Bockhampton, a village near the small city of Dorchester in the southern shire of Dorset—an area that was known as Wessex in ancient times and that has many historical associations with the Druids, the Celts, and the Romans. Hardy's father, a music-loving building contractor, was ambitious for young Thomas; thus, after he completed his education through grammar school, Hardy was apprenticed at age sixteen to an architect. Whatever of his education did not pertain to his vocation he had to pick up on his own, and it was in this fashion that he continued to study Latin and Greek. He also began writing poetry during his late teens, imitating the style and substance of the dialect verses of the Reverend William Barnes, a local curate and poetaster.

Hardy's apprenticeship under the ecclesiastical architect John Hicks lasted until 1862, after which he went up to London at the age of twenty-one to study architecture further. Under the tutelage of John Blomfield, Hardy became proficient enough in his professional life to win a prize given by the Royal Institute of British Architects for an essay on the use of ancient building materials in modern architecture. Hardy's expository talent was further demonstrated in a sketch, "How I Built Myself a House," in *Chamber's Journal*. During this period, Hardy's life was somewhat inchoate. He began at this time, however, to become more deeply interested in literature, writing stories as well as poetry and availing himself of the cultural opportunities London provided. He used his free time to visit the British Museum and the art galleries and spent his evenings at King's College, studying French. The routine of work and study and the rigors of urban life placed a strain on Hardy's health, which had been delicate since his childhood, and after five years, he sought rustication, returning to Bockhampton to recover. While he was at home and employed only part-time with church restorations, he began to write his first novel, "The Poor Man and the Lady." He sent the manuscript to a publisher, but it was rejected because the story lacked plot and suspense. Despite this disappointment, Hardy was encouraged by the editor's praise, and he attempted a second novel, *Desperate Remedies*, which satisfied the requirement for plot ingenuity and was published anonymously in 1871. This book was quickly followed by *Under the Greenwood Tree* (1872) and *A Pair of Blue Eyes* (1872-1873); neither novel was a popular success, but both received positive notice from the reviewers.

At the time, Hardy was encouraged by the editor of *Cornhill Magazine* to write a serial novel. The result was Hardy's first popular and financial success, the pastoral novel *Far from the Madding Crowd* (1874). Success with this book enabled Hardy to marry Emma Lavinia Gifford in the same year. He also gave up his practice as an architect, for he was assured of an income from his writing. After a honeymoon trip to France, Hardy settled down at Max Gate, his home near Dorchester, where he spent the next twenty-five years writing stories and novels. Although he wrote continuously and preferred a retired life, Hardy was by no means a recluse. He made many friends in literary circles and was active on the London social scene as his reputation as a major writer grew. During these decades, when Hardy's creative productivity was at its peak, he published the five major novels that he came to call stories of "Character and Environment": *The Return of the Native* (1878), *The Mayor of Casterbridge* (1886), *Tess of the D'Urbervilles* (1891), and *Jude the Obscure* (1895).

Although Hardy's career as a writer was flourishing throughout the 1870's, the 1880's, and the 1890's, his marriage to Emma was not. The couple was childless, which put a strain on their relationship, and the evidence points to sexual difficulties between Hardy and his wife. Although Emma was a conventional helpmate as a wife, tending to Hardy's business affairs and making fair copies of his manuscripts, she was not a mate to him in the full sense. As the years passed, each was embittered against the other, and the difficulties of their marriage increased. Emma Hardy's death in 1912 was an occasion of mixed relief and bereavement for Hardy, but after two years of mourning he married, at age seventy-four, for a second time. His new wife was Florence Emily Dugdale, who was a longtime friend of the Hardys and had served as his secretary following Mrs. Hardy's death.

During the later years of his writing career, after the hostile reception of *Jude the Obscure* in 1895, Hardy turned again to poetry and worked primarily in this medium for the rest of his life, producing two experiments in drama—the epic drama in verse, *The Dynasts*, and a second verse play, *The Famous Tragedy of the Queen of Cornwall*.

Honors and recognition came to Hardy in abundance in his later years. He was awarded the Order of Merit by King Edward; his home of Max Gate was a shrine visited with veneration by the literati of the English-speaking world. Although Hardy had wished to be buried in his native Dorset, at his death in 1928, he was honored by the nation with a burial in the Poets' Corner of Westminster Abbey. His heart, however, was taken home, where it was interred in the village graveyard of his native heath.

Analysis

Thomas Hardy's *The Dynasts* is, along with John Milton's *Samson Agonistes* (1671) and Percy Bysshe Shelley's *Prometheus Unbound* (1820), one of the longest closet dramas in English literature. This vast epic drama, consisting of nineteen acts and 130 scenes, traces the Napoleonic Wars from 1805 to 1815. Upon its publication, *The Dynasts* was hailed as a major achievement, but subsequent generations have found the massive work more problematic. Indeed, while Hardy's novels continue to be read and are available in numerous editions in any bookstore, only Victorian scholars are likely to plough their way through the 10,553 lines of *The Dynasts*. As Hardy's importance as a novelist increases, his importance as a dramatic poet seems to be fading, despite pleading by some critics to justify *The Dynasts* categorically either as an epic or as a drama.

The Dynasts, which was published in three separate parts in 1903, 1906, and 1908, was initially untitled and was referred to simply as "A Drama of Kings." When all three parts of the completed work were published together in 1910, Hardy labeled it an epic drama and gave it the title by which it is now known. Hardy's title comes from a line on the last page of the final act: "... who hurlest Dynasts from their thrones?" As to his choice of this title, Hardy wrote, "it was the best and shortest inclusive one I could think of to express the rulers of Europe in their desperate struggle to maintain their dynasties rather than to benefit their people."

It is not really surprising that Hardy should have turned his talents to the production of dramatic poetry. There are many indications of an early and lifelong interest in the drama—both folk and professional. Hardy enjoyed plays both in the study and on the stage, and he read widely among the classical Greek, Elizabethan, modern Continental, and modern English playwrights. He was a frequent playgoer in London and knew many theatrical people, among them Harley Granville-Barker, Sir James Barrie, George Bernard Shaw, and John Galsworthy. In fact, at one point in his life Hardy had thought of becoming a playwright himself, and as early as 1867, he was considering writing plays in blank verse but postponed this project after being discouraged by the realities of a stage production.

Hardy's interest in playwriting lay dormant for many years, but, having abandoned the writing of fiction, disgusted by the adverse critical reaction to his later novels, he turned to poetry and drama—his interest in the latter whetted by stage adaptations of *Far from the Madding Crowd* and *Tess of the D'Urbervilles*. Thus, near the end of the 1890's, Hardy plunged into the writing of a verse drama; "nothing could interfere with it," as he said, for it was intended for a "mental performance."

The Dynasts required all of Hardy's skills as a writer. Written in a variety of verse forms, the drama tells an epic story with a cast of thousands. Hardy's forte as a novelist was his ability to tell a story with interest and suspense, and his talent with plot did not desert him here. *The Dynasts* relates a well-known story—the rise and fall of Napoleon—with vivid and fresh appeal. There are scenes of battle, of political intrigue, and of the ordinary life of the people that provide spectacle on the scale of the films of the late Cecil B. De Mille. Unlike previous closet dramas, such as Lord Byron's *Manfred* (pb. 1817), Shelley's *The Cenci* (pb. 1819), or Alfred, Lord Tennyson's *Harold* (pb. 1876), Hardy selected a recent historical event as his subject, as he did in his novels, in which the setting is generally only a few decades removed from the telling; in *The Dynasts*, the time of the action is 1805-1815. Whereas in his fiction Hardy was concerned with the fate of common people in the grips of an indifferent destiny, in the epic drama his concern was to show how princes and powerful men, who often seem to control the fate of the masses, are in turn moved and influenced by the same blind forces that govern the humblest of men.

Hardy's epic drama was the result of his lifelong interest in Napoleon's character and career, a subject that had attracted many other writers of his own and earlier generations. It was his intention to do more than dramatize the turbulent period of the Napoleonic Wars; Hardy's purpose was to show how the events that led up to the period of conflict had been shaped by blind causes rather than human will; the major premise underlying *The Dynasts* is that all human thought and action are predestined—an expression of the anthropomorphic force that Hardy called the "Immanent Will," rather than of Divine Providence. While this was an advanced idea for 1904, it seems to make the drama passé to modern readers, who are not as concerned with questions of ultimate causation as were the post-Victorians.

The cast of characters in Hardy's drama, epic in proportions, is arranged on three levels: first, the celestial abstractions—the Will, the Ironies, the Spirit Sinister, the Shade of the Earth, and the Earth of the Years; next, the great historical figures—Napoleon, the Duke of Wellington, Lord Nelson, George III, William Pitt, the Younger, and the various kings, princes, and generals of Prussia, Austria, Spain, and Russia (these are the dynasts of Europe, all of whom are concerned only to maintain their rule); and finally, the ordinary people, the suffering masses who are puppets caught in the grip of political and historical forces beyond their control. Hardy makes these lower-class characters his collective protagonists, the heroes of the play. On the other hand, the conquerors and kings, the so-called dynasts, are cast as the antagonists, indifferent to the plight of the people and concerned only with expanding their borders; they side with Napoleon when he is up and combine against him when he is down. In the struggles on the human level among the dynasts and their nations, only England stands above the sordid schemes of the Continental kings as the British defy Napoleon's design for world conquest. Among the British generals, Wellington emerges as a worthy rival, whose tenacity will prove to be a match for

Napoleon's brilliant strategies.

Of all the characters in the drama, Napoleon is by far the most interest-ing. He is a complex and evolving personality, whose career as depicted by Hardy is a working out of the Immanent Will in the history of the world. At first, Napoleon functions as an agent of order as he imposes his dream of a unified Europe upon the chaos unleashed by the French Revolution. When he crowns himself emperor, however, his decline into egotistical meg-alomania begins. His march of conquest across Russia is undertaken only for selfish reasons, and from this point on he is pursued by a Nemesis-like retribution for his overwhelming hubris. The human actions in *The Dynasts* culminate in Napoleon's defeat at Waterloo, the battle scenes being pre-sented from a panoramic perspective to which only a motion picture could do justice in visual terms. Hardy's careful historical research, which included interviews with surviving veterans of the battle of Waterloo, is particularly evident here as every battalion and regiment are cataloged in the best epic tradition. Hardy lavishes admiring detail on the exploits of the Scots Greys, the Black Watch, and the British Grenadiers as they hold the thin red line against the furious but futile charge of the French Im-perial Guard.

As the numerous acts of the historical drama are played out, scenes are interspersed in which the spirits play their part, acting as symbols of abstract powers that are personified as actual characters. The Immanent Will influences events through its attendant spirits—the personified Pities, the Years, and Ironies—but the Will itself, because it stands for the all-inclusive mind or ultimate reality of the universe, is never depicted. Its operation is keenly felt at numerous points in the drama when its human puppets, including Napoleon himself, act on impulses or instincts that they cannot resist.

The Pities, Years, and Ironies are indicative of human traits, attitudes, and perspectives. The Spirit of Pities symbolizes sympathy and altruism. The Spirit of Years stands for rejective reason as time places distance between emotions and events. His outlook on human affairs is rationalistic and unsentimental. The Spirit of Pities, with all its compassion, is the ob-vious foil of the Spirit of Years, who has no feeling.

The debate between the spirits creates the effect of a Greek chorus and lends a traditional dramatic ingredient to the otherwise unique drama. Other allegorical characters, such as the Spirit Sinister, the Spirit of Ru-mor, and the Shade of Earth, enter the scene and attempt to interpret the meaning of the unfolding historical events. Their debate, however, is in-conclusive, and though their final chorus ends with a weak note of op-timism, on the hope that the current "rages of the ages shall be cancelled," to be followed by a future period when human reason will overcome selfish aggression and destructive impulses, it is clear that it will take ages of

evolution to turn human instincts of passion into compassion. This evolu-
tionary process, which Hardy termed "meliorism," was his faint but larger
hope for humankind.

The foregoing summary can only suggest the total scope of Hardy's *The
Dynasts*, which in volume exceeds all the other poetry that he wrote during
his career. The work is no less than a poetic representation in dramatic
terms of Hardy's personal philosophy and understanding of history. The
magnitude of Hardy's poem, however, makes it difficult to come to terms
with critically and even artistically. Though Hardy issued the caveat that
The Dynasts was written for a "mental" staging, he agreed in 1914 to an
abridged version that was adapted for a theater production by Granville-
Barker, who cut the original to a tenth of its size. The operation was necessary to bring *The Dynasts* within the practical range of time for a theatrical performance, since it is estimated that it would have required two entire
days and nights of consecutive stage time to dramatize the whole text. As it
was, Granville-Barker's abridgment was a strain on audiences and actors,
and it caused some reviewers to conclude that *The Dynasts* was an
"unplayable play." Its excessive length was not the only fault found with the
stage version: The chopped-up plot lacked any sense of progression, and
the play had no climax; even more debilitating was the replacement of
Hardy's philosophical concerns with an overlay of patriotic sentiment that
was devised by Granville-Barker to fit the nationalistic mood fostered in
England by the outbreak of World War I.

Hardy's final attempt at a dramatic work was a one-act play entitled *The
Famous Tragedy of the Queen of Cornwall*, which was published in 1923. In
this play, Hardy's aim was exactly opposite from the purpose of *The Dynasts*: Here, he aimed at concentration rather than expansiveness in his
choice of plot, characters, and setting, as he consciously tried to observe
the unities. His subject for this play is the tragic love story of Tristram and
Iseult, whose story attracted a number of nineteenth century authors, most
notably Tennyson, Matthew Arnold, and Algernon Charles Swinburne,
who had all written versions of the ill-starred romance.

Hardy dedicated his one-act verse drama to the memory of Emma
Gifford, his first wife, and the play has associations with the courtship that
took place in the spring of 1870 when he and Emma visited King Arthur's
castle, Tintagel, in Lyonnesse—a place he called "the region of dream and
mystery." The legends associated with this area lingered in his mind for
fifty years and led to the composition of *The Famous Tragedy of the Queen
of Cornwall*, which he began in 1916 but did not finish until 1923.

Hardy develops the Tristram story in a unique way, though his basic
conception of the romance depends upon Sir Thomas Malory's *Le Morte
d'Arthur* (1485). The use of the dramatic format forced Hardy to compress
a good many details in his version. For example, to maintain unity of place,

he has all the action take place at Tintagel. Furthermore, Hardy begins his drama immediately before the catastrophe, the events of his play taking place during the last hours of the lovers' lives. Moreover, Hardy adds several original details to the story of the doomed couple who are victims of the irresistible and fatal force of love. He employs a chorus (termed "chanters") and Merlin, the wizard, to provide necessary exposition at the start of the play. We learn that while King Mark has been away on a hunt, Queen Iseult has been called to come to Brittany by Tristram, her lover, who, she believes, is dying. She is prevented from seeing him by Iseult of the White Hands, Tristram's wife, who informs her falsely that he is dead. Queen Iseult returns to Lyonnesse thinking that her suspicious husband is none the wiser about her flight to Tristram's bedside; informants, however, have told Mark of her actions. In a subsequent scene, Tristram recovers and comes to Cornwall, traveling incognito, to see Iseult, who is gratified to learn that he is not dead. He lays bare his heart to her, saying that he has been forced into a miserable marriage with Iseult of the White Hands. Shortly thereafter, a strange ship arrives bringing Tristram's wife, who has followed him upon discovering that he has returned to his former love.

In a poignant scene that was added by Hardy, the deserted wife and passionate mistress meet. It is clearly shown by this episode that the theme of the play is the tragedy of mismatched mates. Queen Iseult cannot love Mark, who is cruel by nature; she is compelled by a love potion to love Tristram. Tristram is loved by both women, but he is too weak to do what is right, his fate also having been sealed by the same love potion. Meanwhile, Mark discovers Tristram's presence at the castle and, catching him in an embrace with Iseult, stabs him in the back with a dagger. The queen plucks the knife from the body of her dying lover and kills her husband with it. Then she leaps over the ledge of the castle and plunges to her death in the sea below, providing to the legendary story an ending that was entirely Hardy's own.

Whatever the intentions of this play, Hardy's revision of the legend created a great deal more sympathy for Iseult of the White Hands than had previous versions. Hardy was able to renew, in this, his last work, the old formula of tragedy that ruled so many of his own doomed pairs of lovers, from Eustacia Vye and Clem Yeobright in *The Return of the Native* to Jude Fawley and Sue Bridehead in *Jude the Obscure*—lovers whose destinies were shaped, like Tristram and Iseult's, by the dual compulsion of character and fate.

The Famous Tragedy of the Queen of Cornwall was Hardy's only work written expressly for the stage. It was first produced by the Hardy Players in Dorchester on November 21, 1923. There was also an operatic version produced in 1924, which Rutland Boughton scored. In writing *The Famous Tragedy of the Queen of Cornwall*, Hardy was perhaps trying to meet the objections of those critics who had indicted him for an inability to write a concentrated play in *The Dynasts*. In the case of this short poetic drama, Hardy proved that he could indeed create plays for the commercial theater. It is ironic in the best Hardyesque fashion that he succeeded at last with a genre that had been his first aspiration as a literary artist—the poetic drama.

Other major works

NOVELS: *Desperate Remedies*, 1871; *Under the Greenwood Tree*, 1872; *A Pair of Blue Eyes*, 1872-1873; *Far from the Madding Crowd*, 1874; *The Hand of Ethelberta*, 1875-1876; *The Return of the Native*, 1878; *The Trumpet-Major*, 1880; *A Laodicean*, 1880-1881; *Two on a Tower*, 1882; *The Mayor of Casterbridge*, 1886; *The Woodlanders*, 1886-1887; *Tess of the D'Urbervilles*, 1891; *Jude the Obscure*, 1895; *The Well-Beloved*, 1897.

SHORT FICTION: *Wessex Tales*, 1888; *A Group of Noble Dames*, 1891; *Life's Little Ironies*, 1894; *A Changed Man, The Waiting Supper and Other Tales*, 1913; *The Complete Short Stories*, 1989 (Desmond Hawkins, editor).

POETRY: *Wessex Poems and Other Verses*, 1898; *Poems of the Past and Present*, 1901; *Time's Laughingstocks and Other Verses*, 1909; *Satires of Circumstance*, 1914; *Moments of Vision and Miscellaneous Verses*, 1917; *Late Lyrics and Earlier*, 1922; *Human Shows, Far Phantasies: Songs and Trifles*, 1925; *Winter Words*, 1928; *Collected Poems*, 1931; *The Complete Poetical Works*, 1982-1985 (3 volumes; Samuel Hynes, editor).

NONFICTION: *Life and Art*, 1925 (E. Brennecke, editor); *The Early Life of Hardy*, 1928; *The Later Years of Thomas Hardy*, 1930; *Personal Writings*, 1966 (Harold Orel, editor); *The Collected Letters of Thomas Hardy*, 1978, 1980 (2 volumes; Richard Little Purdy and Michael Millgate, editors).

Bibliography
Bailey, J. O. *Thomas Hardy and the Cosmic Mind.* Chapel Hill: University of North Carolina Press, 1956. The purpose of this book is to examine Hardy's drama, particularly in the light of Eduard von Hartmann's *Die Philosophie des Unbewussten* (1870); *The Philosophy of the Unconscious*, 1884). Bailey considers this work as an informing force on Hardy's own philosophy. This discussion leads to an examination of Hardy's interest in psychic phenomena, a new interpretation of the spirits in his drama, a definition of Hardy's meliorism, and an understanding of his treatment of Napoleon in the work.
Chakravorty, Amiya. *"The Dynasts" and the Post-War Age in Poetry.* London: Oxford University Press, 1938. Although dated, this volume is an insightful and scholarly work. The author argues that the dominant problem in modern poetry is the problem of self-consciousness. A period of nineteenth century history is then used to depict the forces of nature and

consciousness as involved in the integral process of Hardy's drama.

Dean, Susan. *Hardy's Poetic Vision in "The Dynasts."* Princeton, N.J.: Princeton University Press, 1977. Dean undertakes an approach to the drama that interprets it as vision in action. She tests the visual approach against Hardy's own critical prose writing, in which she finds passages that provide evidence to support a "visual reality" in Hardy's work. Dean's purpose is to shed light on the obscure power and complexity of the work.

Maynard, Katherine Kearney. *Thomas Hardy's Tragic Poetry: The Lyrics and "The Dynasts."* Iowa City: University of Iowa Press, 1991. This study examines the question of tragic literature's vitality in a secular age and explores the philosophical underpinnings of Hardy's tragic vision in his lyric poetry and in *The Dynasts.* It also examines Hardy's efforts within the context of nineteenth century poetry.

Orel, Harold. *Thomas Hardy's Epic-Drama: A Study of "The Dynasts."* Lawrence: University Press of Kansas, 1963. This brief but insightful work explains the meaning behind Hardy's description of the work as an "epic-drama." Retraces Hardy's career up until the time he gave up novels to become a full-time poet. Orel attempts to analyze Hardy's work in the light of the author's views on nature and the universe.

Wright, Walter F. *The Shaping of "The Dynasts."* Lincoln: University of Nebraska Press, 1967. The author argues that Hardy's epic-drama epitomizes his worldview after he had secured from the philosophers the metaphysical structure for expressing what he had long believed to be true. The book is concerned with what went into shaping the drama. More than any of Hardy's major works, Wright states that this drama is artfully conceived, containing within it recurring themes and artistic perspectives similar to those in the novels or lyric poems. Contains an appendix on Hardy's philosophy of art and a bibliography of Hardy's sources.

Hallman B. Bryant
(Updated by *Genevieve Slomski*)

DAVID HARE

Born: Bexhill, England; June 5, 1947

Principal drama

Inside Out, pr. 1968 (with Tony Bicat; adaptation of Franz Kafka's diaries); *How Brophy Made Good*, pr. 1969, pb. 1971; *What Happened to Blake?*, pr. 1970; *Slag*, pr. 1970, pb. 1971; *The Rules of the Game*, pr. 1971 (adaptation of Luigi Pirandello's play); *Lay By*, pr. 1971, pb. 1972 (with Howard Brenton, Brian Clark, Trevor Griffiths, Stephen Poliakoff, Hugh Stoddart, and Snoo Wilson); *Deathsheads*, pr. 1971; *England's Ireland*, pr. 1972 (with others); *The Great Exhibition*, pr., pb. 1972; *Brassneck*, pr. 1973, pb. 1974 (with Brenton); *Knuckle*, pr., pb. 1974; *Fanshen*, pr. 1975, pb. 1976 (adaptation of William Hinton's book *Fanshen: A Documentary of Revolution in a Chinese Village*); *Teeth 'n' Smiles*, pr. 1975, pb. 1976 (music by Nick Bicat, lyrics by Tony Bicat); *Plenty*, pr., pb. 1978; *A Map of the World*, pr., pb. 1983; *Pravda: A Fleet Street Comedy*, pr., pb. 1985 (with Brenton); *The Bay at Nice*, pr., pb. 1986; *Wrecked Eggs*, pr., pb. 1986; *The Secret Rapture*, pr., pb. 1988; *Racing Demon*, pr., pb. 1990; *Murmuring Judges*, pr. 1991.

Other literary forms

While continuing to work in the theater, David Hare turned to television in 1973 to write and produce *Man Above Men* for the British Broadcasting Corporation (BBC), followed by *Licking Hitler*, which Hare authored and directed for the BBC in 1978, *Dreams of Leaving* (1980), and *Saigon: Year of the Cat* (1983). In 1985, Hare adapted his play *Plenty* for the motion-picture screen and also wrote and directed *Wetherby*, which some critics regarded as a better film than *Plenty*. *Wetherby* demonstrated that Hare could work effectively in the medium of film as a total artist. Other Hare films are *Paris by Night* (1988) and *Strapless* (1989).

Achievements

Hare has been identified as a Socialist playwright, a committed artist whose concerns are predominantly moral and often satiric. His work reflects the stance of the "angry" writers of the 1950's carried forward into a second generation of "furious" playwrights, as Jack Kroll has aptly described them. Hare's English characters are shaped by the postwar realities of British life; some of them (such as Susan, the central character of *Plenty*) have not properly adjusted to a changing world, while others (such as Curly, the central character of *Knuckle*) have adjusted at the expense of becoming hardened and cynical or morally complacent. Hare has a genius for drawing strong, distinctive characters who often behave outrageously. Although many of the plays are set in his native England, his concerns are global, as reflected by increasingly international and exotic settings for the later plays: New York, Leningrad, Saigon, India, and the People's Republic of China, for example. He has also extended his work from the stage to film and television. Hare has a unique talent for dramatizing people under pressure and confronted with crises—social, commercial, moral, revolutionary, and political. His scope is impressively broad, and his concerns in general involve issues of truth, honesty, and integrity. Indeed, the title of one of his most successful plays of the 1980's, *Pravda*, means "truth." Hare has been favorably compared with Bertolt Brecht (for *Fanshen*, his documentary play about the Chinese Revolution, "the nearest any English contemporary writer has come to emulating Brecht," in the estimation of Michael Coveney) and Harold Pinter, perhaps the most gifted playwright of the previous generation. Among younger talents, the volume and quality of his work may perhaps be matched by Tom Stoppard, but few others. After the success of *Slag* in 1970, Hare won the *Evening Standard* Award for Most Promising Playwright. In 1974, *Knuckle* won for him the John Llewellyn Rhys Award. In 1979, the British Academy of Film and Television Arts voted *Licking Hitler* the Best Television Play of the Year. In 1985, the film *Wetherby*, which Hare both wrote and directed, won the Berlin Film Festival's Golden Bear Award. *The Secret Rapture* was named the best play for 1988 by *Drama Magazine.*

Biography

David Hare was born in Bexhill, England, on June 5, 1947, the son of Clifford Theodore Rippon and the former Agnes Gillmour, his wife. Hare was first educated at Lancing College (among his classmates were future playwright Christopher Hampton and lyricist Tim Rice) before going on to Jesus College, Cambridge, where he earned a master's degree, with honors, in 1968. Hare began writing plays at the age of twenty-two. In 1970, his first full-length play, *Slag*, about three women teachers locked into a power struggle over a failing English boarding school, won for him the Most Promising Playwright Award granted by the *Evening Standard*, even though the play was not favorably received by some feminists, who considered the playwright to be sexist; others went so far as to call him a misogynist. *The New York Times* drama critic Clive Barnes described *Slag* as a metaphor for the decline of English society, following Hare's suggestion that the play was not so much about women as institutions. Also in 1970, Hare married Margaret Matheson, a marriage that produced three children before ending in divorce in 1980.

From the beginning of his theatrical career in 1968 when he cofounded the Portable Theatre Company (with Howard Brenton and Snoo Wilson), an experimental troupe that toured Great Britain, Hare demonstrated an interest in creative dramatic collaboration and in theatrical direction, as well as in writing plays. In 1969, Hare became literary manager of the Royal Court Theatre, and in 1970 he was appointed resident dramatist. (*Slag* was first produced at the Hampstead Theatre Club before being moved to the Royal Court.) After working at the Royal Court, Hare served as resident playwright at the Nottingham Playhouse, where his play *Brassneck* (written in collaboration with Howard Brenton), which traced corruption through three generations of a Midlands family, premiered in 1973. In 1974, Hare cofounded Joint Stock, another fringe company; *Fanshen* was done as a Joint Stock production in the city of Sheffield.

As a young man, Hare once worked for Pathé Pictorial and went on to write for television productions after having established himself as a successful playwright. *Saigon: Year of the Cat* was directed by Stephen Frears for Thames Television in 1983, for example, but his earlier award-winning teleplay, *Licking Hitler*, Hare wrote and directed himself for the BBC in 1978. In 1985, his film *Wetherby*, which Hare also wrote and directed, earned the Golden Bear Award at the Berlin Film Festival and received a large measure of critical acclaim internationally. Hare wrote the screenplay adaptation of *Plenty*, one of his most successful plays, for a major motion picture that starred Meryl Streep, Charles Dance, and Sir John Gielgud and was directed by Fred Schepisi and released by Twentieth Century-Fox. Having earned a reputation as a sometimes controversial national playwright during the 1970's, Hare had established himself by the mid-1980's as a multifaceted writer and director of international scope and importance.

Analysis

David Hare's creative work can be sorted into three categories: plays he wrote and directed himself, scripts written for film and television productions, and plays written in collaboration with Howard Brenton and others. In discussing Hare for the journal *Modern Drama*, C. W. E. Bigsby described the playwright as having been shaped by his times, the political turmoil and social upheaval of the student rebellions of 1968 and the growing dissent over Western policy in Southeast Asia. Bigsby also noted that 1968 was the year that "marked the beginnings of the theatrical fringe in London." Active in fringe theater from the beginning of his dramatic career, Hare became one of the architects of the fringe movement.

Early in his career, for example, Hare became interested in dramatic collaboration, which later led to successful partnerships with Howard Brenton—*Brassneck* in 1973 and *Pravda* in 1985. At the Royal Court Theatre in 1971, Hare instigated an experiment in group collaboration that resulted in the play *Lay By*, a group effort of seven writers (Trevor Griffiths, Brian Clark, Stephen Poliakoff, Hugh Stoddard, and Snoo Wilson, along with Brenton and Hare), stimulated by a *Sunday Times* feature by Ludovic Kennedy, concerning an ambiguous rape case that might have resulted in an erroneous conviction. The Royal Court rejected the play, but Hare's colleagues in the Portable Theatre Company mounted a production directed by Snoo Wilson in conjunction with the Traverse Theatre at the Edinburgh Festival Fringe. The Portable Theatre also produced another collective effort in which Hare was involved as a writer, *England's Ireland*, in 1972.

The rationale for the Portable Theatre was political. The idea was to have a touring company that would address working-class audiences, an "antagonistic theatre," as Brenton described it, designed for "people who have never seen the theatre before." The plays produced were intended to be controversial in nature (*Lay By* was an exercise in sexual politics, for example, reconstructing a rape and interspersing the reconstruction with a pornographic photo session) and to challenge conventional assumptions and the traditional forms and methods of the established theater.

In this context, Hare may be regarded as a social critic functioning as a practicing dramatist with a flair for satire. His play *The Great Exhibition* is a political satire treating a Labour M.P., Charles Hammett, swept into office during the great Labour victory of 1965 and swept out of office when the Conservative Party returned to power in 1970. Peter Ansorge has called the play a parody of "middle-class playwrights who have turned to working-class communities both for inspiration and as an escape from the more subtle dilemmas of their own environment and class."

Hare's interest in politics is also obvious in *Fanshen*, a play based on a book by William Hinton, an American who went to China "as a tractor technician," as Hare has described him, "both to observe and help the great land reform programmes of the late 1940's." Hare felt "an obligation to portray Chinese peasants" of the village of Log Bow "in a way which was adequate to their suffering," but was "not interested in portraying the scenes of violence and brutality which marked the landlords' regime and its overthrow." After seeing the play, Hinton objected to Hare's "liberal slant" and urged the playwright to revise the play so as to provide a clear Marxist emphasis, but Hare incorporated only a few of Hinton's list of 110 suggested emendations. *Fanshen* (the title is translated as "to turn the body," or, alternatively, "to turn over") was written for the Joint Stock Company in 1974 and opened in Sheffield before moving on to the ICA Terrace Theatre in London in April of 1975.

As has been noted, Hare's artistic sensibilities were no doubt influenced by the events of 1968, and his early work suggests a theater of political commitment and protest, carried into the 1970's. His play *Teeth 'n' Smiles*, produced in 1975 at the Royal Court Theatre, has been called "a metaphor for British society," and in the way it treats rock music and popular culture, "an elegy for the vanished visions of the late Sixties."

The action is set at Cambridge on June 9, 1969, and centers on a performance of a rock band for the May Ball of Jesus College. This concert proves to be a disaster when Maggie, the lead singer of the group, gets drunk, insults the audience, and is finally sent to prison on a drug charge. The musicians regard their privileged audience with contempt: "Rich complacent self-loving self-regarding self-righteous phoney half-baked politically immature evil-minded little shits." Interviewed about the play by *Theatre Quarterly*, Hare claimed it was intended to question "whether we have any chance of changing ourselves."

In his survey *British Theatre Since 1955: A Reassessment* (1979), Ronald Hayman criticizes the play for setting up Cambridge as symbolizing a repressive capitalist system, concluding that "this kind of play bases its appeal on giving the audience a chance to believe that there is a common enemy which can be fought." Hare's targets in this play are self-delusion, class guilt, and class war, but the play mainly attacks the upscale educational establishment, represented by Cambridge (which Hare knew at firsthand), and has been regarded as an indictment of the detached university intellectuals.

The protagonist of *Knuckle*, which opened at London's Comedy Theatre in March of 1974, is far removed from the privileged setting of Cambridge. He is a tough-minded vulgarian who is pragmatic and cynical about the hypocrisy of his world and his own family. Curly Delafield has returned to his home in Guildford seeking information about the disappearance of his sister Sarah, who had worked as a nurse in a psychiatric hospital. Curly is a blunt and brutal man. He had not seen his sister in twelve years, but he is determined to discover what has happened to her.

Sarah's overcoat was found on the beach at Eastbourne, famous for a ghastly murder that was committed there in the spring of 1924. Apparently Sarah either committed suicide or was murdered. The play therefore involves a process of detection, as those close to Sarah, a journalist named Max, her friend Jenny, and her father, are subjected to Curly's relentless interrogation. The mystery of her disappearance is solved at the end, after a sordid story of scandal and blackmail has been brought to light.

Curly is extremely cynical, a man who has been involved in selling arms, and in this regard he resembles in his amoral outlook the character of Andrew Undershaft in George Bernard Shaw's play *Major Barbara* (1905). Curly is habitually skeptical of men and their motives, including his own father. His view of the world is revealed by his motto: "Every man has his own gun. That's not a metaphor. That's a fact." In a mean world, Curly does not "pick fights" but merely provides weapons: "They're going to kill each other with or without my help," he claims. London is viewed as the corrupt center of a corrupt and fallen world, and the corruption has spread to Guildford. As Curly remarks at the end of the play, "In the mean square mile of the City of London they were making money. Back to my guns." Nearly everyone in this play is contaminated by money.

Knuckle is experimental in the way it mixes genres. The play develops as an apparent murder mystery, a whodunit that leaves open the possibility of suicide but turns out to be merely a parody of a conventional thriller. The sleuth Curly is like a stripped-down, plain-spoken Andrew Undershaft wearing a Mike Hammer mask, a very private eye. In fact, however, the play is an allegory of family betrayal, capitalist greed, and corruption. Hare's declared intention in writing it was "to subvert the form of the thriller to a serious end."

Curly is not a likable character because he is so cynical and so crude, but his character, shaped by the world that has molded it, is at least redeemed by his brutal honesty. He is not self-deluded, as so many of Hare's characters seem to be. One of Hare's most ambitious plays that attempts to take on human delusion on a global scale is *A Map of the World*, first performed at London's Lyttleton Theatre in January of 1983. The title comes from Oscar Wilde: "A map of the world that does not include Utopia is not worth even glancing at. . . ," and the central conflict is a philosophical argument between a Marxist idealist, Stephen Andrews, and a conservative "realist," an expatriate celebrity Indian writer named Victor Mehta; the two have been invited to address a UNESCO conference on world poverty in Bombay.

The play is complicated by the way it is framed, with the action shifting from the original confrontation to a filmed reconstruction being shot in London, as the audience realizes when scene 1 gives way to scene 2. This polemical play has been criticized for being too experimental in its framework and conception and too ambitious in scope, taking on issues of artistic freedom, world poverty, Third World nationalism, political compromise, and the decline of Western civilization, in the midst of a rhetorical contest partly based on sexual jealousy. "Unarguably," Hare has confessed, "I was trying to do too many things at once, and although I have now directed three productions of the play, I cannot ever quite achieve the right balance between the different strands."

Hare describes *A Map of the World* as a "disputatious play" that intended "to sharpen up people's minds, to ask them to remember why they believe what they do." Perhaps this goal was better achieved in the earlier play, *Plenty*, despite the puzzlement over motivation evident in the reviews of the later film version. *Plenty* was one of Hare's most successful plays but also one of his most ambiguous. It was first performed at London's Lyttleton Theatre in 1978, starring Kate Nelligan as Susan Traherne, the protagonist, before going on to Broadway. In 1985, Hare reshaped the script for the motion picture adaptation. The film version rearranged the opening, starting the action at St. Benoît, France, in November of 1943, rather than in the Knightsbridge area of London in 1962, presumably to establish Susan's character from the start as a young Englishwoman serving the French Resistance behind enemy lines during World War II.

Thereafter, in general, the film follows the chronology of the play, which mainly concerns Susan's difficulty in adjusting to civilian and domestic life in England after the war in the time of "plenty" that was to follow. The play seems to document a movement from innocence to insanity, as Susan restlessly moves from one job to another and from one relationship to another, presumably trying to recapture the excitement she knew with her wartime lover, a British agent in France known only by his codename, Lazar. After a brief flirtation with a working-class lover named Mick, whom she had selected to father a child in a liaison that only proved frustrating to both of them, she agrees to marry a career diplomat, Raymond Brock, whose career she later destroys for no clearly explained reason.

With regard to Susan, Hare has written that he was struck by a statistic "that seventy-five percent of the women flown behind the lines for the Special Operations Executive were subsequently divorced after the war." The play, which dramatizes Susan's restlessness in this context, has been criticized for its failure to explain her motives. After all, Raymond Brock seems to be a decent character who sincerely cares for his disturbed wife. Hare describes him as a young man of "delightful ingenuousness," and has noted that it would be a mistake to play him as a fool. His character is blemished, however, by the corrupt institution he serves, the Foreign Office. In a less obvious way than Andrew May in *Pravda*, Brock is ruined by his professionalism and his dedication to an unworthy career.

On the surface, Susan may appear to be maladjusted and irrational. She expresses the need to "move on" several times during the course of the play, but at first glance it seems that she is only able to "move on" from one job to another or from one relationship to another. Psychologically, she does not seem to be able to "move on" from the excitement of love and life behind enemy lines during the war. When she is much later reunited with Lazar in England, she discovers that he has "moved on" to shabby domesticity and a life without joy or enthusiasm. The danger of "moving on" in the sense of adjusting to a changing commonplace world is that this could mean nothing more than accepting banal conformity.

Susan's character is vibrant because she resists that kind of commonplace adjustment. Hare has written that men "are predisposed to find Susan Traherne unsympathetic." The commonplace judgment likely to be made about Susan is that she is emotionally unstable, if not completely deranged. "It's a common criticism of my work," Hare notes in his postscript to the play, "that I write about women whom I find admirable, but whom the audience dislikes."

The case against Susan "makes itself, or is made by the other characters," Hare adds, but the character is remarkable in her fierce independence and quite extraordinary in her behavior, which Hare believes should create "a balance of sympathy" throughout the play. Hare has written that he intended to show through Susan "the struggle of a heroine against a deceitful and emotionally stultified class." Her motives are submerged and complex, no doubt, but if that is a criticism of the character, it is one that could also be leveled at Hamlet. The mystery of motivation is not necessarily a flaw in a complex and enduring drama.

Hare's most critically acclaimed play after *Plenty* was *Pravda*, a biting satire of farcical dimensions on the newspaper industry in Great Britain and the dangers of collusion between Whitehall and Fleet Street, between government and the press. *Pravda* was written with Hare's earlier collaborator Brenton and appears to be a not-so-thinly-veiled attack upon the brand of journalism represented by the Australian press tycoon Rupert Murdoch, who took over *The Times* of London, just as *Pravda*'s central character, Lambert Le Roux (from South Africa rather than Australia) takes over the most influential establishment in Brenton and Hare's fictional London, *The Victory*.

Pravda premiered at the National Theatre in 1985, with Anthony Hopkins gaining rave notices for his caricature of Le Roux. Murdoch was reportedly angered by the play. Trevor Nunn, enjoying the limelight of *Les Misérables* (1985), which he directed and adapted as a musical from Victor Hugo's novel, told *Newsweek* that Murdoch "was extremely incensed and sent out the word to get the National and the RSC [Royal Shakespeare Company, whose London home is the Barbican Arts Centre], the two subsidized theatres" in Great Britain. Nunn and Peter Hall, who was instrumental in creating the three-auditorium National Theatre complex on London's South Bank, were both disappointed that the government of Margaret Thatcher did not support the integrity of the National Theatre in the "totally corrupt campaign" (as Hall described it) that followed. When government subsidies to the arts were cut (threatening to close down the National's smallest experimental auditorium in the complex), the director of the National must have sensed political pressure nearly as bizarre and dangerous as what is imagined in the Brenton and Hare play.

Pravda shows Hare's skill as a gadfly, questioning not only journalistic ethics but the larger issue of truth in journalism as well. This "comedy of excess" (as Hare described it) concerns the monopolizing of newspapers in England by the ruthless Lambert Le Roux. The action opens with Le Roux's takeover of a provincial paper, the *Leicester Bystander*, hardly a paradigm for journalistic ethics even before Le Roux's bid. Moira Patterson, a local shop-owner maligned by the newspaper by mistake, goes to the editorial offices to demand a retraction. The cynical editor, Harry Morrison, and his subordinate, Andrew May (soon to become the new editor-in-chief) tell her "we . . . don't publish corrections," because "what is printed must be true," and so "to print corrections is a kind of betrayal" of the public trust. May considers this perverse logic a matter of journalistic ethics.

This satiric introduction to an already corrupt world of journalism hardly inspires confidence in the *Leicester Bystander* and what it represents. The corruption of this provincial paper, however, pales in comparison to Andrew's later experiences as editor of *The Victory*, a national paper, a "paper for England."

Although billed as a comedy and often howlingly funny, *Pravda* is an extremely bitter satire that manages to strike out at corruption in high places and to spoof newspapers at all levels and television journalism as well. Besides *The Victory*, Le Roux owns a gutter tabloid (famous for its nudes) called *The Tide* and also attempts to take over a Left Wing paper called *The Usurper* (shades of *The Guardian*?). Once in power, Le Roux fires underlings with the gleeful abandon of the Queen of Hearts in Lewis Carroll's *Alice's Adventures in Wonderland* (1865). A fired journalist from *The Victory* regrets most that he will never again appear on a television talk show called *Speak or Shut Up*. Now, he will have to "sit at home shouting at the television like ordinary people."

In his bluntness, Le Roux resembles the unsentimental Curly of *Knuckle*, blown up to monstrous proportions, a vindictive Citizen Kane running amok. There is no clever Hamlet to counter the villainy of this Claudius, as Hare's satire seems to be moving in the direction of tragedy. The tragic vision depends on a sense of justice, however, and finally all that appears in Hare's bitter satiric world is a sense of the absurd so total that railing against it is clearly pointless.

Andrew's wife, Rebecca, gives him a "leaked" document that indicates a breach of public trust by the Minister of Defence concerning the transport of plutonium in flasks that are demonstrably unsafe. When Andrew decides to print the story in *The Victory*, Le Roux fires him. When Andrew and other fired journalists from *The Victory* take over *The Usurper*, Le Roux and his subordinate trick them into running libelous stories about their former employer, then threaten Andrew with litigation and bankruptcy.

At the end, Andrew is humiliated into begging Le Roux's forgiveness and editing *The Tide* as a means of penance. Practicing journalism is more important to him, finally, than ethics, integrity, truth, or love. A muddled idealist not fully understanding his presumed convictions, Andrew deserves to become a lackey to the demonic Le Roux, devoting his skill to purveying falsehood and smut, the foreman of what Le Roux calls his "foundry of lies."

Rebecca, who loves Andrew, is forced to abandon him after he succumbs to his bloodlust for revenge against Le Roux (his tragic flaw, if this play could be a tragedy) and after he finally sells his soul to the demon magnate who believes "No one tells the truth. Why single out newspapers?" Rebecca is the only character clever enough to see through Le Roux's deviousness, but she is powerless to take action against him. Otherwise, this bitter, satiric world is populated by mean-spirited, unscrupulous, dishonest people.

Hare has a particular genius for designing ingeniously constructed, unpredictable plots and strong, ambiguous characters that defy immediate classification and interpretation. The male characters tend to be flawed, either because they are infirm of purpose and self-deceived, or because they are all too purposeful and self-assured, in some instances even brutal. In Hare's male characters, civilized behavior and even signals of basic decency can be signs of weakness. Andrew May's apparently "good" qualities (bourgeois ambition, a dedication to the work ethic, a capacity for moral outrage) are in fact merely the product of an unthinking liberal idealism, which easily gives way to his monstrous hatred for Le Roux and his absolute thirst for vengeance. Brock, the diplomat in *Plenty*, is also misled by his emotions.

"Decent" people are not survivors in the kind of world Hare imagines, a world that requires intellectual toughness for survival. The idealist, like the sympathetic Darwin of *Plenty*, cannot stand a chance when countered by the unfeeling pragmatists who operate the machinery of State. Hare's men, often dominated by career ambitions, gradually lose their integrity while serving the corrupt and corrupting Establishment of government and big business. They give themselves to these enterprises and are transformed into cogs in the machinery of State, disposable and interchangeable parts. The career diplomat Darwin of *Plenty*, for example, has given a lifetime of loyal service to the Foreign Office but is betrayed by his superiors during the Suez Crisis. Determined to speak his mind and tell the truth, an honorable course of action, he is crushed and his career ruined. This is the sort of career from which Susan extricates her husband, but Brock, lacking her perspective, can only regret the career loss and resent Susan's interference.

The male characters, then, are driven by ambition and the lure of professional success; their vision will be clouded and their integrity compromised. Brock is not a fool, but he will not conclude, as Susan apparently does, that a state bureau that will betray a career loyalist such as Darwin and make a scapegoat of him is not worthy of one's service. In *Pravda*, with its broad, satiric distortions, Andrew can be seen as a fool because his self-betrayal is expanded to farcical proportions. In a more restrained context, Andrew might be seen as a parallel figure to Brock. In the end, Andrew's integrity is compromised when he goes back to Le Roux to edit the sleaziest tabloid in England, but the man is so stupidly devoted to his profession that he hardly seems to care that he has lost his integrity and self-respect. Rebecca has attempted to clarify his decision and to explain the consequences, but to no avail. In a more subtle way, Susan performs a similar function for Brock in *Plenty*, but Brock is so ordinary, so average, and so typical in his ambition that audiences may miss the point.

Plenty may be mistaken for domestic melodrama (even though Susan is hardly a typical melodramatic heroine), but the movement is toward pathos and tragedy in the way men allow themselves to be transformed and corrupted into banality. The meaning of *Pravda* is the more easily recognized by its satiric approach and farcical distortions. Even so, Gavin Millar, in *Sight and Sound*, praised *Plenty* as "one of the few recent texts, in theatre or cinema, that undertakes an unpretentious but serious review of postwar Britain's decline."

Hare's later plays and films continued to advance his criticism of Tory society and Thatcherism. His films *Paris by Night* (starring Charlotte Rampling and Michael Gambon) and *Strapless* (starring Blair Brown, Bridget Fonda, and Bruno Ganz) extended his interest in conflicted women characters trying to resolve the contradictions in their lives. To prepare himself for *Paris by Night*, Hare attended the annual party conference in Blackpool to observe closely the "new Tory woman," as he described, in his introduction to the screenplay published by Faber & Faber in 1988, the new breed of women who entered conservative politics in Great Britain during the Thatcher years. Also in 1988, he created his most sympathetic woman character, Isobel Glass, for his play *The Secret Rapture.* Isobel is set in conflict with her sister, Marion French, who has become a Thatcherite junior minister and who believes that not to make money is "worse than stupid; it's irresponsible." The humanistic Isobel is saintly and is ultimately destroyed by the morally corrupt world that she inhabits.

Hare then began a trilogy of plays dealing with British institutions. The first play of the trilogy, *Racing Demon*, is about ecclesiastical betrayal and the Church of England and focuses on a well-meaning minister who lost his faith in God but found purpose in serving the needy. The minister's career, however, is threatened and ruined by his superiors for political reasons.

Another play, *Murmuring Judges*, concerns the legal system. A note on the curtain of the Olivier Theatre explained the title: "In Scottish law, a form of contempt, meaning 'to speak ill of the judiciary' or 'to scandalize the court.'" Hare added in a note to the play, published by Faber & Faber, "It is still an offense in Scottish law."

The published text of *Murmuring Judges* begins with a quotation from Ogden Nash: "Professional people have no cares/ Whatever happens, they get theirs." The play is about moral corruption and compromise in the prison service (a young Irishman is jailed and brutalized unjustly) and about an idealistic woman lawyer who is taught a lesson about how justice operates in England. Hare therefore continued to write from a position of political outrage, satirizing and dramatizing the foibles of his time.

Other major works

SCREENPLAYS: *Plenty*, 1985 (adaptation of his stage play); *Wetherby*, 1985; *Paris by Night*, 1988; *Strapless*, 1989; *Damage*, 1992.

TELEPLAYS: *Man Above Men*, 1973; *Licking Hitler*, 1978; *Dreams of Leaving*, 1980; *Saigon: Year of the Cat*, 1983; *Heading Home*, 1991.

Bibliography

Gussow, Mel. "David Hare: Playwright as Provocateur." *The New York Times Magazine*, September 29, 1985, 42-47, 75-76. A substantial evaluation of Hare's career anticipating the opening of *A Map of the World* at New York's Public Theater. Gussow concentrates on the controversial nature of Hare's works that polarize both audiences and critics because of the playwright's political concerns: "the collapse of the English empire, the debilitating effects of the class system, the myths of patriotism, the loss of personal freedom."

Hare, David. "Hare Apparent." Interview by Steve Lawson. *Film Comment* 21, no. 5 (September/October, 1985): 18-22. Hare was interviewed after the theatrical success of *Pravda* as he was planning a film project entitled *The Butter and Egg Man* (finally completed as *Paris by Night*). Lawson begins with a concise career survey that targets Hare's major themes, "choices of honesty." About the films *Wetherby* and *Plenty*, Hare notes, "I'm obsessed with the cost of telling or *not* telling yourself the truth." Hare goes into detail, explaining the changes that he made in adapting *Plenty* to the screen. The interview concentrates on *Plenty* and *Wetherby*, the latter being the first film he directed as well as wrote.

_____. "Joint Stock: A Memoir." *Granta*, no. 18 (1986): 247-255. Concerns the forming of the Joint Stock company with Max Stafford-Clark, David Aukin, and Bill Gaskil after the collapse of Hare's Portable Theatre Company in 1973, and the creation of Hare's *Fanshen*, based upon William Hinton's book about Hinton's experience on a communal farm in China. When Joint Stock was turned into a cooperative after *Fanshen*, Hare parted company with the cofounders and here explains his reasons.

_____. *Writing Left-Handed*. London: Faber & Faber, 1991. A collection of essays linked by "an autobiographical thread," written since 1978, and covering the playwright's student period, his work as literary manager at the Royal Court Theatre during the late 1960's, and his work in the film industry. "A play is not actors, a play is not a text; a play is what happens between the stage and the audience," Hare writes of the theatrical experience. "The play is in the air."

Hayman, Ronald. *British Theatre Since 1955: A Reassessment*. New York: Oxford University Press, 1979. Hayman covers Hare's early career; the influence of Raymond Williams, the Marxist don under whom Hare studied at Jesus College; the Portable Theatre; the Royal Court; and a number of plays, from *Teeth 'n' Smiles* to *Plenty*. An appendix surveys the plays produced year by year from 1955 to 1978. Chapter 3, "The Politics of Hatred," concentrates on Hare's work.

Kramer, Mimi. "The Theatre." Review of *The Secret Rapture*. *The New Yorker* 65 (November 13, 1989): 106-113. This extended review describes

The Secret Rapture as an "anti-nuclear-family drama." Kramer criticizes the way Hare turns a family drama into "an allegory of what has happened to political idealism in England and America" because of an alleged lack of plausible motivation and objects to the play's anti-Thatcherite position.

Poole, Mike, and John Wyver. *Powerplays: Trevor Griffiths in Television.* London: BFI, 1984. Chapter 3 covers Griffith's collaboration with Hare, Howard Brenton, Snoo Wilson, and others in the experimental *Lay By*, an exercise in group writing mounted by Hare's Portable Theatre Company in Edinburgh after it had been rejected by the Royal Court. The goal of the Portable Theatre is explained: to reach working-class audiences through oppositional and committed drama.

James M. Welsh

LORENZ HART

Born: New York, New York; May 2, 1895
Died: New York, New York; November 22, 1943

Principal drama

Fly with Me, pr. 1920 (lyrics; libretto by Milton Kroopf and Philip Leavitt; music by Richard Rodgers); *The Melody Man*, pr. 1924 (libretto, with Rodgers and Herbert Fields); *The Garrick Gaieties*, pr. 1925, pb. 1951 (lyrics; sketches by Sir Arthur Sullivan, Morrie Ryskind, and others; music by Rodgers); *Dearest Enemy*, pr. 1925 (lyrics; libretto by Fields; music by Rodgers; based on Jean Gilbert's operetta *Die Frau im Hermelin*); *The Girl Friend*, pr. 1926 (lyrics; libretto by Fields; music by Rodgers); *Peggy-Ann*, pr. 1926 (lyrics; libretto by Fields; music by Rodgers); *A Connecticut Yankee*, pr. 1927 (lyrics; libretto by Fields; music by Rodgers); *Chee-Chee*, pr. 1928 (lyrics; libretto by Fields; music by Rodgers); *Present Arms*, pr. 1928 (lyrics; libretto by Fields; music by Rodgers); *Jumbo*, pr. 1935 (lyrics; libretto by Ben Hecht and Charles MacArthur; music by Rodgers); *On Your Toes*, pr. 1936 (lyrics; libretto, with Rodgers and George Abbott; music by Rodgers); *Babes in Arms*, pr. 1937, pb. 1951 (libretto, with Rodgers; music by Rodgers); *I'd Rather Be Right*, pr., pb. 1937 (lyrics; libretto by George S. Kaufman and Moss Hart; music by Rodgers); *I Married an Angel*, pr. 1938 (libretto, with Rodgers; music by Rodgers; adaptation of James Vasarzy's play); *The Boys from Syracuse*, pr. 1938 (lyrics; libretto by Abbott; music by Rodgers); *Pal Joey*, pr. 1940, pb. 1952 (lyrics; libretto by John O'Hara; music by Rodgers); *By Jupiter*, pr. 1942, pb. 1951 (lyrics; libretto, with Rodgers; music by Rodgers; adaptation of Julian Thompson's play *The Warrior's Husband*); *The Complete Lyrics of Lorenz Hart*, pb. 1986.

Other literary forms

Lorenz Hart is known primarily as a lyricist. Although he collaborated on several librettos for stage comedies, he wrote more than a thousand song lyrics for those and twenty-four other stage comedies and revues and for ten motion-picture musicals, of which *Love Me Tonight* (1932) is representative. Hart also translated plays, operettas (such as Jean Gilbert's *Die Frau im Hermelin*), and lyrics (such as those to the 1934 motion picture *The Merry Widow*, often without receiving credit).

Achievements

Lorenz Hart played a major role in advancing the musical theater from the level of vaudeville, revue, and spectacle to that of musical drama. He was not the first to take this step, nor did he take it alone, but he was one of the pioneers in an era that included such other musical-theater giants as

George and Ira Gershwin, Herbert and Dorothy Fields, George M. Cohan, Irving Berlin, Arthur Schwartz and Howard Dietz, Oscar Hammerstein II, Cole Porter, and Hart's partner Richard Rodgers. In the early 1900's, W. S. Gilbert and Sir Arthur Sullivan were writing their satiric light operas in England; Sigmund Romberg, Vincent Youmans, Victor Herbert, and Rudolf Friml were writing operettas in the romantic Viennese tradition; and the team of Jerome Kern, Guy Bolton, and P. G. Wodehouse had just begun to adapt these European forms to an American form influenced by music-hall traditions. The satiric lyrics of Gilbert and Wodehouse strongly influenced the young Hart, and the stories that held these musicals together inspired him to want musical comedies in which the songs were closely integrated with the plots and characters.

When Hart and Richard Rodgers met, they found that they shared this vision of the musical theater, and their partnership thrived on their commitment to it. Their attempt to integrate song and drama began in the early shows, as with "Old Enough to Love," a song for mature lovers in *Dearest Enemy*. It continued improving throughout their partnership to the Amazon's defiant "Nobody's Heart" in *By Jupiter*. In their early shows, the integration was not entirely successful, but the partners learned quite a lot about musical integration from their motion-picture experiences in the 1930's. When they returned to Broadway from Hollywood, they began writing their own librettos in which the songs could be inherent parts of the action and dialogue. The epitome of Hart's achievement in integrating lyrics into drama is considered to be *Pal Joey*, with its character pieces, Joey's hypocritical "I Could Write a Book" and Vera's cynical "Bewitched, Bothered, and Bewildered."

In addition to their importance in integrating the music into the drama, Rodgers and Hart also pioneered the use of subjects and stories that had previously been disregarded for the musical theater. For example, *Dearest Enemy* was based on a historical incident of the Revolutionary War; *Peggy-Ann* was the first musical to use Freudian dream theories; *A Connecticut Yankee* used Mark Twain's satire on Yankeeism; *I'd Rather Be Right* was the first musical satire of in-office government officials; *The Boys from Syracuse* set a Shakespearean comedy (*The Comedy of Errors*) to music; and *Pal Joey* dealt with sleazy, small-time nightclub entertainers and criminals. Rodgers and Hart were determined to turn musical comedy away from the stock plots and characters of the early stage. *Pal Joey*, which was not well received at its introduction, is now considered to be the masterpiece that brought Broadway musicals to maturity. Its 1952 revival won the New York Drama Critics Circle Award for Best Musical and eleven out of sixteen Donaldson Awards.

Hart was equally concerned with breaking the "June, moon, soon" mold of the Tin Pan Alley rhyme. An avid reader, he had an understanding of rhyme theory and poetic rhythm that allowed him to write witty, subtle, complex lyrics that impressed nearly everyone who heard them. One has only to compare his "Manhattan" lyrics ("Manhattan" rhymed with "Staten," "Coney" with "baloney") with those of another song, "East Side, West Side" ("town," "down," "O'Rourke," "York") to see the difference. He had an excellent understanding of dialect and could range from the slangy in "The Girl Friend" to the archaic in "Thou Swell" through the romantic in "Isn't It Romantic" and the tender in "My Funny Valentine," from the ironic in "I Wish I Were in Love Again" to the satiric in "Dear Old Syracuse" and the impudent in "Girls, Girls, Girls." Hart may have been the first truly literate American lyricist; certainly he was the first to achieve equal credit with the composer for the songwriting and to have his name, along with those of the author and composer, in lights on the theater marquee.

Biography

Lorenz Milton Hart was born in New York City on May 2, 1895, to Max Hart and Frieda Isenberg Hart. He had one brother, Theodore Van Wyck Hart, who also gained theatrical fame, as comic actor Teddy Hart. Lorenz Hart was educated at Columbia Grammar School, DeWitt Clinton, Weingart Institute, and Columbia University. In school, he belonged to literary societies and wrote for and edited the school papers.

Hart grew up in a highly literary environment. His mother, Frieda, had wanted to be an actress, and from the age of six, he was taken to the theater. He began to write poetry when he was six, and he wrote and performed skits and satires of plays he had seen both on and off Broadway. He loved the Gilbert and Sullivan and Kern-Bolton-Wodehouse musicals, but he never liked Herbert's "schmaltzy" music. At the Weingart Institute summer school, he belonged to the Weingart Literary Society and wrote articles for the literary magazine, often satires and humorous essays. In 1909, he became the editor of *The Weingart Review*. Also at Weingart, he acted in school dramas, farces, and minstrel shows. At fifteen, he began to attend Paradox Lake Camp, where he was active in weekly shows. He was nicknamed "Shakespeare" because he brought to camp a trunkload of books, including a fifteen-volume set of William Shakespeare's works, and performed Hamlet's soliloquy in one of the camp shows.

In 1917, Hart became the dramatic counselor at Brant Lake Camp; there he wrote comedy acts for small-time vaudeville shows. While he was there, Arthur Schwartz (who later composed "That's Entertainment" and "Dancing in the Dark") heard some of Hart's lyrics and took a job at Brant Lake Camp in order to meet Hart and work with him on camp productions. While working at Brant Lake in the summers, Hart also worked for United Plays, a reading and translating company associated with the Shubert theaters. Between 1920 and 1925, he translated and adapted French and German plays and Viennese operettas. Notably, he translated *Die Frau im Hermelin* by Jean Gilbert as "The Lady in Ermine," which was never published or produced but from which he adapted material to use in *Dearest Enemy*. He also is recognized to have done part of what is now the standard translation of Ferenc Molnár's *Liliom*, although he did not receive credit. Schwartz claims that Hart also wrote lyrics for three songs by Billy Rose for which he did not receive credit or royalties. Hart was working in both instances for salary, and his material became the property of the employer.

In 1919, he was introduced to Richard Rodgers by a friend who knew that Rodgers was looking for a lyricist. Hart was twenty-three, Rodgers sixteen. The two collaborated on a number of amateur shows. One of their early songs, "Any Old Place with You," was purchased by Lew Fields for *A Lonely Romeo* (pr. 1919); this was their first song performed on Broadway. While Hart (and later Rodgers, too) was at Columbia University, he and Rodgers collaborated on musicals produced in New York hotel ballrooms. These amateur university productions were often clever enough to attract theatergoers and critics; they provided excellent training for potential theatrical talent.

Rodgers and Hart created more than twenty-five preprofessional musicals. The partners were unable to sell any of their work to Broadway producers for about four years. Hart was continuing to translate, and Rodgers was considering changing his career goal, when Rodgers was offered the chance to write songs for *The Garrick Gaieties*, and he insisted on having Hart as lyricist. They were not paid for this work, but the show was on Broadway, produced by the Theatre Guild, and attended by professional critics. The show, intended for two performances, was so original and witty that it received rave notices and was extended for a six-month run. The hit of the show was the Rodgers and Hart song "Manhattan," which established their reputations on Broadway. Their first big success, however, was "My Heart Stood Still," which was written for the British show *One Dam Thing After Another* (pr. 1927). Its popularity preceded their return to the United States, and the song was then introduced to Broadway in *A Connecticut Yankee*. After that hit production, with few exceptions, Rodgers and Hart's musicals enjoyed one success after another.

After the Crash of 1929 depressed Broadway production, the songwriting team worked in Hollywood periodically in the early 1930's. Their film experiences, particularly when working with Rouben Mamoulian, taught them much about enhancing their story with music and making songs a part of the dialogue. These were ideas which they had already used in such musical dramas as *A Connecticut Yankee*. Innovations in the use of song in the motion picture *Love Me Tonight* prompted improvements in the music of the great Rodgers and Hart Broadway shows of the late 1930's and early 1940's. Motion-picture production techniques, however, were frustrating to them, being so different from their ingrained Broadway techniques. They were unhappy with the long periods of inactivity enforced by studio contracts, with the arbitrary and unexpected rejection or substitution of songs, and with the cancellation of entire film projects deemed noncommercial. They missed their customary participation with their Broadway colleagues in other aspects of stage production: interpreting, staging, choreographing, revising, and directing. When they read "Whatever happened to Rodgers and Hart?" in the Los Angeles *Examiner*, they were convinced that they should return to Broadway.

Drinking had already become a problem for Hart. Indeed, when Hart began his collaboration with Rodgers at age twenty-three, Rodgers' mother had predicted that Hart would not live to be twenty-five. Hart grew up in a fun-loving family. His father had plenty of money most of the time, and the family lived in large New York apartments and had two maids, a chauffeur, and a footman. Max Hart enjoyed living well and indulging his sons. Although Frieda Hart was a good housekeeper, she never minded disruptions caused by her sons and their numerous friends, who made the home a center for games, parties, poetry readings, and dramatic and musical performances. From childhood, Hart developed a taste for high living, conviviality, and incessant activity. He inherited a small size: He was only five feet tall, and his brother was only two inches taller. Furthermore, his head was slightly large for his body, so that he had a somewhat dwarfish look. Although people said they did not notice his size and proportions because his personality was so charming, he remained sensitive about his appearance all of his life. Still, Rodgers recalled that Hart was actually handsome, with animated features and warm brown eyes. When he was young, his father unstintingly gave him money for dates and treating his friends, and it is possible that his father's largess taught him an unintended lesson—that he could gain love and friendship only by paying for them. Certainly he delighted throughout his life in picking up the check for whatever group he was with or even for everyone in the room.

Hart's friend Mel Shauer, however, believed that Hart's drinking was an attempt to quiet the incessant, restless activity of his brain. As boys, Hart and his friends joked that his vertical growth was held down by the size of his brain. He read voraciously, was fluent in three languages, loved conversation and entertaining, and kept constantly on the move, motoring, attending the theater, the opera, the ballet. George Balanchine, commenting about Hart's quick mind, said that whatever was needed on a show Hart would do in a moment, and then he would be off doing something else; he had a certain intuition about what techniques and what talents would work. He was described as "impish" and "puckish"; he might disappear in the middle of a conversation; he loved to tease; he laughed easily and readily. His vocabulary was immense and expressive; as far as anyone knew, he never used a rhyming dictionary. He was a perfectionist about lyrics and shows.

Whatever the reason, Hart's drinking increased during the 1930's, although it did not yet interfere with his work. After he and Rodgers returned from Hollywood, they wrote the songs for eight of their greatest musicals. For four of these, they also coauthored the librettos. These were the years of *On Your Toes, Babes in Arms, I Married an Angel, The Boys from Syracuse,* and what is now considered Rodgers and Hart's masterpiece, *Pal Joey.* Hart, however, became increasingly undependable; he would disappear and be inaccessible for lengthening periods of time. Rodgers sometimes had to track him down and stay with him to get a lyric written. Hart would not discipline himself to write until a rehearsal simply could not proceed until he did. Still, he would turn out brilliant lyrics under these adverse conditions.

By the onset of the 1940's, Hart's alcoholism was becoming a serious detriment to his work. After *By Jupiter,* Hart no longer wished to work with Rodgers, and he went to Mexico to avoid the pressure of doing *Oklahoma!* (pr. 1943) because he did not like the original play. When he returned, although in ill health, he was enthusiastic about working with Rodgers again on an adaptation of Henry Fielding's *Tom Jones* (1749), but he was unable to carry it out. Rodgers had already begun working with Oscar Hammerstein II. The former partners did collaborate on a 1943 revival of *A Connecticut Yankee,* and Hart's last song was "To Keep My Love Alive," a new one for that production. Its quality and critical acclaim proved that his lyric ability was still unimpaired. He developed pneumonia after attending the opening of the revival on November 17, and died at Doctors Hospital on November 22, 1943.

Analysis

"Amusing, breezy, contagious, energetic, fresh, gay, impudent, joyful, sophisticated, unhackneyed, versatile, witty, youthful, zestful"—such are the critical reactions to the works of Rodgers and Hart. Perhaps Lorenz Hart's failure to grow up physically and emotionally, a failure that destroyed him personally, was also what gave his lyrics and plots those fun-loving qualities which contributed to his success professionally. Youthful vitality and wit are the first characteristics common to all the shows of Rodgers and Hart. Hart evidenced a satiric turn of mind from his earliest attempts at writing, and he kept it until his death; Rodgers commented that Hart "really didn't know how not to be clever." All of their plots, those they wrote and those they set to music, were witty satires, in which Hart's irreverent lyrics could play their role.

Another characteristic of Rodgers and Hart's shows is their variety. Both partners believed in avoiding formulas, other people's or their own, and in never doing the same thing twice in a row—or twice at all, if possible. Subject matter for their shows includes anything from grand opera, the Depression, and long-distance bicycle racing to Freudian dreams, Chinese eunuchs, and Amazons. In the six librettos that they wrote themselves, there is a somewhat more consistent use of show business themes. Nevertheless, they made a deliberate policy of turning to a story quite different from whatever they had just completed, no matter how successful. For example, the political satire *I'd Rather Be Right* was followed by the fantasy *I Married an Angel*, which was followed in turn by the Shakespearean farce *The Boys from Syracuse*.

A third important characteristic of Rodgers and Hart's artistry was their effort to make the musical comedy a more completely integrated musical drama, in which the songs advanced the plot and portrayed character. As youngsters, both were impressed with the Kern-Bolton-Wodehouse musicals, in which the plots were not episodic or situational but were motivated by the characters, and the songs were not interludes but were part of the drama. Both writers wished to emulate and indeed surpass what they had admired. Their first Broadway comedy, *Dearest Enemy*, was such a drama, and the history of their songs and librettos is the history of improvements in song as drama.

Dearest Enemy was based on an incident in American history: Some ladies of New York entertained the officers of British General William Howe's staff with cakes and ale, enabling American forces to make a strategic retreat. The show was turned down by several producers who could not imagine the commercial success of a musical based on American history. Rodgers and Hart, however, could see the possibilities of an element of sexual enticement in the delay of the British, and the situation allowed them to counterplay a genuine love affair between a young American girl and a British officer against a strategic flirtation by an older woman. Two contrasting love songs were used to emphasize the differences between these relationships: "Here in My Arms" and "Old Enough to Love." Tired of the traditional love ballad, typically a stock love song with little appropriateness to the singer, the composers were looking for new ways to sing about love. "Old Enough to Love" allowed two variations on the theme; first, it was a love song between mature adults rather than ingenues, and second, it ironically used a tender lyric as a medium for a harsher emotion. (The latter was a technique which Rodgers and Hart used again in many later shows.) Furthermore, Hart suited the dialect of each song to the character singing it. In translating "The Lady in Ermine" a few years earlier, he had researched the eighteenth century, and in writing *Dearest Enemy* he was able to draw on this research in creating dialogue and lyrics that suggested the period. *Dearest Enemy* was one of the first musical comedies to achieve such authenticity; in general, comedy had simply placed a modern story in period costumes and settings. Besides the period dialect, Hart also used simple, ingenuous language for the girl's song and more complex, sophisticated language for the woman's. Thus he began his adaptation of lyric to the portrayal of dramatic character. *Dearest Enemy* also introduced the type of spunky, resourceful females that typically populate Rodgers and Hart musicals.

Although *The Girl Friend* was one of Rodgers and Hart's most popular and profitable productions, it did not add a great deal to their growth as artists. *Peggy-Ann* was the next significant step in their career. Based on a popular play, *Tillie's Nightmare*, in which the heroine had a series of comic dreams, the Rodgers-Hart-Fields team reinterpreted the dreams as Freudian fantasies. It was one of the first musical comedies to use Freudian theory. It also made use of a non-Broadway, balletic style of dancing, which along with the music was an integral part of the dream action. The dream, in turn, constituted the main plot, for the frame story was simply a young girl's coming to terms through her fantasies with the unromantic realities of her everyday life. In accordance with the Freudian background, the songs featured sexual innuendo to a degree unusual for the time, as in "A Little Birdie Told Me So" and "A Tree in the Park."

Chee-Chee, Rodgers and Hart's worst flop, was nevertheless one of their most daring experiments. It was based on a story about a young Chinese man who is trying to avoid inheriting his father's office as Grand Eunuch; the subject of castration was even more daring than the Freudian content of *Peggy-Ann*. The comedy did not appeal widely to critics or audiences; indeed, the satiric treatment of the subject impressed critics as tasteless and sophomoric, at best. This reception was vastly different from the raves Hart usually received for his witty words. Nevertheless, *Chee-Chee* integrated music and drama more completely than did any other Rodgers and Hart musical. So completely did the music become a part of the dialogue that only six songs had titles, compared with between ten and fifteen songs in most musicals. Most of the music consisted of snatches of songs and brief bits of musical dialogue interwoven in the progress of the plot. If the story of *Chee-Chee* had been more palatable to the public, it might have become one of Rodgers and Hart's most highly admired works, but even its failure taught the partners several important lessons: first, that music alone cannot make an unpopular subject acceptable; second, that having at least one and preferably more popular favorites among the songs is almost essential to the success of a musical comedy; third, that it is possible to achieve a nearly complete integration of music and drama; but, fourth, that they had not yet mastered that art. As a result of *Chee-Chee*'s failure, the next five Rodgers and Hart shows were far less venturesome. On the other hand, without the failure, the partners might not have been so receptive to some of the lessons which they learned from motion-picture techniques.

The Depression took Rodgers and Hart to Hollywood, which was less affected by hard times than Broadway had been. They did not enjoy working on films, but they were impressed by the technique by which a song was made to seem a natural extension of the dialogue; they were to use this technique in many of their subsequent stage shows. In *Love Me Tonight*, they also adapted the musically accompanied preliminary dialogue into a form they called "rhythmic dialogue" or "musical dialogue," a form of nonmelodic singing which they used again, as did many other musical comedy writers. For example, the technique was very useful in *My Fair Lady* (pr. 1956) and *Camelot* (pr. 1960) for Rex Harrison and Richard Burton, neither of whom had singing voices. A camera that moved about as a song was playing very likely gave Hart the idea for using the reprise to show character development. In *Love Me Tonight*, the camera moved across seven characters whistling or singing "Isn't It Romantic?" Three different sets of lyrics presented three different attitudes toward love. Hart had the reprise of "There's a Small Hotel" in *On Your Toes* serve a similar purpose. Later, he extended the technique to emphasize plot and character change. In *Pal Joey*, for example, Vera's reprise shows she is no longer "Bewitched, Bothered, and Bewildered." Another lesson came from Mamoulian, director of *Love Me Tonight*, who insisted that Rodgers write not only the songs but also all the background music, in order to achieve musical coherence throughout the film. What was true of musical coherence might also be true of literary coherence, and it was after this experience with Mamoulian that Rodgers and Hart began to write their own books. The ones they wrote themselves—the products of their fully matured talents—are accounted the best of their collaborations.

On Your Toes, the first of their books, did not have a very original plot, but it did bring together all that Rodgers and Hart had learned from their twenty-three years of collaboration. It was a fairly standard show-within-a-show plot, but it made ballet as well as song an essential part of the plot and characterization. The story concerns a former vaudeville dancer with classical yearnings, who becomes involved with a ballet company, fumbles traditional ballet in a comic travesty of classical dance forms, but finally introduces a jazz ballet in which his style succeeds very well. The ballet serves as the climax to the story, and not merely in the traditional "would-be star makes good" sense: In a confusion of identity, two gangsters are trying to shoot the hero, and at the conclusion of the jazz ballet performance, he signals the orchestra to continue playing so that he can keep on dancing and avoid being a stationary target for their guns. Meanwhile, his girlfriend calls the police, who arrive at the moment he becomes too exhausted to continue dancing. Thus, the satiric ballet, the jazz ballet, and the songs advance the plot and show the hero realizing his abilities.

Babes in Arms was a return to the type of joyous revue that had succeeded so well in the 1920's. There is not much to be said about the book, which Rodgers and Hart wrote this time without a collaborator. It is, however, notable that not one or two but five of their greatest songs came from this one show: "Where or When," "My Funny Valentine," "The Lady Is a Tramp," "Johnny One-Note," and "I Wish I Were in Love Again." Their songwriting skills had obviously reached an apex at this time, along with their dramatic skills.

I Married an Angel was a triumphantly witty account of an angel trying to adapt to the ways of this faulty world. In this show and in *By Jupiter*, all of their dramatic and lyric skills came together in what are still among the most memorable productions of musical comedy entertainment.

It was *Pal Joey*, however, that made the greatest impact on the Broadway musical tradition. The idea of doing this cynical, gritty show instead of the usual lighthearted comedy was suggested to them by John O'Hara, who wrote the book, and Rodgers and Hart were quick to see its possibilities. *Pal Joey* concerns a small-time nightclub entertainer who aspires to greater success. He is a handsome but unscrupulous opportunist who lies and seduces his way nearly to the top. Through a liaison with Vera, a wealthy older woman who is willing to pay for sexual excitement, he acquires his own nightclub. Upon a threat of blackmail, however, she quickly becomes disenchanted and drops him. There are no likable characters in this story, with the exception of a girl whom Joey attracts at the beginning of the play but drops in favor of Vera's money. The satire in *Pal Joey* is bitter and disillusioned instead of gay and youthful, and the wit is found in the slangy dialogue and sharp repartee. The show songs are designed to be trite and shoddy, as one might expect in a low-class nightclub, and even the love songs are hypocritical mockeries of genuine love songs. Critical reception of *Pal Joey* was mixed. Some critics found it distasteful; others recognized it as excellent drama and a trailblazing departure from the Broadway traditions. The latter critical opinion was supported by the show's success. It had a long initial run and an even longer run on its revival in 1952, when it also won the New York Drama Critics Circle Award for Best Musical. As Rodgers observed, "The show . . . forced the musical comedy theatre to wear long pants for the first time."

Indeed, this witty observation perhaps best sums up Rodgers and Hart's contribution to the musical theater. Along with Ira Gershwin and Cole Porter, Hart set a new standard in musical comedy for poetic excellence, semantic and phonetic appropriateness, and perfect rhythmic phrasing of lines to his partner's music. Together, Rodgers and Hart, with their collaborators, dared to break the mold of musical theater tradition and open the way to the great musical dramas of the 1950's and 1960's.

Bibliography
Gottfried, Martin. *Broadway Musicals.* New York: Harry N. Abrams, 1979. Gottfried combines a lavish, oversized, richly illustrated volume with a critical history of the Broadway musical. In his chapter entitled "Lyrics," he briefly describes the contribution of Hart to theater lyrics, proclaiming him (with Cole Porter) the supreme lyricist of the American musical theater. Reference is made to Hart's wit and unique contribution throughout the book. Index.

Green, Stanley. *The World of Musical Comedy.* 4th rev. ed. New York: DaCapo Press, 1980. The chapter "Rodgers and Hart" demonstrates how the two formed the first composer-lyricist team for which each man received equal recognition. Green provides standard biographies and traces the two artists' development, show by show. He provides critical commentary on their artistic growth and on their contribution to the Broadway musical, detailing *Pal Joey* as the pinnacle of their collaboration. Index, illustrations, and a complete listing of musicals with credits and discography.

Hart, Dorothy. *Thou Swell, Thou Witty: The Life and Lyrics of Lorenz Hart.* New York: Harper & Row, 1976. A poignant biography by Hart's sister-in-law, lovingly but truthfully telling the story of Hart's tortured life. It includes several reminiscences by friends and associates such as Irving Berlin and Richard Rodgers. Contains the lyrics for more than ninety of Hart's songs, a complete listing of his plays and films with the songs he wrote for each, and numerous personal and theatrical photographs.

Lerner, Alan Jay. *The Musical Theatre: A Celebration.* New York: McGraw-Hill, 1986. Lerner provides biographical and critical information about Hart from the perspective of a friend in the business. Of special interest is his description of Hart's physical challenges and how they caused the melancholy and pessimism in his life and lyrics. Illustrations, bibliography, and index.

Marx, Samuel, and Jan Clayton. *Rodgers and Hart.* New York: G. P. Putnam's Sons, 1976. This popular, anecdotal double biography of Rodgers and Hart chronicles their lives, collaboration, and achievements. It contrasts Rodgers' storybook life with Hart's sad and troubled life and examines how those difficulties influenced their work. Illustrations and index.

Carol Croxton
(Updated by *Gerald S. Argetsinger*)

MOSS HART

Born: New York, New York; October 24, 1904
Died: Palm Springs, California; December 20, 1961

Principal drama

The Hold-up Man, pr. 1923; *Jonica*, pr. 1930 (with Dorothy Heyward); *Once in a Lifetime*, pr., pb. 1930 (with George S. Kaufman); *Face the Music*, pr. 1932 (libretto; music by Irving Berlin); *As Thousands Cheer*, pr. 1933 (revue; music by Berlin); *The Great Waltz*, pr. 1934; *Merrily We Roll Along*, pr., pb. 1934 (with Kaufman); *Jubilee*, pr. 1935 (music by Cole Porter); *You Can't Take It with You*, pr. 1936, pb. 1937 (with Kaufman); *I'd Rather Be Right*, pr., pb. 1937 (with Kaufman; score by Richard Rodgers and Lorenz Hart); *The Fabulous Invalid*, pr., pb. 1938 (with Kaufman); *The American Way*, pr., pb. 1939 (with Kaufman); *The Man Who Came to Dinner*, pr., pb. 1939 (with Kaufman); *George Washington Slept Here*, pr., pb. 1940 (with Kaufman); *Lady in the Dark*, pr., pb. 1941 (music by Kurt Weill); *Winged Victory*, pr., pb. 1943; *Christopher Blake*, pr., pb. 1946; *Light Up the Sky*, pr. 1948, pb. 1949; *The Climate of Eden*, pr. 1952, pb. 1953 (adaptation of Edgar Mittelholzer's *Shadows Among Them*).

Other literary forms

Moss Hart is known primarily for his plays. He also achieved success as a screenwriter; among his best-known screenplays are those for *Gentleman's Agreement* (1947) and *A Star Is Born* (1954). In 1959, Hart published his autobiography, *Act One*, which was made into a film in 1963, as were many of his plays. Finally, Hart published a handful of miscellaneous articles on theater subjects.

Achievements

Moss Hart was one of the great comic playwrights of American drama. In works such as *Once in a Lifetime*, *You Can't Take It with You*, and *The Man Who Came to Dinner*, he gave the theater some of its most amusing moments. He was awarded the Roi Cooper Megrue Award in 1930 for *Once in a Lifetime* and in 1937, with George S. Kaufman, the Pulitzer Prize for *You Can't Take It with You*.

Since Hart's best works are his collaborations with Kaufman, his critical stature will always be obscured by that of the older, more famous dramatist. It would be a mistake, however, to think of Hart as simply Kaufman's collaborator. Kaufman worked with several partners in his career, including such talents as Ring Lardner, Alexander Woollcott, and Edna Ferber, but none of them produced such fine results with Kaufman as Hart did, nor were any of the Kaufman and Hart plays the work of one man more than the other. Theirs was a true collaboration, with each man contributing equally to the final product. Moreover, Hart's solo works, such as *Lady in the Dark*, with its innovative staging and probing of psychological conflicts, show that he could create significant drama on his own.

In addition to playwriting and screenwriting, Hart directed such plays as Alan Jay Lerner and Frederick Loewe's *Camelot* (pr. 1960) and *My Fair Lady* (pr. 1956); the latter won for Hart a Tony Award.

Biography

Moss Hart was born in the Bronx section of New York, the son of Barnett Hart, a cigar maker who was left without a trade when a cigar-making machine was developed. The family survived as best they could, but Hart's early life was dominated by a sense of poverty. The two most important influences in his childhood were his grandfather and his Aunt Kate. These impractical, domineering people, though a great drain on the family finances, were the only sources of color and vitality for the young Hart. Aunt Kate, an avid theatergoer, introduced Hart to the world of drama, which formed in his mind a desire to escape from his squalid surroundings via the glittering stage.

At the age of seventeen, Hart got his first theatrical job as office boy to Augustus Pitou, a touring-show producer known as "the King of the One-Night Stands." While reading plays that were submitted to Pitou, Hart began writing a play of his own, replete with the sentimental and hackneyed elements of those he had read. He presented the play to Pitou, who was enthusiastic about it and agreed to produce it. Entitled *The Hold-up Man*, it opened in Rochester in 1923 and flopped.

The failure of his first play also cost Hart his job. He worked as a director for little theater companies and as an actor, once playing the role of Smithers in Eugene O'Neill's *The Emperor Jones* (pr. 1920) to glowing reviews. He spent his summers as a social director in various resort camps. During this time, he still nursed a desire to write plays in the manner of O'Neill and George Bernard Shaw, but he learned that his talent lay not with serious drama but with light comedy. In the late 1920's, Hart began writing a comedy in the manner of his idol, the comedic writer George S. Kaufman, dealing with the advent of sound in motion pictures. Producer Sam Harris agreed to do the play only if Hart collaborated on it with Kaufman himself. The play, *Once in a Lifetime*, after dubious early showings and several major rewrites, was a smash hit and marked the beginning of one of the greatest writing teams in American drama. It also marked Hart's escape from the poverty of his early years. After reading the enthusiastic reviews of *Once in a Lifetime*, Hart moved his family from their Bronx apartment to rooms in the fashionable Edison Hotel.

In the following years, Hart wrote some of his best plays. These

included musicals with Irving Berlin and Cole Porter and further collaborations with Kaufman, including their greatest works, *You Can't Take It with
You* and *The Man Who Came to Dinner*. With the money from these plays,
Hart was able to buy a large country estate in the Poconos, yet he found
that success did not bring the solution to all of his problems. In 1934, he
began seeing a psychiatrist and came to believe that he was too dependent
on Kaufman. Finally, Hart, acting on the advice of his psychiatrist, broke
off his collaboration with Kaufman, although the two remained friends.

Hart's first play after the break, *Lady in the Dark*, proved that he could
write without Kaufman's support. He went on to write other successful
plays but never with the popularity of his work with Kaufman. In 1945, he
married actress Kitty Carlisle; they had two children. After World War II,
Hart wrote some of his finest screenplays, including *Gentleman's Agreement* and *A Star Is Born*. Hart served as president of the Dramatists Guild
from 1947 to 1955 and of the Authors League from 1955 to 1961. Hart also
returned to directing, winning a Tony Award in 1957 for *My Fair Lady*. In
1961, he died of a heart attack.

Analysis

Those who approach the plays of Moss Hart as literary products to be
analyzed and placed in some dramatic category will be disappointed. Hart
wrote his plays to give pleasure to large crowds. He learned early in his
career that his talent lay in witty light comedy rather than serious drama.
Though his plays satirized every institution of the time, from the New Deal
to the motion-picture industry, their prevailing tone is one of wild spoofing,
not serious criticism. This is not to dismiss Hart as merely a pleasant hack.
With Kaufman, he created some of America's funniest plays. Hart stayed
within the limits of the popular theater, though he did try to extend those
limits. As a result, he created superior entertainment that continues to
delight audiences even today.

A good example of the Kaufman and Hart comedy is their first
collaboration, *Once in a Lifetime*. It concerns three down-and-out vaudeville actors: the likable-but-dumb straight man George Lewis; the tough,
clever May Daniels; and the enterprising Jerry Hylands. They sell their act
and travel to Hollywood in the first days of sound pictures to open an
elocution school for movie actors, who must now be heard as well as seen.
The school, operating in Glogauer Studios, is a failure, but when George
repeats some unflattering comments on motion pictures in general and
Glogauer in particular (comments that he has picked up from Lawrence
Vail, a disgruntled playwright hired by Glogauer to turn out film scripts),
he is taken by the producer to be an outspoken genius and is made studio
supervisor. With Jerry and May as his assistants, George oversees the production of *Gingham and Orchids*, a movie that has the script of another

film, a set only half-lit, and the noise of George incessantly cracking Indian nuts throughout the sound track. To everyone's surprise, the film becomes a financial and critical success, and George is the hero of the hour. Jerry and May, realizing that George does not need their guidance in order to get along in pictures, return to New York to get married.

There is scarcely any facet of Hollywood in the early 1930's that *Once in a Lifetime* does not ridicule, whether it is the "early De Mille" architecture, vapid movie columnists, temperamental German directors, or stars who cannot act. Many of the authors' opinions are put into the mouth of Lawrence Vail, a representative figure among the successful Broadway dramatists who went to Hollywood to write for the studios and then were given nothing to do. (Vail's part was played in the original run of *Once in a Lifetime* by Kaufman himself.) According to Vail, the film industry is "the most God-awful thing I have ever run into."

Given the topsy-turvy nature of movies, the success of George Lewis is perfectly logical. George takes everything at face value and therefore is perfect in a business that runs on hype. He is incompetent and thus is able to excel in a business that cannot tell the difference between a good film and a bad one. Ironically, Jerry and May decide to leave Hollywood, even though it was Jerry who suggested that they go there and May who came up with the elocution idea. Hart and Kaufman imply that intelligence has no value in pictures.

The major targets of the play's satire are stupidity and vanity, rather than the darker flaws revealed in such a work as Nathanael West's *The Day of the Locust* (1939). The only hint of such depths in *Once in a Lifetime* comes when Jerry denies any involvement with the making of *Gingham and Orchids* because the movie looks initially like a flop, but Jerry's duplicity is soon atoned for when he nobly tells off Glogauer and gets himself fired. Even Glogauer, though he is as inaccessible and arbitrary as an Eastern potentate, is not genuinely corrupt; he is simply a silly, vulgar little man puffed up with money. The play does not try to expose Hollywood as much as it tries to have fun at its expense. The film industry was not particularly offended by the play and even made it into a movie.

Another example of Kaufman and Hart's good-natured humor is *The Man Who Came to Dinner*. The main character, Sheridan Whiteside, was largely based on the authors' friend Alexander Woollcott, radio commentator, wit, and man of letters. Whiteside slips on a piece of ice on the doorstep of the Stanleys, a prominent family in Mesalia, Ohio, and fractures his hip. Convalescing for several weeks in the Stanleys' home, he turns their lives inside out. He does his radio broadcasts from the library, sends and receives messages from all over the world, and populates the house with murderers, penguins, and other exotic creatures. Worse, he encourages the Stanleys' son and daughter to direct their lives independently of their parents' wishes and blackmails Mr. Stanley into submitting. Whiteside also tries to break up and then restore the romance between his secretary, Maggie Cutler, and Burt Jefferson, a Mesalia reporter. Just as the play ends and Whiteside is leaving, he slips on the ice again and announces that he is suing Mr. Stanley for $350,000.

The comedy in *The Man Who Came to Dinner* is based on the fantastic characters that populate it, the greatest of whom is Whiteside. In fact, the personality of Whiteside, his eccentricities, his talent for insults and witty repartee, his scheming mind, and his carefully concealed streak of compassion dominate the play and win the audience to him in spite of his boorishness and his impositions on the Stanleys. Whiteside is supported in his comic antics by such figures as the nymphomaniac actress Lorraine Sheldon, the playwright Beverly Carlton (based on Noël Coward), and the movie clown Banjo (based on Harpo Marx). These figures are part of the great world in which Whiteside lives, the world of such figures as Mahatma Gandhi, Walt Disney, and H. G. Wells, all of whom provide some of the play's fun.

Hart and Kaufman's finest play is probably *You Can't Take It with You*, which to some extent resembles *The Man Who Came to Dinner*. Both plays portray the collision of a group of wild eccentrics with a respectable family. The eccentrics in *You Can't Take It with You* are Martin Vanderhof and his family. Martin, called Grandpa in the play, was once a businessman who felt that he was missing the fun of life. For thirty-five years, he has dedicated his life to enjoying himself, and his family has done likewise. While Grandpa collects snakes and attends commencements, his daughter Penny Sycamore writes plays; her husband, Paul, makes fireworks; their older daughter, Essie Carmichael, studies ballet with an expatriate Russian tutor; and Essie's husband, Ed, plays the xylophone and operates a small printing press. The only "normal" member of the group is Penny's younger daughter, Alice, a secretary for a Wall Street firm who has fallen in love with Tony Kirby, Jr., her boss's son. Even though she loves the members of her family, and even though Tony himself is charmed by them, Alice fears that their somewhat anarchistic life-style will clash with the values of the ultra-respectable Kirbys.

Alice's fears are justified when the Kirbys arrive for dinner on the night before they are expected. A drunken actress flirts with Mr. Kirby, Penny tells Mrs. Kirby that the Spiritualism in which she devoutly believes is a fake, and Kolenkhov, the Russian dance instructor, wrestles with Mr. Kirby. At the evening's climax, federal agents, suspecting Ed of subversive activities, arrest everyone just as Paul's fireworks go off. Alice and Tony's wedding seems doomed until Grandpa explains his way of life to Mr. Kirby. According to Grandpa, the quest for material success and social acceptance should never be pursued at the cost of personal happiness. When Tony reminds his father that he once dreamed of being a trapeze artist and later a saxophone player, the elder Kirby becomes reconciled to the Vanderhofs' unusual ways and his son's refusal to follow in his footsteps, and he joins his future in-laws for dinner.

You Can't Take It with You contrasts two families who have in different ways achieved the American Dream. The Kirbys, through hard work, sobriety, and duty, have attained wealth and respectability. The cost of their success has been the sacrifice of their personal happiness. Mr. Kirby suffers from indigestion and regrets that he has lost his youthful ideals. Mrs. Kirby takes solace in the fashionable humbug of Spiritualism and, in a game of word-association, responds to "sex" with "Wall Street." Tony feels that his parents do not understand him and plans to leave his father's firm to become a bricklayer. Even Mr. Kirby's hobby of growing orchids has been taken up as a refuge from business cares and not for its own sake. His remarks concerning the orchids center on the time it takes to grow one, as the Kirbys' lives are, in general, centered on time and schedules.

The Vanderhofs are another side of the American Dream, the individualistic side of the Dream represented by Walden Pond. They do exactly as they like and live off the money from Grandpa's land. They have no desire to make money or to win other people's respect, only to be happy and to make others happy. Their hobbies are taken up spontaneously; Penny became a dramatist only because a typewriter was accidentally delivered to the house. Their meals are largely impromptu affairs. The house is shared by various people, including Donald, the boyfriend of their housekeeper Rheba, and Mr. De Pinna, who used to be their iceman. While the Kirby's live by the clock, time is not quite real to the Vanderhofs; when Alice asks the time, her family's replies are confused.

Like many radical individualists in American history, the Vanderhofs are at odds with the government. Not only is Ed thought to be a subversive, but also Grandpa is harassed for not paying his income tax. Mr. Kirby calls their way of life Communism, but it is really closer to the American ideals of life, liberty, and the pursuit of happiness than is his own way of life. The play does not really answer the arguments against living exactly as one pleases, nor is it meant to do so. What attracts the audience to the Vanderhofs is not the cogency of their arguments but the delight in seeing people do things that others would like to do and the charm with which the Vanderhofs succeed. In this sense, the play is an American pastoral presenting an idyllic world to relieve the frustrated Kirbys in the audience. Interestingly, *You Can't Take It with You* was not originally as successful in England as in America; perhaps its celebration of individualism was too extreme for English tastes.

No survey of Moss Hart's work would be complete without notice of his solo plays, of which the best is *Lady in the Dark*. Lacking the slapstick situations and witty dialogue of his best work with Kaufman, the play examines the psychological state of Liza Elliot, editor of *Allure*, the most popular women's magazine in the country. Liza has reached the top of her profession yet is going through a psychological crisis. She undergoes analysis to find the cause of her problems, and her psychological states are dramatized in a series of fantasy sequences. In one sequence, Liza is a glamour girl adored by every man, even though in real life, she tries to appear totally unglamorous. The fantasy ends when a man resembling Charley Johnson, the advertising manager, paints a portrait of Liza as she really appears.

As Liza's analysis continues, she realizes that her problems relate to a sense of inferiority as a woman, derived from an unconscious belief that she can never be as beautiful as her celebrated mother, who died when Liza was young. Thus, Liza tries to make other women beautiful while remaining plain herself. Her lover, Kendall Nesbitt, is a married man for whom Liza does not have to compete; when Kendall gets a divorce, Liza does not wish to marry him. Similarly, she has a brief romance with Randy Curtis, an insecure movie star who looks to Liza as a mother figure rather than as a lover. Only when Liza understands her neurosis can she love the man who really loves her, Charley Johnson, who appears in her fantasies as her nemesis. Charley sees behind Liza's unfeminine pose and infuriates Liza until she realizes that he is the only man who can fulfill her needs as a woman.

Lady in the Dark, with its concern for psychological complexity, its innovative dramatic techniques, and serious theme, was a marked departure from Hart's previous work, although similarities to the earlier plays exist. Like *Once in a Lifetime* and *You Can't Take It with You*, this play explores the somewhat dubious value of success. Hart comments in his autobiography, *Act One*, that, as sweet as success is, it does not bring personal happiness and indeed often makes unhappiness more noticeable and difficult to bear. Just as success has given no joy to Mr. Kirby, so it has given none to Liza, since it is largely a flight from her unconscious fears. Only when Liza faces these fears can she achieve happiness.

Hart's technique of alternating fantasy and reality in the play through the use of four revolving stages is a brilliant and innovative method for dramatizing what occurs in Liza's mind. Especially effective is the device of using people from the real world as characters in Liza's dreams. Thus, Charley Johnson exposes Liza's self-imposed plainness in her glamour fantasy, exactly as he destroys her unglamorous competent-executive image in reality. The technique's effectiveness is weakened, however, by having Dr. Brooks explain what the fantasies mean rather than having the audience interpret them on its own.

Lady in the Dark demonstrated that Hart could work alone as well as in collaboration and in serious drama as well as in comedy, yet it also proves that his real talent lay in comedy, for although the play received popular and critical praise, it does not have the bite or sparkle of *The Man Who Came to Dinner* or *You Can't Take It with You.* It is good serious drama but not superlative entertainment, and it is for his superlative work that any artist should be remembered.

Other major works

NONFICTION: *Act One*, 1959.

SCREENPLAYS: *Flesh*, 1932; *The Masquerader*, 1933; *Broadway Melody of 1936*, 1935; *Frankie and Johnny*, 1936; *Winged Victory*, 1944; *Gentleman's Agreement*, 1947; *Hans Christian Andersen*, 1952; *Prince of Players*, 1954; *A Star Is Born*, 1954.

Bibliography

Atkinson, Brooks. *Broadway.* New York: Macmillan, 1970. This general survey of the Broadway stage, written by the famous drama critic of *The New York Times*, explores the personal and professional dimension of the writer as well as the collaboration between Hart and George S. Kaufman. Atkinson enumerates their contributions to Broadway theater and maintains that they presided over an era. According to Atkinson, they wrote comedy that was unprecedentedly iconoclastic. Contains numerous illustrations.

Ferber, Edna. "A Rolling Stone Gathers Considerable Heart." *Stage* 14 (December, 1936): 41-43. Ferber, a contemporary of Hart as a writer of Broadway plays and fellow collaborator with George S. Kaufman, describes her impressions of the man and his work. She gives him much credit for his iconoclastic artistic triumphs.

Goldstein, Malcolm. *George S. Kaufman: His Life, His Theatre.* New York: Oxford University Press, 1979. In this standard work on the Broadway theater of the period, Goldstein gives an insightful portrait of Kaufman as a man and an artist. Offers an interesting account of the period of collaboration between Kaufman and Hart. Contains numerous illustrations.

Hart, Moss. *Act One: An Autobiography.* New York: Random House, 1959. In this insightful rendering of his personal life and artistic development, Hart provides the reader with an otherwise inaccessible view into his struggles, triumphs, and influences. Hart details his collaboration and eventual artistic breakup with George S. Kaufman and describes his progression into theatrical direction. Illustrations.

Mordden, Ethan. *The American Theatre.* New York: Oxford University Press, 1981. This chronicle of the American stage from its beginnings to 1980 discusses Hart's 1936 play *You Can't Take It With You* in the context of the Broadway stage in the midst of the Depression years. According to the author, a major feature of American drama in the 1930's was its interpretations and affirmations of the democratic system.

Sievers, Wieder D. *Freud on Broadway: A History of Psychoanalysis and the American Drama.* New York: Hermitage House, 1955. In this work on the relationship between the theories of Sigmund Freud and American drama, Sievers suggests that Hart achieved his psychological insights into character in part from personal psychoanalysis. Hart himself describes Freud's theory of the unconscious as the most influential of Freud's concepts on his work.

Wilson, Lloyd. *Curtain Time: The Story of the American Theatre.* New York: Random House, 1953. In this general overview of the history of American theater, filled with anecdotes and numerous illustrations, the author briefly discusses Hart's collaborations with George S. Kaufman.

Anthony Bernardo
(Updated by *Genevieve Slomski*)

LILLIAN HELLMAN

Born: New Orleans, Louisiana; June 20, 1905
Died: Martha's Vineyard, Massachusetts; June 30, 1984

Principal drama

The Children's Hour, pr., pb. 1934; *Days to Come*, pr., pb. 1936; *The Little Foxes*, pr., pb. 1939; *Watch on the Rhine*, pr., pb. 1941; *The Searching Wind*, pr., pb. 1944; *Another Part of the Forest*, pr. 1946, pb. 1947; *Montserrat*, pr. 1949, pb. 1950 (adaptation of Emmanuel Robles' play); *The Autumn Garden*, pr., pb. 1951; *The Lark*, pr. 1955, pb. 1956 (adaptation of Jean Anouilh's play *L'Alouette*); *Candide*, pr. 1956, pb. 1957 (libretto; music by Leonard Bernstein, lyrics by Richard Wilbur, John Latouche, and Dorothy Parker; adaptation of Voltaire's novel); *Toys in the Attic*, pr., pb. 1960; *My Mother, My Father, and Me*, pr., pb. 1963 (adaptation of Burt Blechman's novel *How Much?*); *The Collected Plays*, pb. 1972.

Other literary forms

In addition to her original stage plays, Lillian Hellman published original screenplays, a collection of the letters of Anton Chekhov, her adaptations of two French plays (*Montserrat*, *L'Alouette*) and of an American novel (*How Much?*), an operetta adapted from Voltaire's *Candide*, many uncollected articles, and several volumes of memoirs, the first two of which have received as much acclaim as her best plays.

Achievements

Hellman was the most important American follower of Henrik Ibsen after Arthur Miller. Like Ibsen in his middle period, she wrote strong, well-made plays involving significant social issues. Like Ibsen, she created memorable female characters, some strong, some weak; and her most important female character, Regina Giddens of *The Little Foxes* and *Another Part of the Forest*, seems at least partially modeled on Ibsen's Hedda Gabler. Both Hellman and Ibsen were exceptional in depicting believable, memorable children. Like him, though more frequently, she used blackmail as a dramatic ploy. Her plays, like Ibsen's, can be strongly and tightly dramatic, and, like his, some, notably *The Little Foxes*, have a question ending: one, that is, in which the eventual outcome for the major characters is left ironically uncertain.

Her last two original plays, however, recall Chekhov more than Ibsen in their depiction of feckless characters and, in one of the two, an apparent, though only apparent, plotlessness. She has been blamed for her employment of melodramatic plot elements, but her use of them is often valid and essential and does not interfere with accurate character analysis, convincing dramatic dialogue, and adroit handling of social issues. Hellman was, after Tennessee Williams, the most important dramatist writing primarily about the American South. Two of her plays, *Watch on the Rhine* and *Toys in the Attic*, won the New York Drama Critics Circle Award. Hellman received many other awards, including the Brandeis University Creative Arts Medal and the National Institute of Arts and Letters Gold Medal.

Biography

Lillian Florence Hellman was born in New Orleans of Jewish parents. Her father was also born in New Orleans, and her mother in Alabama, of a family long established there. Part of her mother's family moved to New York, and when Hellman was five years old, her parents moved there and commenced a routine of spending six months of each year in New York and six in New Orleans with her father's two unmarried sisters. As her memoirs make clear, Hellman's plays are strongly influenced by her Southern, urban background; her mother's family was a source for the Hubbards in *The Little Foxes* and *Another Part of the Forest*; her paternal aunts, for the sisters in *Toys in the Attic*. All of her original plays except the first two (*The Children's Hour* and *Days to Come*) are set in the South: in the Washington area, in Alabama towns, or in New Orleans. Hellman was graduated from high school in New York in 1922, attended New York University from 1922 to 1924, and briefly attended Columbia University in 1924, without completing a degree at either school. She worked for a time thereafter in New York and Hollywood in the areas of publishing, book reviewing, and reading manuscripts of plays and movie scenarios. In 1925, she married Arthur Kober; they were divorced in 1932. Two years later, her first play, *The Children's Hour*, was a tremendous hit, achieving a longer original run (691 performances) than any of her later plays. From that success until her last play in 1963, she was primarily a playwright and occasionally a scriptwriter, though she was never really happy in the theater.

Over the years, Hellman made various visits to Russia, to Civil War Spain, and elsewhere in Europe, including a very dangerous visit to Nazi Germany to take money to the underground at the request of a friend. For many years, she was the companion of the novelist Dashiell Hammett, though they lived together only sporadically. Congressional investigations of Communism in the United States in the early 1950's caused serious trouble for both her and Hammett, though she denied having sufficiently consistent or deep political convictions to belong to any party. As a result of the investigations, Hellman and Hammett were both blacklisted in Hollywood; she also lost the home she owned and shared with Hammett in upstate New York, as well as various friends. Hammett was imprisoned; soon after his release, he became ill, and Hellman took care of him until his death in 1961. In her later years, Hellman devoted herself to her four books of memoirs and taught at Harvard University, the Massachusetts Institute of Technology, and the University of California at Berkeley. She died on June 30, 1984, on Martha's Vineyard.

Analysis

The Children's Hour, Lillian Hellman's first play, was based on an actual lawsuit, the Great Drumsheugh Case. The play displays almost all the dramatic characteristics for which Hellman is noted: crisp, forceful, realistic dialogue; clear character construction and analysis; a clear-cut plot line in the tradition of the well-made play, with fast movement and adroitly handled suspense which kept (and can still keep) audiences enthralled. Some of Hellman's later plays display these characteristics with greater skill, but they are all there in her first. *The Children's Hour* and most of the others can also be called melodramatic, because of the suspense, because of the use of violence and of blackmail, and because of obvious authorial manipulation to achieve a neat conclusion. The plays are never, however, pure melodrama, since pure melodrama would not include valid, well-drawn characters or significant themes. *The Children's Hour*, like many of Hellman's plays, concerns the destructive power of evil, its ability to erode human relationships and destroy lives. In this play, evil is manifested by a child's malicious lie and its repercussions in the lives of two women.

The Children's Hour opens on a class in progress at a girls' boarding school in Massachusetts. The teacher, Lily Mortar, is the aunt of Martha Dobie, one of the two young women who own and operate the school. Presently, Mary Tilford enters, very late for class, carrying a bunch of flowers with which she appeases the teacher. Then the other owner, Karen Wright, enters. Karen has lost her bracelet and asks one of the girls, Helen, if she has found it, an important issue in the play. Karen asks Mary where she got the flowers. Mary repeats her claim that she picked them. Karen, apparently recognizing them, says Mary got them out of the garbage pail and has been lying. Mary's response is, and continues to be, that the teachers are against her, that they never believe her, and that she is telling the truth. Karen grounds her for two weeks. Mary says her heart hurts and pretends to fall into a faint. She is carried to her room.

Martha enters, and she and Karen discuss Mary as a troublemaker, send for Karen's fiancé (Joe Cardin, who is a doctor and also Mary's cousin), discuss getting rid of Mrs. Mortar, and discuss Karen's plans to marry Joe as soon as school is out. Martha is clearly upset at the imminent marriage, although she likes Joe. She hates interference with a friendship that has gone on since college and hates the possibility that Karen might leave the school. Joe arrives and goes off to examine Mary.

At this point in the play, the audience cannot be sure of the meaning of Martha's jealousy, of whether Mary's feelings are in any sense justified, of whether the events thus far are more taut with emotion than what might be expected on a day-by-day basis in a girls' boarding school. Mrs. Mortar, deeply insulted at Martha's desire to get her away from the school and at her offer to send her to London and support her there, indirectly accuses her niece of homosexual feelings toward Karen. Mary's two roommates are caught eavesdropping. Joe has a friendly confrontation with Martha, who apologizes and falls into his arms, weeping. It is reasonably clear that she does not recognize her feelings for Karen as homosexual, if they are. Mary comes in, and it is clear that Joe considers her a troublemaker, as do the women. Then, as the adults leave and the audience sees Mary for the first time alone with other girls, her character becomes only too clear.

Indeed, one becomes more and more convinced that Mary's lies, her manipulation, her dictatorial attitude toward her schoolmates, and presently her outright blackmail of one of them and her cruelty to another represent more than mere naughtiness or adolescent confusion. Mary is psychotic, and dangerously so. Feeling no affection for anyone, she lives for manipulation and power. As soon as the teachers leave the room, she throws a cushion at the door and kicks a table. Apparently, her one genuine feeling other than hatred is the belief that the teachers hate her as much as she hates them. She tells her roommates that if she cannot go to the boat races (since she has been grounded), she will see to it that they do not go either. She forces a girl named Rosalie to do some work for her by hinting of knowledge that Rosalie stole the bracelet that Karen asked about earlier. She forces her roommates to report the conversation that they overheard, and while Mary certainly does not completely understand its import, she nevertheless recognizes it as a weapon she can use. She immediately announces that she is going to walk out and go home, and by physical force, she makes one of the girls give her the money to get there. On this moment of tension, typical of a well-made play, act 1 closes.

The Children's Hour is unusual among Hellman's plays in that it does not all take place in one setting. Act 2 takes place in the living room of the home of Mary's grandmother in Boston. As scene 1 of the act opens, Mary arrives and is admitted by the maid, Agatha, who clearly does not trust her for an instant. Left alone while Agatha goes to fetch Mrs. Tilford, Mary tries with the aid of a mirror to make herself look sick. Mrs. Tilford enters, and Mary dashes into her arms, in tears. It soon becomes clear that Mrs. Tilford is an intelligent woman but that, unlike Agatha, she can be taken in by her granddaughter. It is an irony of the play, however, that she cannot be taken in easily. Had Mary been able to deceive her by simple lies, there would have been no play. Her usual tricks—tears, stories of being mistreated—do not work. Mrs. Tilford has supported Martha and Karen in their establishment of the school, has encouraged her friends to send their daughters there, and certainly trusts the schoolmistresses. Mary, therefore, begins to use the story she has heard secondhand, mentioning it at first vaguely and uncertainly, but then, as she sees that it is having an effect, more positively and specifically. Mrs. Tilford is deeply disturbed and obviously finds it difficult to believe that such a story could be invented. She starts to phone Karen but decides against it. She calls Joe and urgently asks him to come over; she calls a friend, perhaps one with a daughter or granddaughter at the school, asking her to come over as well. Scene 2 opens with Agatha telling Mary that Rosalie is coming to spend the night; a few moments later, Rosalie arrives. The audience learns, partly now and fully later, that Mrs. Tilford has communicated with the parents of all the girls and told them Mary's story, with the result that all the girls have been called home. Rosalie is spending the night with Mary because her mother is in New York.

These circumstances represent significant flaws in the structure of *The Children's Hour*, though they are not as noticeable in performance: First, it is difficult to believe that a woman of Mrs. Tilford's maturity and intelligence would take such drastic action on the basis of her granddaughter's word alone; second, it has to be Rosalie, among all the students, whose mother is out of town, or the play would simply grind to a halt. About the first, one might say in Hellman's defense that it would be emotionally and even intellectually difficult for Mrs. Tilford to believe that her granddaughter would have either the desire or the knowledge to invent such a lie; that to seek external verification of the story would be, even if it were true, almost surely fruitless; and that, given the time and place, it would have been irresponsible of her not to inform the other parents. Problems remain, even so. Surely Mrs. Tilford could have spoken with Joe first. True, Hellman arranges that Joe arrives late, on the plausible ground that he had to stop at a hospital, but would one more night have mattered so much? Doubtless, Mrs. Tilford's urgency is partly emotional, on the ground that most, if not all, of the girls have been at the school on her recommendation. This does not explain, however, her calm assurance later in the play that the story is true. She takes the logical attitude that Martha's, Karen's, and Joe's denials are meaningless, since they are to be expected regardless of whether the story is accurate. She is also a woman who, given her class, her money, and her intelligence, is not prone to being wrong. Perhaps one should regard her attitude as a typical Hellman irony: It is her very sense of responsibility that has made her act irresponsibly. Less defense can be offered for the presence of Rosalie. All one can say is that her presence is essential to the play, and that in a well-made play this represents perhaps the minimum of manipulation.

The scene develops very dramatically. Mary blackmails Rosalie into being prepared to support her lies if necessary. Joe arrives, and very soon he and his aunt are battling. Karen and Martha arrive, and the battle enlarges, with strong emotions on one side and calm assurance on the other. Mrs. Tilford is not even moved by the threat of a libel suit. Finally, Joe insists that Mary be questioned and, against Mrs. Tilford's wishes, brings Mary in. Mary, genuinely nervous, tells her story, making it more and more circumstantial, until finally the circumstances catch her in a lie. She has said that she has seen things through Karen's keyhole, and Karen announces that her door has no keyhole. Mary is therefore forced to say that it was Martha's room, not Karen's; Martha announces that she lives on a different floor, at the other end of the house, and, moreover, shares her room with Mrs. Mortar. Mrs. Tilford is severely shaken. Backed into a corner, Mary says that it was not she but Rosalie who saw them, and that she saw them because Karen's door was halfway open. Rosalie is summoned and at first denies the story, but when Mary makes it plain that she will, if necessary, expose Rosalie as a thief, Rosalie agrees that the story is true and collapses in tears. The curtain falls.

After so tense a moment, act 3 is almost anticlimactic. It opens on the same scene as act 1. Karen and Martha are alone in the house. They have lost their case; the townspeople are against them; they feel so persecuted that they refuse even to answer the phone; and they have not even dared to leave the house. In a rather surprising anticipation of Samuel Beckett and the Absurdists, Martha says that they are "waiting," with the implication that that is all they—or at any rate, she—will ever do. Martha hopes that Karen will escape through marrying Joe, but Karen seems doubtful. Mrs. Mortar, who had left when told to by Martha, unexpectedly enters, and the audience learns that she would have been the key witness at the trial, that she refused to return, and thus the case was lost. Her failure to return was owing to her reluctance to become involved in such a scandal. She returns now because she has run out of money, but Martha has no more to give her. She leaves the room, and Joe enters. He is planning for the marriage and for all three of them to leave together permanently, even though he would thus be giving up a promising career. Martha leaves, and in his words and attitude toward Karen it becomes clear that Joe is uncertain of the truth. Karen quietly denies any homosexual relationship, and he apparently accepts the denial, but it is uncertain whether his doubts have been laid to rest. Karen asks him to think things over for a day or two and make a decision. He reluctantly agrees and leaves, insisting that he will come back, though Karen is sure that he will not. Martha returns and, in a scene of high emotion, tells Karen that, though she had not previously been aware of it, the story that has been told about them was, at least so far as her feelings went, true. She loves Karen "that way." She leaves the room, and presently, a muffled shot is heard. Karen opens the door and sees that Martha has killed herself. Mrs. Mortar rushes in, sees what has happened, and expresses her remorse. The doorbell rings, and she answers it. It is

Agatha. Mrs. Tilford is waiting in her car. Mrs. Mortar tries to keep her from coming in, but Karen allows her to enter, and Mrs. Mortar rushes out sobbing.

The final dialogue is between Karen and Mrs. Tilford. Mrs. Tilford has learned the truth. The bracelet was found among Rosalie's things, and Rosalie confessed. Apparently, Mary has confessed, too. The judge at the trial will arrange a public apology and explanation, and Mrs. Tilford will pay the amount of the damages and as much more as they will take. Karen announces Martha's death and expresses her bitter feelings toward Mrs. Tilford and her attempts to relieve her conscience through money. Gradually, however, Karen recognizes Mrs. Tilford's sincerity and sees that the old woman will be the greater sufferer, since she has refused to commit Mary to an institution and will hence have to live permanently in her company, and since Martha's suicide will inevitably burden her memory. Karen agrees to accept Mrs. Tilford's money. She disagrees with Mrs. Tilford's hope that she and Joe will marry. The two separate amicably, and Karen is left alone at the play's end.

Hellman expressed the feeling later that the final scene was unnecessary, that it was simply evidence of her personal compulsion to spell things out. Certainly none of her important later plays spells things out so thoroughly, but in *The Children's Hour*, the final scene provides desirable satisfaction for the audience. The only valid objection to the scene is that it raises a new possibility: Mrs. Tilford appears soon after Martha's suicide, rather than earlier, perhaps in time to prevent it. Once Martha's feelings are clear, however, it seems doubtful, given the time and circumstances, that anything could have kept her alive, and Hellman properly leaves Karen with an uncertain future. Karen's belief in Joe's permanent defection may be wrong; it may not. The possibility of a happy outcome for her is a valid comfort to an audience after so much bitter emotion, but the certainty of a happy ending would be difficult to accept.

The play was in part a *succès de scandale* on Broadway, since open treatment of homosexuality was very unusual at the time. Hellman wrote the scenario for the first film version, *These Three* (1936), in which the homosexuality was changed to a traditional triangle. A later version restored both title and content.

The Little Foxes is, and almost surely will remain, Hellman's standard play. It represents significant advances in technique over *The Children's Hour* and is in various ways more typical of Hellman's overall production. First, it is set in the Deep South (small-town Alabama), as are three of Hellman's four most significant later plays. Second, the characters are more sharply distinguished and more deeply realized, and the dialogue is more individualized. Third, Hellman displays three significant qualities which are not fully realized in *The Children's Hour*: compassion, humor, and irony.

Fourth, *The Little Foxes* displays more clearly a sociopolitical theme than does the earlier play: These are "the little foxes who spoil the vines" (a quotation from the Song of Solomon), whom Hellman sees as twentieth century capitalists in embryo.

The Little Foxes concentrates on a rapacious small-town Alabama family, the Hubbards, and on some of their victims. The year is 1900. As the play opens, Regina Giddens is giving a dinner party for a businessman from Chicago, William Marshall, with whom her brothers are negotiating to join them in opening one of the first cotton mills in the South. All the characters in the play are present except Regina's husband, Horace, the town banker, long confined at The Johns Hopkins Hospital with a bad heart. The remaining characters are Regina's brothers, Ben and Oscar Hubbard; Oscar's wife, Birdie, the last member of an aristocratic family impoverished by the Civil War; Oscar and Birdie's son, Leo; Horace and Regina's daughter, Alexandra; and the servants, Addie and Cal. Unlike the Hubbards, Birdie has cultural interests; she is a frightened woman, bullied by her husband. Ben is a jovial hypocrite whose hypocrisy has become so practiced that he is sometimes almost unaware of it. He and Regina are the dominant Hubbards. Oscar is relatively weak, obtuse, and blustery, while Leo is a lesser version of Oscar. Alexandra shares Birdie's cultural interests and seems not at all Hubbard-like. Regina herself is a handsome woman, a smooth and clever conniver, who takes in Marshall to a degree that Ben, for all of his hypocrisy, cannot.

When the deal for the cotton mill has been struck, the young couple drive Marshall to the station to return to Chicago. The Hubbards are triumphant, looking forward to being rich. One problem remains: The three siblings are supposed to contribute equal sums to the mill project, enough to make them together the majority shareholders, but while Ben and Oscar are ready to put up their share, Regina must get hers from Horace, who has ignored all letters on the subject. In a piece of typical Hubbard trickery, Regina declares that Horace is holding out because he wants a larger share, and Ben finally agrees that he should have a larger share and that the difference will come out of Oscar's. Oscar is furious, but he is mollified by Regina's quite specious assurance that she will consider something that Oscar very much wants: a marriage between Leo and Alexandra. A plan is then made to send Alexandra, who is devoted to Horace, to bring him home.

Many modern plays, including several of Henrik Ibsen's, involve the return of someone long gone, but the return is almost always early in the play. In *The Little Foxes*, the audience must wait, with anticipation, for what Horace's return in the second act will bring. Before Horace's arrival, Oscar and Leo conceive a plan to steal eighty thousand dollars' worth of bonds from Horace's safety deposit box, to finance their venture. (If they can do this, they will not need Regina as a partner.) Horace then arrives, stiff and ill, accompanied by Alexandra, who has his heart medicine. During the course of the act, it becomes clear that Horace and Regina are, and have been, at odds during most of their marriage, that Horace will not agree to finance the proposed project, and that he will not consent to a marriage between Alexandra and Leo. It is also clear that Regina will not be thwarted and that Horace is too physically frail to withstand her will.

In act 3, Horace, who has discovered the crime, informs Regina about the theft and tells her that he will pretend that the theft was a loan. Moreover, he will change his will, leaving Regina the bonds and all of his other property to Alexandra. Regina will thus lose the opportunity to invest in the business venture (since the partners will no longer need her money), and she will lose her inheritance from Horace. Furiously, she tells him that she married him only for money. He becomes distraught, reaches for his medicine, spills it, and asks her to get his new bottle. She simply stands there as he collapses and dies. Regina is now in a position to blackmail her brothers into assigning her a seventy-five-percent interest in the mill, lest she prosecute them. Regina is triumphant; nevertheless, she now faces a life of loneliness because Alexandra has discovered her mother's treachery and will leave her.

The play ends with a question and is the better for it, since, if the ending represented a total and final triumph, it would emphasize the play's kinship to pure melodrama, and since, given the characters, an ending that had finality would be unlikely. Ben is too clear-sighted, too ironically aware, too psychologically healthy to give up. Alexandra's potential for fighting is probably small, but one cannot be sure. Moreover, the Hubbard siblings are more complex than a recital of the plot might make them seem. Ben retains an incompetent servant because she has always been in the family. Ben and Oscar both seem genuinely moved by Horace's death. Ben and Regina are both capable of viewing their own, and others', behavior ironically, and there is humor in some of their dialogue. Regina is frightened at what she has done, or rather not done. Wicked as the two may be, and much as they might remind one of nineteenth century melodramatic villains, they are human beings, complex enough to be believable.

The play, moreover, has other ironies which remove it from total melodrama. It is ironic that Leo should be Birdie's son and Alexandra Regina's daughter, because Leo is an extreme version of Oscar, and Alexandra has the outlook of Horace. For most of his life, however, Horace has been weak, yielding to his wife, as Birdie has to her husband. Birdie, for whom one is made to feel compassion, gains enough strength to tell Alexandra the truth, and Horace gains enough strength to stand up to Regina. These are highly individualized human beings, and the play is skillfully constructed, absorbing, and genuinely insightful.

Like *The Little Foxes, Watch on the Rhine* contains murder and black-mail, but it is a very different kind of play, peopled with a very different set of characters. It takes place entirely in the living room of Fanny Farrelly, in her country mansion near Washington, D.C. Fanny is a wealthy, eccentric matriarch in her sixties, a character typical of comedy of manners: basically good-hearted, sparklingly alert, and accustomed to having her own way. The time of the play is the spring of 1940. Germany is Nazi-ruled, and there is war in Europe in which the United States has not yet become involved.

The pattern of the first two acts of the play consists of alternating conversation of three kinds: humorous and witty, at times gossipy, as is appropriate to comedy of manners; affectionate; and tense, either because of personally threatening political maneuvers or because of the triangle that is a subplot in the play. The shifts from one type to another can be sudden, but they are always appropriate. Tension can lapse into humor, or an unexpected remark can turn humor into tension.

The characters include, besides Fanny, the other permanent residents of the mansion: Fanny's son, David, a lawyer in his deceased father's firm in Washington, in his late thirties; Fanny's longtime companion Anise, a Frenchwoman; and one of the servants, Joseph. There are also two house-guests who have long overstayed their welcome, Marthe de Brancovis, the daughter of an old friend of Fanny, and her husband, Teck, a Romanian count. Fanny's daughter Sara, her husband Kurt Müller, a member of the anti-Nazi underground and a German in exile, and their children arrive. The audience learns that Kurt has collected twenty-three thousand dollars to aid the resistance in Germany. In brief, Teck discovers the money and threatens to expose Kurt to the German embassy officials unless he is paid ten thousand dollars. Kurt is forced to kill Teck and flee the country, aided by Fanny, who during the course of the play has come to realize the Nazi threat and to be lifted above her own private concerns. The killing is presented, strangely, as an absence of the need to fight evil on all fronts, whether on a conventional battlefield or in one's own environment.

Watch on the Rhine is probably the best American play concerning World War II. It demonstrates that war is not limited to battlefronts and that the world is too small for anyone, anywhere, to be unaffected by large-scale violence. It demonstrates that such violence affects the cultured and the humane, whether they are poor, like Kurt, or wealthy, like Sara's family. The play is highly unusual in being a comedy of manners in which the central subject is war. In spite of the attempted blackmail and actual murder which figure prominently in its plot, it is among the least melodramatic of any of Hellman's plays, and to call the murder melodramatic has its own irony, since this particular murder constitutes an act of war.

The characters in *Watch on the Rhine* are developed with clarity and depth. Fanny is a far more individualized portrait of a wealthy, dominant older woman than is Mrs. Tilford in *The Children's Hour*. Unlike Mary Tilford or Ben and Regina, Teck is a flaccid, unwilling villain. Unlike Birdie, Horace, and Alexandra, the good people are strong, and for the only time in all of her plays, Hellman presents, in Kurt, an admirable hero and a marriage based on strong and permanent love. A believable presentation of either of these is indeed a rarity in modern drama. The children in *Watch on the Rhine* are more fully portrayed than those in *The Children's Hour*. The theme has universal validity; oppression is indeed a major issue throughout Hellman's plays. In *The Children's Hour*, it is oppression by the established rich, by a psychotic child, by established standards of behavior. In *The Little Foxes*, it is anticipated oppression on a broad scale by a rising class of capitalists, and actual oppression on a narrower scale by moneyed Southerners against blacks, poor whites, fallen aristocrats, and one another. *Watch on the Rhine* widens the range in dealing with oppression by Fascists and would-be Fascists. Blackmail itself, in all three plays, is a form of oppression. Later in Hellman's work, in *The Autumn Garden* and *Toys in the Attic*, she showed that even generosity and love can be forms of blackmail; those plays, like *Watch on the Rhine*, give the theme a universality which Hellman's first two successes lack. *The Little Foxes* will probably remain the most popular Hellman play in dramatic repertory, but *Watch on the Rhine* is certainly among her most effective.

Other major works

NONFICTION: *The Selected Letters of Anton Chekhov*, 1955 (editor); *An Unfinished Woman: A Memoir*, 1969; *Pentimento*, 1973; *Scoundrel Time*, 1976; *Maybe*, 1980; *Eating Together: Recipes and Recollections*, 1984 (with Peter Feibleman); *Conversations with Lillian Hellman*, 1986.

SCREENPLAYS: *The Dark Angel*, 1935 (with Mordaunt Shairp); *These Three*, 1936; *Dead End*, 1937 (adaptation of Sidney Kingsley's play); *The Little Foxes*, 1941 (with Dorothy Parker, Arthur Kober, Alan Campbell); *Watch on the Rhine*, 1943 (with Dashiell Hammett); *The North Star: A Motion Picture About Some Russian People*, 1943; *The Searching Wind*, 1946; *The Chase*, 1966.

ANTHOLOGY: *The Big Knockover: Selected Stories and Short Novels of Dashiell Hammett*, 1966 (editor, with introduction).

Bibliography

Adams, Timothy Dow. *Telling Lies in Modern American Autobiography*. Chapel Hill: University of North Carolina Press, 1990. The chapter on Hellman (pp. 121-166) is an excellently argued defense against charges that Hellman was virtually a pathological liar. Based on intelligent analyses of the memoirs.

Adler, Jacob H. *Lillian Hellman.* Austin, Tex.: Steck-Vaughn, 1969. This volume, part of a series of short publications, is a concise, well-written discussion of Hellman's work through the 1960's. Adler, a professor emeritus, is an authority on Southern literature.

Dick, Bernard F. *Hellman in Hollywood.* Rutherford, N.J.: Fairleigh Dickinson University Press, 1982. An account of Hellman's years as a screenwriter, with analyses of her adaptations and her original screenplay *The North Star.* Select bibliography, filmography, index.

Falk, Doris V. *Lillian Hellman.* New York: Frederick Ungar, 1978. Falk discusses Hellman's characters as despoilers or bystanders.

Feibleman, Peter. *Lily: Reminiscences of Lillian Hellman.* New York: William Morrow, 1988. The author, the son of old New Orleans friends of Hellman, became her close friend and companion in her last years, a relationship he describes in this book. His accounts of renovating the house on Martha's Vineyard inherited from Hellman can be found in his column in *Lear's* magazine. Contains a sadly riveting account of Hellman's illness. Some of the anecdotal accounts of their time together are in Hellman's section of *Eating Together*, a collection of Southern recipes selected by both writers, in page proof when she died in 1984.

Hellman, Lillian. *Conversations with Lillian Hellman.* Edited by Jackson R. Bryer. Jackson: University Press of Mississippi, 1986. Consists of newspaper and magazine interviews with Hellman from 1936 to 1981. Extended chronology, index.

Lederer, Katherine. *Lillian Hellman.* Boston: Twayne, 1979. Part of Twayne's United States Authors series, this volume provides a good general introduction to Hellman's work. Annotated bibliography, index.

Rollyson, Carl. *Lillian Hellman: Her Legend and Her Legacy.* New York: St. Martin's Press, 1988. A readable and scholarly biography of Hellman. Photographs, bibliography, index.

Jacob H. Adler
(Updated by *Katherine Lederer*)

BETH HENLEY

Born: Jackson, Mississippi; May 8, 1952

Principal drama

Am I Blue, pr. 1973, pb. 1982; *Crimes of the Heart*, pr. 1979, pb. 1981; *The Miss Firecracker Contest*, pr. 1980, pb. 1982; *The Wake of Jamey Foster*, pr., pb. 1982; *The Debutante Ball*, pr. 1985, pb. 1991; *The Lucky Spot*, pr. 1986, pb. 1987; *Abundance*, pr. 1990, pb. 1992; *Beth Henley: Four Plays*, pb. 1992.

Other literary forms

In addition to her works for the stage, Beth Henley has written screenplays, including *Nobody's Fool* (1986); *True Stories* (1986), in collaboration with David Byrne and Stephen Tobolowsky; and the film versions of her plays *Crimes of the Heart* (1986) and *The Miss Firecracker Contest* (1989). She has also written the teleplays *Survival Guides* (1986) and *Trying Times* (1987), both with Budge Threlkeld.

Achievements

Henley is often compared to fiction writers Eudora Welty and Flannery O'Connor for her sympathetic portrayals of eccentric characters who lead deceptively simple lives in small Southern communities. Her work has also been identified with the literary traditions of the grotesque and the absurd. Henley's unique achievement, however, is the intermingling of absurdism and realism. Her plays realistically capture the Southern vernacular and take place in authentic Southern settings, yet they also exaggerate the recognizable and push the bizarre to extremes to reveal the underlying absurdity of the human condition. Whereas Henley's characters are rooted in her Southern heritage, the meaning of their experiences is not limited to time and place. Loss and renewal, the vulnerability of loving, and the frail but indomitable human spirit are among her recurring themes; Henley delivers these serious concerns, however, through unpredictable characters, outrageously witty dialogue, and offbeat humor. It is her insistence on the value of laughter in the face of adversity that places her within the tragicomic tradition of modern dramatic literature. Another of Henley's strengths is that she approaches her craft with a keen insight into what is stageworthy. This awareness, no doubt, is one of the reasons that her first full-length play, *Crimes of the Heart*, won the Pulitzer Prize in drama in 1981 with the distinction of being the first play to win the coveted award before appearing on Broadway. *Crimes of the Heart* also received the New York Drama Critics Circle

Award in 1981, and, in the same year, Henley captured the prestigious George Oppenheimer/*Newsday* Playwriting Award.

Biography

The second of four daughters, Elizabeth Becker Henley was born May 8, 1952, in Jackson, Mississippi. Her parents, Charles Boyce and Elizabeth Josephine Becker, were reared in the neighboring communities of Hazlehurst and Brookhaven, locales that Henley adopted for two of her plays. Henley's father, an attorney, served in both houses of the Mississippi legislature. A shy child plagued with chronic attacks of asthma, Henley, often bedridden, entertained herself by reading play scripts that were in production at the New Stage Theatre in Jackson, where her mother, an amateur actress, regularly performed.

Henley attended high school in Jackson. During her senior year, she took part in an acting workshop at the New Stage Theatre, an experience that influenced her decision to become an actress. Selecting drama as her major, Henley enrolled at Southern Methodist University in Dallas, Texas, in 1970. While a sophomore, she wrote her first play as an assignment for a playwriting class. The play, a one-act comedy titled *Am I Blue*, was produced at the university under a pseudonym in her senior year. After graduation from Southern Methodist University in 1974 with a bachelor of fine arts degree, Henley taught creative dramatics and acted for the Dallas Minority Repertory Theatre. She earned a livelihood at odd jobs as a waitress, file clerk, and photographer of children at a department store. In 1975, she received a teaching scholarship from the University of Illinois, where she taught acting classes while pursuing graduate studies in drama. In the summer of 1976, she acted in the *Great American People Show*, a historical pageant presented at the New Salem State Park.

Hoping to break into films as an actress, Henley moved to Los Angeles in the fall of 1976. Failing to get auditions for parts, Henley turned to writing screenplays as a creative outlet, but without an agent to represent her, the studios would not read her scripts. Thinking that stage plays would have a better chance of getting performed, especially in small theaters, Henley began working on a comedy (set in Hazlehurst, Mississippi) about a crisis in the lives of three sisters. With production costs in mind, she deliberately limited the play to six characters and one indoor set. She finished *Crimes of the Heart* in 1978 and submitted it to several regional theaters without success, but Henley's friend and fellow playwright Frederick Bailey had faith in the play. Without Henley's knowledge, he entered *Crimes of the Heart* in the annual drama competition of the Actors Theatre of Louisville, Kentucky, where it was selected as a cowinner for 1977-1978. In February, 1979, the Actors Theatre produced the play as part of the company's annual Festival of New American Plays. The play was an immediate success. After productions in Maryland, Missouri, and California, *Crimes of the Heart* opened to full houses on Off-Broadway on December 21, 1980. The public's high regard for the play was matched by critical acclaim. In April, 1981, at the age of twenty-eight, Henley was awarded the Pulitzer Prize in drama for *Crimes of the Heart*, the first woman so honored in twenty-three years. In the fall of 1981, after having been recognized by the New York Drama Critics Circle as the best American play of the season, *Crimes of the Heart* premiered on Broadway; it ran for 535 performances. Subsequent productions were staged in England, France, Israel, and Australia.

Meanwhile, Henley was writing a television pilot entitled "Morgan's Daughters" for Paramount Pictures and a screenplay called *The Moon Watcher* about a historical pageant set in Petersburg, Illinois. She also took a small role as a bag lady in Frederick Bailey's *No Scratch*, produced in Los Angeles in the summer of 1981. In January, 1982, the New York Repertory Company staged Henley's *Am I Blue* with two other one-acts under the collective title *Confluence*. Theater critics found weaknesses in the playwright's student effort but also acknowledged that the comedy showed the promise of her later work.

Within the next three years, two other comedies written before Henley won the Pulitzer Prize were produced in New York City. *The Wake of Jamey Foster* opened on Broadway on October 14, 1982, but closed after only twelve nights. Critics found the play, which was also set in Mississippi, too repetitious of *Crimes of the Heart*. Written before *The Wake of Jamey Foster*, *The Miss Firecracker Contest* was staged in New York in the spring of 1984. Again critics faulted the play for its similarity to her earlier works. Undaunted by these box-office failures, Henley kept writing for the stage. In the spring of 1985, the South Coast Repertory Theatre in Costa Mesa, California, produced her next play *The Debutante Ball*. In the following year, Henley's *The Lucky Spot* (set in a dance hall in Pigeon, Louisiana, in 1934) premiered in New York City. Reviews of the play varied, but one critic considered *The Lucky Spot* to be Henley's best play since *Crimes of the Heart*. In 1990, *Abundance*, Henley's drama about two mail-order brides whose lives become entangled in the American West of the late nineteenth century, opened in New York City to mixed reviews. Later in the same year, the New York Stage and Film Company staged a workshop production of Henley's *Signature* in Poughkeepsie, New York.

As a Pulitzer Prize winner, the playwright-actress also found herself in demand as a screenwriter. While continuing to write stage plays, Henley wrote the screenplay for the acclaimed film version of *Crimes of the Heart*, released in late 1986; the script for another film, *Nobody's Fool*; and a screenplay based on her drama *The Miss Firecracker Contest*. Henley also collaborated with David Byrne and Stephen Tobolowsky on the screenplay entitled *True Stories*, and with Budge Threlkeld on two television scripts,

Survival Guides and *Trying Times.*

Henley's plays have reached audiences far beyond the regional theaters for which she first wrote, making her a significant contributor to American dramatic literature. Although the plays written after *Crimes of the Heart* have failed to bring her the critical praise she earned with that first full-length comedy, her dramatic output as a whole reveals a consistency in tone and theme unsurpassed by her American contemporaries.

Analysis

While the plays of Beth Henley are well constructed and provide ample conflict and suspense, the playwright's keen sense of place and character and her humorous yet compassionate view of the human predicament most typify her work. Her plays are set most often in her home state of Mississippi, where the innocent façade of friendly small-town life belies the horror and lunacy within. The dark side of humanity—the unpredictable, the irrational, the abnormal—attracts Henley, and her plays abound with stories of sickness, disease, and perversions. Ironically, however, Henley creates comedy out of the grotesque and shapes endearing characters out of eccentricity.

Usually, Henley's plays depict the family in crisis joined by a close circle of friends and neighbors. From this basic situation, Henley makes her case for emotional survival. Guilt, despair, and loneliness are typical experiences of Henley's failed heroines, but each continues to search for some measure of happiness and often finds it, if only momentarily, in the community of others. Whereas Henley doggedly exposes human frailties, in the final analysis her view is a charitable one and her plays are optimistic, despite the fact that they offer no lasting resolutions to her characters' problems. The key to understanding Henley's optimism lies in the laughter that her plays evoke; laughter functions to undercut that which is horrifying in life—to render it less horrifying.

Henley's reputation as a major American playwright was established with three full-length plays, *Crimes of the Heart*, *The Miss Firecracker Contest*, and *The Wake of Jamey Foster*. These plays also best illustrate the qualities that shape her unusual talent: a uniquely comic but sad voice, a distinguishing preoccupation with the bizarre, and a gift for working out variations on the themes of loneliness, guilt, loss, and renewal. Set in Hazlehurst, Mississippi, five years after Hurricane Camille, *Crimes of the Heart* is about three sisters—Lenny, Meg, and Babe MaGrath. The immediate crisis is that the youngest sister, Babe, has shot her husband, Zackery Botrelle, who is the richest and most powerful man in the community. The plot is fairly easily resolved when Zackery recovers and his threat to confine Babe in a mental institution is thwarted. This, however, hardly accounts for the sisters' bizarre tale, which Henley unravels through exposition that is brilliantly interspersed with the main action. Babe's trouble is only one more disaster among many that the MaGrath women have experienced, beginning with their father's desertion and their mother's suicide (she hanged herself and the family's cat). The mother's death left the sisters under the supervision of their grandfather, and now the care of the sick old man has fallen to Lenny, the oldest sister, because Babe married young and Meg escaped to California to pursue a singing career. Growing up in the shadow of their mother's inexplicable suicide and the notoriety it brought, each of the sisters suffers silently and alone. Meg was especially affected. Fearing to show pity as a sign of weakness, she tested herself as a youngster by staring at a book full of pictures of people with horrible skin diseases. Remarkably, Henley wrings laughter out of the MaGrath's misfortunes: The sisters suspect that Mama MaGrath killed herself because she was having a bad day; Lenny's prospects for marriage are bleak because she has a deformed ovary; and Babe shoots Zackery because she does not like his looks. To Henley's credit, the laughter is never at the expense of her characters, and there is a kind of bizarre logic to their eccentric behavior that makes the incredible credible. After Babe attempts suicide twice (because she, too, is having a bad day), she learns why her mother hanged the cat: She was afraid to die alone.

Of the same eccentric mold as the MaGrath women, twenty-four-year-old Carnelle Scott, the central character of *The Miss Firecracker Contest*, seeks to overcome her well-earned reputation as the town trollop by becoming Miss Firecracker at the annual Fourth of July celebration in her hometown of Brookhaven, Mississippi. Since Carnelle's determination to succeed is exceeded only by her lack of talent, the outcome is predictable. Carnelle loses (she comes in fifth in a field of five), but she manages to overcome her despondency over the loss and joins her friends to watch the fireworks display at the close of the play. Henley enlivens the simple plot with a number of very odd characters, all of whom, like Carnelle, seek redemption from their unhappy pasts. Delmount Williams, Carnelle's cousin, is a former mental patient who wants to be a philosopher; his sister Elain finds it easier to desert her husband and sons than to abandon her clock collection; and Carnelle's seamstress, Popeye Jackson, who learned her trade by making dresses for frogs, hears voices through her eyes. Henley's propensity for the grotesque is even more marked in *The Miss Firecracker Contest* than in *Crimes of the Heart*. Carnelle recalls a childhood bout with ringworm, the treatment for which was to shave her head and cover it with a disgusting ointment; Delmount's last job was scraping up dead dogs from county roads; and all fondly remember Ronelle Williams, Delmount and Elain's mother, who died looking like a hairy ape after having her cancerous pituitary gland replaced by one from a monkey. Although in *The Miss Firecracker Contest* Henley tries too hard to be amusing at times, her characters are distinctly drawn and believable despite their whimsicality.

Henley pushes the morbid to extremes in *The Wake of Jamey Foster*, which is set at Easter time in Canton, Mississippi. The inevitability of death, an underlying theme in Henley's earlier work, is the central focus of this very black comedy in which Marshael Foster, the thirty-three-year-old widow of Jamey Foster, endures the embarrassment of holding the wake of her estranged husband in her home. Marshael faces the ordeal with anger and remorse; she has only recently filed for divorce because her alcoholic husband left her for another woman. The widow finds little comfort from the strange group of friends and relatives who gather to pay their last respects to Jamey, who is laid out in the cheapest pine box available and dressed in a bright yellow sports coat. Among the mourners are Marshael's brother, Leon Darnell, a turkey jerker in a chicken factory; the orphan Pixrose Wilson, Leon's betrothed, who is planning a career washing dogs; Collard Darnell, Marshael's promiscuous sister, whose whole life has been marred by a low score on an IQ test that she took when she was twelve years old; Jamey's brother, Wayne Foster, a successful banker, and his wife, Katie, who turn up their noses at the other guests; and Brocker Slade, a pig farmer who is in love with Marshael. Very little that is significant happens in the play. As the group waits for morning and Jamey's funeral, they eat, drink, play cards, and take pictures of the corpse, but mostly they talk about gruesome things that have happened to them or others they know: arson, brain damage, miscarriages, automobile accidents, the cow that kicked Jamey in the head and killed him, and exploding pigs. Although plot is subsumed by character and character borders on caricature, *The Wake of Jamey Foster* is both entertaining and convincingly human, especially in the solace the characters find in the calamities of others.

Beth Henley's rise to prominence in the American theater is remarkable considering the regionalism that characterizes her work. The weaknesses of her plays, a penchant for telling tall tales that stretch credulity and a tendency to write gags that force laughter, are overcome by her gift for creating memorable characters. Whereas Henley's dramatic material is confined to small Southern towns and the misfits who inhabit them, her humorous but sympathetic treatment of human foibles has a universality and originality that make her one of the most imaginative dramatists writing for the American theater.

Other major works

SCREENPLAYS: *Nobody's Fool*, 1986; *Crimes of the Heart*, 1986 (adaptation of her play); *True Stories*, 1986 (with David Byrne and Stephen Tobolowsky); *Miss Firecracker*, 1989 (adaptation of her play).

TELEPLAYS: *Survival Guides*, 1986; *Trying Times*, 1987.

Bibliography

Haller, Scot. "Her First Play, Her First Pulitzer Prize." *Saturday Review* 8

(November, 1981): 40-44. Critiques the Off-Broadway production of *Crimes of the Heart* and attempts to account for Henley's idiosyncratic voice. Henley combines elements of the naturalistic play with characters from absurdist comedy and writes "with wit and compassion about good country people gone wrong or whacko." Some attention is given to Henley's biography.

Harbin, Billy J. "Familial Bonds in the Plays of Beth Henley." *Southern Quarterly* 25 (Spring, 1987): 81-94. Examines Henley's plays through *The Debutante Ball* but gives *Crimes of the Heart* the most attention. Recurring themes concern "the disintegration of traditional ideas, such as the breakup of families, the quest for emotional and spiritual fulfillment, and the repressive social forces within a small southern community."

Hargrove, Nancy D. "The Tragicomic Vision of Beth Henley's Drama." *Southern Quarterly* 22 (Summer, 1984): 54-70. Analyzes *Crimes of the Heart*, *The Miss Firecracker Contest*, and *The Wake of Jamey Foster* and finds that the plays "are essentially serious, although they are presented in the comic mode" and that the value of love, especially family love, is Henley's predominant theme. Hargrove's is the first scholarly article to examine Henley's work.

Jaehne, Karen. "Beth's Beauties." *Film Comment* 25 (May/June, 1989): 9-12. Highlights the film version of *The Miss Firecracker Contest* and quotes Henley extensively. Henley's plays analyze "the ways women conform to or rebel against standards of femininity." Although she likes to read tragedies, Henley says "in my own writing I can't see the situations I look at without laughing. I back into comedy. I can't help it."

Jones, John Griffin, ed. "Beth Henley." In *Mississippi Writers Talking*. Vol. 1. Jackson: University Press of Mississippi, 1982. Interviews Henley about her family background, education, and playwriting. Henley says that she likes to write about the South "because you can get away with making things more poetic." About the meaning of her plays, Henley confesses, "I don't think very thematically. I think more in terms of character and story."

McDonnell, Lisa J. "Diverse Similitude: Beth Henley and Marsha Norman." *Southern Quarterly* 25 (Spring, 1987): 95-104. Compares Henley's *Crimes of the Heart*, *The Miss Firecracker Contest*, and *The Wake of Jamey Foster* and Norman's *Getting Out* (pr. 1977) and *'night, Mother* (pr. 1983). Whereas both writers use the family as a framework and employ gothic humor, their plays differ remarkably in tone and style. Henley "writes comedy with serious dimensions, Norman, serious drama with comic overtones." Henley's plays demonstrate a "theatrical" orientation, while Norman's show a more "literary" bent.

Simon, John. "Sisterhood Is Beautiful." Review of *Crimes of the Heart*. *New York* 14 (January 12, 1981): 42-43. Reviews the Off-Broadway production of *Crimes of the Heart.* Simon calls Henley "a new playwright of charm, warmth, style, unpretentiousness, and authentically individual vision." His analysis connects Henley's characters to those of Anton Chekhov, Flannery O'Connor, and Tennessee Williams. If Henley "errs in any way, it is in slightly artificial resolutions."

Ayne C. Durham

JAMES ENE HENSHAW

Born: Calabar, Nigeria; August 29, 1924

Principal drama

This Is Our Chance, pr. 1948, pb. 1956; *The Jewels of the Shrine*, pr. 1952, pb. 1956 (one act); *A Man of Character*, pb. 1956; *This Is Our Chance: Plays from West Africa*, pb. 1956 (includes *The Jewels of the Shrine* and *A Man of Character*; also as *The Jewels of the Shrine*, pb. 1956); *Children of the Goddess and Other Plays*, pb. 1964 (includes *Companion for a Chief* and *Magic in the Blood*); *Medicine for Love: A Comedy in Three Acts*, pb. 1964; *Dinner for Promotion: A Comedy in Three Acts*, pb. 1967; *Enough Is Enough: A Play of the Nigerian Civil War*, pr. 1975, pb. 1976; *A Song to Mary Charles, Irish Sister of Charity*, pr. 1981, pb. 1984.

Other literary forms

James Ene Henshaw is known only for his drama.

Achievements

As one of the pioneering dramatists in Nigeria, Henshaw was also one of the first to be published outside West Africa. *This Is Our Chance*, which has undergone many reprintings, has been extremely popular in West Africa since its first production by the Association of Students of African Descent in Dublin in 1948. It has been staged by professional companies as well as school and amateur groups.

In 1952, Henshaw's dramatic talents were acknowledged when his play *The Jewels of the Shrine* won the Henry Carr Memorial Cup as the best one-act play in the All-Nigeria Festival of the Arts. Henshaw's reputation was enhanced when *A Man of Character* was mentioned in *Nigeria 10*, the tenth-anniversary commemorative publication in honor of Nigerian independence compiled by the Federal Military Government.

Henshaw's influence, impact, and success as a dramatist in Nigeria stem from the fact that he is a very direct, matter-of-fact dramatic artist. Compared to such contemporary Nigerian writers as Wole Soyinka and John Pepper Clark, Henshaw's work is less intellectually oriented. His plays are straightforward, not bookishly philosophical, and are written in simple language. Most of the works are aimed both at the adult reader and at schoolchildren. The beguiling simplicity of plot and style facilitates the staging of his plays, making him one of the most frequently produced playwrights in West Africa. He is also adept at stagecraft (although some critics have complained of implausibility in this regard), giving precise, detailed directions and analysis as to how his work is to be produced at every stage, whether for a school production or for adults.

Henshaw's dramatic philosophy contributes greatly to his popularity. His subject matter, which deals directly with African culture and traditions, focuses on major issues familiar to both his African and his Western audience. For this reason, Henshaw prefaces most of his plays, in the manner of George Bernard Shaw, with elaborate introductions which discuss thematic concerns and other ancillary matters connected with the work. Thus, both the foreign and African producer/reader are helped to see the proper perspective from which the work is to be approached, studied, analyzed, and evaluated. Henshaw himself views the function of his drama, in part, as providing a positive impact upon his society. Joseph Bruchac believes that Henshaw's cardinal aim in writing is to forge, through the dramatic medium, a unity and understanding among Africans, who share closely related traditions and heritage, rather than "explaining the African to the non-African."

Biography

James Ene Ewa Henshaw was born in 1924 in Calabar, South Eastern Nigeria, West Africa, into a large family, the youngest of nine sons. His father was of royal ancestry, descended from the Efik lineage in Calabar, where in the days before independence his importance gave him a position within the colonial Nigerian Legislative Council, an august lawmaking body.

Having been brought up by his eldest brother, Dr. Lawrence Eken Richard Henshaw, following the death of their father, James Henshaw was encouraged to continue his schooling at the Sacred Heart Primary School in Calabar. He then went on to Christ the King College, a secondary school in Onitsha, a well-known commercial center in what was then the Eastern region (now known as Cross River State) of Nigeria.

Upon graduation from Christ the King College, Henshaw traveled abroad to Ireland and in 1943 enrolled as a medical student at the National University of Ireland in Dublin. He took bachelor of science and bachelor of medicine degrees and in 1949 qualified as a physician. In 1954, Henshaw had the opportunity to pursue a course for specialized training in cardiovascular diseases and was awarded the T.D.D. degree by the University of Wales.

Henshaw's professional practice as a physician began in earnest upon his return to Nigeria in 1955, where he first served as a senior consultant in tuberculosis treatment for the government of Eastern Nigeria, in Port Harcourt, until 1978. From 1968 to 1972, he served as the First Controller of Medical Services in Cross River State. Thereafter he became medical consultant in thoracic medicine to the Ministry of Health at the chest clinic in his hometown, Calabar.

In 1973, Henshaw was appointed senior consultant on tuberculosis control at Rivers State, a post he held until 1978. He has since been interested in participating in national programs connected with the medical profession in Nigeria and has held membership in the National Council of Health (1968-1972) and the Nigerian Medical Council (1970-1972). In spite of his demanding professional commitments, James Henshaw is a family man. He married Caroline Nchelem Amadi in 1958; they have eight children.

Analysis

Most of James Ene Henshaw's early, short plays share two thematic threads: tradition and its conflict with modern life, and the worldwide problems of corruption, crime, and materialism. *This Is Our Chance*, one of Henshaw's most popular plays, revolves around Kudaro, the Crown Princess; her father, Chief Damba; her mother, Ansa; her suitor, Prince Ndamu; her tutor, Bambulu; and other village folk whose offices bring them into the story. Set in the royal household and village-kingdom of Koloro and in the rival village of Udura, the play addresses the typically Henshawian preoccupation with the conflict between tradition and modernity and the need to assimilate the best of both African and Western cultures.

From the outset of the play, Chief Damba's obsession with tradition is clear: Tradition compels him to keep the fortune-teller at court, to forbid extravillage marriages, to opt for age-old customs instead of experimenting with new ideas. In Damba's opinion, Koloro's strict adherence to tradition is the key to the village's superiority. He will declare war on any village that threatens traditional values. Yet when the conflict of interest compels him to take his daughter's life—in eloping with Ndamu, the prince of the rival village, Udura, she has broken one of the most important tenets of Koloro tradition—Damba bends tradition to fit the circumstances, thereby opening new avenues for progress in his village.

Ajugo, Damba's prime minister, is a diehard protector of tradition, convinced that the old ways must never succumb to new ideas, no matter what the cost. Ajugo states categorically that matrimonial links outside the village of Koloro are punishable, in the case of the commoner, by banishment, and, in the case of royalty, by death. Damba, faced with the options of war, his daughter's death, or his own loss of life, must choose. Ajugo, ever faithful to tradition, prepares the hemlock for Damba's punishment. Damba's life is spared, however, by the sudden arrival of Princess Kudaro. Even though tradition now dictates Ajugo's death, the prime minister is spared and a new prime minister, Enusi, appointed. Ajugo remains the uncompromising custodian of the indigenous culture.

There is a dichotomy between those characters who favor modernity (Enusi, Bambulu, Princess Kudaro, Ansa, Ayi the maid, Udura's ambassador, and Prince Ndamu) and those who stand for tradition (Damba, Ajugo, and Chief Mboli of Udura). Princess Kudaro, having lived in the city, where she attended school, is at once sophisticated and down-to-earth. Although she is the Crown Princess, she frequently states how much she detests village life. Her elopement with Prince Ndamu is one of the greatest of village taboos. As a character, she represents progress. Princess Kudaro's elopement and the subsequent events, especially her use of Bambulu's antivenom serum, help to bring about peace between the perennially feuding villages.

The bombastic Bambulu, although a foreigner, wields great influence in the village. An accomplished scientist, educated in the Western tradition, and a good teacher, Bambulu the radical is always dressed in Western style. He refers to himself as the catalyst in the village. Under the cloak of teaching about vitamins, he succeeds in sowing the seeds of revolution which undermine the traditional values of Koloro. He is opposed to the blind adherence to tradition that breeds ignorance, hatred, war, disease, bigotry, poverty, and backwardness. As an apostle of progress, good-neighborliness, and reconciliation, Bambulu is mainly responsible for introducing Western ideas and civilization to the village. With Chief Damba's support, he opens more schools and is given full autonomy to teach basic scientific skills, reading, and writing, as well as agriculture.

Chief Damba thus rises out of adversity and seizes the chance to bring peace, progress, and prosperity to his village. Enusi's metaphoric description of their tradition being a sword of Damocles ties in neatly with the problems raised by tradition in the village of Koloro.

A Man of Character foreshadows in its thematic concerns many of the issues addressed in contemporary African writing. One of the most urgent of these is the problem of corruption. In the play, an honest, sincere, dedicated man—a man of character—who refuses to be corrupted in a corrupt society must suffer the consequences of his decision.

As in most Henshaw plays, with the exception of *Magic in the Blood*, when the protagonist runs into an intricate problem, he manages both to extricate and to vindicate himself. In this play, the serene, happy family life of Kobina and his wife, Ayodele, is disrupted by the negative influence of Ayodele's mercenary, domineering sister, Serinya, and her venal husband, Anosse. Kobina, a God-fearing man, refuses to be influenced by Anosse's offer of a bribe. His moral position is that West African society needs people of conscience and that appointments and promotions should be based on merit, not on nepotism or bribery. His refusal to enter into this system of institutionalized corruption breaks apart the family, since Serinya's values have influenced the once content Ayodele. Ayodele now desires a house of her own, new clothes, money for trips abroad, and security for their child, Ibitam. Kobina obviously cannot afford all of these luxuries, since his modest income is being used to educate his daughter. After a quarrel, Ayodele and Ibitam leave Kobina, whose misfortunes are compounded by the suspicious loss of five hundred pounds from his office safe. He becomes the prime suspect, and the onus of proof of innocence rests upon him. In fact, Seboh, Kobina's servant, together with Seboh's crooked, vicious-looking brother, has engineered the entire plot. Seboh, who is referred to as the "stranger" in the play, attempts to blackmail Kobina and his associates (the lawyer Diyego, the magistrate Kopechi, and Sergeant Mbedu), but the judge's quick thinking neutralizes the stranger's malevolent plan. Seboh, the servant, filled with remorse, is apprehended by the police as he attempts to return the money. The two Seboh brothers are hauled off to prison, with the stranger's strong avowal to turn over a new leaf.

The series of coincidences in the play dilutes the plausibility of the plot somewhat, since it is unlikely that all of Kobina's important associates would suddenly and simultaneously converge, uninvited, upon his home. The moral preoccupations of the protagonist render him rather too saintly, even somewhat self-righteous, although his depression and subsequent drinking do indicate that he is indeed human and vulnerable.

As many critics have remarked, the language in the play is inflated and bookish; the characters hardly speak as typical Nigerians do. The ending, as in Henshaw's *Companion for a Chief, Children of the Goddess, Dinner for Promotion*, and *This Is Our Chance*, takes the form of a happy reconciliation. Equilibrium is restored. The moral lesson that *A Man of Character* teaches is the age-old adage that crime does not pay. The upright are vindicated, truth stands, and honesty is shown to be the best policy. The characters become wiser and more determined to continue living in an upright way.

Medicine for Love, subtitled *A Comedy in Three Acts*, is a humorous examination of politics, politicians, and political practices in modern West Africa. It also explores the concept of the African marriage system, examining the issue of traditional wives and arranged marriages—an ancient custom being forced upon a modern city-dweller, Ewia Ekunyah. Henshaw, in his introduction to the piece, succinctly sums up these motifs: monogamy, polygamy, medicine men, tradition, and the African.

Ewia Ekunyah, the hero of the play and would-be politician, finds his life complicated by the unexpected arrival in the city of no less than three traditional wives, Bekin Wari, Ibiere Sua, and Nene Katsina, married to him through the agency of various relatives. According to tradition, these wives cannot be returned. Naturally, rivalry and suspicion are rampant among the three women and their assorted relatives, who resort to medicine for love in order to win Ewia Ekunyah's favor. The machinations begin when Ibiere Sua and Bekin Wari team up against Nene Katsina, the youngest, best educated, and most beautiful of the three. Apart from Nene

Katsina, who displays the characteristics of good humor, romance, and seriousness, the women are eminently unsuitable as wives of a prospective politician. Auntie Dupeh, a dowager-duchess type, is too domineering and aggressive in trying to push Ewia's interests. Auntie Dupeh's imposition as chairperson of Ewia's political planning committee and her recommendation of Agatarata the medicine man as spiritual adviser destroy Ewia's political career.

The array of Ewia's dishonest advisers clearly indicates that the political policymakers active in urban affairs are no better than the candidates themselves. Mr. Joss, Ewia's political agent, using his Machiavellian expertise, spends eighty-one hundred pounds and manages to swindle the poor Ewia into selling his last house to finance the campaign; the Reverend Sanctus Kyei cannot, in times of trouble, give Ewia any sensible advice regarding Ewia's concrete, everyday problems; Agatarata's ignorance of the chemical composition of the ink that becomes invisible on Ewia's application form leads to Ewia's downfall. Henshaw touches here on the very delicate interconnection between Christianity, tradition, and politics. That a modern educated African politician such as Ewia Ekunyah thinks he can win an election or solve his marital entanglements through a juju priest or a Christian minister is preposterous and ironic; these services, in fact, cost Ewia the election.

Henshaw has given a comic look at the operation of politics in contemporary Africa. The fundamental concept of democracy does not seem to be fully understood by the politicians, who tend to think that the survival of the fittest, by any means, foul or fair, is a more appropriate tenet. Instead of honest people of integrity and dignity, there is a multiplicity of crooked, politically self-serving, corrupt candidates and political advisers. The unqualified Ewia resorts to bribery to edge out honest, sincere, and dedicated rivals such as Mr. Sonrillo.

There is no poetic justice in *Medicine for Love*. At the end, all characters, good or bad, gain: Ewia and Nene Katsina gain marital bliss; Auntie Dupeh marries a VIP, Kiudu Bonga; Bekin Wari marries Ewia Ekunya's secretary, Olu Ita, who finds a new job; Ibiere Sua marries Dr. Sigismond Marsey. Finally, Papa Garuka marries Mama Ebunde, Ibiere Sua's mother. The matrimonial ceremony of the entire cast is presided over by the Reverend Kyei.

Dinner for Promotion, as the title implies, centers on the plans of Tikku and Seyil, two young and ambitious employees of Sipo Amalgamated, to get to the top. In the play, promotion depends upon a sumptuous dinner for the Sipo family and upon marrying the boss's daughter rather than upon merit. *Dinner for Promotion* thus touches upon the relationships between employer and employee, between friends, between parents and children, and between in-laws, and deals with the life of the young, educated urban group. Through *Dinner for Promotion*, Henshaw portrays the callous disregard for decency or ethical behavior or even loyalty among friends when personal interests are at stake.

Each character seems to have an ulterior motive. Tikku has his eye on Sharia, the boss's daughter, but his interest is purely selfish; he sees her only as a means for promotion. Seyil, not knowing Sharia's family connections, courts Sharia and takes the advice of Tikku to speak ill of Mr. Sipo, their employer. Naturally, Sharia takes offense as Seyil heaps insults upon her father's head, then promptly walks into Tikku's waiting arms. Through a series of deceptive moves, Seyil plots Tikku's downfall both as suitor to Sharia and as prospective executive in Sipo Amalgamated by sabotaging Tikku's "dinner for promotion," but his plans backfire. In spite of all this confusion and hostility, the ending of the play is typically amicable: The two sisters-in-law, Madam Pamphilia Sipo and Madam Una, are reconciled; Tikku and Sharia, blessed by their parents, are about to be married; Tikku does get his promotion and material gain; and even Seyil gains by being offered a much better job elsewhere. A form of equity reigns.

Enough Is Enough is a contemporary drama set in a detention camp during the last weeks of the Nigerian Civil War. The play documents the incarceration and plight, both psychological and physical, of six detainees and their guards. Henshaw's introduction to the work concentrates upon the personal attitudes and feelings of the detainees, the reactions of Nigerians to the war, and the complex human emotions which permeated the detainees' existence.

Set against the prison backdrop, *Enough Is Enough* centers upon the notion of reconciliation, the woes and gloom of the war, and the role of charitable and relief organizations at that time. The outcry "genocide and pogrom," which became the Biafran slogan during the course of the war, is alluded to throughout the work.

Apart from Ufanko, Bisong, and the disembodied voice of Nwakego, the major characters enacting the drama are Peter Emeribe, a very important member of Parliament; the lawyer Linus Nosikeh; Dr. Dagogo, a politician and medical practitioner; and the arrogant Professor Ezuba, who apparently masterminded the rebellion against the revolution. The remaining characters—the Superintendent, the warder, Mother Cecilia, Sister Lucinda, Major Maxy, and others—serve to highlight the suffering and anguish of the main characters. Referred to as detainees, saboteurs, and criminals, the incarcerated men seem to have rebelled against those advocating war and secession. This rebellion is regarded as treason and is the cause of their detention.

Divided into four acts, each with a distinct thematic concern, *Enough Is Enough* gives a concrete insight into the ravages of war, which claims the lives of healthy, innocent, able-bodied people (sometimes civilians). While all wars are destructive, this war is especially so: It is a civil war, with relatives killing one another, creating a generation of orphans and cripples.

Henshaw is here concerned with the brutal treatment of the detainees, the resultant psychological problems of both the long-term detainees and their guards, the economic difficulties, and ecological destruction. There is a general lack of trust, a lack of freedom to speak or even to remain silent, and a very real lack of decent food and water. The detainees are denied such amenities as radios and the right to receive visitors or uncensored mail. Everyone in the camp is vulnerable to the constant attacks from bombing and disease. Survival becomes a critical issue; the detainees, in spite of their former privileged positions, have had to resort to sordid, subservient practices to survive. Part of the irony of Peter Emeribe's case is that the warder is his former houseboy.

The psychological problems range from insanity to alcoholism. The Superintendent, for example, a brilliant zoologist in civilian life, unsure of his competence in his present position, ends up a nervous, alcoholic wreck. Dr. Dagogo becomes moody, embittered, and mentally unstable after four years of detention at Umudali camp. Ufanko has turned into a cynic, while Peter Emeribe burns with a strong sense of injustice. The lack of privacy, and the constant harassment to which they are subject, cause the prisoners, understandably, to lash out at one another. As for Professor Ezuba, his arrogance leads to the eventual destruction of most of the group. Treating the warders as a pack of ignorant, unqualified upstarts, he insults his captors without considering the consequences for his fellow prisoners, always reminding the world of his former importance. On the other side, the presence of Major Maxy—a mere child trying to behave as an adult soldier, a boy who, at the age of fourteen, functions as an undercover agent—points out the absurdity and unprepared nature of the revolutionaries. Ironically, Maxy, in contrast with his dead brothers, displays filial devotion by trying to protect his father.

One important motif present in this drama is that of peace and reconciliation. The war, having taken its impartial toll of destruction, ends with the signing of the Lagos peace treaty. Umudali Camp is disbanded, and some of the detainees are released. As a consequence of the personal vengeance of the Superintendent, however, the most vocal of the detainees are killed, although, unbeknown to them, the war has already been over for four days.

The play's title, *Enough Is Enough*, fittingly expresses a yearning for peace, unity, reconciliation, and a return to normal life; as the first voice in act 3 cries, "Let's waste no further time. Let's spill no further blood. Let's rebuild the nation anew." Dagogo poignantly replies that the fighting should cease because there has been enough of brother killing brother, of suffering, of dying from bullets, of hunger and disease—enough of everything connected with the war and the prisoners' detention. The emotional demands of such a painful, historical moment give this later play an uncharacteristic slant in the Henshaw canon. The language itself strikes a note of pathos and patriotism, while the imagery constantly reverts to horror and bestiality (references to vampires, lizards, boa constrictors, hawks) to underscore the reality of human suffering.

Bibliography

Dathorne, O. R. *African Literature in the Twentieth Century.* Minneapolis: University of Minnesota Press, 1975. Under a chapter entitled "African Drama in French and English," with a subheading, "Recent Staged Drama," Dathorne compares "social reality and the inner life" in the plays of Henshaw and others. Discusses *This Is Our Chance*, saying that the "title play describes a society that is fettered by an outmoded tradition but nevertheless aspires toward western values." The main character is discussed in terms of "tradition" versus "worn-out institutions."

Graham-White, Anthony. *The Drama of Black Africa.* New York: Samuel French, 1974. In the chapter entitled "Drama Seeking Independence," Graham-White places Henshaw with the transitional playwrights, between the British era and the stylistic changes after the independence movement. Graham-White notes that "Henshaw's plays have little artistic value, yet they are often performed in the schools and are popular there for their simple characterization and firm didacticism."

Ogunba, Oyin. "Modern Drama in West Africa." In *Perspectives on African Literature*, edited by Christopher Heywood. New York: Africana Publishing, 1971. Henshaw is placed with R. Sarif Easmon as a playwright whose motive is "as he himself has implied again and again, to make good citizens of his audience." The dramatic situation does not change from play to play: "There is a simple conflict between tradition and modernism," resolved on the side of modernism, "although with an admixture of what is considered good in tradition." Discusses *This Is Our Chance* and *Children of the Goddess* at some length.

Taiwo, Oladele. *An Introduction to West African Literature.* London: Thomas Nelson, 1967. Puts the work of Henshaw in place as the beginnings of Nigerian drama. Describes the one-act plays, "based on one aspect or other of African culture and tradition." Basically school plays for amateur drama groups, they are contrasted with those of John Pepper Clark-Bekederemo and Wole Soyinka, whose work reveals "the cultural achievements of the past, the dangers of the present, and the fears and expectations of the future."

Kwaku Amoabeng
Carrol Lasker
(Updated by *Thomas J. Taylor*)

DuBOSE HEYWARD

Born: Charleston, South Carolina; August 31, 1885
Died: Tryon, North Carolina; June 16, 1940

Principal drama

Porgy, pr., pb. 1927 (with Dorothy Heyward; adaptation of his novel); *Brass Ankle*, pr., pb. 1931; *Porgy and Bess*, pr., pb. 1935 (libretto; music by George Gershwin; adaptation of *Porgy*); *Mamba's Daughters*, pr., pb. 1939 (with Dorothy Heyward; adaptation of his novel).

Other literary forms

In addition to three plays and the libretto for *Porgy and Bess*, DuBose Heyward was the author of poetry, short stories, and novels. In his own time, he probably achieved more recognition as a novelist than as a playwright. In fact, his plays *Porgy* and *Mamba's Daughters* are dramatizations of his novels of the same titles, set in black communities in and around Charleston, South Carolina. Heyward's final novel, *Star Spangled Virgin* (1939), also has black characters, but it is set on St. Croix in the Virgin Islands. Heyward also wrote three novels featuring white characters; *Angel* (1926) is about the mountaineers of North Carolina's Blue Ridge Mountains; *Lost Morning* (1936), set in the Piedmont, deals with an artist trying to regain his artistic integrity; and *Peter Ashley* (1932) is a historical novel set in Charleston at the beginning of the Civil War. *The Half Pint Flask* (1929), Heyward's best short story, was published separately as a book. Heyward also published poetry: *Carolina Chansons* (1922), *Skylines and Horizons* (1924), and *Jasbo Brown and Selected Poems* (1931).

Achievements

Heyward, a famous writer in his own time, is a comparatively obscure figure today. His characters, however, have become part of the American folklore. People who have not heard of DuBose Heyward nevertheless do know Porgy, thanks primarily to the success of what has come to be thought of as George Gershwin's *Porgy and Bess*. It must be remembered, though, that Heyward wrote the libretto as well as many of the lyrics of *Porgy and Bess*. According to virtually all sources, he also helped shape all other aspects of the production of what was undeniably America's first folk opera. Through *Porgy and Bess*, *Mamba's Daughters*, and *Brass Ankle*, Heyward made at least two other contributions to American theater: Arguably, he was the first American playwright to treat blacks as human beings in their own right, not as mere accessories to whites, and to portray them in this way in their own communities; Langston Hughes describes Heyward as one who saw "with his white eyes, wonderful poetic, human qualities in the inhabitants of Catfish Row. . . ." Heyward's plays with black characters also hastened the acceptance of blacks as serious actors. Ethel Waters in *Mamba's Daughters*, for example, was the first black actress ever to be starred on Broadway in a dramatic play.

Biography

Edwin DuBose Heyward was born in Charleston, South Carolina, into an old Charleston family. When he was two years old, his father was killed in an accident, and his mother began a struggle to support DuBose and his younger sister. Both of these events were to shape his work.

Heyward's writing, both his fiction and his plays, often portrays life in Charleston, most notably life in the black quarter. His contact with the black community probably came principally from his employment as a checker on a steamship company wharf, where he developed understanding and appreciation of the lives of the black stevedores with whom he worked. Afterward, he became successful in the real estate and insurance businesses. He was to pursue this career until his decision to commit himself to full-time writing.

Three people, in particular, influenced Heyward's decision to commit himself to writing as a career. He developed friendships with John Bennett, a critic and author of children's books, and Hervey Allen, who was later to write *Anthony Adverse* (1933). From these friendships grew the founding of the Poetry Society of South Carolina and Heyward's serious involvement with writing. Heyward's marriage to Dorothy Hartzell Kuhns also influenced his commitment to a writing career. He met her at the McDowell Colony, a retreat founded by the composer Edward McDowell for the purpose of encouraging artistic achievement. A graduate of the Harvard School of Drama, Kuhns had a play produced in the fall of 1923, the year in which she and Heyward were married. For the rest of his life, she gave her husband encouragement and the benefit of her own expertise as a dramatist, and collaborated with him on two successful Broadway dramas, *Porgy* and *Mamba's Daughters*, although she consistently claimed that his contribution was greater than hers.

Ira and George Gershwin were collaborators with Heyward for *Porgy and Bess*, first produced in 1935. Ironically, though the libretto and part of the lyrics are Heyward's, *Porgy and Bess* has come to be associated almost totally with the Gershwin name, as the opera has gone through numerous revivals over the years.

Heyward and Gershwin discussed yet another collaboration, a dramatization of Heyward's novel *Star Spangled Virgin*, but Heyward's death at the age of fifty-four ended those plans. Heyward died in Tryon, North Carolina, on June 16, 1940, and was buried in Saint Phillips Churchyard in Charleston.

Analysis

DuBose Heyward's contributions to American drama are minor but nevertheless important. He was one of the first American dramatists to portray blacks seriously and sympathetically. The use of black music in his plays, as well as in the folk opera *Porgy and Bess*, helped create acceptance of black folk expression as an art form. His influence helped black writers realize the value of their own culture and experience.

Heyward's plays also provided access to the stage for black performers. In fact, when *Porgy* was being cast, vaudeville performers had to be recruited and trained for their roles in a dramatic play, since at that time there were no black performers with experience in serious drama. The blues singer Ethel Waters, who played Hagar in *Mamba's Daughters*, was the first black woman to be starred on Broadway in a dramatic play.

Despite the pioneering significance of Heyward's work, he had severe limitations as a dramatist. Virtually all of his critics point to his tendency to rely too heavily on melodrama and to a lack of character development. Many also believe that his critique of white society lacks depth. Nevertheless, Heyward provided the American theater with a positive treatment of a black community and its inner spirit—a spirit to which Heyward referred as "rhythm." For him, "rhythm" was the spirit of a people close to their God and the earth and bound together in their community by suffering, hope, and joy.

Porgy was Heyward's first play. Although Dorothy Heyward wrote a first draft of the play, she asserts that her role was minor, that the play versions of both *Porgy* and *Mamba's Daughters* were nine-tenths DuBose's.

The basic plot of *Porgy*, well known because of *Porgy and Bess*, concerns a summer in Catfish Row, the black quarter in Charleston. The time is the 1920's (a change from the turn-of-the-century setting of the novel). Porgy, the central character, a crippled beggar, is drawn about the streets on a cart made from a soapbox and pulled by a goat.

The play centers on Porgy's brief time of happiness and love with Bess. Bess seeks protection and shelter from Porgy after her brutal lover, Crown, murders Robbins at the beginning of the play. Ostracized by the other women of Catfish Row, Bess slowly finds acceptance and a new life with Porgy. From the beginning, though, the couple's happiness is threatened by Sportin Life, a Harlem drug dealer, and by the possibility of Crown's return.

Their summer of love comes to an end when Crown, who is hiding on Kittiwah Island, brutally forces Bess to resume her relationship with him (she has come to the island on a holiday picnic with others from Catfish Row). Shortly afterward, during a great storm, Crown returns to the Row. Although people at first believe that he has died in the storm, he actually returns to the Row later that night, determined to murder Porgy and take

Bess back. Instead, he is killed by Porgy. The storm also orphans a baby whom Bess claims as her own, after the mother leaves it with her and then goes out into the storm.

Although Porgy is not charged with Crown's murder, he is taken to jail to identify the dead man. Terrified by having to identify the man he has murdered, Porgy tries to escape, urged on by Sportin Life. After the police have caught Porgy and taken him into custody, Sportin Life convinces the people of the Row and Bess that Porgy will be in jail for a year. In fact, Porgy is in jail for only a week and comes back happy, bringing money and presents for Bess and the baby and other friends. Joyfully, he searches for Bess and the baby, only to find that Sportin Life has lured her away with lies and a drug called "happy dust." As the play ends, Porgy drives his goat through the gate out of the Row on the way to New York to look for Bess.

The great achievement of *Porgy* (and the novel on which it was based) lies in Heyward's treatment of his black hero and the black community of which he was a part. The play succeeds as theater, primarily through its use of music and group expression—through spirituals, chants, shouts, parading—and the crowd movements associated with all of these. Its saucer burial scene and hurricane scene are, in particular, made powerful through the use of spirituals to express emotion that could not be conveyed by words.

While the play is powerful on the emotional level, it is marred by an excess of melodrama and, more seriously, a failure to provide the characters with adequate motivation. The audience is not prepared for Bess's crucial decision to leave Porgy and go with Sportin Life, whose character is never developed sufficiently to explain his actions. Even Porgy, the protagonist, is essentially a static character. In addition, in adapting his novel for the stage, Heyward minimized the element of racial conflict and added some incidents and characters which give to certain scenes in the play a condescending, minstrel-show quality. Yet the play does succeed, as an expression of "rhythm" and as a depiction of the significance and humanity of its black characters.

Porgy and Bess, the folk opera that made the Gershwins more famous than its librettist, succeeds in the same ways as the play on which it is based, and in some other ways as well. In comparison to that of *Porgy*, the plot of *Porgy and Bess* is simplified—some of the extraneous minstrel-show scenes are cut—but the songs and chants and "rhythm" of the play are retained and heightened, allowing the folk opera to profit "both by its escape from the play's clutter and the opportunity its songs provided for the characters to express their personal feelings," according to William H. Slavick (*DuBose Heyward*, 1981). Indeed, there are critics who were disappointed with the oversimplification of the opera in comparison with the play from which it was taken, yet, as Slavick notes, *Porgy and Bess* was unique in realizing "the rhythms, color, music, movement, and passion" that bestow upon it "more merit than vaudeville."

Mamba's Daughters, like *Porgy* and *Porgy and Bess*, derives much of its success from the use of music and songs. In fact, one of the characters, a black singer named Lissa, transforms the expression of her people into art. The play's central character, however, is not Lissa, but her mother, Hagar. The play focuses on Hagar's loneliness and separation from the daughter whom she has her own mother, Mamba, rear while she is in prison. Men are Hagar's adversaries—the sailors who refuse to pay her for delivering wash, the white men who administer a mockery of justice, but above all Gilly Bluton, whose life she saves at the expense of her freedom, when she takes him to the hospital in Charleston after being forbidden to return to the city from the plantation to which she was sent. In return for this sacrifice, Bluton rapes Lissa and then blackmails her after she achieves some success. The play ends with Hagar protecting Lissa's name by murdering Bluton and then committing suicide.

Aside from the music in the play—Lissa's music and the song with which Hagar consoles herself—*Mamba's Daughters* derives its power from its focus on the suffering figure of Hagar, who is separated from the daughter whom she loves and for whom she sacrifices everything—even her life. The theme of love as a weapon against injustice, and the song through which Hagar (and Lissa) express their love and suffering, give the play its power. Its weakness lies in its overly melodramatic plot.

Unlike *Porgy*, *Porgy and Bess*, and *Mamba's Daughters*, *Brass Ankle* was unsuccessful on Broadway. Also unlike the previous works, *Brass Ankle* was a play from the start, and Heyward had no collaborator. The play is about interracial marriage and passing. The white protagonist, Larry Leamer, must confront the knowledge of his wife Ruth's black ancestry when she bears him a dark-skinned son after previously bearing a blond daughter, June. The play fails primarily because Heyward resolves the conflict through Ruth protecting her husband from the truth by claiming, falsely, that she has taken a lover. Leamer then kills her and their son—and is thus not forced to come to terms with his knowledge of her race.

Judged by the standards of a later generation, Heyward's dramatic portraits of the black community are deeply flawed; the notion of "rhythm" as the defining characteristic of the black spirit is a notorious stereotype, all too representative of Heyward's baggage of cultural assumptions. Judged by the standards of their own time, however, Heyward's works were courageous, pioneering efforts, and they played a significant role in bringing the black experience to the American stage.

Other major works

NOVELS: *Porgy*, 1925; *Angel*, 1926; *Mamba's Daughters*, 1929; *Peter Ashley*, 1932; *Lost Morning*, 1936; *Star Spangled Virgin*, 1939.

SHORT FICTION: *The Half Pint Flask*, 1929.
POETRY: *Carolina Chansons*, 1922; *Skylines and Horizons*, 1924; *Jasbo Brown and Selected Poems*, 1931.

Bibliography

Alpert, Hollis. *The Life and Times of Porgy and Bess: The Story of an American Classic.* New York: Alfred A. Knopf, 1990. Alpert tells the interesting story—flavored with the spirit of the 1920's and 1930's—of how Heyward wrote *Porgy and Bess* as a novel, how his wife, Dorothy Hartzell Kuhns, turned it into a hit play, and, how, finally, George Gershwin presented his own version in 1935. Alpert describes the performances, recounts Gershwin's experiences with the Gullah language, and illustrates the volume with photographs.

Clark, Emily. "DuBose Heyward." *The Virginia Quarterly Review* 6 (October, 1930): 546-556. A recollection of Heyward by one who knew him through the Poetry Society of South Carolina. Clark recalls her first meeting with Heyward, at the Goose Creek Club in Charleston, and tells of her subsequent correspondence and meetings with Heyward. Revealing in its anecdotes of racial attitudes.

Durham, Frank. *DuBose Heyward: The Man Who Wrote "Porgy."* Columbia: University of South Carolina Press, 1954. The first book-length study of Heyward. The introduction, "Young Man in an Old City," provides excellent background material, and three chapters deal well with Heyward and the theater: "*Porgy* on Stage," "*Porgy* and George Gershwin," and "*Mamba* and Ethel Waters."

Harrigan, Anthony. "DuBose Heyward: Memorialist and Realist." *The Georgia Review* 5 (1951): 335-344. Harrigan identifies Heyward as "the finest expression of the Southern literary genius" and finds this genius expressed not in mythmaking about the South but in convincing representations of the Charleston culture in which he thrived. Harrigan finds that race relations were not Heyward's only topic: He also successfully treated the artist's relationship to his or her society.

Slavick, William H. *DuBose Heyward.* Boston: Twayne, 1981. Slavick is excellent at depicting the Charleston world in which Heyward flourished. The cultural history is presented in "A Charleston Gentleman and the World of Letters," and the Charleston ambience is described in "The Irony of Freedom in Charleston: *Porgy.*" The dramatization of *Mamba's Daughters* is analyzed in "The Rhythms of Charleston: *Mamba's Daughters.*"

Doris Walters
(Updated by *Frank Day*)

JOHN HEYWOOD

Born: London(?), England; c. 1497
Died: Louvain(?), Spanish Netherlands; October, 1578

Principal drama

The Play of Love, pr. c. 1528-1529, pb. 1533; *Witty and Witless*, wr. c. 1533, pb. 1846 (abridged), 1909 (also known as *A Dialogue on Wit and Folly*); *The Pardoner and the Friar*, pb. 1533 (possibly based on *Farce nouvelle d'un pardonneur, d'un triacleur, et d'une tavernière*); *Johan Johan the Husband, Tyb His Wife, and Sir Johan the Priest*, pb. 1533 (commonly known as *Johan Johan*; adaptation of *Farce nouvelle et fort joyeuse du pasté*); *The Play of the Weather*, pb. 1533; *The Playe of the Foure P.P.: A Newe and a Very Mery Enterlude of a Palmer, a Pardoner, a Potycary, a Pedler*, pb. 1541-1547 (commonly known as *The Four P.P.*; possibly based on *Farce nouvelle d'un pardonneur, d'un triacleur, et d'une tavernière*); *The Dramatic Writings of John Heywood*, pb. 1905 (John S. Farmer, editor).

Other literary forms

In his own time, John Heywood was best known for his published collections of epigrams, not for his plays, even though the dramas were printed earlier. His first published poetic work was *A Dialogue of Proverbs* (1546), a versified discussion of marriage incorporating more than twelve hundred proverbs. Heywood's reputation was made by his several collections of original versified epigrams, six hundred in all, published beginning 1550 and collected in his *Works* in 1562; these quips and anecdotes, ranging from two to scores of lines apiece, are sometimes turgid, but they often shine with the wit for which Heywood was famous. He also wrote short occasional poems, songs and ballads, and a lengthy and obscure verse allegory, *The Spider and the Fly* (1556).

Achievements

John Heywood was one of the first writers of secular English drama who portrayed not abstractions but individual persons as characters. Most early Tudor plays represented Bible stories or saints' legends, or dramatized the conflict of such allegorical characters as Wisdom and Treason. Heywood's interludes portray husbands, pardoners, scholars, and fools; while most are unnamed types, each is individualized deftly and many have more than one dimension of character. Although Heywood's three disputation plays are heavy with choplogic, his three farces retain their vigor and interest. In plotting, character-drawing, and versifying, Heywood was far more skilled, at his best, than were other Tudor playwrights. It must be said, however, that Heywood's direct influence on later dramatists seems to have been small; the flowering of Elizabethan comedy, some fifty years after his interludes were published, developed without evident influence from his plays.

Biography

The two hallmarks of John Heywood's life were his ready wit and his loyal Catholicism. Through a long life and drastic swings in religious opinion at the English court, he kept in royal favor by his wit until finally, as an old man, he was driven into exile for his faith. His birth, parentage, and early life are obscure. He was born about 1497, possibly in London; he may have been the son of a lawyer, William Heywood, sometime of Coventry. He may have spent some time at Oxford; the early historian of Oxford, Anthony Wood, claimed that Heywood had been a short time at Broadgates Hall but that "the crabbedness of logic not suiting with his airy genie, he retired to his native place, and became noted to all witty men, especially to Sir Thomas More (with whom he was very familiar)."

Heywood certainly became an intimate of the Humanist circle centered on More, and it is probably no coincidence that Heywood first appears as a salaried appointee at the court of King Henry VIII in the summer of 1519, at about the time that More resigned as under sheriff to concentrate on his duties as privy councillor. Heywood's position at court, at first, was as "singer" and "player on the virginals" (an early keyboard instrument); his skills were appreciated by King Henry, himself an accomplished musician, and were rewarded with grants of money and leases on land in addition to his quarterly stipend. The exact time when Heywood became involved with dramatic activities at court is unknown, but it seems likely that his six extant plays were written in the 1520's. He was later renowned for his varied skills as an entertainer. John Bale, for example, wrote in 1557 that Heywood "was accomplished in the arts of music and poesy in his own tongue, and ingenious without great learning; he spent much time in conducting merry dances after banquets and in presenting pageants, plays, masques, and other 'disports.'" In 1528, he received a life annuity of ten pounds and may have left the court; on January 20, 1530, he was admitted to the London company of mercers and appointed to the office of measurer of linen cloths.

Sometime during the period 1523-1529, Heywood married Eliza Rastell, daughter of the Humanist author and printer John Rastell. Eliza's mother was a sister of Sir Thomas More, and thus Heywood by his marriage cemented his relationship to the More circle at the time More was approaching his zenith at court as chancellor. In 1533, Eliza's brother, William Rastell, publisher four of Heywood's plays. These interludes and the poet's epigrams reflect at many points the Humanists' social ideas, critical temper, and harsh clerical satire. The circle was soon to be split, however, divided by the rise of Protestantism in England.

In 1532, More resigned the chancellorship, and in 1535, he was executed for his Catholicism. The Rastell family was torn by the controversy; Heywood's father-in-law converted to Protestantism, while the son, William Rastell, remained loyal to the old faith. Heywood likewise retained his Catholic sympathies, and near the end of Henry's reign the dramatist became involved in a Catholic plot against Archbishop Cranmer that nearly cost him his life. The plot was discovered and several participants were executed. Heywood himself was condemned and his property ordered forfeit, but he "escaped hanging with his mirth," according to the 1596 report of John Harington, since King Henry was "truly persuaded that a man that wrote so pleasant and harmless verses, could not have any harmful conceit against his proceedings." Heywood read a public recantation in London on July 6, 1544.

Not only were Heywood's properties restored to him after his public humbling, but also he was reinstated at court. At the request of none other than Archbishop Thomas Cranmer, he wrote an interlude, "The Parts of Man," of which only fourteen lines survive, recorded in the manuscript autobiography of Thomas Whythorne, the dramatist's secretary from 1545 to 1548. When the Catholic Queen Mary Tudor came to the throne in 1553, Heywood's prospects brightened, for he had been faithful to her through her years of eclipse after her mother's divorce from Henry VIII. In 1534, he had written her a flattering poem, and in 1538, "with his Children" he presented a play before her; later, he delivered an oration at her coronation and penned a fulsome poem about her marriage. She rewarded him with a higher annuity and more gifts of land. Soon, however, it became obvious that the Protestant Elizabeth would succeed Mary, who was in ill health, and only five days before Mary's death, Heywood resigned his annuity and Mary granted him a forty-year lease on the substantial Bolmer manor in Yorkshire. Mary apparently wanted to protect Heywood from possible loss of income under her successor.

Under the new queen, Heywood managed for some time to remain active at court. In 1559, he aided in presenting a play for Elizabeth at Nonesuch during her summer "progress" or tour. Matters became increasingly difficult for Catholics in England, however, and on July 20, 1564, Heywood and his son Ellis fled to the Low Countries. Heywood lived for some time in Malines, then was granted a place at the Jesuit college of his son Ellis at Antwerp. When in 1578 the college was overrun by a Protestant mob, he barely escaped along with the Jesuits to Louvain. It was probably there that, late in 1578, more than eighty years of age, he died. Even on his deathbed, Heywood retained his wit; when his confessor kept intoning "The flesh is frail," the master epigrammatist twitted him: "You seem to be blaming God for not making me a fish." Heywood's career spanned the Tudor age: Linked to Erasmus by wit and to More by marriage, he survived at four Tudor monarchs' courts by his gifts as poet and dramatist; his son Jasper translated three tragedies of Seneca, and his daughter was the mother of the poet John Donne.

Analysis

The six plays of John Heywood's canon fall naturally into two groups: three debate plays, rhetorical disputations on set topics, and three farces, which include considerable argumentation but also feature rudimentary plots and lively onstage action. Of the former three, the simplest is *Witty and Witless*, with only three characters. John and James debate the latter's paradoxical proposition that it is "better to be a fool, than a wise man." James triumphs by showing that the Witless and the Witty equally suffer bodily pain, that Witless suffers lesser mental pain, and that Witless, being innocent, is sure of the supreme pleasure—salvation. At this point, a third interlocutor, Jerome, intervenes; he upbraids John for yielding and proceeds to overturn all three conclusions. He ends in a terse sermon showing that good deeds affect heavenly rewards proportionally—an anti-Lutheran view which at the time would have pleased Henry VIII, who in 1521 was named Defender of the Faith for his anti-Lutheran writing. Heywood's debate is in the ironic Humanist tradition of Erasmus' *Encomium moriae* (1509; *The Praise of Folly*); it also is indebted to a French farce, *Dyalogue du fol et du sage*, but goes beyond this source, which ends with the victory of the fool, to make a pious nonironic ending.

A considerable step up from this play in rhetorical complexity is *The Play of Love*, a disputation in which two pairs of debaters consider the pains and pleasures of love. This play may have been produced about 1528-1529 for a Christmas revel before an Inns of Court audience who would have followed the legalistic arguments with interest. The four characters comprise the possible permutations of love pairings. Lover Not Loved begins by asserting that of all pains, his is the worst. Beloved Not Loving, a woman, challenges him with a claim that her pain from incessant and unwelcome wooing is worse. After fruitless argument, they go off to find an arbitrator. Meanwhile the joyful Lover Loved enters with a song and declares that "The highest pleasure man can obtain,/ Is to be a lover beloved again." He in turn is challenged by the cocky, taunting Vice named Neither Lover Nor Loved, who avers that a lover is always torn by some passion but that he, being passionless, lives in quiet. When Lover Loved goes to find an indifferent judge of their dispute, the Vice relates to the audience his own love experience, in which he and a sweet damsel deceived each other; this story provides plausible motivation (unusual for a Vice character) for his mocking attitude toward all love. Each pair of disputants chooses the other as judges, with the result that both disputes end, anticlimactically, in a tie: Lover Not Loved and Beloved Not Loving are judged to suffer equal pains, while Lover Loved and Neither Lover Nor Loved enjoy equivalent pleasures. While the arguments are tedious, the play has its moment of excitement: At one point, the Vice runs in "among the audience with a high copper tank on his head full of squibs fired crying . . . fire! fire!" His prank has a purpose: He tells Lover Loved that his mistress has been burned, and the Lover's misery amply proves the Vice's contention that lovers are anxiety-ridden.

The third of the debate plays, *The Play of the Weather*, has the largest cast among Heywood's dramas, with ten characters. Heywood makes an entertaining play from the most trifling of subjects: complaints about the weather. When the great god Jupiter resolves to hear and redress grievances about the weather, eight characters representing a cross section of social types come in turn to make their conflicting pleas; in the end, Jupiter decides the issue in the only possible way: He will continue the weather "even as it was." Heywood enlivens this unpromising material in two ways: He arranges for lively antitheses between pairs of petitioners, and he selects as Jupiter's "cryer" (and the play's chief character) a Vice named Merry Report, whose quips and mocks enliven each episode. The successive pairs of petitioners make directly opposed requests; the Gentleman, for example, wants fair weather for hunting, while the Ranger desires terrific storms to level trees for his prerogative of windfall. Some pairs are set off by simultaneous appearance; the preening, fashion-conscious Gentlewoman is disdained for her vanity by the coarse, robustious Launder. The final complainant, a masterpiece of economical characterization, is the boy, "the least that can play," who comically mistakes the jaunty Merry Report for "master God" and then petitions for frost and snow, for all of his "pleasure is in catching of birds,/ And making of snow-balls and throwing the same." The boy's artless egotism highlights the selfishness of all the petitioners.

Though the ostensible topic is commonplace, the real subject of *The Play of the Weather* is social strife among competing interests and the need for a strong ruler to keep the peace. Particularly under the threat of religious innovation, Heywood is suggesting, England needs a powerful monarch to maintain the harmony of the ancient commonwealth.

Quite different from the *débat* plays are Heywood's three farces. These represent Heywood's most distinctive dramatic contribution, yet they are mostly derivative of French originals, two in part and the third substantially. Like any farce, these three feature fast-moving verbal and physical strife, single-line plots, and an absence of theme or idea; they are designed to dissolve all tensions in laughter. All three plays sharply satirize one or more clerics, or, as Francis Kirkman put it in his 1671 playlist, Heywood "makes notable work with the then Clergy."

The simplest and probably earliest of the three, *The Pardoner and the*

Friar, is little more than an extended quarrel between two itinerant preachers. The supposed setting is a parish church, with the dramatic audience as congregation, where the two title characters have come to raise money for their respective brotherhood or almshouse. The Friar begins first; while he prays before his sermon, the Pardoner displays his papal bulls and holy relics. Like Geoffrey Chaucer's pardoner in *The Canterbury Tales* (1387-1400), this pardoner carries a collection of ludicrous relics that includes such treasures as Saint Michael's brain-pan, the arm of Saint Sunday, and "the great toe of the Holy Trinity." When the Friar begins preaching, the Pardoner refuses to yield the floor, so the two harangue in tandem, in rapid line-by-line alternation, pausing occasionally to rail at one another. Finally they fall to hair-pulling, scratching, and biting just as the parish priest, scandalized, rushes in to part them, calling on Neighbor Pratt the constable for assistance. The two charlatans, facing a night in the stocks, thrash their captors and make their escape. The basic situation of the flyting between two itinerants may derive from the short French play, *Farce nouvelle d'un pardonneur, d'un triacleur, et d'une tavernière* (a new farce of a pardoner, an apothecary, and a tavern-girl); the similarities are, however, slight and perhaps coincidental.

The Four P.P. exhibits a lively lying contest among a Pardoner, a Palmer, and a Potyecary, with a Pedler as judge. (This play may also be indebted to the French farce mentioned above.) After considerable quarreling, the Pardoner tells a coarse tall tale of a remarkable cure, topping it with an exotic story of a woman rescued from Hell. Both stories make sport of women; when the Potyecary in reaction swears he never knew "any one woman out of patience," the three others involuntarily exclaim at his monstrous lie and the Pedler immediately awards him the prize. Lest we take the satire of corrupt churchmen too much to heart, the play ends, somewhat incongruously, with the Pedler's advice that we should "judge the best" of clerics and receive them "as the church doth judge or take them." The Palmer follows, speaking for the author, with an apology and disavowal of "all that hath scaped us here by negligence." The apology seems needless; the play's satire is light and harmless enough.

Heywood's most entertaining play is a vigorous domestic farce, *Johan Johan the Husband, Tyb His Wife, and Sir Johan the Priest*; this play has by far the most complicated plot, the most developed characterization, and the liveliest dialogue in the Heywood canon. Most of the credit, however, is not Heywood's, for his play is a fairly close translation of a French original, *Farce nouvelle et fort joyeuse du pasté* (a new and merry farce of a pie). At many points the translation is phrase-for-phrase; in other sections, Heywood shows originality and often improves on the French version. The story is simple enough: A husband vows to beat his wayward wife, but she easily outfaces him, sends him to fetch her lover the Priest, and dallies with the lover, eating a meat pie while poor Johan Johan is kept busy at the fire warming wax to fix a leaky bucket. Tyb the Wife snickers to Sir Johan about her cuckolded mate, who "chafeth the wax" and "for his life, dareth not look hitherward"; she gloats over her "pretty jape" of making "her husband her ape." Poor Johan Johan complains that "the smoke putteth out my eyes two: I burn my face . . . / And yet I dare not say one word" as his wife and her paramour eat his pie and taunt him. Finally his rage spills out and he beats the two of them soundly and drives them out of the house. From this simple situation, Heywood's version develops considerable human interest; the husband's vacillation between boastful manliness and sniveling servility is the mainspring of the action. He is caught in repeated ironies: He goes at his wife's bidding to fetch her lover to dine because he hopes the Priest will quell their strife; he has to beg the apparently reluctant Sir Johan to accept his invitation; he watches, famished, while the guest eats up his share of a pie; he drives wife and lover from the house at the end, only to run after them in fear of what the pair may be up to at the Priest's house. Apart from its picture of a corrupt cleric, the play makes no statement and has no moral; it is simply good fun.

Heywood's reputation as a dramatist rests on these six plays, though he is known to have written others, along with masques at court, and he has sometimes been credited with the authorship of the two-part interlude *Gentleness and Nobility* (pb. 1535), by John Rastell. Heywood's accomplishment was that he detached the interlude from its dependency on allegorical figures and introduced flesh-and-blood people into his simple plots; in his farces, Heywood created vivid characters whose interests and passions the audience shares even while it laughs at them. His plays benefit from his wide metrical range and considerable skills as a versifier; he makes good use, too, of his extensive proverb lore and of his famous facility with the quick quip. Despite the long passages of tedious dispute in some of the plays, at its best Heywood's dramatic dialogue sparkles with vivid homely diction, lively rhythms, and clever rhymes.

Other major works

POETRY: *A Dialogue of Proverbs*, 1546, 1963 (Rudolph E. Habenicht, editor); *The Spider and the Fly*, 1556.

MISCELLANEOUS: *Works*, 1562 (epigrams and poems); *Works and Miscellaneous Short Poems*, 1956 (Burton A. Milligan, editor).

Bibliography

Bernard, J. E., Jr. *The Prosody of the Tudor Interlude.* New Haven, Conn.: Yale University Press, 1939. Reprint. New York: Archon Books, 1969. Bernard's Yale dissertation is a work of cultural archaeology and an analysis of the metrics of seventy-two interludes, the popular entertainments presented during breaks in the more pompous and serious productions of the sixteenth century. Heywood is represented in *The Pardoner and the Friar*, *The Four P.P.*, and other interludes attributed to him.

Bevington, David. *Tudor Drama and Politics: A Critical Approach to Topical Meaning.* Cambridge, Mass.: Harvard University Press, 1968. Bevington's chapter entitled "Heywood's Comic Pleading for Reconciliation" presents Heywood as a "professional entertainer" whose role as jester allowed him greater freedom of speech under Henry VIII than other humanists of Sir Thomas More's circle. Bevington analyzes *The Play of the Weather* for its analogy between the figure of Jupiter the peacemaker and Henry VIII.

Bolwell, Robert W. *The Life and Works of John Heywood.* New York: Columbia University Press, 1921. Bolwell's study is well written and informative. Bolwell provides a concise chronological table, a lengthy bibliography, and six valuable appendices, including a genealogical table, Heywood's recantation in 1545, and "A List of Pageants, Masks, and Other Revels" from 1510 until 1544.

Hillebrand, Harold Newcomb. "On the Authorship of the Interludes Attributed to John Heywood." *Modern Philology: A Journal Devoted to Research in Medieval and Modern Literature* 13 (September, 1915): 267-280. Hillebrand discusses five interludes: *The Play of Love, The Play of the Weather, The Pardoner and the Friar, The Four P.P.*, and *Johan Johan the Husband, Tyb His Wife, and Sir Johan the Priest.* He ignores *Witty and Witless* and judges *The Play of Love* and *The Play of the Weather* "dull and undramatic." He believes that Heywood wrote *The Four P.P.* and *The Pardoner and the Friar* but is unsure about *Johan Johan the Husband, Tyb His Wife, and Sir Johan the Priest.*

Johnson, Robert Carl. *John Heywood.* New York: Twayne, 1970. A fine introduction written for the Twayne series. Johnson characterizes Heywood the dramatist as "a man of his age who consciously looked backward and to his contemporaries, both in England and on the Continent." He is only a secondary figure in literature who founded no school, but he was an admired entertainer who told much about his age.

Reed, A. W. *Early Tudor Drama: Medwall, the Rastells, Heywood, and the More Circle.* London: Methuen, 1926. Reed's overview is comprehensive and well written. His chapter on the Heywoods presents John in the context of his family circle, including his father-in-law, John Rastell. Reed is diligent in consulting documents from Heywood's day to fill in details about the lives of his subjects. A good reference.

Young, Karl. "The Influence of French Farce upon the Plays of John Heywood." *Modern Philology: A Journal Devoted to Research in Medieval and Modern Literature* 2 (June, 1904): 97-124. Young treats three plays—*A Dialogue on Wit and Folly, The Pardoner and the Friar*, and

Johan Johan the Husband, Tyb His Wife, and Sir Johan the Priest—and argues that the French farce influenced them more than the morality play did. Thus Heywood created a completely new English genre, "in model and inspiration wholly foreign."

William M. Baillie
(Updated by *Frank Day*)

THOMAS HEYWOOD

Born: Lincolnshire, England; c. 1573
Died: London, England; August, 1641

Principal drama

The Four Prentices of London, pr. c. 1594, pb. 1615; *Edward IV, Parts I and II*, pr. 1599, pb. 1600; *The Royal King and the Loyal Subject*, pr. c. 1602, pb. 1637; *A Woman Killed with Kindness*, pr. 1603, pb. 1607; *The Wise Woman of Hogsdon*, pr. c. 1604, pb. 1638; *If You Know Not Me, You Know Nobody: Or, The Troubles of Queen Elizabeth, Part I*, pr., pb. 1605, *Part II*, pr. 1605, pb. 1606; *Fortune by Land and Sea*, pr. c. 1607, pb. 1655; *The Rape of Lucrece*, pb. 1608, pr. before 1611; *The Fair Maid of the West: Or, A Girl Worth Gold, Part I*, pr. before 1610, pb. 1631, *Part II*, pr. c. 1630, pb. 1631; *The Golden Age: Or, The Lives of Jupiter and Saturn*, pr. before 1611, pb. 1611; *The Silver Age*, pr. 1612, pb. 1613; *The Brazen Age*, pr., pb. 1613; *The Iron Age, Parts I and II*, pr. c. 1613, pb. 1632; *The Captives: Or, The Lost Recovered*, pr. 1624, pb. 1885; *A Maidenhead Well Lost*, pr. c. 1625-1634, pb. 1634; *The English Traveler*, pr. c. 1627, pb. 1633; *London's Jus Honorarium*, pr., pb. 1631 (masque); *Londini Artium et Scientiarum Scaturigo*, pr., pb. 1632 (masque); *Londini Emporia: Or, London's Mercatura*, pr., pb. 1633 (masque); *The Late Lancashire Witches*, pr., pb. 1634 (with Richard Brome); *A Challenge for Beauty*, pr. c. 1634, pb. 1636; *Love's Mistress*, pr. 1634, pb. 1636; *Londini Sinus Salutis: Or, London's Harbour of Health and Happiness*, pr., pb. 1635 (masque); *Londini Speculum: Or, London's Mirror*, pr., pb. 1637 (masque); *Porta Pietatis*, pr., pb. 1638 (masque); *Londini Status Pacatus: Or, London's Peaceable Estate*, pr., pb. 1639 (masque); *The Dramatic Works of Thomas Heywood*, pb. 1964.

Other literary forms

Thomas Heywood was as prolific in other forms of writing as he was in the drama. Very little of his other work, however, has any particular literary merit. The long poem *Troia Britannica* (1609) was based on material that Heywood had earlier put into dramatic form, but the poetry is generally considered to be poor, Heywood having never shown a particular flair for verse. *An Apology for Actors* (1612), on the other hand, is an excellent critical work that defends the Jacobean stage on didactic grounds. Because Heywood so often used women as the protagonists of his plays, his *Gunaikeion: Or, Nine Books of Various History Concerning Women, Inscribed by the Nine Muses* (1624) is of interest to the modern reader because it suggests even further the degree to which Heywood was interested in the nature of women and their sufferings. None of these works, however, can lay claim to the merit of Heywood's best plays, and they have received little critical attention.

Achievements

In 1633, Heywood claimed to have written either all or most of some 220 plays, in addition to his volumes of poetry and prose. Yet only *A Woman Killed with Kindness* is well-known or anthologized with any regularity. To measure Heywood's significance in such terms would be to ignore the impact he had on the theater of his day and particularly on the development of the theater since the Restoration, both in England and in Europe. Heywood was the first English playwright to demonstrate consistently the potential of the sentimental drama, particularly the domestic tragedy, to produce effective theater. Restoration writers such as Nicholas Rowe and Thomas Otway followed in their "she-tragedies" Heywood's use of the female protagonist, and George Lillo in *The London Merchant: Or, The History of George Barnwell* (pr. 1731) employed the middle-class ethic of *A Woman Killed with Kindness* and *The English Traveler* to effect a similar pathos. Gotthold Ephraim Lessing, Friedrich Schiller, and Denis Diderot also saw the potential of the sentimental drama as Heywood had used it, although they were more directly influenced by the Restoration dramatists. In Heywood, one can find the beginning of a type of drama that has had a profound impact on Western dramatic literature. Although he did not have the dramatic and artistic talents of those who developed his forms, his plays solidly established the notion that pathos built on a foundation of basically bourgeois morality has both popular appeal and literary merit.

Biography

The facts of Thomas Heywood's early life are scarce. Heywood was apparently born sometime in 1573 to the Reverend Robert Heywood and his wife, Elizabeth. Probably a Cambridge graduate, Robert Heywood migrated prior to Thomas' birth from Cheshire to Lincolnshire, where he served as rector first at Rothwell and then at Ashby-cum-Fenley. Thomas was one of eleven children; there is, however, no record of any dealings between him and his siblings after he arrived in London.

The Heywoods were, it would seem, a family of gentility, evidenced by the application of Heywood's Uncle Edmund for a grant of arms. At sixteen or seventeen, Heywood entered Emmanuel College, Cambridge, a stronghold of Puritanism, which may explain the moral thrust in much of his writing, particularly in the pamphlets of his later career. His college work ended early, however, when his father died in 1593. At this point, Heywood, like so many young men with talent and a bit of learning but no degree, accepted the challenges of the London stage and began his career as an actor.

romance, also demonstrates this sense of immediacy; the audience would have found themselves quite at home during the tavern scenes or laughing with recognition at the clown Clem, who, with typical English decorum, takes himself a bit too seriously for his own good. The central plots of *A Woman Killed with Kindness* and *The English Traveler*, however, best demonstrate this point. Such accounts of infidelity and lovers' intrigues were common in the popular literature of the day, materials that certainly would have been familiar to Heywood's audience. They are, moreover, stories of characters from the middle class.

It is in fact the characters more than the plots in Heywood's plays that do the most to break down barriers between the playwright and his audience. In *A Woman Killed with Kindness*, Frankford, though a member of the landed gentry, is not a member of the nobility; his grief is not that brought on by the peculiar circumstances of lofty birth but, rather, the kind of sorrow that anyone in the audience might experience. Anne's sin, moreover, is not one she commits because of some gruesome sense of fate. Hers is the weakness of human nature—again, a weakness shared with the audience. Bess, the heroine of *The Fair Maid of the West*, despite her excessive virtues, would have greatly pleased the audience, as she was a tavern mistress, a member of their own plebeian class. These few examples well illustrate the generalization that the characters of Heywood's plays, at least the better works, held up a mirror to early seventeenth century life.

To depict the experiences of such middle-class characters confronting what were generally the conflicts of the middle class, Heywood used what could well be regarded as pedestrian language. Poetry was the appropriate language for Shakespeare's noble characters, just as Heywood's prose and simple diction are completely in line with the thematic structure of his plays. His characters are lower in stature than are Shakespeare's; his themes are domestic. For his characters to speak in lofty tones would be out of place, and Heywood was enough of a dramatist to realize that his characters should use language and express sentiments appropriate to their station in life and the conflicts they faced.

Clark has labeled *The Fair Maid of the West* the "quintessence of popular literature," referring primarily to its excellent fusion of romantic elements with those of the domestic comedy. Heywood's success in combining these seemingly disparate elements also makes this his best comedy, containing characters from the domestic mode and plot from the romantic. Both work well to illustrate a theme basic to the Heywood canon: that fidelity, chastity, and married love are virtues that ennoble men and women of the middle class.

Bess Bridges, the heroine of *The Fair Maid of the West*, is reputed to be unmatched in virtue as well as in beauty, making the tavern where she works a popular gathering place for a lively crowd of suitors, including the gallant Spencer, who in her defense kills the overbearing Carroll and is forced to flee to Fayal to avoid being arrested. There he is wounded and, thinking that he will die, sends Goodlack to entrust his entire estate to Bess if she has remained faithful to him. She has, and after hearing that her love is dead, she sets out to Fayal to see his grave. While on the sea, she purges it of Spanish pirates until she is reunited with and married to Spencer at the court of Mullisheg.

This summary illustrates the romantic aspects of the play. It includes voyages on the high seas, suggestive of the many chronicles of travel that were popular at the time. Bess takes on heroic if improbable stature as she captures ships that have been terrorizing the English merchant fleet; thus, the play rings with patriotism such as would have been applauded by an audience who had within recent memory seen the defeat of the Spanish Armada. The settings shift from the tavern at Fay, in the domestic comedy tradition, to the court of Mullisheg, in the realm of romance. Yet throughout, the basic theme of the play is that the fundamental chastity of simple characters such as Bess and the faithfulness to love characteristic of Spencer are ennobling—that it is virtue, not birth, which confers true nobility.

In one sense, all of Heywood's plays, including the comedies, are concerned with the nobility of virtue, particularly the virtue of fidelity. In Heywood's terms, this virtue alone could ennoble even the most lowly characters on the social scale. *The Fair Maid of the West* treats this theme in various ways. First, there is the chastity that distinguishes Bess from the beginning. There is, moreover, the faithful love that she and Spencer share and that finally overcomes all the problems they face. There is, as well, the conversion of the two schemers Roughman and Goodlack, effected by Bess's virtue. Under her influence, these two become her true friends and loyal companions in her search for Spencer. Mullisheg, the pagan, serves as the final yardstick by which these characters, particularly Bess, can be measured. Despite his non-Christian frame of reference, he is so overcome with Bess's morality and her nobility of spirit that he ensures her marriage to Spencer and, despite his own loss, rewards all the characters in her entourage.

In *The Fair Maid of the West*, Heywood masks his seriousness of purpose, one that dominates all of his plays, with comedy and occasionally with sheer farce. He was well aware that audiences came to the theater more for entertainment than for enlightenment, but he demonstrates that they could well appreciate homily and entertainment together if the playwright suitably fused the two.

The Wise Woman of Hogsdon is perhaps Heywood's best example of what can legitimately be called domestic comedy. Lacking the ornamentation of romance elements that spice the action of *The Fair Maid of the West*, the play points up Heywood's place as a link in the chain that connects Renaissance and Restoration comedy. His role in linking the domestic tragedy of the two periods is well-known, but too often his role in connecting the comedy of the two periods goes unacknowledged.

The action of *The Wise Woman of Hogsdon* revolves around the antics of the rake Young Chartley, who has deserted Luce from the city, has contracted to marry Luce from the country, and has left his marriage bed to pursue the lovely Gratiana, the daughter of Sir Harry. These intrigues are complicated even further when the country Luce contracts the Wise Woman, whom Young Chartley has insulted, to handle the wedding arrangements; in order to avenge herself on Young Chartley, the Wise Woman mixes wedding partners. All is finally resolved when Young Chartley, who does in fact end up married to Luce from the city, repents, and all the others are satisfied with the mates they have been left holding.

The Wise Woman of Hogsdon is an acknowledgment of the virtues of chastity, fidelity, and married love. Here Heywood's recurring theme is treated within a completely comic framework. Here, moreover, the content is purely middle-class, suggesting strongly the notion that these virtues glorify even the common folk. Two other aspects from the play demonstrate further the fact that Heywood was directing his homily chiefly at a middle-class audience. First, the Wise Woman herself is a character drawn from contemporary life; she is a fraud and a charlatan akin to the witches, alchemists, and other con artists who were constantly being exposed both in the courts and in the popular literature of the day. Her antics are precisely what Heywood's audience would have expected from her; her duping of Young Chartley and the others would have been much to their appreciation. One scene in particular demonstrates Heywood's awareness of his audience. In the combat between Sir Boniface and Sencer, disguised as Sir Timothy, in which the Latin of the farcical schoolmaster is used by Sencer as a weapon against him, Heywood is clearly painting a comic picture of the pedants, the pretenders to learning, who in their own way were seen by the middle-class audience as even more absurd than con artists such as the Wise Woman. This is low comedy perhaps, but the scene works well to illustrate the folly not only of Sir Boniface but of the pretentious Sir Harry as well.

The gulling of Sir Boniface is reminiscent of the slapstick humor that Jonson fell into in plays such as *The Alchemist* (pr. 1610), as when Face and Subtle dupe the Puritans. The overall style of the play, however, is much more in line with the works of Sir George Etherege and William Wycherley; its action is not unlike that of Etheredge's *The Man of Mode* (pr. 1676) or Wycherley's *The Country Wife* (pr. 1675). Young Chartley, too, reminds one a great deal of Horner and Dorimant, whose quests for women trap them in a web of comic intrigue. For Heywood, however, there is a stronger moral bent at the denouement, not the essentially immoral conclusion typical of Wycherley or the amorality typical of Etherege. Young Chartley is penitent, and all the lovers are satisfied that they have ended up with the partners they should have. No character is totally humiliated. Even the con artists of the play have used their talents to ensure a proper resolution to the basic conflict. Thus, whatever this play may have in common with Restoration comedy, its morality sharply distinguishes it from the masterpieces of that licentious period.

A Woman Killed with Kindness is generally regarded as Heywood's masterpiece, and it has ensured him of a lasting place in the history of English literature. It is a sentimental or domestic tragedy constructed, like his other works, to appeal to a popular audience. The play has, moreover, a subplot which causes many of the same distractions caused by the secondary action in works such as *The English Traveler*. There is, however, one significant difference between this play and Heywood's lesser-known works. In *A Woman Killed with Kindness*, the poet in Heywood shines; his language, although appropriate to his domestic framework and therefore still somewhat pedestrian, is used so well to express meaning consistent with the theme and the characters of the work that there is a harmony between language and sentiment which is characteristic only of great literature.

The central plot of *A Woman Killed with Kindness* begins with the marriage of Frankford and Anne, a marriage viewed by their friends as the perfect union. Frankford, however, takes Wendoll into his home, only to have his friend tempt Anne to infidelity. Upon discovering her adultery, Frankford banishes Anne to a secluded cottage on their estate. Anne refuses to eat and soon lies on her deathbed. Frankford, however, comes to her and forgives her, reinstating her to her position as wife and mother.

A Woman Killed with Kindness is Heywood's best statement of his constant theme: the ennobling grace of married love and fidelity. In this work, however, the statement is enhanced by an explicitly Christian sentiment. Frankford overcomes his initial rage and his desire to kill Anne and Wendoll, determined that he will not destroy two souls that Christ died to save. In this way, the revenge tragedy motif so characteristic of Renaissance theater is shattered by Christian sentiment. His punishment of Anne, suggested by the title of the work, is also characteristic of his goodness, as is his final forgiveness of her. Such is Frankford's virtue that scholars generally refer to him as the ultimate Christian hero.

While the goodness of Frankford accounts in part for the overwhelming sentimentality of the play, the genuine repentance of Anne and Wendoll adds significantly to the final pathos. They accept the tortures of their guilt and do not at any point try to justify their actions. Anne dies—Heywood's morality would not have allowed otherwise—but there is beauty in her death, the beauty of justice matched by forgiveness.

What makes *A Woman Killed with Kindness* a superior work, recognized as such even by those critics who do not accept the possibility of domestic tragedy and do not call Heywood's work a tragedy, is the language. The play's powerful fusion of language and sentiment is particularly clear in the scene in which Frankford confronts Anne about her infidelity. With a series of short questions, pointedly delivered, he asks her what failings as a husband he had demonstrated that would make her turn from him. She denies there being any, until at last Frankford explodes with a declaration of innocence from such failings that demonstrates well the grief he feels. This whole scene is built upon the assumption that the marital vows are sacred and that Frankford's faithfulness as a husband should preclude such treachery by his wife.

Of all of Heywood's plays, *A Woman Killed with Kindness* has had the most lasting interest to scholars; more important, the play has had an enormous impact on dramatic literature. Writers interested in the possibilities of sentimental tragedy have taken it as their model; Diderot referred explicitly to the success of *A Woman Killed with Kindness* as justifying the writing of domestic tragedy. Though the bulk of his work has been forgotten, Heywood has achieved a permanent place in the history of drama.

Other major works

POETRY: *Troia Britannica*, 1609; *The Hierarchy of the Blessed Angels*, 1635.

NONFICTION: *Philocothonista: Or, The Drunkard, Open, Dissected, Anatomized*, 1635; *A Curtain Lecture*, 1636.

MISCELLANEOUS: *Oenone and Paris*, 1594; *An Apology for Actors*, 1612; *Gunaikeion: Or, Nine Books of Various History Concerning Women, Inscribed by the Nine Muses*, 1624; *England's Elizabeth, Her Life and Troubles During Her Minority from the Cradle to the Crown*, 1632; *The Exemplary Lives and Memorable Acts of Nine of the Most Worthy Women of the World: Three Jews, Three Gentiles, Three Christians*, 1640; *The Life of Merlin, Surnamed Ambrosius*, 1641.

Bibliography

Adams, Henry Hitch. *English Domestic: Or, Homiletic Tragedy, 1575 to 1642*. New York: Columbia University Press, 1943. Adams analyzes the features of middle-class tragedy by exploring its backgrounds in morality plays and sixteenth and seventeenth century murder plays. Chapters on popular theology and nondramatic literature help fill in the story. *A Woman Killed with Kindness* gets a full chapter as the best-known example of the genre.

Boas, Frederick S. *Thomas Heywood.* London: Williams & Norgate, 1950. Boas emphasizes the lesser-known works, including the early plays *Edward IV* and *The Four Prentices of London*, and places Heywood among a group of playwrights who (like William Shakespeare and the young Ben Jonson) were also actors. Boas admits that Heywood wrote far too much but judges him a master of lucid speech and perhaps the most typical of Elizabethan writers.

Clark, Arthur Melville. *Thomas Heywood: Playwright and Miscellanist.* New York: Columbia University Press, 1958. Reprint. New York: Russell & Russell, 1967. The fullest record of Heywood's life and work available. The first two hundred pages fill in the career, one chapter studies Heywood the dramatist, and eight appendices scrutinize questions of style and authorship. No separate bibliography but much to be gleaned from the notes.

Eliot, T. S. "Thomas Heywood." In *Essays on Elizabethan Drama.* New York: Harcourt, Brace & World, 1934. Reprint. New York: Harcourt, Brace & World, 1960. Eliot finds "no reality of moral synthesis" in Heywood's plays and no vision informing the verse. Heywood's verse is not highly poetic but can be highly dramatic, and he has "very little sense of humour." *The English Traveler*, which contains Heywood's best plot, and *The Wise Woman of Hogsdon* rank just below *A Woman Killed with Kindness.* Heywood writes dramas of common life, not tragedies.

Velte, Mowbray. *The Bourgeois Elements in the Dramas of Thomas Heywood.* New York: Haskell House, 1966. Velte sketches Heywood's life, giving a concise list of extant plays and their dates, and his other lists are convenient: "Lost Plays Ascribed to Heywood," "Heywood's City Pageants," "Semi-Dramatic Works," "Poetic Works," and "Prose Works." Velte divides the works into chronicles, classical dramatizations, romances, and dramas of contemporary life. Good bibliography.

Wentworth, Michael. "Thomas Heywood's *A Woman Killed with Kindness* as Domestic Morality." In *Traditions and Innovations: Essays on British Literature of the Middle Ages and the Renaissance*, edited by David G. Allen and Robert A. White. Newark: University of Delaware Press, 1990. Wentworth shows how *A Woman Killed with Kindness* can be "described as a repentance play or a domestic morality" descended from medieval morality plays such as *Everyman.* (Wentworth also wrote *Thomas Wentworth: A Reference Guide*, 1986.)

Gerald W. Morton
(Updated by *Frank Day*)

ISRAEL HOROVITZ

Born: Wakefield, Massachusetts; March 31, 1939

Principal drama

The Comeback, pr. 1958; *Line*, pr. 1967, pb. 1968 (one act); *It's Called the Sugar Plum*, pr. 1967, pb. 1968 (one act); *The Indian Wants the Bronx*, pr., pb. 1968 (one act); *Rats*, pr., pb. 1968 (one act); *Acrobats*, pr. 1968, pb. 1971; *Morning*, pr. 1968 (as *Chiaroscuro*), pb. 1969 (one act); *The Honest-to-God Schnozzola*, pr. 1968, pb. 1971; *Leader*, pr. 1969, pb. 1970; *Clair-Obscur*, pr. 1970, pb. 1972; *Dr. Hero*, pr. 1971 (as *Hero*), pr. 1972 (revision of *Dr. Hero*), pb. 1973; *Shooting Gallery*, pr. 1971, pb. 1973; *Alfred the Great*, pr. 1972, pb. 1974; *Our Father's Failing*, pr. 1973, pb. 1979; *Spared*, pr. 1974, pb. 1975 (one act); *Hopscotch*, pr. 1974, pb. 1977; *Uncle Snake: An Independence Day Pageant*, pr. 1975, pb. 1976; *The Primary English Class*, pr. 1975, pb. 1976; *Stage Directions*, pr. 1976, pb. 1977; *The Reason We Eat*, pr. 1976; *Alfred Dies*, pr. 1976, pb. 1979; *The Former One-on-One Basketball Champion*, pr. 1977, pb. 1982; *The 75th*, pr., pb. 1977; *Man with Bags*, pr., pb. 1977 (adaptation of a translation of Eugène Ionesco's play); *Mackerel*, pr. 1978, pb. 1979; *A Christmas Carol: Scrooge and Marley*, pr. 1978, pb. 1979 (adaptation of Charles Dickens' story); *The Widow's Blind Date*, pr. 1978, pb. 1982; *The Wakefield Plays*, pb. 1979 (includes the Alfred Trilogy—*Alfred the Great, Our Father's Failing, Alfred Dies*—and the Quannapowitt Quartet—*Hopscotch, The 75th, Stage Directions, Spared*); *Park Your Car in the Harvard Yard*, pr. 1980; *Sunday Runners in the Rain*, pr. 1980; *The Good Parts*, pr. 1982, pb. 1983; *The Great Labor Day Classic and The Former One-on-One Basketball Champion*, pb. 1982; *A Rosen by Any Other Name*, pr. 1986, pb. 1987 (based on the book *A Good Place to Come From* by Morley Torgov); *Today, I Am a Fountain Pen*, pr. 1986, pb. 1987 (based on *A Good Place to Come From*); *North Shore Fish*, pr. 1986, pb. 1989; *The Chopin Playoffs*, pb. 1987 (based on *A Good Place to Come From*); *Semper Fi*, pr. 1987; *Year of the Duck*, pr. 1987, pb. 1988; *Faith, Hope, and Charity*, pr., pb. 1989 (with Terrence McNally and Leonard Melfi); *Henry Lumper*, pr. 1989, pb. 1990; *Strong-Man's Weak Child*, pr. 1990.

Other literary forms

The relish with which Israel Horovitz approaches language has found its way into two novels, *Cappella* (1973) and *Nobody Loves Me* (1975), and a book of poetry, *Spider Poems and Other Writings* (1973). None of these works, however, has approached the effectiveness of his drama. *Cappella* does show a dramatist's flair for vivid monologue, but the Beckett-like stream of consciousness that pervades much of the novel is rather irritating and often impenetrable. Not surprisingly, it is Horovitz's work in film that comes closest to the level of his stage works. His first produced film script, *The Strawberry Statement* (1970), based on the book by James Simon Kunen, conveyed the atmosphere of the Columbia University student riots in the late 1960's with shrewd social and psychological observations. His next major screenplay was the frankly autobiographical *Author! Author!* (1982), one of his most humane and least ironic works. It depicts the problems of a playwright whose second wife leaves him for another man and who must then deal with five children as well as the preparation for his first Broadway play, entitled *The Reason We Eat* (one of Horovitz's own, lesser-known plays). Ivan Travalian's life and work mirror Horovitz's quite closely, but Horovitz can view his own experience with much humor, giving some satiric insights into theater production. The screenplay is filled as well with a great deal of warmth and love between Ivan and the five children (four of whom are not even biologically his). Horovitz has also written a number of plays for television, sometimes with a social message (*VD Blues*, concerning venereal disease, in 1972; *Play for Trees*, on the importance of saving trees, in 1969). His television adaptation of Herman Melville's *Bartleby the Scrivener* (1977) effectively captured the gloom and poignancy of the original. In 1978, Horovitz wrote a cycle of plays for television called *Growing Up Jewish in Sault Ste. Marie*, adaptations of Morley Torgov's novel *A Nice Place to Come From*. Finally, Horovitz has contributed to a number of periodicals, most notably as a lively, refreshing, and personal art critic for *Crafts Horizons* from 1968 to 1970.

Achievements

Horovitz early staked out his claim to a share in the Beckett-Ionesco tradition of modern absurdity. He dramatizes the alienation of characters trapped in their own realities, often at cross-purposes, unable to communicate. Horovitz examines the violent roots of much human interaction; in his plays, submerged fears and hostilities rise to the surface and take concrete shape in often senseless acts of aggression.

Horovitz is a master of modern metropolitan malaise, yet he has also exposed the decay at work in small-town New England, setting most of his later plays either in Wakefield or Gloucester, Massachusetts. A native of Wakefield, Horovitz has returned to it in a series of plays, linked by related characters, similar themes and moods, and even repeated lines. Through these Wakefield plays, he portrays the constriction, pettiness, and desperation of life in a small town, where people are trapped for generations and where those who have escaped return only to be caught up in the same power struggles.

Horovitz's stark view of contemporary human relationships assures him a significant position in the history of Off-Broadway, a theater tradition given to intense engagement of the audience in ways diverging from the more familiar and comfortable realistic tradition of Broadway (and London's West End). Although, as a consequence, most of his plays have gone unreviewed by the national press, his work has been translated into more than twenty languages, and theaters across the United States and around the world are continually performing his plays. His keen vision earned for him Obie Awards for both *The Indian Wants the Bronx* and *The Honest-to-God Schnozzola*, both of which have also been otherwise honored, while awards have also gone to *Line*, *Rats*, and *It's Called the Sugar Plum*. As one of the creators of sketches for the television special *VD Blues*, he received an Emmy Award, and his script for *The Strawberry Statement* won for him the Cannes Film Festival Prix du Jury.

In his prolific career, Horovitz has received many awards, including an American Academy Award, a Rockefeller Fellowship, the Vernon Rice Award, a Drama Desk Award, a National Endowment for the Arts Fellowship, and a Fulbright Fellowship. In 1980, he founded and became the producer and artistic director of the Gloucester Stage Company in his hometown of Gloucester, Massachusetts. He often directs his own plays at his own and other theaters; *Strong-Man's Weak Child* was produced in Los Angeles under his direction in 1991.

Biography

Israel Horovitz was born in Wakefield, Massachusetts, a town of more than twenty thousand people not far from Boston. Its impact upon him is clear in much of his later work—notably *The Wakefield Plays* and *The Widow's Blind Date*, with their evocation of a stifling small-town atmosphere. Although one source, *Contemporary Authors* (1978), says that his father, Julius Charles Horovitz, was a lawyer, a 1982 interview in *New York* indicates that his father was a truck driver. Bright but lower-middle-class, Horovitz did not attend college. When asked in 1972 to teach playwriting at City College of New York, he listed on his employment form, "Harvard, B.A." for his college education. When this falsification was discovered, Horovitz lost the job. Comparison of various biographical sketches in his published works and other sources reveals a number of discrepancies.

Horovitz's first play, *The Comeback*, was written when Horovitz was seventeen and was produced in Boston in 1958, when he was nineteen. He continued to write and to have plays produced throughout the early 1960's. During this period, he was a fellow in playwriting at the Royal Academy of Dramatic Art and was honored as the first American to be selected as playwright-in-residence with the Royal Shakespeare Company's Aldwych Theatre, in 1965. It was not until *Line*, in 1967, however, that his work was produced in New York, by Ellen Stewart's Café La Mama, an important force in the theater scene of the 1960's. For the next two or three years, Horovitz's work was much produced and much discussed, but a hiatus came in his New York work in the early 1970's, and thereafter his work enjoyed only rare major productions there; instead, he offered world premieres of his work to major regional theaters in Chicago, Los Angeles, and other cities, especially those in New England.

Although Horovitz early supported himself by working in an advertising agency (an experience he was able to use in *Dr. Hero*), he soon began making a satisfactory income from his writing, not only because of his early plays' striking successes but also because of his prolific output. He has written more than thirty-five plays, many of them unpublished.

Horovitz is very much a man of the theater. During the early and mid-1960's, he stage-managed in and around New York; he has directed a number of his plays; he has even acted in several of them, sometimes replacing an actor at the last moment. He is active in groups that develop new plays and playwrights, and he has taught playwriting at New York University as well as at other locations.

Horovitz's family life was revealed to audiences across the country in the 1982 film *Author! Author!*, and while certain details were changed, the spirit of the script is accurate. The film's title character has been once divorced and has custody of a son from that marriage; as the film begins, he is in the middle of a separation from his second wife, who has brought into their marriage four children from three previous marriages. Horovitz, on the other hand, was first married in 1959—to Elaine Abber—and divorced in 1960; he was married to Doris Keefe in 1960 and had three children with her, divorcing in 1972; he then married Gillian Adams, an Englishwoman sharing his love of running. Adams is a former British National Marathon champion; they have twin sons born in 1986.

Analysis

In *Waiting for Godot* (pb. 1952), Samuel Beckett created an indelible image of modern humanity: two bums cut off from any reality other than their immediate present and each other. The image of two men bound together in a mutually dependent but uncomfortable relationship was central also in Beckett's next play, *Endgame* (pr. 1957). The tradition continues in the work of Israel Horovitz. In his plays, the most characteristic relationship is not that of man and woman, as in Tennessee Williams and Edward Albee, nor that of parent and child, as in Eugene O'Neill and Arthur Miller. Rather, it is the relationship of two men, generally equals in age, intelligence, and social class but bound by mutual insecurity, the unrelenting need each has for reinforcement of his masculinity and his own sense of identity. Though considered friends, the two men share a deep undercurrent of hostility based on an insecurity related to both work and sex.

Such relationships in Horovitz's work, however, are not homosexual in any sense. In fact, in contrast to Lanford Wilson—who, in a 1984 issue of *The Advocate*, said, "Since ten percent of the population is gay, then every tenth character is going to be also"—Horovitz portrays virtually no homosexuality in his work beyond the transvestite in *The Honest-to-God Schnozzola*, with whom two American executives engage in sex under the impression that the transvestite is really a woman. The disgust and shame that they feel, like the feeling of Murph in *The Indian Wants the Bronx* when he makes his friend Joey take back a joking suggestion that Murph likes men, are evidence of a fear of homosexuality underlying this kind of relationship.

Because of this fear, the men in Horovitz's plays find any expression of affection difficult. A moment of tenderness may occur—even in that most tension-fraught of Horovitz's plays, *The Indian Wants the Bronx*—but it is only a moment, and the "true" masculine stance, hard and aggressive, is bound to return with greater force. When Joey is left by himself at the bus stop with the non-English-speaking man from India, he begins to make friends, instead of merely taunting him, as he and Murph had been doing before. He begins confiding in the Indian, though the Indian can understand only the emotions Joey's face and voice reveal. Joey's anxiety leads the Indian to comfort him with a hug, which Joey accepts as fatherly affection. Yet Joey's propensity for violence, along with the language barrier, betrays this moment: He takes out his knife to show as a cherished possession, but the Indian interprets this act as a threat, and when the Indian begins to move surreptitiously away, Joey believes that he is going to Murph to reveal what Joey had told him in confidence. Thus, the Indian's attempted escape provokes Joey to hit him and triggers the increasing hostility that culminates in Murph's wounding the Indian's hand.

The play, Horovitz's best known and certainly one of his most powerful, is filled with ironies. Like most of Horovitz's work, it explores failed connections: Joey and Murph are friends, yet their friendship is marred by taunts and insults, signs of a constant quest to make the other seem inferior; the Indian is trying to reach his son, and here are two men in their early twenties whom he could reach (one of whom he does reach, for a moment), yet they finally offer him only hostility and bloodshed. The mutual misinterpretation from which Joey and the Indian suffer results in the exact opposite of what each of them actually wants. Most important, the knife that instigates the misunderstanding and resulting violence is actually being shown by Joey in mockery—it and another like it were given to Joey and Murph as Christmas presents by a girlfriend, even though Murph had been arrested for stabbing someone. Joey is not a truly violent person—much less so than Murph is—but his need to prove himself the equal of

Murph, to assert his manhood, outweighs his decent instincts. Murph, too, is acting out imagined male behavior rather than his real emotional responses. Both young men, living basically aimless lives with no real hope for escape, are essentially dispossessed and seek a bogus manhood in tough behavior and aggressive action.

Compassion, in this postmodern world, simply does not pay. Jebbie, one of the title figures in the one-act *Rats*, has been enjoying a blissful coexistence with a human baby, whom he protects rather than attacks, when his territory is invaded by a younger rat, Bobby. Bobby has idolized Jebbie, and he feels betrayed when he sees that the older rat, a hero to numerous rats before him, is keeping company with the enemy. When Bobby tries to get a piece of the action (a piece of baby's flesh), Jebbie stops him—in fact strangling him in order to do so. All should therefore be well—but the baby becomes upset and yells to its parents that there are rats, thus ensuring Jebbie's death. Jebbie's compassion for the human infant is largely a matter of self-protection, a kind of middle-aged complacence and gratitude for being free from worry, struggle, and "the rat race." This desire for peace and comfort, like Joey's deprecation of violence and desire for sympathetic human contact, results ironically in a return to violence and, in Jebbie's case, to his own defeat. An ironic god is looking down and laughing at the intentions that never quite work out, and Horovitz is right there with him, finding as a touchstone these words of Beckett, which he has quoted in his film script *Author! Author!*: "The highest laugh is the laugh which laughs at that which is unhappy."

There is certainly plenty of unhappiness in Horovitz's plays—especially the insecurity reflected in constant one-upmanship, whether involving rats, street punks, the working class (in *The Widow's Blind Date*), the professional class (*The Good Parts*), old men in a rest home (*Our Father's Failing*), or the corporate world (*The Honest-to-God Schnozzola, Dr. Hero*). Some of Horovitz's funniest dialogue comes from the banter between male friends as each tries to come out on top by putting the other down. Sam and Pa, two centenarians sharing their declining years in a home for the aged (or the insane) in *Our Father's Failing*, provide the most memorable scenes in Horovitz's Alfred Trilogy, part of his longer series entitled *The Wakefield Plays*. Constantly mocking each other, cutting in on each other's jokes (far too familiar to them), and mishearing or misinterpreting each other, they provide a hilarious image of old age and the undying competition between two men whose lives have overlapped for decades. Their competition is not without its sardonic side, for it is based on secret upon secret, what they are keeping from others as well as what one is keeping from the other. The long-concealed violence is bound to erupt at last, and it does, with serious repercussions. Such grim consequences—the dissolution of a lifelong friendship, disillusionment regarding other people, and the destruction of several lives—seem inevitable when competition, rather than cooperation, is the prime motivator.

Competition does produce interesting drama, and at his best, Horovitz exploits this potential to the full, dramatizing conflict through superbly observed dialogue that is often inarticulate, ungrammatical, and fragmentary, but also sharp and believable. Characters interrupt one another, stumble and hesitate, repeat themselves, very rarely engaging in typical stage rhetoric. Horovitz has clearly listened to people and their often inconsequential talk and has re-created such talk for his very ordinary characters. Through their talk, their numerous conflicts emerge.

Since much of his work deals with men's relationships to one another, and heterosexual men specifically, a major instigator of conflict and competition is the opposite sex: Friends become rivals for a woman's attentions. *The Good Parts*, for example, presents this rivalry comically, while *The Widow's Blind Date* treats the same theme with great seriousness. Here the motivating sexual rivalry is complex, rooted in the past, about twelve years before the time of the play, when George and Archie, the principal male characters, and several high school friends gang-raped Margie, now a widow, who, as the play begins, has returned to Wakefield, Massachusetts, from a sophisticated intellectual life in New York.

Margie, who has tried to forget the whole rape experience, has returned to be with her dying brother, a friend of George and Archie, and she asks Archie over for dinner, though they have not seen each other for years. George resents the attention that Archie receives from her, and Archie, recalling the distant past, resents the terrible experience of his first (and only) sexual intercourse with the girl whom he had secretly loved, when he went second in the gang-rape after George had coolly taken Margie's virginity. That the past endures is made explicit when Archie kills George by pushing him against a sharp object which, years before, had almost killed another man with whom Archie had fought. Before Margie leaves, she tells Archie that her revenge is still not finished. In return for her gang-rape, she has destroyed not only a friendship but two men's lives.

It is generally difficult in a Horovitz play to label one character the villain, since most of his characters have unappealing traits and are often to be viewed as victims, but in *The Widow's Blind Date*, it is difficult at the end to see Margie as anything but a villain. The increasing tension and violence in the two acts of the play suddenly appear as part of a revenge plot, and it is this widow—like a black widow spider—who is responsible for one man's death and the other's inevitable arrest.

Such characterizations of women are frequent in Horovitz's work. His women exist solely in relation to men; they are often motivated by a desire to get back at a man (or several men) for some sexual injustice in the past. In turn, the men in Horovitz's plays are often motivated by resentment against women, though without this same need to get back at them; they are apparently content merely to feel oppressed by women.

The resentment, conflict, and hostility pervading Horovitz's work find their inevitable result in some act of violence, or several, most frequently as the conclusion to the play—George's death in *The Widow's Blind Date*, the stabbing of the Indian's hand in *The Indian Wants the Bronx*, the shootings ending two of the Alfred plays, a hideous self-brutalization in *Stage Directions*. Horovitz's purpose is to provoke a strong reaction from his audience rather than allow them to sit back and let the play wash over them.

This provocative approach, largely a result of the influence of Edward Albee's *The Zoo Story* (pr. 1959), was effective in the 1960's, when Horovitz began his career, as Albee did, Off-Broadway. A quarter-century after *The Zoo Story*, however, and nearly two decades after *The Indian Wants the Bronx*—not to mention films such as *Bonnie and Clyde* (1967), or the work of Sam Peckinpah and Francis Ford Coppola—such violence, in and of itself, is not sufficient to make a play powerful. David Rabe and Sam Shepard, in plays such as *Streamers* (pr. 1976), *In the Boom Boom Room* (pr. 1974), *Curse of the Starving Class* (pb. 1976), and *True West* (pr. 1983), can revivify the use of violence by giving it mythic or sociological resonance, but the violence in *The Wakefield Plays*, for example, is both predictable and inadequately prepared for by emotional involvement with the characters. Horovitz's work is more potent when presenting instead the psychic violence people inflict on one another.

A Rosen by Any Other Name examines the effects of such psychic violence on a Jewish Canadian family during World War II. Barney Rosen, the family's father, seeks to change the family name to Royal in order to ward off anti-Semitism. Stanley, Barney's adolescent son, is mortified by his father's efforts and by his own approaching Bar Mitzvah, but he nevertheless finds a way to outwit his father and keep his own name. *North Shore Fish*, a social realist look at the day-to-day operations of a fish-packing plant, depicts a foreman who uses the power of his position to extort sexual favors from his female employees.

Horovitz is too much a realist—Absurdist though he may be—to show his audiences a world where destructive competition does not prevail, yet he is capable of evoking real warmth and love, most notably in his screenplay *Author! Author!*, which depicts father-child relationships in a manner both touching and credible. Thus, his sardonic vision of the world is leavened with compassion.

Other major works
NOVELS: *Cappella*, 1973; *Nobody Loves Me*, 1975.
POETRY: *Spider Poems and Other Writings*, 1973.

SCREENPLAYS: *The Strawberry Statement*, 1970 (adaptation of James Simon Kunen's book); *Alfredo*, 1970; *Believe in Me*, 1970; *Machine Gun McCain*, 1970; *Acrobats*, 1972 (adaptation of his play); *Author! Author!*, 1982.

TELEPLAYS: *Play for Trees*, 1969; *VD Blues*, 1972 (as *Play for Germs*, pb. 1973); *The Making and Breaking of Splinters Braun*, 1975; *Start to Finish*, 1975; *Bartleby the Scrivener*, 1977 (adaptation of Herman Melville's story); *Growing Up Jewish in Sault Ste. Marie*, 1978 (adaptations of Morley Torgov's novel *A Nice Place to Come From*).

Bibliography

Cohn, Ruby. *New American Dramatists: 1960-1990.* 1982. 2d ed. New York: St. Martin's Press, 1991. In this update of the 1982 edition, Cohn places Horovitz with Jack Gelber, Jean-Claude van Itallie, Megan Terry, and María Irene Fornés as "actor activated" playwrights because Horovitz was active in the Royal Academy of Dramatic Arts (RADA) and because, working closely with actors, he often wrote plays that became vehicles for the actors' rise to stardom. Cohn concentrates on the Wakefield plays and states that Horovitz is a strong dialogist but "lacks [Eugene O'Neill's] architectonics and . . . probing morality." No critical apparatus.

DiGaetani, John L. *A Search for a Postmodern Theater: Interviews with Contemporary Playwrights.* New York: Greenwood Press, 1991. Horovitz speaks affectionately of his theater, the Gloucester Stage Company. With prompting, he runs through his repertory, citing his favorite plays and summarizing the themes. *Year of the Duck*, which "got almost no notice in New York," dramatizes some of his own theater experiences in the guise of a rehearsal of Henrik Ibsen's *The Wild Duck* (pr., pb. 1884). He concludes his interview with the remark: "I'm suggesting . . . that people take the theater seriously—whether the theater takes them seriously or not."

Horovitz, Israel. "Tragedy." In *Playwrights, Lyricists, Composers on Theater*, edited by Otis L. Guernsey, Jr. New York: Dodd, Mead, 1974. This excerpt from *The Dramatists Guild Quarterly* describes stage tragedy as "grand fiction" that "can take its audience to the outer limits of human possibility." Although Horovitz's work is not discussed here, this piece, especially in the middle section on tragedy in the modern theater, is revealing of Horovitz's use of "the opposition of conflicting goods."

Miller, Daryl H. "Horovitz Pledges Stronger Allegiance." *Daily News* (Los Angeles), June 4, 1990. Fine-tuning his script of *Strong-Man's Weak Child* at the Los Angeles Theatre Center, Horovitz discusses the play's setting in Gloucester and the rest of the nine-play series used "to represent the contemporary American experience." Normally premiered in

Gloucester, these plays represent an ongoing statement of Horovitz's view of life.

Raidy, William A. "Tireless Energy." *Star-Ledger* (Newark, N.J.), December 1, 1991. Comparing the "tireless marathon runner" (Horovitz's hobby for many years was running) with the playwright's prolific career, Raidy places him in the Gloucester environment, which Horovitz says is "a metaphor for life on this earth." Good personal glimpses of the playwright, plus comments on his friendship with Samuel Beckett.

Rosenberg, Scott. "Coming of Age—with a Twist." *San Francisco Examiner*, January 14, 1992. *A Rosen by Any Other Name*, being produced at the Mountain View Center for the Performing Arts, is the springboard for this review, which examines Horovitz's moral: "If your heritage is under attack, the last thing you should do is deny it." Notes the "wry humor rather than soapbox rhetoric" of the piece.

Scott Giantvalley
(Updated by *Thomas J. Taylor*
and *Robert McClenaghan*)

BRONSON HOWARD

Born: Detroit, Michigan; October 7, 1842
Died: Avon-by-the-Sea, New Jersey; August 4, 1908

Principal drama

Saratoga: Or, Pistols for Seven, pr. 1870, pb. c. 1870 (also known as *Brighton*); *Diamonds*, pr. 1872; *Hurricanes*, wr. 1873, pr. 1878, pb. 1941; *Moorcroft: Or, The Double Wedding*, pr. 1874; *Old Love Letters*, pr. 1878, pb. 1897; *The Banker's Daughter*, pr., pb. 1878 (revised; originally as *Lillian's Last Love*, pr. 1873); *Wives*, pr. 1879 (adaptation of Molière's plays *The School for Husbands* and *The School for Wives*); *Knave and Queen*, wr. 1882(?), pb. 1941 (with Sir Charles L. Young); *Young Mrs. Winthrop*, pr. 1882, pb. c. 1899; *One of Our Girls*, pr. 1885, pb. 1897; *Baron Rudolph*, pr. 1887, pb. 1941 (with David Belasco); *The Henrietta*, pr. 1887, pb. 1901 (revised by Winchell Smith and Victor Mapes as *The New Henrietta*, pr. 1913); *Met by Chance*, pr. 1887; *Shenandoah*, pr. 1888, pb. 1897; *Aristocracy*, pr. 1892, pb. 1898; *Peter Stuyvesant*, pr. 1899 (with Brander Matthews); *The Banker's Daughter and Other Plays*, pb. 1941.

Other literary forms

Bronson Howard is remembered primarily as a dramatist. Given his place as the first American to make a profession of writing plays, his comments on playwriting and the theater in America are important for the student of American dramatic literature. In 1906, for example, he surveyed, in New York's *Sunday Magazine*, the accomplishments of American playwrights and their critics after 1890 in an essay entitled "The American Drama." He commented on the art of acting in "Our Schools for the Stage," which appeared in *Century Magazine* in 1900. In one of the most revealing contemporary articles on late nineteenth century American dramatists—"American Playwrights on the American Drama," appearing in *Harper's Weekly* on February 2, 1889—Howard described his own approach to drama. Howard was a man of very definite opinions, and his most significant explanation of his theory of the "laws of dramatic composition" was first given as a lecture before the Shakespeare Club at Harvard College in March, 1886. This speech, in which he discussed at some length the origin and development of his play *The Banker's Daughter*, was repeated for the Nineteenth Century Club in New York in December, 1889, and was printed by the American Dramatists Club in New York and published as *The Autobiography of a Play* in 1914. This volume also included "Trash on the Stage and the Lost Dramatists of America," in which Howard outlined his approach to the theater and expressed his optimism regarding the future of American drama.

Achievements

Bronson Howard's most significant achievement was his ability to earn a living by writing plays. Prior to his time, many Americans had written plays; some were better plays than Howard wrote—plays by William Dunlap, John Howard Payne, Robert Montgomery Bird, Nathaniel Bannister, Cornelius Mathews, George H. Boker, or Epes Sargent and Nathaniel Parker Willis, for example. Although professional in the sense that they made money by writing plays, these writers were unable to sustain themselves with the income from their plays alone.

There is neither an extensive nor an impressive body of dramatic theory from pre-twentieth century American dramatists. Prior to Howard's lecture "The Laws of Dramatic Composition," commentary on dramatic theory was often scattered, slight, and haphazard. Basing his observations on one of his own plays, *The Banker's Daughter*, Howard outlined certain laws of dramatic construction that are significant in the history of dramatic theory in the United States, in particular illuminating those practices that made the melodramas of late nineteenth century America among the best that have been written. For Howard, the laws of dramatic composition were derived from an understanding of the sympathies of the audience as well as from the expected actions and motives of characters; to follow these laws, he believed, the dramatist had only to use common sense—to remain in touch with human nature. An audience will accept as "satisfactory" an occurrence that is, in a sense, deserved. For example, while an audience will accept the death of a good person in a tragedy, this acceptance will not be forthcoming in an ordinary play. Here, the death must be deserved or the audience will not be satisfied. Further, if a character is evil, the audience will not be satisfied unless that character is punished.

Howard's understanding of the importance of American business during the late nineteenth century and his ability to portray this characteristic of society effectively in his plays is both evidence of his insight and an achievement which distinguishes his work. His first work to explore the world of business, and, in fact, the first in its genre, was *Young Mrs. Winthrop*, a play in which business affairs consume the time and energies of the title character's husband, whose neglect of his society-minded wife threatens their life together. *The Henrietta*, considered by some critics to be his most successful play, reflects the stressful life of Wall Street financiers.

A creator of popular social melodramas on both the American stage and the English stage, Howard also left his mark upon the future of professional American dramatists as the founder, in 1891, of the American Dramatists Club, later the Society of American Dramatists and Composers, the forerunner of the Dramatists Guild. Concerned with promoting a sense of community among dramatists, Howard used his prestige as the first president of the club to bring into existence an amendment to copyright laws which threatened severe punishment for any individual who attempted to steal the work of a playwright.

Biography

Bronson Howard was the son of Charles Howard, a merchant in Detroit, Michigan, whose grandfather, Seabury Howard, fought for the English in the French and Indian War and against them in the American Revolution. After a public school education in Detroit, Howard attended an eastern preparatory school, intending to go on to Yale University. Instead, after suffering from eye problems, he returned to Detroit, where he began his writing career with a series of humorous sketches for the *Detroit Free Press*. In 1864, the *Detroit Free Press* published his first play, *Fantine*, a dramatization of a portion of Victor Hugo's *Les Misérables*.

Howard's interest in writing plays made him aware of the need to know and to understand the commercial theater, and he moved to New York in 1865. Although he continued to write plays, his innocence of the demands of his chosen profession rendered his early efforts fit only for the fireplace. He persisted, however, until he learned the accepted theater conventions of his day, eventually evolving his own principles of dramaturgy. As he studied his craft, he attended theatrical performances, observed the society around him in New York, and made his living by writing for the New York *Tribune* and *Evening Post*.

One of the major problems facing American dramatists of this period was the dual demand placed upon them: to satisfy the immediate theater audience while also providing dialogue that could be enjoyed by a literate public. Before Howard, American literary dramatists had generally eschewed the theatrical techniques that brought people into the theaters, while the actor-playwrights gave little thought to anything but the action upon the stage. As a consequence of this split, there were few fully satisfactory American plays. Although Howard started as a journalist writing plays, he soon learned that plays were to be seen and must present interesting spectacles to the eye. At the same time, he was aware of the importance of the written word, particularly of dialogue that would reflect the interests of society.

Like all successful dramatists, Howard realized that his work would have to be judged not wholly as literature but according to the laws of the theater. Indeed, he objected to the publication of his plays and felt a slight contempt for literary people such as William Dean Howells, resenting their assumption that a true American drama might be realized only through their efforts. Late in his life, he went so far as to argue that drama should be absolutely divorced from literature, and he insisted on being called a "dramatist" rather than a "literary man."

Howard's first success in the theater came with the production in 1870 of a farce entitled *Saratoga*, which ran for 101 nights in Augustin Daly's Fifth Avenue Theatre. Two years later, Daly opened another Howard play, *Diamonds*, a comedy of manners which dealt with New York society. *Moorcroft*, also produced by Daly, was not particularly successful, but by this time *Saratoga* had been transferred to English circumstance by Frank Marshall and produced at the Court Theatre as *Brighton*, with Charles Wyndham in the leading role of Bob Sackett. *Brighton* had considerable success on London stages and gave Howard the beginning of a fine reputation which brought him much pleasure during his visits to England. His marriage to Charles Wyndham's sister helped sustain his English popularity; indeed, five of Howard's plays eventually found responsive English audiences, and he was recognized during his lifetime as the first American playwright with a substantial reputation in Great Britain.

Howard's best-remembered play, *The Banker's Daughter*, first produced in 1873 as *Lillian's Last Love*, gained prestige after Howard's 1886 account of its development in his lecture *The Autobiography of a Play*. It was still being produced in 1914. A dozen years after he first came to New York, Howard was an established playwright. *Young Mrs. Winthrop* appeared in 1882; *One of Our Girls*, which stressed the international contrast in social life that was being exploited by Howells and Henry James, opened in 1885 and ran for two hundred nights. In *The Henrietta*, Howard satirized life on the stock exchange, and in *Shenandoah* he provided an exciting sentimental melodrama about love during the Civil War.

Howard wrote fewer plays in his later years. He lessened his stature in the eyes of historians of the drama by writing for the Theatrical Syndicate, an association of businessmen, formed in 1896, which for years controlled most New York theaters and many theaters in other large towns and which gradually exerted a stranglehold over entertainment in the United States. With audiences, however, he remained popular; indeed, Howard was one of the first American playwrights to make a fortune in his profession. A kind and honorable man, wholly without pretense, he enjoyed a long and productive career as a dramatist. When he died on August 4, 1908, at his home in Avon-by-the-Sea, New Jersey, he was widely acknowledged as the dean of American dramatists.

Analysis

Bronson Howard's career as a dramatist developed during that period in American drama when playwrights were turning from dramatizing farcical representations of a stereotyped society, portrayed only in the most obvious ways, to a social comedy in which manners might be clearly distinguished. Prior to this period, the American theater was dominated by spectacles and amusements created either by the person of a star actor or actress or by the ingenuity of a theater manager and his stage carpenter. The Civil War cast a shadow over the American theater, but amid the struggle of social reconstruction the dramatic arts bounced back with astonishing vigor, strengthened by the nationalism of Andrew Jackson's years, stimulated by the social and intellectual revolutions sparked by Karl Marx and Charles Darwin, and tempered by the sorrows of war. By the time Howard stopped writing, the United States had changed, both forcibly and by choice. American society, challenged by the strains upon it, developed its own unique and distinctive character, and the United States was recognized as a nation among nations.

To match these changes, American dramatists needed to create a drama that could both amuse and stimulate the emotions and thoughts of the human mind. Bronson Howard was a major factor in the development of this American drama—as it grew from amusement to art.

Although Howard collaborated on at least three plays—*Baron Rudolph* with David Belasco, *Knave and Queen* with Sir Charles L. Young, and *Peter Stuyvesant* with Brander Matthews—and adapted Molière's *The School for Husbands* (pr. 1661) and *The School for Wives* (pr. 1662) as *Wives*, he is remembered primarily for the originality of his plots and for his sensitivity and insight into American society. Although he was limited by the conventions and requirements of the theater of his time, he was deeply interested in dramatic theory, and he was particularly concerned with questions of dramatic structure. A well-constructed play, for Howard, was a "satisfactory" play—a play that is satisfactory to the audience. Believing that American and English audiences would not accept the death of a heroine in a play, Howard changed the ending of his original version of *The Banker's Daughter*. He made other changes in this play—changes that he claimed were founded on his "laws of dramatic composition." One of these laws, based on Howard's theory of what will satisfy an audience, is that those who do wrong (for example, a wife who has soiled her moral character) must always die before the final curtain falls. Similarly, and for the same reason, a love triangle must always bring disaster.

In the original version of *The Banker's Daughter*, Lillian Westbrook has married an older and wealthy man, John Strebelow, in order to save her father from financial ruin and also as a result of a quarrel with Harold Routledge. Five years later, now living in Paris with her husband and child, Lillian again meets Harold but remains faithful to her husband. The situation is then complicated by the Count de Carojac, who loves Lillian and who forces a duel with Harold. The supposed death of her old lover causes Lillian to reveal her passion and tell Strebelow that she never loved him. As a result, Strebelow takes the child away, and Lillian dies of a broken heart. The revised work shows the influence of Howard's theories of dramaturgy. First, because she has remained faithful, Lillian cannot be allowed to die in the last act, but because a love triangle cannot go unresolved, either Strebelow or Routledge must die. Howard chose Routledge, who is killed in the duel with the Count. Lillian now needs to recognize her own moral strength and save herself through this recognition rather than depend upon her child for that renewed strength. Finally, Strebelow needs to become a much stronger character, the hero of the play, in fact, and an appropriate mate for a mature Lillian, who now recognizes her own love for him.

By the third quarter of the nineteenth century, American society had been strongly affected by the industrial advances that had helped the North to win the Civil War and by the so-called Robber Barons, notorious for their life-style of "conspicuous waste." Howard recognized the growing influence of the businessman in American society, and he foresaw the social pressures that would result. Howard's first play to reveal a conscious use of the social-economic movement against a background of fashionable society was *Young Mrs. Winthrop*. In this play, Howard dramatized the conflict between the world of business and the domestic sphere. The play enjoyed an initial run of 180 performances, and reviews hailed it as a great American dramatic work; indeed, many consider it to be Howard's most important play, if only because it was the first of its kind. Douglas and Constance Winthrop, businessman and society wife, no longer find joy in their married life. When a gossip, Mrs. Chetwyn, arouses Mrs. Winthrop's suspicions concerning Mr. Winthrop's fidelity, Mrs. Winthrop attends a society ball in opposition to the wishes of her husband. Circumstances promote ready suspicions, but Howard added melodrama to social comedy by having the Winthrops' child fall ill and die while they are away. While the early action is enlivened by the careless and amusing Mrs. Chetwyn, the parents' grief in the later stages of the play threatens to overwhelm the initial premise. Mr. and Mrs. Winthrop part, only to be reunited in the final act as Howard superimposes his moral opinion on the problems that can confront the businessman in American society.

In *Young Mrs. Winthrop*, Howard portrayed a businessman but did not present the details of the business world. He would do this most explicitly in *The Henrietta*, which more recent critics have called the first of the American business plays. Linking New York society and the world of finance, Howard created a stage sermon on the vices of commercial gambling and the worship of money. Taking its title from the fictitious Henrietta Railroad, the control of which is the main issue in the melodramatic plot, the play dramatizes the financial rivalry between a father and his son. Nicholas Vanalstyne is known as "the Napoleon of Wall Street"; his son, Nicholas Vanalstyne, Jr., is equally unscrupulous and is monomaniacally concerned with wrenching control of the financial empire from his father—he is even capable of robbing the company safe. To both men, business is "health, religion, friendship, love—everything." Through the activities of a second Vanalstyne son, Bertie, a satiric portrait of the club man of this period, Howard showed that other side of society which looked askance at the feverish and frequently sordid life of moneygrubbers such as the Vanalstynes. The success of young Nicholas is short-lived, and Bertie eventually saves the day for his father, wins the heroine, and, while the villainous son dies of a heart attack, continues his successful operation on the stock exchange, basing his decisions on the flip of a coin. Popular on the American stage for a number of years, *The Henrietta* was revised by Winchell Smith and Victor Mapes in 1913 as *The New Henrietta*. Changed to meet new theater conventions and modern thought, the play was surprisingly successful.

As the international comedy of manners became a strong social theme for American writers, Howard began to plumb its possibilities in his plays. His first such work, *One of Our Girls*, illustrates his mastery of the international theme. *One of Our Girls* ran for two hundred nights after its opening. The action of the play takes place in Paris, where the Fonblanque family is arranging the marriage of their daughter Julie to the Comte de Crebillon, known well as a scoundrel and as a fine duelist. Opposed to this situation is Fonblanque's niece, Kate Shipley, the forthright and confident daughter of an American millionaire, who not only would not tolerate this arranged marriage of her cousin but also finds no good qualities in the Comte. The complications include a British Army captain who falls in love with Kate and Julie's lover, Henri Saint-Hilaire, but these are finally resolved through the good sense and actions of Kate. Julie is united with her lover; Kate and the Captain have a promising future; and the Comte, having confessed that he killed his first wife, is proved to be a villain. There is strong melodramatic action in the duel in which Henri is wounded and in the scene in which Kate protects Julie and allows herself to be caught in an embarrassing situation with Henri. Kate's American speech patterns provide some humor, as do the chatter of the gossips and the witticisms of the doctor. The main subject of the play, however, is the contrasting pictures of French and American marriage customs.

Howard tried again but failed to dramatize an international contrast in *Met by Chance*, in which part of the action takes place in the Adirondack Mountains. In *Aristocracy*, however, he effectually combined his interests in international society and the business world. The hero is Jefferson Stockton, a California capitalist and millionaire whose power and self-confidence precede him into every room. When his young wife reveals her social ambitions, he knows exactly how to satisfy them. Millionaires, he explains to her, are graded according to years and grandfathers, and in New York the newly rich man who thinks himself impressive is a fool. As he once ordered ten thousand tons of iron in New York, he will now order about five tons of good society for his wife, but it must be done carefully. The way to enter New York society is to take a house in London, and this Stockton does—after a few farcical episodes in London among the money-hunting European nobility. Although the caricatures of the financier and of the society he encounters weaken the overall effect of the social melodrama, the play has an interesting basic idea, and it held the stage for a respectable run.

Bronson Howard came into the theater at an opportune time—a time when American rather than English actors and managers were beginning to control American theaters and were looking for American playwrights. As a writer-journalist rather than an actor or manager, Howard tried new approaches in order to learn about the theater. His subsequent comments reveal that literary dramatists and elitist critics tried his patience. This was a transition period—Howard's life in the theater—and when it was over, the writing of drama in the United States had undergone a change. Clyde Fitch was making a fortune in New York and elsewhere; Langdon Mitchell and William Vaughn Moody were successful playwrights, while Rachel Crothers and Edward Sheldon were about to appear on the scene. During that transitional period, other dramatists added to the development of an American drama, but no one matched Howard's accomplishments in social melodrama, dramatic theory, and service to American playwrights.

Other major works

NONFICTION: "American Playwrights on the American Drama," 1889; "Our Schools for the Stage," 1900; "The American Drama," 1906; *The Autobiography of a Play*, 1914.

Bibliography

Mayorga, Margaret. *A Short History of the American Drama.* New York: Dodd, Mead, 1932. Mayorga comments that Howard linked the historical play with the play of manners. She analyzes *Old Love Letters, The Henrietta*, and his most important play, *Shenandoah*, concluding that Howard established American plays as artistically viable.

Meserve, Walter J. "Comedy and Social Drama: Caricature, Comedy, and Thesis Plays." In *The Revels History of Drama in English, 1865-1920.* Vol. 8. London: Methuen, 1977. A brief introduction to Howard as the first professional American playwright. Meserve focuses on Howard's depiction of businessmen and describes his "Laws of Dramatic Composition." Howard pioneered the awareness of the new social, middle class in the United States.

_____. *An Outline History of American Drama.* Totowa, N.J.: Littlefield, Adams, 1970. This volume provides highlights of Howard's professional contributions, briefly examines his theory of drama and his social themes, and analyzes four primary plays.

Moses, Montrose J. *The American Dramatist.* Boston: Little, Brown, 1925. This brief biography and introduction to the plays justifies Howard being named the "dean of American drama," because he established American drama. Describes Howard's dramatic theory as exemplified in *Young Mrs. Winthrop.* Complemented by an illustration and a chronology of Howard's major productions.

Thomas, Augustus. Introduction to *Autobiography of a Play,* by Bronson Howard. New York: Dramatic Museum of Columbia University, 1914. Thomas praises Howard's perception, human sympathy, proportion, construction, and his ability to generalize. His social themes are told through human stories by an "artistic general" turned philosopher.

Vaughn, Jack A. *Early American Dramatists.* New York: Frederick Ungar, 1981. A brief biography and introduction to the major plays. Contrasts Howard's early comedies with his later social dramas, focusing on *The Henrietta* and *Shenandoah.*

Walter J. Meserve
(Updated by *Gerald S. Argetsinger*)

SIDNEY HOWARD

Born: Oakland, California; June 26, 1891
Died: Tyringham, Massachusetts; August 23, 1939

Principal drama

Swords, pr., pb. 1921; *Casanova*, pb. 1921, pr. 1923 (adaptation of Lorenzo de Azertis' play); *S.S. Tenacity*, pr. 1922, pb. 1929 (adaptation of Charles Vildrac's play *Le Paquebot Tenacity*); *Bewitched*, pr. 1924 (with Edward Sheldon); *They Knew What They Wanted*, pr. 1924, pb. 1925; *Lucky Sam McCarver*, pr. 1925, pb. 1926; *The Last Night of Don Juan*, pr. 1925 (adaptation of Edmond Rostand's play *La Dernière Nuit de Don Juan*); *Morals*, pr. 1925 (with Charles Recht; adaptation of Ludwig Thoma's play); *Ned McCobb's Daughter*, pr., pb. 1926; *The Silver Cord*, pr. 1926, pb. 1927; *Salvation*, pr. 1928 (with Charles MacArthur); *Olympia*, pr., pb. 1928 (adaptation of Ferenc Molnár's play); *Half Gods*, pr. 1929, pb. 1930; *The Late Christopher Bean*, pr. 1932, pb. 1933 (adapted from René Fauchois' play *Prenez garde à la peinture*); *Alien Corn*, pr., pb. 1933; *Yellow Jack*, pr., pb. 1934 (with Paul de Kruif; based on de Kruif's book *Microbe Hunters*); *Dodsworth*, pr., pb. 1934 (adaptation of Sinclair Lewis' novel); *Paths of Glory*, pr., pb. 1935 (adaptation of Humphrey Cobb's novel); *The Ghost of Yankee Doodle*, pr. 1937, pb. 1938; *Madame, Will You Walk?*, pr. 1953, pb. 1955.

Other literary forms

Although best known for his plays, Sidney Howard also translated and adapted a number of works. In his early years, Howard worked as a literary editor and wrote, with Robert Dunn, a collection of articles on strikebreaking agencies entitled *The Labor Spy* (1921). In 1924, he published four stories under the single title *Three Flights Up*. Like Robert E. Sherwood and Clifford Odets, Howard devoted much of his time to writing screenplays, primarily for Samuel Goldwyn's studio. With Wallace Smith, he wrote the script for *Bulldog Drummond* (1929), based on stories by the British writer H. C. McNeile, who wrote under the pen name "Sapper." Howard also adapted two novels by Sinclair Lewis, *Arrowsmith* (in 1931) and *Dodsworth* (in 1936), to the screen. For his 1939 film adaptation of Margaret Mitchell's *Gone with the Wind*, Howard won an Academy Award.

Achievements

While Sidney Howard contributed little that was unique to American drama, his reputation rests chiefly on his ability to focus on limited, narrow subjects and, in the process, to reveal something essential about the human condition. He created a number of substantial and effective plays, characterized by sound craftsmanship, honesty, and skill. In limiting himself to dramatizing concrete, specific situations, he created sharp, telling vignettes about particular people in varied yet specific settings.

Howard's achievements are seen in his expert characterization and in his emphasis on social perspective, which helped his plays transcend the limitations of contemporary drama. In 1925, his efforts were recognized; he was awarded the Pulitzer Prize for *They Knew What They Wanted.*

Biography

Sidney Coe Howard was the son of John Lawrence Howard and Helen Louise Coe. His paternal grandfather, born of English parents, had emigrated from Antrim, Ireland, in 1848 and had settled in Philadelphia. After attending public schools in Oakland, California, Howard was graduated from the University of California in 1915 and then attended George Pierce Baker's Workshop 47 at Harvard University. During this time, Howard began his early collaborative efforts with Edward Sheldon, who had a great influence on the development of American drama. In 1916, Howard received a master of arts degree from Harvard.

World War I interrupted Howard's creative career; inducted into the service in 1916, he served first as an ambulance driver in France and in the Balkans and then as a captain and fighter pilot in the newly formed Air Service. In 1919, Howard joined the editorial staff of the old humor magazine *Life* in New York. Three years later, he became the literary editor of *Life* and was writing and adapting plays. In 1921, he married Clare Eames, an actress, and they had a child, Clare Jenness Howard.

Howard's determined interest in the daily lives of people led him to work in 1923 as a special investigative reporter and fiction writer for *The New Republic* and *International Magazine*. Before settling into the style of social drama that eventually brought him success, Howard wrote his first play, *Swords*, which failed, and collaborated with Sheldon on *Bewitched.*

Following Howard's recognition as a playwright for *They Knew What They Wanted*, he continued over the next five years to write or translate and adapt several plays. Three of these, *Dodsworth*, *Paths of Glory*, and *The Late Christopher Bean*, are among his best contributions to American drama.

Lucky Sam McCarver opened at the Playhouse Theatre in New York on October 21, 1925, and capitalized on the spectacle of affluent life among New York's socialites. The play is an ironic statement on that society and those who aspire to it. *Ned McCobb's Daughter* and *The Silver Cord* both came to New York theaters in 1926. With its well-drawn characters, *The Silver Cord* is one of the outstanding social-thesis plays in American drama. Neither *Salvation* nor *Half Gods* was successful, and after 1929 Howard concentrated on writing screenplays. During the last ten years of his life, Howard continued to write for the stage and achieved moderate success with his adaptation of *The Late Christopher Bean* and with *Alien Corn*. Active in theater affairs, Howard served from 1935 to 1937 as president of the Dramatists Guild, and in 1938—along with Sherwood, S. N. Behrman, Maxwell Anderson, and Elmer Rice—he formed the Playwrights' Company, organized to produce their plays without interference from commercial producers.

In 1930, following the death of Clare Eames, by that time his former wife, Howard married Leopoldine Blaine Damrosch, the daughter of musician Walter Damrosch. They had two children: a daughter, Sidney Damrosch Howard, and a son, Walter Damrosch Howard. Sidney Howard died on August 23, 1939, as a result of a tractor accident on his Massachusetts farm.

Analysis

Sidney Howard was neither an innovator in dramatic form nor a particularly profound writer, and he readily admitted these facts. He was content to "get a kind of glamour around reality," to dare less and achieve more. He was nevertheless a substantial playwright of considerable theatrical skill and imagination who stepped into the ongoing stream of social drama in America and produced at least two major plays in that genre.

Despite a tendency toward preachiness, *They Knew What They Wanted* is an important play for its humanity and for its insight into social morality. A modern version of Dante's story of the love of Paolo and Francesca, it demonstrated Howard's ability to write a compact, effective play.

Tony, a sixty-year-old Italian winegrower, proposes by mail to Amy, a young waitress, whom he has seen once and admired. They correspond, and Amy asks for a photograph of him. Instead, he sends one of Joe, his handsome young hired hand. On his way to the station to pick up Amy, Tony has an automobile accident and is injured. When Amy arrives at the house, she mistakes Joe for Tony, and on discovering that Tony is to be her husband, she is shocked. After the wedding party, Amy, miserable, is left alone with Joe, and they make love. The discovery three months later that Amy is pregnant, Tony's resultant anger, his struggle with his pride, and his final acceptance of and triumph over the trouble, as well as the resolution for all three characters of this dilemma, comprise the heart of the play. All three characters, in the end, know and get what they want, and all are, in the end, satisfied.

In Tony, Howard created his most successful character. The most appealing and most real figure in the play, Tony is also the one most able to deal with the exigencies of the world. He discovers that he can accept Amy's child, love Amy, and find joy in his new family. He becomes not the most miserable of men but a "most happy fella." The other two characters make similar discoveries: Amy discovers that she really cares for Tony and wants to be his wife, and Joe finds that he really values his freedom. The play ends satisfactorily, for the characters and for the audience.

The Silver Cord, although it also suffers from preachment, has a profound effect upon audiences, delving into a deep and often hidden layer of human emotion. Mrs. Phelps, a domineering mother, is in a struggle to possess the love of her two sons and to exclude from their affections the women whom they love. She successfully destroys the love of Robert and his fiancée, Hester, but fails to break up the marriage of her older son, David, and Christina, a more determined woman than Hester and more of a match for Mrs. Phelps. Howard expresses his antipathy toward filial duty grounded on pathological dependence through Christina, who says, "An embryological accident is no ground for honour," and through Hester, who says of children, "Have 'em. Love 'em. And then leave 'em be."

The play dramatizes this conflict—between a "professional" mother and an independent and ambitious wife. Both deserve some sympathy even as each struggles desperately for the fulfillment of her own selfish needs. Christina, however, is not morally disfigured, as is Mrs. Phelps. Christina's concern for her own career is balanced by her more healthy concern for the life of her unborn child and for the freedom to live that she knows is necessary for her own happiness and for David's.

Mrs. Phelps is singularly diabolical, and this makes her a very interesting character; she stalks her sons like prey, weakening their other loyalties with innuendo and crafty appeals for sympathy, then pouncing when these loyalties have been sufficiently worn down. The play is marred, however, by too much weakness in the sons, by the lack of any real dramatic discovery on Christina's part, by the lack of credibility in David's late and undermotivated decision to leave in the end, and, finally, by the playwright's preachiness. By the end of the play, the audience is satisfied: Christina has defeated the villainess after an intense battle, she has helped to free innocent Hester, and she has gained her own personal objective. Christina, however, seems a bit too much like Mrs. Phelps for comfort, and David may well be merely stepping out of one trap and into another. As a social drama with a Freudian thesis, however—the level on which the play was most generally understood—it was successful and powerfully dramatic on the stage.

During the 1920's, Howard adapted several plays and wrote several more. Both *Lucky Sam McCarver* and *Ned McCobb's Daughter*—one a theatrical failure and the other a success—show elements of the social drama at which Howard excelled. Each is concerned with a strong character who faces a series of frustrating social situations and who reacts powerfully to those conditions and frustrations.

Lucky Sam McCarver starts as an analysis of cold, materialistic Sam McCarver but is more effective as the story of a woman who desperately wants love from a man who has only money to give. Sam, who is hardened in his worship of money, frankly uses his wife and her name and sees nothing beyond his growing empire. Having lost human compassion and the ability to feel, he can only think and contrive; in Howard's world, which is essentially a world of action and feeling rather than thought, Sam has no value.

Unlike the comedy *Ned McCobb's Daughter*, in which social conditions provide the background for Carrie to show her superiority of character and her Yankee determination, *Lucky Sam McCarver* is an unhappy social drama about irresponsible people: a frustrated woman and a materialistic man who will always be "disappointed in the universe." Howard's characters usually know what they want, but Howard invariably controls their destinies. Although he frequently tempers his moral judgments with true mercy, within his definitions of right and wrong he is completely conventional in meting out rewards and punishments, emphasizing his preference for a "satisfactory" ending to a play.

In the 1930's, Howard wrote and adapted several plays, bringing his total output to more than twenty-five plays. Worthy of mention is *Yellow Jack*, written with Paul de Kruif and based on de Kruif's book *Microbe Hunters* (1926). It was not a popular success when first staged, but it has been frequently revived since that time. Set in and around an army barracks near Havana, Cuba, it follows Major Walter Reed and his colleagues' fight to isolate the cause of yellow fever, quietly tracing the events and highlighting the nobility of the characters involved in the enterprise and the sacrifices they made. Again, Howard keeps the focus of the play narrow, allowing no extraneous "love interest" or other episodes to interfere with the progress of the action.

Howard found his greatest success in creating social drama from a mixture of realism, melodrama, and comedy. His major interest in his plays, however, was his characters. Psychological interpretation of character is an essential part of his best plays. More exuberant than thoughtful, he was frequently satisfied to have his characters simply react emotionally to strong stimuli.

In *They Knew What They Wanted*, for example, Tony tells Amy: "What you have done is mistake in da head, not in da heart." For Howard, emotion is more important than intellect. Similarly, Christina in *The Silver Cord* at first relies upon reason to resolve her difficulties with Mrs. Phelps, but her attempts fail; intellect is not enough.

Although he generally followed an established trend in American drama, Howard, in his best plays, created strong, compelling characters, interacting in situations that allowed his drama to transcend the limitations of the merely personal. The individualistic, life-affirming spirit of his work was a welcome addition to the social drama of the 1920's.

Other major works

SHORT FICTION: *Three Flights Up*, 1924.

NONFICTION: *The Labor Spy*, 1921 (with Robert Dunn).

SCREENPLAYS: *Bulldog Drummond*, 1929 (with Wallace Smith; based on stories by H. C. McNeile); *Arrowsmith*, 1931 (based on Sinclair Lewis' novel); *Dodsworth*, 1936 (based on Lewis' novel); *Gone with the Wind*, 1939 (based on Margaret Mitchell's novel).

Bibliography

Bonin, Jane F. *Major Themes in Prize-Winning American Drama.* Metuchen, N.J.: Scarecrow Press, 1975. This insightful analysis of Howard's plays shows that he was interested in staging the self-made man and the success ethic as well as depicting women in various roles in marriage and society. Marriages are grim, yet American women are pragmatic; they need a husband for security, no matter how intelligent and strong they might be.

Dusenbary, Winifred L. "Myth in American Drama Between the Wars." *Modern Drama* 6 (December, 1963): 294-308. Howard figures among the playwrights of his generation who used myths as a vehicle for the expression of contemporary issues. While he showed some understanding of how myths work, he failed to identify the essence of those that he used in his plays.

Isaacs, Edith J. R. "Sidney Howard." *Theatre Arts Monthly* 23 (October, 1939): 686, 723-733. The editor notes that Howard died the day that this article was submitted and apologizes for not acknowledging his great contribution to the theater. Isaacs discusses the elements that make Howard's plays enjoyable and analyzes their theatricality. Contains a photograph of Howard.

Krutch, Joseph Wood. "Sidney Howard, Storyteller." *Theatre Arts* 41 (February, 1957): 31-32, 91-92. Conversations that Krutch and Howard had aboard a ship returning to New York inform this article. Krutch identifies the purely American characteristics of Howard's plays and addresses the question of foreign influences. Includes photographs of scenes from three plays and a drawing of the playwright.

Meserve, Walter. "Sidney Howard and the Social Drama of the Twenties." *Modern Drama* 6 (December, 1963): 256-266. Expert analysis of the realism in Howard's plays shows that his social perspective, individualist ethos, and artistic mastery helped define social drama in the United States. While there are traces of Ibsenism, Howard did not offer Americans "food for thought."

White, Sydney Howard. *Sidney Howard.* Boston: Twayne, 1977. This well-conceived monograph offers a biographical and critical survey of the early essays and stories as well as of the major stage plays and screenplays. Quotations from letters, articles, and reviews help to shape the final evaluation of Howard's corpus. The endnotes present information on performances. The chronological table and the bibliography are useful.

Walter J. Meserve
(Updated by *Irene Gnarra*)

TINA HOWE

Born: New York, New York; November 21, 1937

Principal drama

Closing Time, pr. 1959; *The Nest*, pr. 1970; *Museum*, pr. 1976, pb. 1979; *Birth and Afterbirth*, pb. 1977; *The Art of Dining*, pr. 1979, pb. 1980; *Appearances*, pr. 1982 (one act); *Painting Churches*, pr. 1983, pb. 1984; *Coastal Disturbances*, pr. 1986, pb. 1987; *Approaching Zanzibar*, pr., pb. 1989; *One Shoe Off*, pr. 1993.

Other literary forms

Tina Howe is known primarily for her plays.

Achievements

Howe has earned distinction as one of the leading American dramatists of the commercial theater, and she has received some of the highest awards for playwriting. In 1983, largely in response to her most studied and successful play, *Painting Churches*, she captured an Obie Award for Distinguished Playwriting, the Rosamond Gilder Award for Outstanding Creative Achievement in Theatre, and a Rockefeller Playwright-in-Residence Fellowship. In addition to the Outer Critics Circle's John Gassner Award for Outstanding New American Playwright and a National Endowment for the Arts Fellowship in 1984, she received a Guggenheim Fellowship, a Tony nomination for Best Play (*Coastal Disturbances*), and an honorary degree from Bowdoin College.

Biography

Tina Howe, reared in New York City, was born into an aristocratic and celebrated family. Her grandfather, Mark Antony DeWolfe Howe, was a renowned poet and Pulitzer Prize recipient. Her father, Quincy Howe, was an eminent radio and television broadcaster, and her mother, Mary, was a painter. After attending private schools in New York, Howe went to Sarah Lawrence College in Bronxville, New York, where she received a baccalaureate degree in 1959. Howe tried her hand at playwriting during her undergraduate studies and had a play produced (*Closing Time*) at Sarah Lawrence College, with Howe directing and Jane Alexander, Howe's classmate, starring in the production. She did not seriously consider becoming a dramatist, however, until the year after her graduation, when she traveled to Paris and had the opportunity to meet aspiring young writers and, more important, to see various experimental, absurdist theater productions, in particular Eugène Ionesco's *La Cantatrice chauve* (pr. 1950; *The Bald So-*

prano, 1956) and *Rhinocéros* (pr. 1959; *Rhinoceros*, 1959). This experience was a turning point for Howe, for the absurdist dramas appealed to her own antic, comic spirit, and these plays would later influence her dramaturgical style. She returned to New York, married writer Norman Levy in 1961, and taught high school English in Maine, where she also served as drama coach for the school's club. This position helped her learn her craft, for the rigors of writing one-act plays for the club's production season helped her gain the discipline and focus that she needed as a writer. During the late 1960's and early 1970's, Howe and Levy took various teaching positions at colleges in Chicago, Madison, and Albany. Howe continued to write plays, with *The Nest* receiving a professional production. In 1973, the couple settled in New York City with their two children, and in 1983, Howe began working as an adjunct professor of playwriting at New York University.

Analysis

Tina Howe's plays are remarkable for their absurdist depiction of life and their female perspective. Her playwriting style closely allies her with the absurdists, to whom she admits her indebtedness. In particular, she borrowed the absurdists' use of surreal details, incongruous actions, bizarre situations, and farcical characters, for these devices suited her interest in exploring the passions, drives, fears, and anxieties that lie below the surface in all persons. As a result, her plays are, on the one hand, wildly comic, replete with pratfalls, sight gags, and much physical and verbal comedy, and yet, on the other hand, are rueful and poignant, exposing the emotional pain of characters who battle life's unavoidable tragedies and suffering. This tragicomic view of life has sparked comparisons between Howe and Anton Chekhov, specifically for Howe's ability to capture "the same edgy surface of false hilarity, the same unutterable sadness beneath it, and the indomitable valor beneath both." Howe presents her absurdist view of life from the female perspective: The central protagonists of her plays are women, and it is through their experiences that Howe explores such universal concerns as the ravages of time, the ineluctable human process of deterioration, the basal anxieties over death, and the human need to find meaning and permanence in an ephemeral world.

Howe's first two comedies, *The Nest* and *Birth and Afterbirth*, are her most overtly feminist and absurdist plays. In these works, Howe draws biting satirical portraits of women as they struggle to find autonomy in a world demanding that they live according to the traditional roles of wives and mothers. *The Nest* depicts a trio of young women battling one another for the prize of an ideal husband, and the inanity of their actions culminates in a highly charged, symbolic moment, when one of the women removes all of her clothes and dives into a seven-foot-tall wedding cake. *The*

Nest was panned by critics and closed after one performance. *Birth and Afterbirth* looks at women's choices concerning childbirth. Through Sandy, mother of a four-year-old son with behavioral problems (played by an adult actor), who grows increasingly disillusioned and enraged over the demands that her family places on her, Howe shows the physical and emotional toll that child rearing takes on women and attacks the myth that marriage and motherhood fulfill women's lives. On the opposite pole, Mia, a married anthropologist with no children, fears the physical pain of childbirth, and although she has tried to find personal fulfillment through her job, she feels inadequate as a woman because she has no children. With this play, Howe said she wanted "to show how threatening women on either side of the fence can be to each other." The play implies as well that women, regardless of their choices regarding marriage and children, continue both to define and to judge themselves according to the myths of motherhood and family life. *Birth and Afterbirth* has proved so incendiary that Howe has had difficulty getting it staged.

After the failure of these two plays, Howe made a conscious effort to alter her playwriting style. She took note of the successful Broadway plays at the time and concluded that audiences wanted escape, so she set out to find settings that had not been used onstage before, something that audiences would find novel. More important, she decided to tone down her feminist voice by couching it in less threatening dramatic terms. As a result, Howe took women out of their domestic arena, placed them in such exotic and unlikely locales as museums, restaurants, and beaches, and made her central protagonists women artists. When Howe hit on this idea and wrote her first successful play (*Museum*) as a result of her new writing strategy, she knew that she hit her stride: "I had found my niche at last. I would write about women as artists, eschew the slippery ground of courtship and domesticity and move up to a loftier plane." Her later plays are still full of comic exuberance, zany characters, and outrageous situations, but her female characters, in the main, now seek their creative and intellectual potential through nontraditional roles, most particularly as artists.

As the play's title suggests, *Museum* takes place in a museum gallery with three modernist exhibits: five life-size, clothed figures hanging from a twenty-five-foot clothesline and a basket of clothespins on the floor, a series of sculptures made from animal bones and feathers displayed on pedestals, and a group of three, totally white paintings along one wall. *Museum* has no traditional plot; it is a collage of conversations by some forty gallery visitors who meander about studying the exhibits, some expressing their disgust and confusion over such abstract drivel, others completely enthralled and postulating the meaning of each work and the purpose of art in general. The climax of the action occurs when Tink Solheim, a friend of Agnes Vaag (the sculptor of the animal-bone exhibit) begins frantically to search for the special secret that Agnes said was hidden in one of the sculptures. Tink finds a hidden switch, and when she turns it, the lights dim, floodlight illuminates the statue, and music by Johann Sebastian Bach swells out from a hidden speaker. The crowd stands entranced for several minutes, experiencing a communal epiphany. This spiritual awakening leads to pandemonium, as the play concludes with the gallery visitors running about in a frenzy, ripping apart the exhibits, and stealing parts of them in their desire to own at least a small part of something artistic, spiritual, and eternal.

The communal and spiritual experience brought about by a woman's work of art in *Museum* has its parallel in Howe's next play, *The Art of Dining*. The artist in this play is Ellen, a gourmet chef and partner with her husband in a trendy restaurant. Where people coveted art in *Museum*, in this comedy they wish literally to devour it. Starving diners from the surrounding area come to the restaurant to feast voraciously on Ellen's famous culinary masterpieces. The symbol of spiritual starvation in the previous play is made more literal in *The Art of Dining*, and, similar to *Museum*'s finale, Howe brings all the visitors together in one communal, ritual moment brought about by the female creator. Everyone huddles together to feast on Ellen's complimentary dessert. The symbolism of this closing moment of shared community is articulated by one of the diners, Elizabeth Colt, a young anorexic novelist, who stands apart as the diners eat with gusto and explains that centuries ago people gathered together in a shared celebration to enjoy the feast. Through their collective communion brought about by Ellen's gift, this group of strangers comes together in one common humanity, "purified of their collective civilization and private grief."

Painting Churches, Howe's most successful comedy, returns to the world of the artist. It explores parent-child relationships, children's need to gain parental acceptance and approval, and, especially, the larger and more serious issues of life's ineluctable process toward deterioration and the ultimate movement toward death. In this play, Mags Church, an impressionist painter, visits home after a long absence to paint a portrait of her aged parents before their imminent move from their Boston family home and just prior to her first solo show in a famous art gallery. Mags needs her parents' recognition of her creative genius (something they have never given her), and she hopes that her portrait of them will gain their respect for her as an artist and an adult. Once home, however, Mags sees the debilitating effects of time on her parents; her father, Gardner, once a renowned poet, is now addled, and her mother, Fanny, has been reduced to a life of taking care of her senile husband. Mags must face the shattering reality that all children encounter: Her parents are nearing death. After some difficulty getting her parents to sit still long enough to pose, Mags finally finishes her portrait, and it is this gift to her parents that brings all three together in a celebratory moment at the end of the play. When Fanny and Gardner look at their portrait, they compare it to one of Pierre-Auguste Renoir's works, and eventually they envision themselves as figures in a Renoir café scene with couples dancing. A Chopin waltz begins to play, and they start to dance about the room, oblivious to Mags, who stands watching them, her eyes filled with tears. Through Mags's painting, her parents have been rejuvenated, if only for a moment, for in effect they have been transformed into the painting. For a brief, magical moment, time stands still. Mags has locked her parents in time, capturing and immortalizing them by her portrait. Although her parents will soon die, they will continue to live not only in her memory but also forever on her canvas.

Coastal Disturbances includes various short scenes that form a collage, a series of impressions about love from different points of view, from an elderly couple who have withstood infidelities and other marital tragedies to a young couple caught up in sexual infatuation. The play's heroine, Holly, is a professional photographer who has come to a private beach in Massachusetts for a two-week vacation to take photographs and to forget a disastrous affair with her agent-boyfriend in New York. Holly becomes enamored of a compassionate and lovable lifeguard, but when her former boyfriend tracks her down and begs a reconciliation, she capitulates to his charm. While Howe is concerned with the passage of time, which is made quite visible by the ever-changing and gorgeous sunrises and sunsets on the beach, she does not explore this theme as vividly and dramatically as in *Painting Churches. Coastal Disturbances* is atypical of Howe's work; it is a love story that attempts to teach that forgiveness, compassion, and tenderness can calm any emotional disturbance and heal the heart.

With *Approaching Zanzibar*, Howe returns to her previous preoccupations with life's ephemerality, death, art, and rebirth. The Blossom family (husband Wally, wife Charlotte, and two children, Turner and Pony) take a cross-country trek from Hastings, New York, to Taos, New Mexico, to visit Charlotte's dying aunt, Olivia. On this two-week trip, the Blossoms enjoy a typical vacation, camping out, fishing, visiting relatives, and meeting some interesting strangers. At every turn, however, the realities of life's brevity and ultimate closure through death forms a palpable background. Not only is the trip itself a metaphor for the journey of life with its end in death (symbolized by Olivia), but also, throughout, characters make repeated references to the passage of time and the loss of youth and its promise of a future. Charlotte is menopausal, and her anguish over her inability to have more children causes her nightmares about abandoned babies. Wally, once a famous composer, lost his creative energy when his parents' deaths the year earlier traumatized him, forcing him to confront his own mortality. Howe underscores her theme of the inexorable cycle of life (birth, death, rebirth) not only through dialogue with numerous allusions to evolution and reincarnation but also through the Blossom children. Although Charlotte and Wally face midlife, their children are their source of hope and touch with immortality. Turner is a musical prodigy with great promise of carrying on his father's talent. Pony possesses the most miraculous and powerful counter to death, her potential progeny. The celebration of the female's ability to create life and rejuvenate her species as the ultimate defense against death forms the play's closing tableau: Pony, alone at Olivia's bedside, rejuvenates the dying woman; soon the two hold hands and begin jumping on Olivia's bed (a trampoline) while crying out "Paradise." All the others rush into the room, freeze at the sight of them leaping into the air, and then gather around the bed to join their euphoric shouts of "Paradise." Here again, Howe ends her play in a highly charged, theatrical moment of spiritual communion, an affirmation of life, nurturing, and humanity, with the female at its core.

Howe is not only one of the most prominent female playwrights from a new generation of American dramatists who emerged during the second women's movement but also a representative of a group of dramatists whose works characterize the postmodern theater movement that began in the early 1970's. Her plays blend traditional domestic drama with the experimental techniques that deploy considerable theatricality. On the surface, they appear naturalistic, slice-of-life comedies, but she injects an element of surrealism throughout her plays by inserting unexpected, outrageous actions: the frenetic destruction of artworks, an old lady jumping on a trampoline. Like the absurdists, Howe focuses on existential issues, but she lacks their darkness and nihilism, preferring that her characters, and the audience, laugh at life's reversals and accept them with valor and courage. Her language can be, at turns, everyday conversation with dialogue overlapping, or elegantly poetic arias and soliloquies. Through comedy, Howe probes the most basic of human emotions, forces laughter and compassion for those who suffer agonies familiar to all, and reminds viewers that life is full of both tragic and comic events. She celebrates life's everyday, ordinary events—the sunsets, the family vacation, the reunion with relatives—those special ephemeral moments that can be captured perhaps on canvas or with a photograph but can never be relived. Between birth and death is life in process. Howe reminds the audience to live it to the fullest.

Bibliography
Backes, Nancy. "Body Art: Hunger and Satiation in the Plays of Tina Howe." In *Making a Spectacle*, edited by Lynda Hart. Ann Arbor: University of Michigan Press, 1989. Women writers' use of food has become a major area of research, and this essay adds to that body of scholarship by incisively examining Howe's abundant use of food imagery relative to

cultural inscriptions about women's bodies, self-image, self-control, and nurturing.

Barlow, Judith E. "The Art of Tina Howe." In *Feminine Focus*, edited by Enoch Brater. Oxford, England: Oxford University Press, 1989. Barlow discusses one of the central motifs in Howe's plays, the importance of art in daily life. Barlow pays particular attention to Howe's use of women as artists, and her insightful comments clarify Howe's interest in celebrating the unique and powerful creativity of women artists.

Betsko, Kathleen, and Rachel Koening. *Interviews with Contemporary Women Playwrights.* New York: Beech Tree Books, 1987. This interview contains the most biographical information on Howe, her writing habits, her views on the arts, her absurdist roots, and her thematic concerns from *The Nest* to *Painting Churches.*

DiGaetani, John L. *A Search for a Postmodern Theatre: Interviews with Contemporary Playwrights.* Westport, Conn.: Greenwood Press, 1991. In this interview, Howe discusses her indebtedness to the absurdist playwrights, her concerns as a feminist writer, and autobiographical aspects of her plays and characters. Contains a photograph of Howe.

Howe, Tina. "Antic Vision." *American Theatre* 2 (September, 1985): 12, 14. Although numerous published interviews with Howe provide firsthand information from the playwright, this essay by Howe, written after the success of *Painting Churches*, offers the most insight into her views about comical playwriting, her feminist vision, and her aesthetic voice. Contains photographs from production scenes of *Painting Churches* and *The Art of Dining.*

Kachur, B. A. "Women Playwrights on Broadway: Henley, Howe, Norman, and Wasserstein." In *Contemporary American Theatre*, edited by Bruce King. New York: St. Martin's Press, 1991. This chapter on four prominent women playwrights includes information on Howe's metadramatic techniques and her feminist perspective, particularly her use of women both as central protagonists and as artists.

Wetzsteon, Ross. "The Mad, Mad World of Tina Howe." *New York* 16 (November 28, 1983): 58. Wetzsteon surveys Howe's plays through *Painting Churches*, discusses biographical details, and provides a brief analysis of Howe's playwriting style and themes.

B. A. Kachur

DAVID HENRY HWANG

Born: Los Angeles, California; August 11, 1957

Principal drama

F.O.B., pr. 1978, pb. 1983; *The Dance and the Railroad*, pr. 1981, pb. 1983; *Family Devotions*, pr. 1981, pb. 1983; *Sound and Beauty*, pr. 1983 (two one-acts, *The House of Sleeping Beauties*, pb. 1983, and *The Sound of a Voice*, pb. 1984); *Broken Promises: Four Plays*, pb. 1983; *Rich Relations*, pr. 1986, pb. 1990; *As the Crow Flies*, pr. 1986; *Broken Promises*, pr. 1987 (includes *The Dance and the Railroad* and *The House of Sleeping Beauties*); *M. Butterfly*, pr. 1988, pb. 1989; *One Thousand Airplanes on the Roof*, pr. 1988, pb. 1989 (musical; music by Philip Glass); *F.O.B. and Other Plays*, pb. 1990; *Bondage*, pr. 1992 (one act); *Face Value*, pr. 1993.

Other literary forms

David Henry Hwang is known primarily for his plays.

Achievements

Hwang is the first Asian-American playwright to bring specifically Asian and American themes to Broadway and Off-Broadway theater. Within the first decade of his career as a playwright, he staged six major productions in New York and abroad, garnering four Off-Broadway "Best Play" nominations and awards. *M. Butterfly*, his first Broadway play, won both the New York Drama Desk Award and the Tony Award for Best Play as well as a nomination for the Pulitzer Prize in drama. His plays explore issues of ethnic identity, gender, and imperialism, with often stunning theatrical flair.

Biography

David Henry Hwang was born in Los Angeles on August 11, 1957, the son of Henry Yuan Hwang, a banker, and Dorothy Huang Hwang, a professor of piano. His father grew up in Shanghai, China, and emigrated in the late 1940's to California, where he enrolled in the business program at the University of Southern California. His mother, born in southeastern China, had grown up in the Philippines.

Hwang received his A.B. degree from Stanford University in 1979, having majored in English, and he briefly taught writing in a high school in Menlo Park, California, before attending the Yale School of Drama in 1980 and 1981. His first play, *F.O.B.*, was performed at Stanford University before being accepted for production at the National Playwrights Conference at Connecticut's O'Neill Theatre Center in 1979, when he was twenty-one years old. The following year, Joseph Papp brought it to the New York Shakespeare Festival's Public Theater, Off-Broadway. It won an Obie

Award for the best new play of the season.

Like *F.O.B.*, Hwang's next two plays focused on the Chinese-American experience. *The Dance and the Railroad* depicts two nineteenth century immigrants working on the transcontinental railroad, while *Family Devotions* is a bizarre farce set in contemporary California.

His next two plays, jointly titled *Sound and Beauty*, are stylized one-act plays set in contemporary Japan; they were produced Off-Broadway in 1983. The first, *The House of Sleeping Beauties*, reinvents a novella by Yasunari Kawabata, making the author a character in a version of his own work. The second, *The Sound of a Voice*, involves a conflict between a samurai warrior and a bewitching female hermit whom he intends to kill.

In 1983, Hwang received a Rockefeller playwright-in-residence award and a National Endowment for the Arts artistic associate fellowship. A Guggenheim Fellowship followed in 1984, as did fellowships from the National Endowment for the Arts and the New York State Council on the Arts in 1985. On September 25, 1985, he married Ophelia Y. M. Chong, an artist, from whom he was later divorced.

Rich Relations, produced Off-Broadway in 1986, was his first work not about the Asian experience and his first critical failure, though it recapitulated various themes from his earlier plays. Nevertheless, Hwang has termed this failure exhilarating, freeing him from undue concern about critical reaction.

M. Butterfly, produced in 1988, brought Hwang international renown, a Tony Award for the Best Play of 1988, the Outer Critics Circle Award, and a nomination for the Pulitzer Prize in 1989. Based on a true story of a French diplomat and his Chinese lover who turned out to be not only a spy but also a man, the play explores issues of gender, identity, racism, and political hegemony. The same year, he collaborated with composer Philip Glass on *One Thousand Airplanes on the Roof*, a science fiction work concerning a character who may have been kidnapped by visiting aliens.

In 1992, Hwang's one-act play *Bondage* premiered at the Humana Festival of New Plays at the Actors Theatre of Louisville, Kentucky. Set in a parlor frequented by sadomasochists, its two characters are completely covered in black leather, so that their respective races cannot be discerned.

Analysis

Images of Asians and Asian Americans in modern culture have been relatively rare and often stereotypical; few have been created by Asian Americans themselves. On-screen stereotypes ranged from Charlie Chan (performed by a white actor), an image of wise but humble, ultimately "knowing" inscrutability, to the cook Hop Sing on the television series *Bonanza* (1959-1973). Contact between Eastern and Western cultures had been depicted in such works as David Belasco's *Madame Butterfly* (pr.

1900, pb. 1935, the basis for Giacomo Puccini's opera of the same name), Richard Rodgers' and Oscar Hammerstein II's *The King and I* (pr. 1951) and *Flower Drum Song* (pr. 1958), John Patrick's *The Teahouse of the August Moon* (pr. 1953; pb. 1954), and Paul Osborn's *The World of Suzie Wong* (pr. 1958, based on the novel by Richard Mason). Whatever their merits, however, none of these plays offered a genuinely Asian perspective on the events portrayed. By the early 1970's, literature by and about Asian Americans began to emerge; a decade later, its first critically acclaimed and commercially successful such playwright was David Henry Hwang. From his earliest plays about the Chinese-American experience to his Broadway hit *M. Butterfly* and the subsequent one-act play *Bondage*, he has progressively explored issues of ethnic cultural identity, gender roles, the East/West relationship, and the effects of imperialism—and has done so with deftly constructed plots, a number of which incorporate elements of Chinese opera.

In his introduction to *F.O.B. and Other Plays*, Hwang identified three phases "in attempting to define [his] place in America," and his early plays correspond to these. The first is an "assimilationist" phase, in which one tries to "out-white the whites" in order to fit in with the majority culture. Dale, the central character of his first play, *F.O.B.*, is a second-generation American of Chinese descent who dresses like a preppy and particularly disdains Chinese immigrants who are "Fresh Off the Boat," abbreviated "F.O.B." One such, named Steve, is the target of his scorn throughout the play, in part because he reminds Dale of his ancestry, the nonwhite, non-American past that he prefers to ignore, discard, or deny. Steve's cousin Grace, a first-generation Chinese American, functions as an intermediary between the two men, with insight into the plight of both the newly arrived and the all-too-assimilated "A.B.C.'s," meaning "American-Born Chinese." Steve announces himself as the great god Gwan Gung, the Chinese folk hero, the "god of warriors, writers, and prostitutes." Grace tells him that in the United States, Gwan Gung is dead; nevertheless, her contact with Steve reawakens her own fantasy, Fu Ma Lan, a great woman warrior. Dale repudiates both myths, having struggled for so long to overcome his Chineseness, but Steve's presence forces him to reexamine his values. Following Dale's attempts to humiliate the immigrant, Steve becomes in monologue the embodiment of "ChinaMan," the immigrant Everyman who helped build the American West, particularly its railroads. Such cultural kinship finally binds Steve and Grace, who transmutes him from dead god to living warrior. Dale is left behind at the end of the play, uncomprehending, unrepentant, and alone.

Gwan Gung also figures significantly in *The Dance and the Railroad*, Hwang's second play, a product of his "isolationist-nationalist" phase, in which he wrote primarily for other Asian Americans, having rejected "the assimilationist model" as "dangerous and self-defeating." Set in 1867, *The Dance and the Railroad* is a two-character, one-act play whose characters, Lone and Ma, are workers building the transcontinental railroad but are currently on a nine-day laborers' strike. Although conflicts between white management and Chinese labor underlie the action, personal differences between the characters and the traditions of Chinese opera and culture become increasingly prominent. Lone, a refugee from the Chinese opera, isolates himself from the other workers, practicing his art in solitude on the mountainside, above the strike and commercial toil. Ma, a gullible F.O.B. laborer who believes in the promises of the Gold Mountain in America, ascends in search of Lone, discovers his austere artistic training regimen, and yearns to learn opera to "become" Gwan Gung in the new land. To learn the discipline that artistry requires, Ma maintains the "locust" position all night, a metaphor for immigrant experience. Finally worthy to study Gwan Gung, Ma rejects doing so and returns to the work below when the strike ends. The play's later scenes are performed in the style of Chinese opera. The actor playing Lone—his namesake, John Lone—had trained with the Peking Opera for eight years; he also directed the play, choreographed it, and provided its music.

Hwang's third play, *Family Devotions*, is a nine-character farce set in contemporary California. The action centers on three generations of a thoroughly "assimilated" Chinese-American family satirically based on Hwang's own; they are visited by their "second brother" Di-gou, a doctor and former violinist who has lived for thirty years under the Communist Chinese regime. His sisters, ardent fundamentalist Christians, are shocked to find out that he is an atheist and that he rejects the legend of See-Goh-Poh, a Christian "Woman Warrior" who allegedly saved his soul at age eight. He, in turn, is baffled by the family's crass materialism and conspicuous consumption and has come to ask his sisters to renounce their faith and return home with him. The first act ends with one of them, Ama, delivering a fiery testimonial from a rolling, neon-lit pulpit as the "Hallelujah Chorus" blares away. In the second act, the sisters and their daughters tie Di-gou to a table, assailing him with the word of God and See-Goh-Poh. He breaks his bonds in a holy fit of possession, speaks in tongues, and exposes See-Goh-Poh as a fraud whose crusade was a ruse to conceal an unwanted pregnancy. As the grotesque exorcism proceeds, the sisters die in their chairs as Di-gou continues his vehement speech. Di-gou and the young child of the family depart, leaving the house a spiritual wreck, torn between the Chinese past and the California present, between myth and reality. The play shows the influence of American playwright Sam Shepard, to whom it is dedicated, but many of its thematic preoccupations—assimilation versus origins, lost ethnic awareness, a core conflict of incompatible values—are recognizably Hwang's own.

In the third phase of his writing, Hwang sought to move beyond his personal experience. *The House of Sleeping Beauties* is an adaptation of a story by Yasunari Kawabata, who is himself one of the play's two characters. The play is set in a brothel where elderly men learn to accept their mortality by sleeping beside comatose, nude, drugged young virgins. In Hwang's version, Kawabata comes there to research a book but becomes spiritually (platonically) involved with Michiko, the elderly proprietress. The play ends with his suicide by self-poisoning, and he is rocked to his final eternal sleep in her lap.

The companion piece of *The House of Sleeping Beauties* is *The Sound of a Voice*, a fable of a samurai warrior who goes into a forest to kill a bewitching female hermit but instead falls in love with her. The role of the witch was originally written for an *onnagata*, a male actor specializing in women's parts in Japanese Kabuki theater, but in the initial production it was played by a woman, Natsuko Ohama.

Rich Relations, produced in 1986, was Hwang's first play with all Caucasian characters and his first critical and commercial failure. Like *Family Devotions*, it lampooned Evangelical Christianity, deathbed resurrections, and crass materialism within a suburban Los Angeles family, but it offered little that was new in technique or ideas.

M. Butterfly, two years later, was a commercial and critical triumph on Broadway. The play is based on an article that appeared in *The New York Times* about the conviction of espionage of a French diplomat, who aided the Communist Chinese government by turning over embassy documents to his mistress of twenty years, a Chinese opera singer whom he had mistakenly believed to be an extremely modest woman. Hwang, however, sought no additional details from the actual case so as to avoid writing a docudrama; he was struck by the story as an inversion of the plot of the play and opera *Madame Butterfly*, in which a Japanese woman falls in love with a Caucasian man, is spurned, and commits suicide. In Hwang's play, the diplomat, René Gallimard, is the counterpart of Puccini's Westerner, Pinkerton, as he falls in love with opera singer Song Liling, unaware that she is the Chinese counterpart of an *onnagata* and an agent of the Communist government. The role of Song Liling is played by a man (B. D. Wong in the original production), though this fact is not revealed to the theater audience until the beginning of the third act when, in a moment of startling theatricality, Song Liling removes her makeup and changes clothes on stage, dispelling the illusion for the audience before disclosing her true gender and identity to Gallimard in a nude scene near the end of the play.

In many ways, *M. Butterfly* continues the thematic preoccupations that became apparent in Hwang's earlier plays: the use of Chinese opera from *The Dance and the Railroad*, the role for an *onnagata* and the unorthodox sexuality of *The Sound of a Voice*, the clash of Asian and Western values that recurred in all of his earlier plays. Incorporating both Puccini's music and Chinese opera, *M. Butterfly* also explores issues of gender and racial stereotyping, of dominance and submission (political as well as sexual), and of the morality of the Western presence in Asia. Furthermore, the play audaciously questions the nature of love and illusion, undermining any certainty about the ultimate knowability of another person or, indeed, of the world itself. While that theme is not new in twentieth century literature—having been particularly prominent in Ford Madox Ford's novel *The Good Soldier* (1915), for example, seldom, if ever, has it been presented with such dramatic effectiveness and theatrical flair.

M. Butterfly also marks a considerable advance in Hwang's dramatic technique over the earlier plays, which were chronologically presented on realistic sets. The play begins with a retrospective monologue by Gallimard in his prison cell; many flashbacks to European and Asian locales are introduced throughout twenty-seven brief scenes in three acts. The stylized set, designed by Eiko Ishioka, is dominated by a gently sloping, curved ramp, enabling a flexible use of the stage space. the original title, *Monsieur Butterfly*, was shortened to *M. Butterfly* (at Hwang's wife's suggestion) to seem more mysterious and ambiguous.

Following the phenomenal success of *M. Butterfly*, Hwang worried that whatever he did next would be considered a disappointment; accordingly, following a collaboration with the composer Philip Glass on a work entitled *One Thousand Airplanes on the Roof*, he worked primarily on film scripts, including a planned screen adaptation of *M. Buttterfly*. In 1992, his one-act play entitled *Bondage* opened in Louisville, Kentucky. *Bondage*, like *The House of Sleeping Beauties*, is set in an exotic brothel: one that caters to sadomasochists, where a dominating female is paid to humiliate a male clientele. The play begins with Terri, the female dominatrix, in a session with Mark; both are covered from head to toe in black leather so that their faces as well as their ethnic identities are concealed from the audience. The play consists of a fantasy game in which their races continually change, further exploring themes of gender, racial, and political stereotyping, as well as the intricate power relationships that Hwang continues to dramatize with startling, provocative, and highly original theatrical effectiveness.

Other major work

TELEPLAY: *My American Son*, 1987.

Bibliography

Bernstein, Richard. "France Jails Two in Odd Case of Espionage." *The New York Times*, May 11, 1986, p. K7. The original news account on which *M. Butterfly* is based. It recounts the sentencing for espionage of

Bernard Bouriscot, a forty-one-year-old French diplomat, and Chinese opera singer Shi Peipeu. During their twenty-year relationship, Bouriscot mistakenly believed Peipeu was a woman. He also believed they had a son, Shi Dudu.

Gerard, Jeremy. "David Hwang: Riding on the Hyphen." *The New York Times Magazine*, March 13, 1988, 44, and 88-89. This biographical profile, preceding the Broadway debut of *M. Butterfly*, focuses on Hwang's crossover from ethnic to mainstream commercial theater with a play that violates conventions of commercial theater in its treatment of sexism, racism, and imperialism, plus its inclusion of Chinese opera, its scandalous plot, and its brief nudity. Hwang comments on the self-doubt that accompanied his sudden fame.

Hwang, David Henry. "*M. Butterfly*: An Interview with David Henry Hwang." Interview by John Lewis DiGaetani. *The Drama Review: A Journal of Performance Studies*, 33, no. 3 (Fall, 1989): 141-153. In this extensive interview, Hwang discusses *M. Butterfly*, Edward W. Said's *Orientalism* (1978), the mutual misperceptions of West and East embodied in Giacomo Puccini's *Madame Butterfly*, and his play's implications about homosexuality, heterosexuality, and fantasy in love. He also suggests that René Gallimard knows "at some level" that his lover is a man. Photographs.

Pace, Eric. "I Write Plays to Claim a Place for Asian-Americans." *The New York Times*, July 12, 1981, p. D4. This biographical profile was published shortly after *The Dance and the Railroad* opened in New York. Among his attributes as a playwright, Hwang discusses his ability to listen to people with opposite views and empathize with both, his interest in myth and legend, and his concern that Chinese-American characters be presented not as polemics but as people.

Skloot, Robert. "Breaking the Butterfly: The Politics of David Henry Hwang." *Modern Drama* 33, no. 1 (March, 1990): 59-66. Skloot discusses the ways in which *M. Butterfly* brings its audience "into complicity with the discovery, dismantling, and re-establishment of theatrical illusion." Though within the limits of "old-fashioned playwriting," it also challenges traditional assumptions about gender politics, cultural politics, and theatrical politics, which are discussed in separate sections of the article.

Street, Douglas. *David Henry Hwang.* Boise, Idaho: Boise State University Press, 1989. This fifty-two page study, the first book to have been written on Hwang's work, provides a useful introductory overview of his plays through *M. Butterfly* and contains a concise but detailed biography of the playwright. Bibliography.

William Hutchings

WILLIAM INGE

Born: Independence, Kansas; May 3, 1913
Died: Los Angeles, California; June 10, 1973

Principal drama

To Bobolink, for Her Spirit, pb. 1950 (one act); *Come Back, Little Sheba*, pr., pb. 1950; *Picnic*, pr., pb. 1953 (expansion of the fragmentary "Front Porch"); *Bus Stop*, pr., pb. 1955 (expanded version of his one-act *People in the Wind*, pb. 1962); *The Dark at the Top of the Stairs*, pr., pb. 1957 (originally as *Farther Off from Heaven*, pr. 1947, pb. 1950); *Four Plays by William Inge*, pb. 1958; *The Tiny Closet*, pr. 1959 (in Italy), pb. 1962 (one act); *A Loss of Roses*, pr. 1959, pb. 1960; *The Boy in the Basement*, pb. 1962 (one act); *Bus Riley's Back in Town*, pb. 1962 (one act); *Summer Brave*, pr., pb. 1962 (revision of *Picnic*); *Summer Brave and Eleven Short Plays*, pb. 1962; *Natural Affection*, pr. 1963; *Where's Daddy?*, pr., pb. 1966 (originally as *Family Things*, pr. 1965); *Two Short Plays: The Call, and A Murder*, pb. 1968; *Midwestern Manic*, pb. 1969; *Overnight*, pr. 1969; *Caesarian Operations*, pr. 1972; *The Love Death Plays: Dialogue for Two Men, Midwestern Manic, The Love Death, Venus and Adonis, The Wake, The Star*, pr. 1975.

Other literary forms

William Inge was fundamentally a dramatist. Atlantic/Little, Brown published two of his novels, *Good Luck, Miss Wyckoff* (1970) and *My Son Is a Splendid Driver* (1971). Bantam published his earlier scenario for *Splendor in the Grass* (1961). The manuscript of his final novel, "The Boy from the Circus," was found on a table in his living room after his suicide. The manuscript had been rejected by a New York publisher and returned to him; he had not opened the envelope containing it. His two published novels and his first screenplay are set in Kansas and are populated by the same sort of lonely, frustrated people found in his major dramas.

Achievements

Although Inge cannot be said to have advanced the technique of modern drama, as Eugene O'Neill did, for example, he was the first notable American dramatist to write seriously and sensitively about the Midwest, much in the tradition of Theodore Dreiser and Sherwood Anderson among novelists, of Carl Sandburg and Edgar Lee Masters among poets, and of Grant Wood among painters. Inge's first five Broadway plays—*Come Back, Little Sheba, Picnic, Bus Stop, The Dark at the Top of the Stairs*, and *A Loss of Roses*—are set in the Midwest and examine in believable and accurate detail the pent-up frustrations of living in the sort of midwestern small towns that Inge knew intimately from his childhood and youth.

The Liberty of some of his plays is the Independence, Kansas, of his childhood; great irony underlies his choice of that place-name.

The decade beginning in 1950 was a remarkable one for Inge. It is unique for an unknown playwright to emerge on Broadway with the sort of critical and commercial success that *Come Back, Little Sheba* commanded and then to be able to produce in rapid-fire succession three more commercial triumphs. Inge did just this, following the 1950 production of *Come Back, Little Sheba* with *Picnic* in 1953, *Bus Stop* in 1955, and *The Dark at the Top of the Stairs* in 1957. *Come Back, Little Sheba* ran for 190 performances; the next three plays ran for more than 450 performances apiece.

Come Back, Little Sheba won for its author an award from the New York critics as the most promising playwright of the season. *Picnic* won the Pulitzer Prize, a New York Drama Critics Circle Award, and the Donaldson Award, which it shared with Arthur Miller's *The Crucible* (1953). Even though Inge's next two plays won no awards, they were highly successful. Inge's reputation as a serious dramatist was assured; in addition, his first four full-length plays were made into films that succeeded both critically and commercially.

In 1958, just as Inge crested the wave of popularity to which his first four Broadway plays had brought him, *Four Plays by William Inge* was issued by Random House, which had previously published each of the plays separately. It was followed by Heinemann's British edition in 1960. Inge's next play, *A Loss of Roses*, into whose production the author put a considerable amount of his own money, reached Broadway in 1959 and was rejected by critics and audiences alike. It closed after twenty-five performances, leaving Inge, who was singularly sensitive, severely depressed as well as financially strained.

The failure of *A Loss of Roses* caused Inge to leave New York permanently. At the strong urging of Elia Kazan, a close friend since he had directed *The Dark at the Top of the Stairs*, Inge moved to the West Coast and turned his talents to screenwriting. His first attempt, *Splendor in the Grass*, which Warner Bros. produced, again focused on small-town midwestern life and was so successful that it received the Academy Award for Best Original Screenplay of 1961.

Splendor in the Grass was to be Inge's last artistic triumph. He followed it in 1963 with *Natural Affection*, which played on Broadway for only thirty-six performances and was the subject of even harsher criticism than *A Loss of Roses* had received. Hurt and distraught, Inge returned to California, where he worked on screenplays. He also did a final original screenplay, based on one of his one-act plays entitled *Bus Riley's Back in Town*, about which he wrote (in a letter to R. Baird Shuman of May 20, 1965): "As for *Bus Riley*, the picture is a loss. I took my name off it. I haven't even seen the version they are showing."

Inge died a broken and defeated man, convinced that he had nothing more to say. His legacy to American drama is nevertheless great. He dealt with the Midwest as had no American playwright before him. As his close friend Tennessee Williams had focused dramatic attention on the South, so had Inge focused dramatic attention on the Midwest. He created a gallery of memorable characters, particularly female characters, because he understood the female mind remarkably well.

Inge's Broadway successes and his screenplay for *Splendor in the Grass* have secured his position as an American dramatist. Although he generally lacked the pioneering genius and willingness to experiment with form of a Eugene O'Neill, a Clifford Odets, or a Tennessee Williams, Inge still ranks high among the significant contributors to American theater in the twentieth century.

Biography

William Inge's understanding of the female personality is not surprising in view of the fact that he came from an emphatically female-dominated home. As the youngest of Luther Clayton and Maude Sarah Gibson Inge's five children, Inge identified more closely with his mother and sisters than he did with males. His father was a traveling salesman who spent little time at home during Inge's formative years. The young Inge, much dominated by his mother, early developed an interest in acting, largely through his initial school experiences with recitation.

Popular as a teenager, Inge was a cheerleader and was active in his high school's dramatic programs. He enjoyed acting and continued his studies after high school at the University of Kansas, where he majored in drama and frequently acted in university productions. Still provincially midwestern at the time of his college graduation, Inge feared going to New York to pursue his first love, acting, and went instead to George Peabody College for Teachers in Nashville to prepare for teacher certification and to take a master's degree in education. Inge taught high school for one year in Columbus, Kansas, where he surely met numerous teachers such as those he depicts with such accuracy in *Picnic* and students such as those in *Splendor in the Grass*. For the next ten years, except for a crucial three years as art, music, book, and drama critic for the St. Louis *Star-Times*, Inge taught English and drama at the college level, first at Stephens College in Columbia, Missouri, and then at Washington University in St. Louis.

It was the crucial years away from teaching, from 1943 to 1946, that led Inge into his career as a playwright. In his position as a three-year replacement for a friend on the *Star-Times* who had been drafted, Inge interviewed Tennessee Williams, who was resting at his parents' home in St. Louis after the 1944 Chicago opening of *The Glass Menagerie*. A friendship blossomed, and Williams persuaded Inge to do some serious writing. *Far-

ther Off from Heaven, the prototype for *The Dark at the Top of the Stairs*, was the result, and in 1947, Margo Jones, whom Inge had met through Williams, produced the play in her theater in Dallas. The production was well received, and Inge was encouraged by its success to continue writing. By 1949, he had abandoned teaching in order to devote himself fully to his writing.

During this period, Inge had become a heavy drinker, and in 1948, he joined Alcoholics Anonymous. Through his association with this organization, he came to understand much more about alcoholism and about alcoholics, information which finds its way directly into *Come Back, Little Sheba* in the person of Doc Delaney, the play's frustrated protagonist.

Similarly, Inge, continually beset by depression, self-doubt, and concern about his homosexuality, which he was never able to accept, began a course of psychoanalysis in 1949, and he was in and out of analysis through the 1950's. Although one may question whether psychoanalysis made Inge any better able to cope with his own fears and frustrations, its influences and effects are clearly seen throughout his work, particularly in *A Loss of Roses*, *Natural Affection*, and *Where's Daddy?*

Despite the successes he had known, by 1973 Inge felt that he was "written out," that he had nothing more to say. Although he enjoyed his work in theater workshops at the University of California campuses at Los Angeles and Irvine and was successful in them, he was unable to deal with the artistic frustrations that plagued him, and on June 10, 1973, he took his own life.

Analysis

All of William Inge's best instincts as a playwright are at work in *Come Back, Little Sheba*, the story of Doc and Lola Delaney, who are twenty years into a marriage that was forced upon them when the eighteen-year-old Lola became pregnant while the promising young Doc was a medical student. Their hasty marriage was followed by Doc's dropping out of medical school and becoming a chiropractor as well as by the loss of the baby through the bungling of a midwife, to whom Lola went because she was too embarrassed to go to an obstetrician. Lola ends up sterile and, as the action of the play begins, fat and unattractive. Doc has become an alcoholic, but as the play opens, he has been dry for a year.

Come Back, Little Sheba is a study in contrasts. It presents thesis and antithesis but seldom any satisfying or convincing synthesis, which makes it a sound piece of realistic writing. Little Sheba is Lola's lost puppy, who "just vanished one day—vanished into thin air." More than representing a surrogate child, Little Sheba represents Lola's lost youth, and only when Lola stops looking for Sheba is it clear that some resolution has taken place, even though the resolution is not presented as a cure-all for Doc and

Lola Delaney's problems.

The play revolves largely around four characters: Doc; Lola; Marie, their boarder; and Turk, the recurring priapic figure whom Inge later used to keep the action moving in *Picnic* and in other of his plays. Marie, although she is engaged to someone else, is having a brief affair with Turk (significantly, a javelin thrower) prior to the arrival of her fiancé from out of town. Lola is titillated by this tawdry affair and actively encourages it, even though she is planning to fix a special meal for Marie's fiancé, Bruce, when he arrives. Doc, who sees Marie as the daughter he never had, is appalled by the whole misadventure. He falls off the wagon and gets roaring drunk. His drunk scene, in which he threatens passionately to hack off all of Lola's fat, cut off Marie's ankles, and castrate Turk, is the dramatic climax of the play; but he falls into a drunken stupor before he can accomplish any of these vile deeds and is taken off to the drunk tank. So terrified is he by the drunk tank that he returns home chastened, but not before Lola has attempted to go home to her aging parents, only to be rebuffed when she telephones them with her request that they allow her to come home for a while.

As the play ends, Doc pleads with Lola, "Don't ever leave me. *Please* don't ever leave me. If you do, they'd have to keep me down at that place [the drunk tank] all the time." Doc and Lola are back together, not for very positive reasons, but rather because neither has any real alternative.

The characterization and the timing in this play are superb; the control is sure and steady. The business of the play is well taken care of early in the action as Lola, a lonely woman unhappy with herself and with what she has become, talks compulsively to anyone who will listen—the milkman, the postman, the next-door neighbor, and Mrs. Coffman, who in contrast to Lola is neat, clean, and well-organized, as a woman with seven children needs to be. Lola tells the audience all they need to know about her history while convincing them of her loneliness by reaching out desperately to anyone who comes into her purview. The resolution for Lola comes in the last act, when she begins to clean up the house, pay attention to her appearance, and write a note for the milkman rather than lurk to engage him in conversation.

Lola's dream sequences, which hold up quite well psychologically, are skillfully used to handle more of the necessary business of the play. The final dream has to do with Turk and the javelin, which Turk has already described as "a big, long lance. You hold it like this, erect." In Lola's dream, Turk is disqualified in the javelin throwing contest and Doc picks up the javelin "real careful, like it was awful heavy. But you threw it, Daddy, clear, *clear*, up into the sky. And it never came down." Inge's exposure to Freudian psychoanalysis certainly pervades the dream sequences.

Inge does not give the audience an upbeat or hopeful ending in *Come*

Back, Little Sheba; rather, he presents life as it is. Perhaps Lola has matured a little. Perhaps both she and Doc have gained some insights that will help them to accept their lives with a bit more resignation than they might otherwise have, but nothing drastic is likely to happen for either of them. They will live on, wretchedly dependent upon each other. If their marriage lasts, as it probably will, the mortar that holds it together will be dependence more than love. At least Lola has faced reality sufficiently to say, "I don't think Little Sheba's ever coming back, Doc," and to stop searching for her.

Inge's second Broadway success, *Picnic*, started as a fragmentary play, "Front Porch," that Inge wrote shortly after *Farther Off from Heaven*. The original play consisted of little more than character sketches of five women in a small Kansas town. The play grew into *Picnic*, a much more fully developed play, and finally into *Summer Brave*, which is little different from *Picnic* except in the resolution of the Madge-Hal conflict.

Four of the five women in *Picnic* live in one house. They are Flo Owens; her two daughters, Millie, a sixteen-year-old tomboy, and Madge, the prettiest girl in town; and their boarder, Rosemary Sydney, a schoolteacher in her thirties. Madge is engaged to marry Alan Seymour. Their next-door neighbor is sixty-year-old Helen Potts, who also participates in the action of the play. These women are all sexually frustrated; although Madge and Rosemary both have suitors, the relationships are specifically delineated as nonsexual.

Into this tense setting is introduced an incredibly handsome male animal, Hal Carter, who exudes sexuality. As insecure as he is handsome, Hal is down on his luck and has arrived in town looking for his friend Alan Seymour, who might be able to give him a job. Hungry, he exchanges some work in Helen Potts's yard for a meal. He works bare-chested, much to the consternation of the women, whose upbringing decrees that they feign shock at this display but whose natural impulses are in conflict with their conservative upbringing.

Hal, reminiscent of Turk in *Come Back, Little Sheba*, causes chaos, as might be expected. The play focuses on the women, and Hal serves as the catalyst. Inge's ability to draw convincing characters, particularly female characters, is particularly evident in *Picnic*. He maintains his clear focus on the women in the play, using Hal precisely as he needs to in order to reveal these women as the psychologically complex beings they are. Never does the focus slip; never does the control over material and characters waver.

As the action develops toward a climax in the second act, Hal's physical presence more than anything else pushes the conflict to its dramatically necessary outcome. Millie and Rosemary start drinking from Hal's liquor bottle after Hal turns his attention from Millie to her more mature sister. Both Millie and Rosemary are soon drunk. Flo vents her own frustrations by upbraiding the two of them, but not before Rosemary, humiliated that Hal is not available to her and distressed that she finds him so attractive, shrieks at him that he came from the gutter and that he will return to the gutter. This emotional scene heightens Hal's insecurity, which is necessary if the play is to proceed convincingly to a love affair between Hal and Madge, an outcome that seems inevitable.

The screaming fit also forces Rosemary to face reality and to realize that her erstwhile suitor, Howard, is probably her only realistic out if she is not to continue teaching and if she is not to become frustrated and grow old alone. She goes off with Howard and yields to him, after which she asks, then begs him to marry her. In the play's final version, he will go only so far as to say that he will come back in the morning but when he does, Rosemary has already spread the news that she and Howard are going to marry, so that when Howard arrives, everyone congratulates him, and he has no choice but to leave with Rosemary, presumably to marry her. Inge is intrigued by the theme of forced marriage, which recurs in nearly all of his major plays, and *Picnic* offers a striking variation on the theme.

Back at the picnic, Alan and Hal have engaged in fisticuffs and Alan has reported Hal to the police, forcing him to leave town in order to avoid arrest. In *Summer Brave*, Hal leaves and Madge stays behind; at the urging of Joshua Logan, Inge changed the ending of the play, so that in *Picnic*, Madge packs her suitcase and follows Hal a short time after his forced departure.

Bus Stop, despite its popular acceptance, does not have the stature of *Come Back, Little Sheba* or *Picnic*. An expanded version of Inge's one-act *People in the Wind*, *Bus Stop* is set in a small crossroads restaurant between Kansas City and Wichita, where the passengers on a bus are stranded because of a blizzard. Among the passengers is Bo Decker, a twenty-one-year-old cowpoke from Montana who is traveling with Virgil Blessing, a middle-aged father surrogate (suggestive of Pinky in *Where's Daddy?*), and with a brainless little singer, Cherie, whom he met in a Kansas City nightclub, where she was performing. Bo was pure until he met Cherie, but now, in a comical role-reversal, he has lost his virginity to her and is insisting that she return to Montana with him to make him an honest man. Cherie joins Bo and Virgil, and they are on their way west when the bus is forced by the weather to pull off the road.

Cherie has second thoughts about going to Montana, and after thinking the matter over, she accuses Bo of abducting her and the police become involved in the situation. Bo has a fight with the sheriff. He is humiliated and apologizes to everyone in the restaurant, including Cherie. Before the play is over, however, Bo asks Cherie to marry him, she agrees, and they set out for Montana, leaving Virgil Blessing behind and alone.

The development of *Bus Stop* is thin, and the characterization, particularly of Bo, is not close to the high level reached in *Come Back, Little Sheba* and *Picnic*. Although Bo is similar in many ways to Turk and Hal, he is made of cardboard and lacks the multidimensional elements that make Turk and Hal convincing.

The play is stronger in the presentation of its minor characters, particularly the lonely, frustrated Grace, a middle-aged woman who lives at the small crossroads where the bus has stopped and who works the night shift in the restaurant. She has sex with a truck driver not because she loves him but because he keeps her from being lonely. In the end, she and Virgil Blessing are left alone in the restaurant. The bus has pulled out, and one might think that Grace and Virgil are the answer to each other's loneliness, but Inge does not provide a double resolution in this play. He permits Bo and Cherie to leave on a somewhat optimistic note, much as he allowed Hal and Madge a future in *Picnic*, but he wisely backs off from providing the pat resolution that a romance between Grace and Virgil would have provided, because the psychological motivation for such a relationship has not been built sufficiently throughout the play.

The original play, *People in the Wind*, contained two characters who were not included in *Bus Stop*. They are two older women, apparently both unmarried and seemingly sisters, who are going to visit their niece. It appears that they want the niece to take them in in their old age, but they are not sure she will do so. They are nervous, drinking bicarbonate of soda to calm their stomachs. They represent the fate that can befall people who do not form close family ties early in their lives. In dropping them from *Bus Stop*, Inge was clearly opting to make the focus of the later play love rather than loneliness, which was the central focus of *People in the Wind*.

The Dark at the Top of the Stairs, the finished version of *Farther Off from Heaven*, is Inge's most autobiographical play. In it, the author returns to a plot centering on a family, and this time, it is clearly Inge's own family that he is writing about. Rubin Flood is a harness salesman who travels a great deal, leaving his children, Sonny and Reenie, in a mother-dominated home. The setting is a small town in Oklahoma.

Inge, who had been in psychoanalysis for several years when he wrote *The Dark at the Top of the Stairs*, paid particular attention to the Oedipal elements of the mother-son relationship in this play and in two subsequent plays, *A Loss of Roses* and *Natural Affection*, although not with the success that he achieved in this earlier presentation.

Rubin Flood and his wife, Cora, were married early, propelled into marriage by Rubin's unmanageable libido. The marriage has encountered difficulties, which come to a head when Rubin, having lost his job—a fact he keeps from his wife—discovers that Cora has bought Reenie an expensive dress for a dance given at the country club by the nouveau riche Ralstons. He demands that the dress be returned for a refund, and a heated argument ensues, during which Cora taunts Rubin to strike her. He obliges and then leaves, vowing never to return. In act 2, Cora's sister, Lottie, and her dentist husband, Morris, have arrived for a visit. Cora hopes that she will be able to persuade Lottie to take her and the children in now that Rubin has abandoned them. In this scene, also, Reenie's blind date for the dance, Sammy Goldenbaum, arrives. A cadet at a nearby military academy, Sammy is meticulously polite and none too secure. His exquisite manners charm Lottie and Morris before he and the pathologically shy Reenie depart for the dance. Once at the dance, Reenie introduces Sammy to the hostess, who is drunk, and Reenie leaves the dance, not telling Sammy she is going. He tries to find her but cannot.

In act 3, Reenie's friend Flirt appears with the news that Sammy took the train to Oklahoma City, rented a hotel room, and killed himself, presumably because the drunken Mrs. Ralston, on discovering that Sammy was Jewish, had asked him to leave the party. Sammy's suicide forces the principal characters to reconsider their lives, and the play ends somewhat on the upbeat. Rubin has returned home. He is tamed, as is evidenced by the fact that he confesses to Cora, "I'm scared. I don't know how I'll make out. I . . . I'm scared," and that he leaves his boots outside, not wanting to dirty up Cora's clean house.

Sonny Flood, who has been an obnoxious child throughout the play, apparently has turned the corner by the end of it. He volunteers to take his distraught sister to the movies, and when his mother tries to kiss him good-bye, he declines to kiss her, giving the audience an indication that his Oedipal tendencies are now coming under control.

Inge tried to do something daring in *The Dark at the Top of the Stairs*, and although he failed, it was a creditable attempt. He juggled two significant conflicts, the Rubin-Cora conflict and the Sammy-society conflict. As the play developed, the conflict involving the suicide was not sufficiently prepared for to be wholly believable. Inge's admitted purpose was to use the suicide subplot to divert the attention of the audience from the conflict between Rubin and Cora, so that they could return to this conflict in the last act with a fresher view.

The suicide subplot has been severely attacked by critics. It is, however, a serious misinterpretation to view the suicide as an event which the author intended to present realistically. It can succeed only as a symbol, serving the useful function of promoting the resolution of the main conflict. This is not to justify the suicide subplot, which is a weakness in the play, but rather to demonstrate the artistic purposes Inge envisioned for it.

None of Inge's later plays achieved the standard of his four Broadway successes. Some of his most interesting work is found in his one-act plays, fourteen of which are available in print. Had Inge lived longer, probably some of the materials in these plays would have lent themselves to further development as full-length dramas; particularly notable are *To Bobolink, for Her Spirit, The Tiny Closet,* and *The Boy in the Basement.*

Inge understood both the people and the social order of the Midwest, particularly the matriarchal family structure common to much of the area. Inge's midwestern plays reverberate with authenticity. His first four Broadway plays depict their commonplace characters with extraordinary sensitivity, building through accounts of their prosaic lives toward a pitch of frustration that is communicated to audiences with enormous impact. By capturing so deftly this pervasive sense of frustration, Inge presents the universal which must be a part of any successful drama. Audiences left Inge's early plays with an internalized sense of the gnawing isolation and conflict that his characters experienced. This is his legacy to American drama.

Other major works

NOVELS: *Good Luck, Miss Wyckoff,* 1970; *My Son Is a Splendid Driver,* 1971.

SCREENPLAYS: *Splendor in the Grass,* 1961; *All Fall Down,* 1962; *Bus Riley's Back in Town,* 1964.

Bibliography

Centola, Steven R. "Compromise as Bad Faith: Arthur Miller's *A View from the Bridge* and William Inge's *Come Back, Little Sheba.*" *Midwest Quarterly* 28 (Autumn, 1986): 100-113. A Freudian analysis of Arthur Miller's and Inge's themes and characters in these two plays. Focuses on the "corrosive effect" of compromise when linked to sexual repression. Notes the irony of Sigmund Freud's assertion that repression is necessary to safeguard society when juxtaposed to Miller and Inge's picture of the destructive effects of repression in their characters' lives.

McClure, Arthur F. *Memories of Splendor: The Midwestern World of William Inge.* Topeka: Kansas State Historical Society, 1989. The focus is the "regional quality" of Inge's work. Unusual features include photographs and posters from stage and film productions (some in color) and reminiscences from those who served as models for Inge's characters and from actors who played them. Information on Kansan memorials to Inge underscore his midwestern roots.

McClure, Arthur F., and C. David Rice, eds. *A Bibliographical Guide to the Works of William Inge, 1913-1973.* Lewiston, N.Y.: Edwin Mellen Press, 1991. An attempt to "present a complete picture of Inge's work as a teacher, journalist and author." Divided into works by Inge, including his journalistic articles and reviews; biographical information, among them obituaries; critical articles and reviews of Inge's work; and brief chapters on his forays into film and television. Sporadic annotations.

Shuman, R. Baird. *William Inge.* Rev. ed. Boston: Twayne, 1989. An updated version of Shuman's 1965 book, this volume focuses primarily on summarizing and analyzing the plays. Shuman's stated goal is "to present a balanced view of William Inge and . . . show the inroads . . . public expectations make upon the private and creative life" of a sensitive artist. Index, select bibliography.

Voss, Ralph F. *A Life of William Inge.* Lawrence: University Press of Kansas, 1989. A carefully researched "reconstruction" of Inge's life, with numerous photographs, most of Inge at various stages of life. Voss's examination reveals a troubled man whose life was a "pattern" of secrecy, especially concerning his homosexuality and alcoholism. Voss concludes, " 'Inge Country' was never just the state of Kansas or the midwestern prairies . . . [but] almost always a troubled state of mind."

R. Baird Shuman
(Updated by *Elsie Galbreath Haley*)

ALBERT INNAURATO

Born: Philadelphia, Pennsylvania; June 2, 1948

Principal drama

Urlicht, pr. 1971, pb. 1980; *I Don't Generally Like Poetry but Have You Read "Trees"?*, pr. 1972 (with Christopher Durang); *The Life Story of Mitzi Gaynor: Or, Gyp*, pr. 1973 (with Durang); *Wisdom Amok*, pr. 1973?, pb. 1980; *The Transfiguration of Benno Blimpie*, pr. 1973, pb. 1976; *The Idiots Karamazov*, pr., pb. 1974, augmented pb. 1981 (with Durang, music by Jack Feldman, lyrics by Durang); *Earth Worms*, pr. 1974, pb. 1980; *Gemini*, pr. 1976, pb. 1977; *Ulysses in Traction*, pr. 1977, pb. 1978; *Passione*, pr. 1980, pb. 1981; *Bizarre Behavior: Six Plays*, pb. 1980; *Coming of Age in Soho*, pr., pb. 1985; *Best Plays of Albert Innaurato*, pb. 1987; *Magda and Callas*, pb. 1989; *Gus and Al*, pr., pb. 1989.

Other literary forms

In addition to his dramatic works, Albert Innaurato has become a regular reviewer of, and commentator on, opera, publishing articles about directors and reviews of recordings in *The New York Times*. He has also written several teleplays, including *Verna, USO Girl* (1978) and *Coming Out* (1989).

Achievements

Innaurato enjoyed enormous popularity with the simultaneous success of *Gemini* and *The Transfiguration of Benno Blimpie* in 1977: Both plays received Obie Awards. Since that time, Innaurato has struggled to fulfill the high expectations of his audience, and none of his subsequent efforts has met the high level of critical acclaim that the earlier plays enjoyed. Innaurato has received Rockefeller and Guggenheim grants and has served as resident playwright at the Circle Repertory Company and The Public Theater. *Coming of Age in Soho* underwent a widely publicized revision during the course of its Public Theater production and received a measure of praise, as did his next play *Gus and Al*. Nevertheless, Innaurato continues to be remembered for his first two New York productions, which established his place as an important contemporary dramatist.

Biography

Albert Innaurato was born and reared in Philadelphia, the son of Italian immigrants. The ethnic world of south Philadelphia provides the background for his most successful plays; though precise autobiographical parallels have not been revealed by Innaurato, the events and characters in the plays are transformations of his own experiences and acquaintances. His portrayals of Italian-American life are sufficiently realistic that Innaurato's opinions about ethnic identity have been sought out by reporters.

Many of Innaurato's plays were begun when he was quite young; a version of *Urlicht*, for example, dates from his late teens. He continued to write prolifically during his undergraduate years at Temple University, where he received his B.A. Many of these early works were lost or destroyed, though some of the titles are known. Innaurato develops scripts rather slowly, so some of the material may eventually surface again in new plays.

Perhaps the most persistent early influence on Innaurato was his taste for opera. He taught himself to play the piano and made some early experiments in operatic composition, but its influence lingers mostly through frequent allusions to opera in plays such as *Gemini* and in the leitmotif structure of the plays, which also feature set speeches designed as arias. Innaurato collects opera recordings and has written about his fascination with the form for *The New York Times*.

After attending Temple University, an experience transposed into *Ulysses in Traction*, the young writer spent a year at the California Institute of the Arts. His education there was unsettling, causing him to question his assumptions about art, politics, and society, and he left the school to return to the East Coast.

During the early 1970's, Innaurato studied playwriting at Yale University under Howard Stein and Jules Feiffer. The discipline of regular writing and constructive feedback seems to have provided an unusually productive routine for Innaurato, who developed his serious dramatic talents in plays such as *Earth Worms*. Feiffer's influence seems important to Innaurato's development as a satirist, too—his concern for grotesque, seriocomic characters who exist beyond social conventions.

Equally important to Innaurato's development at Yale was his association with Christopher Durang. The two young writers shared a virulent anti-Catholicism, most concisely demonstrated in the famous monologue by the title character of Durang's play *Sister Mary Ignatius Explains It All for You* (1979). Durang is more important to Innaurato for having collaborated with him on a number of madcap comic satires. The ridiculous mayhem of *Gemini* does not seem eccentric in Innaurato's oeuvre when considered in relation to plays such as *The Idiots Karamazov*, *I Don't Generally Like Poetry but Have You Read "Trees"?*, and *The Life Story of Mitzi Gaynor: Or, Gyp*, all written during the Yale years with Durang. These works also provided the experience with allusion and the manipulation of theatrical conventions that Innaurato used later in *Ulysses in Traction*.

In 1974, Innaurato was graduated from Yale with a master of fine arts degree in playwriting. He had also directed and acted in some of the plays, which even in their student productions featured talented, capable casts. His work was published in Yale's *Theater* magazine and was produced by the Yale Repertory Theatre. Some of his plays also received readings and critical feedback at the Yale summer session, the O'Neill Theater Center's National Playwrights' Conference.

In 1975, Innaurato received a Guggenheim Fellowship and began his career as a full-time playwright. The first production of *Gemini*, at the PAF playhouse in Huntington, Long Island, was so successful that a subsequent production was arranged at the Circle Rep. When this Off-Broadway staging was acclaimed by critics, the play was moved downtown to a small Broadway house where it ran for 1,778 performances. This bona fide hit, following close upon the heels of a heralded performance by James Coco as Benno Blimpie, made Innaurato the most talked-about young playwright of the season. His work received especially close scrutiny from the gay press, where Innaurato's theme of sexual confusion was furiously debated.

In the mid-1970's, Innaurato's progress became uneven as he tried to support his playwriting activity through a series of odd jobs, including work as a commentator on opera broadcasts and as a television writer. *Ulysses in Traction* was very coolly received, as were productions of some of the early plays. Innaurato directed the Playwrights' Horizons production of *Passione* in 1980, which was then transferred to Broadway, with Frank Langella supervising the performance. The personal financial and health problems that have slowed Innaurato's production were eventually made public in 1985, during his work with Joseph Papp on the production of *Coming of Age in Soho*. Still, Innaurato's commitment to dramatic writing seems strong, and he continued to produce new material—two plays in 1989—despite the lack of a major later success and his continuing public statements against the power structure of the critical press in New York.

Analysis

Albert Innaurato's plays alternate in their effect from farcical comedy to unrelenting pathos. The consistent aspect of his work is not a matter of genre or formula, but one of theatrical style. Innaurato populates his plays with grotesque misfits, vivid personalities that depart from traditional theatrical types. The settings are drawn from contemporary lower-class dwellings and ground the desires of his sympathetic characters in a run-down atmosphere that predicts their eventual defeat. Actions, too, are frequently grotesque, particularly when the plays' themes combine death, eating, and debased sexuality. Innaurato's vision disturbs and fascinates audiences because he has created new voices for the expression of obsessive concerns, new ways to dramatize important themes through characterization. Innaurato's work is uneven, however, almost equally divided between adeptly constructed scripts that shift cleanly from one scene to the next and plays that diffuse his obsessions into shrill, unfocused energy. If any single work can be said to predict the themes and style of Innaurato's work, it is John Guare's _The House of Blue Leaves_ (1971).

The Innaurato hero is usually unhappy, from a depressed family, sexually confused, but in love with beauty. The most concise expression of this character's unhappiness comes in Innaurato's _The Transfiguration of Benno Blimpie_, perhaps his best work. Benno, "an enormously fat young man," narrates his story while seated on a stool apart from the main acting area. Benno's desire for love and beauty, expressed by his passion for great paintings, is contradicted by everything around him. His combative Italian parents ignore and abuse him, his grandfather carries out a sordid affair with a foul young Irish girl, while Benno, eventually raped by a gang of schoolboys, takes solace in eating.

The performance begins with Benno's announcement that he plans to eat himself to death. The plot then proceeds through a series of flashbacks, which establish in turn the cruelty of his parents, the depravity of his grandfather's sexual activity, and the incongruity of his passion for art. Much of the story is narrated by Benno, who remains stationary and participates in the flashback action only vocally, altering his voice to indicate youth while the other actors behave as if a Benno figure were present in the scene. This choice to disrupt the conventional structure of the acting event causes the behavior of the other characters toward the phantom Benno to be more noticeable than usual. When they ignore his needs and requests, or send him away, the audience is conscious of the theatrical parallel that objectifies his rejection. Once Benno's story is complete, Innaurato repeats the first scene; this time, however, Benno adds a gesture with a cleaver, showing that he will literally eat himself—consume his own body until he dies.

The economy of construction and unrelenting plot progression in _The Transfiguration of Benno Blimpie_ are especially impressive when compared to Innaurato's other early works, such as _Wisdom Amok, Urlicht,_ and _Earth Worms_. In the first two of these plays, Innaurato's anti-Catholic feelings are so virulent that the plays surrender any pretension of credible mimesis to a free-associative, vengeful attack on the Church. Nothing like reality, the plays also fail to achieve any internal, formal coherence, dissolving instead into a disintegrated barrage of images. In _Wisdom Amok_, there are no sympathetic characters; the action begins with grotesquely disrupted public events, then immerses itself in a sacrilegious madhouse. The power and fascination of charismatic madness were important themes in other plays popular at the time of _Wisdom Amok_'s composition, such as Peter Weiss's _Marat/Sade_ (1964), but Innaurato's attempt to explore the plunge of a cleric into insanity and murder sheds no new light on the repressive qualities of religion, nor is his character sufficiently interesting to maintain sympathetic attention. _Urlicht_ is slightly more compact, substituting the extravagance of opera for the decadence of the Church but still surpassing credibility with its grotesque extremes of imagery and action.

In *Earth Worms*, Innaurato's work remains diffuse, but the characters evolve along with the dramatic events to create a number of unique, fascinating personalities. The most flamboyant of these characters is Bernard, an aged transvestite and retired English professor who takes the dominant role in the action, performing a Pygmalion-like transformation on the central female. This character, Mary, who reappears in *Passione* as Aggy, is an uneducated young Appalachian woman who becomes mature enough eventually to push the other crippled characters away. Innaurato's trademark of sexual confusion is stamped not only on the professor but also on Arnold, Mary's serviceman husband. He brings her back to his childhood home, now grown filthy and decayed, then abandons her when his guilt over the death of their child overcomes him. These roles and a few others make *Earth Worms* a fascinating play for actors, and its challenges have been met in the professional production by Robert Goldsby at the Berkeley Stage Company.

The anti-Catholic theme is communicated in a different, symbolic mode in *Earth Worms*. Nuns who resemble Furies or the witches from *Macbeth* terrorize the husband and perform actions that reflect back upon the play's dramatic events. The most terrifying of these is the surreal dance they perform with the dead infant impaled on a cross. Innaurato's alternation of these horrible symbolic gestures with squalid realistic scenes provides a loose form that supplies striking effects almost at random.

In *Gemini*, Innaurato deals with a similar group of people but shows them at an earlier age, when their environment is less decayed, their dreams still intact. This shift, accompanied by the change into a quick, complex, but more conventionally comic dialogue structure, transforms the same themes and grotesque character images into the material of farce. The audience, no longer directly addressed by a Benno figure, gains some perspective on the action; this distance from the bizarre world of Italian south Philadelphia is at least partially supplied by the introduction of two visitors from Harvard. The consternation of these attractive outsiders at the rude characters and strange twists of action guides the audience's response. In addition, Innaurato finally omits his obsessive, distracting attack on Catholicism, allowing full attention to be focused on the construction of the play itself.

The title character of the play, Francis Geminiani, is probably the most autobiographical hero in the playwright's first group of plays. A young Harvard (not Yale) student whose name symbolizes his split sexual inclinations, Francis acts out his sexual indecision in the playwright's old neighborhood. The hero also loves opera, using the music to express his moods and provide inspiration for important decisions. While Francis, like the playwright, thinks that he is pudgy, the genuinely grotesque traits of Benno Blimpie have been foisted off onto Herschel, a young next-door neighbor who is still childish enough that he arouses more laughter than pathos. In the serious plays, all

HENRY JAMES

Born: New York, New York; April 15, 1843
Died: London, England; February 28, 1916

Principal drama

Daisy Miller, pb. 1883 (adaptation of his novel); *The American*, pr. 1891, pb. 1949 (adaptation of his novel); *Theatricals: Tenants and Disengaged*, pb. 1894; *The Reprobate*, pb. 1894, pr. 1919; *Theatricals, Second Series: The Album and The Reprobate*, pb. 1894; *Guy Domville*, pb. 1894 (privately), pr. 1895, pb. 1949; *The High Bid*, pr. 1908, pb. 1949; *The Other House*, wr. 1909, pb. 1949; *The Outcry*, wr. 1909, pr. 1917, pb. 1949; *The Saloon*, pr. 1911 (one act); *The Complete Plays of Henry James*, pb. 1949 (Leon Edel, editor).

Other literary forms

Henry James was a prolific writer, most lauded for his fiction. His best-known novels, on the intersection of American and European manners and morals, include *The American* (1876-1877), *The Europeans* (1878), *Daisy Miller* (1878), *The Portrait of a Lady* (1880-1881), *The Wings of the Dove* (1902), *The Ambassadors* (1903), and *The Golden Bowl* (1904). He combined his study of mannered society with an evaluation of social and political justice in *The Bostonians* (1885-1886) and *The Princess Casamassima* (1885-1886); in *The Tragic Muse* (1889-1890), he produced his one novel about the theater. James also wrote more than one hundred short stories and tales (now collected in Leon Edel's twelve-volume *The Complete Tales of Henry James*, 1962-1964). James was a perceptive critic of his own fiction as well as that of others; his study *The Art of Fiction* (1884) is a seminal work of its kind. He prefaced many of his novels with long discussions of fiction writing (collected by R. P. Blackmur in *The Art of the Novel: Critical Prefaces*, 1934) and wrote essays on other fiction writers, both contemporaries and predecessors, among them Nathaniel Hawthorne (*Hawthorne*, 1879), Honoré de Balzac, Anthony Trollope, George Eliot, Robert Louis Stevenson, Ivan Turgenev, and Charles Dickens. He also wrote theater reviews and essays on playwrights from William Shakespeare to Henrik Ibsen, which are collected in *The Scenic Art* (1948; Allan Wade, editor). James was a major travel writer of his day, contributing his essays on England and Europe to American publications such as *The Nation*, *Atlantic Monthly* and the New York *Tribune.* After a return visit to the United States, he wrote *The American Scene* (1907), a reflection on American life. He wrote a biography of his sculptor friend, *William Wetmore Story and His Friends* (1903), and completed two volumes of memoirs, *A Small Boy and Others* (1913) and *Notes of a Son and Brother* (1914). An edition of his letters has been edited by Leon Edel (*Henry James Letters*, 1974-1984).

Achievements

James's novels detail the complexities of human relationships; his exploration of consciousness and of narrative viewpoints led, in his more mature works, to the psychological realism for which his novels are chiefly remembered. James's reputation as a dramatist never equaled his reputation as a novelist. James saw five of his plays professionally produced and five others published, but of his fifteen completed plays, none was both produced and published during his lifetime. Most of James's plays became a part of English dramatic literature only in 1949, some thirty-three years after James's death, when they were collected by Leon Edel in *The Complete Plays of Henry James*. Consequently, James's importance as a playwright stems neither from influential productions nor from timely publications. He is a minor but unique figure in English-language drama, valuable for his ability to treat common turn-of-the-century dramatic themes and forms in an uncommon way. While he borrowed liberally from the French well-made drama he admired, his plays are best understood as English comedies of manners. James took the British stage tradition of William Congreve, William Wycherley, Sir George Etherege, Oliver Goldsmith, and Richard Brinsley Sheridan, refined its upper-class milieu, and in doing so clarified the comedy of manners' conflation of manners and morals. As James's characters struggle for a livable synthesis of manners and morals, James focuses on understanding the special social skills, limitations, and perceptions of women. James realized the full dramatic potential of his innovative comedy of manners only once, in *The High Bid*, a play which stands as an emblem of his successful distillation of the dramatic tradition. While James's plays often suffer from oblique dialogue, melodrama, and flimsy plots, his dramatic works that came after *The American* are generally more graceful and are often more substantial than is the successful West End fare of such contemporaries as Arthur Wing Pinero and Henry Arthur Jones.

James's theater interests were encouraged by such important figures as actresses Elizabeth Robins and Fanny Kemble, writer and producer Harley Granville-Barker, and playwright George Bernard Shaw; his work was commissioned by the actress Ellen Terry and by producer-managers Augustin Daly, Charles Frohman, Edward Compton, Sir John Hare, and Sir Johnston Forbes-Robertson. James's achievements as a playwright, however, remain limited. While his plays are stageable (two were successfully produced in London in the late 1960's), his work has found success on television, stage, and screen only through the adaptations of his fiction by other writers. When he first edited James's plays, Leon Edel suggested that they were most important as experiments in the "dramatic method" which enabled James to write his last novels. Many critics join Edel in finding the plays most important as adjuncts to James's fiction.

Biography

Henry James, Jr., was the second of five children born to Mary Robertson Walsh and Henry James, Sr. A friend of Ralph Waldo Emerson and a follower of the Swedish philosopher-theologian Emanuel Swedenborg, Henry James, Sr., advocated a "sensuous" rearing of his children. This amounted to showering his five children with educational opportunities and encouraging them to adopt an individual morality. While much of the young James's education occurred at home and through extensive foreign travel (his first trip abroad came when he was five months old and was followed by several more stays during his childhood and adolescence), he also had tutors and attended various schools in the United States and in Europe, including Harvard Law School. James's family was of great importance to him throughout his life. He was close to his parents until they died in 1882 and remained close to his siblings—especially William, his older brother and greatest rival, who gained fame as a psychologist and philosopher, and his only sister, Alice, whom James helped care for during her many long illnesses. The frequent, long, newsy, philosophical letters which passed between James and his brother and sister suggest the interests, love, and concern the three shared.

When James traveled to Europe in 1872 at the age of twenty-nine, he began the first of his extended stays abroad. He lived in the United States only for brief stretches of time after this, settling permanently in Europe in 1875. His preference for foreign residency led him, in 1915, the year before his death, to become a naturalized British citizen. James spent the longest stretches of time in England—both in London, where he set up several residences, and in Rye, Sussex, where he took out a long lease on Lamb House. He also paid lengthy visits to France and Italy. James documented such foreign living in the many travel pieces he wrote for American readers but put it to best use in his fiction and drama, where the American abroad and the clash of American and European manners were his special terrain. During his early years in the United States and abroad, James published stories, reviews, essays, and novels while he developed important literary friendships with William Dean Howells, Henry Adams, Robert Louis Stevenson, Ivan Turgenev, Gustave Flaubert, and Émile Zola.

From the publication of his first novel, *Roderick Hudson*, in 1875, the greatest share of James's life was devoted to his fiction writing. Writing was a daily concern, for most of James's work, even his novels, appeared first in magazines such as *Macmillan's Magazine*, *Century Magazine*, *Atlantic Monthly*, and *Harper's Weekly*, which had demanding deadlines. James's preoccupation with his writing was also an aspect of his concern about money; he appears to have had enough money to live comfortably, but he constantly worried about income and expenses. The course of his career has generally been measured by the fluctuating success of his fiction. James gained his early reputation from novels such as *The American, Daisy Miller*, and *The Portrait of a Lady*, in which he developed his world of cross-cultural confrontations and integration. During the 1880's, however, with the publication of the more overtly political novels *The Bostonians* and *The Princess Casamassima*, James lost public favor. While production of his stories continued to be prolific, it was in the first decade of the new century, with the publication of his last, long novels—*The Wings of the Dove, The Ambassadors*, and *The Golden Bowl*—that he gained his stature as "the Master." James's American tour in 1904, when he returned after a twenty-one-year absence, occasioned *The American Scene*, a volume of essays on his homeland. From 1907 to 1909, James prepared the prefaces and revisions of his life's work for the twenty-four volumes of the New York edition, issued by Scribner's. Although sales of this collected edition disappointed James, his literary reputation had been secured.

While producing novels, stories, travel pieces, reviews, and critical essays, James also managed a full social life. He was a welcome guest at English country-house weekends and a seemingly essential addition to American expatriate households in London, Paris, Rome, Florence, and Venice. His friendships with Americans James Russell Lowell (United States ambassador to Great Britain), Grace Norton and the Curtises (Bostonian socialites), Francis Boott and his daughter Lizzie (Bostonians with European art interests), John Singer Sargent and Edwin Abbey (American artists), and others were cemented by extensive correspondence as well as social visits. Late in life, James traveled and corresponded with American novelist Edith Wharton and was neighbor to H. G. Wells. James's brother and sister, William and Alice, remained James's most life-sustaining connections after their parents died in 1882. James traveled in Europe and to the United States to visit and care for both, and he mourned them deeply when they died (Alice in 1892 and William in 1910). James never married, finding marriage anathema to his art, though he was romantically pursued by Constance Fenimore Woolson, a fellow American writer who was James's close friend from 1880 to her death in 1894. Late in his life, James had close attachments to several of his young admirers, including Jocelyn Persse, Howard Sturgis, and Hendrik Andersen.

James's interest in the theater culminated in the five years from 1890 to 1895, when he considered himself mainly a playwright, but lasted throughout his life. Some of James's most vivid childhood memories include early trips to Broadway and productions of Shakespeare, Dickens, and Harriet Beecher Stowe's *Uncle Tom's Cabin* (1852). As a teenager, he dabbled in playwriting, and one of his first pieces of critical writing was in response to the absorbing performance of an actress. James's several extended stays in Paris in the 1870's convinced him of the vitality of the French theater, and in his essays on the Théâtre Français and on French playwrights such as

Victorien Sardou and Alexandre Dumas, *fils*, he displayed his respect for the well-made play he would use as an early model for his own drama. After James completed *The Tragic Muse*, his novel about the London theater, he devoted the next five years of his life to theatergoing and playwriting; biographer Leon Edel contends that James never wrote with greater intensity. The embarrassment of the opening night of his play *Guy Domville* in 1895 provoked James to declare that he would never write for theater again, but during the remaining years of his life he continued to write plays, attend the theater regularly, and maintain his friendships with actresses, producers, and playwrights. In 1909, James even found himself lobbying the British Parliament for a relaxation of stage censorship.

Some of James's last writings were memoirs of his childhood, in which he recorded his vivid memories of early theater experiences. He continued to write fiction to the last, leaving two unfinished novels at his death. His final years were shadowed by the outbreak of World War I, which James saw as a negation of the world and the art in which he believed. After he had sustained a stroke in 1915, William James's widow, Alice, and her son and daughter, Harry and Peggy, came from the United States to nurse James until his death in February of 1916. The British government bestowed the Order of Merit on James shortly before he died.

Analysis

Henry James's legacy to drama is a perspective on American and British upper- and middle-class social life that no one else could imitate. He brought to his drama the multicultural understanding that was the basis of his best fiction. Onstage, as in a narrative, he tracked turn-of-the-century Americans and their English counterparts through courtship and marriage, leisure and business, money and art. The drama that resulted was not always successful but was an instructive experiment in dramatic style. Concentrating his effort on the creation of a social milieu where manners function as they should, James offered a world where morality is not a matter of right and wrong but a negotiating between individual wants and society's needs. The two most important components of the milieu, or atmosphere, in James's plays are the women who are in control and the missions of social and moral salvation on which they embark.

James was influenced by two dramatic traditions—those of the French and the English theaters. James's intimate knowledge of French theater that he acquired in Paris convinced him that the well-made play was the model to imitate. In his earliest plays, he tried to approximate the neat plots, the series of climaxes, and the easy identification of right and wrong he found in the French drama. As James himself showed in his comparative studies of English and French drama, however, the French model could not be translated neatly into English. James had often complained of the crude morality of English theater audiences, going so far as to label its tastes immoral, yet as he practiced his own playwriting skills in the 1890's, it became clear that he was finding the English tradition of the comedy of manners as useful a model as the French tradition of the well-made play. Borrowing from the English tradition both a striving to balance opposites and a stylized concentration on wit, social artistry, and women, James wrote his best plays.

James's theater career is divided in two by the ill-fated production of *Guy Domville* in 1895. In the first part of his career, while still in his twenties, James wrote three short plays which were published as short stories, "Pyramus and Thisbe," "Still Waters," and "A Change of Heart," which suggest his attraction to witty, comic dialogue and romantic plots. These were followed by adaptations of his novels *Daisy Miller* and *The American*, the first commissioned for an American production with Daniel Frohman in 1882 but never produced, and the second commissioned by British manager Edward Compton in 1889 and produced in 1891. Neither adaptation was successful, but James's lifelong desire to write for the theater had been awakened and he went on to spend the five years from 1890 to 1895 consumed by drama. These years, which Edel has labeled "the dramatic years," are marked in James's letters, notebooks, and life by the great hopes and disappointments tied to the stage. Although James completed at least six plays and parts of several others during these years, only *The American* and *Guy Domville* were produced. When James was hooted offstage during the curtain call of *Guy Domville* in January of 1895, he pronounced himself done with theater. James's letters of early 1895 are full of his feeling that drama (the written product) must be separated from theater (the onstage product), but, as his later involvement with the theater attests, he could not relinquish the hope of seeing his plays produced. While the second half of James's theater career, after 1895, was not marked by the great energy, commitment, and concentration of the earlier period, the plays of this period are more mature and natural. James wrote an early version of *The High Bid* immediately after the *Guy Domville* debacle and completed four plays after 1895, his best among them.

The failures in James's plays are of two extremes, represented by his earliest (*The American*) and latest (*The Outcry*) full-length dramatic works. When James adapted his novel *The American* for the stage in 1890, his decision to use the French well-made play as a model led him to simplify the cultural collisions of the story, so that in the play, the cultured French become everything bad and the innocent American Christopher Newman is everything good. James's imitation of his French model also produced superfluous entrances and exits and melodramatic dialogue and confrontations, and necessitated the addition of a neat, happy ending. Later, James would build a synthesis out of the meeting of European and American morals by borrowing from the comedy of manners, but in this play he offered only a stalemate. By the time of James's last full-length play, *The Outcry* (written in 1909), he had mastered the basics of dramatic construction, but the play is nevertheless a failure, the wit and repartee of its dialogue obscured by oblique references and convoluted thinking. *The Outcry* is too much art and too little life. James's best plays—*The Reprobate, Guy Domville,* and *The High Bid*—offer believable social milieus and delightful characters and dialogue.

The Reprobate is the best of the four plays James published in 1894 in his two-volume series, *Theatricals: Tenants and Disengaged* and *Theatricals, Second Series: The Album and The Reprobate.* The play's two main characters, Mrs. Freshville and Paul Doubleday, are former lovers who meet by chance at the Hampton Court villa of Mr. Bonsor. Mrs. Freshville is there chasing a new love, Captain Chanter, although she eventually ends up with a third man, Pitt Brunt. Doubleday lives there as a ward of Mr. Bonsor; Doubleday is the "reprobate" of the title, whose past indiscretions have necessitated his now being closely guarded. In the course of the play he matures, aided by both Mrs. Freshville and his new love, Blanche Amber. The play is the earliest example of James's mastery of dramatic form. The tight construction of the play is suspenseful, not artificial, and melodrama has become a technique James uses to good effect at the end of his acts. James has also adapted the milieu of the comedy of manners successfully. The dialogues are enticing mixtures of wit, innuendo, and manipulation, and the comedy-of-manners emphasis on social decorum and romance is believable.

James also developed, in *The Reprobate*, the controlling female character who would become the hallmark of his drama. Mrs. Freshville assumes control of the play's events from her first entrance, displaying her understanding of her social world as one where a person gains power by knowing how to play social games. Blanche Amber is, in many ways, a younger Mrs. Freshville, just learning how her world operates and practicing her newfound social skills. Together, Blanche Amber and Mrs. Freshville direct attention to the issues of the play as they set out to "save" Doubleday. They teach the overprotected Doubleday that social power lies in an understanding of manners, and they teach him how to use that power. By the end of the play, he has learned his lesson well, and his message is James's: Good, bad, and freedom are relative concepts which must be negotiated in the world of manners. The play's first production came in 1919, in London, after James's death. It received both praise and criticism but established the stageworthiness of James's delicate brand of manners comedy.

Guy Domville is the best known of James's dramas, although it is remembered for its melodramatic stage failure rather than its artistic merits. James wrote the play in 1893 for George Alexander, the popular actor-manager of London's fashionable St. James's Theatre, and worked closely with Alexander and his cast during rehearsals. On the play's opening night, January 5, 1895, however, James was too nervous to watch the production of his own play and spent the evening at a production of Oscar Wilde's *An Ideal Husband*. In his absence, James's first act met with great approval, but his second act was jeered, and the third merely tolerated. When James returned to the St. James's Theatre, he was encouraged by Alexander to acknowledge the curtain-call applause, completely unprepared for the vicious disapproval and hooting with which the audience greeted him. He left the stage "green with dismay" (in the words of actor Franklyn Dyall) and vowed to friends that he would abandon the theater altogether. The play continued its run for four weeks and did not, in the end, mark the conclusion of James's playwriting career, but James's attitude to playwriting had been irrevocably changed. He would never again write plays in which he made such a personal investment.

As even the first-night audience knew, however, the play had its merits. Although *Guy Domville* is not a comedy of manners, James had created for this serious drama a mannered milieu which had a grace, charm, and delicacy rare on the English stage. Reviewers including Arthur B. Walkley and George Bernard Shaw, applauded a dialogue that was witty and playful while allowing the characters to discuss the play's serious issues. While the play, like most of James's other plays, has a love interest, that love is a platonic one between Guy Domville, a young man about to enter the Church, and Mrs. Peverel, a widow whose child Guy is tutoring. Instead of detailing this love, James focuses on the choice Guy must make between entering the Church and accepting his family's call to join them in the fast-paced social world. The play is marred by the melodrama of an unbelievable scene in act 2 in which Guy and another character, George Round, feign drunkenness to trick each other, but generally its topics, seriously expressed, are those of James's other plays: the potential artificiality of mannered life, the saving of individual freedom and morality, and the connection between manners and morals. The play is atypical of his work in that it is not a comedy and is not centered on a powerful woman, but it is the first of James's plays in which his central character is portrayed as a social "artist" who masters the "art" of living.

Also in 1895, shortly after the stage failure of *Guy Domville*, James wrote the one-act "Summersoft" for British actress Ellen Terry. Terry never performed the play, but James expanded it to the full three-act play *The High Bid* in 1907 and saw it successfully performed both in Edinburgh and London by Sir Johnston Forbes-Robertson and his company in 1908. The play is James's best because in it he combined the clean dramatic lines that he mastered in his earlier plays with the cultural insights of his last years. The key to the play's success is Mrs. Gracedew, an American widow who uses her position as a cultural outsider to show the play's Britons why their society's traditions and manners are sacred. Mrs. Gracedew comes to Covering End, the family home of Captain Yule, merely to visit, but finds herself obliged to save the majestic home from the greedy Mr. Prodmore. She also saves Prodmore's daughter, Cora, from a bad love match and successfully engineers her own love match with Yule.

Specific structural techniques James had garnered from his long apprenticeship to the well-made play—suspenseful act closings and ups and downs in a character's fortunes—embellish one of the simplest of James's play plots in *The High Bid*. Such simplicity is balanced by the rich comedy-of-manners milieu, with characters aware of decorum and full of politeness and well-timed deference. Because Mrs. Gracedew—as an American—is an outsider to this mannered world, she has learned its ways almost better than the natives. More than any other character, she commands this world of nuance through innuendo and indirection, wit and wordplay. In her, James created his fullest portrait of the social artist and social savior. What Mrs. Gracedew must save is upper-class British society, a mission accomplished in part through her alliance with young Cora, in part by detailing for others, primarily Yule, the ideals of mannered life, which preserve culture and civilization. While the progressive Yule raises important questions about inequities in this system that Mrs. Gracedew defends, she is successful in her mission: She saves a world where manners are morals and life is a delicate art, as James himself sought to save the comedy of manners as a viable dramatic form. In a series of letters that he exchanged with George Bernard Shaw in 1907, James defended his dramatic art as a rarefied and complex image of life, valuable precisely because it challenges audiences to strive for the most that they can possibly achieve in life. In *The High Bid*, James created such a dramatic world, where life is an art worth saving.

Other major works

NOVELS: *Roderick Hudson*, 1875; *The American*, 1876-1877; *The Europeans*, 1878; *Daisy Miller*, 1878; *An International Episode*, 1878-1879; *Confidence*, 1879-1880; *Washington Square*, 1880; *The Portrait of a Lady*, 1880-1881; *The Bostonians*, 1885-1886; *The Princess Casamassima*, 1885-1886; *The Tragic Muse*, 1889-1890; *The Spoils of Poynton*, 1897; *What Maisie Knew*, 1897; *The Awkward Age*, 1897-1899; *The Wings of the Dove*, 1902; *The Ambassadors*, 1903; *The Golden Bowl*, 1904; *The Outcry*, 1911; *The Ivory Tower*, 1917; *The Sense of the Past*, 1917.

SHORT FICTION: *A Passionate Pilgrim*, 1875; *The Madonna of the Future*, 1879; *The Siege of London*, 1883; *Tales of Three Cities*, 1884; *The Author of Beltraffio*, 1885; *The Aspern Papers*, 1888; *The Lesson of the Master*, 1892; *The Real Thing*, 1893; *Terminations*, 1895; *Embarrassments*, 1896; *The Two Magics: The Turn of the Screw and Covering End*, 1898; *The Soft Side*,

1900; *The Better Sort*, 1903; *The Novels and Tales of Henry James*, 1907-1909 (24 volumes); *The Finer Grain*, 1910; *A Landscape Painter*, 1919; *Travelling Companions*, 1919; *Master Eustace*, 1920; *Henry James: Selected Short Stories*, 1950; *Henry James: Eight Tales from the Major Phase*, 1958; *The Complete Tales of Henry James*, 1962-1964 (12 volumes, Leon Edel).

NONFICTION: *Transatlantic Sketches*, 1875; *French Poets and Novelists*, 1878; *Hawthorne*, 1879; *Portraits of Places*, 1883; *A Little Tour in France*, 1884; *The Art of Fiction*, 1884; *Partial Portraits*, 1888; *Essays in London*, 1893; *William Wetmore Story and His Friends*, 1903; *English Hours*, 1905; *The American Scene*, 1907; *Views and Reviews*, 1908; *Italian Hours*, 1909; *A Small Boy and Others*, 1913 (memoirs); *Notes of a Son and Brother*, 1914 (memoirs); *Notes on Novelists*, 1914; *The Middle Years*, 1917; *The Art of the Novel: Critical Prefaces*, 1934 (R. P. Blackmur, editor); *The Notebooks of Henry James*, 1947 (F. O. Matthiessen and Kennneth B. Murdock, editors); *The Scenic Art*, 1948 (Allan Wade, editor); *Henry James Letters*, 1974-1984 (5 volumes; Leon Edel, editor); *The Art of Criticism: Henry James on the Theory and Practice of Fiction*, 1986; *The Complete Notebooks of Henry James*, 1987.

Bibliography

Anesko, Michael. *"Friction with the Market": Henry James and the Profession of Authorship.* New York: Oxford University Press, 1986. The most thoughtful and well-researched specialized study available. It covers with great skill the social and economic aspects of James's career as a novelist, essayist, dramatist, and critic. It is erudite but still quite useful for the general reader.

Edel, Leon. *Henry James: A Life.* New York: Harper & Row, 1985. The standard account of the United States' most celebrated but often unread novelist. Edel includes much detail, many illustrations, and a definitive bibliography. This biography focuses on the American/British novelist, short-story writer, and literary and art critic as his career evolved from nineteenth century realism to impressionism and modernism. Edel also covers James's career as a theater and art critic for London and New York journals and newspapers.

Edel, Leon, and Ilse Dusoir Lind, eds. *Parisian Sketches: Letters to the New York Tribune, 1875-1876.* New York: New York University Press, 1957. This volume reveals the important role of James as an art critic in London and Paris, despite his florid and elite style that American newspaper editors and readers in the 1870's found unusual.

Freedman, Jonathan L. *Professions of Taste: Henry James, British Aestheticism, and Commodity Culture.* Stanford, Calif.: Stanford University Press, 1990. A later scholarly account of James the exile novelist. James explores the clash between American and European cultures, but his neutrality forces the reader to appreciate the moral codes and social structures of both societies.

Habegger, Alfred. *Henry James and the "Woman Business."* New York: Cambridge University Press, 1989. This book is part of the Cambridge Studies in American Literature and Culture series. It is the best account of how James's fiction and plays presented women, feminism, and sex roles in the light of the rapidly changing political and social views of the late Victorian age and pre-World War I era.

Putt, Samuel Gorley. *Henry James: A Reader's Guide.* Ithaca, N.Y.: Cornell University Press, 1966. A concise and useful introduction to the novels and short stories of James. The dramatic tension in his writing occurs when Americans misunderstand British and European moral codes, roles, and social classes. James, who is often misunderstood as an "aesthete," offers a sharp view of the private mentality and identity hidden by social and ideological conventions.

Seymour, Miranda. *A Ring of Conspirators: Henry James and His Literary Circle, 1895-1915.* Boston: Houghton Mifflin, 1988. A shorter but comprehensive biography, more useful for the general reader. James's father was a well-known Swedenborgian and Fourierist philosopher and his brother, William James, was an even more famous pragmatist philosopher at Harvard University, but Henry's life took a very different path. After his father's death in 1882, James became a cosmopolitan expatriate and (in 1915) a naturalized British subject. In the 1890's, he wrote unsuccessfully for the theater, at the same time producing fiction, essays, criticism, and travel books. Only after his death in 1916 has his reputation as a literary master become established.

Susan Carlson
(Updated by *Peter C. Holloran*)